Hey

I think this topic will interest you! Written and just published by a friend here at P.S. She is 9 yrs!

♡, mom

ADVANCE PRAISE FOR *Talk to Text*

"High-spirited and deliciously erudite, *Talk to Text* is a fascinating journey through what Gwen Groves Robinson calls the 'turmoiled development of prose.' She makes clear that the art of writing prose didn't just appear full blown; it had to be invented, and 'the history of prose's sluggish take-off is full of drama and conflict—and all too often sheer nuttiness.' Robinson's sly wit, clever phrasing, and vivid examples, from Greek and Latin literature and beyond, restore grammar to its long-lost etymological cousin, glamor."
—Christopher Benfey, Andrew W. Mellon Professor of English,
Mount Holyoke College

"Gwen Groves Robinson's *Talk to Text* is a substantial and fascinating book. It traces the transition from orality to literacy in Ancient Near Eastern and Greek cultures, and then more explicitly the ways in which the characteristics and strengths of spoken language were preserved in texts, making literature something deeper and more beautiful than mere literacy. With thorough scholarship, dealing with authors famous and not so, it traces this and related themes in ancient Greek through Latin culture, deep into the Western Middle Ages. There is much of historical interest, much of contemporary relevance."
—James H. Stam, Scholar-in-Residence, Philosophy,
American University

"Though writing is the craft of artificially representing speech, it now competes with speech for clarity and precision. In *Talk to Text* Gwen Groves Robinson traces the contentious and often misguided trajectory of writing from the earliest visual symbols to the most complex and nuanced contemporary sentences. With grace and humor, she analyzes the contributions of our most influential authorial ancestors, so that all those who write can appreciate this precious literary inheritance—and how, in our technological age, we are throwing it away."
—William T. La Moy, former editor of *Printing History* and curator of rare books
and manuscripts, Syracuse University and the Peabody Essex Museum

Talk to Text

This book is part of the Peter Lang Humanities list.
Every volume is peer reviewed and meets
the highest quality standards for content and production.

PETER LANG
New York • Bern • Berlin
Brussels • Vienna • Oxford • Warsaw

Gwen Groves Robinson

Talk to Text

Ancient Origins of Western Prose and the Transition from Oral to Written Culture

PETER LANG
New York • Bern • Berlin
Brussels • Vienna • Oxford • Warsaw

Library of Congress Cataloging-in-Publication Data

Names: Robinson, Gwen Groves, author.
Title: Talk to text: ancient origins of western prose and the transition
from oral to written culture / Gwen Groves Robinson.
Description: New York: Peter Lang, 2020.
Includes bibliographical references and index.
Identifiers: LCCN 2018058166 | ISBN 978-1-4331-6151-3 (hardback: alk. paper)
ISBN 978-1-4331-6152-0 (ebook pdf)
ISBN 978-1-4331-6153-7 (epub) | ISBN 978-1-4331-6154-4 (mobi)
Subjects: LCSH: Writing—History. | Written communication—History.
Classification: LCC P211 .R633 | DDC 302.2/24409—dc23
LC record available at https://lccn.loc.gov/2018058166
DOI 10.3726/b14652

Bibliographic information published by **Die Deutsche Nationalbibliothek**.
Die Deutsche Nationalbibliothek lists this publication in the "Deutsche
Nationalbibliografie"; detailed bibliographic data are available
on the Internet at http://dnb.d-nb.de/.

With Special Assistance From Mary Beth Hinton

The paper in this book meets the guidelines for permanence and durability
of the Committee on Production Guidelines for Book Longevity
of the Council of Library Resources.

© 2020 Peter Lang Publishing, Inc., New York
29 Broadway, 18th floor, New York, NY 10006
www.peterlang.com

Printed in the United States of America

IN MEMORIAM

JOHN ALAN ROBINSON

CONTENTS

Section 4: The Roman Catholic Church

Section 5: The Medieval Period in Western Europe

FIGURES

CHRONOLOGY

Focusing on Greek

Anaximander	610–546/545 BCE
Anaximenes	fl. 545 BCE
Heraclitus	540–480 BCE
Aeschylus	525/524–456/455 BCE
Pindar	518/522–438 BCE
Hecataeus	fl. early 5th century BCE
Sophocles	496–406 BCE
Protagoras	485–410 BCE
Herodotus	485/4–430/420 BCE
Euripides	484–406 BCE
Gorgias	483–376 BCE
Antiphon	480–411 BCE
Socrates	470–399 BCE
Democritus	460–357 BCE
Thucydides	460–404 BCE
Aristophanes	450–388 BCE
Lysias	445–380 BCE

Isocrates	436–338 BCE
Xenophon	431–350 BCE
Plato	428/27–348/347 BCE
Demosthenes	384–322 BCE
Aristotle	384–322 BCE
Zenodotus	fl. 280 BCE
Demetrius	fl. 2nd century BCE
Dionysius of Halicarnassus	fl. early 1st century BCE
Dionysius Thrax	fl. 1st century BCE

Focusing on Latin

Plautus	254–184 BCE
Cato	234–149 BCE
Terence	195–159 BCE
Varro	116–27 BCE
Cicero	106–43 BCE
Julius Caesar	100–44 BCE
Sallust	86–35/34 BCE
Livy	64/59 BCE–17 CE
The Emperor Augustus	63 BCE–14 CE
Seneca the Elder	ca. 55 BCE–ca. 39 CE
Seneca the Younger	4 BCE–65 CE
Quintilian	35–96? CE
Trajan	53–117 CE
Tacitus	56–120 CE
Pliny the Younger	61/62–113 CE
Hermogenes	160–ca. 225 CE
Donatus	d. 355 CE
Jerome	ca. 347–ca. 420 CE
Augustine of Hippo	354–430 CE
Patrick	late 4th century–ca. 460 CE
Theodoric	454–526 CE
Boethius	470/475–524 CE
Cassiodorus	490–585 CE
Gildas	early 6th century–570 CE
Priscian	b. late 5th century

Columcille	521–597 CE
Augustine of Canterbury	d. 604/605 CE
Columban	543–615 CE
Isidore	560–636 CE
The Faminator	fl. mid-7th century CE
Aldhelm	639–709 CE
Bede	672/673–735 CE
Alcuin	732–804 CE
Charlemagne	742–814 CE

PREFACE

If talking is the 'natural' mode of human communication, how did the artificial mode of writing come to substitute so deftly and satisfyingly for it? *Talk to Text: Ancient Origins of Western Prose and the Transition from Oral to Written Culture* attempts to answer that question. Starting from crude messages scratched on bone, stone, and pottery shards, writing has become a man-made extension of our birthright of speech, and has reached an astonishing level of capability over time. Centuries of corrective nitpicking have repaired and refined its early awkwardness and rendered it up today as a robust adjunct to our powers of communication. How did it happen that a mere handful of alphabet letters came to be so richly efficient at conveying description, argument, and wit? The story is replete with both heroes and fools. The historic struggles and arguments that impeded writing's quick advance were often well intended, but just as often mulishly wrong-headed.

I first began thinking about these matters some 40 years ago when, as the editor of the *Syracuse University Library Associates Courier*, I found myself championing (on grounds of sound sense and accuracy) the British management of quotation marks—without success, of course. Being much stirred by these matters, however, I proceeded to write 10 articles on the developing potentials of punctuation, whose beginnings in the ancient world had *not* been a popular consideration. During my years of working with writers, I became more and more involved in the hows and whys of what constitutes clarity, and so it was that I gathered my thoughts for this volume of *Talk to Text*.

My plan was to go back to the origins of literary prose, that is, to writing whose goal is a pleasing and clear expression of the thought that conceived it. In searching through early texts and manuscripts, I was amazed to discover that the history of prose development was so full of uncertainty and conflicting opinion. Propriety, style, and beauty of expression dominated ancient literary discussion as much as did word meanings, pronunciation, spellings, and pedagogy—and all of it seemed subject to unending correction and redirection. The writing skills that we now practice so casually were never a human entitlement. Our literary ancestors worked hard for them. Out of speech for the ear, they found a secondary route for the transfer of thought—and that route was through the eye.

The psychological impact of this shift from ear to eye proved to be spectacular. The result of the eye's participation in the act of conveying and receiving information was the refinement of word-use. Vision put the focus on accuracy and hence on precision of meaning. The progress was bumpy, drawn-out, and frequently misdirected—yet withal, it was thrilling. The impact of the eye's exacting perceptions, and its influence on the developing artistry of prose writers are the twin topics of this book.

Knowing something of the ancient Greek and Latin languages, I initiated my plan with a study of the literary beginnings in early Greece, where the development of the easy-to-learn and handy-to-use alphabet redirected the goals of communication away from the ear's fondness for metered sound to the niceties on offer by sight—hence, away from the music of intoned poetry towards the press of hard thinking into script. It was fascinating to witness writing's slow breakthrough towards fluency and precision, and to meet the various literary personalities as they wrangled over matters of style and set the rules for grammar, spelling, pronunciation, and the various aspects of manuscript copying. In the early years of writing's development, it seemed that no detail was unworthy of argument. The tug of war between beauty and clarity set the scene initially. The follow-up natter of background commentary could be rancorous as well as sharp and effective. When all is considered, what Greece did for written communication and the polished literature of subsequent generations is astonishing.

Rome followed in the footsteps of Greece. In admiration for all that the Greeks had done, it maneuvered its own less flexible language to the forefront of Western literature. It was the Latins who codified grammatical rules so expertly that their language would last and spread throughout Europe to become the long-lived, sacrosanct paradigm of perfection. When barbarians invaded the continent and the levels of literacy declined, it was the Celts in the North, with their strange syntax and passion for words, who saved the Western world's cultural inheritance and exported it back to the continent. There, under the rule of Charlemagne, literacy thrived briefly once again.

This is a vast area for study. The cast of characters is large and multifarious. While some are quite jolly to know, others are clearly beyond the pale. The history of prose development includes names that most are only vaguely aware of—Thucydides, Gorgias, Varro, Cassiodorus, Gildas, Aldhelm, and Alcuin—and yet we owe them much, for they advanced the capabilities of the written prose that we enjoy today. They, with many better known others (I think of Herodotus, Cicero, Seneca, St. Jerome, St. Augustine, and Bede), turned writing into a flexible and powerful means of communication, and thereby encouraged the growth of reading, both for information and for pleasure. Against habit and ignorance, some by example and some by dictate, they bequeathed to us a treasure that we should sincerely thank them for.

Obviously, the materials for such an extensive undertaking must include names and concepts that are not broadly familiar. In aid to those who are new to this undomesticated monster subject, the opening chapter introduces and explains a number of concepts needed for later chapters—along with their accompanying, perhaps unfamiliar, vocabulary. Throughout the book I have tried hard to supply all the uncommon terms with explanation and example. I have tried, too, to provide the relevant historical background for each step forward, along with the apposite opinions of recent psychiatrists, psychologists, physiologists, professional linguists, physicians, academic cognitivists, and both ancient and modern literary critics and writers. In and amongst, I have pointed out current rhetorical ploys that derive from early oral-aural days, and illustrated their continuing use with modern examples.

The history of language and its push towards a clear transmission of thought requires a wide canvas, for so many things need to be taken into account. The expression of meaning begins with the brain as it spins its holistic contents into strings of wordage, first for speech and then for the page. This process being still not entirely understood, my tale will necessarily embrace both fact and speculation. In almost every area of this immense topic, scholars of history and language will wish to delve more deeply. But I have chosen to address my gleanings to all those who write, and while writing, might wonder about the origins of their craft: about what they are actually doing and why they are doing it *this way* instead of *some other way*.

ACKNOWLEDGMENTS

If I were to thank all the people who have encouraged me to battle on through the thickets of this vast topic, I would have to write another book-length treatise. This I do not propose to do. Therefore, like so many before me, I will confine my expressions of appreciation to those who through many years of searching and reading labored to keep me on track: who hunted down sources, located books, checked through my many drafts, corrected my various errors, remodeled my explanations, and discussed, endlessly discussed, the various aspects of my chosen subject.

At the very top of any possible list must be my classically trained, electronically skilled, and philosophically inclined husband. He fed my energies and disputed my ideas. He sharpened my thinking. He introduced me to word-processing and gladly labored to resolve my computer entanglements. For all these reasons and so many more, I am dedicating the finished result of my efforts to him.

Other members of my family have been generous as well. To my daughter, Gwen Owen Robinson, who from her early teens shared my hobby of grappling with the meanings of words, and to her husband, Hartmut Kuhlmann, for his ready wisdom and knowledge, I owe immense gratitude. Their interest in books and writing, their willingness to seek out materials, suggest resolutions to snarls, and all too often, rescue me from ruination were unfailing. My son Hugh Robinson has nobly overseen the acquisition of illustrations. He first accompanied me to the Parker Library in Cambridge, England (a wonderful experience for us both), and later elicited the aid of Dr. Anne McLaughlin (Sub-Librarian, Parker Library, Corpus Christi College), who has so willingly responded to my needs. My eldest son, Alan Robinson, and especially his wife, Margaret, despite their busy lives, have throughout the many years of gathering materials been unendingly helpful in expediting my access to the collections of the Five College Libraries, clustered near Amherst, Massachusetts. Phoebe DeVries, my granddaughter, has essentially 'been in charge' of untangling my more recent computer snarls, while improving (though I doubt that she noticed) my formatting skills along the way. My grandson Peter Richer and granddaughter Theodora Richer have joined in the effort of educating me in the sublime potentials of the computer.

Primary among the many others to whom I am indebted are Christopher Benfy, Andrew W. Mellon Professor of English at Mt. Holyoke College, and Professor James H. Stam, Scholar in Residence, Philosophy, American University in Washington, DC. Both of these gentlemen took time out from the more important aspects of their busy lives to read my manuscript and generously proclaim its one or two virtues. Jennifer Hoit is another to whom I am obligated. She was immensely helpful in organizing the Greek and early Roman sections of the original drafts. I am very grateful, too, to my wise and generous consulting editor, William T. La Moy, who was the curator of rare books and manuscripts at Syracuse University and at the Peabody Essex Museum, where he also served as director of publications. With tremendous kindness he volunteered his expert help in reviewing the final manuscript, making suggestions, and then helping to organize it for publication.

But it was Mary Beth Hinton, my editor, and a friend of many years, who read the manuscript in raw form, persuaded me to work it into shape for publication, and then connected me to the Peter Lang publishing house. I am blessed beyond measure for her wise advisements regarding the current endeavor. She has been exceedingly patient, incisive, kind in her criticisms, and unerringly able both in spotting errors and suggesting improvement. For all of that I owe her my very sincere gratitude. Happy the moment when she first walked into my office in the approximate year of 1989!

·SECTION 1·
A PRELIMINARY OVERVIEW
OF THE COMMUNICATION PROCESS

· 1 ·

WHAT ARE WE TALKING ABOUT?

From Thought to Speech to Writing: *What Goes Wrong?*

Yellow?—We call this yellow color "yellow."...It just seemed like a different color than you kind of expect from a big network launching a season....It was kind of like, well, let's try not to look like every other network has looked every year, and we came up with yellow.[1]

This speech, transposed into print from a television interview, was probably annoying to hear, but it is even more annoying to read—unless, of course, you are hooked on the commercial possibilities of yellow.

Ideally, talk should consist of a balanced exchange in which the speaker works to make his message assimilable and the listener works to assimilate. The courteous listener will accept some mental backing and forthing, for the aural-oral world is exceedingly tolerant; but rarely will a reader put up with incessant shifts of direction. When thought-scraps are transposed to paper, a laborious effort to extract sense becomes the lot of the reader.

To discuss writing, which is the artificial dimension of our communicative powers, we must for obvious reasons deal first with speech, which is the natural one. Speech is the outering (or uttering) of our thinking selves, of that arcane mental brew of emotion and reason that feeds our personalities, and makes us *us*. Even the most casual talk requires some split-second forethought. Before we open our mouths, we will have perceived our listener's psychological needs, his intellectual level, and likely areas of interest. To all of that, we will adjust our approach. If our listener is in mourning for a beloved family member, we will refrain from recounting the joke we heard at last night's orgy. We will not ask a sweaty farm hand if he finds ploughing "enervating" or "spiritually unfulfilling." Having settled our mode of address, word choice becomes our primary focus. We must now burrow into the seethe of our mental scenery to select and transpose *into words* what we want to convey. Therein lies effort. We discover we must precede speech with thought. And what precisely we mean by *thought* is very hard to define. Is it the intake or the analysis of a perception? The figuring out of a quandary? An evaluation of experience? A mental reconstruction of a remembrance? Perhaps it is any or all of these and more; but however viewed, thought is the wellspring of what we then say and later attempt to write.

The tension we feel when we speak increases as we move from the family breakfast table to the office, where, for example, we are charged to persuade an adversely inclined finance committee to increase our departmental budget. Such an assignment accelerates the struggle to impress. To succeed, we will need to be clear and to the point. We must lay out the argument with words that our listeners can easily handle, words that are in keeping with expectation. And we must embed those words in a syntax that is direct and clear.

The intensity of concentration that we apply to important oral verbiage increases substantially when we come to write it down. The dangers we had merely sensed suddenly become real, for our reader will have time to scrutinize the words we set down—time to examine our grammar, wince at our misspellings, disprove our argument, question our motives, and so on. Writing must with all possible accuracy convey the intention that drives it. Everyone knows that *writing words* and *saying words* are two different skills, and that writing, because it does not come naturally and is more permanent, is, for most, the more worrisome one to handle.

A Word About Words

It is rather a shame that we have to bother with words, for they are poor coin for all that we sometimes wish to convey. How much more complete it would be if we could just beam our emotional, practical, and conceptual signals into the receptors of our choice, and fly on! Instead we have words and more words. Though their meanings are limited, let alone inconstant, their individuality—as well as their capacity for reuse and rearrangement—make them convenient. In general terms, a word is a single, distinct, linguistic element that is used to build larger, thought-evoking constructs. Speakers instinctively reposition words to express different ideas. Communication would be impossible if a never-before-used sound was needed for each transmission of an idea.

In the word group 'run,' 'slowly,' 'dogs,' 'fat,' we find: a verb, an adverb, a noun, and an adjective. Each is what is known as a *content word*, in that it conveys to the mind some inkling of an idea. When shuffled into a different order, the same words can render up an actual thought: that is, they can make a statement: 'Fat dogs run slowly.' Though now a completed proposition, this short sentence may itself be only a part of a yet bigger thought: 'Because fat dogs run slowly, it is better to choose thin ones for dogsled racing'—which may lead us onward to further enlargements about competitions in Greenland, or the international availability of thin dogs, and so on. Simple as the words may sound, they can slither and slide in their usage. *Fat* and *run* may become nouns, and *dogs* may be used as a verb, as in: The *run* in her stocking *dogs* her memory. Even *slowly* can be made a noun, as in: His old man's *speedily* took longer than her youthful *slowly*.

There are also *function words* or *particle words*—like *but, however, moreover, on the one hand*—words whose duty is to manipulate the grammatical relationships among the *content words* so that some varied, fuller, or more explicit meaning can be reached. Communication (particularly when written) owes much of its success to the guiding power of such words; for words are not only associated with meanings, they are associated with one another.

When speaking, we meld word groups into seamless clusters; we enforce meaning with intonation and pause to mark a completed notion. When writing, we individualize words and punctuate groups of them with points and stops (commas, colons, etc.). In general, the precise boundaries of all words are more obvious when written than heard. It is the spaces we see between them that make them so. In the oral mode, the spots we choose for pause and termination can be surprisingly varied, for as speakers we are freer to shift the emphasis and recluster the words with pitch or volume.

Though we all feel that we know what words are, their functions are tricky and their transmissions capricious. Though commonly thought of as peepholes into the thinking mind, words can as effectively be viewed the other way around: that is, as inhibitors of the full output of the thinking mind.

With their limitations, they in no way ensure the yearned-for goal of a pure
and perfect transfer of meaning.

It is difficult to describe the intake of our senses. All too often, words
fall short. Though in the hands of some they may seem on target, the goal
of a complete and precise communication is rarely achieved. It is only ap-
proximated. The fact that words are common enough to be negotiable among
millions of users tends to depersonalize them and to extract their emotional
potential. Howls and hugs can be more telling. Yet for a word to communicate
at all, it must previously have been used—otherwise, it is only an arbitrary
noise. In being used (elsewhere, by others), it may acquire a nuance from
an extraneous context that does not match our own experience with it. The
discrepancy between what we intend and what is understood when we funnel
our thoughts into words exposes their wobbling capabilities. The entire legal
profession could be viewed as founded on this fact.

Along with error and ignorance, time plays a part in the blurring of word
precision. An inspection of the *Oxford English Dictionary* (*OED*) pages reveals
a quarry of historical change. Consider the word *shady*. It is recorded in our
English literary history as early as 1579, when it meant simply *affording shade*;
and again, as *shaded*, or *protected by shade*; and slightly later as being *uncertain*,
or *indefinite in outline*. In 1807, *on the shady side* became a witty way of saying *on
the far side* when speaking of one's age. Thus: She made a lovely bride, albeit
on the shady side of 40. From there, it was no great leap to *uncertain*, *unreliable*,
and our now familiar connotation of *disreputable*—as in *a shady character*.

There is also the loss of specialist words that fade as various trades become
obsolete and the names of their tools and ranks are forgotten. Some have
been selectively dropped by lexicographers who have been limited by the demands of space. Robert Macfarlane in his book *Landmarks* reports that in a
recent edition of the *Oxford Junior Dictionary*, a number of nature words were
dropped on the grounds that youngsters these days preferred electronics to
nature. Thus, such words as *acorn, dandelion, heather, pasture, lark, ivy, willow,
mistletoe* (to name a few) had given way to such as *blog, chatroom, voice-mail,
cut-and-paste, broadband, celebrity, committee, attachment*[2]—all so depressing to
those old enough to remember climbing trees or searching for four-leaf clovers
in the grass.

Meanwhile, readers will be gratified to know that the word *grammar*, in
use in one form or another for some two and a half millennia (and probably
more), is the source of today's word *glamor*. The line of descent must have
begun with the early scrutiny of habits of speech. In subsequent centuries, the

prestige of having writing skills and book learning brought with it an aura of occult knowledge, wonderment, and admiration. Thus, by the late fifteenth century (with the slight modification of *r* to *l*, whose two separate sounds require only a minimal movement of the tongue) was born the word we now use for hair styles and couture.

Despite the facetious characteristics of words, writers like to think about their values and history, for the more one knows about a word, the more one can play with its resonances. Word knowledge inspires wit and is the storehouse for poetic statement. And whether we are prose writers or poets, we all aspire to having that knowledge. We sense its power.

Yet word drift remains persistent. Lexicons of classical Greek and Latin, let alone the dictionaries of medieval languages, can testify to this everlasting fact. Grammarians of modern languages are kept busy noting (and lamenting) 'slippages' from previous meanings and modifications of words. Writers must accept that in time or in some faraway place the word they choose may not precisely mesh with younger, local usage that has replaced it, metaphorized it, modified its function, or simply confused it with a similar word. Over time, the results of street talk, jargon, ignorance, and carelessness lead to new usages that by enduring will eventually qualify for lexicographic attention.

For all these reasons, the disciplines that must be practiced with a high degree of precision (like music, science, and mathematics) have given up on words, favoring more explicit notation. Arabic numbers and the symbols of logic convert rigorously into a stable, universally understood meaning. The pitch-and-time marks on a musical staff are equally rigorous, though they offer no incontestable instruction for a perfect musical interpretation. Other subjects like philosophy and theology that deal in conceptual thought and require (or ought to require) the strict separation of intellect from emotion are poorly served by words, for common usage will have contaminated their transparency. Ideographic road signs, being free of words, can transmit an idea in a flash—be it an oncoming vista or a moose crossing—but never with any specificity. They are useful for emergencies, however, in that they short-cut the human aural system and all the tedious words that clutter it.

Even if words could be made to broadcast an idea more efficiently, the mere passage of time would tend to blunt the subtlety of their meanings. Because they are such deficient tools, a communicator (either speaker or writer) must limit himself to the pinnacles of his topic, however skimpy they may seem to be when compared to the rich scenery of his mind. With words so weak and inefficient, the recipient of them is forever obliged to interpret their signals *according to his own lights.* All communication works this way. One seizes a holistic, three-dimensional mental abstraction out of a stream of many, conceptualizes it, and compresses the result into a string of wobbly words to be fired into somebody else's mental environment. Much may go wrong in that radical transformation from A's interior image into his ulterior wordage and on to the interior image that B will end up with. Translations from one language to another expose the most obvious instances of this failure of two word-dependent minds to connect snugly. Here is George Steiner's analysis of that famous lament:

> Each and every human being speaks an "idiolect": this is to say a language, a "parlance" which remains in some of its lexical, grammatical, and semantic aspects his or her own. With time, with individual experience, these aspects incorporate associations, connotations, accretions of intimate memory, privacies of reference singular to the speaker or writer. For each one of us, there are tone-clusters, particular words, phrases either embedded in our consciousness or branching, as it were, into the subconscious, whose patterns of sense, whose specific charge is deeply ours. These elements translate only partially in even the most scrupulous proceedings of shared communication. All exchanges remain incomplete.[3]

A more recent description of our imperfect powers of communication is that of George Dyson. He is describing the matter of books and authors. Books, he tells us, have mysterious properties—like strings of DNA.

> Somehow the author captures a fragment of the universe, unravels it into a one-dimensional sequence, squeezes it through a keyhole, and hopes that a three-dimensional vision emerges in the reader's mind. The translation is never exact.[4]

But the news is not all so frustrating. If we go back to the quoted passage on the first page, we will see that, despite the confusion of language, something in the way of information has come through: namely, that yellow will have an impact on the TV viewer. ABC will benefit. Likely millions of dollars will change hands. In short, we know—in a *sort of* sort of way—what is meant. In churning his topic as one might churn a laundry tub in search of a sock, the advertising executive has said enough to spark in us a responding recognition of his basic idea. With very little in the way of precision, he has managed to ignite our receiving imaginations, which then take over. It would seem that, where words peter out, some allowance of intuitional beam is accorded us after all. Though intuitional beams may cut neatly to the target, we would not want too many of them. A total replay of alien perception would eat us up. We would have no time to perceive things for ourselves, and so would not exist. Imagine, if you can, that yellow theme in the fullness of its possibilities—a complete recall of all the potentials of yellow as viewed through the lens of him who loves it. Only a mother could stand it.

Against such a threat, words offer an unappreciated virtue. They preserve our individuality. They deter human society from amalgamating into a single pulsing mass, by separating us as they themselves are separate. Words fortify our personal terrain. They give us privacy. Being both discrete and time restricted, they cannot radiate our every thought to swamp the atmosphere. Thus, we are freed from the incessant buzz of what everyone else is thinking. But the primal importance of words is that they make language possible. It is language that transforms our experience, allows us to hold abstract ideas in mind, juggle images, hypothesize, and reconsider possibilities. Because words define, enumerate, and allow manipulation of experience and perception, they enable us to move from an environment of objects and images to one of generalizations, concepts, and theories. For those who cannot deal with words, it is a dark world indeed.[5]

With Imagination the Gap Is Reduced

It is hard to guess what ancient readers might have gleaned from their ancient texts. Early manuscripts, being handcrafted and without a stable uniformity, would seem to resist being read. With writing conventions not broadly fixed, it was a struggle to determine what the author wished to have understood. Nevertheless, the ability to read and write was highly admired. Being expensive to acquire, it quickly became the key to legal, governmental, and educational control. Later, in the early Christian era, when the writings of saints and learned churchmen could be accessed and interpreted only by those who could read, literates continued to hold privileged positions. Until Gutenberg's printing press democratized it, literacy was the primary key to power. In such an atmosphere the author of a lengthy treatise or document would assume tremendous prestige. Whatever he wrote and however awkwardly he wrote it, he was assured of adulation. Acclaimed as 'a man of knowledge,' he knew that his work, however set down, would be tackled by reverent, applauding, and desperate-to-understand readers. With admiration assured, why change?

Self-satisfaction is *not* a goad to improvement. And so it was that the reader's difficulties lasted for far too long.

For centuries readers had only the short end of the stick—and initially, hardly any stick at all. It was up to them to divide the run-on, unpunctuated, and crabbed ink marks into meaningful phrases; to hunt down the verbs, locate possible cadences, and supply the required emphases. Readers were assisted by the fact that so many early texts tended to deal with themes already familiar from oral tradition: myths and legends, the feats of renowned heroes, military actions, and biblical and hagiographical topics. Each of these realms generated its own checklist of expectations that helped the reader to anticipate an appropriate meaning from a sea of textual uncertainties.

In those early years the formation of an alphabet letter was in no way standard. Unsettled spellings slowed a reader's quick comprehension. The lexical content of words was often unsettled. Nor was 'white space' to separate the written words a reliable constant. Indication for cadence (either pause or termination) was not routinely obvious. Punctuation did not exist as we know it; in its place, the reader was directed by succinct mechanisms embedded in the infrastructure of a composition. Slowly, as time passed, rules developed to eliminate these difficulties. But for centuries, with nothing made easy, there was little to do but *suppose* the meaning where the puzzle pieces were missing or did not quite fit. We should think of ancient readers as deeply concentrated, murmuring as they proceeded and backtracked along the densely scripted lines.

That kind of imaginative overdrive is not required of modern-day prose readers. Writers have been exercising their craft for a long time, and the press of their efforts has been towards tightening the connection between the intended meaning and its reception. The desire for precision is most evident in the modern how-to manuals that we must all wrestle with from time to time. There (one hopes), instructions are ordered in keeping with the logic of the steps to be made and in pace with the passage of time: first you do this, then you do that. Details are finely calibrated: items are weighed to the final ounce, or measured by degree, calorie, pixel, millimeter, or an eighth of a teaspoonful. If you can read, then you will have a handle on all the needed practicalities for raising bees or tailoring an overcoat. Indeed, if the presentation of your handbook is clear—and sometimes it is and sometimes it isn't—you cannot go wrong. Literate explicitness can guide the dumbest of us through the mechanical, computational, and legal entanglements of contemporary living, for which the glory of success depends entirely on the clarity of the how-to description.

Though often useful, particularized detail is not always desirable, and certainly not in the old, old art of storytelling. Too much is too slowing. It is only the counter-to-norm that interests us. The rest, if it is standard, can be intuited. Be it amorous, adventurous, or even murderous, when the subject matter relates to the dealings and doings of humankind, we can be counted on to emote as intended without the guidance of minute detail. As listeners and readers, our experienced imaginations simply 'fill it in.'

The dangers of heavy reliance on imagination lie in an increased likelihood of misperception. In the case of writing, how truly have the reader and the author connected? If the writing is sloppy, the chances of a sound connection are not good. But if the author has supplied enough information, he will usually succeed in getting his reader somewhere near the intended target. But then, if the reader is imaginatively hyperactive, or unresponsive to nuance, or as willfully recalcitrant to suggestion as an adolescent, then misunderstandings are likely to occur. A perfectly reasonable eight-year-old, with decisive experiences that do not match those of a poet, might, for example, churn up a volley of unpleasant connotations from Shakespeare's "Shall I compare thee to a summer's day?" Instead of soft skies and flowering shrubs, he might think of hay fever and sneezing—or worse: cowpats, sweat, ants in his sandwich, and so on.

Art galleries have taught us to see comparable distinctions between the exact and the general: as between a highly detailed Canaletto, say, and an impressionistic, broad-brush Renoir. Though both require an adaptation of the mind, Renoir, being more subjective in his outlook and more dependent on our visualizing things he has left out, makes the greater demand on our imaginations. And, we are able to meet it. Guided by experience, the interpreting mind has become quite flexible. It can cope with the exactitudes of photography and technical and medical drawing, as well as the deceits of perspective, pigmentation, and shading. We owe this stretch of capability to an enduring dissatisfaction with the status quo: to a desire to rearrange it, freshen it, and enlarge its range of impact—in short, to make it different and to teach others to see it differently. With one success building on another, artists have led us from the simplistic body shapes of prehistoric fertility idols through the distorted anatomies of tenth-century Virgin Marys to the muscular aesthetics of Michelangelo, whose measurements of the human body are more in accord with what we feel ourselves to be. But we have always known where to direct our imaginations when confronting imperfect depictions of familiar material. It would seem as if whatever a human says or draws, some interpretable element will emerge.

Since painters have the same problems as writers when it comes to conjuring up facets of human experience by artificial means, it is interesting to see what the art world has to say on the matter of creating acceptable illusion. We turn for this exercise to the art historian E. H. Gombrich, whose artistic observations cast light on literary challenges as well.[6] To begin, we must accept that the amount of information reaching us from aural and visual sources is incalculably large—so large that neither words nor paint can begin to render it up in toto. One must rely on appropriate suggestion and an instructed receiving imagination. Just as the word *bull* in no way resembles the snorting, dirt-pawing beast we are wise to run away from, so too does the tree painted on canvas fail to be really 'real.' It is flat to begin with, and unresponsive to most of the things we think of when we think of trees. Birds, insects, wind, even the prospect of being axed, do not relate to that rigid painted image. And yet, the blob of green with the streak of brown beneath proclaims itself a tree, and we accept it—even from the hands of a child. We do this, says Gombrich, because we, like the artist, have had experience in the real world. We have touched trees, sawed them down, plucked their leaves, and picnicked under them. Out of the vast variety of tree-related possibilities, we have extracted generalities—the *schemes* of them, if you will. We learned their common traits from our senses as we grew and moved about in the real world. Our experiences have given us a conceptual knowledge, *which then dominates over the process of sight.* We test every new artistic signal against experience. Shared experience provides the schemes, and the mind preserves them for all the subsequent variations.

In the world of artistic depiction, our experience-honed imaginations are constantly at work. When we see a profile portrait, we know that the painter is not telling us that his subject has only one eye, one ear, and half a mouth. Experience tells us to imagine from the clues that are offered a complete and normal head. Chinese painting is deliberately spare in respect to schematic clues. Large spaces are left vacant in order to increase opportunity for the imaginings of the beholder.

Literary experience has taught the public how to make the same sort of imaginative leap to arrive at an authorial intent. As we examine the history of art and compare it with that of writing, we will see this give-and-take process stabilize in steps—each step incorporating a rise in expectation with its responding readjustment. In the interplay between painter and viewer, or writer and reader, the always-incomplete offering—the quick stroke, the sparsely worded clue—must somehow give the necessary punch to activate the imagination. In the past, thousands of schemes have been developed to support the hoped-for transfer of an idea. As those schemes built up over the centuries, so the public became more familiar with as well as reliant on them.

The imagination, thus educated, overrides what the eyes actually see or the ears actually hear. It leaps to interpret an artist's picture, or a speaker's or writer's words—for words, too, are shortcut tools for coping with the vastness of reality. The flexibility of words, in both representing generally and failing to represent fully, makes them practical equipment for human communication. Though less quick than icons to inject an idea into our skulls, they are more explicit—which is to say: they are explicit enough to inform in some detail. Equally, they are sufficiently *in*explicit to protect us from a complete, blow-by-blow reenactment of everybody else's passing thought.

As for the ancient write-read dyad, it was up to the early reader to decipher an author's written lines, to imagine the missing elements and derive meaning from imperfectly formulated clues. The interpretive gap was wide, the signals unstable, cumbersome, and all too often absent. In time, principles and rules would develop to support the retrieval of authorial intention and to make a page of writing less reliant on the excessive energies of readers.

Convention: A Source of Comfort

It seems odd that common 'street talk' should have been the wellspring of all the world's great literatures. Yet, however much we may disdain its wayward habits, when we undertake to communicate, we must keep its norms in sight, for they are the sources of our commonality. Though words may block and blur, we have agreed that within the precincts of our communication game, they will convey some *scheme*, if you will, of meaning. And so, we pitch them out and trust them to 'connect.' Centuries of practice have taught us the rules for this imperfect sport. Those rules are our grammar. By measuring ambiguous speech against grammatical rule, we know when to expunge an inappropriate interpretation; or, how to interpret a meandering utterance. Practice has taught us to compensate for incomplete structures, guess the referents of pronouns, and fill in "the missing steps of an argument"[7]—like those of our yellow-loving ABC expositor. When speech grows sloppy, we are sustained by those reference points of established oral usage, among which we have lived from early childhood. Because they are there, we can often comprehend even the slimmest of hints.

However sporty words may be, they are no match for the life of the mind. Sensing a word's inherent deficiencies, the speaker plays within the broad rules of his language, seeking the intuitive range of his listener. As the speaker speaks, the listener works to supply the missing nuts and bolts of whatever is being said. In a linguistic terrain common to both, there is still space for imprecision—for lexical errors, defective cadences, new slang, and so on. But in the end, a well-chosen schematic clue will convey at least some idea of the intended meaning.

About Grammar

To speak or write in a manner from which sense can easily be gleaned by another, we must follow our grammar's conventions of relationship and order. Even our prehistoric ancestors must have felt this need. We can assume this because the earliest samples of any text in any language show signs of attempting to organize the elements of its flow. Rules about subjects and objects, verb tenses, inflections, prepositions, about where each word should slot into the syntactical line, and how that syntactical line should be brought to conclusion—all these rules are the result of speaker-listener adjustments made over the many millennia that *homo sapiens* has sapiently been talking. Without some rules for combining words—even if everybody had agreed on their meanings—we would understand little of what we say (let alone write) to one another.

An interesting glimpse at the formation of a new language and how people almost unthinkingly seek to order it with grammar can be found in the transformation of pidgin languages into creoles. At the stress points of two peoples coming together—be it through migration, commerce, or conquest—the initial means of communication is through an awkward mix of both native languages. That first-generational *lingua franca* is called a "pidgin" language, and it is helped along, one supposes, with body language and environmental context somewhat in the following manner:

Imagine many, many years ago: An English speaker is standing alongside a Mediterranean two-masted lugger filled with fruits and vegetables, and is considering the purchase of tomatoes. The three-language mix (English, French, Italian) runs as follows:

"Pomodori? [Tomatoes] Questi sont molto molto bons!" [These are very very good!]
"Si?" [Yes?]

"You like? Vedete. See? Bellissimi sont." [Look. They are beautiful.]

"Hmm. Very well. Cinq." [Five.] (*Holds up five fingers.*)

"A vous [To you] I sell six. Is good. Non sont molto cari." [They aren't very expensive.]

(*Glowering.*) "Cinq. Non più." [Five. No more.]

"Okay. Okay. Cinque. Cinque beauts per voi. [Five beauties for you.] Molto nice. Guardate." [Very nice. Look.]

"Si, si. Va bene. [Yes, yes. Very good.] Hmmm. I take six." (*Holds up six fingers.*)

"Ah! Verr buon'idea!" [Very good idea.]

Here we see a collision of Italian, French, and English. The dominance of any single language over another would depend on where the scene takes place and which speaker knows more of the other's language. In the European past, Greek, Latin, German, and French were the dominating languages at meeting points. Now in the Western world, of course, it is English.

But what is most interesting about pidgin speakers is that their children can take up that awkward mix of languages and, without instruction or apparent effort, cultivate from it a sophisticated, expressively pliant, grammatically complete *creole*. And it is this fact that so strongly fortifies the validity of Noam Chomsky's thesis—that the modern human brain is born physiologically prepared for full-bodied linguistic activity.[8]

To convey meaningful thoughts, word strings must be governed by some sort of grammatical rule. Without set standards, the verbalization of our opinions and ideas would result in a bewildering confusion of unrelated representations—a puzzling, disordered word-train, embodying no proposition, and hence uninterpretable.

About Agreement for Word Meanings

Convention also rules the semantic side of language. There are lexical restrictions and extensions that we must know about if we are to communicate successfully with others in our community. If, when we use words, we do not exactly adhere to common habit, we risk being misunderstood, or, like Mrs. Malaprop, even laughed at. As we have seen, lexical quirks and values are honed by usage. Custom dictates how a word may fit into a sentence. We know, for example, that *below* is never a verb. Nor is *beautify* an adjective. Most words have long histories that affect their substance and present-day boundaries. The aspects of a word's complexion we learn by listening to others speak. If we have done our listening fastidiously and wish to be smart and up-to-date, we will not order *bovine thyroids with disintegrated potatoes* in a restaurant, nor complain to our personal trainer that winning the decathlon not only *confiscated our health* but also *impecuniated our purses*. We would certainly wrinkle our noses if a friend wrote us that his *preprandial swim in the billowing deep off the tempestuous headlands of Brittany was fraught with terror*. Words are not happy when they stray beyond the boundaries of convention. We must know how others use words and what they will expect when we use them too.

Some Diverse Linguistic Conventions

Grammatical and semantic conventions differ amongst the world's languages. Our use of *it*, as in 'Since *it has* rained, *it will be* wise to wash the mud from your hubcaps' must be very hard for budding Cambodian linguists, as must our huge vocabulary for Turks, who prefer to attach syllables to a limited number of core words in order to extend their meaning. Thus: yat=lie down; yatmak=to lie down; yatik=leaning; yatak=bed; yatay=horizontal; yatir=lay down; yatir-mak=lay something down; yatirim=deposit, investment; yaterimci=depositor, investor. Though the core-word collection is not large, the additional bits provide a full and pliable vocabulary.[9] Latin, Greek (both ancient and modern), German, Swedish, Icelandic, Danish, and Norwegian wordmongers work with inflections to mark the duties of the words they use. An inflection is (usually) a suffix that indicates the function of a basic word root within the sentence. It tells us whether it is a *noun* or a *verb*; and if a noun: Is it the *subject* or *object* of the verb? And if a verb: Is it *you* or *she* acting in future or past? In English the plural 's' and the past-tense '-ed' are samples of inflection. Agglutinative languages (like Turkish) do not use inflections.

The Germanic languages tend to put the past participle of a verb last. As does Japanese, German negates at the end of a statement, thus making it extremely difficult for instantaneous translators to handle, since they don't know if the many words that precede the verb are to be considered true or untrue. Though an everyday German word arrangement will not be very different from an English one, when it seeks formality, it can become quite snarled.

Steven Pinker, in the chapter entitled "The Horrors of the German Language" (in his book *Words and Rules* [New York: *Basic Books*, 2015], 225), gives an example of everyday speech:

Ich habe einen grünen 'KACH' gegen meine Erkältung genommen.
Meaning: I have a green 'KACH' for my cold taken.

But here is a more formal sample:

Bezug nehmend auf Ihr Schreiben vom 18. dieses Monats, freue ich
mich Ihnen mitteilen zu können, dass die nächst gelegene Apotheke
in der Tat von einem sehr dicken Apotheker geführt wird.

For which a word-for-word translation reads thus:

Reference taking to your writing from the 18th of this month, please I
myself you inform to can that the next located pharmacy in the deed
by a very big pharmacist led [operated by] is.

Mark Twain's delightful essay on "The Awful German Language" is very
much to the point.

The evolving Romance languages (thank heavens!) chose to shed the
heavy use of inflection, and English followed suit to benefit by their example.
Icelandic, like all its Germanic cousins, did not; and moreover, it continues
to mystify non-natives with some very remotely referenced kennings. A *ken-
ning* is a metaphoric phrase that through constant usage is adopted to replace
the original prosaic thing it was intended to poeticize. *Feeder of the raven,*
for example, substitutes for 'warrior'; *field of the golden rings,* for 'women'; *sea
fowl's bath* and *realm of the monster,* for 'sea.' One wonders if *Fields of the Golden
Rings* might occasionally be used in Iceland to identify a ladies' room. These,
though they were devised more than a thousand years ago, are still meaningful
(possibly even enjoyable) to the conservative natives of Iceland. But education and practice have taught their nimble minds to jump like frogs amongst
the hordes of circumlocutions as they scramble for the 'real thing.'

Hawaiian, until recently an unlettered tongue, uses the Roman alphabet
in its written form. With a mere eight consonants and a collection of mu-
tating particles (small words or, in this case, word bits that hop around to
organize relationships and modify meanings), Hawaiian offers yet another set
of linguistic entertainments. Heavily reliant on repetition and vowel sounds,
it is initially very hard to gather in for less aurally oriented English speakers. To them, who count on the stability of distinct syllable forms, Hawaiian
seems all sinew and no bone. Though many Hawaiian words will stay intact
when used, they must maintain their integrity against a bluster of additional
melodious particles, each of which affects the sense and resembles (to English

ears, alas) all its mates. The effect is pure, endlessly flowing, ungraspable song. Nevertheless, even Hawaiian can offer access to understanding, if one masters its habits.

Numerous features of American Indian languages are to us both strange and fascinating, as are even some quirks of our Indo-European cousins—like the Celtic and Slavic languages. The variety of paths and channels that humans have developed in their intense desire to communicate is amazing.

Some Interesting Features of Far Eastern Languages

High on the list of useful linguistic tools is the Japanese *wa* particle. *Wa* follows the opening words of a sentence to mark off what the context will be and thereby focus our wandering minds. It operates thus: *Concerning this mess on the floor (wa), I'm tired. Concerning road rage (wa), if Uncle Bert drives, I'm not going.* More daring yet, Japanese does not bother with the gender differentiation between husband and wife, so that a telephoned request for *Watanabe-san* might bring either Mr. or Mrs. Watanabe to the receiver, or even any of Mr. Watanabe's seven post-adolescent sons and unmarried daughters, his brother, mother, father, grandfather, grandmother, uncles, nephews, or any unmarried female family members. If Papa claims some significant professional achievement, he will be addressed as '*sensei*' (thus: Watanabe-sensei). For his dual-sexed brood of preadolescent children, '*chan*' or '*kun*' will be attached to the family name (thus: Watanabe-chan for girls; and for boys: Watanabe-chan until about age seven, then Watanabe-kun.) Yet even with these complicated distinctions, the resourceful, imaginative, possibly even psychic Watanabes—along with their friends, relatives, and children—somehow manage.

Despite their complexities, Far Eastern languages are rich in capability and well worth a quick pause for inspection. In the fifth and sixth centuries CE, when the Japanese wished to become literate, they adopted the ancient Chinese logographs, known as *kanji*, which offered (and still offer) the benefit of being combinatorial—that is, one may be combined with another to create a new concept. The interaction of their combined images thus fires up a third meaning. For example, the notion of *autumn* is conjured up by the juxtaposition of the radical symbol for *crops* (禾) with the one for *fire* (火), resulting in the single-*kanji* (秋).[10] The original Chinese shapes (dating from the second millennium BCE) are considered to have been pictographic, though remodeled over time under the press of a needed simplicity, a desire for speed, and a fondness for calligraphic artistry. Thus, an early depiction, say, of a *bed* to elicit a *buh* sound would over the centuries have modified as the *buh* signal gradually replaced the *bed* signal in reader's heads. With the hearing relationships to pictographs in this way diminished, Chinese script today is considered to be 'phonetically seriously deficient.'[11] In other words, since it has retained some minimal but recognizable sound signals, modern Chinese writing (which is made up entirely of kanji) is assessed as merely *leaning heavily towards* being ideographic. The sounded origins of the original visual components now lie mostly buried in linguistic prehistory, far out of earshot and inaccessible to modern investigation.

But the oral side of the Chinese language is made up of monosyllables with meanings accorded by tone and sentence position. The stand-alone, sharply focussed kanji that represented them in writing were ill-suited to the flow of the polysyllabic and inflected Japanese language. The result of the kanji adoption by the Japanese was to turn their writing system into one of the most complicated writing systems in the world. To perfect a more complete written transmission of their own indigenous language, the Japanese connected those imported kanji with their own additions of two *kana* syllabaries for the representation of their particle words, as well as the verbal and adjectival endings. Those kana are: the *hiragana* (developed in the eighth century CE) and the *katakana* (developed in the fourteenth century CE)—the latter being mostly to translate foreign imports, like today's *hotel* and *baseball*. To illustrate in hiragana, the list of syllables beginning with a *k* sound reads as follows: *ka* as か; *ki* as き; *ku* as く; *ke as* け; and *ko* as こ. The kana symbols can be strung together to spell any Japanese word, though a written sentence without a kanji or two will be considered childish. The result of all this is a line of script composed of mixed stimuli, some today mostly visual (the original Chinese kanji) and some aural-based (the Japanese kana). The finished sentence is laid out to be read across from right to left, or top to bottom, moving right to left across the page. Often, in Japanese, a kanji will have an original Chinese meaning and pronunciation as well as one, two, or even three Japanese meanings and pronunciations.

In the Chinese, totally-kanji script, there is no alphabetic or syllabic system to represent new concepts, or to transliterate foreign words or signal future or past, plural or singular. There are no sound-related *additives* (like the kanas) to modify a meaning. There is no subjunctive verb form to present 'counterfactual' ideas, as in: *Were you to hammer that nail with an axe, you would smash your thumb*. It is not surprising that in situations where we say, "That's Greek to me!" the Greeks say, "That's Chinese to me!"

Literary professionals tell us that early, free-flowing, intimate novels— like the Japanese eleventh-century classic *Tale of Genji*—were written only by women, because women (with their endemic weakness of brain) were thought too mentally frail to be taught the difficult Chinese kanji. And so, while their menfolk squinted over the complexities of immutable ideographic kanji in order to set down the temporary governmental, military, and judicial edicts of their generation, women scrawled their yearning hearts out in lissome, aural-based, syllabic kana, and thereby achieved enduring fame.

As to *spoken* Chinese, its salient characteristics are handily described in Leonard Shlain's book *The Alphabet versus the Goddess*. Shlain tells us that spoken Chinese has no distinct parts, but is instead made up of some

> 400 to 800 monosyllabic sounds or, as linguists call them, "vocables," none of which signifies a specific word. Instead, the meaning of each syllable depends *entirely* on the place (syntax) it occupies in relation to the preceding and following vocables. The meaning of the vocalization that signifies "mother," for example, can change depending on what precedes and follows it. There is no word for the word *word* in Chinese, because the Chinese language has no words! Besides the holistic nature of its syntax, spoken Chinese depends heavily on musicality. Each Chinese vocable [vowel] has four to nine "tones" [or pitches: four for Mandarin and nine for Cantonese]. The meaning of each vocable can vary according to the singsong manner in which it is spoken....By varying tone and context, a Chinese speaker can use vocables as nouns, verbs, adjectives, or adverbs.[12]

Thai is especially difficult for Westerners who were bred on the alphabetical manifestation of words. That its 69-plus million users make daily use of its 44 consonant and 32 vowel differentiations as well as its five tones is mind boggling to a tone-deaf Westerner. It is the tones that differentiate the multitudinous homonyms. The effect can be illustrated in English with the word *trunk*. Imagine that if you said *trunk* in low C it would carry the 'luggage' meaning; if in middle C, then the 'stem of a tree'; if in high C, the narial extension of an elephant. Two more notes and two more meanings would be needed to equate with the Thai complication and thereby Thai the score. Also strange to us is the fact that those 32 vowels do not consist of an individual letter-size symbol, but of a small mark written above, below, before, or after the consonant with which it is pronounced. Words are not separated from each other and the configurations representing consonants generally flow uninterruptedly until the idea changes.[13]

Consensus for Textual Formation

As nighttime dreaming tells us, the unguarded mind is home to teeth-grinding chaos. With morning's awakening, the need to make sense of things takes over. Indeed, our daytime practice (compulsion, actually) is to distinguish, separate, classify, and arrange. Orderliness is a necessity for coping with life—let alone communicating any ideas about it. In keeping with the desire to be comprehended, we have learned to divide our output of speech (and writing) into units—in speech with pauses of silence and drops of the voice; in writing with punctuation, paragraphing, chapter divisions, and so on. Our propensity to fragment wordage and arrange the fragments in predictable patterns has its roots in the limitations of human physiology and is conjectured to have been a feature of prehistoric speech.[14] Certainly, organized language—language that is decipherable by the modern mind—is fully manifest both in cuneiform and hieroglyphics; and also, very definitely, in the alphabetized writings of Homer and Hesiod (ca. eighth century BCE) and in the earliest recorded legal defenses of sixth-century-BCE Athens. Thereafter, the growing numbers of pedagogical treatises began to advocate *structural* principles in order to optimize the comprehensibility of whatever it was that one wished to say, and from there, of whatever one wished to write. During the subsequent centuries, as confidence grew in alphabetized Greece, matters of style took hold.

The early mandates for optimal communication were essentially a collection of rhetorical rules for an orderly and expectable presentation: one that the listening (and eventually reading) side of the action could count on. In oratory as in subsequent manuscript writing, the first thing to make clear was the general nature of the oncoming word mass. Clues, or *schemes*, were developed to answer this need. Their job was to inform the recipient hearer of *the type* of material being presented. Would it be allegory? History? Legal defense? Would it be celebratory, political, inciting, or funereal? Each type had its identifiable characteristics. Once the signals of overall intention were in place, subsequent conventions emerged to structure the meat of the piece. Some were devised to render the style in keeping with the desired level of magniloquence, outrage, or exhortation; others to offer appropriate ideas for introductions and endings. In and amongst the considerations were the pow-

ers of rhetorical question and the value of exclamation and direct address.
And very stirring these could be. *Oh Men of Athens! What shall we do now?*
Though we turn ourselves into slaves, should we not agree to surrender for the sake
of our children?

Particularly clarifying to meaning was the ancient (and undoubtedly prehistoric) use of *parallelism* and *antithesis*—two structural modes for categorizing
human perception, since all things are either alike or not alike. The Bible's
Old Testament is full of both modes. Parallelism is the restatement of a proposition in fresh terms, in order to enlarge or reinforce a meaning. In Psalm
55 we find, for example: "Give ear to my prayer, O God; and hide not thyself
from my supplication" (verse 1). In other words: "Hear me, O God, and hear
me." Antithesis is the negative restatement of a positive proposition, and its
purpose is to stress a contrast, as in "The light of the righteous rejoiceth: but
the lamp of the wicked shall be put out" (Proverbs 13:9). (The Psalms date
mostly from the sixth century BCE, though some are thought to be from the
fifth. The rest of the Old Testament writings were later—from the second and
third centuries BCE.)

For dealing with the superficial textural details, ancient rhetoricians spoke
of *tropes*—from the Greek meaning 'turns'; that is, turns away from the normal, and familiar today as in "That was an interesting turn of phrase." Tropes
are figures of speech like metaphor; simile; personification, as in *The sky wept*
buckets; and metonymy (a much used figure, wherein an aspect of something is
substituted for the whole, as is, for example, *suits* in "The bar was packed with
suits" [i.e., *businessmen*]; or, "fourteen *sails* [*ships*] were approaching the island
fortification"). Tropes such as these broaden the communicative powers of
language by intimating unstated relationships. All figurative language——as
in *Her hair was spun of gold; the angry seas; daffodils dancing in the breeze,* and
words like *doves* and *lambs* (as symbols of peace and innocence)—falls within
this category. Other textural considerations were *How complicated should a*
sentence structure be? How compact or extended? How elevated in style? How
exalted in word choice? Appropriateness, consensually arrived at, was critical.
One did not toy with conventions of propriety.

Because they were so useful (as well as essential), both the structural
and textural rules for speechmaking were formalized and eventually codified.
Known in the Greek world as the 'rhetorical arts,' they ruled over the word
flow of Greek oratory and literature. Over time they became more specific as
well as more numerous. Amongst them were the settled arrangement of inter-
acting words within a statement—notably, the SOV (Subject-Object-Verb)

pattern as well as some forms of punctuation to indicate the termination of discrete units within a lengthy text. Deriving from ear-oriented orality, these signals for stopping were *not* line-dots (commas or periods) or virgules (slashes), but instead, finalizing rhythms and the positionings of verbs. The protocol for signaling clausal and theme boundaries established by early oratory passed with ease into written prose. The descendants of those signals, in their various and modified guises, have directed verbal traffic right up to contemporary sermonizing, speechmaking, and textual formatting (as in the laying out of books and newspapers).

Turning now to the matter of written beginnings: The world has agreed that large tracts of prose need to be 'introduced,' for the reader must know what kind of a bog he is about to slip into. In ancient times, an historical or scientific essay usually began with some sort of enticement to proceed: a dedication, perhaps to god or emperor; or a statement to allure, such as "I tell things never told before"; or, "It is my duty to impart this unique possession of knowledge"; or "Since idleness is to be shunned, allow me to enrich your mind with the following astonishing facts."

Today's writers have discarded such cumbersome introductions. Being more confident, we pace our prose more briskly. We tweak the conventions to seek fresh, more stimulating routes into the minds and imaginations of our readers. In general, the significant thing to remember is that ancient word-mongers, having formulated conventions to hold their listeners' attention, later clung to those conventions to ease readers into text. We who write today, being literately trained and experienced readers, feel no need for such obvious guideposts. Our long acquaintance with literacy has freed us from the impositions of yesteryear. We have veiled their presence on the page and often maneuver without them at all. We have generally agreed on how to express ourselves in writing.

In writing for strangers, we revert towards established grammatical levels, so that those who are unacquainted with the private lingoes of youth, family, or neighborhood can process what we say. We write more freely in notes and letters to friends. The more closely we adhere to the standards of consensually established or 'educated' speech, the greater the radius of our communicative reach. Colloquialisms that wander from 'accepted' parlance may create an initial sense of clubbiness and fun, but they mean nothing over broad spaces and tend not to last. When expressing difficult thinking—be it scientific, legal, political, philosophical, or contractual—one tends to follow formal usage, *especially when it is to be written.* Although in real-life confrontation we can stretch the nuance of our meanings with nonce words (temporary or ephemeral words), pitch, gesticulation, and facial expression, the source of all successful transfer of thought, both spoken and written, lies in the conventions arrived at through the truces and treaties of linguistic history.

Context

Along with *words, imagination,* and the trusty support of *convention, context* is crucial to communication. Context reinforces the words we actually say, and within its schematic boundaries, a speaker/writer can enjoy an increase of freedom. Conversation recorded out of context is virtually opaque. For the reader, a clear view of the oncoming subject matter is a necessity.

If, for example, I admire a certain view, I might say *Lovely!* to myself and record a mental picture. The rest of my reaction will transmute into a silent scrutiny of pleasing particulars, which I bundle into my memory for possible wording at a later time. If somebody else is with me, I might exclaim, "Look at the shades of sky over there!" The agreeing response would induce in both of us a sense of communion. Later, however, I might wish to write to a distant friend about that view and the sensations evolving from it. For that, an immense conversion of approach must take place, for context must be supplied at a distance in deficient, never up-to-scratch words—in this case, unsounded words. I must write *where* I enjoyed so much beautiful sky. Was I standing on the summit of Mt. Parnassus? or gazing through my dirty office window? And in either case, how did I come to be there? Once all that has been settled, I must tackle the management of my description within that context. Shall I depict the scene scientifically? poetically? in a moralizing manner? Shall I turn it into a symbol of personal nostalgia? of grief for the dying? of God? Whatever I choose to do, I shall be careful to dress my words in appropriate hues of modesty, introspection, sympathy, empathy, humor, encouragement—*whatever*—for to please someone else I must respond to his interests and intelligence level, and thus keep my own self attractive. It would not do to describe those sun-rimmed thunderheads with sneering sarcasm or vulgar slang. My demeanor is a relevant factor.

Settling smoothly into a comfortable contextual relationship with an imagined reader is the hardest part of writing. The introductory paragraph (wherein context and relationships must be made clear) is a common site for editorial criticism. Within a few lines the authorial self must establish a mutually acceptable safety zone in which to entertain (or beguile, inform, admonish, attack) his reader. He must identify the topic and clarify his approach to it. An intimate letter will take shortcuts and idiomize in ways that will not do for formal composition. We must adjust our address to the level of our relationship. The better we know our correspondent, the better we can count on him to intuit our meaning, and the more we can play with grammatical and lexical conventions. In intimate talk, we can expunge and compress as much as we find workable. In nose-to-nose confrontation with strangers, the context—be it a hurricane or a malfunctioning elevator—is usually obvious, or, if misjudged, then speedily corrected by voice, gesture, or facial expression. Writers, however, must match output with expectation *on a single try*.

Because it is so necessary to establish context immediately and to secure attention as soon as possible for what it is that one wishes to talk or write about, most languages open their sentences with the doing or done-to subject. Thus, in English, Italian, French, and modern Greek, we find the predominating structure to be subject, verb, object (SVO). In ancient Greek, Latin, German and Japanese, the verb comes last (SOV), while the subject matter still comes first. But with expectations firmly established, folk can permissibly rearrange to achieve a particular effect, as in "Fast falls the eventide"; or, "Since the traffic was dense, I turned off at Oak St."

It would seem that an established context has always been crucial to the standard communication. Writing simply makes the need trickier to satisfy, in that absent realities must be supplied artificially. On paper, demonstrative references are not useful. *This* tree *here*, *those* trees over *there*—are not the words of a writer. A writer's world is a distant world, both in time and in space. Nevertheless, a writer has his armory of weapons: primarily, an overwhelming vocabulary, a catalogue of ancient-to-modern ploys to choose from, and a trained readership that seeks to be enlightened. To achieve their wanted results, writers of prose can fiddle and substitute, rearrange and invent. Nevertheless, they must *seem* to be candid and assured.

* * * * *

The progress of thought into speech and on into writing has developed slowly. Even today, with so much science at hand, we can only conjecture about what goes on in our brains as we move from a thought to the communication of it. Writing and reading offer synthetic imitations of speaking and hearing, and for success rely on oral custom. Whereas languages have developed their complicated systems from a desire for fuller expression, their actual limitations are set by the brain's physiology. It is significant that we are designed to take in speech far faster than any other noise.

> The sounds of human speech can be recognized at an extremely rapid rate, up to 25 phonetic segments (approximating to letters of the alphabet) per second. By contrast, non-speech sounds cannot be identified at rates exceeding 7–9 items per second.[15]

The development of visual signals to represent sound is a comparatively recent aspect in the lifetime of communicating humans. Yet today we manage both to impart and to comprehend complicated full-bodied thoughts and emotions by means of the pen and the eye. We have invented and used these 'seeing' techniques for their convenience, and with practice we have pushed them to approximate the flexibility and ease of their natural parent sources. Though the written word does not move with real time, it offers compensations.

With all that said, we turn now to the difficult early years of writing's development towards the sophisticated write-read interplay that we enjoy today. To acquire some encompassing view of this massive subject, we begin with an overview of the awkward prealphabetic years as reflected in cuneiform and hieroglyphics. We move then to an inspection of the Greek emergence from an oral background into full-bloom literacy; and then, of the similar succeeding struggles and successes of early Latin-speaking societies: beginning with Classical Rome; then on to the Early Church; then the Irish, Scots, and English; and finally, Charlemagne's realm. In sum, this is a multifaceted history of the march from thought to speech and from speech to writing as it processed through the ancient Western World.

The lack of acquaintance with ancient languages should not be a problem. All is translated, explained, and illustrated.

Notes

1. An oral exposition of the ABC television network's 40-million-dollar deal to use yellow for its logos and ads. Lee Clow, quoted in Maurine Dowd, "What Price Aubergine?" *New York Times*, July 23, 1997.
2. Robert Macfarlane, *Landmarks* (London: Penguin, Random House, 2015).
3. George Steiner, *Errata: An Examined Life* (New Haven: Yale University Press, 1998), 105.
4. George Dyson, *Turing's Cathedral: The Origins of the Digital Universe* (New York: Pantheon Books, 2012), 312.
5. Cf. Oliver Sacks, *Seeing Voices: A Journey into the World of the Deaf* (Berkeley: University of California Press, 1989), 40–8, and passim.

6. Cf. E. H. Gombrich, *Art and Illusion: A Study in the Psychology of Pictorial Representation* (Princeton: Princeton University Press, 1989), with particular reference to pages 195–219.

7. Steven Pinker, *The Language Instinct* (Cambridge: MIT Press, 1994), 228. The chapter "Talking Heads" has been particularly useful in dealing with these ideas.

8. An additional fact that favors the Chomsky theory is the enormous complication of verb structures and the elaborate network of rules and laws and word relationships evident in the languages of many non-industrialized societies. For interesting examples see Mark Mably's *Spoken Here: Travels Among Threatened Languages* (London: Arrow Books, 2005). The complexity of this topic is huge. Cf. also the views of Derek Bickerton as discussed in Bernard Comrie, "Before Complexity," in *The Evolution of Human Languages: Proceedings of the Workshop on the Evolution of Human Languages*, Santa Fe, New Mexico, August 1989, *Santa Fe Institute Proceedings* 11, ed. John A. Hawkins and Murray Gell-Mann (Reading, MA: Addison-Wesley, 1992), 201. Henceforth I refer to this book as *SFI Proceedings* 11. Bickerton suggests that speakers who inherit the syntax of more than just two languages have no firm syntactical example to follow, and must rely on an innate syntax, that is, a 'bioprogram.'
The *SFI Proceedings* 11, which supplies so many of the references for this subject, is the publication of lectures delivered at a workshop organized to speculate on this mysterious and complex topic. The participants could make but few provable claims, but their rigorous reasoning on the subject is both fascinating and thought provoking.

9. Wikipedia, s.v. "Turkish Language," accessed June 3, 2016.

10. Also helpful in these matters was Steven Roger Fischer, *A History of Language* (London: Reaction Books, 1999), 102–5 passim.

11. Andrew Robinson, in "Writing Systems" in *The Oxford Companion to the Book*, 2 vols., eds. Michael F. Suarez and H. R. Woudhuysen (Oxford: Oxford University Press, 2010), 1:4, explains: "The higher proportion of phonetic representation in a script, the easier it is to guess the pronunciation of a word. In English the proportion is high, in Chinese it is low. Thus, English spelling represents English speech sound more accurately than Chinese characters represent Mandarin speech sound; but Finnish spelling represents the Finnish language better than English spelling represents spoken English."

12. Leonard Shlain, *The Alphabet Versus the Goddess* (New York: Viking Press, 1998), 182–3.

13. *Encyclopaedia Britannica*, 15th ed., s.v. "Thailand."

14. Cf. Terrence W. Deacon, "Brain-Language Coevolution," *SFI Proceedings* 11:76. He also reminds us of the generally accepted fact that the hominid's "brain-language co-evolution proceeded for a long time without a vocal tract capable of generating the modern range of vowel sounds." Thus, human language in its very early stages must have consisted primarily of the sharp pulmonary expulsions of consonantal sounds and cheek clicks.

15. John A. Hawkins, "Innateness and Function in Language Universals," *SFI Proceedings* 11:87.

References

Comrie, Bernard. "Before Complexity." In *The Evolution of Human Languages: Proceedings of the Workshop on the Evolution of Human Languages*. Santa Fe, New Mexico, August 1989. Edited by John A. Hawkins and Murray Gell-Mann. Reading, MA: Addison-Wesley, 1992.

Deacon, Terrence W. "Brain-Language Coevolution." In *The Evolution of Human Languages: Proceedings of the Workshop on the Evolution of Human Languages*. Santa Fe, New Mexico, August 1989. Edited by John A. Hawkins and Murray Gell-Mann. Reading, MA: Addison-Wesley, 1992.

Dyson, George. *Turing's Cathedral: The Origins of the Digital Universe*. New York: Pantheon Books, 2012.

Encyclopaedia Britannica, 15th ed., s.v. "Thailand."

Fischer, Steven Roger. *A History of Language*. London: Reaction Books, 1999.

Gombrich, E. H. *Art and Illusion: A Study in the Psychology of Pictorial Representation*. Princeton: Princeton University Press, 1989.

Greenberg, Joseph F. "Preliminaries to a Systematic Comparison Between Biological and Linguistic Evolution." In *The Evolution of Human Languages: Proceedings of the Workshop on the Evolution of Human Languages*. Santa Fe, New Mexico, August 1989. Edited by John A. Hawkins and Murray Gell-Mann. Reading, MA: Addison-Wesley, 1992.

Hawkins, John A. "Innateness and Function in Language Universals." In *The Evolution of Human Languages: Proceedings of the Workshop on the Evolution of Human Languages*. Santa Fe, New Mexico, August 1989. Edited by John A. Hawkins and Murray Gell-Mann. Reading, MA: Addison-Wesley, 1992.

Mably, Mark. *Spoken Here: Travels Among Threatened Languages*. London: Arrow Books, 2005.

Macfarlane, Robert. *Landmarks*. London: Penguin, Random House, 2015.

New York Times. "What Price Aubergine?" July 23, 1997.

Pinker, Steven. *The Language Instinct*. Cambridge: MIT Press, 1994.

———. "The Horrors of the German Language." In *Words and Rules*. New York: *Basic Books*, 2015.

Robinson, Andrew. "Writing Systems." In Vol. 1 of *The Oxford Companion to the Book*. Edited by Michael F. Suarez and H. R. Woudhuysen. Oxford: Oxford University Press, 2010.

Sacks, Oliver. *Seeing Voices: A Journey into the World of the Deaf*. Berkeley: University of California Press, 1989.

Shlain, Leonard. *The Alphabet Versus the Goddess*. New York: Viking Press, 1998.

Steiner, George. *Errata: An Examined Life*. New Haven: Yale University Press, 1998.

Wikipedia, s.v. "Turkish Language." Accessed June 3, 2016. https://en.wikipedia.org/wiki/Turkish_language

·SECTION 2·

EARLY HISTORY:
GREECE AND ALEXANDRIA

· 2 ·

LITERACY BEGINS

A Few Prealphabetic Considerations

The conventions of language are *acoustically*, not visually, encoded in the human brain. We are wired to *hear* words from the very start and to process discourse through the ears long before we can deal with it by eye. If, as infants, we are deprived of the necessary grammatical imprint from the rhythms and intonations of speech-sound, we will be seriously handicapped throughout our lives. Human dependence on orally transmitted and aurally received communication has cut the pattern for all human sociability, including the procedures for interaction through writing.[1]

Writing is extraneous to our fundamental selves. John the Evangelist's biblical 'Word' was perforce an oral word, for "In the beginning" (of the beginning he was thinking of), the communicating mind had only the medium of speech at its disposal. What was said rang into the head through the ear. Literary custom has obscured the fact that language *is* speech, that the most elevated literary styles owe their viability to grammatical codes tempered by countless generations of *illiterate* speakers.

It is easy to imagine how, in a world of distantly separated peoples, mystical fears, and poor transport, proto-writers might have invented simple visual signals to warn or inform, and that those signals gradually grew in their offerings of detail. Though prehistoric animal drawings, rock cuttings, and notched bones may suggest attempts to honor a deity, record a fact, or communicate information, scholars know of no genuine pre-Hellenic writing—that is, no full or fluent transmission of message by visual symbol—before the Sumerian cuneiform syllabaries, which date from 3100 BCE. Prior to the invention of a fluid script, the keeping of tribal affairs had been entrusted to the memories of 'learned' members, whose sacred task was to recount them in some poeticized form at ceremonial gatherings. Over generations, the agglomerating perspectives of those priestly bards must have distorted the original renditions, and thereby introduced confusion, ambiguity, and even incomprehensibility.[2] Entrusting facts to mental recall is not a sure-fire way of keeping them intact. For that, writing is more certain.

Moving (Slowly!) Towards an Alphabet

Scholarly speculation about the origins of human speech is more or less this: that some 50,000 years ago there was a sudden and marked shift in early anthropoid behavior, for it was from that time that a surge of cave art, bone artifacts, and more sophisticated hunting tools begins to appear. This spurt of innovative activity, it is thought, relates to the early development of some kind of language that enabled our ancestors to engage in abstract thought. Philip Lieberman, a professor of linguistics at Brown University, tells us of evidence (from fossils) of a repositioning of the larynx in the throats of early post-Neanderthal humans. The subsequent change in the vocal tract, he reasons, allowed a greater variety of sounds (particularly vowel sounds) to be made voluntarily.[3] Lieberman also considers the matter of division of the human brain into two hemispheres. Since 90 percent of the human race is right-handed, he conjectures that the dominating right-handedness played a part in the hemispheric split of the human brain, thus causing a division of response to emotion and reason. He supports this theory by pointing out that the right hand's more-complex task of tool control (for sewing, scraping, cutting, molding, etc.) would have been more concentration-demanding than the left hand's customary job of merely holding in place the object being worked on.

The brain and vocal tract evolution would (says Terrence W. Deacon, professor of anthropology at the University of California at Berkeley)

> indicate that language is not a recent addition to human culture but is on the order of 2 million years old. This is time enough for many

features of language to have arisen, flourished, and perished without a trace. It is also time enough for there to have been many stages of archaic languages and for each of them to influence and be influenced by brain and vocal tract evolution.[4]

The topic, we see, is thick with speculation. It draws on fossil facts as well as the study of modern brain structure and its capabilities, on anthropology, archeology, linguistics, comparative modern languages, and physiology—on anything, in fact, that it can lay its hands on.

Because our knowledge of that prehistoric era is so sketchy, we begin our story of how a thought was anciently remodeled for speaking and again for writing with the early kingdom of Sumeria in the southerly reaches of the Euphrates valley; for it is there that we find the site of the earliest known, fully expressive writing. Known as cuneiform (*cuneus* meaning 'wedge' in Latin), its sense-symbols evolved in the form of small clustered wedge shapes pressed onto clay tablets that were then baked to hardness (see fig 2.1). Experts tell us that those wedges were originally (ca. 3000 BCE) arranged to represent pictorial forms of simple items (both nouns and verbs) like *eat, come, greet, hand, pot, fish,* and so on. This was the initial move towards full expression in the 3,000-year lifetime of cuneiform writing. Commercial, administrative, and elitist interests all encouraged the expansion of those simple pictographic configurations in order to refine their meanings and enlarge their scope.[5]

Over time, with the increase of confidence and ambition, Sumerian scribes elaborated their wedge-clusters to the point where they could record considerable subtlety with both individuality and style. The resulting complexity of their renderings escalated exponentially. In their logo-syllabic (words from syllables) system of cuneiform script, one can spot groups of 30 or 40 wedges, variously patterned to represent either a single word *or even a single syllable.* As nuances of basic ideas were perceived to be needed, so each wedge-group became more complicated, thereby outgrowing its original pictorial intention. With that, its form became less pictographic and more idea-bearing. In scholarly terminology, one would say that such a group of wedges became more of a logogram or logograph (*logos* here meaning 'word' in Greek, and the *gram* and *graph* from the Greek word for 'write'). Being so intensely complicated, the mastery of Sumerian script required years of specialized training. The hard working commoner, having neither the time nor the money for guidance to learn it, remained illiterate. Thus, though it came to be used (as is the alphabet) across linguistic borders, Sumerian cuneiform remained essentially a medium for the privileged: for royal administrators, government officials, and priests[6]—and though there were exceptions, most of those who mastered cuneiform were undoubtedly men, as was the case with the Chinese kanji.

Fig. 2.1: Sumerian clay tablet

This tablet (MS Doc. 829) was written by a Sumerian scribe in an administrative office around 2200 BC. The full translation follows:

18 jars of pig fat—Balli.
4 jars of pig fat—Nimgir-ab-lah.
Fat dispensed (at?) the city of Zabala.
Ab-kid-kid, the scribe.
4th year 10th month.[7]

Reproduced by kind permission of the Syndics of Cambridge University Library.

An interesting step towards accessible, full expression was achieved with the application of the rebus principle, in which the depiction of an object was embedded in the script, to be interpreted either for itself or for its phonetic value. To play the rebus game in English, the depiction of a hand in a lineup of other inscribed symbols might directly mean *hand*, or it might represent the initial syllable in the word *handsome*. One must guess which. In Sumerian, on an undated tablet, we find the abstract word 'reimburse,' which was represented "by a picture of a reed, because 'reimburse' and 'reed' shared the same phonetic value, *gi*, in the Sumerian language."[8] This rebus romp with its sound-see, aural-visual compound of pictographs and script was a staple feature of Egyptian hieroglyphics, some samples of which also date back to 3000 BCE. Thus, like the modern Japanese with their kanji-kana mixture,[9] ancient Egyptians had constantly to use both eye and ear to work their way through a line of 'writing'—a demanding exercise that, by causing momentary ambiguity, would have increased the effort of decipherment.[10]

Compared with the cuneiform and hieroglyphic systems, the Phoenician alphabet with its vast reduction of symbols-to-be-memorized (i.e., 22 as against cuneiform's 600-plus wedge-clusters) must have seemed a gift from heaven. While scholars still argue over how it came into being, most favor the theory of commercial need for simplicity, for the Phoenicians were noted merchants throughout the Mediterranean. In matters of trading, a speedy record-keeping method was useful—especially one based solely on phonetic principles that could cut through the babble of Mediterranean languages and their dialects. As we note from the modern surge in smartphone texting: where the desire for speed is pressing, busy folk will find shortcuts.[11] It is interesting that the progression of invention for encoding sound has moved from the complex—as in cuneiform clusters and hieroglyphics, where many symbols (or 'pen' strokes) were needed to represent a word or syllable—to simpler syllabaries like the Japanese kana, where syllables are represented by symbols of only one or two 'pen' strokes; and then again, to the Greek alphabet letters with their quite sufficient, often one-stroke (in Greek), 20-plus sound representations. Of all these methods, an alphabet empowers by far the most flexible, easy to learn, and quick indication of sound.

It was the far-ranging Phoenician traders from areas along the coasts of modern Lebanon and Syria who first had the idea of simple signs to symbolize phonemes: that is, the distinct units of a sounded syllable. For example, the word PAN has three phonemes, whereas SPLIT has five; however, the word PHLEGM, despite its six letters, has only four. What the

Phoenicians devised was a system whereby the consonant sounds of speech could be represented by what came to be known as 'letters.' Initially, each letter-shape was the modified representation of a specific sound-related object in the manner of B is for bull, C is for cup, D is for dog, and so on—a sound-to-sight-development that seems to have been the kick-off method for a number of scripts: cuneiform, kanji, and the alphabets. In the case of the Phoenician alphabet, once its pictorial origins were forgotten, what remained was a flexible abstract system, relieved of historical baggage and readily adaptable to most languages. In short, it was a thing of beauty—*almost*. The hitch was that it dealt only with consonants, which in practice made the words decipherable but only with effort, as it failed to complete the full sound representation. Nevertheless, the Phoenician alphabet was both useful in itself and an inspiration to the Greeks, who claimed the prize (sometime around the eighth century BCE) by supplying symbols for the missing voiced (vowel) elements. It was thus that the Greeks, whose flexible, fully expressive and easy-to-use consonant-plus-vowel alphabet kicked off our age of informing and entertaining one another by means of reading and writing. The combined Phoenician-Greek assault on previous writing methods eventually enforced the demise of cuneiform (whose last inscription is dated 75 CE) and the Egyptian hieroglyphics (whose last inscription is dated 394 CE).[12]

We now shift our grateful attention to the Greeks and the rise of writing.

The Greek Alphabet

In the Greek alphabet (as in our Roman one of today) each letter is used to represent a linguistically meaningful sound (or phoneme), be it a vowel (which is sung out through the open throat) or a consonant (which inhibits that vocalization by means of lip, tongue, teeth, or contraction of throat). It is, in short, a notation for 'recording' speech to the degree that the reading eye can intuit a missing nuance as it follows the succession of clues.[13] Gesticulation and facial expression play no part in this silent exercise, though ways (like italics and underlines) would develop in time to suggest emphasis. Punctuational guidance, such as we count on today, remained for a long time uninvented. For the quick intake of text that we now enjoy, the human brain would need training, practice, and even physiological adjustment.

In the wake of the Greek alphabetical advance, writing reached an immediate new level of expressiveness. Letter representations for the vowels that were so prominent a feature of the Greek language allowed speech bytes to be represented with far less ambiguity. Instead of drawing an arbitrary cook pot or seashell to represent a signature, people could write their names as they were sounded, thus: 'Meg' or 'Bob' instead of Mg (Mig? Mog?) or Bb (Bab? Bub?). Abstract nouns like *love, hate,* and *honor* could be transcribed directly, easily, and without reliance on memory or the use of rebus teasers. Whatever words were *sayable* could be *translated into letters* and quickly understood.

With that momentous birthing of a full alphabet, the whole body of cultural 'knowledge,' hitherto embedded in melodic poetry and cluttered with clichés, maxims, and mnemonic rhymes (like our "*i* before *e* except after *c*"; or "thirty days hath September, April, June," etc.) was dislodged from its acoustical matrix and began its drift into visual space, where time plays a different game. Fixed on the page, what is kinetic becomes still, allowing contemplation and analysis; for in quiet the reading eye can gather up facts to question and catalogue, to consider objectively and compare.

The alphabet opened a new frontier of distant, unexplored spaces. With this simple tool a common man could scribble anything. And whatever it was that he scribbled would endure into the next hour, into the next month, and be comprehended by those who had not even seen him do it! Evidence of man's expanding self-assertiveness has come down to us scratched in alphabet letters on the shards of oil flasks and drinking cups—baked clay being nearly unpulverizable. Studying these fragments in today's museum cases, one can almost hear the voice sounds and feel the sense of astonishment, self-satisfaction, and delight: "I wrote this!" "Tleson, son of Nearchos, made this!" "Athenodotos is handsome!" Also handsome were Panaitios, Epidromos, Leagros, and no doubt thousands of others whose sounded names had never been written before.

Later mid-sixth-century BCE inscriptions manifest a diminishing egocentricity in the writings of ordinary people. Instead of astonishment, inscriptions begin to convey unemotional, third-person information. "This is the tomb of…" "Here lies…" Such evidence suggests that writing was internalizing—that writers were gaining the confidence to separate from immediate reaction and offer an objective view. It is a moment to notice. Ancient voices incised on stone are telling us facts, without the intrusion of exuberant ego or the traditional use of prosodic rhythms. In the years before this development, the assumption had always been that 'true' knowledge (in the form of primordial ancestral memory) was sacred and therefore required to be set into verse, whose sources were clouded in mysticism and contoured by oboes and dance. Versified chant with its easy-to-remember rhythmic beats and repetitious phrasings had from time immemorial been the medium for conveying past doings and religious instructions to current and future generations.[14]

Now, alphabet writing was offering a new possibility. It could set down information in unmetered prose that related more closely to the way humans actually talk. When people found that they could say and write more accurately *what they really meant* if they were not obliged to comply with poetic dictates, then prose began to take hold. Initially, it was considered a less worthy medium for matters of high import—a conveyance only for plain and practical matters, for setting down laws and lists of commodities, and for the give-and-take of daily message sending and document making. But during the fifth and fourth centuries BCE, grammatical and semantic refinements were developed, and it was these that turned prose into a worthy vehicle for exacting historical, philosophical, and scientific treatises.

It was during that period that a succession of historians settled the direction that unmetered, purposeful, and elegant prose would eventually take. Put end to end—from the awkward, tongue-tied Hecataeus to the rambling Herodotus, then on to the difficult density of Thucydides and finally to the lucid, relaxed command of Xenophon—their four diverse writing styles span a critical time of literary growth. Their successive outputs stand witness to the emerging powers of prose writing to transmit precise fact in a graceful and lucid way.

The Joyful Athenians

Learning to write with an alphabet was so simple that children could do it, and did. Even Athenian girls were taught their letters so that they might better run the household. Extant graffiti attest to the fifth-century popularity of letter making. There is proof of expanding literacy in the contemporary mention of 'bookshops,' the city's book-mart quarter, and the large collections of 'books' (that is, ungainly-to-handle papyrus manuscript rolls, some longer than 20 feet) in temples, in the houses of rich men, and amongst the possessions of students. Fifth-century Greeks were clearly able to read and write. We know of the existence of libraries and schools, of the sending of letters as if they were in no way unusual, and that there thrived an export trade in books copied by slaves. The tragedian Euripides (d. 406 BCE) was reputed to have acquired for his own pleasure and personal use a library of considerable size. By the early fourth century BCE, Plato had established his Academy, with a library, followed in time by Aristotle, whose Lyceum claimed a large and diverse collection of books. Beneath the lighter soils of busy message sending, graffiti, legal bulls, commercial contracts, and ledger keeping, we see a more profound literacy sinking its roots and yearly growing stronger.

The novelty of a vibrant alphabetizing public was so remarkable that it soon provided meat for jokes. The works of Aristophanes (ca. 448–ca. 388 BCE) contain numerous references to 'books' and reading. By way of example, here is a chorus from *The Frogs* (406? BCE). It is singing exuberantly about the audience it faces—an Athenian audience of some four to seven thousand—which is not to say they could all read effortlessly, but only that most would be sufficiently initiated to enjoy a flattering tease:

> They've all got textbooks now
> However high your brow,
> They won't be shaken.
>
> No talking down to these:
> That's all outdated!
> For native wit alone
> They're highly rated;
> But now they've learnt to read
> It's real tough stuff they need;
> They don't want chicken-feed—
> They're educated![15] (Ar., *Frogs.* 1112–19)

With practice came ease and with ease came numerous indications of increasing alphabetized volubility—on pots, tombs, steles, and walls—arousing, one might have supposed, intimations of uniformity: uniformity of the letters themselves, their alignment, the spacing and separation of words, and a protocol for cadence. *But no.* Constancy in these matters would need more time to settle. The ride from a thought into speech and on into writing was proving to be bumpy. How lucky we are today, in that both writers and readers have learned to work so smoothly in harness.

Some Practical Considerations
for Setting Pen to Paper

To appreciate how a misalignment between a writer's intention and his reader's understanding might have surfaced in the wake of early alphabetic literacy, imagine the following statement in its spoken form.

My mother said your father stole my pig and ran away.

Unaware of the benefits of consistency, even in matters of letter formation, an early scribe might have dealt with our sentence like this:

$$\mathcal{M}_Y {}^M {}_O {}^{\Upsilon} {}_{H} {}^{\boxminus} {}_{R}$$

But suppose the message was intended to convey this:

"My mother," said your father, "stole my pig and ran away."

or:

My mother said, "Your father stole my pig and ran away."

Talking voices have little trouble distinguishing such differences. But writing can easily fail us. Without punctuation points to indicate pauses, or quotation marks to differentiate the speaker from his speech, intended meanings can crash.

Though letter making grew more uniform over time and lines became straight, not all scribes saw reason to individuate words. Still very much orally oriented in those early times, they wrote the language as they heard it: from the grinding monotone of dictation or in their heads as they murmured what they were copying and sometimes did not understand. It is easy to see how the slow advance of the writing tool on papyrus might have flattened the rise and fall of a scribe's murmuring intonation, obliterated his sense of pause between word groups, and moved his attention from meaning towards getting the sequence of phonemes into consistent alphabet letters.

A modern reader should take a moment to appreciate how speaking aloud tends to favor syllable groups over words. Speech puts great emphasis on vocality—that is, the voice sounds of the vowels when not stopped by consonants. As in a song, the spoken syllables flow seamlessly, playing havoc with the integrity of words while relying heavily on pitch and rhythm to achieve the wanted transfer of meaning. For exercise, pronounce this statement:

Fair love you faint with wandering in the wood.

You will most likely find that, if you speak to bring out the meaning, what you actually say is more akin to this:

Fairlove youfaint withwanderinginthewood

in which the words seem melded into groups.

Where a word string contains syllables with sounds that smoothly combine, the words themselves will flow in groups when spoken. In the sample sentence above, the amalgamated syllables are easy to pronounce as a group. Note how easily the *r* and *l* in the address "fairlove" unite; they blend their sounds as naturally as do the *n* and *d* in "wandering." But that is not the case with the *nt* (of "faint") and the *w* (of "with").

To experience the visual confusion transpiring from a compacted unpunctuated line, try this one:

It'ssounlikeherleavingherbasketinthebullrushes!

Here, it takes the reader a moment of adjustment before his eye can gather up the meaning of *It's so unlike* with its low-lying, minim-prone letters *o*, *u*, and *n*—which, when subjected to the idiosyncrasies of script, tend to look confusingly alike. Once those opening letters have been sorted out, the remaining bit can be broken apart more easily, thanks to the consonantal risers in the letters *l*, *k*, *h*, and *l* that swoop above the body of the letter and in some hands trespass into the line above. The letter *g*, on the other hand, has a descender, which also helps the meaning to percolate intelligibly. But even with its risers and descenders, the above letter-compacted line can still project possible other words (words incompatible with the intended sense) and distract our attention with irrelevant choices. Here, with little effort we can pick out unwanted words: *herb, ask, as, tin, tint.* In the world of sound, those potential intrusions remain quiescent. In the given example, even syllable interpuncts (mid-letter-height dots often found in ancient inscriptions and epigraphs) would have illumined the meaning of our sentence more helpfully.

It's·so·un·like·her·leav·ing·her·bas·ket·in·the·bul·rush·es!

Be that as it may, word separation is not so crucial to a beginner reader, who, unless taught otherwise, will tend to tackle an alphabetized statement letter by letter, relying on his aural memory to recognize the moment when a word has been formed.

Though plainly interrelated, writing and reading are fundamentally in opposition. In early years a would-be writer, once he had mastered the newly invented alphabet, could begin immediately to extrude his preoccupations into letters, phoneme by phoneme, and henceforth shower the world with them, because he *knew what he wanted to say*. For a reader tracking the unknown, the task was never so easy, for the alphabetized words demanded of him a persistent neurophysiological reference to the *unheard* sound signaled by each rarely uniform handwritten letter. Let us consider more closely the labors of an ancient murmuring novice reader. If word meanings are to be decoded from the individual phonemes of lettered clues, then a complex cerebral networking will be involved, for the mind must operate through a circuitry of eye and ear, memory and tongue. A slow-motion replay of the action might turn out to be something like this:

"This letter," says Eye to Ear, "is a *b*."
"It will make a *buh* sound," prompts Memory.
"Gotcha," says Ear.
"Say '*buh*,' Tongue."
"*Buh*," says Tongue.
"Tongue just said '*buh*,'" says Ear.
"OK," says Memory. "Keep going, Eye. Let's try the next one."

As we have seen, a message made up of ideogram-logographs (like Chinese kanji) works differently. With its ancient oral-pictorial aspects worn away, a kanji routes more directly into the mind's memory bank via the eye. That same logographic access may also be achieved by an alphabetically written word when it lies distinct in a surround of white. There, with repeated practice, the eye will perceive it as a discrete image and hence skip the slowing vocal interface.[16] A child learning to read will fight each phoneme of the word C-A-T for a short time, but then begin to pick up the meaning by glimpsing the whole word-image as a logographical lump. Words whose letters are bunched, or do not lie on the line and are not uniformly shaped, impede this immediate logographical intake.

Extant pieces of early writing show that, initially, uniformity of design and layout was not a valued benefit. Scribes seemed oblivious to the wants of their readers. They formed their letters every which way. They lined them up from bottom to top; top to bottom; left to right; right to left; or back and forth and back again, from margin to margin as an ox plows a field (in 'boustrophedon' style); or spiraled them prettily outwards from center to margin. Indeed, at the inception of alphabet writing, reading was plagued by the lack of consistency, and deciphering a text seemed akin to working a puzzle. The rapport between eye and ear was not yet a smooth one.

On the Powers of Grammar

All languages are made up of bits of sound that human physiological systems are able to handle. Noam Chomsky's *deep structure grammar* is grounded on the human's underlying, universal, linguistic capability—a capability activated by a kind of neurological power source that is in place and ready for action shortly after birth. It is a genetic endowment whose function is to shield us against that birthing-time onslaught of perception and relates us to the outer world. As it sifts and sorts the mess of new sensations, teaching us how to differentiate, so it readies our newborn minds for a lifetime of talk in the *surface grammar* of our environment, be it England, or anywhere else. Strengthened by linguistic interaction, that native surface language more or less fixes during adolescence.

It is interesting to notice that Chomsky imagines the activities of his substructural grammar as somewhat resembling those of the visual cortex, which has well understood innate devices for ordering perception. Especially relevant to our topic is the binary aspect of the eye's physiology, namely its cones and rods. The eye-to-brain system works by the superimposition of a particular figure (say, a tree) sharp-focused by the retina's cones against its background (say, a forest) scanned by its rods. This play of contrasts—the specific against the general—would appear to be basic to our perceptual intake.[17]

We shall be increasingly aware of our pairing 'specific against general' inclinations as we move on with our story. Being somewhat dual ourselves—twinned in limb as well as brain—we are in thrall to dualities: light against dark, left against right, sound against silence, movement against stillness. Both visually and aurally we cope best when faced with *something* that is relieved by *something else*, and that in turn can be *nothing*. The ancient use of antitheses and parallels (as in the Old Testament) tells us that the human mind has long been comfortable with its two-way mode of perceiving reality.

Surface grammars—that is, the grammars of the world's various mother tongues—are very different from Chomsky's deep structure grammar. Surface grammar is the product of environment; whereas the so-called deep-structure grammar is innate in all humans. There are many hundreds of surface grammars—each with its own set of conventions and rules. The systematized languages that humans actually speak are the result of concurrence amongst people who have over time been geographically close and so have interacted with each other. The characteristics peculiar to each of these surface tongues were initially determined by the group experience of their speakers as they strove to communicate with increasing degrees of specificity.

Like that of any spoken language, the grammar of English is a surface grammar. Its rules are learned so that communication may succeed within its area of jurisdiction. The output of each surface grammar is retrievable by fellow speakers. In the case of languages in the Indo-European family, kindred grammatical conventions control the syntax (i.e., the arrangement of words and word-strings within a statement), verb tenses (past, present, future, etc.), their moods (imperative, subjunctive, indicative, etc.); and the use of inflection instead of agglutination. As Lewis Carroll so well illustrated in his poem beginning "*'Twas brillig, and the slithy toves / Did gyre and gimble in the wabe…*," grammar is the activating propellant of all languages; its force is separate from its semantic partner. We can see this truth more readily, perhaps, in the following light-hearted analysis:

> Suppose someone were to assert: The gostak distims the doshes. You do not know what this means; nor do I. But if we assume that it is English, we know that the doshes are distimmed by the gostak. We know too that one distimmer of doshes is a gostak. If, moreover, the doshes are galloons, we know that some galloons are distimmed by the gostak. And so we may go on, and so we often do go on.[18]

The validity of Chomsky's thesis—that the human brain is born neurologically prepared to participate in full-bodied linguistic activity—is fortified by the way that hybrid languages appear to be formed, as well as by the fact that sign languages for the deaf are governed by complete grammars. Like hearing children, young signers acquire a marvelous, totally facile communicating ability when they, too, engage with their grammar early enough—that is, during their critical first four years.[19]

Grammar controls our talk by interconnecting the ear, the mouth, and the mind. Its source, we conclude, must be regulated by some kind of logic. What exactly that logic might be, we do not know. Cognitive science peters out at this twilit frontier, leaving us to pick our way from insight to insight. Until our scientists and neurosurgeons can fully illumine the mysteries of the human brain, we are obliged to think of grammar only vaguely, as a responding reflex to our inherent, ill-understood need for order.

In general usage the word *grammar* covers the principles for sentence structure (namely, matters of formation, syntax, governance, reference, and cadencing) as well as the diction evolved from the received practice of 'proper' word use.

Scriptura Continua: **An Impediment to Literacy**

Word separation (that is, the separation of written words by means of white space) was a 'natural feature' of writing in Chinese kanji, but common as well in the scripts of other recorded languages—such as Sumerian, Phoenician, and Hebrew. It would seem that from earliest times the integrity of all words was a recognized feature. Their distinct, individual identity was markedly exposed in writing. Given that, it is a mystery why the Greeks began to connect their letters into long strings with no spaces between words—a style of writing that came to be known as *scriptura continua* (see fig. 2.2). Perhaps the inclusion of vowel representation (the unique feature of their alphabet) was a culpable factor, since it allowed the inner or mental voice to ride along as it does in speech, without imperative breaks between consecutive words. Greek was a notably vocalized language, full of vowels that united syllables into unbroken song. If you try pronouncing the first line of the *Iliad* (herewith transcribed), you will see how the many vowels needing to be pronounced almost force you to sing.

> May-nin a-ei-de, the-a, Pay-lay-i-a-do Ak-i lay-os
> Anger sing, goddess, of the son of Peleus Achilles
> (Sing of the wrath, O goddess, of Achilles, the son of Peleus)

Another culprit in inspiring word jamming might have been the labor required to smooth a stone's surface for writing. Once the space had been prepared, it was surely obvious that more letters could be inscribed by closing the gaps between words. But however it happened, *scriptura continua* became a revered precedent and the increasingly common arrangement for setting down text on papyrus. Even when papyrus was easily procurable and making space massively available, the revered custom of cramming continued. As time passed and readers became more numerous, orderers of 'books' continued to prefer that all page space be packed with as much verbiage as possible; for even good quality papyrus was never as cheap or handy to deal with as paper is today. 'Books' at this stage would have been papyrus sheets glued together and wound into scrolls—functional, but ungainly to handle. The handier codex (the form of book we know today) became popular later when papyrus was hard to find and reading was a more universal skill. When the breakup of Egypt in the seventh century CE diminished the commercial production of papyrus, parchment (prepared skins of goats and sheep) was used to replace it. Being extremely expensive, its use in cheaper editions encouraged a multitude of skimping frugalities, such as the reduction of alphabet letter size, the cramming of words on a line, the elimination of verbs of *being*, the abbreviation of common words and their inflections, and for an extra squeeze, the contraction of margins. In the fullness of its glory, *scriptura continua* amassed pages of un-interrupted, handwritten lettering with the occasional marginal paragraphic signal to indicate a new topic, and a few questionable scatterings of marks to indicate pause.[20] With the easy delineation of words no longer possible, a reader was forced to roll up his sleeves and fight for comprehension.

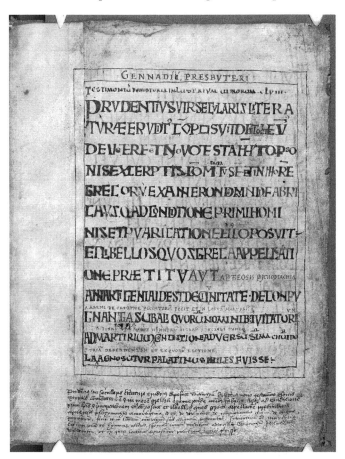

Fig. 2.2: *Scriptura continua*

The page shown here (from MS023) is a presentation inscription, recording the gift of this book, a late tenth-century English manuscript containing the works of Prudentius (fl. 384–410) and Orosius (fl. 375–418), to Malmesbury Abbey. The squeezed-to-gether words give a good idea of the difficulties a reader might have had deciphering scriptura continua. *Courtesy of Parker Library, Corpus Christi College, Cambridge.*

The aura of intellectuality emanating from a compacted Greek *scriptura-continua* text would become an attraction for the culture-craving Roman literaries of the second century BCE. 'Tam educati quam illi sumus' ('We're as educated as they are'), said they, and promptly jammed their Latin lines to prove it. But alas for the poor reader, whose eyes for centuries would now have to struggle to match what his ears could so easily do. "Weneryegoin?" is inelegant to hear, but assimilable. Visually, it is more of a puzzle.

In the early centuries of Greek writing, the positioning of words for their sound was extremely important—even for matters of urgency—for it was still an oral-aural world. An ideal statement, one that would successfully please, instruct, or persuade, required both music for the ear and sense for the mind. A shift in 'natural' word order for the achievement of that goal made the extraction of meaning harder. When 'unnatural word order' is embedded in a tract of *scriptura continua*, the effort required to gather in its meaning quite plainly increases.

English poetry has its own history of rearranging, inverting, and condensing phrases in order to create rhymes and maintain rhythms. The following lines are taken from John Donne's address to Death:

> From Rest and Sleep, which but thy picture be,
> Much pleasure, then from thee much more must flow...

Here the poet is counting on the reader's ingenuity to extract his ingenious meaning. He has dropped the understood opening 'Since/Because' as well as the verb (possibly 'flows') and, moreover, attached the 'which' clause to the already out-of-position prepositional phrase and moved the lot to precede the subject 'much pleasure.' Thus, for the sake of sound, Donne has encased a meaty conceit in a hard-shelled brainteaser. In naturally ordered, fully expressed English, the meaning is essentially this: *Since, O Death, much pleasure flows from rest and sleep (which is nothing more than a shadowy image of you), then, much more pleasure must flow from the actual you.*

In ancient Greece where the spoken word was everything, not only poets *but also prose writers* reorganized the 'natural' flow of the language in search of sonorous ear-gratifying effects. Imagine, then, the reader's plight when scribes began to jam those crucial inflections (the very keys to decipherment) against neighboring but unrelated words, and then, perversely, confusingly, *insanely*, dropped and/or abbreviated them. Yet despite its contortions, *scriptura continua* enjoyed a long and hardy life in the history of literature. Requiring huge effort to decipher the meaning, such writing impeded the development of the reading eye for many, many centuries.

The fundamental tension between eye and ear—our two most powerful instruments for the intake of information—is well documented by the outcomes of schoolroom punctuation exercises, where the perceived need for commas and periods can often vary. In cultures where the writing does not provide an individuating space between words, the procedures are more difficult, for the children must be drilled *to distinguish words*. The syllabic kana of a modern Japanese text, for example, are strung—sometimes in lengthy groups without significant spaces between—here and there amongst the stand-alone, whole-word, logographic kanji. The reader is expected to scan the line, differentiating the meaningful kana units as he goes along. He is helped by particles, those essentially meaningless words (like *wa*) that are inserted into a statement to act as guides to the overall wanted meaning. In English, a particle, like *when*, indicates a time function of a sentence segment; *but* or *however* give notice of contrariness; the words *and, moreover,* and *furthermore* tell us that something will be added to whatever has already been said. In Japanese a reader is also helped by the convention that the subject-predicate-verb order will generally obtain; and modernly also, by paragraph indentations, commas, and periods. Word boundaries are obvious only in the visual integrity of each kanji logogram, and *not* in the aural-based kana syllable-strings. Japanese youngsters *must be taught* how to extract the integral words from a *continuum* of such kana syllables when they occur amongst the more eye-demanding messages of the kanji logograms. A line of Japanese kana (hiragana in this case) may looks like this:

ゆみこはしょくどうにいってすしをたべます。

It is a full sentence which means, "This evening Yumiko will go to a restaurant and eat sushi." In its second rendering beneath, the individual words are separated by slashes (virgules).

ゆみこは／しょくどうに／いって／すしを／たべます。
[yu mi ko wa/ sh yo ku do-u ta/ it su te/ su soi o/ ta be ma su.]

There are many ways besides that of creating space to guide the eye in marking off words and phrases. Slashes (or virgules) have done the job in the past, but parentheses, too, could be used (as in the computer language Lisp), as well as varying type sizes. Interpuncts can still be found embellishing the title pages of classy books. Alfred Knopf was devoted to them. In the world of computers, letters are coded as numbers (known as the ASCII code numbers), and in order to save space in computer document storage, several word processing programs have been designed with alternative means of separating the words. A notable one, for example, identifies the last letter in each word by the addition of 128 to its ASCII code number. The result is effectively like this:

jim128wants128three128beers128.

Interestingly, the eventual acceptance of sheer space (interpretable as 'nothing') suggests the silence (again, a kind of 'nothing') that surrounds words when they are spoken emphatically or purposefully, one at a time. However, the artificiality of that between-word white space becomes immediately apparent with the realization that in the aural domain (the home site of all language), word clusters are the full-bodied structures of meaning, whereas individual words are only their parts. For example, within a spoken sentence, the phrase *in order to* (pronounced *inorderto*—with the rhythm *de-dee-de-de*) easefully guides the receiving mind to a specific expectation. You might even say *I'm going to the market dedeedede buy peaches* and be successfully understood—understood, for the reason that the three words (which can be broken apart and used in a multitude of other phrases) are compacted into a single meaningful lump with an easily recognizable rhythm and sentence position. On the other hand, if you were to say *"in* (pause) *order* (pause) *to* (pause)" with no variance of rhythm or pitch, the hearer would be pushed to work harder than he would thank you for. The insubstantiality of what English speakers consider to be words is in this way faintly reminiscent of the more extreme Chinese syllabic vocables as described previously (by Shlain).

* * * * *

We may now zoom in on ear-eye interactions and thus begin the story of their enforced marriage in the opening market for alphabetic writing. The ear will come first, for in the world of communication, it was the first to deal with words.

Notes

1. Fischer, *A History of Language*. Fischer provides a splendid account of the features of animal communication.
2. Nicholas Ostler, *Empires of the World: A Language History of the World* (London: Harper Perennial, 2005), 10–11.
3. Philip Lieberman, "On the Evolution of Language," *SFI Proceedings*, 11:21–39.

4. Deacon, "Brain-Language Coevolution," *SFI Proceedings*, 11:77.

5. Andrew Robinson, "Writing Systems," in *The Oxford Companion to the Book* (Oxford: Oxford University Press, 2010), 1:2.

6. University of Cambridge Digital Library, cudl.lib.cam.ac.uk/view/MS-DOC-000829.

7. Robinson, "Writing Systems," 1:2.

8. Ibid.

9. The kanji was originally pictorial and the kana purely aural.

10. Victor H. Rosen, "Strephosymbolia," paper presented at the New York Psychoanalytic Society meeting, January 11, 1955. The subject deals with the not-uncommon failure to synthesize the function of the phonetic qualities of a word with its visual elements. The author identifies this same kind of failure as a contributing source for one aspect of dyslexia.

11. As in u for "you," 4 for "for," r for "are," etc. But because of the dearth of commercial evidence in the early alphabetized inscriptions in Greece, a number of scholars have postulated that the alphabet was not invented for commerce but to record the oral epics of Homer in the eighth century BCE. (See Robinson, "Writing Systems," 6.)

12. Robinson, "Writing Systems," 1:7.

13. Alphabet letters being only 'rough draft' indicators for speech sound, phoneticists have developed an International Phonetic Alphabet, based on the "principle of strict one-to-one correspondence between sounds and symbols" (*Oxford English Dictionary*, 1st ed.). The symbols of this extensive alphabet attempt to track all the minute variations of mouth sounds in all languages—a very ambitious goal and, of course, not perfectly attainable.

14. Rosalind Thomas, *Literacy and Orality in Ancient Greece* (Cambridge: Cambridge University Press, 1995), 64. In matters of early alphabetic literacy, I have been especially helped by the scholarship of Rosalind Thomas in her two classic studies, *Literacy and Orality in Ancient Greece*, and *Oral Tradition and Written Record in Classical Athens* (Cambridge: Cambridge University Press, 1989); and also that of Gregory Crane, *The Blinded Eye: Thucydides and the New Written Word* (Lanham, MD: Rowman & Littlefield, 1996).

15. Aristophanes, and David Barrett, *The Frogs, and Other Plays* (Baltimore: Penguin Books, 1964), 146–97. The audience figures come from the calculations of Eric Csapo, "The Men Who Built the Theatre: The Theatropolai, Theatronai, and Arkhitektones," 96–100, in *The Greek Theatre and Festivals Documentary Studies*, ed. Peter Wilson (Oxford: Oxford University Press, 2007).

16. Paul Saenger, *Space between Words: The Origins of Silent Reading* (Stanford, CA: Stanford University Press, 1997), 4. When writing this, Mr. Saenger was the rare book curator at the Newberry Library in Chicago, and his excellent book is essentially a learned history of silent reading.

17. See Richard Gregory, "The Grammar of Vision," *Listener* 83 (February 1970): 242–6; and reprinted in his book *Concepts and Mechanisms of Perception* (London: Duckworth, 1975), 622–9.

18. This passage, by an unidentified "able but little known writer," is found in C. K. Ogden and I. A. Richards, *The Meaning of Meaning: A Study of the Influence of Language upon Thought and the Science of Symbolism* (London: Ark Paperbacks, 1985), 46.

19. Oliver Sacks, *Seeing Voices: A Journey into the World of the Deaf* (Berkeley: University of California Press, 1989), 118. According to Sacks, the "acquisition of Sign grammar occurs

in much the same way and at much the same age as the grammar of speech, it seems likely that the deep structure of both is identical. Certainly, the propositional power…and formal properties of both are identical, even though they involve…different types of signals, different kinds of information, different sensory systems, different memory structures, and perhaps different neural structures."

20. Saenger, *Space between Words*, 9–10.

References

Aristophanes, and David Barrett. *The Frogs, and Other Plays*. Baltimore: Penguin Books, 1964.

Crane, Gregory. *The Blinded Eye: Thucydides and the New Written Word*. Lanham, MD: Rowman & Littlefield, 1996.

Csapo, Eric. "The Men Who Built the Theatre: The Theatropolai, Theatronai, and Arkhitektones." In *The Greek Theatre and Festivals Documentary Studies*. Edited by Peter Wilson. Oxford: Oxford University Press, 2007.

Deacon, "Brain-Language Coevolution." In *The Evolution of Human Languages: Proceedings of the Workshop on the Evolution of Human Languages*. Santa Fe, New Mexico, August 1989. Edited by John A. Hawkins and Murray Gell-Mann. Reading, MA: Addison-Wesley, 1992.

Fischer, Steven Roger. *A History of Language*. London: Reaction Books, 1999.

Gregory, Richard. "The Grammar of Vision." *Listener* 83 (February 1970): 242–6. Reprinted in his book *Concepts and Mechanisms of Perception*. London: Duckworth, 1975.

Lieberman, Philip. "On the Evolution of Language." In *The Evolution of Human Languages: Proceedings of the Workshop on the Evolution of Human Languages*. Santa Fe, New Mexico, August 1989. Edited by John A. Hawkins and Murray Gell-Mann. Reading, MA: Addison-Wesley, 1992.

Ogden, C. K., and I. A. Richards. *The Meaning of Meaning: A Study of the Influence of Language upon Thought and the Science of Symbolism*. London: Ark Paperbacks, 1985.

Ostler, Nicholas. *Empires of the World: A Language History of the World*. London: Harper Perennial, 2005.

Robinson, Andrew. "Writing Systems." In Vol. 1 of *The Oxford Companion to the Book*. Edited by Michael F. Suarez and H. R. Woudhuysen. Oxford: Oxford University Press, 2010.

Rosen, Victor H. "Strephosymbolia." Paper presented at the New York Psychoanalytic Society meeting, January 11, 1955.

Sacks, Oliver. *Seeing Voices: A Journey into the World of the Deaf*. Berkeley: University of California Press, 1989.

Saenger, Paul. *Space between Words: The Origins of Silent Reading*. Stanford, CA: Stanford University Press, 1997.

Thomas, Rosalind. *Literacy and Orality in Ancient Greece*. Cambridge: Cambridge University Press, 1995.

———. *Oral Tradition and Written Record in Classical Athens*. Cambridge: Cambridge University Press, 1989.

· 3 ·

ORALITY—ITS CHARACTERISTICS

Oral Habits Have Deep Roots

Although spaces between words can be seen on extant seventh-century BCE Greek inscriptions and subsequent papyri, they were not consistently or even commonly used in texts until more than a millennium later—so much does habit mesmerize the mind. The slow adoption of what would have made reading easier supports recent opinion: *that the impact of early writing on oral attitudes was not very extensive.* It would seem that despite the substantial presence of literate intellectuals, Classical Athens—the Western world's hub of intellectuality and pre-Christian culture in the fifth and fourth centuries BCE—remained essentially a talking city: that is, a city that relied on its read-write capacity only superficially and preferred oral attestation for matters of consequence. Until the establishment of the Alexandrian library (ca. 200 BCE), we have little evidence of literacy in the sense that we think of it today. The modern word 'literacy' includes in its meaning an ability to write and read easefully; and with that, a confidence in handling associated literary activities: cataloguing, record-keeping, dating, and retrieval. One must not assume too much when 'books' and 'documents' are mentioned in extant inscriptions, texts, and graffiti from earlier periods.[1] Those uneven scribblings, mentions

of laborious decipherments, and the persistent faith in the mystical empower-
ment of letters do not signal a true and broadly adopted literacy.

'Literate' early Greece was in fact steeped in oral habit. How else might
we account for the fact that the direction of writing did not (even in the
classical fifth century) flow regularly from left to right? that spacing between
words, though it appeared sporadically in the early alphabetized years, did
not take hold vigorously across the board? that the continuing fashion of in-
scribing individual alphabet letters in an ornamental grid pattern (known as
stoichedon) broke words at line endings in an interruptive and disconcerting
way? that the dating of documents by Olympiads (as in *The year that Menippus
raced his horses to victory*) did not begin until 500 BCE nor develop thereafter
in helpful, unambiguous ways? that despite the establishment (in the late fifth
century) of a so-called central archive, there were no lists of citizens nor were
there land registers until the late fourth century? Perhaps most telling of all
are the clay shards of popular curse tablets, on which the lettering of the name
of the one to be cursed was often reversed or turned upside-down or deformed,
as though to transmit to him or her some extra dose of evil.

Despite these deficiencies, there is some evidence of literacy in the mid-
sixth century BCE as well as small schools (for boys); but a general facility
with the written word was slow-growing and more prevalent by far amongst
the privileged. However much acquainted with the formalities of writing
some might have been, before 325 BCE (the beginning of the Hellenistic
Period) there were in fact no centralized, or government sponsored, or sub-
sidized school systems in Attica to initiate or support a high level of general
public literacy.[2] In flourishing Classical Greek cities, access to a schoolmaster
was limited to the upper social levels. Though one cannot know for sure,
scholarly conjecture tells us that during that time, only some 20 percent of
Greek-speaking city populations were full-fledged reading and writing literates and that for the most part they were the privileged members of wealthy
and socially elite families.[3]

Nevertheless, we owe much to that 'some 20 percent.' They took the tentative first steps into the world of literature, and it was they who made it
habitable. By the mid-fifth century BCE, it was thought that if a legal affair
was expected to be large and detailed, one would be compelled to commit it
to writing, since the person reporting on it would be unable to recall it in its
entirety. By the last decades of the fifth century, literates had increased in
numbers and were becoming more and more dependent on the written word.
But because a usable archival system was so beyond the ken of the times, the

developing legal practice was to have the written versions of contracts *supple-ment* (not duplicate) the oral ones, and to have both versions attested to by live witnesses. When the time came to consult and enforce those agreements, the words could then be reinterpreted jointly, both by readers of what had been written and by 'rememberers' of what had been spoken.

Indeed, the tide was turning. Yet 'book'-oriented and 'pen'-fluent cultivated literates were still obliged to conduct their affairs with folk who were not, and hence in an ambiance that was fluid and changeable. The lack of document storage technology, for example, in the fifth and fourth centuries meant that much went on by announcement and hearsay. That, in turn, meant that government decrees could vary or conflict, or be delayed, outmoded, or even *un*proclaimed without notice or warning, in outskirt sections of the city.

Imagine the feeling. At cock's crow, Kurios Petros lifts himself from his couch in a sweat. *Will yesterday's transaction in the markets of Athens' downtown agora be recognized as legal today in his Kephisia neighborhood? And if not, will he be accused of deceit and thrown into prison?* The sense that nothing holds, that whatever one strives to do might in a flash and without warning be undone, is intolerable to a highly literate mind. The very word 'literate' subsumes some sense of stability and likely fulfillment of expectation. For those straddling the oral-literate borderline, it was both natural and wise to keep hold of the traditional, ear-oriented skills.

And indeed, we find that that is what they did. Well into the fifth century BCE, even among those who could handle their letters, writing was viewed with suspicion. To some, undoubtedly, it represented a kind of opportunity, but for many it was considered entrapping in a way that the spoken word never was. Agreements, promises, and treaties, when inscribed on stone *stelai* (monumental pillars) for the public to examine and adjudge, were less flexible, less deniable, less re-interpretable than the early classical mind could easily come to terms with. Whereas the spoken word could be recanted, denied, or (with a shift of emphasis) modified, the written word seemed intolerably fixed, whether it was true to the original intention or might be inconvenient to deal with later on. In his *History of the Peloponnesian War*, Thucydides reports the popular anger aroused by the trickery that some written statements were perceived to conceal.[4]

We cannot with certainty gauge the overall importance of written language in fifth-century civil administration because of the impermanency of papyrus on which government concerns would have been set down. Nevertheless, scholars of these matters assure us that the number of inscribed stones erected to inform the man on the street of official happenings grew by leaps and bounds between the years 470 and 430 BCE. Originally, these stones had been cut to mark real-estate boundaries or to record the memorable sayings of great men and poets. But as their usefulness became more apparent, their numbers increased rapidly to include civic and business matters: tribute lists (for taxes owed), building specifications, edicts, remembrances of martial exploits, ledger accounts of the colonies, and so on.

As time passed, of course, dependence on the written word grew. A landmark moment was reached in the fourth century, about the year 337 BCE, when Lycurgus, at the height of his power in the Athenian government, commanded that the works of the great fifth-century Attic tragedians (Aeschylus, Sophocles, and Euripides) be written down in definitive, authorized versions, from which actors in the future might not lawfully depart.[5] This fourth-century historic edict stands witness to the superior claim that reading and writing were increasingly exercising over memorization and speech. Yet despite all, fourth-century Athens continued to be a city of commissioned heralds who *orally announced* commands, news, and invitations. Between performances, the classical tragedies were still commonly *read aloud* by the secretary of the polis. The growing body of written materials was generally the work of official logographers ('word writers' who prepared legal notes and recorded speeches, edicts, geographical discoveries, and the like) and scribes (whose job was to write letters and read back ledgers).

In such a scene, it was not a needful thing to be exquisitely calligraphic, for it was not likely that your fellow citizens would disdain some little roughness in your letter-making skills. Literacy being still very young, the influence that it would grow to have, both on the mind and on the eventual habits of speech, had barely begun. Meanwhile, writers of prose sought their effects from the familiar ear-biased medium of oratory, whose ploys and conceits, exalted diction, formalities, and layout of argument were the artistically crafted extensions of speech. Good orators were admired for the beauty of their rhythms, the purity of their word choice, their application of imagery, and for the avoidance of unattractive consonantal juxtapositions (as in, say, the word pair 'old thrushes' with its awkward adjacency of *ld* and *th*). While they spoke in prose and connived to outwit, they had all been honed on the subtleties of poetry.

Poetry, with its collection of rules to pleasure the ear, had infected the habits of orators, whose elegant speeches were the admired precedents for important prose—and particularly that of history. Basically, there were two kinds of oratory. In *civil oratory* (where the goal was to persuade one's political opponents or to curry favor from a jury), it was good practice to package one's argument neatly, in assimilable structures that could elicit emotion with controlled stateliness. *Epideictic oratory* was a different sort of animal—its purpose being to praise a victory or the achievements of someone deceased, and while doing so to set an inspiring example. For that, sweeping rhythmical phrases and exalted language were used. But epideictic rhetoric could expand or contract, for it was useful too in advertising one's personal skills, for lecturing, or selling something. When unshackled, the epideictic practitioner could let loose with sweeping rhythmical phrases in a mode closer to poetry than to ordinary speech. But of course, a mix was always acceptable; for it is better to speak with some degree of eloquence when persuading, as well as with some degree of sound sense when trying to be eloquent.

These differing oratorical intentions (the civil and the epideictic) may reasonably be considered to be the progenitors of two (still hotly alive) contrasting writing styles: the plain sort of prose ('Be terse, be exact—lean, not fat'); and the grand one ('extend for the pleasure of beauty and wit—time can wait'). In evaluating the oratorical successes of each of these styles, it is worth noting that a mix of interesting rhythms, imagery, careful repetition, paraphrasing, antithesis, and rhetorical questions to engage the audience *actually does* increase the ease with which long stretches of speech-making can be aurally absorbed. With the inception of writing, those helpful devices (inherited from oral poetry by way of a speaker's podium) were transferred to the page, where they rained their blessings in visual form for many centuries and even now (though repressed) influence the practice of writing. In early days, their exuberant presence dominated prose manuscripts—usefully, one must suppose, since writing was by custom re-rendered aloud. We shall inspect some of those tricks-of-the-trade shortly, and while doing so, take note of the long, complicated written structures they tended to generate—structures not disciplined by today's dot-on-the-line full stops (which had not yet been adopted), but instead by *other dividing and cadencing signals*.

Turning again to the root causes for the long-lived, word-jamming *scriptura continua*: along with the previously mentioned effects of monotone dictation was the ever ready-to-swell intellectual ego. As a member of the privileged elite, an orator, politician, philosopher, poet, or historian would have viewed himself as something of a guru informing the ignorant multitudes. It was up to *them* to retrieve the meaning of whatever he wrote, not up to *him* to invent some newfangled writing rule to accommodate their dim wittedness. Words encoded in letters have always aroused a worshipful attitude in those who cannot easily read—a useful truth, not lost on wily ancient authors. Also to be blamed for the lingering acceptance of *scriptura continua* is the 'why-bother?' presumption that everybody would know what those cramped letters were about anyway. Since the canon of literature was derived from old and familiar oral materials, their textual versions could to some extent be viewed as mnemonic—mere reminders, so to speak, as to whether it was Thursday or Friday that Paris whisked Helen off to his waiting ship.

In early times, to learn a prayer, a speech, or a poem, or to recall the already familiar details of a contract or an edict, the solitary reader needed only enough reading experience to winkle out the familiar syllables, and tongue them for his ear. A man who was to read aloud to others would prepare his rendition (his *praelectio*, as the Latins would come to call it) in advance by converting each alphabetic symbol back into sound and practicing it for easy replay.[6] Thus, tediously, through trial and error, he would restore the integrity of each word in its word group and arrive by spurts at the sense. Aside from a small portion of that literate 'some 20 percent,' it is unlikely that anyone read, or was expected to read, with immediate comprehension.

For all these reasons, early literacy might best be thought of as a 'phonetic literacy' whose exercise lay in rooting out sense from an avalanche of undifferentiated words, and sentence structures without boundaries. To improve one's chances of comprehension, long practice was needed—as was the mastery of grammar, the foreknowledge of context, and some instinct for the ways of language. More than a passive pleasure, reading was an arduous exercise: first to exhume what the text might mean, and then to argue about it with all one's disagreeing friends.

Whatever the high or low purpose of cramming words might have been, it assured the good health of oral attitudes and interfered with the progress of easy reading. The deciphering skills that readers acquired in their unremitting battle with compacted lines might well have discouraged scribes from improving their scribal techniques. But gradually, in different localities and epochs, improvements in clarity and retrievability developed. Texts came to be fractured (or, as Saenger says, "aerated") in a succession of ways: by groupings of letters or syllables between white spaces; by marking off (usually by virgules, or slashes) the recognized phrasal and clausal units; and by the device of *per cola per commata* (through *colons* and *commas*—a technique to be discussed later). Thwarting these moves came the popular use of ligatures (the connecting strokes that tied letters together as modernly found in such as *fl, ff,* and *ae* when rendered in print), abbreviations, and the leaving out of 'obvious' verbs. It was as though some sumptuary edict were in force to restrict readerly comforts. In Latin, space between words did not become an expectable feature until the tenth century CE. In Greek, serious vacillation from division to nondivision of words would continue much longer. Even today, in the Peloponnesus and Cycladic islands, eighteenth-century CE writings on church walls stand witness to the durability of *scriptura continua*. Its very venerability would seem to have made it holy.

For too long a time, punctuation points and spaces would not regularly be present to indicate the pauses and cadences of the speaking voice. Aurally biased scribes did not sufficiently appreciate the fact that words, however tightly strung when sounded, represent separate concepts and retain those concepts even when being recombined. Not until the scanning eye had matured would that fact succeed in giving the boot to *scriptura continua*.

The Ear-Eye Split, as Recorded in Punctuation

In the artificial environment of writing, punctuation is the big-league broker for the exchange of ideas between author and reader. Thoughtful authors, who keep their stalking readers firmly in mind, break up their word mass for easy consumption.

Personal views of what works best in the way of signaling pause or full cadence in a text is, and has always been, highly varied. There is often more than a single way to present the same lineup of words for the 'outering' of a thought. How one writer may choose to modify, emphasize, or suppress a particular aspect of a statement can differ from how someone else might do it. Because writers put so much effort into the sculpting of word arrangements, they have tended to feel rather strongly about their punctuational decisions. And the feelings of editorial opposition have often been just as strong. Indeed, prose history is awash in argument over the cleanest, clearest, and most pleasing way to feed word groups into someone else's head. With that problem came another, even more challenging one: how could one tell when a string of word groups (as in a phrase or clause, or even a full statement) was complete? As we wade into the buzzing fecundity of human conviction, we will see how important to understanding are textual divisions, pause indicators, and full stops. They are the indicators of bonding, separation, and termination.

They are the crucial tools for breaking a mass into the necessary small bits for human consumption.

The punctuational stops (the commas, colons, semicolons, and periods) were born out of a physiological need to rest. The slowdowns and halts they demand are the key substitutes for the lift and drop of the voice. Their message is as needful to writing as diastole is to systole, or exhalation is to inhalation. Through their representation of ebb against flow, they gather words into related groups, and so open a passage towards assimilable meaning. Though the something-backgrounded-by-something-else feature of our human perceiving apparatus is vigilantly searching for possible physiological, anthropological, and literary insights, the study of punctuation is perpetually relegated to the lower orders of the educational process.

If pause played no part in meaning, speech would emerge from our mouths in a continuum, wherein neither the words themselves nor meaningful word groups could be readily distinguished. In writing, the pause marks and stops tell the reader where meaning demands termination. 'White space' (as found between words and in paragraphical indentations, margins, and chapter divisions) increases that sense-exposing mental silence. These two punctuational devices—pause marks and white space—are the critical and easy-to-spot sense-makers of the words we set down for the eye to interpret. As substitutes for the voice-drops of speech, they break up the text into absorbable units for the successful transmission of a writer's thinking.

The reach of punctuation is broader than is generally suspected. The fact that some mark of completion is needed in all step-by-step logical procedures is obvious to computer programmers. To understand is to break into parts; to create is to arrange parts. Working in fragments is a deeply human necessity. It springs from an insoluble conflict: the human compulsion to make order out of chaos and the brain's physiological limitations for doing so. For though the human brain may speculate about infinity and eternity, it is physiologically unable to take in or give out information without letup. We count on division. *We must deal with 'reality' in bits and pieces.* In short, though we cannot handle very many facts at any one time, yet we yearn to see reality beyond the appearance of things and to understand how the world really works.

Punctuation was once an exalted subject for study. Many eminent writers have tackled the subject—Cicero, Ben Jonson, R. L. Stevenson are only a few out of many. By way of example, in 1890, from his lecture platform in Boston, the renowned scholar John Earle proclaimed punctuation to be a system of *ad-*

minicula—a requirement for guarding unwary readers "against confusion and collapse," its province of activity being "the higher region of Grammar" and hence the very "structure and articulation of thought."[7] Though punctuation is no longer so revered or popular a topic, poets as recent as Robert Graves, Ezra Pound, e. e. cummings, and Marianne Moore extensively honored the delicacy of nuance that it can achieve. Vladimir Nabokov and John Updike were very alert to its powers.[8] Indeed, anyone responsibly engaged in setting down thoughts on paper will think deeply about how to break up and arrange his subject matter so as to ensure its full revelation. At lighter levels, anyone who puts pen to paper or fingers to keyboard will need to think where in the flood of his words he should plant the needed pause marks. Though becoming rarer, editorial reverence for thoughtful punctuation has not totally evaporated in these opening decades of the twenty-first century.

For our purposes now, let us agree on some description that will cover all the things that punctuation seems to be about. First of all, we may say that punctuation involves the use of white space and stopping devices to organize written language into comprehensible units. Beyond that, it may seek to refine, illumine, emphasize, disambiguate, or elicit emotion. Described thus broadly, its area of jurisdiction includes matters of word separation, margins, headings, and chapter divisions; the positioning of points ('puncts,' or 'stops': that is, periods, commas, colons, and semicolons); the use of the dash (a pausal sign of varied and subtle intentions) and the hyphen (for which, thanks to Noah Webster, English and American usages differ); as well as marks of quotation, exclamation, ellipses, and question marks. Italics, underlinings, small lettering, capital lettering, parentheses, and counter-to-standard use of bold lettering should also be included, for they too are telling. To abbreviate, let us agree that punctuation will include any division, or separation, or gathered up, or unworded signal that relates to the conveyance of *thought* or *feeling* through writing.

To satisfy this sweep of goals, it will be necessary to consider not only the demands of convention, but also those of changing style; for style and pointing (a word commonly used for 'punctuating with stops') have always gone hand in hand. The arrangement of words on paper, their rhythmic patterns, the method or protocol established for the dealing out of information, whether for the purpose of clarifying facts or heightening emotion—all these things that are monitored by punctuation lie at the very core of style. They are personal and individual. In speech, rhythm (achieved by a cadencing voice-drop or pitch change) will enhance the intake of meaning. The writer will be aware of rhythms too, as he shifts his word order, marks off phrases, and arranges the paragraphic blocks of his argument to make them cohere more intelligibly.

Two basic concepts guide the action of punctuation today, and each has its origin in the deep structure of the human mind. The rhetorical one is more oriented to speech sound. It sinks its message into the receiving mind through signals familiar to the ear. It echoes oral rhythms, inviting emotion to the page and comfort to the ear. Note where the comma lies in the sample below, and how it has little to do with the needs of the grammar-dependent eye, but is so telling for the ear.

In general he does it, and does it thoroughly.

In dealing with this grammatically, one could argue that "In general" is better marked off with a comma to make plain the fact that it modifies the entire statement and is quite different from it in that it represents authorial opinion and is not necessarily a statement of fact. Grammatically, the comma before "and" intrusively divides the subject *he* from its second verb. In any case, for purely informative purposes, it is not necessary.

Emily Dickinson was a notoriously emotional punctator, as may be seen from her archived papers and manuscripts in the Emily Dickinson Collection in the Amherst College Archives and Special Collections.

> I heard a Fly buzz—when I died—
> The Stillness in the Room
> Was like the Stillness in the Air—
> Between the Heaves of Storm—[9]

Abhorring the deathlike finality of a full stop, Dickinson turned to the ambiguities allowed by the dash, with its implicative wisp of suggestion, in place of a more positive finish. The dash, being a vague sort of instrument, was for her purposes a very companionable punct.

The punctuation deriving from such vocal-auditory intention is known variously as rhetorical, elocutionary, or euphuistic. It reached maturity in monastic times, survived in vigor through Shakespeare's era, and is today effectively used for heightening dramatic and emotional effects. One might even liken it to the dynamic signals (< >, *pp* and *ff*) on a sheet of music—in short, a performance instruction. But its presence is rare in scientific or expository writing, for it is too intimate, too exposing—too, if you will, unreliable and personal. One discerns it at play in the renderings of speeches, sermons, poetry, or conversation—wherever meaning is dressed for the ear. Actors have always required its help in performance. "Emphasis is the link which connects words together, and forms them into sentences, or into members of sentences," wrote the actor Thomas Sheridan in 1781. The goal of such a punctuational style is to "reflect the ups and downs of voice sound in the expression of a train of ideas."[10] At the height of punctilious interest in punctuation, a huge array of complicated symbols was devised to guide the declaimer of text towards a more dramatic and intelligible rendition. Strange configurations, embedded amongst the clauses, told him when to smile, to gesture, to lower or raise his voice. Amongst the more entertaining and dramatic punctuational symbols are the following, whose names expose their purpose: a *punctus lamenti* or *planctus* (You have just said something sad, so wipe the tears from your cheeks); a *punctus gaudii cum honestate* (Give a hearty honest laugh); and a *punctus orationis finalis* (For the *finalis punctus* make clear that you have finished at last. But how? Perhaps by folding your arms across your chest and cocking an eyebrow at the audience?) All of the above are from the German late 1800s, and the symbols themselves are visually complicated. In appearance they rather resemble kanjis with a Gothic twist.[11]

Paralleling the rhetorical pointing style is the logical (syntactical, or grammatical) one. Logical pointing offers a second way for the successful intake of written material, a route laid wide by Gutenberg's invention of movable type and the development of a fully democratic literacy. Thereafter, reading aloud (though still a popular activity) was no longer a necessity. Printers took over the task of refining the ways to clarify the meaning of text for the reading eye; and punctuation, the means for breaking text apart, was its focus. The result was the growth of logical pointing. Logical pointing can be profuse in its use of punctuation marks. They are marshaled in droves to illuminate sentence structures, to secure the boundaries of word groups, and to establish their relative importance within a statement. Phrases and clauses are made distinct, so that the eye, recognizing which words go with which, may quickly gather them up in meaningful chunks. This fracturing process provides an eye-to-brain substitute for the sounded ear-to-brain cadences and emphases. Logical pointing is more intellectually oriented than its rhetorical sister, and more objective than intimate. Its reference is to grammatical law, not to the inward voice of the writer. Its allegiance is to clarity and consistency. Below is an example of logical pointing:

Although Ms. Fang Chunhua said she had intended her remarks as a tribute to the Honorable Pang Kong, her translator, all too frequently mistaking her words (perhaps even deliberately), somehow managed to render him up

as a clumsy, albeit pleasant, bumbler; in the end, as is generally agreed,
Ms. Fang's 'tribute' was the cause of his electoral defeat.

Logical pointing was a late achiever. It matured to its present capabilities during the eighteenth, nineteenth, and early twentieth centuries, when exactitude of language became the aspiration of French and English intellectual circles. In the hands of heavy-handed printers, it could become quite dictatorial. Below is a sample of what one printer's rendition did to Emily Dickinson's delicate first-round of composition:

> I Heard a fly buzz when I died; (*bang!*)
> The stillness round my form
> Was like the stillness in the air
> Between the heaves of storm. (*bang!*)[12]

The dreamlike mood is gone. The interruptive punctuation has destroyed the musing atmosphere and rendered the lines more factual, less mystical; and though some might say the result is more understandable, it is certainly less suggestive of Dickinson's emotional state or the actual way the mind throws out thoughts.

The two punctuational branches—the emotional rhetorical and the intellectual logical—though growing side by side and often interchangeable, have flowered in different seasons. Academia today favors the logical style, which still predominates in all expository writing. However, now that literary ambition is content with less exalted statement, and the reading eye has become more practiced in dealing with the syntactical elements of text, pause marks internal to the sentence have become less necessary. Replaced by periods or commas, the ill-understood semicolons are slowly fading away. Commas in adjectival buildups are also tending to disappear, leaving the big tall bushy green tree to be just that, an envisioned whole, and not as previously: a tree that is also big, and tall, and bushy, and green. Again, words like *too* and *of course* seem more and more to include within their own sense boundaries the wanted mental pause. Marker words (or particles) like *therefore, moreover, on the contrary, on the one hand*—previously so much relied upon—no longer signpost every turn in written argument. How shocking all this would have been to eighteenth-century printers, whose eye-driven passion was focused on the rigid, logical, and architectured layerings of text!

No one will be surprised to learn that, in the course of their long histories, the two essential approaches to pointing text have conceived a crowd of hybrid offshoots, even within the pages of a single composition. Though lacking pedigrees, these 'natural' offspring of personal taste might as well be approved (despite the frowns of teachers), for when all is said and done, a relaxed punctuating style is what best delineates our intimate truths as we traverse the experiential gamut from emotion to objectivity. In short, *there is no pure body of 'correct' punctuating law*. Successful reception of the intended meaning is the only measure. If an author is wanting to stir you, he will 'speak' to your ear in aural rhythms. If he is explaining something, he will 'eye' his words from the vantage ground of grammar. It is up to him to mix his styles in good readable taste and never to break his flow where the traditions of speech do not allow it. If he confuses us by puncturing prepositional phrases with commas or planting semicolons after noun subjects, then we will not read him. It is as simple as that. He will do a better job of feeding his thoughts into our heads if he knows what he is doing with his points, and why. More than writers have tended to realize, their 'simple' act of patterning a thought for paper has had a long, fought-over history.

From antiquity up to the late twentieth century, the direction of artistic effort was towards sentential complication, imagery, and, in English-speaking circles, the use of 'sophisticated' Latinate words—along with the increasing use of punctuation to keep it all straight. Even in the years when the world was purely oral, simple signals (perhaps a nod or a press of the lips) must have been used to instruct the listener that what he had heard was in some sense complete and that he might turn his attention to his own response. The human mind wants that signal of finish. Later, particularly after printing got under way, literary punctuation became so intricate and its rules so unyielding and ambitious that even short phrases were marked off to underscore their integrity and rank their importance within the sentence. Gradually, as literacy stabilized, such fussiness gave way to the interests of speed. Though we still have writers with the skills to weave damascene word-textures, the target is now to please the public, for if they are pleased, they will buy more books and magazines. For the modern general public, textual simplicity is a must.

A Paean to Writing:
The Tool That We Made Remakes Us

Writing is neither so direct nor so flexible as speech, yet its gifts are many. Through its offices, complex statements and transitory flights of the imagination can be set down with prospects of permanence and accurate retrieval, whether or not the memory holds. Yet its powers were slow to take hold amongst the masses where education was not made available. Those who could not read preferred to use their heads, *not alphabet letters*, for recalling the particulars of events and whatever had been said. That preference was a common one in early times, yet it was destined to fade with the increasing acceptance of the written word. By the future first century BCE, Diodorus Siculus would be looking back admiringly at the benefits that writing afforded. For it "is writing alone which preserves the cleverest sayings of men of wisdom and the oracles of the gods, as well as philosophy and all knowledge…" Whereas nature may be the cause of life, the "cause of the good life is education which is based upon reading and writing." The unerring fixedness of writing supports the firmness of contracts and laws. Through the services of literacy, the dead can be "carried in the memory of the living," and men be enabled to converse across space "with those who are at the furthest distance from them."[13]

We today are grateful for the glimpses of antiquity that writing has safeguarded for us, and for the vast accumulation of human knowledge that it has made possible. Writing makes history more stable than does narration from memory. With its broad chronological and geographical reach, it is less reactive to contemporary perception, compulsion, or fashions of language. Whereas oral dialects commonly have only a few thousand words of whose semantic histories their users know little, a literary language preserves a wealth of past meanings for hundreds of thousands of words, with all their historical nuances. The *Oxford English Dictionary* records, at the very least, a quarter of a million distinct English words, excluding those with attached inflections or deriving from technical and regional vocabulary. If single words carrying several senses were counted, the total would probably approach three quarters of a million.

But the crowning benefit that writing has bestowed on our present-day world is the chance to classify, to sequence, and to critically examine the propositions of argument. Says Walter Ong, whose writings on this subject were pioneering: "Human beings in primary oral cultures, those untouched by writing in any form, learn a great deal and possess and practice great wisdom, but they do not 'study.'"[14] With the development of writing, knowledge could at last be communicated in language free of the stereotypic norms of oral epic expression—those formulaic repetitions, persistent meters, and heroic epithets (like "Wily Odysseus" and "Rosy-fingered Dawn")—which had previously been relied upon for the poetry that held together cultural memory. When practiced in spacious tranquility, writing found itself able to express new, out-of-the-way, radical, and even iconoclastic ideas. Before the Greek alphabet made writing easier to do and to interpret, science and history as we know them today did not exist, nor was there any variegated, richly vocabu-larized literature.

With the increase of visual stimulation, inherited precepts were ques-tioned. Previous credence in old ways was shaken. The activated eye moved intellectual attention away from the outmoded schematic generalities of oral habit, with results that spread into all areas of human endeavor. 'Bro-ken-stance' statuary, suggesting movement, appeared as sculptors began to relax the stiff postures of their iconic figures and to humanize marble por-traits with features of increasing individuality. The management of space and balance in architecture changed too, as witness the Parthenon, whose designers deceived the eye by softening hard-rock rectilinearity with sub-tle adjustments to rigid measurement. Poetic forms (odes, epodes, elegies, paeans) and segments of oratorical outline (preface, narration, proof, and conclusion) were identified and defined. It was as if human knowledge was being broken into pieces so as to be more closely analyzed for higher goals and better understanding.

Unlike speech, writing is a slow-motion activity and out-of-step with real time. The fact that the medium is static allows a writer to contemplate choices. It was surely a revelation to find that with 'paper and pen' one could rethink, cross out, and fiddle ideas into clearer, more exact, more beautiful, more daring and elaborate formations; and withal, invite a reader to headier heights of beauty and intellectual perspective. As written statements became more assured, more expansive and complicated, so they became more reliant on a stable language whose word meanings, syntax, and grammar would fit with the reader's expectations. For a transfer of meaning in the silent world of writing, agreement about those elements is crucial.

Ancient writers were initially tentative in laying down rules to establish those necessary standards. But once writing had become a somewhat mastered activity, ideas quickly emerged for enlarging its rudimentary scope. As skill developed, writers began to stretch basic statements to incorporate peripheral ideas. They created new words and modified old ones. They experimented with word order, cadence, rhythms, and the styling and placement of phras-es. They decreed a proper position for verbs. They invented new particles to handle the multilayered clausal buildups and thus forced the archaic *and* link off center stage. As writers became more prolific and facile, so their readers became more sophisticated. The communicative power of written language, with side issues of propriety, beauty, and style, were hotly discussed. Discussed too, were what a thought was, how inclusive the setting down of it should be, and how it should end.

With the acceptance of visual perceptions, time came to be viewed differently. The feel of enclosed, present-tense simultaneity that oral societies tend to foster, along with their fatalistic mythologies and amorphous knowledge-hoard, gave way to a new perspective—to a serial view of cause and effect. The act of pressing a holistic thought into linearly worded speech and then into writing is thought to have induced a growing sense of chronological progression that could explain the present in terms of the past and predict the future by reference to the present. Literate culture with its gift of record keeping and retrieval encouraged an appreciation of accuracy, which in turn downgraded the position of the wise old folk upon whose 'said-heard' memories and tribal 'truths,' history had heretofore depended.

Writing, which *we* had invented, began in some sense to reinvent *us*. Though we may insist on its 'artificiality'—its distance from all that we find natural in ourselves—it has behaved more like an incorporated new organism, so profoundly has it changed our way of thinking and dealing with life.

From Orality Into Literacy: The Full Sweep

Nonliterate societies are conspicuously responsive to sensory intake. Their focus of awareness is not so much on the future or past as on the seamless, immediate, engulfing, simultaneously-perceived-from-all-directions *present*. Though they linearize their words in speech, they are not inclined to consider matters in linear sequences of cause-and-effect as do literates, but to explain and predict with myth and to invoke change through communal prayer. Nor do they consciously fragment or objectify their experiences for the purpose of understanding them. Instead, relationships within a social group are dominated by an intuitive and corporate family feeling. Each individual is a participant in whatever palpitates the group, and whatever emotion he feels, he will react to almost instantaneously.

Here is Marshall McLuhan on the subject.

Civilization is built on literacy because literacy is a uniform processing of a culture by a visual sense extended in space and time by the alphabet. In tribal cultures, experience is arranged by a dominant auditory sense-life that represses visual values. The auditory sense, unlike the cool and neutral eye, is hyper-esthetic and delicate and all-inclusive. Oral cultures act and react at the same time....To act without reacting, without involvement, is the peculiar advantage of Western literate man.[15]

Concerning the matter of time in preliterate societies: in his study of the Arabic language, Raphael Patai describes a telling aspect of Arabic verb tenses—a feature from antiquity that has lingered into the present. Where in English there is a rigid correspondence between the form and the meaning of a verb, in Arabic there is not. For example, the form for a perfect tense verb can also represent the pluperfect, the future, and in the most frequently used expressions of everyday life, the present participle. The reason for this is thought to be that Arabic is closely aligned with proto-Semitic (i.e., prehistoric, purely oral Semitic), which is known to have used the imperfect form for all tenses. In other words, it showed no specific breakdown of time into past, present, and future. Time, as the literate mind thinks of it, is a very difficult and disconcerting concept for those brought up in an 'oral' environment with its sense of a broad-scoped continuance. Also interesting on this point is the persistent presence in Arabic of the archaic connective *and* in place of our chronologically more informative *when, after,* or *before,*[16] and the fact that stories and accounts often ended with the word for *and.*

In an oral culture, communication takes place in a dynamic surround of oral-aural, present-tense, face-to-face participation, whose potential is nothing if not explosive. The talk is sharp, restless, and laced with argument, riposte, affirmation, and rebuttal—all of which must, for the sake of meaning anything at all, be guided by mannerly rule. It is true that shouts and fists have been known to quell the voices of opposition in councils of deliberation; but when all is said and done, a vociferous melee rarely leads to sound decision-making. Orderly debate is almost always better.

Concerning orderliness and our inheritance from prehistoric language, modern research and speculation has this to say:

If speech sound distinctions were relatively more vague in the early stages of language evolution, we can assume that the syntactic organization of archaic languages would have included a number of means for amplifying the redundancy....It is probable that most means used for increasing predictability in modern speech would be exaggerated in archaic speech. Thus we should expect to find [early] languages with more highly constrained and stereotypic clause structure, highly redundant and predictable marking of major grammatical functions and semantic categories, and more rigid constraints on phonemic combinations. And we should also expect that speech contexts were more highly ritualized, including greeting and parting rituals, speech initiation, and conversational turn-taking rituals, as well as the use of conventionalized gestures....

It is probable that most means for increasing predictability in modern speech would be exaggerated in archaic speech....Because archaic languages had to function in the context of more severe cognitive and phonological constraints, they were almost certainly more rigidly structured than modern languages.[17]

Since order is more likely to produce a positive outcome than is disorder, we may conjecture that debates in primitive, preliterate days developed principles for regulating the necessary courtesies; for it is unlikely that humans were born with a ready-to-go protocol for the governance of potentially passionate talk. To speculate further, once those courtesies were put into practice and their usefulness was recognized, they became the prerequisites of serious oral exchange.

Samples of ancient Sumerian and Egyptian correspondence manifest a hierarchy of courteous address; and by the time of Homer's *Iliad* (presumed to have been composed ca. 800–1100 BCE) procedural formalities for discussion or debate in Greek are plainly apparent. A common protocol controls the oratorical give-and-take of both Trojan and Argive leaders, whose speeches—even as they move towards quarrel—are attentively considered and then answered. It would seem likely that the body of customs that regulated the flow of speech in councils of war or in the meting out of justice, took on, over time, the aspect of rules—rhetorical rules—for controlling and guiding all public oratory and address. Those rules must have been firmly in place when the facile flow of alphabetic writing came on the scene, for writers seem to have taken up without delay a well-developed system for controlling the potential ramble of prose.

It is in early fifth-century expository prose—in extant historical, philosophical, geographical, and judicial materials—that the regimen generated from what was most likely pre-historic oratorical custom becomes fully manifest. As writing grew to be a more necessary feature of civic life, pedagogical handbooks on writing style and language analysis began to appear, stirring up questions that attracted the attention of philosophers and theorists. Once the transfer of voice-sound to the page was secure and the expectations of readers were sufficiently fulfilled (this being a matter of centuries), then—only then—did ancient rhetorical restrictions, with all their dictatorial detail, relax their grip and begin to fade, leaving us now with only the shades of their earlier palpable presence. Today we find traces of ancient rhetorical rule in the layout of modern narrative, in the procedures for topic introduction and approach to closure, and in the emotion-heightening use of paraphrase and rhythmic patterning.

A Jump Into the Future: Plato's Spell on the Written Word

In the boundary centuries between orality and literacy, a thinker like Plato (ca. 427–347 BCE), who wanted to express difficult, new ideas to a less than semiliterate public, had many things to consider before putting his thoughts into words and then writing them down. Writing required a special treatment; for while it was like speech, yet it was different. Plato, who proved himself a consummate artist and communicator, must have thought deeply about how best to attract a reading public that was accustomed to an oral culture. How did he manage it?[18]

He introduced many of his philosophical ideas in scenes of lively dialogue and confrontational exchange. His characters were people who were prominent in Athenian society—privileged people whom folk admired. He depicted them as they met in familiar Athenian places and conversed in their natural speech. His heroic protagonist was well chosen too. Feisty and notoriously unconventional, Socrates was a well-known figure in Athenian society—a man of tremendous acuity, personality, and influence, who could engage the interest of any audience. As Plato (and later Xenophon) depicted him, Socrates's method of teaching was to query opinion, and then to query the answer, and by taking unexpected stances himself, to elicit deeper thinking. For example, in Plato's dialogue *Phaedrus*, Socrates (though educated and literate himself) is described as stirring up argument by promoting the virtues of memory over those of literacy—a view that favored the old-fashioned ways that conservative folk could trust. Plato (and Xenophon too) described Socrates's questioning mode as being quirky, incisive, instructive, and challenging, yet friendly. Designed to make

people think, it encouraged them to reconsider their unexamined opinions of
difficult philosophical and political matters.

As well as the choice of Socrates as hero, Plato was prescient in other
respects. As a masterly wordsmith, he propounded his views in natural but
graceful, often poetic language that would appeal to the discerning Athenian
ear. He devised stories to clarify difficult conjectures about natural phenomena and human psychology—myths, in effect, that illustrated truths in a way
that novice literates could accept. With enticements such as these, Plato succeeded in luring his ear-bred followers across the aural-visual dividing line,
where philosophical abstractions like morality and truth, death and the nature of being could be discussed in depth, not only then, but for many years
into the future and in faraway places.

Adding to the drama of query and dispute, Plato used another device, a
structural device called *framing*. Framing is especially interesting for the light
it casts on Plato's remarkable intuition for dealing with a newly activated
readership. The ploy he used is still used today, and its purpose is to simulate
the feel of a full surround. It does this by setting previously experienced material within a framework of current material (in a construction akin to Russian
dolls). It is a trick that is very useful in narrative. By embedding a flashback
into an ongoing situation, a writer enlarges his canvas and makes his account
more explicit. Within that flashback might be another flashback. In such a
case, the doubled 'framing' produces a stack of scenes that elucidate the material of the matrix text.

As each of Plato's background frames yielded to the next, so it prepared
the preliterate mindset for an intensified focus on the targeted intellectual
core. Each step made that journey to the ultimate philosophical revelation a
more comfortable experience. In moving from frame to frame, readers were
encouraged by the casual human conversation, by descriptions of familiar
venues, by the references to admired Athenian leaders, by the rhapsodic
flights into myth and tale, and the deepening drama of argument and confrontation—all these things being succinctly deployed to soften the approach
to a difficult and unfamiliar topic. By such means was Plato able to lead his
inexperienced readership, step by step, towards difficult discussions of truth,
love, virtue, and death.

Let us look for a moment at Plato's dialogue *Phaedo*, to see how, by working with frames, he created a here-now, full-surround atmosphere out of linear strings of written words. The critical heart of the *Phaedo* dialogue is its
discussion of immortality and in what form immortality might exist. That

abstract philosophical core is made relevant by its frame, which is the actual setting in which that sober discourse took place: namely, the Athenian prison where Socrates, surrounded by mourning friends, was about to oblige his executioners, drink his infusion of hemlock, and die. *What could be more gripping?* There is the much admired Socrates in the company of his grieving disciples as they ponder the serious matters of life after death. Their exchange of views reinforces the situation they find themselves in and frames the philosophical centerpiece with a simultaneous, earthbound actuality.

The prison scene of concerned friends that frames the philosophical pith—which is the analysis of death—is itself embedded in another frame, one that opens the piece with a lighter, conversational scene between two men who meet by accident in the street of a *different* town at a *later* time. Their dialogue takes place in the present tense. The first man, who was not a witness to Socrates's death scene, asks the one who was, to tell him about it. Their discussion establishes the appropriate mood of gloom, doom, love, and awe that prevails throughout all the subsequent parts. At the conclusion of the *Phaedo*, the reader is back with these two men as they review what had happened. Thus, the dialogue itself is brought to an end by the same voices registering the same sense of regret and concern with which the piece began.

* * * * *

Plato's handling of contemporary ear and eye perceptions was brilliant. His easy flow of language, his beautiful flights of imagination, and easy-to-follow philosophical discussion proved a major force in the development of literature.

With his outstanding achievements in mind, we now move back to the fifth century to inspect the troubles of earlier writers—the better to appreciate the miracle of Plato's leapfrogging advance.

Notes

1. The materials for this section on early Greek literacy (unless otherwise indicated) are drawn from Rosalind Thomas, *Literacy and Orality*, particularly pages 73–94, and 138; and also from Crane, *The Blinded Eye*, 16–21, and 72.

2. "Hellenistic" describes the period that began ca. 325 BCE after the death of Alexander the Great. The term is particularly applied to Greek-speaking Alexandria in Egypt, which after the decline of Athens became the intellectual hub of the Mediterranean world. The preceding fifth and fourth centuries BCE are generally referred to as "Classical" (with the focus on Athens). Working back in time, the sixth to approximately the tenth centuries BCE are

known as "Archaic"; while "Helladic" describes prehistoric Greece. Thus, in sequence by date: Helladic, Archaic, Classical, and Hellenistic.

3. William V. Harris, "Texts and Society in the Roman Empire," abstract of *Escribir y Leer en Occidente* (Valencia: Universidad Internacional Menendez Pelayo, 1993), 2:5–8.

4. Thucydides, *History of the Peloponnesian War*, trans. Charles Forster Smith, Loeb Classical Library (Cambridge: Harvard University Press, 1921), 5.29.2–3.

5. Thomas, *Oral Tradition*, 48.

6. Saenger, *Space between Words*, 4–45 passim. I have relied on Saenger for these materials on the early difficulties of manuscript reading.

7. George P. Marsh, *Lectures on the English Language*, 4th ed. (New York: Scribner, 1863), 415.

8. The *New Yorker* editor Katherine White's correspondence with both Nabokov and Updike are revealing on this point. Nabokov proves himself unassailably firm as to his pausing decisions; Updike is less sure of himself, more inquiring of Mrs. White's opinion, and their discussions are intense. See the Katharine Sergeant White Collection, Special Collections, Bryn Mawr College Library.

9. Emily Dickinson, *The Poems of Emily Dickinson*, ed. by Thomas H. Johnson, Cambridge: The Belknap Press of Harvard University Press. Copyright ©1951, 1955 by the president and fellows of Harvard College. Copyright ©renewed 1979, 1983 by the president and fellows of Harvard College. Copyright ©1914, 1918, 1919, 1924, 1929, 1930, 1932, 1935, 1937, 1942, by Martha Dickinson Bianchi. Copyright © 1952, 1957, 1958, 1963, 1965, by Mary L. Hampson.

10. Thomas Sheridan, *A Rhetorical Grammar of the English Language* (Menston, England: Scolar Press, 1969), 103.

11. For more on this subject, see Gwen Robinson, "The Punctator's World: A Discursion (Part Three)," in the *Syracuse University Library Associates Courier* 24, no. 2 (1989): 70.

12. T. W. Higginson and Mabel Loomis Todd, eds. *Poems by Emily Dickinson: Third Series* (Boston: Roberts Brothers, 1896), 184.

13. Diodorus Siculus, *Library of History*, trans. C. H. Oldfather, Loeb Classical Library (Cambridge: Harvard University Press, 1946), 4:401.

14. Walter Ong, *Orality and Literacy* (London: Methuen, 1982), 8. Dr. Ong (along with Marshall McLuhan) was something of a pioneer in identifying the differences between oral and literate casts of mind.

15. Marshall McLuhan, *Understanding Media: The Extensions of Man* (New York: McGraw Hill, 1964), 81–8.

16. See Raphael Patai, *The Arab Mind* (New York: Hatherleigh Press, 2002), 69–70 and passim.

17. Deacon, "Brain-Language Coevolution," *SFI Proceedings*, 75–7.

18. This section on Plato owes much to Helen H. Bacon's "Plato and the Greek Literary Tradition," her presidential address to the American Philological Association of December 1985.

References

Bacon, Helen H. "Plato and the Greek Literary Tradition." Presidential address to the American Philological Association, Washington, DC, December 1985.

Crane, Gregory. *The Blinded Eye: Thucydides and the New Written Word*. Lanham, MD: Rowman & Littlefield, 1996.

Deacon, "Brain-Language Coevolution." In *The Evolution of Human Languages: Proceedings of the Workshop on the Evolution of Human Languages*. Santa Fe, New Mexico, August 1989. Edited by John A. Hawkins and Murray Gell-Mann. Reading, MA: Addison-Wesley, 1992.

Dickinson, Emily. *The Poems of Emily Dickinson*. Edited by Thomas H. Johnson, Cambridge: The Belknap Press of Harvard University Press. Copyright © 1951.

———. *Poems by Emily Dickinson: Third Series*. Edited by T. W. Higginson and Mabel Loomis Todd. Boston: Roberts Brothers, 1896.

Harris, William V. "Texts and Society in the Roman Empire." Abstract of Vol. 2 of *Escribir y Leer en Occidente*. Valencia: Universidad Internacional Menendez Pelayo, 1993.

Marsh, George P. *Lectures on the English Language*, 4th ed. New York: Scribner, 1863.

McLuhan, Marshall. *Understanding Media: The Extensions of Man*. New York: McGraw Hill, 1964.

Ong, Walter. *Orality and Literacy*. London: Methuen, 1982.

Patai, Raphael. *The Arab Mind*. New York: Hatherleigh Press, 2002.

Robinson, Gwen. "The Punctator's World: A Discursion: Part Three. *Syracuse University Library Associates Courier* 24, no. 2 (1989): 70.

Saenger, Paul. *Space between Words: The Origins of Silent Reading*. Stanford, CA: Stanford University Press, 1997.

Sheridan, Thomas. *A Rhetorical Grammar of the English Language*. Menston, England: Scolar Press, 1969.

Siculus, Diodorus. Vol. 4 of *Library of History*. Translated by C. H. Oldfather. Loeb Classical Library. Cambridge: Harvard University Press, 1946.

Thomas, Rosalind. *Literacy and Orality in Ancient Greece*. Cambridge: Cambridge University Press, 1995.

———. *Oral Tradition and Written Record in Classical Athens*. Cambridge: Cambridge University Press, 1989.

Thucydides. Vol. 5 of *History of the Peloponnesian War*. Translated by Charles Forster Smith. Loeb Classical Library. Cambridge: Harvard University Press, 1921.

· 4 ·

IN THE CLINGING EMBRACE OF ORALITY

A Writer's Key to the Garden of Eden

A speaker can spin a rational thought into words and at the same time show his own emotional reaction to it. Amusement, grief, outrage, urgency, sympathy, reluctance, submission, condescension, disdain, and so on—all can be transmitted by the quality of voice sound, which can reach beyond the power of words. To illustrate this claim: imagine hearing someone say, "I'm going to go to my doctor today." The statement can be said with satisfaction if pain is expected to be relieved; with glee and excitement if romantic interests pertain; or, in a tone of inconvenience or worry. The same words, standing alone on the page and unsupported by additional information, are nothing but factual. It is always the case that words, buoyed by voice sound, are more reflective of the mind's holistic brew than are their cousinly written ones. Trapped in his silent world, a writer must struggle to concoct a voice-like, full-round potency. While speaking can more fully and quickly reflect a 'thought-and-emotion' mixture, writing at least offers time for contrivance to work towards the same goal. With the need to compress *much* into *little*, writers (often unknowingly) will consult their inheritance of ancient artifice and ruse.

To transmit a full account of almost anything, wordmongers must compensate for human limitations. We have inspected framing—the artifice that can render up the events of *there* in the middle of what's going on *here*, or the *past* in the middle of what's going on *now*, leaving the patchwork result to be perceived as whole cloth. This 'meanwhile-back-at-the-ranch' shift of scene with its plot-developing flashback has for centuries been a standard storytelling stratagem. As we have seen in Plato's *Phaedo*, the ploy supplies a focused view of the main one, of which it illumines some aspect. Despite the bump-and-hiccup effects that flashbacks tend to induce in a plot line, they are generally felt to enrich a tale.

But there are other ploys to enrich and compact linear wordage. One potent choice lies in the adroit *juxtaposition or amalgamation of two dissimilar concepts or ideas, each of which comes with its own array of associations*. From such a combination springs to life a third perception, a something new—a broadened view, a definitive insight. Much of poetic imagery works in this way. The pairing of unexpected, unrelated notions can add an informative sparkle to expand a meaning. Consider the following figures of speech and the stretch in meaning they offer:

Simile: The senator dressed *like a hobo*.
Personification: The sun *smiled* on their mud-caked trainers.
Metaphor: By the light of sputtering candles, he *wolfed* her risotto marinara.
Litotes: His muscles were *hardly those of a mouse*.

Throughout history, wordmongers (both oral and literate) have accepted manipulations like these as expanding, refreshing, and appropriately useful. One might conclude that their continuing presence in modern communication points to a lingering attachment to—or is it a hunger for?—that long-ago, preliterary Garden of Eden, when all was one, including us. In that plush and blooming plot of mystical land, Time was immaterial, and we could process our global surround without fragmenting it.

In addition to framing and imagery are many other contra-time, word-mongering ploys, and most are very, very old—older than singing Homer or pen-crafting Plato. Though sometimes awkward by modern measure, ancient literary invention could be both successful and complex. Moreover, it was important to us for the groundwork it set for all modern speakers and writers. For, like the ancients, we who speak and write today must do battle against the flow of time-gulping natural language while trying to keep pace with our thinking. Our subconscious hope might well be to recreate the preliterate's encircling consciousness so as to emulate the reality in our heads where so many flashing intakes seem to occur simultaneously. For example, on meeting a long lost friend, it is well within the reach of human ability to note the spittle on his moustache, smell his sweat, hear him cough, and recognize that while he has the musculature of an ape and the choking laugh he has had since kindergarten, his *r* sounds are now attractively redolent of Scotland. All these disparate things can be registered more or less concurrently. A writer, having time to circumvent his own limitations, will attempt to communicate his bundle of mental responses by amalgamating various of its features. He might even try to piece together the bitty aspects of his whole perception, and make of them a broad mosaic as though they were colorful pebbles, whose aggregate could be swiftly absorbed. Perfect success will elude him, of course, for no artifice can wholly substitute for the real thing.

With a toolbox of nouns and verbs, which so sadly fail to express all the aspects of what one wants to communicate, wordmongers who are doomed to write must convey their ideas with studied contrivance. Structuring a text by framing, and enhancing it with imagery are merely two of our ancient, inherited tricks. Over the centuries a good many other sleights of hand have become so routine that they are hardly recognizable as tricks. (We shall inspect some in a moment.) Perhaps in the future, others will be invented to free us from the bondage of tick-tocking wordage.

What writers crave is to find the means to communicate in a single small package the sensations they feel and the thoughts that they simultaneously think. They are aware of the confusion that a word-mush can create. They are aware too of the choo-choo effect that a lengthy train of words can produce. And so, they pare down their verbiage and work with delusion and suggestion. They manipulate words like reflecting mirrors to evoke the *nonsequenced* thoughts and sensations that riot in their minds. With practice they can succeed in entrapping something of that critical substance—that full sense of complete reality—which they feel to hold in their heads and seek to portray.

The deceits that word-ridden writers have hit upon work because they have been popularly accepted to represent the real and vital thing. When listeners and readers are trained and ready to compensate imaginatively, a wordsmith's reach can be quite remarkable. Let us briefly work through the array of equipment that lies at hand. To sharpen the specifics of a proposition or enlarge the view so as to bring readers in line with authorial perspectives, writers can apply definitive adjectives and nouns that will express more than their handful of letters might at first glance foretoken, thus: *not* just 'a bird in a bush,' but 'a buff-breasted scrub wren on a resin-scented cedar branch.' With metaphor and hyperbole they can hype the basic information to elicit bigger pictures, thus: *not* just 'He went through the crowds,' but 'He shouldered his way through the press of howling enthusiasts.' And again, he was not just 'broad-shouldered and tall'; 'He was a giant of a man.' A juicy adverb will speak volumes, and can stretch the view with a touch of wit, thus: *nepotically awarded, punitively promoted, risibly formal, terminally incurious.* Subtlety and restraint in the use of any of these ploys, of course, is always recommended.

Moving onwards, we discover that clauses (both subordinate and insubordinate) can attach one facet of information to a disparate other, and in that way modify the flavor of the primary proposition. Particles are the links for this coupling maneuver. *When, if, after, who,* etc.—none of which has any particular meaning of its own—are the useful tools for modifying or expanding the sense of the governing statement. In the sentence *She was thinking of something else when she drove John's Mercedes through the drugstore window,* two things are being described, one after the other, but intended to be imagined as simultaneous. The unexpected material of the *when*-clause (set with its verb in the perfect tense) hits the reader's mental screen from a launch pad of blandness reinforced by the verb's imperfect tense. The interjection of a parenthesis that adds relevant information from the past to the ongoing statement can accomplish the same effect. *John's Mercedes (the one she drove through the drugstore window) is now being hauled to the dump.*

In all of this, time is the opponent and enrichment is the goal. With the aid of memory we seek to break up the clock's hold. If we could not do this, words would not be able to handle the deeper textures of our experience—the sources of our thinking—within the time barriers that we have to express them. In the following several racing-on sentences (the kind that skim and never dive), each action follows its predecessor in the lockstep order of real time. We are left with no reasonable background feel for Susie's irrational behavior.

> *Susie was in the Washington zoo and she ran to the bear cages and she waved at the polar bears. She blew kisses at the polar bears and shouted "Hi, polar bears!" at them. Then her mother said, "Let's look at the crocodiles now, dear," and Susie said she did not want to and she clung to the guardrail with all her might and screamed and screamed and screamed.*

Were we required to develop this wispy episode into a full-length novel, we would best begin by deploying some time-collapsing techniques to dispel the tedium of all those yawn-provoking *ands.* Also, we would include some background materials for Susie's behavior. With framing, for example, we might discover the source of Susie's psychotic passion for polar bears and thereby render the tale a touch more edifying. Perhaps her grandfather, the renowned Arctic vegetarian, played a part. In that case, we might frame the account with the adoption of an orphaned polar bear cub during a family hunt for succulent herbage in Svalbard.

The past is part of our present. It is the source of causes. With frames empowering 'meanwhile-back-at-the-ranch' structures; with complex sentences; with specifying adjectives and nouns, telling adverbs, and layered verb tenses; with metaphors, similes, and other figures of speech—with all this ammunition at hand, wordsmiths (be they oral or literary) can envelop their listeners and readers in a simulated surround of sensation and rational thought. While endeavoring to do so, might they not in fact be harking back to the enveloping, natural-state 'reality' in which our preliterate forebears must once have lived their lives?

A Literary Dilemma

Plato revised his own writing extensively, resorting to many of the aforementioned tricks of the trade. But also, as we have seen, he engaged his public by depicting his wise old hero, Socrates, an educated and literate man, as both challenging and unpredictable. In his dialogue *Phaedrus*, we are surprised to find Socrates claiming that the written word is nothing but a lifeless image of the spoken word. What is written, he says, has no vitality nor does it demand reply. If used extensively, it would one day substitute for memory—as indeed it has. Not only does Socrates argue that the written word is lifeless and has an enfeebling effect on the memory, but he is also tentative about the goals of writing in general. It seemed to him a slippery art—one that political and civil orators could employ dishonestly to reshape their statements *after* the fact, and thus distort the truth and mislead posterity. (We experience this simple truth today in the doings of journalists, publicists, and spin doctors.) Socrates held that truth lay in what was *said* in the heat of the moment, and not in a subsequent account of it.

And indeed, the oral word has much to offer. Live word sparring, when abetted by copious memory and a farsighted focus on the argument's target, was (and is still) considered to be an exciting skill. Plato depicted Socrates as being agile with language, brimming with novel ideas, witty, and seemingly untroubled by the limitations of memory and orally recorded knowledge.

Plato's use of dialogue to expound his philosophy, and his exclusion of poetry from his own ideal state (as set forth in *The Republic*), marked a turning point for the full acceptance of prose that was both informative and artistic. Indeed, prose had begun to grow cocky, and was now flaunting its powers to challenge the ear. Although information recorded in rhythmic chant was easy enough to remember and pass along to future generations, it could be pliant with factual matters. Historical epics and poeticized scientific reports, while formerly appealing, seemed now to be shackled by the rules of prosody with its inclusion of cliché. Though writing was silent, static, and deprived of the thrills of wrangle and bicker, it could claim exactitude. It could also travel far and survive the passing years.

This surprising instance of Socratic-Platonic confrontation—surprising in that Plato was using the written word to describe the literate Socrates's statement of oral preference—marks a critical period of change. To appreciate the thrust of readjustment taking place, the modern reader should be reminded that throughout Classical Greece audiences commonly gathered around their poets (as they had done for centuries) to *hear* them recite. They *listened* to orators and to those who could read aloud from books of history and drama. They got their news from rumor and heraldic announcement. They were accustomed to taking in the flow of sound—and did so with passion and discrimination. They delighted in fine-turned phrases and could be vociferously critical *ad hoc* about meters, about the purity of diction, the appropriateness of words, the harmoniousness of composition, and the relevancy of content. Greek ears were highly sensitized through long acquaintance with rhapsodic subtleties and all the elusive, exquisite aspects of oral-aural artistry.

In Thrall to the Ear

In Plato's era in the first half of the fourth century BCE and for centuries after, literates would still be interpreting dense text for those not-fully-literate who were seeking knowledge—a fact that satisfied the needs of an essentially oral world but may be said to have prolonged the adolescence of writers. For why should they change if the public seemed satisfied? We should think of that listening public as adeptly assimilative of mouth-sound, from the haphazard bounce of common speech to its ceremonious counterpart, the language of oratory, epic, and special occasions.

While the public's ears were practiced in processing words, their eyes were not, though the alphabet offered wide vistas of free and easy expression. Because the act of setting down a lengthy prose treatise was an obscure occupation and unfortified by historical precedence or by fully settled views about structure and vocabulary, the early pre-Plato, fifth-century prose writers turned for precedents to the traditional formulas of Athens's prize oratory—the pinnacle of oral, nonpoetic endeavor. The essential and highly acclaimed features of a perfect speech were these: a formalized program of beginning, middle, and end; the use of repetition and rolling rhythms; and the clarifying presence of both rephrasings (parallelisms) and contrasts (antitheses). Even with these matters settled, the move from hearing to seeing could be fraught with mistakes. The ear's adaptability allows loose play with logical structures, which are, if only by mental reference, the bones of lucid communication and the sine qua non of eye-directed prose.

As literacy grew, the incompatible wants of ear and eye became more evident. What was a writer to do? How, with a pen, could he best inject his thinking into someone else's orally-oriented head? By favoring the sensuous, sociable, extrovert ear? or the implacable, distancing eye? It was this basic rivalry—so remindful of Manichean dark and light, of body against soul, intuition against intellect, id against ego—that generated the predicaments of style and cadencing choices that live on today.

The Word-Loving Sophists

The basic meaning of the word 'sophist' is 'wise man,' and the ancient use of it was twofold. Its 'smarty-pants' connotation derived from the sophistic tendency to deprecate ancestral religious 'truths.' The word also implied a genuine expertness. In that more admirable mode, it was used as an honorific title for the professional educators who traveled to leading Greek cities and (for a hefty price) lectured ambitious young men on how to win a debate. Skill in word use was the key. In the fifth century, as democracy was encouraging public participation in civic decisions, an attractive and purposeful delivery—a delivery of fluid eloquence founded on a logical sequence of argument—became the target for those wishing to shine. Thus, the analysis of language and the development of verbal ability became the specialty of the education-minded sophists, whose ranks came to include not only the deep thinkers and genuine teachers, but also their money-grubbing hangers-on, pundits, imitators, and quacks—all of whom added fresh aspects to the meaning of 'sophist.'

The analytic abilities of the best peripatetic sophists had a huge impact on the development of literature, rhetoric, and philology.

> [The sophists] developed the concepts and categories of the parts of speech, moods, genders and diction; they contributed to the artistic qualities of literary prose; they elaborated paradoxes and common-places useful…to writers; they sharpened logical reasoning, and they laid a foundation for literary criticism.[1]

Protagoras (probably born around 485 BCE in the remote northeast of Greece) was active in Athens from the 450s to the 420s, and generally thought to be the first to claim the title of 'sophist.' What we know of him and his fellow thinkers, most of whom came from Ionia (on the Aegean coast of modern Turkey) tells us that humankind was at last beginning to penetrate the mists of the old religions and reject their mythopoeic orderings of the universe. Before then, Nature's quirks and threats had been seen to derive from the passions of hot-blooded gods and goddesses. 'Knowledge' came in the form of epic stories featuring Zeus, his thunderbolts, quarrels, and love affairs—all accepted as inherited 'fact' from oral-aural animistic prehistory. Neither Homer, nor any pre-fifth-century writer, had supposed a real division between god-oriented decree and the fate of man—which is to say, they viewed nature's law and man's law as one.[2] But now, the sophists enter the picture. They are helped by the presence of alphabetic writing as they begin to analyze nature's phenomena more objectively.

Protagoras maintained that all is relative; that there is no absolute reality, no difference between appearing and being; that each man is the judge of what is true for himself; and that *there exist two opposite arguments for every subject.* Protagoras claimed to be able, through artful debate, to make the weaker cause the stronger. Accomplishing this ambition required a facility with words and a familiarity with grammar—indeed, with whatever linguistic finaglings lay at hand to win a point. *Persuasion was the goal.* For that, subsequent eastern 'professors of wisdom' continued to investigate the capabilities and shortcomings of language, seeking to improve its flexibility, clarity, and stability of form, whether spoken or written. Over time they prescribed rules of grammar, syntax, word order, and compositional arrangement. They analyzed the meanings and nuances of words and taught how one should conduct oneself on the podium—how and when to gesture and where to pile on the emphasis. All these things made up the art of rhetoric: that is, the science of using words effectively in speech and then later in writing. It was Protagoras who propounded the theory that leadership virtues were reflected in clear speech, which itself reflected clear thinking—and that the result would lead to orderly living.

Generally speaking, the word-loving, detail-addicted, hair-splitting sophists were the first to put Greek prose on track for the highly finished, pleasing word-flow of such as the later, fourth-century Plato; and their influence would be lasting. Though Plato, the consummate sculptor of verbal material, benefited from sophistic discovery, he despised the sophists themselves. Their hold on the public purse and imagination was too strong. Their wordy cleverness and passion to win the argument seemed in no way directed to hunt down truth or support political justice—let alone instill virtue. By Plato's time, sophistic lectures had become an intellectual fashion, and while costing the moon, they inspired an expensive show-off activity for the young male members of wealthy families. In Plato's view, knowledge with all its aura of virtue and truth had meandered off course. But as we have seen, sophists could be a variety of things. Some were intellectually principled, others money-grasping, ignorant, and deceitful. What they were, in short, was a mixed bag.

Modern scholars have divided the sophists into two camps: east and west. The Protagoras eastern group, whose high purpose was to achieve accuracy, analysis, and logical cohesion, had its roots in Greek-speaking Ionia. *Why there?* one wonders. A speculative answer is that westward-working commercial influences from more-advanced eastern civilizations had begun to intellectualize the Mediterranean's Greek-speaking eastern fringe. In any case, it is certain that by the Archaic early sixth century BCE, the Greeks on the Ionian coast had produced a number of inspired and literate Greek-speaking philosophers, who, repudiating Zeus, addressed the real workings of the universe. We shall shortly inspect the intellectual and linguistic accomplishments of these eastern sophists. But because the emotional right hemisphere of the human fetal brain develops before its reasoning twin, and because prosodic orality is for the moment our topic, let us first address the western contingent.

The western sophists made their impact on Athens slightly after the eastern sophists. Originating in Sicily, they held to the traditions of ceremonial rhetoric—that is, the high-flying, inspirational, exhortative rhetoric that required eloquence and kept its focus on the beauty of style and the emotional responses that euphonious speech could elicit, *and not so much* on the logic needed for legal argument or civil debate. As far as is known, Korax in Sicily was the founder of prosodic rhetoric with its penchant for beautiful phrasing. He was the teacher of Tisias, who in turn taught the influential Gorgias.

The impact that these Sicilian rhetoricians had on the manipulative possibilities of the language of prose was astonishing.

Gorgias—in Every Sense of the Word

Our first real glimpse of the 'shadier' type of prose word use—that is, the rhythmic, aural type that plays to the emotions—comes from what is known of the early rhetorical teachings of the Sicilian sophist Gorgias of Leontini (ca. 483–ca. 376 BCE: a long life), of whose grandly styled output (frowned upon by Plato's Socrates) very little survives. Regarded as the creator of 'artificial Greek prose,' Gorgias urged his disciples to decorate their diction with poetic conceits—florid images and pleonastic phrase-pairings that jingled like verse, delayed comprehension and lulled the brain like a gurgling brook. Gorgias disdained the Protagorean view that word skill would open the mind to a virtuous and orderly life, or that it might help to discover the truths of reality. Instead, he focused his efforts on the art of clever and beautiful speaking, the mastery of which, he claimed, would empower a man to dominate the experts in any sort of field.[3] To ensure that one's flow of words would not run dry, Gorgias advised his disciples to commit to memory (as had he) copious passages of beautiful oratory that could be drawn upon extemporarily to advance their own arguments *and keep them coming.* His prescription for persuasion was deluge, and the mastery of persuasion (he quite rightly perceived) was the key to *pure power.*

The need for rhetorical finesse in those times was great. Eminent men devoted their lives to advising the young (if their fathers could afford it) how to achieve 'effective speech' and thereby become famous. Gorgias, the Star Mouth of Sicily, was sovereign at that. He especially prided himself on having (without a scrap of medical knowledge) more successfully prevailed upon a patient to undergo an operation than had the patient's brother, who was the actual physician. What beauteous things he managed to say we have not been told, nor do we know if the patient survived his brother's knife.

Gorgias was vastly admired in his time. He was sent from Sicily to Athens in 427 BCE to plead the cause of his oppressed fellow Leontinians against their tyrannical neighbor, Syracuse. Athenians adored him. His high-flying rhetoric made a tremendous hit with their rhythm-loving ears. That his bizarre prose style should have so dazzled the Athenians is today rather mysti-fying, for Athens at the time was the very nest of logic-oriented civil oratory. While its citizenry responded almost electrically to the music of speech, for political and judicial arguments they demanded sound logic as well. From the popular public readings and dramatic performances, they knew the well-fo-cused oratory of Homeric heroes. They had savored the cogent eloquence of Aeschylus, Sophocles, and Euripides. Nevertheless, history records that the Athenian public positively reeled with pleasure whenever Gorgias opened his mouth.

What was this man's gift perceived to be? In a word, it was this: he was the first to bring to prose all the artistry that had previously been reserved for poet-ry. From his time on, prose composition would be viewed as a formal craft with a musical elegance all its own—and hence a facile and worthy competitor for poetry, which up to then had been the vehicle of 'knowledge.' By enlarging the aesthetic scope of prose, Gorgias supplied a joy much craved by Atheni-an audiences. Politicians, rhetoricians, and literary aspirants—all seized on the new possibilities. Henceforth, philosophers and explicators would be less inclined to squeeze their arguments into meter, as Xenophanes, Parmenides, Empedocles, and the theologue Hesiod had done. All in all, by encouraging 'beautification,' the Gorgianic style removed what had heretofore been a com-plaint against all prose language—that it could not compete with melodious Homer and wasn't in truth very beautiful.

Though the fame of Gorgias was enormous, it quickly became apparent that his ornate, gushing-faucet style would need some toning down, for it soon began to offend the Athenian sense of measure and clarity. In his early dia-logue *Gorgias*, Plato reaffirmed the rule that decoration should not deform the form, and described Socrates as disdaining overblown rhetoric on the grounds of its being a dangerous knack, more akin to cooking and flattery (the special-ty of women) than philosophy (a man's domain).

The Gorgianic excess of aesthetic ploy would in time be tempered by Isocrates and Cicero. Nevertheless, its inflated verbosity would have a long ca-reer, one that stretched on and on, beyond Englishman Lyly's sixteenth-cen-tury novel *Euphues* and into the church oratory of today. By way of more modern example, one can find it in the speech mannerisms of the Reverend Jesse Jackson. But to sample this early BCE moment, let us join Agathon's drinking party (described by Plato in his dialogue *Symposium*) and listen to Plato's takeoff on Gorgianic swell. Agathon (playing the part of Gorgias) is describing for the benefit of wise old Socrates the attributes of Eros (the god of carnal love). The repetitive thumps of positive-negative phrases (so tedious!) was a growing complaint against Gorgias.

> This is he [Eros] who empties men of disaffection and fills them with affection, who makes them to meet together at banquets such as these: in sacrifices, feasts, dances, he is our lord—who sends courtesy and sends away discourtesy, who gives kindness ever and never gives unkindness; the friend of the good, the wonder of the wise, the amazement of the gods; desired by those who have no part in him, and precious to those who have the better part in him; parent of delicacy, luxury, desire, fondness, softness, grace; regardful of the good, regardless of the evil.[4] (Plato, *Symposium*, 197d)

Recognizing at last that a perspicuous communication cannot after all be achieved in this way, those sharp Greeks invented a new word, "gorgiaze," and used it derogatorily.

In remarking on Gorgias's style and the influence it would have on subsequent Greek prose writers, J. D. Denniston, an authority on the subject, tells us this:

> What he did was, in fact, to take certain qualities inherent in Greek expression, balance and antithesis, and exaggerate them to the point of absurdity. To his doctrinaire mind, balance meant mathematical equality. And this was more readily obtained, and more blatantly obvious to the ear, if the clauses were short. Hence his writing is throughout chopped up into the smallest possible units.... Gorgias, the ancient authorities tell us, was the first writer of Greek prose to exploit consciously the use of rhyming clauses. Whereas in earlier prose, rhymes naturally arose out of symmetrical structure, in Gorgias and Isocrates, and other writers under the Gorgianic influence, they are deliberately sought out. Double rhymes, too, are not infrequently found.[5]

In this discussion of the differing influences of emotion and reason in the human brain, it should be stressed that, since the dawn of history, the healthy human has assuredly operated with both. It is only *a shift in emphasis* that we talk about in these pages. While literacy drew identifiable new responses from the brain's left hemisphere, we may assume that some sort of grammar and syntactical rule has always guided human speech. Even melodious Gorgias could not do without logical order to move his singsong blather along. The progression of argument in his only wholly-extant piece, the overwrought *Encomium of Helen*, is, for example, impeccable. Was Helen rightly blamed for leaving Menelaos? No, says Gorgias, since the choice was not hers. She was *obliged* to accompany Paris to Troy, the compulsion being one (or perhaps all) of the following: (1) fate or divine will; (2) muscular force; (3) ineluctable persuasion (for who can resist sweet words?); and (4) uncontrollable sexual desire. Throughout the *Encomium*, the arguments are burdened with paraphrased repetitions, acoustical symmetries, rhymes, and pairs of parallel and antithetical phrases.

Nevertheless, beneath all the foam of his effervescing mind, we find a solid infrastructure. The steps of his argument, though silly to us today, are well signposted. Though the *Encomium* is only an exercise to amuse himself (so he claims), Gorgias takes care to announce what he is going to say; he then says it; and moreover, having said it, says that he has said it—a tedious procedure. Even the most inept amongst us are left *in no doubt* about the progress of his argument, for despite the overload of trinkets and bells, meaning does emerge. Along with his bubble-headed topic (though a popular one in his time), Gorgias also offends our intelligence by hammering us into a daze with the same artistic precepts he seeks to recommend.

Despite all, his work presents techniques that would in time be useful to serious prose writers with more important matters to discuss than the hairdos of Helen. Since style is such an important part of expression, Gorgias must be thanked for his wide-swinging efforts. Isocrates and Cicero, both men of solemn purpose, will soon be on stage to show how to practice rhetorical artistry at a more acceptable level. Meanwhile, anti-Gorgias criticism would be gathering on its own. Socrates, Plato, and Aristotle, being the champion triad of serious fifth- and fourth-century intellectuals, railed against the vitiation of meaning for the sake of gratifying the senses. That the measure of a man's worth is his intellect seemed to them unarguable. One should guard against devices that relate too obviously to bodily sources—heartbeats, breathing, and the pairings of limbs and organs. Prosody, music, dance, and emotional rhetoric all catch their energies from our basic physical beings and should, said those critics, have no influence on the search for truth. Sound pedagogy must encourage the *powers of reason*. Nevertheless, in those early years of literacy, even Plato seemed somewhat respectful of the tricks and turns of Gorgianic habit; for in later dialogues, neither Socrates as depicted by Plato, nor Plato as reflected in Socrates, appeared to loathe Gorgias totally; and everyone admired the work of his disciple Isocrates (436–338 BCE), who wrote his prose with comely good sense.

Nevertheless, with respect to the arts of communication, uncertainties would continue to multiply. The scientific inquiries of the Ionians and the objectifying effects of alphabetic writing were only beginning to generate their powerful logical influence.

* * * * *

The next chapter, chapter 5, will conclude our exploration of the emotional ear-driven responses that helped to prepare prose for artistic acceptance.

Notes

1. George A. Kennedy, "Sophists and Physicians of the Greek Enlightenment," in *The Cambridge History of Classical Literature*, ed. P. E. Easterling and Bernard M. K. Knox (Cambridge: Cambridge University Press, 1985), 1:473.
2. W. K. C. Guthrie, *The Sophists* (London: Cambridge University Press, 1971), 55.
3. Guthrie, *Sophists*, 29.
4. Benjamin Jowett, *The Dialogues of Plato* (New York: Random House, 1937), 1:523 and 1:323. The above Platonic materials have been drawn from Benjamin Jowett's translations and commentary.
5. J. D. Denniston, *Greek Prose Style* (Oxford: Clarendon Press, 1952), 10. Mr. Denniston was a renowned scholar of ancient Greek literature and language. His scholarship is referred to frequently throughout this treatise.

References

Denniston, J. D. *Greek Prose Style*. Oxford: Clarendon Press, 1952.

Guthrie, W. K. C. *The Sophists*. London: Cambridge University Press, 1971.

Jowett, Benjamin. Vol. 1 of *The Dialogues of Plato*. New York: Random House, 1937.

Kennedy, George A. "Sophists and Physicians of the Greek Enlightenment." In Vol. 1 of *The Cambridge History of Classical Literature*. Edited by P. E. Easterling and Bernard M. K. Knox. Cambridge: Cambridge University Press, 1985.

· 5 ·

PROSE CLAIMS ACCEPTANCE

Our Physiological Responses to Rhythm

What do we know about our physiological responses to rhythm and melody? It is quite plain that the prosodic features of speech are separate from the grammatical ones.[1] Emotions can be aroused by serial noun-based word pictures if the atmosphere is supportive. When listening to the sometimes impossible-to-parse verses of a song, we can be held by the pulsing repetition of mind-catching images. Human response to such stimuli seems to be universal. The semantic content of noun images dealt out rhythmically can excite the mind as well as inform it. We find a good example of such power in John Masefield's poem "Cargoes," in which there is no completed sentence. (Here, the forms *rowing, dipping, butting* are gerundives: that is, adjectives derived from verbs and hence powerless to make a full, grammatical statement.)

> Quinquireme of Nineveh from distant Ophir,
> Rowing home to haven in sunny Palestine,
> With a cargo of ivory,
> And apes and peacocks,
> Sandalwood, cedarwood, and sweet white wine.

Stately Spanish galleon coming from the Isthmus,
Dipping though the Tropics by the palm-green shores,
With a cargo of diamonds,
Emeralds, amethysts,
Topazes, and cinnamon, and gold moidores.

Dirty British coaster with a salt-caked smoke stack,
Butting through the Channel in the mad March days,
With a cargo of Tyne coal,
Road-rails, pig-lead,
Firewood, iron-ware, and cheap tin trays.[2]

The Japanese have also worked with this trick of eliciting mental pictures in poems and songs with verbless strings of noun phrases. A chanted, shamisen-accompanied "Blue wisteria, under the moon's thin slice" or "Rain splash on dark waters" followed by similar unintegrated noun images can suggest the yearnings of love on a chilly spring night, or (if you wish) the intimations of mortality in the face of cosmic eternity. Declarative verbs (which are so necessary to a decipherable flow of prose) show intention; they energize and make propositions. Nevertheless, cleverly juxtaposed noun phrases can be powerful without them, and very powerful when enhanced by rhythm or music.

In addition to words for oral communication, tonality, pitch, volume, and emphasis can all carry emotional significance. The crooning, cooing tones and rhythms that a mother uses when rocking her baby are more potent in cementing the relationship between them than the words that actually accompany these vocalizations. It is well known to psychiatrists that infants who grow up in an environment of unresponsive soundlessness are seriously impaired for speech development. It seems that the rhythmic and intoning apparatus for communicating must be in place before words can effectively be brought into play.[3] That generally accepted theory supports the more speculative one, that in human prehistory, some form of music and dancing preceded (or at least accompanied) the development of language. True or not, it should be noted that nonliterate societies especially respond to and enjoy producing rhythmic musical sounds.

Interesting in this respect is the drum language once (and perhaps still) used in parts of Africa to convey simple messages over long distances. In this system, drumbeats imitate the rhythms of commonplace word clusters—commonplace because nothing novel or elaborate can be communicated in this way. Two pitches from two drums render the song line of this surrogate language, and the simultaneous strike of both drums marks a cadence. Understanding is sought by repeating the content of the message in various stereotypic forms.[4]

Similar results can be brought about with the violin. If the context is settled, then apt bowing can imitate the intonation and rhythms of expected speech, such as are found in commands, expressions of disgust, cajoling requests or hot argument: "*Eat your spinach!*" "*No, I won't!*" "*You must!*" "*I don't wa-ant to*"—and so forth. Even more than seeing, hearing is fundamental to our emotional makeup. So embedded in our physical core are the tentacles of our auditory apparatus that small children up to the age of four or five have difficulty holding still when music is sounding. Volume, rhythm, pitch, melody, and even harmony physically affect us all. They arouse and intensify feelings; they help us to structure time. Physiotherapists, being aware of the power of musical stimulus, have on occasion been able to elicit dance from a person who cannot walk and song from a person who cannot talk. That we are so in sympathy with the effects of sound is well known to filmmakers, who stir us up smartly with their mounting tempi and percussive accompaniments. Rhythm—so deeply incorporated into the human system with heartbeats, breathing, lovemaking—is of particular importance to writers. It dominates the aural need for cadence and informs the visual need for punctuation. Dogs, pigs, cows, ants, lizards, etc., show no response to rhythm.

The fact that there are two basic ways of punctuating text—the rhetorical, which is related to emotion and music, and the logical, which is related to reason and grammar—arises from the way we are physically put together. To simplify the matter for the layman, Dr. Storr explains the behavior that derives from our complicated duality as follows:

> Music and speech are separately represented in the two hemispheres of the brain. Although there is considerable overlap, as happens with many cerebral functions, language is predominantly processed in the left hemisphere, whilst music [is] chiefly scanned and appreciated in the right hemisphere. The division of function is not so much between words and music as between logic and emotion. When words are directly linked with emotions, as they are [most particularly] in poetry and song, the right hemisphere is operative. But it is the left hemisphere which deals with the language of conceptual thought.[5]

Leonard Shlain, surgeon and professor of medicine (also the author of *The Alphabet versus the Goddess*), tells us that the right hemisphere is the older, more basic half of the human brain.

In utero, the right lobe of a human fetus's brain is well on its way to maturation before the left side begins to develop....The right brain integrates feelings...[is] non-verbal...comprehends the language of cries, gestures, grimaces, cuddling, suckling, touching and body stance....[It] generates feeling-states, such as love, humor, or aesthetic appreciation, which are non-logical [that is, not based on reason]....Standing in the shadows of our ancient beginnings, feeling-states overwhelm the brain's more recently evolved glib facility with words....Feeling-states do not ordinarily progress in a linear fashion, but are experienced all-at-once.

About the left side of the brain, Shlain has this to say:

The left brain's primary functions are opposite and complementary to the right's....The left lobe controls the vital act of willing. In right-handed people, 90 percent of language skills reside in the left hemisphere. Speech gave the left brain the edge to usurp the sovereignty of the mind from its elder twin....Speech is abstract and depends upon the left brain's unique ability to process information without the use of visual images.[6]

Shlain also tells us that the brain's left lobe controls analysis of speech and that *the reduction, or fracturing, of the components of a sentence into their separate parts is essential to understanding speech.* Speech is perforce linear. The beginning segments of a statement must be held in the memory to fit with the requirements of middle and end. In contrast, emotion is processed *holistically* by the right lobe. Objective thinking is enhanced by this dimediation of our brains. It gives us perspective by creating a distinction between *me-in-here* and *world-out-there.* These sorts of generalizations make useful rules of thumb for the layman; but it is important to understand that the brain is more plastic than this strict lobe formula might suggest. Nevertheless, it is true that if for some reason the lobes do not properly synthesize during the growing period, then the visual-ideographic functions will not correlate with the oral-auditory ones. Readers who suffer from a persisting poor coordination between the cerebral hemispheres have to fight hard to master our sacrosanct visuo-phonic alphabet. Herein is a source of dyslexia, a frustrating but common problem.

On the matter of music, Oliver Sacks adds this:

Musical perception is chiefly a right hemisphere function in pre-
dominantly "naïve" listeners, but becomes left hemisphere in professional musicians and expert listeners who grasp its grammar, and
for whom it has become an intricate formal structure.[7]

Speculating scholars believe that tribal laws, prayers, and accounts of ancestral feats were chanted in early preliterate ceremonial gatherings, and
would therefore have been more melodic and poetic than prosaic. If that
is accepted, then it is likely that the right lobe of the brain was the more
active one and was perceiving intuitively, without analysis. By sensing and
immediately emoting, it created a feeling-state that tended to view 'reality'
through metaphoric myth-making and stories. By comparison, it is the left
lobe that dominates today in literate parts of the world. Unlike its sister
lobe, it views the world with a specificity that favors strict evaluation of perceptions, one by one, following the footsteps of time. Critical analysis and
the formulation of thoughts into coordinated sequences are prime features
of a literate culture. They have been fortified by the intensity of focus that
literacy requires—a focus so concentrated that it can separate thought from
feeling, object from subject, and mind from body.

In summary, the right-left lobe confrontation is this: for the right,
an I-Thou pantheistic and incorporative relationship with the phenomenal
world through myth; *versus* for the left: a rational I-It relationship, wherein
the goal is to make experience coherent by dealing with the intake of information bit by bit—whether in linear bits (like words), in graphs, or with bits
represented by symbols arranged in a branching tree-like structure. Though
the human mind works in both brain-lobe modes, the cultural emphasis
can swing between them, and does. In less literate societies, myth-making
reactions to natural phenomena have predominated. In highly literate ones,
reason probes the factual origins of whatever mystifies. All known civilizations before the seventh century BCE were mythopoeic in that they relied
on stories rather than physical analysis to explain the causes of the things
that terrified them—like thunder, earthquakes, floods, droughts, epidemics,
and death. It was the Ionian Greeks who invented the easy-to-use, vow-
el-included linear alphabet and developed the sophistic rationalism that
changed the Western world.[8]

We shall inspect the rational side of the cerebral split shortly. Meanwhile, back to the topic of ear-oriented, emotion-stirring rhetoric.

Rhetoric Moves Onto the Page

The oral arts were formulating rules for well-ordered speech long before literature came on the scene. By the fifth century BCE, Athenian orators, the admired paragons for those aspiring to fame and power, were plainly strategizing both to be clear and elegant. For that, some system of arrangement was necessary, not only amongst phrases and clauses, but also amongst the contributing segments of overarching argument. Meaningful content is laid out to lead somewhere. Its parts are not randomly scattered but must follow custom; for words and phrases are more readily understood when their positions in the lineup have been standardized. Orderliness supports the speaker-writer's intended connection with the listener-reader. That being the case, one may conjecture that from earliest times some standardized presentation of subject and content would have been sought. With the contours of exposition being familiar, a listener would know by the cut of the language where the speaker was in his presentation of ideas—the *proemion* (introduction)? the *diegesis* (narration)? the *pistis* (proof)?, or the *epilogos* (conclusion)?[9]

The body of precepts and rules for top-notch oratory came to be known as the 'art of *rhetoric*' (with the italicized Greek stem relating to speech). Since early writing was viewed as the mirrored form of an actual utterance, instructions for composing top-grade words on papyrus simply followed the directives of its most esteemed oral counterpart—top-grade oratory—whose own inherited guideline was to arrange words in ear-pleasing ways, and to strive for the order and graciousness originally inspired by poetry and dance. But as literacy grew in confidence, it encouraged a more critical analysis, and that sharpened the game. With the development of writing, the 'art of rhetoric' turned its attentions to syntax, grammar, imagery, word-meaning, and division of topic.

Since tyrants, royals, and dictators prefer to *impose* their wills rather than to *discuss* them, democracies became the usual sites for heated rhetorical exchange. As we have seen, democratic Sicily was the beehive source of honeyed speech, and like their more reasoning Ionian cousins, Sicilian sophists practiced widely. Starting with Korax (ca. 467 BCE), they set about *writing* handbooks called *technes*. Initially, these were only collections of ideal speeches, but they came in time to include specific recommendations for word use, and information on the parts of speech, optimal word order, and grammar—in short, how to perfect a spoken performance and, by extension, how to perfect its written version as well. Sublimity of utterance was crucial, for in the ancient world the expressed word, be it spoken or written, was deemed to be soul exposing. Writing's enduring stability encouraged a studious, concentrated striving for beauty and clarity.

Thus it was that in pursuit of linguistic perfection, sophistic rhetoricians from both camps, east and west, began to refine particulars: to suggest special meters for mini-cadences, measure out sentence proportions, and (vainly) advise restraint. Their attentions brought to light clauses (called *colons*: plural *cola*) and initiated discussion of their definitions (*What were they?* and *how to make whatever they were perfect?*); all of which worked towards isolating idea-bearing segments from the swell of unending verbiage at a time when terminal cadences (full stops) were scarcely mentioned. Phrases (called *commas*: plural *commata*) were not specifically dealt with until Rome's early Christian era. In sum, Protagoras's boost to textual progress lay in his adherence to logical and analytical processes; Gorgias's gift lay in the attention he brought to the sensual aspects of rhythm, repetition, and balance that words can be made to incite.

While writing pressed slowly on, extemporized oral rhetoric continued to flourish, almost as a popular entertainment, in disputatious Athens. In the general atmosphere of hearsay—without telephones, microscopes, film, computers, or indeed any device of modern scientific exactitude—public opinion was shaped by the force and appeal of the spoken word, and the apparent trustworthiness of the speaker. In civil courts or political musters, it was worth your property, your reputation, your life, to defend or accuse with maximum skill. Addressing a jury was no small thing. Imagine yourself confronting a multitude of some five-hundred doubting compatriots, all staring at you judgmentally—their stern faces reflecting the thinness of your case. How do you best disclaim your guilt? By babbling and blubbering? Certainly not. One must not count on sympathy. This hard-nosed citizenry must be *dissuaded* from suspicion, and for that, a *techne* in the pocket was worth its weight in gold. A man must appeal to those who would judge him, not only by the acceptability of his argument but also by the nicety of his diction. With so much at stake, it was easy to see the benefit of memorizing apt phrases (as Gorgias had advocated), or, yes! even of jotting down notes before facing the court or mounting the podium. Clever speech could not only sway judges, *it could deceive them.*

The practice of preparing notes for any rhetorical ordeal was already common before the time of Socrates. By the mid-fifth century BCE, the custom had stretched to the writing down of one's entire speech before delivering it—or more likely, to hiring someone else to do the writing job for you. Professional speechwriters (called "logographers") like Antiphon (fl. ca. 460 BCE) were increasingly resorted to. From that sort of help, it was no great step to repair for publication one's *already given* speech; and from there, to simply write the whole of it afterwards, in pretense that those beautifully organized and rhythmic phrases were what one had actually said on a vital occasion. *All was not as it seemed.*

Nevertheless, writing was there. People were using it, and it had to be dealt with. The chasm that separated the 'beautifully spoken' from the 'awkwardly written' narrowed as writers busily honed their skills to please posterity and gratify themselves. Homeric perfection was their target. Indeed, Homer's artistic yet rational management of his topic set an extraordinary example for all future poets and writers of prose. For centuries Homeric levels of perfection were the yardsticks for measuring the success of all ambitious wordmongers.

At this level of prose history, we stand between the paradigms of Homer's epic poetry—with its sensual-logical balance—and Plato's fourth-century amalgam of reason and beauty for prose. Lingering still on the sensual side of the fence, we next meet Isocrates, a man who was able to make considerable improvement over the mesmerizing lilt and pulse of his teacher, Gorgias. But first, a quick glimpse at that interesting phenomenon—the *periodos*.

Introducing the *Periodos*

As the *technes* from both eastern and western sophistic camps spread the news, so a desire for verbal sophistication grew. Educated Athenians began to reject the archaic, *and*-ridden, running-on-forever style of statement in favor of what came to be known as *periods*, that is, statements that 'completed a full thought.' The so-called 'full thought' was an expansion of the core message to include related subsidiary aspects of it. Importantly, however, *periods* also included a sense of termination. Though 'wholeness' and 'full circle' were the operating concepts, *periods* also differentiated the levels of importance amongst their many parts. In sum, they were elaborate sentences that brimmed with varying levels of subordinate structures. Particles were the critical tools for differentiation amongst the parts. Particles allowed the *periods* to grow, and in growing to *dis-equate* the relationships of all the participating ideas. The segment that carried the governing verb was the designated nucleus. It carried more weight (though not necessarily more information) than the other segments. As can be imagined, arranging a collection of related mini-ideas around their core idea demanded both a focused attention and a facility with language.

The term *periodos* in Greek means 'road around' or 'racetrack,' but precisely when the term was first applied to a sentence structure is uncertain. We know only that its basic elements were in practice long before the late fourth century when Aristotle called it by name and recommended its powers. Later, the *periodos* would become a major topic for all the ancient expositors of literary style.

In broad terms the *period's* purpose was to build a solid unity from a collection of associated thoughts—thoughts that would otherwise be joined in a rambling train by *and* or *then* connectives. The *period's* unifying ambition was achieved with particle words such as *since, when, while, but, that, who, on the contrary*, and so on. Particles tightened the relationships amongst the segments of a *period*ic sentence and marked their level of importance within the whole. Whether written or spoken, the *period* worked to resolve the problem of words having to be delivered linearly—in a one-dimensional, time-dominated lineup even when the 'well head' thought with its variegated extensions was felt to be whole, integrated, and indivisible. Conceptually, the *period* proved an ambitious substitute for the global and all-incorporative levels of mental experience. For shape more than intention, one might think of an ancient *period* as an overly-upholstered complex sentence.

The period's growth and various transformations became extensive as time passed, but for present purposes, one should view the *period* as the Greeks taught the world to do; that is, as a statement whose primary message is enlarged by a quantity of supporting linearly laid-out materials, known as *cola*, or clauses, and by the later-noticed and thereafter defined *commata*, or phrases. It is from the ancient *comma, colon*, and *period* that we get our terms for modern punctuation.

Isocrates Constructs a Splendiferous *Period*

In the practice of Beautiful Persuasion, Isocrates (436–338 BCE) cut a notable figure. Moderate in temper and congenial as well, Isocrates was less subject to excess than was his teacher Gorgias. As a result, his work would find its admirers well into future centuries. Nearly two millennia after his demise, his imposing style burst into bloom again as a model for such influential Renaissance English prose writers as Lyly, Elyot, and Ascham, for whom the rhetorical music of classical times was best represented by magniloquent sentence structures, still being called *periods*.

What makes Isocrates especially important for our purposes is that, unlike other Greek orators of his time, he *composed his discourses to be read rather than spoken.* His own published *Art of Rhetoric* has been lost, though it is pretty clear what he would have said in it. Isocrates advocated embellishment of language on the grounds that it tended to calm restive minds and would successfully persuade them to embrace truth and just causes. Fortunately, the influence of Socrates (whom he admired) restrained him from total ear-directed lavishness and turned his creative energies in the direction of factual content. Though he was certainly responsive to Gorgianic sound, Isocrates is considered to have surpassed his teacher with his more subtle control of an argument. His writings became the paradigm of 'artistic' rhetoric during his own Classical Greek period, for they brought music to the page without obscuring the subject matter. Isocrates was an outstanding figure among the many famous men of his time, and the teacher of eminent leaders both in Athens and in Greece at large. The school that he opened in 392 BCE came to represent Athens herself in the eyes of literate men abroad. We are told that Isocrates made more money from academic work than anyone else in his time. (The earlier Protagoras and Gorgias are also known to have become rich.)

Isocrates was born in the fifth century, in Pericles's time, and lived (like Gorgias) on and on. In the year 380, he achieved tremendous fame with his publication of *Panegyricus,* considered to be the very essence of 'fine writing.' We may imagine Isocrates as a willowy, not very healthy gentleman whose ambition was to be acclaimed the 'wisest man' in Greece. Luckily, by his time writing was an established art, for his voice was too weak for the podium. The subjects Isocrates chose to expound with his pen were not trivial judicial cases to settle local squabbles and minor theft, but Big Issues: Hellenic affairs, and political and constitutional matters. His mission was to improve the management of cities and the characters of those who inhabited them. In and amongst, he condemned the money-grabbing sophists, whose disquisitions he thought had grown aimless and impractical—far too much biased towards clever speech and mythological topics. His own teachings included more serious matter. His declamation on the standard topic of Helen, for example, is weightier in content than that of Gorgias, in that it incorporates materials on the practical and political reforms said to have been instituted by Theseus, the legendary founder of Athens. Such topics, he felt, not only sharpened the rhetorical prowess of young students, but improved their behavior and broadened their civic scope as well. Education, according to Isocrates, should give moral direction to human activities.

In time Isocrates's attention would turn almost wholly to politics and to the defeat of his vibrant rival, the renowned orator Demosthenes. Whereas Demosthenes wished to combat the threatening armies of Macedonian Philip (father of Alexander the Great), Isocrates wished to accept Philip's rule, reasoning that only Philip could unite all of Greece. It was plainly a time of great urgency, with interests at stake that were far more vital than the morals of Helen. A persuasive argument required rhetorical finesse, for it is no small thing to manipulate an impatient crowd with only words. To win one's point, phrasing, imagery, rhythm, reason, clarity, and sound psychological assessment—all must be managed with skill.

Much has been written about Isocrates over the centuries, but the critic we shall now turn to for appraisal is also from the ancient world, though several centuries later than Isocrates. Dionysius of Halicarnassus (Halicarnassus was the ancient name for modern Turkey's Bodrum) migrated to Rome ca. 30 BCE (shortly after the death of Cicero) and dedicated himself to supporting the purity of Classical Greek. In his studies of the stylistic achievements of ancient Greek orators, Dionysius tells us that Isocrates set the confused inheritance of oratorical studies on a new course.[10] That confused inheritance, he said, had derived from the conflicting pedagogies of the sophistic, nit-picking, dialectic East (Ionia) and the flamboyantly rhetorical West (Sicily). In a somewhat extended embrace of the two, Isocrates was seen to have written well-argued political discourses in beautiful rhythmic language.

Dionysius compares Isocrates's style to the unadorned style of earlier speechmakers, which is to say, before the logical eastern Protagoras and the melodious Sicilian Gorgias put their oars in. Previously (up to half a century before the arrival of these 'foreigners' in Athens), the untutored, home-grown speechmaking had been considered quite acceptable, and folk seemed satisfied with the quantities of clarity and beauty being put into play. Even the legendary heroes of Homer's *Iliad* and *Odyssey* had addressed and persuaded each other in clear, soundly argued, terse, albeit 'poetic,' diction. It would seem that Isocrates was inching towards those purer forms and back from the brink of Gorgianic extravagance—just enough back, in fact, to be acceptable to modern minds.

As we have noted, the *period*'s task was to gather diverse but related ideas into a unified, single construction. Isocrates had a penchant for large, even mountainous periodic constructions. Though often involved and many lines long, they were controlled grammatically and were aurally pleasing as well. Isocrates crafted his cornucopian statements to avoid the clash of harsh consonants or unseemly clusters of vowels and to maintain the music and balance with unobtrusive rhythms. Concerning the specifics of Isocrates's style, our guide Dionysius of Halicarnassos finds much to praise. He tells us *on the one hand* that not a word is used at random, and that the actual language conforms closely with the most ordinary and familiar usage, avoiding the banality of archaic and obscure words. Though the use of figurative language is evident, a happy balance is struck. Isocrates's writing is lucid and vivid, as well as moral, convincing in tone, and appropriate to its subject.

On the other hand (Dionysius continues):

> [I]t is not a compact, closely-knit style...and is therefore ill-suited to forensic purposes: it sprawls and overflows with its own exuberance. Again, it is not so concise, but seems to drag its feet and move too slowly....Nor again does it display a natural, simple and vigorous arrangement of words...rather it is designed to create an effect of ceremonious and ornate dignity, so that it may at times be more attractive, but at other times it seems laboured. For this orator [Isocrates] seeks beauty of expression by every means, and aims at polish rather than simplicity. He avoids hiatus [as in 'a orange,' or 'a action'] on the ground that this breaks the continuity of utterance and impairs the smoothness of the sounds. He tries to express his ideas within the framework of the rounded *period*, using strong rhythms which are not far removed from those of verse, thus rendering his work more suitable for reading than for practical use. For the same reason his speeches will bear recitation on ceremonial occasions, and private study, but cannot stand up to the stresses of the assembly or the law-courts. This is because such occasions demand intensity of feeling, and this is what the period is least capable of expressing. Clauses ending with similar sounds and having equal length, antithesis and the whole array of figures of this kind, are found in Isocrates in great numbers, and often spoil the rest of his artistry by obtruding themselves upon the ear.[11] (Dion. Hal., *Isoc.* 2)

Along with his avoidance of hiatus, Isocrates also rejected the short (very oral) breathless phrasings and re-phrasings favored by Gorgias (as caricatured in Plato's account of Agathon). Tightly knit *cola* were his preference. It was a preference that was much aided by the inflectional powers of the Greek language and the growing batch of newly invented particles. Inflections enabled Isocrates to disarrange word order and make statements flow with fewer breaks for breath intake. The particles provided the directional signals for all the verbal traffic. (We shall examine the powers of both inflections and particles later, to see how they actually worked.) Isocrates could manage these complexities because of his devoted interaction with writing, which allows ample planning time for what is to come next. Though an abundance of artistic devices can become wearisome to impatient modern readers, Isocrates maintains a control that (with minimal readerly patience) does satisfy. What remains of his work tells us that his arguments were principled and clearly presented.

The sample below is the finishing *periodos* from his masterpiece, *Panegyricus* (a treatise said to have taken him a decade of writing and revising). In it, he contradicts Demosthenes, and successfully persuades all the city states of Hellas to unite under Philip in order to defeat the Persians. Note how particles, balance of antitheses, and predictable rhythms can, also in English, force the sense to emerge *even if one eliminates the modern punctuational stops*—which is the way it must have been preserved and read through many centuries.

And you must not depart to your homes as men who have merely listened to an oration; nay, those among you who are men of action must exhort one another to try to reconcile our city with Lacedaemon [Sparta]; and those among you who make claims to eloquence must stop composing orations on "deposits" [of money] or on the other trivial themes which now engage your efforts, and centre your rivalry on this subject and study how you may surpass me in speaking on the same question, bearing ever in mind that it does not become men who promise great things to waste their time on little things, nor yet to make the kind of speeches which will improve no whit the lives of those whom they convince, but rather the kind which, if carried out in action, will both deliver the authors themselves from their present distress and win for them the credit of bringing to pass great blessings for the rest of the world.[12] (Isoc., *Paneg.* 4.188–9)

With Isocrates's timely modifications of Gorgianic frills, we may at last turn our attention to the Protagorean side of the equation: that is, to our developing grammar-enthralled, eye-fed, objectifying capabilities, whose source has traditionally been thought to lie in the left lobe of the human brain. While today's learned opinion warns against too much simplification in ascribing activities to separate parts of the complicated brain, linguists still find the dif-

fering lobe characteristics—the left lobe's penchant to reason and the right's
to emote—useful in discussions of the human neural makeup.

Notes

1. See Anthony Storr, *Music and the Mind* (London: HarperCollins, 1992), particularly pages
   9–47. Dr. Storr is a distinguished English psychiatrist with a special interest in the sources
   of creativity.
2. Grateful acknowledgment is made to the Society of Authors, as the Literary Representative of the Estate of John Masefield, for permission to reproduce John Masefield, "Cargoes," in *Ballads* (London: E. Mathews, 1903).
3. Justin D. Call, "Some Prelinguistic Aspects of Language Development," *Journal of the
   American Psychoanalytic Association* 28 (1980): 259–89.
4. Walter J. Ong, *Interfaces of the Word* (Ithaca: Cornell University Press, 1977), 92–120.
5. Storr, *Music and the Mind*, 35.
6. Leonard Shlain, *The Alphabet Versus the Goddess* (New York: Viking, 1998), 18–23.
7. Sacks, *Seeing Voices*, 105–6.
8. Alan B. Lloyd, *Herodotus* (Leiden: E. J. Brill, 1975), 1:152–60.
9. George A. Kennedy, "Oratory," *The Cambridge History of Classical Literature*, 1:498–9.
   Though the four-part format would change over the years, this particular divisional structure probably comes from the early Syracusan rhetorician Tisias, the teacher of Gorgias.
   The term *rhetorike*, however, did not apparently come into usage until Plato's *Gorgias*,
   usually dated to the 380s BCE, and might well have been coined by Plato, whose penchant
   for "coining technical jargon is well documented, particularly with respect to terms denot-
   ing verbal arts." See also, Edward Schiappa, *The Beginnings of Rhetorical Theory in Classical
   Greece* (New Haven, CT: Yale University Press, 1999), 14–15.
10. Dionysius of Halicarnassus, "Isocrates," in *Critical Essays*, trans. Stephen Usher, Loeb
    Classical Library (Cambridge: Harvard University Press, 1974), 1:105. The opinions of
    Dionysius will appear from time to time throughout this section on the Classical Greek
    world.
11. Ibid., "Isocrates," trans. Usher, 1:107–9. One senses the passage of time (some 300 years!)
    in this assessment of style. It is a sophisticated piece of analysis, made possible by mature
    experience with the written word.
12. Isocrates, *Panegyricus*, in *Isocrates*, trans. George Norlin, Loeb Classical Library (Cam-
    bridge: Harvard University Press, 1980), 1:241.

References

Call, Justin D. "Some Prelinguistic Aspects of Language Development." *Journal of the American
    Psychoanalytic Association* 28 (1980): 259–89.
Dionysius of Halicarnassus. "Isocrates." In Vol. 1 of *Critical Essays*. Translated by Stephen Ush-
    er. Loeb Classical Library. Cambridge: Harvard University Press, 1974.

Isocrates. *Panegyricus*. In Vol. 1 of *Isocrates*. Translated by George Norlin. Loeb Classical Library. Cambridge: Harvard University Press, 1980.

Kennedy, George A. "Oratory." In Vol 1. of *The Cambridge History of Classical Literature*. Edited by P. E. Easterling and Bernard M. K. Knox. Cambridge: Cambridge University Press, 1985.

Lloyd, Alan B. Vol. 1 of *Herodotus*. Leiden: E. J. Brill, 1975.

Ong, Walter J. *Interfaces of the Word*. Ithaca: Cornell University Press, 1977.

Sacks, Oliver. *Seeing Voices: A Journey into the World of the Deaf*. Berkeley: University of California Press, 1989.

Schiappa, Edward. *The Beginnings of Rhetorical Theory in Classical Greece*. New Haven, CT: Yale University Press, 1999.

Shlain, Leonard. *The Alphabet Versus the Goddess*. New York: Viking, 1998.

Storr, Anthony. *Music and the Mind*. London: HarperCollins, 1992.

· 6 ·

THE OTHER LOBE

Logical Perspectives

As the Greek alphabet made writing more accessible, so it prompted a concentrated application of the eye. Language itself came under focus and was seen to need sharpening. Clarity, flexibility, and precision became the new goals. Writing's gift of time encouraged detailed exposition, stabilized the public's perception of what true knowledge was, and gave a boost to exactitude. It inspired the initiation of record-keeping, not only for business, but also for medicine, geography, astronomy, politics, law, and—of special interest to us—history.

We are not surprised that the preference for accuracy began in the Ionian east—far, far from Sicily. There, in the city of Miletus (on the west coast of what is now Turkey), the first known Greek treatise in prose was written (ca. 546 BCE) by the astronomer-philosopher Anaximander, whose disciple, Anaximenes, followed suit in "a simple Ionic prose."[1] Their move to prose from poetry took hold and opened up a better means for transmitting complicated thinking. Their example gave a boost to the acceptance of prose.

To avoid the risk of being misunderstood, the serious prose-writing conveyor of information attended to his layout of words. Words made visible on the page allowed time to muse over exact meanings, time to analyze the formulation of sentence structures and to notice options that might make better sense or be less ambiguous if crafted in a different way. As writing became more and more a familiar form of communication and was increasingly counted on to encode abstract and complicated thoughts, so the task of composing a statement became more onerous. Authors became less centered on their own satisfactions and more alert to readerly reaction. Once the process began, a slow escalation of writer-reader skills developed. As each new device fell into place and was accepted, some new aspiration would emerge to push the levels even higher.

It remained, however, a difficult exercise to liberate words from their matrix of prosodic custom—to train them away from the vagaries of oral habit and prepare them for the precision-seeking mind. As natural speech tumbled onto the page and lay there dumb and still, so possibilities of a misconstruing eye emerged. Without the advantage of gesticulation, facial expression, the loud and soft of voice-sound, or the ability to retract and readjust during the flow of an explanation, written words seemed stiff and stony. They were easy to misinterpret. They had no innate elasticity, no bounce, no sinuosity or emotive color. *Saying* things was so much easier!

Nevertheless, writing had much to offer, and ambitious folk took to it eagerly. They began to experiment with what they wrote, both to enliven it and to force it to convey with clarity highly complicated ideas. Blessed with the gift of time and the opportunity to correct imperfections, they could try new things. And this they did. They invented new words, new particles to direct them, and new signals to highlight a change of scene or a finish to argument. They standardized letter shapes, the spellings of words, and how best to lay them out. Matters of cadence—of where and how to assure a visual assimilation of what could orally be done with a rise or drop of the voice—remained for a while unaddressed and bound to their oral inheritance. But because writing kicked up so many linguistic quandaries and focused so intently on the best way to 'outer' a thought, serious writers increasingly turned their attention away from the mesmerizing impact of 'beautiful speech' to consider a logical management of words for the page.

Discovering the Logic in Oral Epic Poetry

In 427 BCE when Gorgias arrived in Athens, he encountered—though perhaps did not notice—a local tradition of soundly sensible rhetoric in play. Its terse and intense character had been shaped by the speeches of Helladic (prehistoric) heroes (like Nestor, Agamemnon, and Odysseus) in the epic poems of Homer, which everyone in the mid-fifth century BCE would probably have heard many times, and in portions have known by heart. Some few *might even have read them.*[2] But how? How would the earliest readers of those primary manuscripts have managed to hack through the mass of all the word-jammed, unpunctuated, variously spelled and possibly uneven lines?

The first step was to decipher a few words. These would expose remembered subject matter and establish the context needed to arouse expectations. After that, the recognition of whole lines would have been possible, as familiar rhythmic meters and semantic patterns emerged into view. One thinks, for example, of the repeated epithetical phrases: 'wine-dark sea,' 'soft-hearted Menelaus,' and 'laughter-loving Aphrodite'—each with its own rhythmic beat. Critical, too, would have been the recognition of the several available particle signals that directed the reader's focus from word group to word group.

To see how it all might have worked, let us examine a passage from Nestor's address in the *Iliad* to his fellow Argives. Set out below in *scriptura continua*, without respect for meaningful line breaks (which did not come into being until ca. 200 BCE), the conglomerated English lettering will at least suggest how daunting a task confronted the ancient reader of manuscripts.

NESTORTHENBELLOWEDAGREATSHOUTTOT
HEARGIVESOHBELOVEDDANAANWARRIORSSQ
UIRESOFARESLETNOMANLUSTINGFORSPOI

Two challenging aspects not demonstrated here were the idiosyncrasies inherent in scribal writing and the fact that, without paragraph markers, the passage would not immediately have stood out as an integral whole. That is to say, there was nothing overwhelmingly obvious to indicate that the preceding episode was over or that the subsequent one had begun. Without quotation marks or indentation, how could a reader divine where Nestor's words began, or ended? Solutions lay in the words themselves. By identifying them, one could crack the code and pluck out the meaningful kernel.

A view of the speech, laid out *colon* by *colon*, however, shows us how simple a bundle of rhythm, conciseness, visual evocation, and logical ordering we have before us.[3]

Νέστωρ δ' Ἀργείοισιν ἐκέκλετο μακρὸν ἀΰσας·
[Nestor then to the Argives bellowed a great shout:]

"ὦ φίλοι ἥρωες Δαναοὶ θεράποντες Ἄρηος
["Oh beloved Danaan warriors, squires of Ares!]

μή τις νῦν ἐνάρων ἐπιβαλλόμενος μετόπισθε μιμνέτω
[let no man now lusting for spoil hang back]

ὥς κε πλεῖστα φέρων ἐπὶ νῆας ἵκηται,
[in order to go to the ships bearing the greatest load [of loot];]

ἀλλ' ἄνδρας κτείνωμεν· ἔπειτα δὲ καὶ τὰ ἕκηλοι
[instead, let us slay men: thereafter at your ease]

νεκροὺς ἂμ πεδίον συλήσετε τεθνηῶτας."
[you will strip the corpses [lying] dead over the plain."]

The foundation of this urgent exhortation rests on the tensions of antithesis. After the customary address with its defining standardized epithet "*warriors of Ares*," the *negative* imperative *Let no man hang back* disposes the mind to its *positive* resolution, *instead, let us slay men*. At the same time, the *now* of the *present* treacherous situation predicts rewards for the *future*. The movement throughout is from negative towards positive: thus, warning to hope, rejection to promise. These counterbalancing internal relationships hold the several lines of script together as an identifiable unit. They distinguish it from the matrix text, even under the inherent adversities of *scriptura continua*.

But there is more. When we analyze the passage more closely, imagining our modern selves battling an endless tide of early Greek penmanship, we come up with the following clues to guide us: Nestor is the first word and his verb of bellowing follows close behind, after the intervening particle **de** (written δ') ('Nestor **de** bellowed'), which tells us that something new is about to happen. **De** signals us to turn away from the previous scene towards the one confronting us, in which Nestor will figure. Even though there are no quotation marks to trumpet the fact, we know when we are actually into his shout to the Argives, because of the **ō** (written ὦ) [read *Oh!* as in: *Oh Lord, Father of us all*, or, *Oh James, you slob, what have you done with my car keys?*], which is used in address and habitually followed by a string of more or less standardized epithets—in this case "beloved Danaan warriors, squires of Ares."

Once the rhythms of Nestor's invocation have thumped to an end, we meet the particle **mē** and so expect something quite different to think about. **Mē** is a negative subjunctive indicator. [Subjunctives suggest *possibility* instead of *fact*.] In this case, that negative subjunctive indicator **mē** (Greek μή) introduces a negative command [May it not be that]: *Let no man lusting for spoil now* *hang back*. The terminus of this *colon* is marked by the 'delay' verb *mimnetō* (μιμνέτω) on the next line.[4] *Mimnetō* tells us that some portion of sense has been achieved. Once we are satisfied about that, we move on to confront the next words, *ōs ke* (ὥς κε), a pair of particles meaning *in order that* (Nestor is commanding his men *not to hang back in order that*—in order that *what?*). We have been deftly led to another clause-ending subjunctive verb, *iketai*, meaning *he may go*. We now have *in order that he may go*. Having reached *iketai* (ἵκηται), we are greeted by the particle *alla* (ἀλλ') meaning *but* and indicating a reversal—a reversal, that is, from the negative command to a positive command: *but men let us slay*. This exhortation to kill men is the climax. The excitement subsides as we are drawn back to the tonic by the succeeding three particles *epeita de kai* (ἔπειτα δὲ καὶ). These slowing-down words are individually translatable as *then, on the other hand, and*; though in combination they were often used to introduce an important last item of a series. Once that last item is finished, our mental voice will drop, and we are permitted a deep breath in preparation for meeting the next bit. The governing verb of Nestor's final utterance carries a very positive future inflection, *you will strip*. In the Greek, *you will strip* is the next-to-final word of the speech, yielding pride of closure to *the dead*. The finality of the words resolves the tension set up at the beginning. With the enemy's deadness, the passage appropriately ends.

In the Loeb edition the entire little speech (both in Greek and in English) is pocked with pause marks (especially commas) and demarked as a whole by a full stop, quotation marks, and the follow-up indentation of a new paragraph. Yet even without this modern triple defense against confusion, an ancient reader could have realized that a change of focus was on its way, for the next line (the first of the Loeb's new paragraph) begins: Ōs eipōn (*So saying*), and is followed immediately by a third person singular governing verb *otrune* (ὄτρυνε) (*he aroused*). *So saying he aroused* leads by convention to new material, even in English. *So saying, he slammed the door and raced down the stairs.* With that, we know that the scene will shift.

In place of modern punctuation, particles have assorted and connected the components of Nestor's speech. Because there was only a handful of particles in Homer's time, they were necessarily helped by the antithetical balances, and the position and type of verbs. All of these indicators, which oral custom might have emphasized with rhythm, gesture, volume, and pitch, became immediately crucial once the word-flow was manuscripted into silence. Without sound to help, the reading eye was obliged to work only from those indicating signals for recreating all the excitement and hullaballoo of Nestor's high moment—the rise of his shouting voice as he moves into the spotlight of our attention, and the drop-back into narrative flatness when he is done. Though the Loeb rendition is fortified by the points of modern punctuation, we are grateful to those early directional signals even today, as our aural memories stir us to 'hear' the dramatic rise of Nestor's shout and the purposeful ring that it carries. Interestingly, upon close inspection, not a word seems out of place. There is no real need for oral emphasis to override a potential aberration in the grammar.[5] All is neat and complete. As we immerse ourselves in the drama of the occasion, we appreciate how well emotion and logic can be made to work together, when neither is unduly falsified by haste, ambition, or forced artistry.

It is clear that both our cerebral hemispheres participate in relating our human selves to outer 'reality.' In persuading his warrior colleagues to contain their impetuous greed, Nestor himself applied reason. Indeed, sensible persuasion must always have been rooted in logic. If I should want you to jump off the town bridge, I would be wise to think up some convincing reasons why you might enjoy the water: it is cleansing; it is cool; spectators will video your prize-winning breaststroke, and so on. Though my hexametric rhythms and euphonious consonantal juxtapositions may enthrall you, they are not likely to persuade you to plunge.

That he could so perfectly clothe sound reasoning with prosodic beauty was Homer's unique achievement. In the form of poetry, he spoke to the full man: to the emotions as well as to reason. Later emendations of Homer's work have made it impossible to know if Nestor's words, as laid out in the oldest writing that survives, were those that Homer or his immediate followers actually 'sang.' Nevertheless, the general makeup of the speech and all the other speeches and episodes in Homer's epics show a similar tight coordination of oral dramatic effects and logical sound sense—proof that even so long ago the human brain was fully able to balance emotion with reason.

Logic in Early Judicial Oratory: Antiphon

There is nothing like a crisis to focus the mind. During the early fifth century BCE, when Persian forces were threatening to invade the Greek mainland, Athenian citizens came to their political and diplomatic decisions through hard public debate. It is from this sober period that well-reasoned written prose began to flourish. The orator-logographer Antiphon preceded Gorgias by half a century and Isocrates by almost a whole one. Antiphon was born ca.

480 BCE, during the Persian War years (the subject of Herodotus's *Histories*), and lived in Athens through the heady moments of Athens's glory (the era of Pericles), through the Peloponnesian Wars (Thucydides's topic), and into the Athenian political decline (recorded by Xenophon). He died ca. 411, around the age of 70, leaving behind not only a reputation for clever argument but also documents of interest to us today. He was in fact the first logographer whose works we know. Influenced by the Ionian sophists and their leading figure, Protagoras, Antiphon's youthful preoccupations are said to have included language analysis and the acquisition of knowledge. He became, in time, the teacher of Thucydides, who, two decades later, would begin to ready the Greek language for an objective account of history. Antiphon's few surviving logographic speeches are believed to have been written either for student practice or for his nervous clients to memorize and deliver in their own defense before a jury in court. But in either case, the presentation of materials built on sound sense was an obvious need.

It is interesting that all of Antiphon's extant pieces begin with complex, well-reasoned, *periodic* statements, the purpose of which was to dazzle the jury and lay the groundwork for subsequent argument. In the following example, taken from *On the Murder of Herodes*, Antiphon launches his young client Euxitheus's defense with an intricately constructed, psychologically canny appeal for sympathy. The ambitious intention of so much complexity was to establish an attractive yet modest posture for poor Euxitheus, one that would confirm his candor and modesty yet win the hearts of a jury that relished displays of oratorical wit and fine turns of phrase. Antiphon tackles the task with the following complex (modernly fractured by punctuation), expansively inclusive, and multifaceted *periodic* statement.

> I could have wished, gentlemen, that my powers of speech and my experience of the world were as great as the misfortune and the severities with which I have been visited. Instead, I know more of the last two than I should, and am more wanting in the first than is good for me. When I had to submit to the bodily suffering which this unwarranted charge brought with it, experience afforded me no help; while now that my life depends upon my giving a truthful account of the facts, my case is being prejudiced by my inability to speak. Poor speakers have often before now been disbelieved because they spoke the truth, and the truth itself has been their undoing because they could not make it convincing: just as clever speakers have often gained credit

with lies, and have owed their lives to the very fact that they lied. Thus the fate of one who is not a practised pleader inevitably depends less upon the true facts and his actual conduct than upon the version of them given by his accusers.[6] (Antiph., 5.1–3)

In this quoted passage, Antiphon has cleverly generalized a personal situation. *Poor speakers are to be pitied not punished*—so this bewildered youth tells us, in an artful entwinement of parts that suggest the written aspects of its origin. Indeed, Antiphon has constructed for his client a complicated cluster of cross-referenced and related ideas—a *periodos*, no less. Once that epigrammatic survey is over, the tone deflates and business proceeds at a faster clip. A straightforward narration of what had happened then follows.

Built of ideas more abstract than the previous oral Nestor piece, Antiphon's *periodic* fistful of *cola* are arranged in a pattern of opposites that displays considerable forethought and wit. Though the punctuation in the above excerpt is modern, the semantic interdependence of the *cola* is evidence that Antiphon presented the passage as a single hunk. Viewed as a whole, we may say that we have before us a nice example of an early, much-labored-over, written-down *periodos* that might possibly have been marked off in the original by a *paragrafos* signal in the margin.

The intricacy of this opening *period*, with its projection of callow wistfulness, compels the approval of the jury. *Ah ha!* they say. *What a sparkling fellow! So young! So modest and unassuming!* With the atmosphere thus established, attention shifts to the specifics that will supply the defendant with unassailable responses to the accusations being made. He must above all things appear to be honest. To achieve that indispensable goal, Antiphon now presses Euxitheus's words into an oral-oriented narrative run, in which the pyramidal *periodic* construction loosens its hold and breaks apart to simulate unguarded natural speech. There, the *cola* (or clauses) come one after the other, and are linked by *ands* and *thens*. Laid out in this way, inter-sentential relationships are ignored and the *cola* are left to indicate only the passage of time: first *this* and then *that* and *that* and *that*. In this urgent narrative mode, Antiphon's *cola* become shorter, evoking the anxiety of a speaker who is straightforward rather than conniving—yet not so sternly unconniving as to fail to balance his positive *cola* with negative ones, in the antithetical mode to which the Classical Greeks were so addicted.

Euxitheus, we learn, was a wealthy young man from Mytilene on the isle of Lesbos, who had been accused of murdering the Athenian Herodes. The two had found themselves embarked together on a small craft bound for Aenus on the Thracian coast. When the weather turned and the seas became dangerous, their captain was forced to run for a protected bay, where other boats, too, had gathered. There, the pair transhipped to the rain-protected hold of a larger boat to wait out the storm. With hours to spend and nothing much to do, they and the other passengers proceeded to the pleasures at hand, namely wine, which was ample. In the subsequent conviviality, Herodes out-did himself and for some reason decided to stagger ashore. From that moment he was never seen again. In court, Euxitheus is speaking:

> It has nowhere been shown that I persuaded Herodes to accompany me; on the contrary, it has been shown that I made the voyage independent-ly on business of my own. Nor again, as is clear, was I making my voyage to Aenus without good reason. Nor did we put in at this particular spot by prearrangement of any sort; we were forced to do so. And the tran-shipment after coming to anchor was similarly forced upon us, and not part of any plot or ruse. The boat on which we were passengers had no deck, whereas that on to which we transhipped had one; and the rain was the reason for the exchange. I will produce witnesses to satisfy you of this.[7] (Antiph., *On the Murder of Herodes*, 5.21–22)

Though Herodes quitted the boat, Euxitheus says of himself, "I did not leave the boat at all that night." Instead, the next day, he anxiously joined the search. The jury's acceptance of this account is not known, but since the speech survived and was admired as an example of Antiphon's skill, let us assume its success—for we feel rather sorry for this young, candid, sparkling, modest, wealthy (and probably handsome) Euxitheus—and besides, Herodes shouldn't have gone wandering off in the dark, dead drunk. Intriguing to no-tice is how, once that flashy, intellectually contrived, introductory *periodos* ends, the pen is driven by oral energies. Suddenly, a succession of short, crisp *cola* are conjuring up quick images of consecutive actions, and coaxing the jury to believe that their childish rush *reflects the unworked, unpolished, honest-to-God facts.* Reeking of the simple, talk-propelled, running-on writing style, they pound at us to take part, to empathize and emote on behalf of this inno-cent (we hope) young man.

Having finished his narration of events, Euxitheus then sheds his youthful hesitancy and emerges as quite a persuasive and confident debater. Guided by Antiphon, his assertions are shrewd, incisive, and rooted in logic. He con-cludes his defense with a fireworks display of impressive and well-reasoned arguments, for which (aside from the facts) he uses common-sense sophistic reasoning about motive and likelihood. Herewith, a few examples:

> Let it be enough for me to prove my innocence of the crime; and that depends not upon my discovering how Herodes disappeared or met his end, but upon my possessing no motive whatever for murdering him.... (Antiph., *On the Murder of Herodes*, 66)

> Remember too that it is pity which I deserve from you, not punishment. Wrongdoers should be punished: those wrongfully imperilled should be pitied....(Antiph., *On the Murder of Herodes*, 73)

> Moreover, whereas involuntary mistakes are excusable, voluntary mistakes are not; for an involuntary mistake is due to chance, gentlemen, a voluntary one to the will. And what could be more voluntary than the immediate putting into effect of a carefully considered course of action? Furthermore, the wrongful taking of life by one's vote is just as criminal as the wrongful taking of life by one's hand.... (Antiph., *On the Murder of Herodes*, 92)

> There is nothing remarkable in the fact that the prosecution are misrepresenting me. It is expected of them: just as it is expected of you not to consent to do what is wrong. I say this because if you follow my advice, it is still open to you to regret your action and that regret can be remedied by punishing me at a second trial: whereas if you obediently carry out the prosecution's wishes, the situation cannot be righted again....[8] (Antiph., *On the Murder of Herodes*, 94).

Some Specifics About Particles

J. D. Denniston, who wrote the six-hundred-page scholarly classic on particles to which we now turn, tells us that a Greek particle is a word (usually a small word) that may have two functions, though rarely a significant meaning of its own.[9] The first function is to intensify the degree of emphasis, approval, doubt, or emotion that will affect the word group falling within its jurisdiction. For example, *ē*, coming first in a word group, solidly emphasizes the author's conviction about what comes after, as in: *ē polloi touto poiousi* (*in truth* many do this). *Dē*, like many of the particles, affects the preceding word. On occasion it also is used to affirm, as in *polloi dē touto poiousi* (*really many* do this), where it adds energy to the mere *mala polloi* (*very* many). ***Ge***, while sometimes affirmative and intensifying, is the most commonly used particle in all of classical Greek literature for concentrating the attention on one out of many ideas. It is perhaps a bit like our *most importantly*, as in: 'He was first up at the starting line, sailed close to the wind, and (***ge***) won the race.' Confusingly, a single particle may be used for multiple effects; and this must have been particularly the case before the demands of writing inspired the invention of many more. For example, aside from emphasizing (as shown above), *ē* can also indicate interrogation, where it will add force to a simple question, as in: 'Do you really do this?' in place of the simple 'You do this?' or 'Do you do this?'

But more important to the matter of syntax is a particle's second function, in which it establishes a relationship between separate *cola* (think: clauses) as it connects them. This is quite a different matter from connecting the *cola* with *and*. When *and* is used to yoke a pair of expressed ideas, it equalizes the importance of their contents. When more *ands* tack on yet more ideas, a chain of equally valued ideas is formed. When writers wrote in chains of *and-cola* they were said to be writing in the 'running-on' or 'continuing' style—in any case, a monotonous and primitive style. As literacy developed, that style came to be downgraded. In its place the more challenging, more succinct, indeed *more informing* way was to join the *cola* in ways that would subordinate one to another, so as to indicate the relative values of each. Sometimes it might be just a simple ***ge*** that could handle the job. To antithesize for balance and contrast, the Greeks used (perhaps overused) the paired ***men...de*** particles, meaning *not only x but also y* (*on the one hand x, on the other hand y*).

For the purpose of pinning down with further description, we English speakers use either adjectives or subordinating linking particles (*which, who, that, after, because,* etc.). Both ways can be used to alleviate monotony, but more importantly they can be used to rank the elements within a statement and so establish a hierarchy of importances. To illustrate the action, here are three ways of stating more or less the same thing. The two-idea sentence 'Logs filled the tub and the tub was made of copper' may become either: (1) 'Logs filled the copper tub' (in which case *copper*, being demoted to the rank of adjective, spotlights *tub*); or (2) 'Logs filled the tub that was made of copper' (in which case, *copper*, again a noun, still subserves the *tub*).[10] Fans of particle gymnastics will appreciate how deftly the responsive particles *the...that* have improved the *copper* interests without overwhelming the tubbish ones.[11]

Particles are useful for tying together the otherwise loose-ended components of a statement or even, in larger terrain, the components of a saga. To bond his episodes, Homer favored the particle **oun** (meaning: 'In accordance with what I have said,' or 'With that said and done'). It is interesting that so many of our English particles (such as *thereafter, because, so that, in order to, on the one hand, meanwhile,* etc.)[12] are so encumbered with syllabic baggage; whereas in the famously multisyllabic Greek, **oun**, **ē**, **de**, and their likes stay sleek and slim.[13]

In ancient Greek there are many forward-looking particles that inform the listener-reader of the path he is about to travel. And there are backward-looking ones to secure the coherence of a previous thought before launching into a fresh one. Thus, a connection can be expressed reciprocally—or, as Denniston put it, "from rear to van and from van to rear."[14] There are also the **men** and **de** particles ('on the one hand this: on the other hand that'), which offer an oppositional means of combining without the *and* word **kai**. Either singly or in groups, these uninflected particles may have referential, corresponding, or coordinating duties. The same particle may have in one place many duties, and in another hardly any at all, or more confusingly, different ones.

In dealing with particles like **de**, which (rather rare for us) rule over what has preceded, one should note that a number of languages make use of their own similar ones, notably the Japanese with their sweeping-up *wa*. An early western example is the Latin enclitic **que**, meaning 'and.' Thus: *arborque* means 'and [the] tree.' Modernly, English too has a few back-referencing particles: *withal, to boot, also, as well.* In any language, the use of such particles—indeed, of all cross-referencing particles, whether within or between sentences or paragraphs—emit a whiff of ancient oral simultaneity, in that they bind extensions of wordage to make a tighter temporal and spatial whole. In preliterate societies, where reading and writing have not imposed their strong sense of temporal and spatial direction, the human emotional responses and reasoning abilities react more as one; and life is less organized in terms of past, present, and future time.

The fixed linearity of writing has impressed on our minds concepts of purpose and outcome. It has reinforced our temporal perceptions. It has encouraged us to set up differentiating and divisive propositions (such as *Whereas this, not that*), and taught us to see the world in terms of *If this, then that*. It has required an explicitness that we shall see develop commandingly over the centuries. Those backward-looking particles simply perform the task of sweeping up (or bundling) previous words. Although forward-thinking, English-speaking folk may find a profuse presence of them a little trying, the sensation of dealing with them need be no worse than driving around the block backwards. In the end, you will get there.

However, even the more stable-looking Greek particles seem to transmogrify a little too willingly. They can appear in one place with one meaning and reappear on the same page with another. And that, of course, is why Mr. Denniston, so long ago, needed 600 (instead of 20) pages to describe them; and even then, felt obliged to apologize for not having space to tackle them all. Still, his work remains foundational to the topic. One notes that the categorization of the huge number of Greek particles has become an enormously interesting topic to today's scholars, whose attentions now focus on the minute, delicate, often untranslatable distinctions of Greek particles as they guide the voice through the sense and music of text.

What Do the Philosophers Have to Say?

It is time to consider what the philosophers contributed towards promoting the cause of intelligible and gracious prose, for along with the high-pressured judicial-political orators, and the literary-minded historians that we shall soon be discussing, they too may claim some credit. Ancient philosophy embraced many of the separate disciplines that we speak of today: botany, theology, ethics, medicine, astronomy, anatomy, geography, physics, and so on.[15] Early fifth-century Ionians began the action with their speculations on the universe: on the mysteries of the night sky, on the origin of man, and the makeup of matter. Without chemical or physical laboratories, without the benefit of x-ray, microscopes, telescopes, computers, cameras, or calculators—without even a facile numerical system—all of these prospectors for knowledge had to reason their way to truth and explain their findings *in words*, though like Euclid, they may also have used diagrams.

As literacy spread amongst the elite, encouraging a focus on the objective over the subjective and the particular over the general, so attitudes to knowledge changed. Wanting to know factually what was going on in the world around them, intellectuals began to reject the old poeticized tall tales. The most effective way to inform others of Truth was to set it down, fact after fact, in sound, clear, well-connected prose.

As far as we know, the first toddling attempts towards this goal were those of the sixth-century philosophers Anaximenes and Anaximander, both of Ionia, who were said to have written their theories of the universe in 'book'-length prose, of which only fragments of content have survived the ages.[16] Heraclitus of Ephesus (ca. 540–ca. 480 BCE) was the most notable subsequent philosopher to reject verse in favor of prose. As he was the first to identify and discuss the two sides of the 'soul,' Nature (emotion) and Reason (logic), it should not surprise us to discover that his writing style was heavy on antithesis, or that he described the universe in terms of conflicting opposites. In the surviving fragments of his thinking, there is much wordplay, paradox, and imagery—the sum of which reveal a continuing attachment to the habits of early prosody. Still, one might say that Heraclitus was the priming spirit of sophistry in general and of Ionian sophistry in particular; for his writings were like April showers to the start-up of philosophical inquiry as we know it today.

Democritus (460–ca. 357 BCE) was born 20 years after Heraclitus had died, and lived into old age. He is generally regarded as the most versatile and constructive philosopher of his time. Though he too abandoned the strictures of poetic meter, he was vastly admired for the 'poetry' of his prose—a fact that again tells us that the literate intelligentsia (even into the early fourth century) actively relished 'beautiful language,' even in analytic treatises. The extant fragments of Democritus show a mastery of style, a style that is polished, forceful, and rich in the rhetorical customs of ancient oral habit—that is to say: balanced phrasings, repetitions, parallelisms, antitheses, and the repeated use of emphasizing particles. Yet throughout, his authorial voice is clear, individual, often wry, and epigrammatic. Having developed an atomic theory of matter, Democritus was far and away the greatest scientist of his era. He wrote on all manner of things, from science to morals, and—interesting to us—linguistics and grammar. Taking his cue from the antithetical views of Heraclitus, he made 'the senses converse with reason,' and by this means, gave a fillip to the everlasting discussion about Emotion and Reason.[17]

Amongst those striving to encapsulate difficult ideas in writing, it had become clear that prose allowed a greater precision than did verse. One could be more exact in a medium that, when matters came to a head, favored meaning over verbal music. By discarding (or even diluting) the edicts of poetry, one could expand more precisely and liberally on the complicated matters of medicine, philosophy, science, history, or politics. Yet neither Heraclitus nor Democritus, with so much to say, really grasped the moment. Neither seemed able to cut loose from the poetry-saturated atmosphere in which he lived, nor to concentrate solely on structuring written information so as to make it fully communicable. That was a skill not yet developed. It was not for a long time a recognized goal.

When compared to the levels of poetic maturity, even middle-fourth-century scientific writing seems awkwardly adolescent, though not much of it has survived to be inspected. The practice of easing the intake of knowledge by gathering ideas according to subject matter was not as yet common. Surviving remnants of these early technical endeavors allow only a peep, and according to Denniston, the scene is one of struggle.

> And the cause of this lies in the quality of the [philosophers'] thought. They expound truth in oracles rather than proceed to it by the ordered march of logic. Hence [to the modern mind] their writing gives the effect of stiffly piled-up masses: it is static, not dynamic. *And it is safe to say…that the unit was the sentence rather than the paragraph.*[18] [The italics have been added.]

Thus, even well into the fourth century, the most exalted thinkers were still having trouble gathering up their findings to expound a covering theory. Reflecting the 'full-surround' customs of preliterate times, they simply presented their ideas more or less as they came to mind, for unlike the historians, they had no narrative thread to follow. In any case, these pioneers of modern science did not find it easy to decouple scientific explanations from inherited habits of communication. They had not yet learned to assort their findings and relegate them to the construction of full topical statements. With this failure to categorize, their discoveries emerged as scattered ideas that made retrieval by others very difficult. All of this tells us that the analyzing influences of literacy, though beginning, had not by the mid-fourth century taken full hold in the sciences.

* * * * *

The release from poetic tentacles came more quickly to history, where the timeline of events made the telling of happenings easier. And so it is there that we will delve more deeply. Where philosophy developed in the direction of modern-day sciences, history moved more in the paths of interpretation of events and the literary aesthetics of narration and style. Deriving from origins of sacred tribal lore, it also trailed clouds of sanctity. While requiring a degree of reverential treatment, it was also charged with the task of dealing in facts. For such a spread of responsibility, history pushed at the boundaries of ordinary prose—though it was sluggish in becoming a *bona fide* literary medium. Even in the fourth century BCE, popular terms for prose continued to be *psilos logos* (naked language) and *pedzos logos* (language that walks on foot), from which opinions came our modern word *prosaic*. Among literaries, the earthy lowliness and foot-soldierly aspects of prose could not compare with star-studded poetry.[19] It was an attitude that did not die easily. Some eight centuries into the future, St. Jerome will be kicking himself for not having put the Vulgate Bible into poetry.

Though very little of his work survives, the earliest prose-writing historian that we know about was Hecataeus of Miletus, who lived in the early fifth century BCE. Hecataeus wrote treatises on geography, distant peoples, plants, astrology, geology, and the origin of man—most likely in short, pamphlet-length pieces. Next was Herodotus (ca. 485—ca. 425 BCE), who wrote an extensive account of the Greek wars against Persia. Drawing from the example of the poet Homer, who wrote with a sweeping bird's-eye view of the legendary Greek-Trojan war and the Olympian squabbles that drove its zigzag course, Herodotus wrote his war-chronicling prose on a vast, all-inclusive canvas. Though he claimed to have winnowed out all unreliable rumor, his was a very chatty account, infused with marvelous happenings, digressive anecdotes, and gossipy hearsay about this or that king. The landslide of detail with its portrayal of Persians and sidetracks into Persian history, its descriptions of tribes, places, and peoples who occupied the world of this time (whether or not the Persians had anything current to do with them) gives the effect of a surging effusion of irrelevancies. The loosely-connected themes and interruptive presentations of new subject matter are generally hard for modern readers to stick with. Interestingly, the works of both Hecataeus and Herodotus were referred to in antiquity as *historiai* ('researches,' or matters that have 'to do with facts and actual events'). Their efforts were surpassed by Thucydides (460–404 BCE), who, in his unfinished account of the Peloponnesian Wars, raised the bar for linguistic flexibility and set more serious standards for the concept of history. His work represents a genuine rejection of the habits of oral-world thinking. This account of the Greek emergence into thoughtfully crafted and easy flowing literacy—a literacy that respected both beauty and fact—will end with the historian Xenophon (431–350 BCE). His writings tell us that by the mid-fourth century, a full mastery of supple prose writing—on really any subject—had at last been achieved. With a few exceptions, Xenophon shows himself to be almost entirely on the modern side of the oral-literate divide.

An Overview of the Historian's Progress

Throughout the fifth century, even as the Greek military was being distantly engaged, Athens was passionately cultivating the disciplines of philosophy, history, oratory, architecture, and art. It was only a few decades after Herodotus had completed his rambling account of the Greek wars against Persia that Thucydides began his great *History of the Peloponnesian War*.[20] When the first of these wars broke out in 461, Pericles, upon whose lips "Persuasion was said to have sat," was the political leader of Athens. His orations, as recorded with admitted artistic license by Thucydides, would long be revered for their beauty, balance, and good sense.

It was more or less during Pericles's lifetime that Athenian intellectual activity reached its ebullient peak—where it would stay for the rest of the fifth century and for most of the fourth. The building of the Parthenon was begun. The plays of Aeschylus, Sophocles, Euripides, and Aristophanes were being performed to huge, enthusiastic audiences. The Ionian sophist Protagoras was lecturing to Athenian youths about grammar and language. Gorgias was rhetoricizing and Antiphon was active in the law courts. Meanwhile Socrates, Plato, Xenophon, and Isocrates were shedding their babyhoods and developing muscle to dominate the end of the fifth century and the approaching, equally productive, first half of the fourth. Aristotle, Demosthenes, and Menander (the dramatist) would trail after, to finish off the cultural buzz of the 300s with a final flourish. Such a prolonged burst of creativity brought fresh inquiry and deepening knowledge with every passing decade.

When we come to compare Herodotus's *History* with that of the younger Thucydides, we shall see how in a mere few decades oral attitudes seemed to be fading. The differing perspectives of the two historians tell us that in that short interim, readers and listeners had experienced some sort of oral-to-visual mental shift that readied them for a stricter cause-and-effect analysis. Where the orally oriented Herodotus saw fit to include everything remotely pertinent to his subject, including myth, lore, and hearsay, Thucydides did not. Thucydides chose to hunt down the root causes of adversity—the mistakes of judgment, the pressures deriving from ambition, passion, and fear—in order to examine and assess their influence on the outcome of events. Where Herodotus delights us with his tales of long ago, Thucydides is hard at work to warn us and teach us, and while teaching us, to impart the authentic feel of confronting desperation. He invites his readers to stand witness at his side,

while wartime leaders address the populace and build their cases for a winning
strategy against Sparta. To simulate the tension, Thucydides adheres (so he
claims) to the sentiment—if not the very words—of the proposals under debate in the councils of war. His descriptions of action are lean and delivered
without authorial comment. He is mirroring reality. *This is the truth*, he is
saying. *This is how and why it happened.*

Thucydides, before his exile, had been a general and had participated
in much of the action he describes. His writing rings with the authority of
knowing, and what interested him particularly was the swing of the political
pendulum as it affected Athenian fortune. As his account ends abruptly in
the middle of the second war, it is assumed that he died and was not therefore
around to deal with the end of the fighting. That task would be taken up by
Xenophon, who (like so many others) was vastly admiring of Thucydides's
breakthrough *History*.

Thucydides knew very well how to pay out suspense and tell an exciting
tale. He avoided the customary colorations of high drama, though in the
realm of thrills, his accounts of the retreat from Syracuse, the race to Mytilene, and the plague that later swept through Athens are classic. He did
not, for example, imitate dialects, record sentiment, nor indulge in descriptions of blood, grief, temper, or physical appearance. By eschewing details
that were extraneous to the march of his chronicle, he achieved a clean
view of motive, opportunity, choice, and result. Though it may sound to be
a dry sort of procedure, it is in fact gripping; for the whole *History* is laid out
to develop—episode after episode—the oncoming, logic-driven downfall of
Athens.

Thucydides repeatedly contains his own horror at the erring decisions
arrived at by his short-sighted compatriots. What he writes of the character
and impulses of those in charge is to illumine wider issues of ambition, fear,
expediency, and deceit. In this mode, he proceeds, blow by blow, towards the
inexorable outcome. It is a cerebral, secular exercise that disclaims all reference to the erotic whims of Zeus or the shrieks of freshly widowed womenfolk.
The paying out of each episode to its logical finish leads us onwards through
the book. As breath-holding readers, we are left thinking: *Oh my God, Men of
Athens! Why did you do this, when you could have done that?*

When we come to compare Thucydides more closely with his predecessors Hecataeus and Herodotus, we shall see how modern a man he actually
was. Unbiased reportage and certifiable facts are his stated objectives. And to

do the job in the way he saw fit, *he revitalized the language he had to work with.* We shall look into this matter shortly.

Concerning historical truth, Thucydides has this to say of his goals:

> [The] endeavour to ascertain…facts was a laborious task, because those who were eye-witnesses of the several events did not give the same reports about the same things, but reports varying according to their championship of one side or the other, or according to their recollection. And it may well be that the absence of the fabulous from my narrative will seem less pleasing to the ear; but whoever shall wish to have a clear view both of the events which have happened and of those which will some day, in all human probability, happen again in the same or a similar way—for these to adjudge my history profitable will be enough for me. And, indeed, it has been composed, not as a prize-essay to be heard for the moment, but as a possession for all time.[21] (Thuc. 1.22.2–4)

The *History of the Peloponnesian War* represents a significant step away from the works of his two predecessors—from the tongue-tied awkwardnesses of Hecataeus and the garrulous, mytho-panoramic storytellings of astonishment-prone Herodotus. In the case of Thucydides, a profound intellectuality has suddenly appeared, one might almost say, out of the blue, for he seems to have had no precedent. Unlike Herodotus, Thucydides stands apart from his tale—like a detached spectator himself. By depersonalizing himself, he allows (indeed *invites*) us to search through each event for some universal law that will be useful for the future. Though it is Herodotus who must be honored for having put together the first-ever, modern-book-length historical account in prose, it is Thucydides (so shortly afterwards), who first strove to untangle a mass of eclectic happenings into a cause-and-effect network. Where the chatty, digression-addicted Herodotus rushed hither and yon propelled by his own enthusiasms, Thucydides concentrated on the confluence of events that would (and did) lead to disaster. *This is what happened at this juncture and the result led to that, which led to that,* and so on. In this manner he guided his readers from quandary to decision to action to result, nexus by nexus, towards Athens's sad defeat.

* * * * *

Thucydides is our first prose writer with modern literate aspirations. In his historical account of the First Peloponnesian War, he extended the reach and flexibility of the Greek language. His objective approach broke through ancient custom and led the writing of history towards goals of precision and truth. Others soon followed along—most famously Xenophon. With so many linguistic problems having been resolved by his time, Xenophon's language shows an elastic simplicity that unfolds plainly, yet gracefully, with a realistic adherence to facts. Though he is not generally considered to have been a great literary artist, the display of assured ease in Xenophon's output owes much to the pioneering experimentation of his predecessors. Sadly, the work of other historians of his period has either been lost or has survived the years only in fragments.

Notes

1. A. A. Long, "Early Greek Philosophy," in *Cambridge History of Classical Literature*, 1:245. Only fragments of these two men's writings have survived.
2. Scholars still argue about the dates for when the *Iliad* and the *Odyssey* were set down in written form, but an acceptable guess would be around 800 BCE.
3. Here presented with modified translation: Homer, *The Iliad*, trans. A. T. Murray, Loeb Classical Library (Cambridge: Harvard University Press, 1946), 1:266.
4. In ancient Greek, verbs tended to come at the end of clauses (*cola*); whereas verbs that governed an overarching statement, that is, main verbs, were allowed a bit more freedom.
5. Josef Taglicht's *Message and Emphasis* (New York: Longman, 1984) is interesting on this point. Vocal emphasis can, and often does, correct or broaden the scope of a particle's control, even when that particle is logically out of place in the traditional syntactical lineup. Thus, though the raised voice can override the sense of what the arrangement of the words is actually imparting, in writing, *all words must slot into the line* where meaning, syntax, and grammar dictate. A common example of this oral phenomenon is with the word *only*, whose grammatical misplacement within a sentence can be (indeed, often is) overridden by heightening the voice. In writing, however, placement alone assures the wanted semantic differentiations, as in: "*Only* I wanted to taste the champagne" (Sam didn't want to, and Myrna was drunk already); "I *only* wanted to taste the champagne" (I did not want to dance or steal the spoons); "I wanted *only* to taste the champagne" (not finish the bottle or pour it out the window); "I wanted to taste *only* the champagne" (not the gin or the beer); or, "I wanted to taste the champagne *only*" (not race Jim to the dock or check out what George was doing in the garage).
6. Antiphon, *On the Murder of Herodes*, in *Minor Attic Orators*, trans. K. J. Maidment, Loeb Classical Library (Cambridge: Harvard University Press; London: William Heinemann, 1941), 1:161.
7. Ibid., 1:175.
8. Ibid., 207, 211, 227, 229.
9. The material in this section is especially dependent on J. D. Denniston's *The Greek Particles* (Oxford: Clarendon Press, 1954), xxxvii–lxxv, and on his *Greek Prose Style*, 84, 90.

For these pages, the Greek letters have been transposed to English ones for easier intake. Although in the past 30 years scholars have developed new concepts about particles and their applications, Mr. Denniston's work is still highly appreciated and considered to be foundational.

10. Interesting to writers is what to do if between two tubs, one iron and one copper, the wish is to disregard an unappealing empty iron tub in favor of the log-filled copper one. In that case, a written 'Logs filled the copper tub' is not enough. Though an emphasizing voice can make the selection of *copper* stand out clearly, writing cannot. The only real options open to writers who want such a thing are to boldface *copper*, change its font, underline it, enlarge it, italicize it—or, if enthusiasm is unquellable, to do all five. In the case of the more extended 'Logs filled the tub that was made of copper,' another chance to give copper the edge over iron lies in changing the current grammatically approved *that* to a more prominent modernly unapproved but traditionally acceptable *which*, and hope that the reader will get it.

11. 'Both…and' and 'either…or' are also responsive particles that produce interlocking constructions; but their use is to equalize, not subordinate.

12. In our English particle collection, *if* and *but* are unusual in being so brief.

13. Note, too, the *ua, e, i* of Hawaiian and the *wa, ga, ka* of Japanese—all so short.

14. Denniston, *Greek Particles*, xli–xlii.

15. Along with 'scientific' prose in the sixth century BCE were the home-spun Aesop fables. These will not be dealt with here for two reasons: (1) they do not represent the energetic endeavor of saying precisely what is in the writer's mind to say (in recounting a story, one can always bypass that rocky path); and (2) over the centuries they have been much replenished with apocryphal materials from numerous hands.

16. Interestingly, the contemporary philosophers from the western Greek world of southern Italy and Sicily—Parmenides and Empedocles—continued to versify their theories in Homeric hexameters.

17. This material comes largely from Long, "Early Greek Philosophy," 254–8; and also from James Romm, *Herodotus* (New Haven, CT: Yale University Press, 1998), 14.

18. Denniston, *Greek Prose Style*, 2.

19. Romm, *Herodotus*, 13.

20. The two consecutive, fifth-century wars between Athens and Sparta, the first from 460–445 and the second from 431–404 BCE. Thucydides's account ends abruptly in 411.

21. Thucydides, *History of the Peloponnesian War*, trans. C. F. Smith, 1:39–41.

References

Antiphon. *On the Murder of Herodes*. In Vol. 1 of *Minor Attic Orators*. Translated by K. J. Maidment. Loeb Classical Library. Cambridge: Harvard University Press, 1941.

Denniston, J. D. *The Greek Particles*. Oxford: Clarendon Press, 1954.

———. *Greek Prose Style*. Oxford: Clarendon Press, 1952.

Homer. Vol. 1 of *The Iliad*. Translated by A. T. Murray. Loeb Classical Library. Cambridge: Harvard University Press, 1946.

Long, A. A. "Early Greek Philosophy." In Vol. 1 of *The Cambridge History of Classical Literature*.
    Edited by P. E. Easterling and Bernard M. K. Knox. Cambridge: Cambridge University
    Press, 1985.
Romm, James. *Herodotus*. New Haven, CT: Yale University Press, 1998.
Taglicht, Josef. *Message and Emphasis*. New York: Longman, 1984.
Thucydides. Vol. 1 of *History of the Peloponnesian War*. Translated by Charles Forster Smith.
    Loeb Classical Library. Cambridge: Harvard University Press, 1921.

7

FIFTH-CENTURY HISTORIANS
GIVE A FILLIP TO PROSE

Three Ways of Structuring a Sentence

Three types of sentence structure are described in ancient handbooks on style. They are hypotaxis, parataxis, and asyndeton. Hypotaxis, being the most complicated, is the one most reliant on particles.

For referring to sentences built from subordinated relationships, *hypotaxis* was the ancient insider's word. Under the rule of *hypotaxis*, a pyramid, or hierarchy, of importances is established. A primary assertion (whose verb governs all) provides the foundation for all the elements of its superstructure. A hypotactic sentence, in short, is like a modern 'complex sentence,' as in: When you get to the fork in the road where the hay wagons are, *bear left*. Here, the governing core has been italicized; the when and where clauses merely specify details relative to it. *Hypo* (the prefix we find in 'hypodermic' or 'hypothermia' means 'below'); and *taxis* means 'arrangement' (as in 'taxonomy'). Antiphon's opening *period* in *On the Murder of Herodes* and Isocrates's ending *period* for the *Panegyricus* are both examples of what was anciently thought of as hypotactic (multilayered) statements. Indeed, any extended *period* is by its very nature hypotactic.

The contrary to *hypotaxis* is *parataxis* (*para*, as in 'parallel' or 'paramedic,' meaning 'alongside.') *Parataxis* connects ideas without evaluating them. All elements being equal in parataxis, *and* is the usual link (with additions of *then*) in the manner of Susie at the zoo. Paratactic verbiage moves in a rush. It is *not* associated with hard thinking. As the years passed, so the *and*/*then* monotony of parataxis came to be considered childish.

Extant literature tells us that even in early Classical prose, the incumbent running-on style (parataxis) showed signs of retreat as the more sophisticated, more complicated hypotactic structures advanced. These younger sentential arrangements consisted of several (sometimes numerous) *cola* that were directed and controlled (since modern punctuation was not yet invented) by a handful of particles (modernly called 'connectives'), such as *when, but, after, before, on the contrary*. For the larger paragraphic or chapter-length parts of a treatise or historical account, the connectives would be longer: *As has been previously said; In keeping with their stated intentions*, etc. As writing skills improved and empowered the pen to explore opportunity, a good many content words were charged with particle duties, so as to increase the particle supply and thus support ambition.[1] With an enlarged body of particles, one could now begin to weave the offshoots of a thought into a broad *periodic* tapestry, and in that way, out of many bits, make a more interesting and informative whole. The boost that particle proliferation gave to the potential of a statement was critical to prose development.[2]

In early examples of writing (such as Antiphon's inaugural *periodos* for the accused Euxitheus), we are well into hypotactic activity. Though *periods* are said to have been practiced even on preliterate podiums, writing in alphabet letters (much encouraged by the invention of papyrus in ca. 700 BCE) heightened the levels of elegant showmanship to what we saw in Isocrates's *Panegyricus*. With aspirations soaring, pedagogues (in accordance with their nature) emerged in droves to devise theories of literary style and to dictate rules for what came to be known as a proper classical *periodos*—which is to say, a hypotactic statement in full stretch.

At this point in the story, the especially significant thing about the whole particle caboodle is the diminishing appearance of the very oral *kai* (and) and *de* (then). Both the *kai* and *de* particles can be found in profusion in Homer, whereas only *de* exuberantly persisted in early prose, most notably in Herodotus. Eventually, however, even the ubiquitous *de* was obliged to restrain itself, as subtler particles joined the fray. With so many directional indicators now at his command, a writer could more adroitly steer his reader through the uncharted swells of free-ranging prose.

It would appear that particles are highly active in most (if not all) languages and often prolific in their numbers. In some languages (like Hawaiian) they seem unduly profuse as well as overburdened. Hawaiian is not of Indo-European origin and was until recently a totally oral language to boot. Particles in Hawaiian "may indicate whether the nearby content words are nouns or verbs, whether action is completed or going on, whether a noun is subject, object, agent, possessor or locative"[3]—which is to say that they impart the sort of grammatical information that in Latin and Greek is usually provided by inflectional endings. Hawaiian, in contrast, has no inflections. The Greeks, so eager to explore truth and explain their perception of it, *used both particles and inflections* to control their increasingly refined output of written wordage.

In contrast to the disjointed, Susie-type parataxis and the *periodic* hypotaxis à la Isocrates, stands a third way to construct a sentence—*asyndeton*, the King of Disconnection. *Asyndeton* (the *a* meaning *not*, as in 'asymmetrical' and the rest meaning 'bound together') is popularly used today in the form of exclaiming imperatives for clothing catalogues, as in *Come, startle your friends! Make waves in this hand-stitched burlap swimsuit!* Travel brochures, too, lean heavily (and tediously) on asyndeton: *Come to Samoa,* they bark. *Relax, exercise, dance with the happy natives on uncrowded beaches!* Dragging our dazed attentions back to the glamor of grammar, we note also that *asyndeton* is essentially *the non-use* of the old-fashioned *and*. In today's usage, *asyndeton* has been gifted with punctuation marks. Whether early commentators in Caesar's time used raised dots or virgules for his swaggering *Veni vidi vici* is not known. In any case, he did not separate the words with *et* (and) nor with particles such as *when* and *then*. *When I came, I saw, then conquered* lacks excitement. By treating the statement asyndetically, he made his claim more compelling.

It is interesting that by late Classical times asyndetic starkness had become a recognized artistic device, effective for speeding up narrative, or heightening emotional effects; for it implied that the feelings being set into words were too deeply engaged to allow the time to think about links and hierarchies. Especially in the silent world of writing, the 'unnatural art,' where particles were counted on for so many jobs, their absence could create something of a shock. Some five (possibly more) centuries into the future, Longinus would write (in Greek) that disconnected (asyndetic) *cola* gave 'a sense of agitation.'[4] To illustrate, he quoted the historian Xenophon (fourth century BCE):

And locking their shields, they pushed, fought, slew, fell.

Yes! The style can agitate us, especially when spoken. At the very least, it arouses attention. It adds yet more thrills to the semantic aspects of a thrilling topic. Note how the implants of paratactic *ands* destroy the emotional punch:

And locking shields, they pushed and fought and slew and fell.

as do, even more so, the implants of hypotactic particle connectives:

Once they had locked their shields one with the other, they then pushed until they were forced to fight, whereupon they slew and finally fell.

Emotion, we see, is more truly aroused when artifice lies out of sight. Early prose writers (like Thucydides and the conservative Isocrates, both of whom were deeply engaged with the initial process of 'artificial' writing), rarely employed asyndeton; whereas the much younger Demosthenes, the greatest orator of all (despite the above-mentioned defeat by Isocrates) felt confident to exploit it to the full. Caesar, as noted, would come to use it too. Asyndeton, we see, can be a powerful tool. Though it may not actually agitate us, it definitely alerts us. Its contrariness to the standard, whatever the content, puts us on our guard and arouses our attention—even when the subject is peaceable, as in The baby yawned, smiled, shut his eyes, slept.

The overused *and* and *then* particles of very early times might well have played a part in eking out poetic lines to their wanted metric length. True or not, they faded with the development of increasingly ambitious prose, and their simplicity lost its appeal. Instead, a fresh array of particles was generated to guide the reader through the complexities of written lines. Acting at times like a kind of punctuation, the particle hoard soon doubled, then tripled. The goal throughout was to sharpen up the wanted distinctions so that the reading eye might move more easily through densely textured text.

As one looks down from these heights of achievement, one realizes that, apart from connecting *cola*, the repetitive *ands* of primitive paratactic continuousness can also be seen *as breaking apart* the *cola*, for in essence they do little but interject meaningless signals between individual propositions that do not necessarily relate to their neighbors. Paratactic habits tend to prevail in primitive storytelling, where the *logical* aspects of plot progression are seen to relate to the passing of time: thus, *First this and then that and then that and then that.* What most surprises the modern mind, however, is the realization that those ancient paratactic *cola* would sometimes snap apart at an *and*-joint to make room for insertions of totally new material. It was as though the sto-ryteller had suddenly received some piece of extraneous information and did not know where to insert it—*So why not here?*

In early Greek writing, snippets of suddenly remembered fact or anec-dote were sometimes wedged between the ongoing members of a paratactic lineup—a sure-fire recipe for unlimited, possibly eternal, development. And though development of *one* theme in the middle of an ongoing *other* theme can impart considerable depth and complexity to a text or a speech, it can hardly be said to contribute to its dramatic tension.[5] Since words (unlike thoughts) are rigidly time controlled and whether spoken or written must arrive and depart in linear mode, interruptions in a paratactic string of words are not really so great for argument or storytelling. One does not come across these irrelevant insertions in hypotactically structured prose. There, the writing is too tightly woven to allow disruptions of this sort. In the following paratactic 'episodette,' the italicized words mark the intrusions.

> Bullets rained from behind the rock and several bore mercilessly into his thigh. Bill dropped his gun and fell to the ground with a heart-rend-ing thud and his horse rose up in terror. *The horse's name was 'Fire-fly.'* Quickly, Bill seized the right stirrup with both hands and calmed the horse with soothing words. He was unable to stand. He directed the horse to drag him through the snow to a distant Indian camp. At last they reached the Big Chief's tent. *The tent was the finest one in all of Canada. It was made of blood-spattered bison pelts draped over a stand of shaved oak boughs and it smelled rankly of musk.* The horse stopped and Bill lay like a frozen log at the Big Chief's naked feet. "Get out," said the Big Chief.

Nevertheless, the earliest prose historian, Hecataeus of Miletus (early fifth century), wrote in this same unfocussed, *one-thing-brings-to-mind-an-interest-ing-distantly-related-other-thing* style (most noticeably in his accounts of human customs, animals, and geography). So too did the slightly later Herodotus in his rosters of military and marine forces, campaign lists, and ethnographic and dynastic materials. Though parataxis gets the job done eventually, its accept-ance of interruption is often irritating to modern literate minds. We consider it childish. While the interruptions are primarily semantic, they distort the grammatical substructure of the entire piece. Their sudden bobbing-up ap-pearances destroy the even advance of the principal topic.

Parataxis, and asyndeton too, interest us for their emanations of archa-icness and the feel they give of mirroring our simplest, unconniving selves. Their habit of shifting goals tells of the flighty, untargeted mental processes by which our minds, when unguarded, actually work. When we are alone with our truest, deepest selves—alone with nothing to explain and no one to impress—we can be aware of the past, scan for the present, and plan for the future all at the same time. Our inner lives are seamless. When we break into that wholeness for the sake of putting our thoughts into words—even unspo-ken, unwritten words—cracks and divisions perforce occur. Is it not possible, then, that paratactic and asyndetic utterances reflect the process of setting thoughts into words? Even today, stylists consider that asyndeton's quirky ef-fects offer the closest representation of the intellectual and emotional com-plexities of the thinking mind. Asyndeton would in fact eventually come to be prized in the elegant prose-writing circles of seventeenth-century England.

An imperfectly shaped word-string *can be* understood when said aloud to others, for it follows a basic human norm that is well in tune with the ear. Writing, however, and particularly expository writing, wants more than an asyndetic hiccup or a paratactic *and*-link for relating ideas. A comprehensive thought is not best transmitted with bits and bats lying on a static piece of paper. To be meaningful, its subsidiary parts must be organized to be easily retrievable. A writer's job today is to recompose those artless first impressions and arrange them in elucidating, logically sequenced, and (one hopes) inter-esting sentences. That is what readers expect. Literary traditions, built up over the centuries, have taught us that a sound logical progression is best for giving word strings and full statements the feel of *going somewhere*.

To assure another person's comprehension, book-length materials are best arranged in paragraphs and chapters in a hypotactical manner that builds to-wards some goal, shows growth in its offerings of information, and distinguish-es the finish of an old topic from the onset of a new one. What is the point, for example, of detailing life in an uncomfortable home if we delay telling our reader that the home we are yattering on about is an igloo? Or again, of describing the difficulties in a fast-moving scherzo performance, if we fail to mention the fact that it is a pianist we're talking about? The same need of timely information will apply to the construction of a story. We should, at the very least, tell our listener-readers *who* Bettie is if we want them to thrill later on when Joe finally suggests cohabitation. If we fail in this, we shall be withholding all the incremental excitements of the developing Bettie-Joe pas-sion. With suspense gone, the urge to hear more or read further will collapse beyond the powers of resuscitation. Where a speaker can quickly adjust for what he has said or carelessly failed to say, a writer must calculate for the future and strive for a logical growth of the meaning he seeks to impart. Writers can no longer use paratactical insertions to 'catch up' on information they have inadvertently left out. Speakers can do that to a degree and children do it all the time. But good speakers pay out their words so that they don't have to backtrack for left-out material. *Critical information is best supplied in time so that the recipient of our words may build up a structured, mental 'knowledge base.'* When it comes to writing, an appropriately sequenced laying out of facts becomes a positive duty. Words fixed on the page cannot be queried. Both for speaker and writer, experience has taught that a wave-like motion from beginning, to middle, to end should be sought in order to give the listener-reader a pattern that will feed the requirements of reason and order.[6] By now we are accustomed to satisfying these expectations, and do so (for the most part) with assurance. But we were not always like that.

The Evolving *Period* and What It Tells Us

The literary *periodos* emerged from the mists of time as a recognized entity in the late-Antiphon, early-Isocratean era. Though later critics wrote of early orators as having spoken in *periods*, it was not until Aristotle approved it that we can be sure that a *period* was a sufficiently mapped-out structure for writers to announce 'I am herewith writing a *period*.' But long before 330 BCE (the assumed date of Aristotle's *Rhetoric*), Ionian sophists and Athenian orators and logographers (like Antiphon) had prepared the public brain to admire the cleverness of hypotactic formulations. Perhaps 375 BCE is a good date for the emergence of the full-fledged, confident, and deftly handled literary *periodos*: that is, around the time of Isocrates's *Panegyricus* publication.

That writing encouraged the desire to include more information within the confines of a sentence would seem irrefutable. The growing numbers of pamphleteers and logographers had undoubtedly noted the *dynamis* of interlocking clausal relationships while hearing them from the lips of top-notch orators. With writing's bonus of holding still for examination, they were able to recast an assemblage of *cola* and build related ideas into an even larger intricate statement. Thucydides fiddled with the *period* (sometimes successfully, sometimes not) in his great *History*. As we shall soon see, by the time of Cicero in the first century BCE, the fully developed *period* proved to be the perfect format for the display of wit and intellect.

The scholarly surmise that Helladic verse consisted of racing trimetric lines suggests that *asyndeton* would have been the dominating spirit of earliest utterance. If that be true, then the ascending line to a celestial prose statement would have been, first, asyndetic *unbonded* responses to a whole-earth swirl of sensations; second, paratactic *loose-bonding* (stringing perceptions together with repeated *ands* and time-related *thens*); and third, hypotactic *tight-bonding*, which explored relationships and would, through trial and error, eventually generate the mature *period* with its aura of incorporated relevancies and its feel of sophistication. That sequence—from raw simplicity to increasing complication—is, after all, the way that children progress with speech. With that likely development in mind, we may conclude that our earliest literary roots lay in the same emotion-nourishing soils that we find in Xenophon's asyndetic little battle scene. There, we noted that the *rat-a-tat-tat* progression of active verbs were ordered as they occurred in time. It would never have done, had Xenophon written: *They pushed, fell, slew, fought, locked shields.* While hypotaxis seeks to escape the rules of time, neither parataxis nor asyndeton even try.

Asyndeton's fragmentation of idea-flow, with its time-ordered parts and imperative demand for attention, is suggestive of our quick, jerky reactions to circumambient sensory intake. That intake is satisfyingly complete until one tries to communicate it in a lineup of words. History tells us that the more we relied on the eye, the more hypotactic our written language became (and by metastasis, our formal speech as well). Might it be possible that in building their all-inclusive structures, orators and writers were unconsciously reaching to recover the long-gone feel of our preliterate selves—that same kind of intense, simultaneously perceived, global experience that our ancestors seem to have known so well? Unlike speech or writing, mental functions (perceptions, ideas, reactions) are neither time-ridden nor linear in structure. They are holistic and, unless purposefully elicited, unpredictable. They flood our minds from all directions, and the closest imitation of them in speaking and writing is the hypotactic *periodos*.

How Herodotus Sought to Control
His Paratactic Floods

Given the nature of early scribal output, one is left to wonder: specifically, how in ancient times did readers manage to make sense of the manuscript lines of Herodotus, whose unpunctuated prose not only meandered in the 'continuing' oral style but very likely appeared in *scriptura continua* as well?[7]

In imagining Herodotus setting down so vast a tract, one must remember that he was dealing with papyrus scrolls, a material that must have made revising or editing immensely difficult and would have required considerable planning in order to keep the contents in the wanted sequence.[8] Since many of the detailed segments appear to interrupt the overall historical narrative, it has been suggested that Herodotus initially organized his material into several separate works, and later spliced the scrolls to make a lengthier whole.

Despite the seeming randomness, *there was a method* to Herodotus's chronicle of Persian aggression. Upon inspection one sees that the text, which covered the reigns of Cyrus, ca. 550 BCE, down to Xerxes's invasion of Greece in 481–479, was not sheer ramble, but succinctly organized, with topics well integrated and a system for demarking them. Deriving in part from the ploys of poetry, prose had adopted an archaic kind of punctuation—though not yet in the form of dots, virgules (slashes), ivy leaves, paragraphic indentations, or even chapter headings. We speak now of words: not only particle words, but also word groups, repetitions of words, and even whole statements—words so planted as to gather and divide materials, and to steer the reader from one account or scene to the next. Herodotus relied on such 'word mechanisms' to differentiate the serial unities of his long, long tale so that a reader could, with some diligence, distinguish the beginnings and endings of episodes, topics, or even statements—and so be led along. Homer's Nestor speech, though presented in poetry, suggests the way.

A prominent Herodotus ploy was to wrap up an episode by actually repeating some of its more memorable opening words so that the reader would be reminded of what had been said before. In short, by having 'the mouth bite the tail,' he turned a linearly meandering account into a cohering circular one—a device known as *ring composition* (also found in early poetry)—and in this way, could be said to have communicated with his audience in a manner familiar to their experience as recent members of an oral society. Making the end of an episodic segment bring to mind the beginning of it was a way of saying, "Let's move on. I've finished with that lot." In storytelling, ring composition works rather like the balladic refrain, which brings verses of wide-ranging materials repeatedly back to the tonic thought. The technique derived from the same impulse that produced the *periodic* sentence: namely, the urge to gather, connect, and distinguish disparate ideas for the sake of making a unified whole.

Ring composition worked with signaling reminders, more or less as follows. To initiate an episode Herodotus might say (but didn't): "Under *thunderous clouds* they crossed the *man-eating sands*," and expect that when he later mentions *threatening clouds* and/or *treacherous sands*, the reader will know that a unified story has been achieved. Or, in variation, Herodotus might summarize certain aspects of the preceding narrative with a participial phrase so that the terminus of a finished item would relate to the beginning of the next[9] (thus: "Bob having hacked Jack into small pieces, the feast continued and the ambassadors…"). Yet again, he might simply end a finishing sentence with a word, perhaps in the dative case,[10] and begin the next with the same word in its nominative form (as subject), using the 'pivot' word to launch a new action or thought (thus: "…and he lopped off the villain's head with his shining sword [*sword* marked by the inflection for the dative case]; followed by [in the nominative case]: "A sword that is not too blunt answers well to the hand, for there was once a king, living in the hot deserts of Egypt, many many years ago when…who…"). Here is Mr. Denniston:

> When a sentence is beginning to straggle, and the structure of the thought is thereby becoming obscured, the picking up of a cardinal word by repetition often restores clarity. There is a certain naivëté about this way out of a difficulty, and it is not surprising that repetition of this kind is commoner in Herodotus than in other [later] writers.[11]

Programmatic patterns for prefaces, advice-giving, omens, and predictions—all of which were already established in poetry—gave additional boosts to the groping reader of early prose.

The organization of the whole "consists of a number [or string] of *logoi* [meaning, in this case, accounts or stories]…which in turn consist of a series of smaller *logoi* in a kind of chinese-box technique," each one opening and closing in the awkward manner described earlier.[12] The perceptual experience is one of simultaneously apparent realities. We have seen a more sophisticated collapsing of time in the later 'framing' technique used by Plato in his *Phaedo*.

As for the decoding of individual words and *cola* within the *logoi*, Mr. Immerwahr, the Herodotus scholar, tells us that a reader worked in the same general way, by recall and anticipation. For picking apart the sentential segments, the meagre collection of particles were a help, as were phrasal rhythms, correspondences, verb forms, semantic rhyming (with word-pairs like *bleak* and *barren*, *pale* and *wan*, for which, once you've figured out the first half, the other comes quickly), antitheses, the familiarity of topic, and most importantly, a sense of the logical progress. At deeper levels lay the rhythmic ebb and flow of major themes: the buildup and decline of empires; happiness followed by grief; desperation before success; and verbalized planning before action.

Mr. Immerwahr describes Herodotus as reaching out to find connections with other events, "especially at the beginning and end of a story." He is hampered in this because he writes in a primitive single chain rather than the more complex, particle-controlled manner of hypotaxis.

> There is no clear-cut subordination; instead repetition, anticipation, and summary create units of unequal length. These in turn form a chain, with certain interruptions attached at definite points. It is well not to apply to these latter the term digression, since it is frequently impossible to say whether the digression is more or less important than the main narrative.[13]

In the following excerpt (also taken from Mr. Immerwahr's *Form and Thought* (see note 13), one sees at work the principle of interruption for the purpose of including more information—the same awkward device as was illustrated in our Big Chief episodette. The quaint intrusion (below italicized) creates space (space with a punctuational force) between old and new material. The reference to the poet Pindar and his epigrammatic "Law is king of all" objectifies the view and is intended to ready us for change.

> Such then now are these customs, *and Pindar appears to me to have been right in saying that Law is king of all*, but while Cambyses had been fighting against Egypt, the Lacedaemonians had also waged a war against Samos and Polycrates...[14] (Hdt. 3.38.4–39.1)

Carolyn Dewald, in her essay in the book *Classical Closure*, tells us that Herodotus's *Histories* was structured throughout as a "series of loosely connected and approximately sequential, semi-discrete narratives"; and that formal closure was "a conspicuous part of his narrative technique from the very beginning of the work."[15] Each new state of the narrative, however long it might be, is presented as a self-contained whole, set off from what has come before by an introductory sentence; and in most cases, brought to a definite end, whether by a formulaic end-sentence, an authorial reflection, some interruptive materials, a brief summary of the preceding narrative sections, or a gnomic aphorism (that is, a generalizing remark of practical wisdom like *Well, it's always been hard to kill two birds with one stone*). Here below are a few samples of the many episodic ending sentences Professor Dewald has found in Herodotus's Book 1:

This was the way it was concerning the rule of Croesus and the first
conquest of Ionia. (1.92.1)
The Lydians, then, were enslaved by the Persians. (1.94.7)
Now concerning the end of the life of Cyrus, although many stories
are told, this one has been narrated by me as the most credible.[16]
(1.191.6)

Features such as the ones described above can be found in both Hecataeus
and Herodotus; but whereas Hecataeus (in the little that remains of his writing) connects only where he must, Herodotus connects wherever he can,
and with considerable variety. Seeking subtlety, he varies his terminating
signals. He avoids when he can a common ploy of oral epic poetry: namely,
to end a *logos* (episode in this case) by repeating the actual opening words
of it. To complete a frame, or to end a *logos*, Herodotus will even shun the
main feature of a story and refer instead to some minor detail of it. The fact
that he has gone to the trouble of embedding subtle dodges like that into
his predominately paratactic formulations gives evidence of an artistic aspiration, which would have been hard to manage without the benefit of 'pen'
and 'paper.'

   To give an idea to the modern reader of the footwork required to follow
Herodotus down the paths of Persian conquest, here is an imagined string of
Herodotean episodes in which the matters addressed are handled (more or
less) in the following way. A geographic passage introduces a battle scene
that once took place there. That battle portion of the text concludes with a
not too obvious phrase or idea taken from the introductory geographic passage and by this means turns our attention to an account of the ruling figure
within that geographic area. From mention of that ruling figure, we might
then be led back to a history of his forebears with associated anecdotes about
the power-acquiring gumption that got them the empire that the present
stupid ruler is about to lose for all the following anecdoted reasons. Once
those have been dealt with, repetitions and references of one sort or another
will lead us back to the geographical beginning, from where the author then
moves on.

   It was in this way that Herodotus's history proceeded, frame within
frame, *logos* within *logos*—rather like a hypertext novel, where every detail
offers the possibility of expansion (though in this case, the reader is without
option links). Once an episode is complete, it takes its place, like a new
knot along a rope of other knots, following which more rope is hauled in to

continue the procedure. As the pattern is exposed, one sees how ingenious Herodotus was in compressing so much material into retrievable linearity. Despite the appearance of panoramic sprawl, the informed eye can uncover a mass of information—and when all is said and done, find real enjoyment.

To appreciate the simplicity of Herodotus's story-telling technique, we look now at a translated (word for word) sample passage. The subject it deals with is the death of Atys, son of Croesus. In studying it, one can see how related words are gathered into groups (punctuated here for readerly ease), and how they follow one another in a way not too dissimilar from the way we might speak to a child. The prevalence of the old-timey connecting particles is striking: the paralleling *kai* (for *and*), and the antithesizing *men* and *de* (for *on the one hand/ on the other hand*), along with hammerings of *dē* (for *very* or even *very very*). The essential indicator of new material is *de* (*then*), and its presence would have been very useful to the reader of unpunctuated *scriptura continua*, since it kept both the paratactic narrative elements in temporal order and broke up the solidity of text with the feel of a mini-pause.

To highlight their numbers in this short passage, the particles most common to the habits of orality have been bold-faced and set into square brackets. The several instances of hypotactic connectors have straightforward and simple duties: 'because,' 'for,' 'how,' or 'that.'

> After then [**de**] Solon's departure, great vengeance from God seized Croesus so it-seemed, because he-considered himself to be of all men most-fortunate. Suddenly then [**de**] to him while sleeping a dream stood over, which showed to him the truth of the future evils to happen to his son. There were then [**de**] to Croesus two sons: of them the one on the one hand [**men**] was defective for he-was exceedingly [**dē**] speechless [unable to speak]: the other on the other hand [**de**] was of those of his own age by far in all things the first [best]: the name then [**de**] to him was Atys. This being the very [**dē**] Atys showed to Croesus the dream how he would lose him, shot by an iron spear-point. He then [**de**], when he had waked and [**kai**] to himself the-meaning considered, dreading the dream, presented on the one hand [**men**] to his son a wife: him accustomed on the other [**de**] to lead the-army of the Lydians, nowhere anymore to such doings did he send.[17] (Hdt. 1.34)

The language, we see, is simple and the meaning delivered quite straightforwardly.

Two Assessments of Thucydides:
One Modern, One Ancient

In his book *The Blinded Eye*, Gregory Crane compares the styles of Herodotus and Thucydides, the one so oral and the other so visual. In their two works (which are of similar length), Herodotus used words related to 'hear' some 1,537 times, and Thucydides only 490 times. For verbs of 'see,' Herodotus has the higher number, but the tallies are much closer. However, Herodotus uses words expressing 'marveling at' and 'miracle' almost four times as often as Thucydides, and his characters tend to "gaze upon" new phenomena with dropped jaws, whereas Thucydides's are more inclined to speculate on what those phenomena might mean. They 'skept-,' meaning 'scrutinize' or 'study the evidence.' Thucydides uses 'skept'-derivative words some 50 times to Herodotus's mere three. The Thucydidean narrative, far more frequently than its Herodotean counterpart, expresses an opinion as to why someone pursued a particular course of action and how an event derived from its cause. Mr. Crane goes on to say:

> Thucydides wrote for readerly observers, contemplating in their mind's eye the phenomena, "seeing," but with a sight that transcends physical appearance and that uses evidence as the starting point for calculation....[W]here Herodotus aimed at *atrekeia*, a faithful representation of what had happened, Thucydides went a step further, searching for *akribeia*, a level of accuracy aimed not simply at recovering the past but also at analyzing the reader's present, and forecasting his future. Thucydides' razor excluded families and kinship from the narrative. Irrational beliefs in oracles and religious activities were banished. Such elements clouded the observer's vision, playing into the ancient traditions that saturated *logoi* [stories, accounts] with emotion.[18]

Thucydides is famous for his tight and cogent reasoning; yet his syntax is often so austere, his thoughts so compacted, and his words so defiantly idiosyncratic as to be difficult to understand. On occasion, they can seem incomprehensible. Though one can spot the age-old antitheses and Gorgianic touches of balanced phrasing, it is plain that Thucydides was setting aside the paradigm of rhetorical enchantment in favor of concise, factual information. More difficult, perhaps, for the outsider to appreciate is how he manipulated an essentially oral language system into a tightly-knit written one. With an oral-aural audience to instruct and a tradition of simplistic historical writing to draw from, how did Thucydides come to attempt such a pioneering literary goal? He must have counted on *someone*—someone literate, austere, and intellectual—to be able to understand it.

Mr. Crane tells us that there did indeed exist an elitist predilection for learned obscurity, of which the much admired lyric poet Pindar (who was born some 60 years before Thucydides) had been a master. Both Pindar and Thucydides "*challenged* their audiences to comprehend their meaning."[19] But where Pindar wrote in verse, to be sung (or intoned), Thucydidean discourse was designed to be read, scrutinized, debated, and to endure—'a possession forever'—a different medium entirely. Though contemporary praise for Thucydides is not abundantly extant, appreciation for his achievements soon grew. A hundred years later, the orator Demosthenes, for example, is said to have copied out the *History* eight times. Nevertheless, it is not until Rome's literary heyday that Thucydides's achievement would become truly appreciated. And even then, native Greek speakers would still be finding some passages too complex to figure out.[20]

Particularly admired are the speeches that Thucydides composed on behalf of the war-leaders. They were far longer than our previously quoted speech by Nestor. Their substance was involved, detailed, and closely argued. To follow all the steps of debate—the proposals and rebuttals of ambassadors, generals, and politicians—a mature attention span was required, and in many cases, hard study; for their contents could deal with abstract projections as well as narrated accounts of events. Though supposedly spoken, their polish bespeaks the finishing touches of a studious literary endeavor.

Thucydides used the decision debates of war leaders as the climactic pivots from which new action would spring. His imitations of present-tense argument heighten the atmosphere of doubt and urgency, and at the same time enliven the less emotional tenor of the background, past-tense narrative pace. In that sense, their structural function becomes grandly punctuational, for when they appear, they set up a rhythm of marking out sections of text by episode and thereby provide the cadences that Herodotus had less successfully sought by means of anecdotal inserts. Despite their textual complexities, the mere fact of *their being speeches* must have appealed to the sociable Athenians.

With all this in mind and ignoring (if possible) the modern punctuation, let us now 'listen' to the Thucydidean Pericles, a "man who was at that time the first of the Athenians, most powerful in word and action."[21] Pericles, here, is pleading for Athens to stand firm against the Spartans. (Again, ignore the modern punctuation.)

> But as regards the war and the resources of each side, make up your minds, as you hear the particulars from me, that our position will be fully as powerful as theirs. For the Peloponnesians till their lands with their own hands; they have no wealth, either private or public; besides, they have had no experience in protracted or transmarine wars, because, owing to their poverty, they only wage brief campaigns separately against one another. Now people so poor cannot be manning ships or frequently sending out expeditions by land, since they would thus have to be away from their properties and at the same time would be drawing upon their own resources for their expenses, and, besides, are barred from the sea as well. Again, it is accumulated wealth, and not taxes levied under stress, that sustains wars. Men, too, who till their own lands are more ready to risk their lives in war than their property; for they have confident hope of surviving the perils, but no assurance that they will not use up their funds before the war ends, especially if, as may well happen, the war is protracted beyond expectation.[22] (Thuc. 1.141.2–6)

Pericles's speech, which carries on for several pages in the same purveying, reasoned manner, won the vote, and Athens engaged in war.

Because Thucydides did so much both to improve the art of historiography and the flexibility of the Greek language, one is surprised to learn that some four hundred years later, Dionysius of Halicarnassus,[23] should be so critical of him. Of course, Dionysius is right in discovering imbalances of arrangement and curious skippings-about throughout the *History of the Peloponnesian Wars*; he is right to note that not all the speeches were perfectly reasoned and that no speeches at all were provided for a number of occasions when they should have been. He is right to point out that Pericles's renowned funeral speech was devised for a less deserving occasion than later military losses would come to provide. Dionysius shows great confidence in his own powers when (again rightly) he suggests a more logical layout for the opening book: namely, to transplant the concluding section to the end of the introductory section. Can it be that Thucydides, the darling of Hellenophiles, was not so great after all? *What's going on?*

It would seem that we, who have now inspected the early oral-rhetorical atmosphere out of which Thucydides grew, can better appreciate his remarkable accomplishment. We admire his brave premiere performance, his pioneering aspirations to precision. The complaints of Dionysius come after some four centuries of literary experience to draw from, and they represent a retrospective point of view. By his time, much work had been done to make written prose flexible. Nevertheless, he is impatient with Thucydides's occasionally imperfect logical approach—that very approach that we at the pre-Thucydides end of the time-scale were so pleased to see not only developing, but frequently soaring. In sum, Dionysius's criticisms demonstrate the advance of literacy during the intervening years—that is, from Thucydides's fifth century BC to his own first century BCE.

We note, as we read of Dionysius's disapproval, that he supports his remarks with exact quotations and references. He has been *studying, researching, rereading, and taking notes!* Given the gap of some four-hundred-plus years, we should have expected as much. Nevertheless, not even the advance of literacy could make Dionysius as deep a thinker as was Thucydides, for he was fixed on the theory that *history itself* was somehow sacred. An historical account, he felt, should be agreeable, full of human interest and anecdote à la Herodotus, or 'gracious' like the subsequent Xenophon. *History's duty was to inspirit, not to downgrade.* Of Thucydides, he grumbled that, instead of enrapturing his readers with Athenian victories, he had submerged them in the inglorious decline of Athens—a repugnant topic!

Alas, it did not occur to Dionysius that there is more to learn from the analysis of defeat than from self-glorification. Though he recognized that Thucydides, who died before finishing his great work, probably intended to fix some of the annoying rough spots in his otherwise almost okay manuscript, the very selection of those long-drawn-out and degrading Peloponnesian Wars for a topic was (for Dionysius) an ineradicable and demeaning error. For our purposes, Dionysius's opinion gives a good measure of the discrepancy level between two eras of literary attainment and perception, and a rather increased admiration for Thucydides.

Comparing Thucydides With His Predecessors: A Review of Fifth-Century Historiography

During the five decades in which Hecataeus, Herodotus, and then Thucydides were writing, the parataxic *and* became less and less used. Something new was happening in the career of written expression. The goals for achievement had shifted, and with them the organization of selected materials, the manipulation of syntax, and the enlargement of the word hoard. The reach and complexity of a statement had increased. One senses a heightened sophistication—with refinements achieved for the purpose of being more explicit, truer to fact, and clearer in its description.

We turn again to Thucydides, who, as commander of an Athenian fleet, had failed to prevent the Spartan capture of Amphipolis. For this, he was exiled and so spent the next 20 years (probably until death) in exile. It was during this time that he wrote his historic account of events, planned its purpose, shape, and content, and battled the literary limitations of the early Greek language. In an outburst of energy, he enlarged its scope, forcing it to deal with what he wanted to say and how he wanted to say it. He created new words, disarranged the word order, and compressed and hierarchized sentential components in new ways—all in the interests of making it *do his will*. His high seriousness allowed no room for reporting casual hearsay. Far more than Herodotus, he systematized the presentation of his material. He was, in short, more intellectually oriented. As Sir Kenneth Dover points out in his *Evolution of Greek Prose Style*, in a Thucydidean speech

> we often find that a generalization is derived from a factual datum and leads into another factual statement, which in turn generates another generalization [in contrast with Herodotus], where...the generalizations are heaped together.

Furthermore, within those generalizations

> we are struck by his [Thucydides's] fondness for treating the neuter singular adjective with the article as a noun [that is, to make a particular into an abstract: as in "The Awesome," "The Beautiful"].[24]

Plainly apparent is a move towards a more ordered presentation of material and a greater reach for a clear written prose language. In addition, Thucydides made his characterizations psychologically acceptable. He described in orderly progression how a man moves from the moment of receiving information, to the consideration and scrutiny of it, and then on to action and its result. He unified and rounded off his episodes decisively, most frequently with "a firm *ta men*, a prepositional phrase, then *outos*, and a verb in the past tense."[25] To illustrate such strong finality in today's lingo, we might say: *Those things about the New York City public school system then in this way have been reported.* Thucydides's episodes rode one after the other, towards a single point, so that a sense of 'whole cloth' prevails. About this, Mr. Connor says in his *Thucydides:*

Throughout the History episode recalls episode and language echoes earlier phrases and ideas. Such recurrences shape not only the form of the work but also the responses and attitudes of its readers. We pause, interrupt the forward movement of our reading, break through the surface linearity of the text to recognize underlying patterns and structures.[26]

A Telling Comparison of the Three Historians

To evaluate the achievements of Thucydides, we now turn our attention back to the pre-*periodic* Hecataeus (fl. 520–480 BCE), the great-grandfather of modern history, who so bravely chose unmetered prose to say what he had to say. It was time, Hecataeus had said, to be accurate about things: to put an end to the proliferating uncertainties of word-meaning and the conflicting accounts of Zeus's escapades, of which only one version could possibly be true—and even that unlikely. We like this gentleman. His reach for objectivity in a world belabored by myth and rumor is refreshing. Nevertheless, Hecataeus could not free himself entirely from the sticky ignorance of his era, and so remains, as we see from the extant fragments of his works, a striving but archaic figure. As for his writing, his unmetered lines were essentially in the 'running-on' style, the mix of asyndetic and paratactic that Aristotle would soon be telling us was the style of "everyone in former times."[27]

Below, in a passage from a first-century stylist and critic (Demetrius, whom we shall meet again shortly), we are lucky to find the surviving opening sentence from Hecataeus's now lost *Genealogies*. It is a sentence about which Demetrius has nothing pleasant to say. Being some five centuries ahead on the road to full literacy, he finds the simplicity of Hecataeus's style both archaic and irksome. We shall shortly inspect the opening sentences of Herodotus and Thucydides to see how they compare. Here then, with the Loeb punctuation included, is Hecataeus, from the very early part of the fifth century BCE.

> Hecataeus of Miletus speaks as follows. I write these things as they seem to me to be true. For the stories told by the Greeks are, as it appears to me, many and absurd.

About which, Demetrius disdainfully comments as follows:

> Here the clauses seem thrown one on top of the other in a heap without the connections or buttressing or mutual support which we find in *periods*.[28] (Demetr., *On Style*, 12)

Half a century later, Herodotus (ca. 500 BCE–ca. 430 BCE) was still enmeshed in that choppy, non-*periodic* style, for which reason (a century-plus
into the future) he would earn the contempt of Aristotle, who disliked the
running-on style with its tangle of sense and interruptive materials. Later, in
keeping with changing attitudes, the critic Dionysius of Halicarnassus would
find the *Histories* of Herodotus delightful. Modern critics find its archaic narrative style enjoyably quaint and full of historical interest.

But what is most interesting is how Herodotus would occasionally turn to
what appears to have been a primitive *periodic* effort: that is, an attempt to
take stock, to abstract some apical perception from all the multifariousness of
possibility. At those few critical moments of choice, he hierarchized the *cola*
to give a sense of their relationships. The resultant hypotactic constructions
seem to reflect his hardest thinking—that is, the very moment in which he
is selecting several elements from many and laboring to unite them. A handsome example of what would come to be called an 'historical *period*' (noted for
its big head and long dwindling tail) is the opening sentence of his *Histories*.
It is herewith translated without the addition of punctuation and in the word
order of the original Greek.

> Of Herodotus of Halicarnassus of the inquiry a setting forth [*This is
> the 'head' of the statement. The missing 'is' being understood, it is complete
> within itself. We now confront the tail.*] so that not the happenings from
> men by time faded may become nor deeds great and marvelous those
> on the one hand by Greeks those on the other by foreigners demon-
> strated unrenowned [lost to memory] may become and other things
> especially for what reason they fought with each other.[29] (Hdt. 1.1)

In this opening excerpt, English speakers will find the 'disarranged' word order more painful than that found in the Atys episode, where the thrust of
narration was so uncomplicated. In addition, those who are acquainted with
ancient Greek may find the repetitions of word roots (such as, within this
single sentence, **apodex**is and **apodech**thenta, and the triple appearance of
genomena, **genētai**, and **genētai**) rather boring, if not plain simple-minded.
Nevertheless, they were acceptable binding devices in the Greek opinion of
that era.

Despite his awkward ways, Herodotus surprises us, for he also attempted a
number of more advanced 'oratorical *periods*.' To remind: the oratorical *period*
with its delayed completion is thought to demonstrate a somewhat higher

level of psychological finesse for holding a person's attention. In the English sentence below, the delaying phrase is italicized.

> The Reverend Hamish MacNab, *after announcing a somewhat confused instruction for the Sunday Coffee Hour*, vowed to reduce his breakfast dose of Laphroaig.

That *postponed fulfillment* was the underlying requirement for the early Greek oratorical *period*. In the sentence beneath (from Book I of Herodotus's *Histories*), we find one of his several oratorical periods. The italicized portion is the crucial delaying factor.

> But Adrastus, son of Gordias who was son of Midas, this Adrastus, *the slayer of his own brother and of the man who purified him, when the tomb was undisturbed by the presence of men*, slew himself there by the sepulchre, seeing now clearly that he was the most ill-fated wretch of all men whom he knew.[30] (Hdt. 1.45)

Here, we have been given the subject (*Adrastus, this Adrastus*), but are left to wait for the verb *slew*. One may frown at the archaic unwieldiness of this statement, most especially when one compares it with more polished oratorical *periods* of the soon-to-be future. However, Mr. Denniston pleads credit for Herodotus, in that, as measured by what we know of previous writers, he advanced Greek prose style more than had any of his predecessors.[31]

Thucydides was active and writing before Herodotus had died, but the two seem very different. Thucydides, almost haughtily avoiding the trodden paths of his forebears, headed off alone in search of new ways to explain past doings and report facts. To achieve his wanted effects, he would twist the balance of a statement, as though to shake loose all the dangling trinkets of poetry and traditional high rhetoric. He wove loosely associated thoughts into tight relationships with a shorthand language that was much complicated by embedments of parenthetical materials, new word forms, and hitherto uncommon intersentential connections, like participles and genitive absolutes—that is, word groups carrying genitive (possessive) case inflections that are used to create a *when, while,* or *by* clause. It is similar to Latin's later 'ablative absolute.' With so much artifice at large, the resultant and sometimes mystifying congestion demanded (and still demands) much effort from the sense-hungry reader.

In general, ancient Greek prose goes far beyond the reach of modern English prose when it comes to artifice and craft. "The Greeks stylized everything,"

Mr. Denniston tells us, sounding a little depressed. And "it is the most difficult thing in the world to point to any Greek [passage] which may be regarded as 'natural.'" We can barely touch upon this enormous topic here, but it is important to be aware of the Greeks' devotion to artistry. It is as though their dilating intellectuality was pushing at the language, urging it to incorporate more content—varying aspects, broader views, cleverer constructions—within its elastic confines.

For a finishing climax to this comparison of these three early historians, below (word for word) is the opening statement to Thucydides's great masterpiece, *The History of the Peloponnesian Wars*. To provide (somewhat) the experience of total immersion, the commas and semicolons of modern punctuation have been dropped, leaving the task only to sense, inflection, and verb forms. The word order of the original Greek has been left intact to show how bold, leaping, and memory-and-eye-dependent the arrangement is. The following three italicized words are the keepers of order. They are present-tense participles with nominative inflections to indicate that they relate to the subject (i.e., the narrating Thucydides himself). He is the one who is *beginning, expecting, judging,* and *seeing.* It would be hard to imagine such an arrangement being casually *spoken.* Also to be noted is the italicized opening, the trademark of the so-called 'historical *period,*' as already seen in the simpler opening statements of both Hecataeus and Herodotus. (The 'oratorical *period,*' we remember, delays information to trigger suspense.)

> *Thucydides an Athenian wrote the war of the Peloponnesians and Athenians* how they fought against each other *beginning* straightway at the undertaking and *expecting* great it would be and most important of previous [wars] *judging* that at their peak they were for it [the war] both [sides] in total preparation and the rest of Greece *seeing* aligned against each other some straightway of two minds.[32] (Thuc. 1.1)

Amongst the tricky bits in this passage are the paired words used for binding purposes: *kathistamenou* and *xunistamenon,* the first meaning more or less *make a stand* (establish) and the second (apparently invented on the spot) *stand with.* Thucydides was fond of compound pairings, such as this one, in which the stems stay steady while the prefixes are sharply contrasted.[33] Even in English, this device can inject an element of wit, as in, for example, *I can neither understand nor withstand your charms*; or as in, *When I detected the crime, I protected the victim and antitected the perpetrator. In this second example* the third verb is *invented* à la Thucydides—for the sake of emphasis and rhythm. Mr.

Denniston tells us that such compound formulations were popular in Thucydides's time and that Antiphon, the sophist and logographer, who was once Thucydides's teacher, actually gave lessons in the art of creating them.

The lineup of authorial intention amongst the three historians is rather interesting. Hecataeus wants to correct the perception of knowledge, since the myths about Zeus have nothing to do with truth, and truth is what he is after. Herodotus and Thucydides both pick up the theme of truth, but add purpose to their accounts of it. Herodotus wants to discover the causes of the Persian-Greek war and also to preserve the memories of the great deeds of heroes on both sides of it. It is rather as though 'glorious deeds' might be the major topic. But it is Thucydides who speaks of writing down the history of the Peloponnesian War *in order to study the causes and the course of it*, because he felt such knowledge would be important to later generations.

In narrative episodes, Thucydides surprises us with sudden blasts of straightforwardness, for a good story must keep beat with the passing of time. However, when he levitates into the abstractions of philosophy, geography, and anthropology, or the tight logic of political argument, his style immediately becomes less conventional and again more difficult to tease apart, for he seems to have so much to say, yet allows himself so little space to say it in. The following agglomeration of *cola* (written some six decades before *Isocrates* was polishing his *periods* for the *Panegyricus*) seems a likely trial-balloon *periodos*: that is, a *periodos* whose ambitious goal would seem to have led it slightly astray. (Please ignore the Loeb punctuation.)

> For it is plain that what is now called Hellas was not of old settled with fixed habitations but that migrations were frequent in former times each tribe readily leaving its own land whenever they were forced to do so by any people that was more numerous for there was no mercantile traffic and the people did not mingle with one another without fear either on land or by sea and they each tilled their own land only enough to obtain a livelihood from it having no surplus of wealth and not planting orchards since it was uncertain especially as they were yet without walls when some invader might come and despoil them and so thinking that they could obtain anywhere the sustenance required for their daily needs they found it easy to change their abodes and for this reason were not strong as regards either the size of their cities or their resources in general.[34] (Thuc. 1.2.1–3)

Though clearly a single topic, with the ideas and their numerous facets predicating an informative inclusiveness, it has a meandering air about it that weakens the drive of its message. To formulate a full-fledged, healthy, super-duper *periodos*, the clausal topics should connect more tightly.

Thucydides was not above reverting to archaic techniques when it suited him to do so. The following passage is a lovely example of ring composition, here applied to the crafting and marking off (punctuating) of a *period*. Whether to wrap up a lengthy sentential *period* or an historical episode (as in Herodotus), 'ringing' gave the sense of a well bonded group of related thoughts. It succeeded in this by demarking a portion of the whole with the same (or almost the same) word for both the beginning and the end—as we saw Herodotus repeatedly doing. Like a snake biting its tail, the result made a ring with the end remindful of the beginning. It was a favorite device of his predecessors (poets included), but in the case of the following example, Thucydides, by making the ploy less obvious, has brought it to a more sophisticated level. The result is a plainly marked, consolidated nugget that stands out as a densely packed unit from its surrounding word mass. Here, from Thucydides's *History*, '**sphal**entes' ('they stumbling,' meaning 'they coming upon hardship') is the opening word. **Esphal**ēsan ('They stumbled,' meaning 'they came upon hardship') is the last. The Loeb translation ignores this likeness of beginning and end entirely. In any case it would be hard to duplicate in natural English. The word for *stumbling* comes first in the Greek. (Please ignore the Loeb punctuation.)

> And yet, after they had met with disaster [stumbled] in Sicily, where they lost not only their army but also the greater part of their fleet, and by this time had come to be in a state of sedition at home, they nevertheless held out ten years not only against the enemies they had before, but also against the Sicilians, who were now combined with them, and, besides, against most of their allies, who were now in revolt, and later on, against Cyrus son of the King, who joined the Peloponnesians and furnished them with money for their fleet; and they did not finally succumb until they had in their private quarrels fallen upon one another and been brought to ruin [stumbled].[35]
> (Thuc. 2.65.12–13)

One should note how ambitious Thucydides was in juggling his time frames by means of particles. In the above passage, the affiliation of *cola*, each to its neighbor, is effected by a variety of particles that guide the reader across the wide informational spaces they each introduce. At the beginning of the above passage, we find the destitute Athenians in Sicily facing a difficult 10 years; in the middle, their allies are revolting and Cyrus has joined the Peloponnesians; at the end their own private quarrels ruined them. In short, the statement spans an enormous field of historical fact. *Nevertheless, Thucydides himself made it distinctly whole, sharp in its outline of beginning and end.* His purpose, it would seem, was to emblazon a significant truth: that despite a number of setbacks and losses, the real cause of Athens's fall was the mismanagement by its governmental leaders. In other words, *Athens could have won*. It would seem that we have here not only a ring-cadenced statement, but also, from the pupil of Antiphon, an ambitious and successful specimen of an early ring-styled *periodos*.

Because a linear *periodic* statement—whether spoken or written—could relate the numerous elements of a densely packed thought, it remained *the admired mode* for all polished statements throughout the fourth century BCE. Ancient judges and critics and educated readers were appreciative of—indeed could be dazzled by—complex statements. Thucydides was writing at a time when literary perspectives were just beginning to preponderate over oral habits and his pivotal experiments have revealed both struggle and success. The danger was always that early *period*-makers would sometimes become too ambitious, too inclined to over-complicate while still uncertain about the supporting grammar. Yet the literary successes of the not-yet-born Isocrates would soon be showing a way to bring clarity to convoluted statements and thereby sustain a long life for the *period*. Admiration for a full and intricate statement will stay with us well into the years of Roman supremacy, and be revitalized in the centuries beyond.

Notes

1. Mr. Denniston suggests that the evolution of particles probably represents a relatively late stage in the development of expression, as their existence betokens a certain self-consciousness. As we shall soon see, scholars today can use the growing presence of particles to date a Greek manuscript.

2. Denniston, *Greek Prose Style*. He goes on to say (p. xxxvii): "A few Greek particles can be clearly seen to have been, at an earlier state, other parts of speech." We see a similar conversion of meaning in our word *come*, as in, *Come here!* and *Come June, I'll be in Nicaragua*—where a verb becomes a time particle. And again, a double usage of the word *since*, as in, *Since Thursday, they have been promising to leave*; and *since*, as in, *Since you have flunked chemistry, you will not be accepted in medical school*—thus, both a *time* particle and a *because* particle.

3. Mary Karena Pukui and Samuel H. Elbert, eds., *The New Pocket Hawaiian Dictionary* (Honolulu: University of Hawaii Press, 1992), 225.

4. See Longinus, *On the Sublime*, trans. W. H. Fyfe, rev. Donald Russell, Loeb Classical Library (Cambridge: Harvard University Press, 1995), 234–9.

5. Henry R. Immerwahr, *Form and Thought in Herodotus* (Cleveland, OH: Press of Western Reserve University for The American Philological Association, 1966), 47–9.

6. Richard McKeon, *The Basic Works of Aristotle* (New York: Random House, 1941), 1462.

7. In this discussion of Herodotus's methods, I have drawn primarily on the content of Immerwahr's *Form and Thought*; Romm's *Herodotus*; Denniston's *Greek Prose Style*; and Carolyn Dewald's contributions as set down in "Wanton Kings, Pickled Heroes, and Gnomic Founding Fathers: Strategies of Meaning at the End of Herodotus's Histories," in *Classical Closure*, ed. Deborah H. Roberts, Francis M. Dunn, and Don Fowler (Princeton, NJ: Princeton University Press, 1997), 62–82.

8. Romm, *Herodotus*, 58. Also see 57.

9. Immerwahr, *Form and Thought*, 49.

10. Identified by an inflection to indicate that the noun is an indirect object or the object of a preposition.

11. Denniston, *Greek Prose Style*, 4, 96.

12. Henry R. Immerwahr and W. R. Connor, "Historiography," in *The Cambridge History of Classical Literature*, 1:437.

13. Henry R. Immerwahr, *Form and Thought*, 59, 61.

14. Ibid.

15. Dewald, "Wanton Kings," 63.

16. Ibid., 63–4.

17. This is the author's translation of the Greek text in Herodotus, *The Persian Wars*, trans. Alfred Dennis Godley, Loeb Classical Library (New York: G. P. Putnam's Sons, 1921–1925), 1:40.

18. Crane, *Blinded Eye*, 236–47.

19. Ibid., 252. Italics are added.

20. P. J. Rhodes, *Thucydides: History* (England: Aris and Phillips, 1988), 1:3–5 and 1:215–20.

21. Thucydides, *History of the Peloponnesian War*, trans. C. F. Smith 1:215.

22. Thucydides, *History of the Peloponnesian War*, trans. C. F. Smith 1:243–5.

23. Dionysius's more benign opinions about the chronologically-later Isocrates have already been cited.

24. Sir Kenneth Dover, *The Evolution of Greek Prose Style* (Oxford: Clarendon Press, 1997), 3; see also Denniston, *Greek Prose Style*, 36.

25. W. Robert Connor, *Thucydides* (Princeton, NJ: Princeton University Press, 1984), 92.

26. Connor, *Thucydides*, 235.

27. Aristotle, *The "Art" of Rhetoric*, trans. J. H. Freese, Loeb Classical Library (Cambridge: Harvard University Press, 1926), 387.

28. Demetrius, *On Style*, trans. Doreen C. Innes, in Aristotle, Longinus, Demetrius, *Poetics*, Loeb Classical Library (Cambridge: Harvard University Press, 1995), 23:355.

29. This word-for-word translation is my own. The passage is rendered more smoothly by Godley, in *Persian Wars*, 1:2. It reads as follows: "What Herodotus the Halicarnassian

has learnt by inquiry is here set forth: in order that so the memory of the past may not be blotted out from among men by time, and that great and marvelous deeds done by Greeks and foreigners and especially the reason why they warred against each other may not lack renown." Herodotus, *The Persian Wars*, trans. A. D. Godley, Loeb Classical Library (Cambridge: Harvard University Press, 1920).

30. Herodotus, *Persian Wars*, trans. Godley, 1:51.

31. Denniston, *Greek Prose Style*, 4, 96.

32. This is my translation of the Loeb's Greek text in Thucydides, *History of the Peloponnesian War*, trans. C. F. Smith, 1:3. Smith renders the passage as follows: "Thucydides, an Athenian, wrote the history of the war waged by the Peloponnesians and the Athenians against one another. He began the task at the very outset of the war, in the belief that it would be great and noteworthy above all the wars that had gone before, inferring this from the fact that both powers were then at their best in preparedness for war in every way, and seeing the rest of the Hellenic race taking sides with one state or the other, some at once, others planning to do so."

33. Denniston, *Greek Prose Style*, 19; see also 129.

34. To illustrate the meandering aspects of this passage, I have removed the punctuation from C. F. Smith's translation of the Loeb Greek text of Thucydides, *History of the Peloponnesian War*, 1:3–5.

35. Thucydides, *History of the Peloponnesian War*, trans. C. F. Smith, 2:379. The Greek here exposes a rather disconcerting habit of Thucydides. He switches prepositional forms on the reader: sometimes relying on inflections and sometimes turning the whole into a prepositional phrase (as we do in English). Since meter was not a constraint in prose, one wonders *Why the vacillation?* Possibly, it was a desire for variation; or a switch into the modes of conversation where word order held closer to the principles of meaning than to artistry with rhythms, which inflections so easily provided. Suetonius tells us (in his "Divus Augustus," in *The Twelve Caesars*, trans. Robert Graves [London: Penguin Classics, 1957], 91 [Suet., *Aug.* 86.1]) that Augustus in his anxiety to be understood "put prepositions before the names of cities, where common usage omits them"—thus, making 'prepositional phrases' just as we do in English.

References

Aristotle. *The "Art" of Rhetoric*. Translated by J. H. Freese. Loeb Classical Library. Cambridge: Harvard University Press, 1926.

Connor, W. Robert. *Thucydides*. Princeton, NJ: Princeton University Press, 1984.

Crane, Gregory. *The Blinded Eye: Thucydides and the New Written Word*. Lanham, MD: Rowman & Littlefield, 1996.

Demetrius. *On Style*. Translated by Doreen C. Innes. In Vol. 23 of *Poetics*, by Aristotle, Longinus, and Demetrius. Loeb Classical Library. Cambridge: Harvard University Press, 1995.

Denniston, J. D. *Greek Prose Style*. Oxford: Clarendon Press, 1952.

Dewald, Carolyn. "Wanton Kings, Pickled Heroes, and Gnomic Founding Fathers: Strategies of Meaning at the End of Herodotus's Histories." In *Classical Closure*. Edited by Deborah

H. Roberts, Francis M. Dunn, and Don Fowler. Princeton, NJ: Princeton University Press, 1997.

Dover, Sir Kenneth. *The Evolution of Greek Prose Style*. Oxford: Clarendon Press, 1997.

Herodotus. Vol. 1 of *The Persian Wars*. Translated by Alfred Dennis Godley. Loeb Classical Library. Cambridge: Harvard University Press, 1920.

Immerwahr, Henry R. *Form and Thought in Herodotus*. Cleveland, OH: Press of Western Reserve University for The American Philological Association, 1966.

Immerwahr, Henry R., and W. R. Connor. "Historiography." In Vol. 1 of *The Cambridge History of Classical Literature*. Edited by P. E. Easterling and Bernard M. K. Knox. Cambridge: Cambridge University Press, 1985.

Longinus. *On the Sublime*. Translated by W. H. Fyfe. Revised by Donald Russell. Loeb Classical Library. Cambridge: Harvard University Press, 1995.

McKeon, Richard. *The Basic Works of Aristotle*. New York: Random House, 1941.

Pukui, Mary Karena, and Samuel H. Elbert, eds. *The New Pocket Hawaiian Dictionary*. Honolulu: University of Hawaii Press, 1992.

Rhodes, P. J. Vol. 1 of *Thucydides: History*. England: Aris and Phillips, 1988.

Romm, James. *Herodotus*. New Haven, CT: Yale University Press, 1998.

Suetonius. "Divus Augustus." In *The Twelve Caesars*. Translated by Robert Graves. London: Penguin Classics, 1957.

Thucydides. Vols. 1 and 2 of *History of the Peloponnesian War*. Translated by Charles Forster Smith. Loeb Classical Library. Cambridge: Harvard University Press, 1921.

8

MOVING TOWARDS PERFECTION

'Attic' Style Versus 'Asiatic' Style

By the end of the fifth century BCE, literary perspectives had extensively broadened. As prose gathered power, so the influence of poetry became less onerous.

We have seen how fifth-century Sicilian sophists in the West had produced their treatises and pedagogical handbooks on rhetorical beautification, and how Ionian sophists in the east had begun to ponder the distinctions of grammar and discuss how to use words more precisely. Classical Greek (fifth to late-fourth century BCE)—with all its inflections, growing vocabulary, accumulating particles, rhetorical rules, and artistic passions—was full of perfidious traps that coaching could help to avoid. Protagoras, the influential Ionian skeptic and prime instigator of focus on the cognitive aspects of language, recommended 'correct' grammatical forms. He advised on word usage, and gave tips on the ins and outs of logical disputation. One imagines him, finger raised, admonishing the encircling youths not to confuse the dative with the genitive nor apply the plural where the dual was wanted. *We must keep our language Homerically pure!* His teachings would lead to eventual delvings into etymology, division of parts of speech, and the fine distinctions between 'synonyms,' such as *home* and *house; book* and *tome.*

The straightforward, logic-driven language associated with the urgings of Protagoras came in time to be known as the 'Attic' style; whereas the florid, ear-targeted style of Gorgias was (owing to its penchant for decoration) called 'Asiatic,' even though its most notorious practitioner came from Sicily to the west. (Obviously, it is wiser to forget geographic notions in trying to remember all this.) The Attic (Protagorean) style was characterized by simplicity. It favored tight-lipped expression with sparkling wit and well-wired intersentential tensions à la Nestor. It disdained the poetry-derived ideals of balanced clauses, engorged syntax, and the tedium of persistent rhythm. Though by Greco-Roman times Attic writings could seem quite terse, their byword was directness—directness with spin-offs of sincerity, intellect, brevity, and wit. Attic imagery drove to the point; Attic content aimed for wisdom. Attic word choice was rugged and indifferent to dissonance. Its nongabbling plainness allowed intense significance to attach to single words. In the first century BCE, our friend and critic Dionysius of Halicarnassus, would equate the Attic style to an 'ancient and indigenous,' trustworthy and lawful, model Athenian wife. For this we must think of a good household manager and attentive mother, who has, alas, been dispossessed of authority by the greed of her imported counterpart: a wanton, greedy Asiatic harlot for whom good household management was in no way a top priority.[1] Of Attic austerity Dionysius tells us:

> It requires that the words shall stand firmly on their own feet and occupy strong positions; and that the parts of the sentence shall be at considerable distances from one another, separated by perceptible intervals. It does not mind admitting harsh and dissonant collocations, like blocks of natural stone laid together in building, with their sides not cut square or polished smooth, but remaining unworked and rough-hewn.[2] (Dion. Hal., *Comp.* 22)

The Attic style, preferring to be more to the point than pretty, was always thought to have had its roots in antiquity and to have derived from such language as might have been the predecessor of our Nestor example. If indeed its blunt plainness descends directly from the prehistoric asyndetic roughness of speech—and Dionysius, speaking of its 'antique air,' seems to think that it does—we might consult Nestor's shout once again. There, we find that the words are grouped by relationships of meaning—in a natural, straightforward mode. The *cola* lead smoothly from one to the next, and within the actual shout, are directed by particles and finished with a verb—the exception being the final *colon*, where, as we have seen, the last word, "dead," holds for itself the vital result of the scene.

We are surprised that the syntax is so like our own everyday English. Each *colon* is concise, intense, and carries a full burden of meaning. One can well understand how Homer's ancient lines came to inspire all Greek (and Latin) writing, for—*despite the constraints of meter*—they conjured up rich mental images while maintaining an even balance between logic and emotion. There is no reason to think that Nestor or anyone else might have spoken differently on such an occasion. In short, while the concept is dramatically inflated and the rhythm of the lines pleasing, the word order seems natural. The lines are delivered with a commanding punch that is easily comprehended.

Though the Attic style will come to acquire over its lifetime a number of idiosyncratic conceits, it is basically the heir of intelligent practical speech; whereas the Asian style more closely relates to the precepts of ceremony, dance, and religion, and thereby requires greater contrivance. *The Cambridge History of Classical Literature* surmises that pre- and early Helladic (Bronze Age) heroic accounts would have "consisted for the most part of short sentences confined, as in other oral cultures, to verse."[3] Though short asyndetic lines would seem appropriate for the thinking and talking habits of our imagined primitive ancestors, we have no real knowledge of how humans communicated or what they did, or wanted, or were really like, those many thousands of years ago. In our distant beginnings, it has been argued, there was perhaps no division between man's instinctual life and his ability to reason—no division of brain into left and right hemispheres.[4] Proof of such an evocative possibility lies lost in the mists of prehistory. Nevertheless, since artistry can only begin once the practical basics have been settled, it would seem to be true that Atticism is the senior style. In its maturity it wrung out of language all the meaning it possibly could. Its later primary goal was to pare down subsidiary ideas and thereby heighten the essential elements of a statement for a more impactful reception.[5]

When we come to glimpse the confusingly numerous offspring of these two parental styles, bubbling Asian and austere Attic, we find that there was very little that could stay fixed in anyone's mind about either one of them once people began discussing their attributes. Where one says that Thucydides was Attic, another proclaims him the disciple of Gorgias. Indeed, the vagueness that envelops critical discussions of ancient literary styles is extreme. Even so, the underlying principles as described above offer a general rule of thumb that can be useful in distinguishing Asian from Attic; or if not actually useful, then

certainly talked about in terms of being useful. Once Isocrates was finally out
of the way, rhetorical Asianism lay low for a while, then gathered to rampage
again in Alexandria's Hellenistic period. But in the middle of the first century
BCE, the stern Atticists re-rallied and counter-attacked—in the name of language purity and better logic. And so it went (and still goes). The root hairs
of the two approaches to written communication have remained generative,
themselves nourished (as are so many other things) by the counter balances of
emotion and reason. And the real question they raise is this: To what extent
can one or *should one wish to* express meaning with artistic collusion?

By avoiding both excessive emotion and arid reason, Plato (mid-fourth
century BCE) had shown a sound middle way into the world of supreme literature. Yet not all, it would seem, had noticed.

Fledgling Notions for the Aeration of Text

'Aeration' breaks up the visual density of a text so as to expose its segments,
be they words, clauses, sentences, or the chunkier paragraphs and chapters.
In short, the spacious layout provided by aeration is a generic form of punctuation in that it contrasts *something with nothing*. It both manifests and ac-
centuates the opposition of activity to rest. The 'airiness' it provides allows
the reader a speedier comprehension. Originally, the word *and* (even when
embedded in the compacted lines of a *scriptura continua*, like the "128" of Jim's
"thirst128for128beer") gave readers a better-than-nothing substitute space.

When the alphabet first came into being, all seemed excitement and high
activity. Egos burgeoned as opportunities opened up for keeping commercial
accounts, scrawling quick notes (as well as graffiti), and for the setting down
of Homer. Because learning alphabet letters and combining them to make
words was not so hard to do, anyone might have thought that writing would
soon settle into a facile flow of separated words. But even by the end of the
fifth century BCE, when 'the 20 percent plus' cultivated Athenians were
successfully reading, they were apparently doing so without the constancy of
word-spacing or decisive closures. Their hunger to solve the secrets of manuscription must have been intense.

In view of the centuries of subsequent disregard for readerly relaxation,
one is astonished to discover that topic divisions were already being marked
off by a number of fourth-century BCE Greek scribes. This small corps of
scriveners devised and deployed (sometimes) the only punctuation mark of

the time—the *paragraphos* (looking something like a check mark) to indicate absolutely that some set of related thoughts had ended and another set would now begin. Handy ways to flag cadences *between the paragraph* marks remained uninvented, and without them, the old-timey, awkward (not to mention nebulous) methods persisted. Thus, smaller break points internal to the paragraph (all so readily manifest in voice sound) continued to be indicated by signposting particles and the positioning of verbs. Of primary importance too was the rhythmic beat of a word's syllables—that is, the prosodic metrical combinations of long and short syllables such as iambs (de-dee), dactyls (dee-de-de), spondees (dee-dee)—to indicate beginning and end.

While these needful matters were being so impractically addressed, Greek philosophers were beginning to theorize tentatively on the general subject of language formation. Plato (in the mid-fourth century)[6] recognized that a simple statement required at least a subject and a verb, though he failed to discuss the extensions and limitations that might thereafter apply. Being a magnificent stylist himself, he did not bother to pontificate to others on matters of style. That rich career path had not yet opened up. And so it fell to Aristotle, a half generation later, to initiate the practice of analyzing options for putting words on 'paper' and evaluating their effects. By the year 350 BCE (with Isocrates still on stage) the time for theoretical discussion about language was ripe at last, and Aristotle, the categorizing, defining, dictating schoolmaster, stepped up to the podium.

In his *"Art" of Rhetoric*, Aristotle described all writing as being set in one of two opposing styles: the *continuous* or the *periodic*. The first (also called the *running-on* style) was the common, somewhat primitive one wherein, as we have seen, simple propositions are connected *in perpetua* by *and* or *then* until some body of sense is accomplished. In the silent world of writing, such verbal gush seems characterless and tedious. And so, Aristotle urged his pupils towards an alternative style, which he called the *periodic* style. The *period*, said he, broke apart the breathless continuum of *and*-ridden paratactic word-flow into groups of related ideas. Each *period* was distinguished by a discernible beginning and end, so that the magnitude of related ideas might be easily grasped. He recommended rhythms both for closing down a thought and for opening up a new one. Moreover, he decreed what they should be. He limited the size of the resulting *periodic* word-chunks to 'what the memory could keep hold of.' Accepting Plato's observation that a subject-and-verb combination fulfills the sense of unity, he urged writers to end a thought with a verb. It is interesting to note that this collection of advisements will soon transmogrify into a prosody for prose that would prelude what visual space and regularized punctuation would eventually achieve. But for now those opening and closing meters, though quickly mastered by aurally-trained ears, would seem an impediment to a relaxed setting down of one's thoughts. The old *kai* (and) and *de* (then) that had aerated word-flow so easily in the continuous style were, by this time, being broadly frowned upon.

Some of Aristotle's surprising prescriptions will be dealt with shortly, but at this point it is handy to think of a theorized *periodic* sentence as being rather like a shortish modern 'complex' one. Take for example: *Though I don't much care for Sam, I rather admire his technique on the piano.* Despite the fact that each of the above two segments has a subject and a verb, their relationship is not an equal one. The particle *though* in the first segment has a detractive force that directs our focus to the second, more positive, more important one. When the two segments are linked in this way, each adds color to the underlying, so-called full thought and to the sense of finish as well. The feel of the sentence in its paratactic form, however, is quite different: *I don't much care for Sam and I rather admire his technique on the piano.*

One should appreciate that by the time Aristotle was addressing the principles of sentence structures and style, his authoring coevals were already pumping out multiclausal *periods* of three to fifteen-and-more lines. Without the benefit of theoretical analysis or scholarly instruction, they were *simply doing it.* It was, no doubt, in recognition of their success that Aristotle took his stand: roundly deploring the endlessness of the old continuous mode on the grounds that it was "unpleasant neither to foresee nor to get to the end of anything"[7]—let alone have breath for it. As had others, he labeled that mode "archaic." Aristotle's claim that the continuous style was 'no longer popular' tells us, indeed crucially tells us, *that Athenian minds had reorganized to reject it.* A new intellectuality, a search for *reasons why*, was breaking apart the old, immediate 'response-to-sensation' moulds of pre-literate oral habits. Still, it would take centuries for the concepts known as *periods, colons,* and (later) *commas* to stabilize before transmuting into the points (or puncts) we use today.

It is sad to think that the initial gestures towards breaking up or 'aerating' text inspired no massive scribal response. Even Aristotle's recognition that rhetorical pauses in the flow of language were important to the sense brought no real action for indicating them visually on 'paper.' And so it was that early readers were left to labor on without the support of paragraph breaks, sentence-initiating capital letters, indentations, commas, word-division, or even unequivocal signs of full stop—to which we must also add: no headings, no folios (page numbers), no indices nor constancy of lettering.

One is amazed that a vigorous pointing system did not take hold during all the intellectual buzz of the fifth and fourth centuries in Athens. Why, when Aristotle, the most august of living Greek philosophers, was already discussing the brain's ability to assimilate minutiae but not the vast possibilities of infinity and eternity, did working pens not hit upon some practical method for parceling out manuscript lines in manageable pieces? or to accommodate—at the very least—the reading eye with consistent word breaks? There are a number of ways to respond to this question, and some have already been considered. But the overarching answers are these: (1) humans in general expend the lowest possible energy towards changing their habits; and (2) those who are privileged are content as they are.

The fact of punctuation's sluggish lift-off might be added to the reasons for the lack of a facile and comprehensive aural-to-visual handover. By impeding the spread of fact and discovery, those densely packed, unpunctuated texts can be said to have slowed the development of human intellectual faculties. They made reading too hard and too slow, for too long. Unfortunately, those ingrained customs of dense manuscription would come to be reinforced by the early Christian Church, which was for many centuries the jealous keeper of written knowledge. Had the Church decided to break loose from the *scriptura continua* habit, ignorance would probably not have persisted throughout the medieval centuries.[8] As it was, the liberation of the Public Brain would lie far into the future.

Those under Greek influence who had been schooled in reading and writing during the literary flowering of the Classical and Hellenic eras were lucky indeed. They at least had learned how to break *scriptura continua* into words, and to spot the directional particles, cadencing rhythms, and terminating verbs. Since books and learning thrive best in established, well-assured societies, those who lived during the disruptive breakup of Macedonian rule in Egypt were not destined to be so culturally fortunate. Literature, with its cargo of civilized knowledge, became then, more than ever, the property of pompous scholars and uneducated scribes.

Further Developments in 'Attic' Oratory: Lysias

Lysias (445–380 BCE) was an orator in Athens, and active in the turnover decades of the fifth to fourth centuries, that is, more than half a century later than

Antiphon or Pericles, but contemporary with Plato. Lysias is the acclaimed prototypical Atticist,[9] admired through the ages for the purity of his dialect, for his unstilted, prosaic vocabulary, his lucidity, brevity, and vivid representation of character—all of which suggest a growing tendency in which Plato too played a part. The critic Dionysius of Halicarnassus some centuries later says of Lysias that his was a manner of utterance "in which ideas are reduced to their essentials and expressed tersely, a style most appropriate, and indeed necessary in forensic speeches and every other form of practical oratory."[10] We are told (and will shortly see for ourselves) that his 'engaging oratory' was not (except in the opening *periods*) composed of vast, rhythmic structures, but in loosely bound, simple sentences. Like Antiphon, he had come to the conclusion that a scholastic pomp of words and phrases was useless in judicial courts, and that a plain, close-fitting, and vigorous style made the best route to success when trying to persuade. As Plato was also seeking a more relaxed yet gracious style, we may conclude that the unadorned rhythms of common speech had at last found their place in the world of acceptable prose. The word 'natural' comes into play at this point. Directness for quick intake is the crucial element of 'natural' speech or 'natural' word order. It is a mode of communication in which there is no complication of artistry to delay comprehension.

Lysias was considered to have ushered in a healthy new style with the unpretentious simplicity of his prose, which was both attractive and natural. His surviving court cases record 'real people' in realistic, even homely, settings. Nevertheless, despite the aura of unaffected intimacy, his accounts were carefully arranged with preface, narrative, well-argued proof, and a conclusion—all of which followed the steps of public expectation. When (sadly for him) Lysias lost his Athenian privileges, he no longer had the right to address the court himself, and instead (happily for us) began to write out speeches for others to give, as had Antiphon before him. Much of his work has been lost, though extant pieces tell us that humor and caricature played a part in justifying his fame.

In the following passage, taken from his *On the Murder of Eratosthenes*, we note that Lysias's overall manner is similar to Antiphon's, though in general it moves more quickly and offers more detailed description. Supported by an environment of growing literacy, Lysias is clearly at ease with his 'pen.' His style is more 'natural' than that of either Thucydides or the highly rhetorical Isocrates, who was yet (some 23 years later) to publish his *Panegyricus*. The most noticeable artifice that Lysias employs in the specimen piece beneath is antithesis, which imparts a relaxed control over scene and character. Yet his use of oppositional forces avoids the artsy sing-song pairings and constant antithetical relationships found in the writings of Gorgias.[11] In the body of Lysias's defense, the clauses and phrases are brief—like those of Antiphon's Euxitheus. Each rides upon the next with a staccato breathlessness, suggestive of candid earnestness, and are rarely subordinate one to another. There are no unnecessary shifts in the word order—a feature so prominent in ambitious pen-crafted ancient statement. However, when it came to the matter of the opening statement— the usual terrain for *periodic* compression—Lysias, the champion logographer, like everybody else followed in the tracks of precedence.

The defense for his client commences with the requisite network of complex thinking, expressed in only mildly disarranged but common enough Greek words laid out in a series of hypothetical 'if'-*cola* with antithetical balances. Though it may seem a bit difficult to unravel, it initiates an introduction that is extremely brief, *almost 10 times shorter* than the introductory materials that Antiphon had provided for his *Murder of Herodes*. Moreover, we can detect a more easeful and open handling of the wordage. Here now is the opening *period* from the defending speech generally known as *On the Murder of Eratosthenes*, which was composed by Lysias for the accused Euphiletus to memorize and deliver in court. It constitutes about a third of all the carefully wrought introductory material, which is immediately followed by a ripping account of what happened. (To give a better feel for its *periodic* wholeness, the Loeb's colons, full stops, and sentence capitalization have been removed. The commas, however, have been retained for easier intake.)

> I should be only too pleased, sirs, to have you so disposed towards me in judging this case as you would be to yourselves if you found yourselves in my plight, for I am sure that if you had the same feelings about others as about yourselves, not one of you but would be indignant at what has been done, you would all regard the penalties appointed for those who resort to such practises as too mild, and these feelings would be found, not only amongst you, but in the whole of Greece, for in the case of the crime alone, under both democracy and oligarchy, the same requital is accorded to the weakest against the strongest, so that the lowest gets the same treatment as the highest.[12]
> (Lys., *On the Murder of Eratosthenes*, 1–2)

Shortly thereafter, the pace picks up. The first line of the excerpt below translates straightforwardly word for word, thus (Euphiletus is speaking): "And the wife to go I bid and to give to the child the breast." Again, later: "And I on the one hand laughing, she on the other hand got up." Lysias wrote this defense for

Euphiletus, who had killed Eratosthenes after catching him in *flagrante delicto*
with his wife. On behalf of his client, Lysias's job was to prove not only that
there had been no spite, no pursuance of feud or premeditation involved in the
murder of Eratosthenes, but also that Euphiletus himself had acted in trust of and
in accordance with the law, which allowed the killing of marital intruders. Thus,
in Euphiletus's words as written out by Lysias for him to memorize and say, we are
told the whole story with severe clarity and force. The speech was delivered before a court of 51 judges, whose final decision on the case is not known. Note the
home-like atmosphere, the feel of darkness, and the saucy responses of the wife.

> So I bade my wife go and give the child her breast, to stop its howling.
> At first she refused, as though delighted to see me home again after
> so long; but when I began to be angry and bade her go,—"Yes, so that
> you," she said, "may have a try here at the little maid. Once before,
> too, when you were drunk, you pulled her about." At that I laughed,
> while she got up, went out of the room, and closed the door, feigning
> to make fun, and she turned the key in the lock. I, without giving
> a thought to the matter, or having any suspicion, went to sleep in
> all content after my return from the country. Towards daytime she
> came and opened the door. I asked why the doors made a noise in the
> night; she told me that the child's lamp had gone out, and she had lit
> it again at our neighbour's. I was silent and believed it was so. But it
> struck me, sirs, that she had powdered her face, though her brother
> had died not thirty days before; even so, however, I made no remark
> on the fact, but left the house in silence.[13] (Lys., *On the Murder of
> Eratosthenes*, 1.12–15)

Not much remains of Lysias's logographic speeches. But Dionysius of Halicarnassus, who (luckier than we) had many at hand, tells us that Lysias's charms
were great indeed and most evident in the portraits he drew of the litigants.
These highly vivid views, drawn with psychological insightfulness, give us our
best glimpses into the private lives of Athenians during the Classical period.
But what later critics most admired was the effective simplicity of the Lysianic
style—his fast-paced short statements, unstilted vocabulary, and descriptions
of people, families, and homely household topics—all of which, though seemingly artless and candid, "was in fact almost inimitable."[14] His writings were
vociferously acclaimed. Lysias, as did all the known early orators, brought
much to the advance of prose: ease, flexibility, and the acceptance of everyday
common topics. With Lysias, as with Plato, we find ourselves in the world of

natural speech—in Plato's case, beautifully contrived but seemingly effortless arrangements of thoughts and words; in Lysias's case, the familiar feel of street talk, and of café and domestic realities.

Xenophon of Athens

Last in our chain of early Greek historians—Hecateus, Herodotus, and Thucydides—comes Xenophon (431–350 BCE), who amongst his many other works continued Thucydides's unfinished tale of the Peloponnesian Wars with his own *Hellenica*. By Xenophon's time, with considerable credit to Thucydides some 30 years earlier, the act of writing prose for posterity had become a more easeful occupation and a more incorporated part of scholarly activity. Lysias, the admired, plain-spoken logographer, was still on stage, dramatically recounting the doings of felons and murderers while setting fresh goals for a more natural expression in writing.

The wholesome flow of his language, his pace, and his intimate characterizations seem to have been a strong influence on Xenophon, for following suit, he too wrote in straight, unadorned language and dealt in depth with character analysis. Yet he went further. He disdained the custom of formal *periodic* introduction and dived promptly, even abruptly, into his topic. Being almost exactly coeval with Plato, Xenophon, too, befriended the elderly philosopher Socrates, and wrote four works about him, including a *Symposium* and an *Apology* that extended the view that Plato was offering during the same period. One wonders if Socrates's notoriously unconventional and unaffected manner was an influence towards the development of the natural language that all three authors—Lysias, Plato, and Xenophon—were now making so acceptable.

For a sample of Xenophon's no-nonsense directness, beneath is the opening statement to his *Anabasis* (meaning 'a march up-country'). The *Anabasis*, written in reminiscence towards the end of his life, relates his adventures as leading commander of the ten thousand Greek mercenary soldiers who had been stranded, starving and ragged, far from home in foreign territory. Those ill-starred troops had joined the Persian armies of Cyrus, who was hoping to seize the Persian throne from his less able brother. When Cyrus was killed in battle and the Greeks found themselves with all their own generals dead in the eastern edges of Persia, Xenophon himself led them through countless hardships back to Greece and to safety.

Taken from the Greek text of the 1998 Loeb edition, here are the first few more or less word-for-word lines of Xenophon's account. The quick launch of topic and the simplicity of the language are strikingly new to the sacred art of writing history. As will be seen, the passage is in no way awkward (in the manner of Hecataeus), nor rambling (in the manner of Herodotus), nor compacted and severe (in the manner of Thucydides). Instead, it reads plainly and simply as follows. Its guiding (very common) particles have been bold-faced:

> Two sons were born to Darius and Parysatis, the older [*men* = on the one hand] Artaxerxes, the younger [*de* = on the other hand] Cyrus. When then [***Epei de***: in indication of a new subject] Darius felt pain and suspected the end of his life, he wanted to have both his sons to be present. In fact [***ouv***] on the one hand [*o men*] the elder being nearby it chanced, Cyrus on the other hand [*de*] called back from the territory of which him satrap he had made...[15] (Xen., *An.* 1.1–2)

Xenophon continues in the same easy, story-telling manner with interesting accounts and analyses of war. Amongst these he includes political inquiry, as well as descriptions of places, people, their characters, and the hardships they suffered. His portraits of leaders, and particularly that of Cyrus, probe into the essence of sound upbringing, good leadership, good character, and good government. He wrote about men he had known in the field of battle and about events in which he had participated—all of which add a sense of immediacy and factual exactitude to his reports. Unlike Herodotus, he does not continually digress; nor like Thucydides, does he appear to be fighting a recalcitrant language. Instead he writes with an easy-flowing grace. Though educated in a world of rhetorical dominance and plainly sensitive to the powers of artistry, he does not swing out to engage in linguistic feats of cleverness. All of Xenophon's writings proceed with a refreshing flow of clear, straightforward sentence structures, close to the habits of unaffected speech. Though the rhetorical arts would continue to impose rules for prose expression, Xenophon explored a more relaxed way for silent words to convey excitement and meaning, and showed (as had Plato) that simplicity can hold much beauty. In sum, his collective writings expanded the reach of flexible, natural expression and proved a high mark in the maturing of prose.

Though Plato and Lysias must certainly have been an influence on Xenophon, the habits derived from his years of military command, when he would have had to control his exhausted troops with terse and direct language, have also been thought to have led him away from the rhetorical arts that were still broadly influential during his youth.[16] Though there is evidence throughout his writings of familiarity with 'beautiful speech,' what he actually produced for his readership was an attractive simplification of its sometimes obfuscating complexities.

While Xenophon (like his contemporaries Lysias and Plato) was clearly at ease with his pen, there remains still an element of archaism in his work. He was forgetful at times of what his readership needed to know in order to follow the thread of his argument. For example, he would allow new faces to appear on his stage without introduction. Again, he would sometimes fail to provide the background necessary for understanding what he was describing. It was the same old matter of authorial self-absorption—the failure to consider what a reader might need to know. Perhaps the tendency was aggravated by having to deal with awkward papyrus rolls. However it was, it seems that Xenophon sometimes forgot that written words travel broadly both in space and in time, and that his reader of wherever and whenever might not know a crucial supporting fact. But generally, his historical accounts hold together very well. They are pleasant to read and informative on many fronts. One feels to be in the presence of a man of broad experience—a practical, good, brave, and wise man, who was also an excellent teacher.

Despite his hectic military career, his political activities, and his writing down of major historical events, Xenophon found time as well to write a number of interesting shorter pieces—essays and studies: about people, kings, despots, sophists; about household management, marriage, the cavalry, hunting, and horsemanship—proving that prose was now well on its way and that he was a facile master of it. Most important was the fact that he worked his words to impart what he meant and to have it understood. By the end of his long life Xenophon had done for history what Plato had done for philosophy and Lysias had done for oratory. As always, where the aim is earnestly to inform, the language must strive for precision rather than decoration; and the simpler that language is, the more people there will be who understand it. We have seen how Plato, a true artist and an inspired teacher, studiously practiced simplicity; and we shall shortly see how other conveyors of knowledge, though steeped in the knowledge of rhetorical rule, came to apply the same primary rule—clarity first—in their writings. In the oncoming years, the most notable reach for clarity will be found in works designed for teaching.

Xenophon represents the height of achievement in the development of historical writing during the Classical Greek fourth century. By the time of his death, a historiographer would have felt empowered to say what he meant both clearly and gracefully. Interestingly, even within Xenophon's extensive corpus of writings, we can trace a simplifying vocabulary and a more relaxed management of sentence structure. These derive from an increase of confidence, as manifested in his inserts of personal opinion and even jokes; in the in-depth developments of character; and throughout, a growing adoption of particles. That surge in particle increase tells us of two things: the improved ability of those who could read, and the increased authorial concern for successfully transmitting the intended sense of a thought. In addition, the swell of particle presence throughout Xenophon's works gives us a handy chronology for their invention and use.

In a close study of the *Hellenica*, which is believed to have been written at different stages during the latter part of Xenophon's life, Professor Malcolm MacLaren,[17] our mentor for the moment, composed a chart of particle increase organized as they appeared in the four sections of Xenophon's *History*. As we glance down the figures, we can almost see Xenophon grow in competence, assuredness, and deftness in handling subtleties. To illustrate the swell of Xenophon's use of particles over his authoring years, herewith are a few samples. In the case of **men**: in the opening section of the *Hellenica*, this particle was not used at all; over the years it became more fashionable, and appears 47 times in the fourth section. **Kai**...**de** increases from zero to 49; **mentoi** from 2 to 110; **ge** from 7 to 63; **de** from 10 to 125. Additional counts tell us that the instances of the verbal future optative mood increased from 3 to 44, rhetorical questions from 4 to 51, the binding powers of anaphora (as in *both* this *and* that) from 2 to 46.

MacLaren also points out examples of Xenophon's dry wit and jocular sarcasm (signs of a person at ease with himself and enjoying what he can do with the language). We are told that as the lengthy *Hellenica* continues to be written over the years, such instances of fun increase, the first section being practically devoid of humor. To illustrate Xenophon's facile wit, MacLaren translates amongst several other examples the following:

> Apropos of a visit at the Great King's court, the envoy Antiochus observes that while he saw any number of cooks, butlers, and door-keepers, a careful examination failed to reveal any fighting men who would be a match for the Greeks; and as for Persian wealth, it was all an exaggeration, and the famous golden plane-tree, by which they set

such store, wouldn't provide shade enough for a grasshopper. (Xen. *Hell.* 7.1.38)[18]

MacLaren's study of the *Hellenica* gives abundant evidence of Xenophon's expanding confidence and ease. "It has often been observed that Xenophon does not appear in the *Hellenica* in the first person until after Book II, 3, 10."[19]! From that point on he refers to himself 14 times. And again: "No one who studies the speeches in the *Hellenica* can fail to be impressed with their wondrous subtlety of argumentation. Speakers display the greatest resourcefulness in making a case for themselves out of the most unpromising material. They show an extraordinary ability to turn an apparently unfavorable situation to their own advantage; to argue on either side or both sides of a question, as expediency may dictate."[20] There is none of this in the first book of the *Hellenica*.

All of these findings point to an immense and growing ease with the authorial 'pen.' Within a few decades, Xenophon had spanned the gap from his early awkward, tentative stiffness—in which he seems inclined to imitate the great Thucydides—to his later facile confidence in handling any kind of writing. The setting down of the *Hellenica* took many years and was worked on intermittently throughout the latter part of Xenophon's life. The quirks and changes of style through the four consecutive periods of composition point to an increasing independence from precedent. As we follow the trail of particles and note the evidence of growing ease and mastery, we see a tremendous leap forward in the flexibility of the written word. Confidence has lessened the power of rigid rhetorical rule. By the end of the fourth century BCE, written prose was well on its way to being a reliable conveyance for all manner of human expression. It had found the route to elegance and clarity.

Demosthenes: Orator and Writer

A political or judicial oration was in essence a kind of exhortative essay. It was designed to persuade with a lineup of facts illumined with fire and logic. Public admiration for oratorical sublimity assured its influence over the word-artistry of all the contemporary and succeeding historians and philosophers of ancient times.

We have noted the awkwardness of Hecataeus, and the seeming randomness of Herodotus. We have witnessed Antiphon's cleverness in honing a complex opening *period* for his client Euxitheus. We have seen how his pupil, the historian Thucydides, had teased the language of his narrative to higher levels of exactitude and flexibility; and again, how Lysias made a literary virtue of undecorated oral liveliness; and yet again how his younger contemporary Plato refined that groundswell of oral liveliness to create writing of beauty, pliability, clarity, and intelligence—all of which provided a fertile background for Xenophon's easygoing mastery of written prose. At this point in our story, Plato and Xenophon had died, and the aged, still active Isocrates (renowned for his extenuated yet sense-bearing *periods*) had still a decade to live and to argue (in writing). Determined to work in written prose, all of these fifth- and fourth-century beneficiaries of polished oratory worked hard to improve their new medium: to make it more translucent and aesthetically agreeable as well. The philosopher Aristotle (at one time a pupil at Plato's Academy) was at this moment advising and *theorizing* about how to perfect written prose.

Now we must meet Demosthenes, whose fourth-century dates exactly match those of Aristotle (384–322 BCE). Active in the years 350–330, that is, a half century after Lysias, Demosthenes represents the pinnacle of lasting oratorical achievement during the Greek Classical era. His surviving speeches (undoubtedly refurbished later) show us that, by the mid-fourth BC century, written Greek prose was truly off the ground and flying high. It could handle philosophy, history, and accounts of political dispute with a polish that has never been surpassed. Demosthenes, we know, felt himself particularly indebted to Thucydides and studied his work intensely. Not far into the future, he would himself be studied with equal intensity by aspiring Latin orators and writers, and many centuries later by English Parliamentarians. Building on the shoulders of predecessors, Demosthenes succeeded in doing for recorded political oratory what Xenophon had done for history and the essay, and what Plato, too, had done for political analysis and philosophy. That is, he wrote his speeches with aptly apportioned sound sense and rhetorical artistry, and in that way brought the quality of all early Greek prose to new heights. His reputation for brilliance has never diminished.

Like many of his prose-writing fellows, Demosthenes began his career as a litigator and logographer in the law courts of Athens. By exercising his 'pen' before mounting the podium, he kept himself well away from the risks of oral brinkmanship. Plutarch tells us that Demosthenes would not speak *ex tempore* if he could help it.[21] Instead, like Churchill, he wrote down what he intended to say in advance, delivered his speech, and afterwards polished it for posterity. Along with Pericles (about whose literary abilities we know little), Demosthenes is traditionally considered the best of all the ancient Greek orators. His style—deriving from a snappy mix of admonition, logic, analysis, impatience, passion, and cajoling—has retained its literary appeal through the ages, owing special thanks to the admiring support of the yet-to-be-born Roman Cicero.

Interestingly, Demosthenes seemed unaffected by the restrictive rhetorical theories of his admiring coeval, Aristotle. When compared with the syntax of his ultra-literary political opponent (the now-aged Isocrates), Demosthenes's sentence structures seem friendlier, more natural, more consonant with the hodgepodge ways of talk. Always clever, always aware of the built-in restiveness of listeners (and readers), he relieved the monotony of lengthy word flow with structural variety: from rounded *periods* to asyndetic *cola*. He was master of the oratorical *period* with its sophisticated built-in delay factor; and he was quick to shift subsidiary clauses or replant sentential elements to accommodate the drive of his thinking and keep his audience alert. Demosthenes was noted for his varied sentence rhythms, by which, in order to engage emotions and arouse excitement, he kept receptive ears off-balance.[22] He did not reject the use of Gorgianic ornament, as Lysias had seemed to do. In fact, after Lysias had cleansed the oratorical palate, so to speak, we find that Demosthenes could and did risk being quite artistically bold and free. One sees this in his use of parallelism and metaphor, occasional poetical words, and even his freedom with colloquialisms.[23]

Topping all that, Demosthenes sparkles most vividly in his handling of antitheses. No one that *he* talked about "laughed on the one hand" while "somebody else on the other hand got up." His contrasts were broader in scope. He did not dish them out as did his opponent Isocrates, first one and then the other, but arranged ideas around a single thesis, the whole of which he then antithesized against an opposing collection of integrated ideas. This wide-lens treatment required some sophistication of intellect, for to accomplish it successfully a speaker-writer must have perspective—some preorganized view of the whole piece.[24] He must do his thinking a giant step back before opening his mouth or setting pen to paper. This new evidence of thinking ahead so as to bundle together related ideas and intensify the drive of his thesis is a very interesting feature of Demosthenes's work. It was the lack of this ability that had marred the works of the early philosophers (like Heraclitus and Democritus).

We will note that more and more as literacy developed, so did a foresighted treatment of prose materials become more common. In this respect as in others, Demosthenes stands up well under modern inspection. Says our voluble critic and friend, Dionysius of Halicarnassus:

he pretended to no single style and imitated no single orator, but by selecting the best qualities from all of them developed a style with a universal appeal, which is what chiefly distinguishes him from all other writers.[25] (Dion. Hal., *Dem.* 21)

In short, Demosthenes artistically surpassed both Antiphon and Lysias by using 'Asiatic decoration' to embellish 'Attic plainness,' and by that means found a happy medium. Those with logical Stoic leanings claimed him for the Attic team; those who preferred a more florid eloquence called him "middle styled." He was never considered to be Asiatic à la Gorgias, though when he wanted, he could handle prosodic decorations as well as anyone.

Remembering Isocrates, who set out his arguments in swells of elaborate wordage, let us for a moment enjoy Demosthenes's angular counter punch. *Take that, Isocrates!* It reaches our ears in the form of natural sounding, yet sensibly thought out and carefully crafted, written-down talk as it dexterously copes with the demons of exaggerated acoustical pleasure and high-pressured logic. The translation is from the Loeb edition.

> But when our turn comes, what shall we say then? For of course he [Philip] will deny that he is attacking us, just as he denied that he was attacking the men of Oreus, when his troops were already in their territory, or the Pheraeans before that, when he was actually assaulting their walls, or the Olynthians at the start, until he was inside their frontier with his army. Or shall we say, even at that hour, that those who bid us repel him are provoking war? If so, there is nothing left but slavery, for there is no other alternative. Moreover, you have not the same interests at stake as some of the others, for it is not your subjection that Philip aims at; no, but your complete annihilation. For he is well assured that you will not consent to be slaves; or, if you consent, will never learn how to be slaves, for you are accustomed to rule others; but that you will be able, if you seize your chances, to cause him more trouble than all the rest of the world. For that reason he will not spare you, if he gets you in his power.[26] (Dem., *Or.* 10.61–62)

Although Demosthenes (or his scribe) probably wrote in *scriptura continua* using only (perhaps) the *paragraphos* for pointing it, we need not be too worried for his readers' deciphering eyes. By the time that Philip II of Macedon was threatening Athens in mid-fourth century, the clause-concluding verbs, as well as their beginning and ending meters,[27] had become firmly accustomed guides for the well-practiced reader. Also, the collection of signaling particles had grown, and Demosthenes used them abundantly. As always, they flagged the word groups, indicating whether they were to continue in the vein of the previous word group, enlarge its purport, detract from it, or introduce a new time frame, a contrariness, or result—and in this way, steered the eye in and out the *commata* and *cola* towards a fully textured meaning.

Demosthenes's injection of rhetorical questions into his speeches adds an oral zing that the *Panegyricus* of feeble-throated Isocrates sadly lacked. As we read a fast-paced Demosthenes speech, we may imagine the stunned silence that might have followed such questions.[28] Demosthenes is glaring at his audience—*If that is so obvious, why do we delay? Yet how best can we proceed?*—while all those upturned, wide-eyed faces gape back at him as the matter is considered. *Hmmm. How to proceed?* The absence of Isocreatean repetitiveness, euphony, and balance puts the focus on the argument and its urgency. What Demosthenes is saying is *very* important and he lets you know that. His word choice, his syntax, his rhythms, his style—all are gathered to hammer home the importance of his demand: *THINK!*

But an additionally interesting fact is this: that even as Demosthenes was molding his words on the podium and polishing them with great skill and confidence, Aristotle, the great thinker, was theorizing about the art of rhetoric in the clumsiest, most primitive, rigid way—even though he admired Demosthenes and must often have heard him in full blow. The startling Demosthenes-Aristotle contrast will shortly be dealt with.

All in all, Demosthenes proved himself to be a fearless master of the Greek tongue, a consummate stylist at work in an era when style was less a pedagogical topic than was the resolution of specific grammatical enigmas. By giving content the edge over form (but not forgetting the form and never forgetting clarity), Demosthenes ensured that his way of putting words together would in the future become the paradigmatic one. Though he lost the debate with Isocrates about Philip, he won history's laurels for developing a perfect style for communicating.

More Speculations About the *Period*

It has now been shown how particles can direct, assort, connect, and evaluate a series of *cola*. When we enlarge a statement with fresh aspects of thought, we are, figuratively speaking, building an architectural structure—adding a wing here, a garage there, repositioning roofs, and so on. Through the ages, the generic *period* has followed similar principles of addition, adjustment, and modification. Nevertheless, it has remained its essential multifaceted, identifiable self, despite the whims of fashion and the tinkerings of literary experimentalists.

In the writings of all who discussed it, the early *periodic* style represented an improvement over the paratactic (or 'continuing') style, which tended to ramble, was prone to interruption, and was unsteady in its focus. With its flow of serial parts, a paratactic statement gave the overall impression of deluge. Because the driving thought is delivered more or less in fragments, it is incompatible with the highest aims of literature, where form and content must share the limelight. Stick-to-itiveness and fulfillment of thought were the clinching attributes that made *periods* the optimal conveyances of logical thinking.[29]

The *periodic* style is an interesting animal. To understand the principles of a *periodos*, one might start by comparing it to a wooden wagon wheel, whose felloes (i.e., the curved pieces forming the rim) become the idea-bearing, word-group segments, or *cola*. As each felloe-*colon* is fitted to (or 'tongued' with) its neighbor, an interdependency is established, so that in the finished wheel rim a felloe's support is both given and received. The result is a New and Completed Thing with an enlargement of capability. This wheel image strikes close to the essence of a *period*, but fails to hit the bull's-eye, for it does not include the sense of beginning and end, or of swell and cadence. As we have seen from our Isocratean example, the peaks and troughs of an extended *periodic* sentence can be quite oceanic.

It is interesting to think about what might have been an ancestral prototype for the *periodos*. Possibly, as poetic lines gave way to prose ones, the preliterate propensity for a global view (as manifested in habits of antithesis and parallelism) exerted some initiating force. But whatever its source, the mature *period*'s most interesting contribution to literary history was the fillip it gave to the concept of cadence. The *periodic* goal of 'completing a thought' shows a mindset that begins to be truly intellectual. The closely argued logic of Athenian political and judicial oratory (such as we saw in the excerpts at the end of Antiphon's speech) was influential to its development in that it was goal-controlled, driven by logic, and more and more frequently written down to be tinkered with later.

As we watch the *periodos* advance through time, we see its engulfing appetite redefine the boundaries. From Gorgianic choreography, from sophistic teachings and Athenian oratorical debate, into the workshops of experiment, theory, and persnickety Hellenistic scholars—on and on the '*periodic* ideal' progresses like an enlarging snowball to spatter eventually onto the cerebral 'total canvas' of such as Walter Pater and Henry James, some 24 centuries later. Within that time span, we will find many variations. Today, we may think of it (should we think of it at all) as just a great big, moderately well-knit, particle-controlled and visually punctuated, multiplex sentence that comes in time to a definitive end. Modern writers (who can be quite as dexterous with long-windedness as was Isocrates) have been known to design outrageously embroiled *periods*, not only for the pleasure of showing their skills or inducing a frisson of suspense, but sometimes even for humor.

The limitations of the human brain determine the mode of our expression.[30] Comprehension of another person's thinking is predicated on the recognizable integrity of his (the speaker-writer's) thoughts as well as on the order in which they emerge into sound or view. In accordance with the *periodic* theory, each sentential segment must be seen as separate from the mess of other thoughts, yet form a related succession. A communicator finds himself more readily understood, more effective and powerful when, having identified the limits of a mini-thought, he takes the trouble to rank its level of importance amongst the tiers of other mini-thoughts.[31] The value of the burgeoning *periodic* style was seen to lie in its ability to incorporate related aspects and nuances in a similarly effective (though admittedly different) way to that in which voice modulations can extend meaning in speech. It is a matter of giving emphasis. Of course, as rhetoricians got into the act with their various 'How To' publications, rules developed, as witness the division of *period* types, such as oratorical *periods* versus historical *periods*.[32] Later, in post-Classical Hellenistic pedagogy, a *periodos* was not to consist of more than four major segments, or *cola* (thus, as we shall shortly see, up two from Aristotle). Roman edicts would allow more. As writers felt more trustful of prose and less restricted by prosodic rules, so *periodic* architectures were allowed at last to deregularize in order to respond more generously to individual minds as they sought to organize their ideas for exposure. Depending on whether they seemed more given to the mannerisms of ornament or to the push of argument, the resultant writing styles came to be classed as either Asian (read *fancy*) or Attic (read *plain*).

In our earliest surviving samples, the *periodos* adhered to patterns of parallelism and/or antithesis, as thoughts and things were perceived to be, à la Roget, either like each other or different from each other. As we shall shortly see, Aristotle (though possibly only for teaching purposes) dealt mostly with the *period* in these terms—a fact that can baffle, given that his practicing contemporaries had long escaped such restrictions. Repetitive paralleling and antithesizing can soon become tedious. The biblical Psalmic verses (which derived from an oral society) offer a rich supply of example. Though they strike to the heart and are easily memorized (thanks to their rhythms and predictability), one would not wish to subject a serious discussion on, say, 'The Theory of Evolution' or 'The Principles of Actuarial Analysis' to such treatment.

The nice thing about the eventual, fully developed encircling *periodos* was that it fought against being locked into linearity. Even nicer was its recognition of the concepts of beginning and end. And perhaps even nicer than either of those was its willingness to enjoy its space, and by doing so, delay that final silence-demanding full stop that is so unpleasantly remindful of death.

Notes

1. Dionysius of Halicarnassus, "The Ancient Orators," in *Critical Essays*, trans. Usher, 1:5, 7.
2. Ibid., "On Literary Composition," in *Critical Essays*, trans. Usher, 2:169.
3. G. S. Kirk, "Homer," in *The Cambridge History of Classical Literature*, ed. P. Easterling and B. Knox (Cambridge: Cambridge University Press, 1985), 1:46. While the ancient world recognized rhymes and alliteration as rhetorical devices, they did not again become popular until Gothic times.
4. A tempting thesis. Origen, the Christian exegete (see *Contra celsum*, 4.79) argued for man's initial uni-cameral mind; so also would Julian Jaynes, the Princeton psychologist, in *The Origin of Consciousness in the Breakdown of the Bicameral Mind* (Boston: Houghton Mifflin, 1976); and doubtless many others.
5. R. C. Jebb, *The Attic Orators from Antiphon to Isaeos* (London: Macmillan, 1876), 1:27. Also see Kennedy, "Oratory," in *The Cambridge History of Classical Literature*, 1:503.
6. In his dialogue *The Sophist*.
7. Aristotle, *The "Art" of Rhetoric*, trans. Freese, 385–9.
8. Saenger, *Space between Words*, 13.
9. Though Lysias had studied with the Sicilian Tisias, he "found little or no use for the jingling epigrams of Gorgias, and taught himself and his pupils to admire only the precision and euphony" of Gorgias's work. Lysias, *Lysias*, trans. W. R. M. Lamb, ed. G. P. Goold, Loeb Classical Library (Cambridge: Harvard University Press, 1976), xvi.
10. Dionysius of Halicarnassus, *Lysias*, in *Critical Essays*, trans. Usher, 1:31. See also 1:31–5 and the editor's introduction, 1:16–17.
11. Goold, introduction to *On the Murder of Eratosthenes*, in *Lysias*, xvii.
12. Lysias, *On the Murder of Eratosthenes*, 5.
13. Ibid., 9–12.
14. Kennedy, "Oratory," in *The Cambridge History of Classical Literature*, 1:508.
15. Xenophon, *Anabasis*, trans. Carleton L. Brownson, rev. John Dillery, Loeb Classical Library (Cambridge: Harvard University Press, 1998), 47.
16. See Xenophon, *Xenophon* 7, trans. E. C. Marchant, Loeb Classical Library (Cambridge: Harvard University Press, 1968), xli.

17. Malcolm MacLaren Jr., "On the Composition of Xenophon's *Hellenica*," *American Journal of Philology* 55, no. 2 (1934): 121–39.
18. Ibid., 132.
19. Ibid., 135.
20. Ibid., 135–6.
21. Plutarch, "Demosthenes," *The Age of Alexander*, trans. Ian Scott-Kilvert (Middlesex, England: Penguin Books, 2011), 203.
22. Denniston, *Greek Prose Style*, 67–8. In his *The Ancient Greek Historians* (New York: Macmillan, 1909, 112), J. B. Bury has suggested that Demosthenes's famous rhythm changes are a kind of punctuation, comparable to Herodotus's digressions and Thucydides's interpolated speeches.
23. Ibid., 17.
24. Dionysius of Halicarnassus, *Demosthenes*, 1:315
25. Ibid., 1:369.
26. Demosthenes, "The Fourth Philippic," in *Orations*, trans. J. H. Vince, Loeb Classical Library (London: William Heinemann, 1930), 1:302–5.
27. These were called *clausulae* and will be discussed shortly.
28. Connor, *Thucydides*, 95, tells us that the term for the quick question and answer exchange is *brachylogia*. The documentation about fifth-century rhetoric being 'grievously deficient,' the effects of the technique are nowhere fully discussed. However, it is generally accepted that questioning does engage the listener—a fact well noted by Socrates, who considered questioning the most reliable way of getting people to think.
29. Jebb, *Attic Orators*, 32.
30. George A. Miller, "The Magical Number Seven, Plus or Minus Two: Some Limits on Our Capacity for Processing Information," *Psychological Review* 63, no. 2 (1956): 81–97. One of the most highly cited papers in psychology, his thesis is often interpreted to argue that the number of objects an average human can hold in working memory is 7 ± 2—an estimate frequently referred to as Miller's Law.
31. In recognition of this fact, modern usage enjoys such things as bulleted lists, paragraph indentations, chapter headings, and flow charts—anything to illuminate the patterns that organize the details. In the case of paratactic statements, order is usually maintained with respect to the passage of time.
32. The opening statements of both Herodotus and Thucydides were historical *period*s. The historical *period* itself gives the effect of an extended musical phrase, whose initial *forte* diminishes towards a quiet close—a thought suggested by Denniston, in his *Greek Prose Style*, 7–8. The historical *period* is less intellectual than the oratorical *period*, in that it requires less forethought to construct and less effort to take in.

References

Aristotle. *The "Art" of Rhetoric.* Translated by J. H. Freese. Loeb Classical Library. Cambridge: Harvard University Press, 1926.

Bury, J. B. *The Ancient Greek Historians.* New York: Macmillan, 1909.

Connor, W. Robert. *Thucydides*. Princeton, NJ: Princeton University Press, 1984.

Demosthenes. "The Fourth Philippic." In Vol. 1 of *Orations*. Translated by J. H. Vince. Loeb Classical Library. London: William Heinemann, 1930.

Denniston, J. D. *Greek Prose Style*. Oxford: Clarendon Press, 1952.

Dionysius of Halicarnassus. "The Ancient Orators." In Vol. 1 of *Critical Essays*. Translated by Stephen Usher. Loeb Classical Library. Cambridge: Harvard University Press, 1974.

———. "Demosthenes." In Vol. 1 of *Critical Essays*. Translated by Stephen Usher. Loeb Classical Library. Cambridge: Harvard University Press, 1974.

———. "On Literary Composition." In Vol. 2 of *Critical Essays*. Translated by Stephen Usher. Loeb Classical Library. Cambridge: Harvard University Press, 1985.

———. "Lysias." In Vol. 1 of *Critical Essays*. Translated by Stephen Usher. Loeb Classical Library. Cambridge: Harvard University Press, 1974.

Jaynes, Julian. *The Origin of Consciousness in the Breakdown of the Bicameral Mind*. Boston: Houghton Mifflin, 1976.

Jebb, R. C. Vol. 1 of *The Attic Orators from Antiphon to Isaeos*. London: Macmillan, 1876.

Kennedy, George A. "Oratory." In Vol 1. of *The Cambridge History of Classical Literature*. Edited by P. E. Easterling and Bernard M. K. Knox. Cambridge: Cambridge University Press, 1985.

Kirk, G. S. "Homer." In Vol. 1 of *The Cambridge History of Classical Literature*. Edited by P. E. Easterling and Bernard M. K. Knox. Cambridge: Cambridge University Press, 1985.

Lysias. *Lysias*. Translated by W. R. M. Lamb. Edited by G. P. Goold. Loeb Classical Library. Cambridge: Harvard University Press, 1976.

Lysias, "On the Murder of Eratosthenes." *Lysias*. Translated by W. R. M. Lamb. Edited by G. P. Goold. Loeb Classical Library. Cambridge: Harvard University Press; London: William Heinemann, 1976.

MacLaren, Malcolm Jr. "On the Composition of Xenophon's *Hellenica*." *American Journal of Philology* 55, no. 2 (1934): 121–39.

Miller, George A. "The Magical Number Seven, Plus or Minus Two: Some Limits on Our Capacity for Processing Information." *Psychological Review* 63, no. 2 (1956): 81–97.

Plutarch. "Demosthenes." *The Age of Alexander*. Translated by Ian Scott-Kilvert. Middlesex, England: Penguin, 2011.

Saenger, Paul. *Space between Words: The Origins of Silent Reading*. Stanford, CA: Stanford University Press, 1997.

Xenophon. *Anabasis*. Translated by Carleton L. Brownson. Revised by John Dillery. Loeb Classical Library. Cambridge: Harvard University Press, 1998, 47.

———. *Xenophon 7*. Translated by E. C. Marchant. Loeb Classical Library. Cambridge: Harvard University Press, 1968.

· 9 ·

ON MATTERS OF STYLE

The Belated Advice of Aristotle

Scholarly opinion is ambivalent about what Aristotle had in mind to be the dominant feature in *periodic* structuring. Was it rhythm? or thought? Which was the better principle to follow for making a wonderful *period*? To simplify the topic, Aristotle ignored the *period*'s propensity to extend and hence never fully dealt with it. Whereas Thucydides and Antiphon had long ago contrived to construct *periods*, and Demosthenes was still busy pumping them out with Beautiful Abandon, here was Aristotle suddenly prescribing rigid rules for *attaining sublime periodic perfection*. As it was, his linguistic commentaries offer the first analytical insight into the young world of alphabetic literacy. In them, we are witnessing the earliest actual directives for writing elegant prose.[1]

Being further along the road to literacy, more at peace with the written word, and more able to analyze its effects than were his philosophizing antecedents, Aristotle could apply to the investigation of the write-read function the full force of his stupendous rational energies. Moreover, he could handily write them down for the benefit of posterity. Behind him lay a good century's worth of literary growth to draw from and a fund of Ionian grammatical doctrine on which to build. And so, he set his inquiring mind to ferret out the underlying complications of language in general, and to theorize about its communicative and aesthetic capabilities. His *Rhetoric* was the opening salvo in the long history of theorizing about literary style and advising how to perfect it.

First of all, said Aristotle, logic should prevail in matters of grammar. Logic was the key to a pleasing chain of words and to the ease of understanding them. He was critical of the Isocratean tendencies that gave 'loose rein to passion.' He lambasted Herodotus for the open-ended strings of *cola* that paid so little heed to the distinctions of governance. Such stringing together of words was unpleasant, he argued, because it was endless. *What Aristotle advocated* (in what many consider to have been his expanded lecture notes) was his own highly focused, regimented *periodic* style that would feed out meaning in quick, assimilable quantities. Material handled in this way was "easy to learn, because it can be easily retained in the memory."[2]

In Aristotle's view, a logical line of argument was an absolute requirement for the resolution of serious matters, and to him everything was a serious matter—indeed, it is hard to imagine him ever laughing. Not for him the exuberance and bloat of rhetorical trickery! Nevertheless, being Greek, he did not disdain what the Rhetorical Arts were empowered to achieve. Demosthenes's great speeches were exemplary, he felt, because they pushed both the oratorical and literary arts towards strong, rational argument. Only when supported by logic and proof could the arts of rhetoric properly promote truth.[3] Aristotle was practical enough to add, however, that one should take care not to overlook human sensibilities entirely, for language is more powerful if it has some aesthetic force and is delivered in pleasing but not overwhelming rhythms. Eschewing the sprawling *periods* of some of his compatriots, he recommended a style of compact word groups that were logically and pleasingly arranged *to lead directly somewhere.*

Also important, Aristotle advised that a logical statement is best understood when leavened with earthly considerations; for it is an uncontested fact that the minds of the general public are too small to sustain undiluted ratiocination. He therefore urged that syllogisms written in prose not be joined together too tightly, nor logical advance come too quickly for the average mental consumption. (Since canny Greek orators had already reached the same conclusion and had for many years been aerating their arguments with personal reminiscence, anecdotes, and salacious scandal,[4] one wonders if Aristotle was perhaps advising his deceased grandparents rather than his own student contemporaries.) In sum, Aristotle's proposal was an ambitious medley. Let language be clear, yet gracious; and while weighted with good sense, not so dense with information as to become difficult or tedious. To that end he offers the following advice in his The"Art" of Rhetoric (written ca. 330 BCE, some 50 years after Isocrates's Panegyricus[5] and almost 100 years after Thucydides's History).

> Generally speaking, that which is written should be easy to read or easy to utter, which is the same thing. Now, this is not the case when there is a number of connecting particles, *or when the punctuation is hard [difficult], as in the writings of Heraclitus.*[6] (Arist., Rh. 3.5.6)

The italicized words have remained a source of mystery and speculation. What might that punctuation have been? The *paragraphos*? Virgules? Dots? As we see, even in the late mid-fourth century, Aristotle was thinking it necessary to dissuade would-be writers from writing overly convoluted *periods—periods* that relied heavily either on particles or on some kind of unrecorded marks to sort them out. Those interesting punctuational 'marking distinctions' must have been a very early, now lost, attempt to give breathing space to those reading aloud, though there is no way of knowing what they looked like or in what respect they might have failed or succeeded in straightening out complicated areas. In addition to word strings being understandable and pronounceable, Aristotle urged accuracy in word meanings and precision in the correspond-ence of genders and numbers. In other words, one should not ignore subtle differences of meaning between such words as *house* and *shelter* or *food* and *meal*; and should seek to avoid an unseemly mix of masculine and feminine or singular and plural nouns and adjectives. Perhaps the following will help to suggest the crass diction that Aristotle so rightly sought to avoid: *Them ladies sure was piteous after Pericles passed off*—the sense of which rides through even though its conveyance is ugly. Hortatory counsels such as those of Aristot-le suggest that the prevailing literary conditions in Athens were not on the whole so marvelous, despite the previous and contemporary achievements of several authorial giants.

A writer, Aristotle continued, should aim for well-bonded language that flows easily. Words should be arranged so that the thought they contain and the colon that expresses them end together, with a long-vowelled syllable (as in the time required to sound the long *o* in the English word *pole*) to mark their twinned termination. The long-vowel feature was advised on the grounds that a short-voweled syllable (such as *pot*) would mutilate the sense of cadence and cause readers and hearers to expect more. (We are here entering into the as-yet-unresolved matter of punctuation. As it became more and more talked about in Latin times, these rhythmic beginnings and endings for *cola* would come to be known as *clausulae*.) Continuing with the matter of linguistic perfection, Aristotle also recommended that the *colon* should be of an appropriate length for the single intake of breath and, of course, express some unity of sense. The *comma*, or phrase, he left for his successors to worry about.

Aristotle was equally specific about the *period*. It should be compact, that is, of such a size that its meaning may be easily grasped. If the body of what needs to be said does not fit into a fully coherent, free-standing *colon* (hence, a very short sentence), it will become a *period* and will require to be divided into two *cola*—preferably divided so as to bring out an antithetical balance, as in this modern example:

> After the storm, cloud shadows continued to cover the fields of barley,
> whereas the corn stood brightly in sunlight.

However, there should be some similarity of wording in each of the two halves. (By this, he means that a writer should remind a reader of a word or an inflection from the opening *colon* either at the beginning or at the end of the second *colon*—thus to emphasize their unity in combination.) This last injunction casts some light on early punctuational sensibilities, in that it deals with the problem of how to combine, yet keep separate, the segments of a complex statement. We also sense a whiff of the old punctuational ring composition. An example of such an Aristotle-driven formulation might be:

> Cloud *shadows* darkened the *barley fields*, whereas the *corn fields* were
> left without *shade*.

From this medley of essentials—that is: (1) to say things that were important and logically sound with a close regard for graciousness; and (2) to squeeze the result into strict formulations that were preferably antithetic—we can guess that the youths of that time were definitely in need of discipline, rather as they are today. Despite the probability of Aristotle's *Rhetoric* having been only a collection of unfinished instructions on these matters, it still seems strange that the samples he provided (presumably for advanced students of rhetoric) should be so stilted and so poorly representative of the current practice of his two remarkable contemporaries, Demosthenes and the still-alive (though barely) Isocrates.

Aristotle illustrates his notions with a number of 'meritorious' *periods*, not all of which quite coincide with his own thesis. Nor do they always conform with modern notions of verb inclusion for clauses. After a good chat on the virtues of a two-*cola period*, he strangely offers, by way of example, the following tri-partite sentence:

(1) *It often happens in such matters that //*
(2) *the wise fail //* (3) *and the unwise succeed.*[7] (Arist., Rh. 3.9.7)

Scholars still argue over Aristotle's views of the *period*: whether he actually favored definition in terms of meter and rhythm, or in terms of structure of thought. He discusses both, but does so separately—a source, no doubt, of the confusion. Perhaps he had not solved the problem in his own mind.

To succeed at this intricate Aristotelian game is easier than it seems. One merely proceeds as follows. First, find a thought that you wish to communicate. Next, select some words to do so. If the words do not combine nicely with appropriate unifying inversions and terminating signals of long vowels, then, pick up your 'pen' and *force them to accord*. Do not hurry, for in writing, there is always plenty of time. If at the year's end, the unifying inversions and termination-signals match with the completed sense, then you are on the road to fame. You have optimized the chances of easy retrieval, pleasured your recipient, and satisfied Aristotle.

No wayward thoughts came waltzing from Aristotle's inflexible head. To understand the rigid aspects of Aristotelian requirements, we will not be far off target if we think of an ideal *period* as a "syntactic structure with an inner cohesion produced by the logical pre-planned arrangement of its parts according to the requirements of the whole."[8] Beauty will emerge naturally from those logical preplanned arrangements. Thus, Aristotle's analysis of what the best prose might be directs us towards an aesthetic combination: good sense with good sound. We are reminded by this that the best that we can say—hence the best that we can write—comes from the full use of our two-hemisphered brains. When reason and aesthetic sensibility work hand in hand, they can achieve a perfect communication—what Jespersen would in the future call *a successful impression.*[9]

After Aristotle's time, the *periodos* might best be thought of as a 'completed full lap,' for it will at least satisfy us that it has been completed. Our satisfaction may be enhanced by rhythmic cadencing, though not with immoderate, repetitive thumping à la Gorgias. In those early Gorgianic days of its youth, a *periodos* was considered mostly in terms of oratory and necessarily included notions of breathing and sound. It was not the custom, as it is today, to separate emotional responses so rigorously from the reasoning ones.

With so much said and left unsaid, it is easy to see how future grammarians, rhetoricians, and well-practiced literates would come to study Aristotle with both impatience and admiration. His tedious and confusing analysis of what the best prose might be merely reinforces the achievement of Demosthenes. It is a case of analysis and theory limping along in the footsteps of ingenious realization. Nevertheless, for the prose writers following Aristotle, the contemplation of an 'ideal *period*' would remain a mesmerizing occupation.

Two Centuries Later: Demetrius

Preserved from (probably) the second century BCE is an interesting short treatise that shows us how Aristotle's germinal literary directives would grow to maturity. *On Style* is a work presumed to have preceded that of Dionysius of Halicarnassus. It was written (in Greek) by a rhetorician named (probably) Demetrius, whose whereabouts of birth and upbringing are as elusive as the rest of him. Nonetheless, his ideas would live on to proclaim the fact of his phantom existence. They constitute what is probably the earliest post-Aristotelian commentary on literary theory to survive complete.

In the temporal interim between Aristotle and Demetrius, prose-smiths had plainly been hard at work, organizing and testing the varying aspects of literary artistry. Demetrius, we will find, was clearly in touch with the world of books. He seems to have had on hand any number of prose specimens to ponder and compare, to admire or reject; for his scrutiny of the cognitive and aesthetic formulation of written verbiage is both close and detailed. In composing words to explain his thesis, he was far more deft and easeful than Aristotle, but then, of course, his topic had been kicking around for some two hundred years, and the concerns of literaries had moved up a notch. With vocabulary and grammatical structures more or less settled, style in its broadest aspects was what people liked to talk about in his time.

Taking his cue from Aristotle, Demetrius too favored the well-wrought *period* over the ancient 'running-on' style, though he allowed it some fresh liberties to expand and work its will. He described the 'running-on style' as "disjointed," and effectively denigrated it by likening it to stones lying near each other, but loose, scattered, and uncombined.[10] Those same stones, said Demetrius, might better be fitted to cohere in such a way as to create a self-supporting, vaulted dome. And who will not agree? As it is a far lovelier thing to construct a self-supporting vaulted dome than to scatter stones for others to trip over, so is it lovelier, too, to weave free-wheeling ideas into *periods* than to spew them forth as they come to mind.

Demetrius illustrates The Bad Style by essentially trashing the opening statement to the *Genealogies* of the once revered, archaically un*periodic*, historian Hecataeus. That work began—as we may or may not remember—"Hecataeus of Miletus speaks as follows." What particularly irritated Demetrius about Hecataeus was the jerky sequencing of his word-strings and more generally, the piled-up abruptness of his presentation. *So primitive!*

What we must remember is that Demetrius was working with a stronger, more assured prose language. His was a language that writing had stabilized with considerable grammatical particularization, about which Demetrius can now offer many perspicacious remarks. Following on from Aristotle's simplistic treatment of the *periodos*, which vaguely distinguished *cola* and ignored so many other things, Demetrius began his *On Style*:

> Just as poetry is organized by metres (such as half-lines, hexameters, and the like), so too prose is organized and divided by what are called clauses [read *cola*]. Clauses give a sort of rest to both the speaker and what is actually being said: and they mark out its boundaries at frequent points, since it would otherwise continue at length without limit and simply run the speaker out of breath. But the proper function of such clauses is to conclude a thought.[11] (Demetr., *Eloc.* 1–2)

A clausal thought, Demetrius continues, may either be complete and able to stand alone as a simple, fully expressed thought; or incomplete, that is, a component only (be it verbed or verbless) of a medium thought, or even a *huge* thought. (The idea of a verbless word group, or 'phrase,' is being addressed at last.)

> For just as the arm is a whole, yet has parts such as fingers and forearm which are themselves each a whole, since each of these has its own shape and indeed its own parts, so too a complete thought, when it is extensive, may subsume within it parts which are themselves whole… (Demetr., *Eloc.* 2)

He then guides us through a catalogue of style instructions. About the particles, he advises: Don't make your connectives (*on the one hand, on the other*, etc.) correspond too nicely, lest your language sound too artificial, "since there is something trivial about exact precision"; and be sparing of your filler words: *indeed, similarly, generally,* and the like. Demetrius also warns against clauses that are too long ('endless') and ones that are too short ('arid and minced'). Appropriateness to topic and tone is what one must strive for. Whereas we might use an extended clause in religious or philosophical material, we would refrain when giving commands or describing simple realities (such as *how to sharpen a knife,* or *where to find the barber's shop*). According to Demetrius, the clauses of the historian Xenophon are very apt. Xenophon's account of the Greeks' arrival at the river Teleboas is ideal to the occasion, for he says only: "This river was not large, it was beautiful however." The broken rhythm emphasizes both the smallness of the river and its charm. Demetrius explains that if Xenophon had expanded the idea to say: *This river was in size inferior to most rivers, but in beauty it surpassed them all,* he would have failed in propriety, and would have become what is called the frigid writer.

Demetrius was right in preferring terseness. Expansion dissipates the power of the message. This truth is readily made obvious when a proverb is stretched to incorporate detail. A *stitch in time saves nine,* for example, loses its punch if expanded: *If you take the time now to do the job right, then you won't have to spend a lot more time to do it later on* sounds whiney and nagging. Moreover, its lack of punch makes it harder to remember. Length is murder to excitement and emotion. It attracts tedium. The compression of meaning into small spaces is the sign of masterliness (a very Stoic-Protagorean-Attic concept), for one must always remember how little acorns produce big oaks. Demetrius tells us that a *colon* (think clause) is bigger than a *comma* (think phrase). Aha! We have arrived at the concept of a *comma,* by which, of course, we mean not the modern punctuational stop, but rather the several combined words (as in *under Mildred's solid-mahogany executive desk*) whose terminus suggests the need for the mini-pause that we modernly call 'comma.' Opening participial phrases are also a common source for *comma* example, as in: *Before running the marathon, he ate a pizza.*

The *commata,* then, make up or add to the contents of the *colon,* as the *cola* make up or add to the contents of the *periodos.* This ancient perception of a 'sentence' defines the *comma* as a distinct yet not separate entity within a *colon.* Demetrius gives the *comma* less clout than a trimeter (a measure of three metrical feet) and recommends it for parceling out words in the plain (Attic) style, which he praises for its ancestral and heroic resonances.[12] We are told that two trimeters equal more or less half a *colon.*[13] Though his discussions are more facile than those of Aristotle, Demetrius still feels compelled to relate prose to poetry and to evaluate it in poetical terms.

And now for the Demetrian *periodos*. It is formed (as we may have guessed) from a linear arrangement of all the tiny phrasal and medium-sized clausal ideas that feed the big basic *periodic* thought. Ideally, it will finish with a backward flick of the tail, such that the end evokes the beginning. Demetrius's backward flick is less constraining, less rigidly prescribed than Aristotle's. Nevertheless, it too reflects a lingering attraction to ancient ring construction. (Recall the 'stumbling statement' of Thucydides). But, since proportion among the parts must be a crucial consideration in *period*-building, Demetrius wants that backward flick to be the longest segment.[14] Its job is to unify, to round up the previous ideas and put a satisfying termination to the total. If that tail is too short to complete the required full wrap-around, then we have no Demetrian *period*.

Demetrius then illustrates this precept with a tail that is strangely shorter (even in Greek) than what he had earlier recommended. The following lines, he tells us, constitute the ideal *period* in that the words "chiefly because" shout for the tail's governing verb resolution.

> Chiefly because I thought it was in the interest of the state for the law to be repealed, but also for the sake of Chabrias' boy, I have agreed to speak to the best of my ability in their support. (Demetr. *Eloc.* 10)

Whereas, in rearrangement, these following lines *are not ideal*:

> I will speak in their support, men of Athens. For Chabrias' son is dear to me, and much more so is the state, whose cause it is right for me to support.[15] (Demetr. *Eloc.* 11)

In recommending that final flick of a *periodic* tail, Demetrius also reveals a sophisticated appreciation of the 'oratorical *period*.' We see that the world of literary theory has advanced beyond Aristotle's simple (but curiously awkward) formula: namely, a *periodos* is made from two (preferably antithetical) *cola*, unified by inflection, and/or rhythm, and/or word repetition. In his description of the long-in-use 'oratorical *period*,' Demetrius recognizes that writing must flow, as does speech, and that our attentions can be better held when a writer forestalls the completion of a whole thought in order to lure us onward. In contrast, Aristotle's view of the *period*, with its requirement of intense unity, seems static. The excitement aroused by saying that something is *this plus this* or *this and not that* seems no more stirring than putting together two halves of an apple. Though the formula is in some sense satisfying and can suggest the full-round view that the word *periodos* is supposed to impart (namely, a *circuit* or *path going around*), it becomes increasingly trite when used repeatedly and all too soon fails to hold our attention.

Demetrius is not considered to have been stylistically innovative. His recipes for a graceful layout of words are more likely to represent some plateau of thinking in his time. His ready referrals to previous authors and his confident manner tell us that a significant buildup of 'literary conversation' had taken place during the two or so centuries after Aristotle. A storehouse of linguistic knowledge was at hand—a source of advice for writers in search of both cognitive and belletristic satisfactions.

After reading Demetrius, one finds Aristotle's instructions more than ever archaic, stiff, and even deadening, though his tentative speculation that a *period* was basically "a portion of speech that has a beginning and an end" was a wave of the arm in the right direction. With the advance of writing, Aristotle's rules seemed no longer pertinent to a writer's trade, being as they were more corrective, more pedagogical and restrictive than 'literary.' By the time Demetrius came on stage, the rhetorical spotlight was probing the shadowy edges of style, and for that the perfection of a *period* was paramount. Demetrius gave it license to contain three, even four *cola*—beyond which, until Latin takes the lead, succeeding stylists will (for a while) deem it 'gross and unseemly.'

Meanwhile, the value of syntactic variation had become openly important. Demetrius, as had Demosthenes, favored a good mix of sentence types.

> My own personal view is that speech should neither, like that of Gorgias, consist wholly of a series of *periods*, nor be wholly disconnected like the older style [like that of Hecataeus], but should rather combine the two methods. It will then be simultaneously elaborate and simple, and draw charm from the presence of both, being neither too ordinary nor too artificial. Those who crowd *periods* together are as lightheaded as those who are drunk, and their listeners are nauseated by the implausibility; and sometimes they even foresee and, loudly declaiming, *shout out in advance the endings of the periods*.[16] [Italics added.] (Demetr. *Eloc.* 15)

After Aristotle's initial stimulus, Demetrius's small treatise *On Style* gave a fillip to the whole topic of perfectly scripted communication and moved it forever into discussions of style. The precepts of his advice, which seem so childish to us today, should nevertheless be appreciated, for they constitute the first extant aesthetic analysis of prose writing. By the end of the first century, when Dionysius of Halicarnassus was being so persnickety about Thucydides's early-dawn achievements, literary prose will have acquired an exceedingly high opinion of itself.

But back once again to Demetrius. He is urging us now to bear in mind that *periods* come in three flavors. Starting from the top: the oratorical *period* should be compact and circular, and emitted orally with a rounded mouth and appropriate (*but what could they be?*) gestures. He illustrates the oratorical *period* with the previously mentioned *Chabrias' boy* sentence, which makes us wait for the final flick of the tail—the completing wrap-around clause. The historical *period* is less magnificent. It, says Demetrius, should be neither too compact or circular, nor yet not enough compact or circular—its care being to convince us of the immense (almost sacrosanct) dignity of history. Though consensus has customarily given the historical *period* a big head to contain the governing verb (as in the opening sentences of Hecataeus, Herodotus, and Thucydides), Demetrius seems to prefer the simplicity of Xenophon's modest little river scene, and hence, *not the big head*.

We come ultimately to what Demetrius called the 'dialogue *period*.' Its members are disjointed and more or less flung upon each other. Demetrius's illustration comes appropriately from the opening lines of Plato's *Republic*, for which, it is said, Plato sought a deliberately relaxed pose. Socrates (the occasional anti-writing proponent) is speaking:

> I went down yesterday to the Piraeus with Glaucon, the son of Ariston, to pay my devotions to the Goddess, and also because I wished to see how they would conduct the festival since this was its inauguration.[17] (Pl., *Resp.* 327a)

What could be more casual? The dialogue *period* is so lax and simple, says Demetrius, so much the most disjointed and loose of the three styles, that when we reach the end we can hardly realize that the words formed a *period* at all. For sheer insubstantiality, the dialogue *period* rather resembles the phantasmal Demetrius himself.

To modern sensibilities Demetrius seems as dictatorial about the 'perfect' style as Aristotle had (so many years earlier) been about the 'perfect' *periodos*.

A Quick Foray Into the Bogs of Inflection

What is this thing called 'inflection' that is so rarely mentioned in English school grammars? It is merely this: a discrete sound (representable in letters) that is added to a word to modify some aspect of the word's function within a statement. More simply, it makes that word do something other than it would standardly do. Thus: the 's in *girl's* turns *girl* into the possessor of something; or the *s* in *girls* makes her plural; or the *s* in *gives* identifies its *he, she,* or *it* subject. Likewise the *ly* (as in *triumphantly*) can change an adjective into an adverb, while the comparative *er* and superlative *est* may be added to *small* to make *smaller* and *smallest.* Unlike a particle, an inflection, almost without exception in English, clamps onto the back end of the word it seeks to affect.[18] It can be a syllable (in some languages, perhaps two or three syllables) or even a single-lettered phoneme like our English *s*, but its presence is important, for it speaks volumes.

In highly inflected languages like ancient Greek and Latin, an inflection will tell us who or what the subject of a verb is. Is it you, I, or he, who are/am/is racing for the bus? An inflection will tell us about the likelihood and time (present, past, future) when all or any of us might have been doing it, or indeed, actually did it, or might have done it, or will do it, or would do it, or ought do it. In the case of nouns and adjectives, matching inflections can tell us, for example, which employee was the pleasant lady (Italian: *simpatica signora*) and which the pleasant gentleman (Italian: *simpatico signore*).

For a more complex modern example, we turn to Iceland's numerous case endings (noun and adjective inflections), which, surviving the ages, are still being applied in order to indicate whether the noun is acting within the sentence as subject, object, genitive (possessive), etc. Icelandic inflections are empowered in the standard Indo-European way. While maintaining their own integrity, they can attach to different word roots, as the structure of a sentence demands. Thus, the word *hest-ur* (horse) tells us that a horse is the subject; he is *doing* something (snorting, perhaps) or *being* something (skittish). *Hest* tells us that the horse is going to be *the object* of somebody else's action (he will be curried, set out to pasture—perhaps even eaten); *hest-i* that something is going to be *done to* or *by* the horse (we will give a carrot *to* him or be nuzzled *by* him); and *hest-s* (genitive) that the horse *has* something: i.e., something belongs to him (a loose shoe, or a glossy tail).

Today's Italian verbs are organized into three conjugations, with the forms for *I, thou, he-she-it, we, you,* and *they* distinguished by the inflection, which is added to the end of the root verb. In the case of the root verb *ved-* which means 'see,' we have: *ved-ere*, its infinitive form, 'to see'; *ved-o* meaning 'I see'; *ved-i* meaning 'you see' (familiar form); *ved-e* meaning 'he-she-it sees,' and so on. With these endings in place, the subject pronouns (understood from the context) can be, and often are, dropped. Similar inflectional endings are applicable to all the verbs of whichever conjugation.

A highly inflected language allows words to range widely. Within a statement, inflections allow the reordering of words to enhance rhythm, or avoid dissonance, or emphasize an idea, or tempt experiment—all, without demolishing the message. Suppose you were compelled to say or write this:

> The sisters, Gretchen and Griselda, knowing nothing of its grumpy greediness, rushed to greet the groveling grizzly bear.

Then, you could get rid of that gargling gurgle of *g* and *gr* sounds by rearranging the word order. The inflections would show which words related to which and the hearer/reader would know that it was not Gretchen who was growling and grumpy. With inflections to maintain the connections during a swap in word positions, one can reduce the ugly g/gr impact—as in the following rearrangement:

> Gretchen the sisters and Griselda, knowing grumpy nothing of greediness its, to greet rushed the grizzly bear groveling.

Since inflectional systems of literate languages tend to be regular throughout and *hence predictable*, they are not, once learned, too unwieldy to use. Nevertheless, English has graciously dropped most of its inherited Anglo-Saxon inflectional baggage along with yesteryear's annoying masculine, feminine, and neuter nouns and adjectives. Though we are now compelled to adhere to word order and accept ugly sounds, we delight in our freedoms. Our national tongue, being easier to learn, can communicate with less effort than most. And that is a major reason why badly spoken English has outstripped badly spoken other languages to become the politically eminent international *lingua franca* of today.

Hyperbaton

Hyperbaton is a rhetorical term that describes a switch in the usual order of words. It remodels the standard flow of natural speech (that is, speech that is free of aesthetic crafting)[19] by repositioning words whose meanings would ordinarily bind them together. Hyperbaton is used (1) for emphasis, (2) to create a metrical line of poetry, (3) to allow a rhyme to emerge, and (4) in long-ago times only, to establish firm rhythmic cadences (*clausulae*) to *cola* and *periods*. It is in all cases an artistic device, and its presence can give a suspenseful delay to expectation. In English, however, its use requires some special care. It is no good saying "strong" and then a dozen words later, "fort." The image of 'strong fort' will be lost. In ancient Greece, ears tuned to the empowerments of inflection would have captured it. In English the usual use of hyperbaton is for occasional emphasis in prose and for the maintenance of rhythm or rhyme in poetry.

Mr. Denniston suggests a number of reasons why ancient literary prose artists might have relied on hyperbaton the way they did. There was the wish to avoid the tedium of repeated, similarly inflected endings as in, for example, the singsong repetition produced by the Greek *hoi polloi kaloi angeloi* (the many beautiful messengers); or the harshness of a Latin string of dative plurals, for example, *pluribus virginibus tristibus* (to many sad virgins); or, indeed, to avoid any irritating sounds (as in *blubbering blabber* or *scruffily scrambling*) that might grate on the ear. There was also the task of creating *clausulae* (rhythmicized cadences) in accordance with old habit and Aristotelian edicts. But perhaps most important for present-day understanding of early Greek or Latin classical prose is hyperbaton's contribution towards creating *emphasis*.

> Logically connected words stand out in higher relief when spatially separated: and, looking at the clause or sentence as a whole, alternating rise and fall of emphasis produce a pleasing effect.[20]

We find this kind of hyperbatonic emphasis in English, as in, for example: *A champion, he is not*. Or more elaborately: *His policy, despite uproarious opposition, won the day*, where the interruptive insert is sometimes more powerful, more explicit, perhaps even more memorable than the rest of the statement. We see a rare single-word instance of it in today's British *abso-bloody-lutely*.

The pleasure deriving from hyperbatonic disarrangement is in apparent response to some physiological substratum in the human makeup. From earliest times, the exigencies of metered poetry had made it a familiar device, easily achieved in the malleable matrix of highly inflected Greek, where meaning, supported by inflection, can survive amongst words that have been transplanted (even distantly) out of their customary 'natural word order' sequence. Being quite a step away from straightforward street-and-home utterance (that is, what we think of as 'natural speech,' where modifiers stand next to the words that they modify in order to speed the intake), hyperbaton takes a bit of forethought to create and a bit of predisposition to enjoy receiving. It makes communication trickier as well as more interesting. We have felt its pull in the more sweeping instances of oratorical *periods*. It is a sophisticated ploy. Small children don't practice it. It is even today regularly present in the poetic verbiage of uninflected languages. Poets of all stamps rely on the flexibility it allows for escaping from or complying with metrical dictates.

Ancient authoring prose-smiths, noting the presence of hyperbaton in skilled oratory, in poetry, and in poetic drama, picked it up as a familiar, useful tool and fiercely put it to work. We will see much use of hyperbaton as prose artistry gathers steam. Of the early prose writers that we shall be dealing with in these pages, all of whom were working with inflected Greek or Latin, the most hyperbatonically addicted enthusiasts will be the Irish and their fervent imitators.

Notes

1. The works of Aristotle that dealt with specific analysis of semantics and language structure were lost to view for many centuries and did not resurface until the twelfth century. (See the *New Encyclopaedia Britannica*, 15th ed., s.v. "Medieval Syntax.")
2. Aristotle, *The "Art" of Rhetoric*, trans. John Henry Freese, Loeb Classical Library, 373–5, and 387–9.
3. Freese, introduction to *The "Art" of Rhetoric*, xxii.
4. Jebb, *Attic Orators*, lxxvii and lxxviii.
5. It is tantalizing to imagine the extent to which Aristotle might have drawn on Isocrates's now lost *Art of Rhetoric*. As an actual practitioner, Isocrates might have been the more helpful guide.
6. Aristotle, *The "Art" of Rhetoric*, 375–7. The italicized remark about punctuation in the writings of Heraclitus is most intriguing.
7. Author's translation of the Loeb Greek text of Aristotle, *The "Art" of Rhetoric*, 390. In the Greek, the paired antithetical verbs are equal in beat: *atukein* (fail) and *katorthoun* (succeed), and the wise and unwise (*phronimous* and *aphronas*) are, as in English, similar yet sufficiently different to intrigue the ear. Here again is the trick that Antiphon had devised and taught to Thucydides.
8. This succinct definition comes from R. L. Fowler, "Aristotle on the Period," *Classical Quarterly* 32 (1982): 89–99.
9. Otto Jespersen, *Essentials of English Grammar* (London: George Allen & Unwin, 1972), 19.
10. Demetrius, *On Style*, trans. Innes, 345. See also John Edwin Sandys, *A History of Classical Scholarship* (Cambridge: Cambridge University Press, 1903–8), 1:312.

11. Ibid., 359. The sequence of paragraphs on the makeup of a *period* has been drawn from sections 1–34 of Demetrius's text. For easy intake, 'clause' for *colon* and 'phrase' for *comma* have been used.

12. Seeking the casual pace of relaxed speech, Plato used trimeter rhythms for Socrates's opening statement in the *Republic*. Ancient dramatists used trimeter rhythms for dialogue. Trimeters, especially in quick-paced iambics (de-dee de-dee de-dee), being brief and fast, are prominent in common speech.

13. See Doreen C. Innes, "Period and Colon: Theory and Example in Demetrius and Longinus," in *Peripatetic Rhetoric after Aristotle*, Rutgers University Studies in Classical Humanities 6, ed. W. W. Fortenbaugh and D. C. Mirhardy (New Brunswick: Transaction Publishers, 1994), 37, 41.

14. We have here, then, an elaboration of the concept of an oratorical *period* (long in use), whose rule was the suspenseful wait for resolution of the opening proposition. This head-and-tail sort of explanation is typical of ancient commentary on style.

15. See Demetrius, *On Style*, 353–5. The passage, which Demetrius does not quote in full, actually comes from Demosthenes's oration "Against Leptines."

16. Ibid., 359. N.b. how Demetrius's use of the words 'speech' and 'listeners' reflects the continuing orality of his age. For centuries yet to come what was written would more often than not be read aloud.

17. Plato, *The Republic*, trans. Paul Shorey (London: William Heineman, 1930), 1:493. Plato is said to have revised this trimetric opening many times, seeking just the right rhythms to evoke casual talk (cf. Denniston, *Greek Prose Style*, 7; and for longer analysis, 41).

18. The exceptions to this general rule are most notably found in some of our passive past participial formations, which originated in our case in the Germanic languages and have come down to us through Anglo-Saxon, thus: I was much *bepleasured* by his attentions; her hand was *bespoken*; his face was *bedaubed* with cherry jam; I was *beset* with things to do. German and its close northern cousins (Icelandic, Swedish, etc.) are still quite busy with such formations.

19. In his *A History of Language* (p. 48), S. R. Fischer speaks of "syntactic universals." For example, he tells us that all languages in their basic, uncrafted form are constrained to put adjectives (like 'big') next to the nouns they describe (as in 'big cave')—just as all human languages have verbs (action or mode words), and can produce commands, statements, questions, and negatives.

20. Denniston, *Greek Prose Style*, 58–9.

References

Aristotle. *The "Art" of Rhetoric.* Translated by J. H. Freese. Loeb Classical Library. Cambridge: Harvard University Press, 1926.

Demetrius, *On Style.* Translated by Doreen C. Innes. In Vol. 23 of *Poetics*, by Aristotle, Longinus, and Demetrius. Loeb Classical Library. Cambridge: Harvard University Press, 1995.

Denniston, J. D. *Greek Prose Style.* Oxford: Clarendon Press, 1952.

Fischer, Steven Roger. *A History of Language.* London: Reaction Books, 1999.

Fowler, R. L. "Aristotle on the Period." *Classical Quarterly* 32 (1982): 89–99.

Innes, Doreen C. "Period and Colon: Theory and Example in Demetrius and Longinus." In *Peripatetic Rhetoric after Aristotle*. Rutgers University Studies in Classical Humanities 6. Edited by W. W. Fortenbaugh and D. C. Mirhardy. New Brunswick: Transaction Publishers, 1994.

Jebb, R. C. *The Attic Orators from Antiphon to Isaeos*. London: Macmillan, 1876.

Jespersen, Otto. *Essentials of English Grammar*. London: George Allen & Unwin, 1972.

Plato, *The Republic*. Translated by Paul Shorey. London: William Heineman, 1930.

Sandys, John Edwin. Vol. 1 of *A History of Classical Scholarship*. England: Cambridge University Press, 1903–8.

· 1 0 ·

ALEXANDRIA BECOMES THE HUB
OF GREEK CULTURE

Hellenistic Times in Egypt

Following the death of Alexander the Great in 323 BCE, the intellectual leadership of the 'civilized world' passed from Athens to Alexandria, a city soon made both powerful and rich under the rule of the Ptolemys. There, scholars and poets, rhetors, artists, scientists, and philosophers, lured by the prospect of gold, convened from all over the world, bringing their books and know-how with them. It is believed that Theophrastus, Aristotle's successor as head of the Lyceum and the inheritor of his library, made his way there too, and that his library eventually ended up in Rome.

Cultural appetites in Alexandria were voracious. Philosophy, science, and the arts were flourishing, and 'books' (scrolls for the most part) were much sought after. So great was the thirst for knowledge that the city's educated aristocrats set up a museum ('a place for the Muses') within the precincts of the royal palace. Essentially an academy, this Alexandrian Museum became famous as a meeting point for intellectuals, a haven where they could exchange ideas, teach, write, read, debate, and think. Included within its boundaries was a library—the glory of the ancient world—whose visionary mission was to assemble the texts of every known Greek author, past or present, and by that means create a storehouse for all human knowledge.[1] As academic enthusiasms progressed, so they stimulated the copying and borrowing of books, thereby increasing the library's holdings massively. At its peak, the library claimed to have in its keeping nearly half a million scrolls, as well as another forty thousand stored elsewhere.[2] So ambitious was Ptolemaic Alexandria to accumulate scholarly materials, that by royal decree, all ships stopping at Alexandria had to surrender whatever books they were carrying. The need for sorting and classifying books (as opposed to *just listing them*) became urgent. Because scribes were not of a single standard, most manuscripts required editing as well.

To handle what had so quickly turned into deluge, the early and most eminent museum scholar Callimachus (fl. 280–ca. 245 BCE) conceived an idea, an idea so brilliant as to cause a decisive shift in the received perspective of all scholarly work for all time. Callimachus was a man of great learning and intellectual energy. Being not only an encyclopaedist, superb poet, and prolific writer of Attic-styled prose, he was also a practical thinker. His sublime but simple idea was this: *arrange books by subject matter*. Once this new method for book storage was implemented, it replaced forever the confusing and pointless custom of recording accessions by provenance, by value, by purchaser, size, or even by what sort of substance they were written on—which of course had nothing to do with what a scholar wants when he searches for a book. Callimachus's system of assorting books by subject matter would prove to be not only useful to literature, but profoundly consequential to the progress of all human culture.

Specifically, Callimachus divided the Alexandrian library into subject areas: medicine, oratory, drama, history, legislation, and so on, dedicating several shelves (or tables—a fact that would lead in time to the term 'table of contents') to each. That done, he had the longer works recopied from the scrolls into several more easily handled shorter sections, called 'books.' He adopted the custom of alphabetizing—a procedure rarely used in those days. He was also the initiating author of the famous *Pinakoi* (meaning 'tables'), which listed the writings of all those who were eminent in any kind of literature. This bibliographical tract, eventually amounting to some 120 manuscript rolls, included biographies of authors too (*When did this man sleep?!*) and became the main reference catalogue for any ancient scholar seeking information. For us today, it has been the source for a large part of our knowledge about the ancient literary and scientific world. Although Callimachus did not live to bring about the entire range of his ambitions, he bequeathed his vision to a series of able successors, under whom the library remained a scholarly sanctum—an organized reading space where texts could be opened side by side and critically compared.

Zenodotus (fl. 280 BCE), also a noted Alexandrian scholar, was the first 'head museum librarian' and an early emendator of Homeric texts. A century or so later, came the well-known Aristophanes of Byzantium (fl. 200 BCE), who made his particular contributions in the area of punctuation and the fine-tuning of doubtful texts.

Though *periods* and *cola* had long been recognized elements of speech and writing, they had not, as far as existing evidence tells us, been dealt with textually until Aristophanes of Byzantium defined their signals for the scholarly editing of manuscripts. Before his time, run-of-the-mill scribes had no known (let alone consistent) system of punctuation symbols to differentiate word-strings; nor, for a time afterwards, did they consistently apply what they had. From the first century BCE, we begin to find manuscripts with break-marking puncts, though no consensual agreement was yet in place to control their shape or their value. Scribes, being an unhomogeneous group, tended to adopt whatever marks their equally unhomogeneous teachers had taught them. Sometimes they applied those marks with thoughtful intention, but also sometimes, it was said, they merely stuck them in to create a scholarly appearance or—more unconscionably—for decoration. Rarely did they seem to anticipate what a reader might easily take in.

Aristophanes of Byzantium moved to change all this. When he became Alexandria's head librarian ca. 194 BCE, his area of jurisdiction included a community of outstanding scholars (of which he was one), along with an estimated 700,000 manuscripts, in a city that was quickly becoming the stronghold of political as well as intellectual prominence.[3] To appreciate the extent of his prestige, one should realize that in the Alexandria of that era, a royal grammarian was as prized as a champion football quarterback or a star chef is today.

P. M. Fraser, in his extensive study of Alexandrian culture, tells us that Aristophanes's scholarly achievements would for any time be considered enormous. Beyond his invention of a rational colometry (which we shall deal with shortly; but, described briefly, is the breaking off of a written line as in poetic verses), Aristophanes improved contemporary recension (correction) techniques by developing new and systematizing old critical and lectional signs (aids to interpretation). He was especially honored for having put out the best-to-that-date editions of Homer, Hesiod, Anacreon, and most lastingly, Pindar. Also to his credit lies a better-than-ever-before analysis of grammatical elements. At the request of Ptolemy, he devised a workable array of accent marks in order to preserve the traditional pronunciation of the scattering, dialect-prone Greek language, which was by then the language of a threatened civilization. Most famously perhaps, Aristophanes was honored for his three-dot 'punctuating system' which, though much admired, seems to have been less about grammar than about breath-intake when reading aloud,[4] though to render up sense, the two must often have meshed. With no mention of verbs, he presented his formula as follows: two short word-groups (which he called *commata*) equaled a longer word-group (which he called a *colon*); and two *cola* equaled a sentence (which he called a *period*). A sentence could be punctuated as follows:

(1)   A dot after the middle of the last letter (thus: E·) to indicate breathing at the end of a short segment of words, a *comma*

(2)   A dot after the bottom of the last letter (thus: E.) to indicate breathing at the end of a medium-sized segment, a *colon*

(3)   A dot after the top of the last letter (thus: E˙) to indicate the end of the longest segment, a *periodos*

Under these vague rules, it would be hard to compose a proper grammatical sentence. But if verbs are allowed, one can pleasantly kill a few minutes thinking up a grammatical sentence in English that might illustrate Aristophanes's fine sense of balance. Perhaps the following will do.

By doing what I want· I would distress the neighbors on my right. but by failing to do what I want· I would please them more than I want˙

Amongst standard capital letters (majuscules) Aristophanes's three-points offered a discrimination that would come to be lost once minuscule script became popular. Embedded amongst those small, minim-dense stylus or quill strokes, the vertical placements of the three dots could not be readily discerned. In any case, this three-point system was seldom used, though it survived in a number of versions to appear again in Rome, most lastingly in the influential works of pre-Christian Dionysius Thrax and later (CE fourth century) in those of Aelius Donatus—the eponymous source of *donat* (a word rarely used today), meaning 'a student's book of grammar.'

Aristophanes of Byzantium wrote on grammatical and lexicographical topics in addition to a great many other subjects. He was, above all, a scholar-editor—a textualist and grammarian. By developing a new level of critical specialization, he marked the decisive emergence of a professional approach to writing and literature. Orators, philosophers, historians, theologians, poets—all would benefit from the practical farsightedness of this man. He was, in fact, the father of meticulous scholarship and of all the generations of editors yet to come.

Alexandria's Analogy Versus Pergamon's Anomaly

In time, Pergamon came to challenge Alexandria, and a rivalry grew as to which scholarly center would dominate the other. Pergamon not only built a library to house its enlarging collections of manuscripts, but, like Alexandria, fortified its claim to erudition by supporting teams of poets, grammarians, philosophers, and scholars. Though now in ruins, Pergamon's famous library walls still stand, a sightseer's attraction, on the western coast of Turkey; whereas Alexandria's library was long ago completely destroyed, and though rebuilt as a modern working library, continues to be prone to catching on fire. In their heyday, both institutions cherished a passion for language analysis, each championing its own linguistic theory: *analogy* for Alexandria and *anomaly* for Pergamon. For comparing the two theories in modern terms, one might think of *normative* versus *descriptive*. As the two terms intermittently pop up in matters of early language study, perhaps it will be wise to know a little about them.

In those early years of literacy, Alexandrian *analogy* offered a major insight into the study of language, since its primary premise was *the regularity of inflectional endings and parts of speech*—a regularity we count on today in mastering any inflected language. When inflections are predictable and constrained to be constant—that is, they do not change shape at every phase of usage—they become intellectually manageable. The memory retains them. They can be talked about and taught to children and foreigners. In our historical context, *analogy* was the principle of regularity among the inflections and parts of speech. It offered the solace of method and predictability.

Anomaly was developed by the Stoics at Pergamon. It held that *analogy*'s doctrine of inflectional regularity could only be maintained at the expense of a great many exceptions; and that being so, it was wiser to observe the inflectional variations in use, and carry on with life in a more accepting manner. Of the two principles, *analogy* tends to become a little prescriptive (and we all hate that these days); whereas *anomaly* is OK, if *observe* is all you want to do. As a teaching device *anomaly* is hopeless—its precept being more or less that of rejoicing in Nature's infinite variety. While infinite variation is hard to master and grammatical confusion is everyone's dominant enemy, one could say that of the two, the Alexandrian analogists have been kinder to posterity. They opened up their own can of worms but taught them how to behave—for which, nobody seems half grateful enough.

The historical clash between the two centers of scholarship with their opposing linguistic theories might be seen as bearing some relationship to the alphabetic takeover from orality. Whereas *analogy* seems to spring from analysis of the written page—those lists of case endings, etymologies, intransitive verbs, and the budding blossoms of punctuation marks—*anomaly* appears to be more closely allied with the aural world. In that world, whatever noises a speaker emits, his listener will jump to intuit. Imagine speech in the days when there was no backup from books. In an outpost village or sheepherding community, who would have cared if folks sometimes dropped or slurred the final syllable of their dative-plurals, or shifted the vocative *o* to *uh?* In the context of speaking, meaning *is searched for* on the spot and can be queried until it is found.

In general, two things should be remembered about Alexandria's *analogy:* first, that its system of regularity offered for the times a major insight into the study of linguistics; and second, that its precepts famously and enduringly opposed that other theory—Pergamon's *anomaly.*

Alexandrine Scholasticism: Some Aftereffects

After Aristophanes of Byzantium, Aristarchus of Samothrace (born ca. 215 BCE) carried on the Alexandrian Library's legacy of textual scholarship. He developed Aristophanes's thoughts on *analogy* and continued his work of textual correction. He was sufficiently at ease with written words to remind others that the rules for making *periods,* and the divisions within *periods,* cannot be rigid. Rigidity (such as Aristotle had prescribed) is not wise, he said. It inhibits a facile transfer of meaning. Despite the importance of that refreshing observation, there are scholars like Mr. Fraser who are not so sanguine about the achievements of Aristarchus. Fraser tells us that Aristarchus was mistaken in details of syntax, and confused as well about a verb's voice and mood.[5] As contemporary Pergamon scholars were also critical, we must conclude that Aristarchus was not quite the intellectual perfectionist that his predecessors were.

Nevertheless, the Alexandrian Library, for more than one hundred years—from the innovative overtures of Callimachus to the expulsion of Aristarchus with others of the intelligentsia in 145 BCE—fostered a textual exactitude theretofore unknown. Alexandrian attention to editorial precision would fire up a long-lasting interest in linguistics, an interest that would soon sweep through pre-Ciceronian Rome, where a disciple of Aristarchus, Nicanor the Stygmatist (*Stygma* meaning *point* or *mark*—in this case, a punctuational mark, and in modern Greek, *tattoo*)—would soon come to theorize, write, and teach. But for this present panoramic moment, it is interesting to notice this about the big-gun Alexandrian librarians: whereas the great Callimachus and the early head librarians had been poets as well as scholars, their young successors, Aristophanes and Aristarchus, were textualists only—as indeed Nicanor would later come to be. Publishing poetry, we note, was no longer the supreme requirement for literary prestige.

Taken together, the entire group of Alexandrian scholars did us many favors. They developed critical and punctuational signals, and introduced colometry as a viable way to aerate text and elucidate meaning. It is very probable that their activities encouraged the separation of words. Out of a mass of inherited *scriptura continua* they identified and defined strophes and antistrophes, odes and epodes. They divided poetry into lines, and pressed those lines into the shapes that are familiar to us today, with the result that rhythms and rhymes are made to emerge at first sight. Today's lucky readers of Coleridge's "Kubla Khan" can read it with all its prosodic signals exposed and not from a mash, thus:

Inxanadudidkublakhanastatelypleasuredo
medecreewherealphthesacredriverra
nthroughcavernsmeasurelesstomando
wntoasunlessseasotwicefivemilesoffertile *etc.*

We owe much to the Alexandrians for stabilizing the conventions of prose writing. It was their initiative, so long ago, that preserved for us today a glimmering knowledge of the ingenious Classical Greek mind.

With the breakup of political stability and the diaspora of erudites, Alexandria's concentrated intellectuality diffused to regather in other places, though it retained as did Athens much of its reputation for sophistication and learning. Communication being what it was (namely, poor) and human reliability being what it still is (*very* poor), the transmission of knowledge was at best unsteady. The high efforts of bright stars had small chance against the sludge of popular custom. Even in Ptolemaic Alexandria, the very heart of textual industry, the copy-work had been faulty. Because of the laborious and idiosyncratic nature of the scribal task and the spotty education of so many of the scribes, each edition of a text was perforce unique, with subsequent 'copies of copies' varying yet further from their already varied exemplars.

As Alexandria's intellectual prowess diminished under the press of political strife, classical knowledge was maintained (imperfectly) through synopses, commentaries, and spoken tradition—in a popularization remindful of our own modern reinterpretations: the cartoon-pictures, coloring books, films, and abridgments of, say, Shakespeare's *Othello* or Melville's *Moby Dick*. According to Mr. Fraser, "There can be no doubt that texts such as the [official] 'city-texts' and the early recensions of Zenodotus were already, less than a century later, inaccessible to Aristarchus."[6] Ludwig Friedlaender, who was (in mid-nineteenth-century Germany) Nicanor's great scholar and textualist, conjectured the unlikelihood of Nicanor ever having handled the materials of his own teacher, Aristarchus.

One may criticize the Alexandrine editions of ancient texts, and indeed the latest scholarship is tending to do so. It is said that Aristarchus (along with other editing grammarians of the Alexandrine school) so radically altered the already-old, probably-many-times-recopied manuscripts in their keeping that we today cannot sensibly think to be reading the very words (let alone rhythms) that Pindar, for example, composed in the heat of inspiration. The complaint today is that instead of "the real Pindar" we have only his ghost (possibly even his *mangled* ghost) as rendered up by the professionalism of pompous Alexandrian philologists. The only thing we can be certain of is that the final products "fitted the grammatical and ethical standards which these gentlemen had made up for themselves."[7] Happily, ancient intellects were not so perfection-inclined as to bring all to a standstill. We are grateful to them today for the valuable classical residue that they did manage to preserve, so much of which would, and did, survive not only the breakdown of its own nurturing birth site, but also the breakdown thereafter of its adoptive Roman civilization and even the (almost) illiterate millennium that followed.

Alexandria's inspirational fire was itself an inheritance from Classical Athens, the founding center of the Western literary world and the city where ambitious young men first crowded to learn the mechanics of rhetoric. It was their youthful enthusiasms that had compelled their sophistic teachers from Ionia to pursue linguistic inquiry. Accordingly, with Protagoras in the lead, then Aristotle and the Alexandrians following, the elements of grammar were increasingly studied, patterns were noted, and logical connections investigated. As the last in this lineup, the Alexandrians were left to apply the final, pre-Roman, literary burnish. They were the ones who reduced the diverse earlier thoughts and theories to a useful grammatical system. It was in their library that textual criticism and interpretation became a prestigious activity.[8]

But the story, of course, goes on. Crates of Mallos, the Stoic head of the Pergamene school and the hot rival of Aristarchus at Alexandria, assembled for the Greek-speaking world the first known collection of grammatical facts. Thanks to him, etymology became a respected area in the study of grammar, as did orthography (a must for readable manuscript production). His emendations of Homer took a turn towards scientific adjustments, and his revision of Aristarchus's revisions included geographical corrections as well as lexical ones. He further enjoyed undoing some of the Alexandrine *analogy*-driven rules regarding declensions and conjugations, which he looked upon more or less as a waste of time. Interestingly, his own bibliographical *Pinakoi* gave prominence to prose writers, not poets, whereas the *Pinakoi* of Aristophanes of Byzantium had particularly favored poets, though he himself was not one.

Quite by chance, this man Crates becomes important to our chronicle, for when he was sent on an ambassadorial mission to Rome in 159 BCE, he fell into a sewer and broke his leg. Being forced to stay put in Rome for some many months, he spent his convalescence informing his hosts of the linguistic excitements buzzing around back in Pergamon. His lectures were apparently highly stimulating. Because of Crates, Greek and the comparison of it with Latin came to be studied avidly by all the philhellenistic Roman young bloods, for it was a popular opinion of the times that Latin was a dialect of Homer's sacred tongue—whereas, in fact, it was only an Indo-European cousin, and by that time a thoroughly separate language. With the prevailing reverence for all that was Classical Greece, scholarly output from the east was warmly received in Rome.

Dionysius Thrax

With Dionysius Thrax ('Thrax' meaning Thrace) we are close to the end of pre-Christian times. Thanks to the scholars of style (like Dionysius of Halicarnassus and the phantasmic Demetrius) and to those of language and texts (like Aristophanes of Byzantium, Aristarchus, and Crates of Mallos), popular appreciation of prose had vastly increased. The critical output of all these luminaries shows us that written prose had decoupled from poetry and become (despite magnetic Homer) an acceptable and useful alternative to it. *It could even be beautiful.* All that being so, grammarians and rhetors swarmed to instruct the world in the science of prose perfection. Because prose is loquacious and in the fullness of a manuscript page can seem to be unending, the primary move in studying it was to break it apart so as to expose its constituents. Thereafter, it was a matter of justifying the connections amongst them and reconsidering the lot in terms of grace, logic, and cognitive retrieval. To keep an out-of-earshot reader on the right track became at last an acknowledged and worthy goal.

During the intellectual diaspora under Ptolemy VII, Dionysius Thrax (fl. 100 BCE), a student of Aristarchus in Alexandria, settled on the island of Rhodes, a traditional center for philosophy and rhetoric, and a haven for wandering *grammatikoi* (teachers of grammar). There, he wrote his famous *Techne grammatike.* This slim handbook [*techne*], with its codification of various grammatical elements, became the classic instructional text for students up to the fourth and fifth centuries CE, in both Athens and Alexandria. Because it was translated extensively, copies of it survive today. The two most complete extant manuscripts, in Armenian translations, date from the late fifth century CE.

The *Techne* begins with the following definition: "Grammar is the empirical knowledge of what is for the most part being said by poets and prose writers"—a statement that recognizes both the emergence of 'acceptable' ways of putting language together and the fact that some folk wanted to know about them. Grammar was by this time a distinctly desirable topic to master. Dionysius Thrax begins his *Techne* by defining 'reading' (by which he meant 'reading aloud') as the art of rendering faithfully through (spoken) words all that is written, be it in verse or in prose. One must 'read' with discernment, he says, and observe the rules of prosody and division, for it is by such discernment that one can apply to each discourse the appropriate tone. Prosody teaches the modulation of tone and what sounds pleasing and sensible to the ear; division (the clarifying of phrases and clauses) distinguishes the ideas and their relationships. The divisions are marked by points—historically, for the purpose of reading it aloud. Of these there are three: the final point, which lies on the line and indicates that the wanted sense has been achieved; the medial point, which indicates that the sense is about halfway there; the *hypostigma* (in this case, a raised mini-point—from the Greek *hyper* = above), which indicates that an idea has been launched but has yet some need—even quite a lot of need—of completion. We have here the reversal of Aristophanes of Byzantium's program, whose high dot signifies the full finish, while the on-the-line dot signifies a half finish. Nevertheless, we have progressed.

"And how is the medial point distinguished from the *hypostigma?*" asks Professor Thrax. "Ah!" say we, his pupils. "It is, perhaps, distinguished *by duration of pause?*" Hurrah! We are right! The medial designates the longer pause and the *hypostigma* designates the shorter one. *The substance, then, of a textual 'pause' is Time.* (This notion of variously enduring pauses will dominate the pedagogy of punctuation, well beyond Gutenberg. Victorian schoolteachers were positively devoted to it.) Though beginning to separate from the artistic traditions of poetry, prose in its early CE history was still stubbornly bound by the dictates of aural memory. Not until it is free from the constraints of reading aloud will the practiced eye not bother to pause for the puncts. In a quick and silent traversal of a written line, it will merely register the relationships that they indicate.

Having dispatched the matter of pointing, our Thracian professor presses bravely on—through the dense thickets of poetical tropes, obsolete words, epithets, surnames, analogies, and literary criticism—none of which quite tallies with modern ideas of grammar. But not to worry, for once all that is over, he emerges at last onto the smooth terrain of alphabet sounds, the concept of generic and particular, and the various parts of speech.[9] These last are familiar to any young student of grammar today.

Categorizing, which marks the very essence of a literate mind, is Professor Thrax's overwhelming passion. The details he churns up are multitudinous and tend to arouse an appreciation of Pergamene nonchalance about the whole business of inflectional regularities and parts of speech. Nevertheless, in those early days, the minutiae of the *Techne* were considered thrilling. In the final section, in an exercise of classification that today seems overwhelming (let alone useless), Dionysius Thrax ranked the vowel letters according to whether they were long, short, or mixed; then listed possible diphthongs and all the consonants. He next tackled the syllables (long, short, and medium), with discussion of the ways (sometimes as many as eight ways: three from its nature, five from its position, *and so on*) in which they could vary. He again (though without much detail) divided words into eight parts of speech in terms that are familiar to us today: noun, verb, participle, article, pronoun, preposition, adverb and conjunction. He divided verbs into eight categories according to mood, voice, number, tense, etc. He divided nouns into three genders (masculine, feminine, neuter); and words into two groups (primitive words and seven varieties of derived words) and into three forms (simple words, compound words, and double-compound words), then into three numbers (singular, dual, and plural) and once more into the five cases (nominative, genitive, dative, accusative, vocative). About the prepositions, he continued enthusiastically: "There are eighteen prepositions—6 monosyllables and 12 disyllables."[10] We will leave him there.

Because Dionysius's little grammar was all analysis and no synthesis, it did not deal with syntax. One wonders (a little) *what he might have said about that.*

Notes

1. A. W. Bullock, "Hellenistic Poetry," in *The Cambridge History of Classical Literature*, 1:542. Cf. also 1:549.

2. Alberto Manguel, *A History of Reading* (New York: Viking, 1996), 189–92. This book has been especially useful for materials relating to Alexandria's library.

3. P. M. Fraser, *Ptolemaic Alexandria* (Oxford: Clarendon Press, 1972). This entire book has been extremely interesting and helpful, but the reference here is particularly to pages 140–4.

4. Though punctuation grew to mesh well with grammar over the centuries, in early years it was essentially discussed in terms of breath intake during a reading aloud of text. That we owe this three-point invention to Aristophanes of Byzantium is not firmly accepted by all scholars. For example, Rudolf Pfeiffer, in *History of Classical Scholarship from the Beginnings to the End of the Hellenistic Age* (Oxford: Clarendon Press, 1968), 179, conjectures that this pointing system might well belong to the time of Hadrian, three centuries later, and that Aristophanes himself might have used only two points. Nevertheless, the kudos belongs to Aristophanes.

5. Fraser, *Ptolemaic Alexandria*, 463–7.

6. Ibid., 462–3.

7. Anthony Grafton, *The Footnote: A Curious History* (London: Faber and Faber, 1997), 89–91. The scholar whose opinions Grafton is remarking upon here was Godfrey Hermann, the professor who perhaps most of all influenced the great historian Leopold von Ranke "to prefer bare facts and historical sources to derivative later narratives, however well they read."

8. Pfeiffer, *History of Classical Scholarship*, 272.

9. The information herewith provided on Dionysius Thrax comes from Jacques Chahan de Cirbied, *Grammaire de Denis de Thrace*, tirée de deux manuscrits Armeniens de la Bibliotheque du Roi (Paris: au bureau de L'Almanach du commerce, 1830), xxi and 5–9.

10. Henri Irénée Marrou, *A History of Education in Antiquity*, trans. George Lamb (New York: Sheed and Ward, 1956), 171–2.

References

Bullock, A. W. "Hellenistic Poetry." In Vol. 1 of *The Cambridge History of Classical Literature.* Edited by P. E. Easterling and Bernard M. K. Knox. Cambridge: Cambridge University Press, 1985.

Chahan de Cirbied, Jacques. *Grammaire de Denis de Thrace*, tirée de deux manuscrits Armeniens de la Biblioteque du Roi. Paris: au bureau de L'Almanach du commerce, 1830.

Fraser, P. M. *Ptolemaic Alexandria.* Oxford: Clarendon Press, 1972.

Grafton, Anthony. *The Footnote: A Curious History.* London: Faber and Faber, 1997.

Manguel, Alberto. *A History of Reading.* New York: Viking, 1996.

Marrou, Henri Irénée. *A History of Education in Antiquity.* Translated by George Lamb. New York: Sheed and Ward, 1956.

Pfeiffer, Rudolf. *History of Classical Scholarship from the Beginnings to the End of the Hellenistic Age.* Oxford: Clarendon Press, 1968.

·SECTION 3·

THE LITERARY ARTS IN ROME

· 1 1 ·

EARLY YEARS

When the *Techne* Hit Rome

The *Techne* of Dionysius Thrax was published in Rome in the era of Julius Caesar (ca. 60 BCE), a time when linguistic pursuits were all the rage, much as they were in the days of the Grimm brothers, one imagines, or indeed are now under the stimulus of Chomsky, Pinker, and MacWhorter. That the *Techne* was so warmly received is no surprise, for its offerings, coming straight from the lips of a Greek, addressed the very things—grammar and meaning— that Roman rhetoricians and writers were at the time struggling to sort out in their own Latin language. Writing was no new thing on the Italic peninsula it seems, for scholars have found evidence there of rudimentary alphabet writing from the late seventh century BCE, that is, even before Greece became the great power of the Mediterranean world. Early Latin speakers had apparently learned the trick of using visual symbols for sound-representations from the seafaring Phoenicians and Greek-trading Etruscans. It was an easy step to re-adjust the alphabet values to suit their own language.[1]

Cultured Romans agreed that Latin word usage should be standardized, that the wayward running-on style should be discouraged, and that the syntactical components of prose should be structured so as to coordinate logically. 'Correctness' was at a premium, as it always is amongst the unassured. In search of perfect correctness, Romans, like their admired Greeks, split into factions. Again, there were the Alexandrian analogists who favored strict and learnable rules; and in opposition were the Pergomene anomalists who were willing to let usage dictate propriety. There were those who sought Gorgianic plenitude, and those who longed to get to the point; and hence, we find— as in Classical Greece—Asianists opposing Atticists, and Atticists opposing Asianists, with numerous levels of shading between. At the heart of all this was the Atticist-if-ever-there-was-one, Julius Caesar, whose grammatical energies are as surprising to literary moderns as his military energies were to the ancient Gauls. He not only coined the term *ablative* (the bane of youngster Latinists), but also wrote a treatise on the philosophy of language—*De analogia,* now lost.

In a market as verbally smitten as Rome's, the *Techne* of Dionysius Thrax was destined to thrive. So successful a treatise was it that early Latin grammars and studies of rhetoric were for several centuries modeled after it.

* * * * *

In the decades after Alexander the Great's death, while imperial Macedon was fragmenting, Rome was itself on the rise. The Romans, with their practical outlook and penchant for endurance, made stalwart soldiers. They honored the customs of their ancestors and taught their sons—Primus, Secundus, Tertius, Etceterus—to contribute their muscle to the state and to be sensible, thrifty overseers of the food supply. Under the banner of soldierly simplicity, Rome spread outwards like floodwater towards the world's rim. Its armies conquered Hellenic Sicily in 212 BCE, overcame Macedonia in 168 BCE, the mainland of Greece in 146 BCE, and the kingdom of Pergamus in 132 BCE. (Only later did it subdue Cleopatra's Alexandria.) With these aggressions, Rome replaced both Athens and Alexandria to become the dominating military, commercial, and tax-collecting force of the civilized world.

But an interesting thing resulted from Rome's acquisition of these lands and the wealth they contained. As shiploads of booty—gold, jewels, ornaments, books, paintings, statuary, fine cloths, and talented Greeks now made slaves—reached the victorious capital, they awakened Rome's artistic appetite. Soon the city's patrician classes were in thrall to the sophistication of the eastern peoples they now ruled over. By the end of the second century BCE, Rome was busily steeping itself in everything Greek—Greek scholarship, education, and art; Greek dress; Greek mannerisms; and especially Greek rhetoric. How beautifully those Greeks could speak! *How persuasive they were!*

With their Homeric heroes, their knowledge of medicine, their renowned architects, artists, historians, dramatists, poets, philosophers, and athletes—the Greeks seemed glamorously superior to the home-grown stuff. When Romans compared themselves and their compatriots with those sleek and graciously mannered eastern Greeks, they saw how plodding, provincial, stammering, and stick-in-the-mud they themselves were, and quite understandably decided to reinvent themselves.

And so, the snooty upper crusts of Roman society, disdaining the rugged virtues of their more ordinary countrymen, turned with a passion to the study of the Greek language and culture. Once the Greeks who had not been enslaved were apprised of the Hellenophilic market opening up in rich Rome, they also came to take advantage. *And why not?* Along with the private tutoring that was already under way in the houses of the great, Greek began to be taught in small neighborhood schools. Even by the year 167 BCE, there were large numbers of qualified Greek teachers in Rome. Out of that influx, the wealthy Romans supplied their sons, and even young daughters, with Greek grammarians and rhetors, and themselves with Greek servants, Greek grooms, Greek painters, Greek sculptors, and even Greek huntsmen. To give their grown sons the total immersion experience of Greekness, eager fathers shipped them off (around the age of 20) to the still functioning rhetors of Athens, Rhodes, Pergamon, and Alexandria. For those with senatorial prospects, whose futures lay in managing Rome's vast, newly acquired estates, Greek became the second language, and Greek rhetoric the most popular subject for students to study. Cato the Elder (an Atticist of stern, puritanical principle) was disgusted that Rome should be filled "as if by a rushing, mighty wind" with the sounds of Greek eloquence.[2] And so it was that Rome the Conqueror was itself conquered.

Comparing Greek With Latin

In Caesar's period (some decades before Christ), Latin was in the throes of change. Once Rome's military successes had brought droves of Greeks into the city—both slaves and ambitious free men—old stalwarts and purists began to worry that alien learning and language were affecting, indeed *in*fecting, the Latin of their forefathers. Caesar himself was an old-fashioned purist, whereas Cicero was a semi-purist, who rather liked to step over the line when it suited him. Where Caesar chose to recount his soldierly truths in simple, well-rooted

Latin etymons and short syntactical structures, Cicero inclined to flamboyant *periods*. He complained that Latin was not subtle enough to convey what he wanted to convey. Like Thucydides in his time, Cicero felt he must enlarge his native language, make it more malleable, more responsive to his fertile mind and towering ambitions. He was not alone in pressing for change, for many sophisticates of his time were recognizing the deficiencies of their native tongue. And indeed, it is true that until Caesar and Cicero came along, nothing really fine had yet been written in Latin.[3] Poets and prose writers alike deemed Latin a sluggish medium for their rocketing thoughts. It was too stiff, too earthy, too practical. Moreover, it was not 'beautiful.' We should assess these criticisms.

As we know from Quintilian's writings of a century and a half later, in the estimation of learned Romans, Latin could not even by then measure up to Greek. But in its earlier days, it was definitely lacking. It had no extensive philosophical terminology of its own, nor was it as flexible syntactically. For euphony and delicacy, for richness of vocabulary, Greek was the favored language. Gutteral consonant-ridden Latin—with its harsh *b, d, g* and *kw* sounds, its ugly couplings of such as *f* and *l* (as in *floruit* ['it flourished'] and *flosculus* ['floweret']), its *unct* syllables, and syllables that ended in *m*, 'like mooing cows'—could not compete with mellifluous Greek for the sheer beauty of sound.[4] To remind readers of Greek's abundant vowel sounds, here again is the opening line of Homer's *Iliad*, transposed into Roman alphabet letters. One can sing it more easily than say it. As for the *d, p,* and *ch* (the *d* pronounced as a voiced th, and the *ch* as a breathy kh—if modern Greek is any guide in the matter), both the *d* and *ch* would have been airy soft, leaving the plosive *p* as the only eruptive sound in the line.

> ***May-nin a-ei-de, the-a, Pay-lay-i-a-do Ak-i lay-os***
> [Sing the wrath, goddess, of Achilles Peleus's son]

Following are the opening words of Vergil's *Aeneid*, with its more awkward tongue-and-throat adjustments marked out in boldface. (Note that although the English spelling is usually 'Virgil,' 'Vergil' will be used in these pages, since ancient inscriptions tell us that 'Vergilius' was the Latin form.)

> **Arm**a vir**umque** cano Troiae **qui** primus ab oris
> [Of arms and a man, I sing, who first from the shores of Troy]

But more important than rough sounds, Latin lacked the useful active past participle, as well as the definite article—the latter, being an imperative need

in discussing abstractions such as The Good or The Beautiful. It is interesting
to recall that when (four centuries earlier) Thucydides was bothered by similar constraints, he too had attached the Greek neuter *to* (the) to a number of
adjectives in order to universalize their concepts. Plato later added more. Now
in Rome it was Cicero's turn to broaden the scope of his language. And this
he did. To express in a flexible Latin the high-level thinking of his philosophically oriented mind, he coined new words—for example, *qualitas* ('quality'),
moralis (moral), and *beatitudo* (happiness)—and reworked the meanings of
old ones. Chafing at the inelasticity of his beloved mother Latin, yet bound
to it by pride, habit, and affection, he protested the view of old-timers who
thought that 'invented' words might sully the language of their ancestors—
thereby sounding a bit like members of the French Academy, who rejected the
internationally used word 'computer' because it was 'unFrench,' and instead
demanded that 'ordinateur' replace it. New topics always require the creation
of new words, Cicero argued, for even the Greek philosophers in their time
had resorted to invention. As Seneca would later complain: *Quod est* (What
is) is a feeble and phonetically unpleasing substitute for Plato's simple present
participle *ōn* (modernly pronounced 'own'), and meaning 'that which is in a
state of being'.[5]

The Latin world inherited its perceptions of language from the Greeks.
Though the two languages are both derived from a common Indo-European
source, time and distance had long before separated their habits and rendered
them different in both sound and structural formation. Romans yearned for
the elegance of Greek and, in seeking a closer relationship to it, looked avidly
for similarities, claiming them even when there were none. It was a situation
like that which emerged many centuries later in England when grammarians
there, who were steeped in admiration for Latin, began setting out Latin-
ish rules for uplifting and beautifying 'uncouth' English—as in proscribing
split infinitives, prepositions at sentence ends, and dangling participles. Never mind that Greek had articles, a verbal middle voice, an aorist tense and
a third-person imperative, whereas Latin had not; that Greek had singular,
dual, and plural verb forms, whereas Latin had only singular and plural forms;
that Greek had optative and subjunctive verb moods, and Latin only the subjunctive. Latin grammarians, anxious to uplift their language for worldwide
literary acceptance, simply willed themselves over the hurdles.

Perhaps it was because the Romans had such an uphill battle in measuring
up to the Greeks that they persisted so valiantly and painstakingly with linguistic analysis. Aided by the enlarging mass of available world literature, they

made big strides in the codification of language parts—grammar, syntax, vocabulary. They discussed (endlessly) the foibles and potentials of style. In the early years of prose, Greek grammarians and rhetoricians had not talked about syntax (the arrangement of sentence parts), deeming its details to be more or less obvious. The Romans, being less intuitive in matters of style, found it pedagogically helpful to separate and classify all the teeming grammatical, syntactical, and semantic mechanisms—and this, in benefit to the world, they slowly began to do. Whereas, for example, in the first century BCE, Dionysius Thrax had thought to enlighten the world by so uselessly dividing Greek prepositions and inflections into mono- and di-syllable lists, several centuries later, Donatus (of 'Donat' fame) was dividing Latin prepositions and verbs according to the cases they required for their objects (*bravo!*). Matters of syntax had longer to wait. Not until the early sixth century CE would they be addressed systematically (by Priscian).

And so it was that, bit by bit, Latin tackled its problems, found solutions, and eventually constructed a mass of definition and rule. Errors in language use, for example, came to be designated in more exacting ways than just 'errors in language use.' Romans made those errors more noticeable and memorable—more teachable to learners—by grouping them in accordance with their descriptions and effects: barbarisms, solecisms, mispronunciations, instances of excessive fastidiousness, misspellings, and so on. They recognized the concept of puns and drew up tables of inflections for practical usage. All of their meticulously defined items were then sucked into the maw of managed pedagogy, so that students could be nagged to adopt or steer clear of them. 'Rhetoric' was the name of this subject at school, and in classical Roman times a boy first met with it at age 14, after the basic grammar studies were finished. Like the toga, rhetorical studies symbolized one's entry into patricianly manhood.

On Roman Literacy

During the Athenian democracy, political debates had flourished almost as a popular entertainment. We find similar levels of rhetorical excitement once again in the Roman Republic's senate. The time we now face is the final century and a half before Christ—that is, some three centuries after Athenian Antiphon wrote down his court defense for the young Euxitheus. Once again, as Roman public figures became more thoroughly literate, we will witness an increase of interest in the manipulative powers of written words. The training of budding aristocrats would allow no shortcut in matters of reading and writing. We shall look into that training shortly.

There have been endless scholarly debates on the matter of literacy throughout the Roman Empire, and it is clear that in the hinterlands literacy levels were far lower than in cities and towns. Pompeiian graffiti tell us that by the late first century CE, people were clearly enjoying themselves as they scribbled jokes, insults, and scraps of poetry on each other's walls. How much true and fluent literacy developed beyond that is hard to assess. Certainly it spread and grew, but we can only guess how far down the social scale it went.[6]

By the first century BCE, although Rome had not reached the levels of public literacy that were prevailing in Athens, Roman booksellers and copyists were busily trading, and 'books' (in the form of scrolls and codices) were circulating within a limited class of Roman society. Educated elites corresponded in writing with each other and knew the canonical works of literature, frequently in both Latin and Greek. They made their speeches from written notes (called *libelli* or *pugillaria*),[7] and could be fussy about the calligraphy of scribes, yet write their own letters with all the panache of a modern prescribing doctor.[8] While the masses remained illiterate, and the middle stratum (the craftsmen, merchants, and shopkeepers) reached levels sufficient to deal with accounts, messages, inventories, and graffiti, the leisured wealthy were joining literary circles and endeavoring to build up their own private, well-stocked manuscript collections. Julius Caesar himself talked of setting up a public library. It is well documented that the Roman aristocracy of that late pre-Christian era had an academic interest in both literature and language, and that textual criticism (as derived from the Alexandrians) was an ongoing activity.

By the end of the first century CE, the book trade in Rome was flourishing. Public libraries and private collectors were publishing and disseminating books that had been copied in their own private scriptoria. Book acquisition had progressed from its war-booty origins (when books were as prized as was gold) to the quieter activities of recitation, emendation, copying, and lending. Rome's holdings never paralleled the huge, royal collections at Pergamon and Alexandria, nor did the Romans of that pre-Vatican period approach Alexandrian levels of scholarly and critical activity.[9] Nevertheless, intellectual, authorial, and textual aspirations burned ardently amongst the privileged classes of Rome. The first Roman public library was founded in 39 BCE. Augustus founded one in the temple of Palatine Apollo, the prototype for several later foundations, in which the Greek books were housed separately from the Latin ones. By Constantine's time (306–337 CE), Rome had 28 public libraries.

Civilizing Rome: Cato

Cato the Elder (234–149 BCE), whose writings would be posthumously admired by Cicero, was the first Roman to write down and publish on a large scale
his own speeches (now, alas, lost). He was also the first Roman of significance
to depart from the custom of expounding historical, scientific, or theological
revelations in poetry. Moreover, he departed from the custom of writing in
Greek (the language preferred by the sophisticates of his time). Before Cato,
the scope of Latin rhetoric had been more or less limited to formulaic funeral
orations, speeches in the Senate, and military exhortations. But with the establishment of larger juries in this Roman second century BCE, a true and eloquent
prose came to be practiced in the law courts, where trials were held publicly and
crowds convened to enjoy the atmosphere of accusation, connivance, and possible scandal. From the midst of such circumstances, Cato—the strict moralist,
the victorious general, and grand old man of his times—initiated the lift-off of
written Latin prose for all of later Europe. The extant scraps of his oratory show
both a quirky wit and a maximum disdain for the pirouettes and arabesques of
Greekish rhetorical display.[10] In an atmosphere that was being invaded by effete
Greeks, Cato stood firm for austerity. He was an advocate for the Roman tradition of farming, at which young men grew strong, resourceful against adversity,
and able to endure hardship. That, he said, was the nurturing atmosphere that
had made Rome strong. Cato, when in power,

> had tried to outlaw, and then tax prohibitively, various forms of luxu-
> ry, and continued to inveigh against spending on handsome slaves or
> imported food, and adorning one's house with statues of the gods 'as
> though they were pieces of furniture.'[11]

Cato's De agri cultura (written about 160 BCE) is our earliest specimen of an
entire piece of Latin prose and the only complete composition of Cato that
remains for us to inspect. Remembering that Cicero (who would later bring
Latin prose to its paradigmatic pinnacle) is said to have cherished his access
to some 150 of Cato's speeches, we should examine a passage from this early
work. What could Cicero have admired of this austere forefather, who failed
in elegance, clarity, artistic disposition of clauses, and even the quantitative
rhythms for cadencing (known as clausulae)—who was, in sum, impervious to
the art of the well-rounded Isocratean period, of which Cicero himself would
soon become master and later outdo?

To give some sense of the stern stuff—the soldierly side of the Roman character from which Cicero claimed (perhaps as an antidote to his own volubility) to draw nourishment—the passage below is presented. It is the opening statement of the *De agri cultura*, as set out and translated for the Loeb Classical Library's edition. Despite its plainness, one notes the authority that empowers it. Cato is not a man to argue with. He will tell you what he thinks without embellishment. *Rem tene, verba seguentur*, was his advice. ['Hold to the subject; the words will follow.']^[12] Here, then, is the Loeb rendition of Cato's opening *period*, an early example of the Latin *circuitus* (Greek *periodos*). (The modern punctuation should be ignored.)

> It is true that to obtain money by trade is sometimes more profitable, were it not so hazardous; and likewise money-lending, if it were as honourable. Our ancestors held this view and embodied it in their laws, which required that the thief be mulcted double and the usurer fourfold; how much less desirable a citizen they considered the usurer than the thief, one may judge from this. And when they would praise a worthy man their praise took this form: "good husbandman," "good farmer"; one so praised was thought to have received the greatest commendation. The trader I consider to be an energetic man, and one bent on making money; but, as I said above, it is a dangerous career and one subject to disaster. On the other hand, it is from the farming class that the bravest men and the sturdiest soldiers come, their calling is most highly respected, their livelihood is most assured and is looked on with the least hostility, and those who are engaged in that pursuit are least inclined to be disaffected. And now to come back to my subject, the above will serve as an introduction to what I have undertaken.^[13] (Cat., *Agr.* preface)

Note how the first portion of the statement (down to the third line's "honourable") is unclear. The word *more* confuses us. Without telling us first about the virtues of farming, Cato assumes that we know his theme (from the title) and how he will treat it. Trade is more profitable than what? Agriculture, no doubt, though he doesn't actually say so. The fact that trade is hazardous and money-lending is not as honorable (as trade? as it should be?) does not affect the profitability or usefulness of the merchant. And why, if the merchant lives with danger, should the farming class (which doesn't) produce the bravest men? Since his topic is farming, his statement might have been clearer if he had not mentioned merchants and usurers at all. In short, Cato does not rigorously express what he hopes to have understood. His manner is oral. *He assumes too much.*

But we must be careful in our indictments and take note of how much Cato's *periodic* opening strives for a philosophical overview, and how awkward this writing seems when compared to our example of the early Greek logographer Antiphon. Once Cato has completed his overviewing statement, he launches abruptly into his topic. The sudden switch is disconcerting. Having satisfied this duty to established (Greek) literary custom by beginning with an overviewing *period*, he renders the rest of his thesis in the serial mini-thoughts of running-on parataxis. In the birthing years of both Greek and Roman literacy, the driving authorial ambition was to construct the opening words so as to yield a broad and ruminative mental vista. As we have seen with the Greeks (before Lysias, Plato, and Xenophon), educated writers tended to complicate the patterns of natural speech. Cato, who was straddling an oral-visual boundary and wanting to persuade with acceptable elegance, did not find the practice of rhetorical artistry easy. In the words of the *Oxford History of the Classical World*:

> What we know of prose literature suggests that the Romans, like many primitive peoples, found generalization and abstraction hard. It was only from about 100 BCE, too, that they began to use traditional Greek logical structure in treatises, with explicit definitions of the subject and all key concepts, and careful division of the material into parts or aspects, instead of piling up information hugger-mugger like Cato in his agricultural treatise.[14]

Nevertheless, Cato's somewhat confused conversion of a rather complicated idea into the inflexible language of his day preludes an early Latin plain style—also known as Attic—in which no artistic prettiness is allowed to distract from the argument's core. The words Cato used were common and forthrightly repeated. Thus, in this short paragraph, we find *existemarint, existimare; fenerari, feneratorem, feneratorem;* we find *ita* three times, and *tam* twice. His assumption, moreover, is that we will know what he means, whether or not he is precise in exposing it. To gain the full effect of an early reader's difficulty in confronting such tight and unsignposted writing, one must imagine the passage in its earliest manuscript form of *scriptura continua*. When we compare Cato's roughness with the smooth rendition of the above Loeb passage, we note that the translator, Mr. Hooper, was enough concerned for the great Cato's literary reputation to fill out the skeleton clues and substitute for repeated words when he could. The first few lines of the word-for-word translation of the given text (below) will reveal the problem of its decipherment and illumine its inelegance. For a merciless 'full experience,' the modern puncts have been removed. The parenthesized words represent those that either Cato did not supply or that Latin did not require.

> It is (the case) at times (that) to excel in commerce wealth to seek unless/despite so dangerous it is and likewise to practise usury if so honest it is elders our so had (it) and thus in laws set (it) that the thief twice be condemned the usurer four times how much worse a citizen they judged the usurer than the thief from this one can judge and the man good whom they were praising thus they were praising a good farmer and a good cultivator.[15]

After the carefully wrought, but laconically awkward introduction (which is complete as presented), Cato pelts us with asyndetic commands: *Do this, Do that*—as fresh agricultural considerations come to his mind. The effect is as frank as that of a diary, as provokingly direct as a notebook list of memoranda or instruction—which some say it possibly was, though the formalized opening *period* rather belies that intention. The entire piece smacks of laconic militarism. The advisements themselves, deriving as they do from seasoned experience, allow no argument. And yet, by omitting crucial explanations of, for example, advocated equipment, they do not always take a reader's understanding into account. That lack of specificity is particularly archaic in that it represents the oral attitude about finding out what's going on. When compared, for example, with Xenophon's smooth and detailed essay on horsemanship, Cato's effort of some two centuries later seems very primitive indeed.

As for the punctuation of Cato's agricultural handbook, we have no idea how the passage read originally or if in its early years it was punctuated at all; nor do we know whether the Loeb edition's short *cola* reflect quite the way Cato actually set them down. The Bibliotèque nationale in Paris has the earliest known extant manuscript, which dates, alas, from only the thirteenth century—almost 1,500 years after Cato wrote the piece!

In Cato's Latin springtime, a literary perspective was not yet a given. A little parataxis here and there was acceptable, for the goals of Latin prose (so newly unleashed from poetic meter) were in an early stage of maturation. When we come to Varro's advice on agriculture, some 115 years later, we shall see how much more explicit the offerings of wisdom are—how much more graciously and logically organized, as well as comprehensively instructive. As far as Cato's cumbersome introduction is concerned, it was crafted with *cola* that were neither long, nor overly balanced, nor richly vocabularied, nor even euphonious, for his was a '*very* plain style.'

Lusting for Culture

By the time that BCE had become CE, alphabetic writing had been in existence for some eight hundred years, and the body of Western literature had grown extensively. As had the upper-crust Classical and Hellenistic Greeks, so the upper-crust Romans too made rhetoric—the art of using words effectively—its crowning educational achievement. Roman scholars admired the successes of Alexandrian linguistic analysis and tasked themselves with similar codification of grammatical minutiae for Latin. Far into the Latinate future we will see the effect of Alexandria's legacy, most conspicuously in the developing completeness of statements and the erosion of habits responding to oral sensitivities. As writing spread and dependence upon it increased, so did confidence inspire the urge for precision.

By the time of Julius Caesar's death in 44 BCE, strict rules were governing public expression, whether oral or written, and adhering to them was crucial to one's reputation. Declaiming, the practice of speaking under rhetorical rule on specific themes to an audience of critics, became the graduating test for proving a young patrician's manhood. Get-togethers for the purpose of hearing and criticizing a contemporary's authorial efforts were popular. Publication was achieved by a first recitation. Afterwards, the writer would argue out the fine points with the complaining members of his audience, and, if convinced, adjust his manuscript to their suggestions.[16] A friend was not a friend if he did not save you from a dissonance, an illogical cadence, or a cadence with a faulty rhythm.

Upon purchasing a newly copied scroll, a person did not simply tuck it under his arm, seek a shady spot, unroll it, and begin to read. Instead, the new owner would whip out his writing tools and, grinding his teeth, summon his wits to *figure it out*. This decoding battle was called a *praelectio*. It was, in essence, a preparation for reading one's investment aloud to friends and family. But before the proud owner could do that, it was necessary to seek out the dominant verbs, take note of inflectional relationships, and demark the cadences as best he could once he had identified them. Also, he might question (or change) the word-choice or the *clausulae* rhythms for terminus. He might even consult his neighbor about the scribe's spelling, or his uncle about the grammar. It would seem that every new manuscript required a praelectory tussle to lay bare its textual secrets.

With the spreading availability of manuscripts and the intense focus required to deal with them, language study became imperative for those with money who wished to shine. Grammarians and rhetors gathered to instruct the ambitious with their various insights. A major topic for discussion was style. Which was superior? Was it the Attic (descended from practical simplicities), or the Asian (from ceremonial language)? What will be new on the Roman scene is how deeply analyzed and intensely crafted (hence *nonextemporized*) both styles, and all their hybrid progeny, soon came to be.

Notes

1. This information, as does most of the subsequent material on education, comes from the monumental work of Henri Irénée Marrou, *A History of Education in Antiquity*, trans. George Lamb (New York: Sheed and Ward, 1956), 246–51.
2. Plutarch, "Cato the Elder," in *Makers of Rome*, trans. Ian Scott-Kilvert (London: Penguin, 1965), 145.
3. Suetonius, "Divus Julius," *The Twelve Caesars*, trans. Robert Graves (London: Penguin, 1957), 26. Here Suetonius reminds us that Cicero (in his *Brutus)* claims that he knew no "more eloquent speaker than Caesar." He refers to Caesar's style as "chaste and pellucid" and says of his memoirs that they are "cleanly, directly and gracefully composed, and divested of all trappings."
4. Quintilian, *Institutio oratoria*, trans. H. E. Butler, Loeb Classical Library (Cambridge: Harvard University Press, 1980), 5:396–401.
5. Miriam Griffin, "Cicero and Rome," in *The Oxford History of the Classical World*, ed. John Boardman, Jasper Griffin, and Oswyn Murray (Oxford and New York: Oxford University Press, 1988), 459.
6. Cf. Mary Beard, *SPQR: A History of Ancient Rome* (New York and London: Liveright, 2015), 470–1.
7. It is interesting that by this time in the mid-first century BCE, Cicero's secretary (a slave called Tiro) had invented and was using a shorthand of some 5,000 symbols, which he used to take down the dictation of his master. See Wikipedia, s.v. "Tironian Notes," accessed June 17, 2016, https://en.wikipedia.org/wiki/Tironian_notes.
8. Harris, "Texts and Society in the Roman Empire," in *Escribir y Leer en Occidente*, 2:3–17. Concerning the literacy levels of Rome during its heyday, Harris conjectures that, despite the impressive instances of Latin writing found on tablets, shards, wall paintings, coins, papyrus rolls, and fragments recorded in the *Corpus Inscriptionum Latinarum*, adult literacy in the entire Roman Empire as a whole "is unlikely to have ex-

ceeded 10% at any time" (p. 3). Writing as a popular art was still in a state that is better viewed as a "craftsman's literacy" (p. 10). The portraits of refined Pompeiian women holding pens, book rolls, and writing tablets seem more to suggest an elevated social status than an elevated literary ability. These ladies belonged to families that could afford some (perhaps even considerable) education for their female members, even without the expectation of material advantage (p. 16). Mary Beard, in *Pompeii: The Life of a Roman Town* (London: Profile Books, 2010) seems to suggest bigger percentages of literacy (pp. 182–5). Perhaps the differing calculations derive from differing definitions of literacy: Harris meaning "full reading and writing with absolute ease and literary enthusiasm," and Beard meaning "capable of reading and writing both for pleasure and the necessities of living." In any case, it is a tricky subject—and like Homer's birthdate, endlessly intriguing to scholars.

9.   E. J. Kenney, "Books and Readers in the Roman World," in *The Cambridge History of Classical Literature*, 2:22–4.

10. L. P. Wilkinson, "Cicero and the Relationship of Oratory to Literature," in *The Cambridge History of Classical Literature*, 2:234–5.

11. Miriam Griffin, "Cicero and Rome," in *The Oxford History of the Classical World*, ed. John Boardman, Jasper Griffin, and Oswyn Murray (Oxford and New York: Oxford University Press, 1988), 435.

12. A. S. Gratwick, "Prose Literature," in *The Cambridge History of Classical Literature*, 2:143.

13. Cato and Varro, *On Agriculture*, trans. W. D. Hooper, Loeb Classical Library (Cambridge: Harvard University Press, 1993), 3.

14. Griffin, "Cicero and Rome," 435.

15. Note the reversed position of *bonum* in the last line. Rendered in Latin, the text in the Loeb edition reads: Est interdum praestare mercaturis rem quaerere, nisi tam periculosum sit, et item funerari, si tam honestum sit. Maiores nostri sic habuerunt et ita in legibus posiverunt, furem dupli condemnari, feneratorem quadrupli. Quanto peiorem civem existimarint feneratorem quam furem, hinc licet existimare. Et virus bonum quom laudabant, ita laudabant, bonum agricolam bonumque colonum.

16. Kenney, "Books and Readers in the Roman World," *The Cambridge History of Classical Literature*, 2:8, 12.

References

Beard, Mary. *Pompeii: The Life of a Roman Town*. London: Profile Books, 2010.

———. *SPQR: A History of Ancient Rome*. New York and London: Liveright, 2015.

Cato and Varro. *On Agriculture*. Translated by W. D. Hooper. Loeb Classical Library. Cambridge: Harvard University Press, 1993.

Gratwick, A. S. "Prose Literature." In Vol. 2 of *The Cambridge History of Classical Literature*. Edited by P. E. Easterling and Bernard M. K. Knox. Cambridge: Cambridge University Press, 1985.

Griffin, Miriam. "Cicero and Rome." In *The Oxford History of the Classical World*. Edited by John Boardman, Jasper Griffin, and Oswyn Murray. Oxford and New York: Oxford University Press, 1988.

Harris, William V. "Texts and Society in the Roman Empire." Abstract of Vol. 2 of *Escribir y Leer en Occidente*. Valencia: Universidad Internacional Menendez Pelayo, 1993.

Kenney, E. J. "Books and Readers in the Roman World." In Vol. 2 of *The Cambridge History of Classical Literature*. Edited by P. E. Easterling and Bernard M. K. Knox. Cambridge: Cambridge University Press, 1985.

Marrou, Henri Irénée. *A History of Education in Antiquity*. Translated by George Lamb. New York: Sheed and Ward, 1956.

Plutarch. "Cato the Elder." In *Makers of Rome*. Translated by Ian Scott-Kilvert. London: Penguin, 1965.

Quintilian. *Institutio oratoria*. Translated by H. E. Butler. Loeb Classical Library. Cambridge: Harvard University Press, 1980.

Suetonius. "Divus Julius." In *The Twelve Caesars*. Translated by Robert Graves. London: Penguin, 1957.

Wikipedia, s.v. "Tironian Notes." Accessed June 17, 2016, https://en.wikipedia.org/wiki/Tironian_notes.

Wilkinson, L. P. "Cicero and the Relationship of Oratory to Literature." In Vol. 2 of *The Cambridge History of Classical Literature*. Edited by P. E. Easterling and Bernard M. K. Knox. Cambridge: Cambridge University Press, 1985.

· 1 2 ·

THE DEVELOPMENT OF LITERARY POLISH

A Classical Education

In early Classical Greece, education had been especially strong in the oral arts: music,[1] poetry, and oratory. In addition, it heavily emphasized athletic competitiveness. At a tender age, a privileged boy would be handed over to some admired senior, who would henceforth be his mentor. Through constant companionship and affectionate (often *very* affectionate) devotion, the boy would learn quite a lot about sex as well as the arts of proper conduct, matters of culture, and war. The baths and work-out chambers of the *palaestra* (or *gymnasia*) were the venues of a young aristocrat's training.

In the Hellenistic Alexandria of the second and first centuries BCE, schooling was more organized. With the spread of writing, the content of an adolescent's learning syllabus became more literary and intellectual, less physically personal and less compulsory about athletics and military training. As time passed, the *palaestras* metamorphosed into quieter places and began to build up libraries, which grew to contain the works of poets, writers of comedy and tragedy, orators, and philosophers. With the shift of emphasis from sports to scholarship, young men were encouraged to participate in literary competitions for the best prose eulogy or poem. Throughout this period, Athens (though politically and militarily weakening) remained a strong cultural and educational center. Meanwhile Pergamon, Ephesus, and the island of Cos were growing in intellectual prominence—as was Rhodes, where Dionysius Thrax wrote his *Techne*. Meanwhile, the peripatetic sophists continued to be popular sources of knowledge, and there were many schools of medicine.

The preparatory buildup for all these enlightening activities had been going on for some four centuries. Once the alphabet had manifested its potentials, a complete education necessarily included instruction for using it, both to impart information and to accumulate knowledge. Full literacy (meaning the ability both to read and to write with ease) assured a lifetime of privilege. The great Aristotle himself had said that nobody could be knowledgeable without having learned to read and write. And so, in the follow-on Hellenistic scene, grammar and literature, with all their entailments of word use and style, became the eminent features of pedagogical curricula. Literacy was henceforth the *sine qua non* of culture and the basis for the definitive form that classical education grew to have. And so it was that, having taken root in fourth-century Athens, the 'classical' style of early pedagogy came to be formalized in Alexandria during the second and first centuries BCE. Once adopted, it continued to thrive throughout Imperial Rome and into monastic Christianity. Even in the twenty-first century its tenuous reach is identifiable, most notably in the geographical pockets of Catholicism, and particularly in theological seminaries. In France and Italy, primary school grammar and arithmetic are still taught through repetition, often chanted to a sing-song tune. Yet another Alexandrine inheritance is the French literature classroom technique known as the *explication de texte*. Such activities are genuine residue from the old Dionysian *Techne*.

The primary goal in becoming 'literate' was the ability to read texts, which, as we have seen, could require some formidable effort, given the idiosyncrasies of scribal hands, the lack of regularized punctuation or spelling, and the plague of *scriptura continua*. The child aristocrat in a Hellenistic schoolroom was the object of relentless pedantry. He began his primary course of study by learning to say the alphabet, and repeating—again and again and again—the sound that each letter denoted. The teacher, a low-paid fellow (or more likely, a slave) with too much to do, would drill his pupils until he was cross-eyed, before allowing them to practice the letter shapes on wax tablets. Once the shapes had been mastered, then came the exercise of putting them together to make syllables. And so the process dragged on, until perfection at each level was attained. As the months and years rolled by, words were set out for copying, and then more words, first isolated and at last in combination.[2]

Not until the age of 11 did a Hellenistic pupil begin truly to study for his luminous future: first with a grammarian (with whom he would search out all the literal, figurative, etymological, and connotative minutiae of words, their positions and duties in sentence structures, and their consequent inflectional requirements); and finally, at the age of 14 to 15, with a rhetor. It was the rhetor who would teach him the elements of style, persuasion, argument, and comportment on the podium—who would prepare him to become an *orator perfectus*.

The Romans adopted the classical Greek and Hellenistic cultures with speed, for the gifts of literacy were not totally foreign to them. Their Italic ancestors had long before learned about 'visual representation of sound' from the commercial activities of fourth-century BCE Etruscans and the Greeks who had settled around the boot of their peninsula, north along the coast to Marseilles and in nearby Sicily. But even before Rome devised its own alphabet to represent the sounds of Latin, its young men had learned to appreciate the power of a well-presented speech. They knew how to inspire troops, harangue a tribunal, and how to get on the right side of a crowd. In short, Italic soils were quite ready to embrace and nourish literacy. And as we have seen, by the second century BCE, the passion for linguistic study was rampant in Rome. The first highly trained, Greek-educated Latin orators seem to have appeared at the time of Cato and were numerously present in Rome by 137 BCE (i.e., well before Cicero), though rhetoric would not standardly be taught there for another 70 years or so.

The Romans fell in love with Greece. Everything Greek was considered desirable. To assure that their scruffy children could master the crucial elements of culture and grow up to be Greek-like, they set up schools that paralleled the Hellenistic school system. In time rhetors were hired to supply the essential finishing polish—Good Form—for which they would present their pupils with model wedding, birthday, and funeral speeches to learn by heart and repeat from memory. That drive towards perfection (an Alexandrian legacy to Rome) was fully incorporated into the schooling of the young. Because reading and writing were still considered to be tough meat even for mature teeth, the program for mastering them was run in slow motion and remained recalcitrant to innovation or soft-hearted sentiment. Roman pedagogues kept their eyes on the target and that target was Perfection.

In Roman times (with cultural Rome generally lagging behind Athens by some three centuries), top families preferred to educate their offspring at home. But generally, boys and girls whose papas could afford it were sent to primary school at the approximate age of seven, accompanied daily as soon as the sun was up by a slave companion called their *paedagogus* (child-leader). In the schoolroom, the children would sit on stools and work on a waxed board perched on their knees, while the *magister* sat in state on his *cathedra* (seat). The children would learn to say the alphabet forwards and then backwards. With a stylus (shaped like a pencil) each would follow the shapes of letters stamped onto their wax boards, before attempting to imitate them on their own. They would form letters together: AX, BV, TS, for example, and conclude by making syllables. After much practice at that, they worked with single names, moral sayings, short sentences, and finally brief continuous passages.

Professor Marrou provides us with an extant account (from the early 200s CE) of a day in the primary school life of a Roman boy. A child of perhaps nine, who had mastered the letters sufficiently to use them, describes how, as was the custom, his day began as soon as the sun was up. (In winter, he would wake to smoky lamplight.) The following is the boy's own statement, apparently written (in Latin of course) as a school exercise. [The italics and punctuation are Professor Marrou's.][3]

When day breaks I wake up, call the slave, and get him to open the window—which he does at once. I sit up, sit on the edge of the bed, and ask for my shoes and stockings because it is cold. *Otherwise, no doubt, he would have put on his sandals straightaway without bothering about...stockings.*

As soon as I have put my shoes on I take a towel—I have been brought a clean one. Water is brought me in a jug so that I can wash. I pour some of it over my hands and face and into my mouth; I rub my teeth and gums; I spit out, blow my nose and wipe it, as any well brought-up child should.

I take off my nightshirt and put on a tunic and girdle; I perfume my head and comb my hair; I put a scarf round my neck; I get into my white cloak. I leave my room with my pedagogue and nurse and go and say good morning to my father and mother. I say good morning to them both and kiss them.

I go and find my inkstand and exercise book and give them to the slave. Then everything is ready, and, followed by my pedagogue, I set off through the portico that leads to the school. *There is no breakfast. Probably he simply had a...little cake or pie bought as he passed a baker's shop.*

My schoolfellows come and meet me; I say hello to them and they say hello back. I come to the staircase. I go up the stairs quietly, as I should. In the hall I take off my cloak, run through my hair with my comb, and go in, saying, "Good morning, master." The master embraces me and returns my greeting. The slave hands me my writing-boards, my ink-stand and my ruler.

"Good morning, everybody. Let me have my place. Squeeze up a bit." "Come here." "This is my place!" "I got it first!" I sit down and set to work. *Most of the work was done in the morning, but it also went on into the second half of the day.*

I have finished my lesson. I ask the master to let me go home for lunch; he lets me go; I say goodbye to him, and he returns my farewell. I go home and change. I have white bread, olives, cheese, dry figs and nuts; I drink some fresh water. Having finished my lunch, I go off to school again. I find my master reading; he says to us, "Now to work again!"

There was no longer, as at the beginning of the Hellenistic period, any time for physical exercise: the child does not seem to have gone to the gymnasium, but only to the baths; for the day ended with a bath.

I must go and have a bath. Yes, it's time. I go off; I get myself some towels and I follow my servant. I run and catch up with the others who are going to the baths and I say to them one and all, "How are you? Have a good bath! Have a good supper!"

At the age of 11 or 12, those who were to continue their education (boys most likely, while the girls, if they continued at all, probably did so in their homes) began their studies with a *grammaticus*, who continued in a similar, but more elevated vein. Under the tutelage of a *grammaticus*, an adolescent would first learn a text by heart, and only then tackle the actual reading of it. Following a discussion of its contents, and the classification of its elements, the student was quizzed.

In addition to the forms and meanings of words and their relations to other sentence elements, a young grammar scholar was expected to learn all the names and features of his cultural history: who were the heroes, their gods, their enemies; where were the battles fought; what rivers and mountains were crossed; what cities fell or survived—indeed all the details of the great epics, religious mythology, popular legend, and lore. Professor Marrou tells us, for example, that it was essential

to know the names of all the persons who had been restored to life by
the art of Asclepius; to know that Heracles was bald when he came
out of the sea-monster which had swallowed him for a moment.[4]

Happily, a sample catechism on Homer has survived the passage of time. It
was found written out on a page in one of the extant copies of Dionysius
Thrax's little treatise on grammar, and can probably be dated from around the
time of Christ.

Q. Which gods were favourable to the Trojans?
A. (In alphabetical order) Aphrodite, Apollo, Ares, Artemis, Leto,
Scamander.
Q. Who was the King of the Trojans?
A. Priam.
Q. Who was their general?
A. Hector.
Q. Who were their counsellors?
A. Polydamas and Agenor. And so on.[5]

With its small dollop of analytical content, Dionysius Thrax's *Techne* represents a pedagogical pivot; for after its 'publication' in the first century BCE,
scholarly temperament became vigorously responsive to Aristotelian and Alexandrian precepts. Adolescent classes took on a more critical air. Literary
exercises progressed from the vagaries of epic poetry to real grammar and the
study of sentential elements and techniques of communicating. Factual history, medical discovery, mathematics, the physical sciences, and philosophy
soon became topical considerations as well; and enveloping all was the feel
of true scholarship with its habitual fussing over the meaning of words. Until
Dionysius Thrax, grammar had not been taught in order to help youths grasp
the mechanics of their mother tongue. Rather, it had been perceived as an
advanced science, purely speculative and theoretical, yet definitely necessary
for the acquisition of culture.

But now, even the adolescent grammar student was being introduced to
the controlled action of elementary composition. The teacher would tell a
story and the student would set down the core of it as best he could. Mastery
of that exercise (a sort of half-oral sample of précis writing) essentially completed his grammar years and made him officially eligible to begin his course
of rhetoric—the final stage of his formal and expensive education.

Strangely, additions to Dionysius Thrax's *Techne* in later generations were rare, amounting merely to a bit on prosody and meter, and a table of the full conjugation of a verb. Professor Marrou expresses surprise that such a meagre treatise with all its under-described dictates should satisfy the public curiosity for so many years. It was not until the third century CE that one begins to come across school papyri and writing boards that show the performance of practical exercises in inflectional morphology.[6] Thus, for some four centuries, this ubiquitous little volume traversed the ancient world, instructing the young, both in Greek and in translation, without any tables of nouns declined with adjectives, or classification of verbs, their forms, and the cases they governed. Nevertheless, it gave literacy a real boost. No doubt good teachers supplied the missing parts as they figured them out—such minutiae as the different inflections and where and how to use them; verb tenses; how to build towards a cadence; where to put the verb, the particle, the adjective, and so on.

Clearly, the ancient schools knew how to make haste slowly. No upward step was ever taken until there had been a long intensive stay on the level beneath. The pupil was drilled and drilled again—one wonders how he stood it. But literacy, being young and so very desirable, was worth unusual effort and concentration. Only the urgency to acquire perfect accuracy and correctness in word usage will account for the curious practice of having pupils go through all the cases and all the numbers of the words in a short passage or even a whole story. When considering the impatient young of today, an exercise of this nature seems so extraordinary that it is hard to believe the theoretical writers who mention it. Still, there is no doubt that it was commonly practiced. An Egyptian writing-board shows us a schoolboy dutifully declining a passage based on Pythagoras. First in the singular:

> "*The* philosopher Pythagoras, having gone ashore and started giving language lessons, advised his disciples to abstain from flesh meat. [There, the 'philosopher Pythagoras' is the subject and hence set in the nominative case.] We are next told that the opinion *of* the philosopher Pythagoras was…" [the genitive case]. "It seemed good *to* the philosopher Pythagoras…" [dative]. "They describe *the* philosopher Pythagoras as saying…" [accusative]. "O philosopher Pythagoras!" [vocative]. [Then scorning all logic, the sentences had to be repeated in the dual number:] "The [two] Pythagorases, philosophers…" [and then in the plural (i.e., more than two):] "The Pythagorases, philos-

ophers, having gone ashore and started giving language lessons, advised their disciples..." and so on for all the different cases.[7]

After doing this sort of thing, day after day after day, you could begin to think of other things as you guided your stylus through the sun-warmed wax. Nevertheless, the practice was useful, for it made writing a steady-state thing, being in essence a sort of early rendition of the uniformity that printing would eventually bring about. It made clear, mature writing easier to do (one was so used to the many particulars); at the same time the clear and regularized formation of scripted letters eased the life of the reader.

Once the young patrician had completed the grammarian's course, his ambitious father would hand him over to the very best rhetor he could find, or afford—the rhetor being a person who taught, not just correctness, but the *art* of speaking and writing. Hellenistic rhetors had been notoriously finicky. In an environment of mounting literacy, their Roman successors followed suit. Latin-speaking students were obliged to expand into prose the famous stories of epic poetry. But the task was more than just that, for the requirements became suddenly multitudinous and difficult. These poor overstressed youths had simultaneously to seek brevity, clarity, verisimilitude, and correctness; and along with that, introduce six elements: agent, action, time, place, manner, and cause, in three of four species of composition: mythical, poetical, historical, or civic.[8] As may be imagined, rhetorical composition offered no leeway for frank opinion.

Professor Marrou gives us an example of the slow, tentative advance required of such a procedure.[9]

Suppose a student had been given the following topic upon which to expand: "Isocrates says, 'The roots of education are bitter but the fruits thereof are sweet.'" This had to be treated in its proper order in eight paragraphs.

(1.) Introduction to Isocrates and a eulogy on him.
(2.) A paraphrase of his aphorism in three lines.
(3.) A brief defense of his opinion.
(4.) Proof by contrast, refuting the contrary opinion.
(5.) Illustration by analogy.
(6.) Illustration by anecdote—borrowed from Demosthenes, for example.
(7.) Quotations from old authorities in support (Hesiod, etc.)
(8.) Conclusion: "Such is Isocrates's excellent saying about education."

We see here a handsome display of the eye-oriented tendency to divide and study. The rigid dogmatism of micromanaging Roman rhetorical training, with its emphasis on exactitude and repetition, discouraged youthful experiment. Instead, all the lavish advice—even down to a system for gesturing—became a guidebook course for the development of wit, a wit so practiced that it could sprint, dodge, and jump *despite the swarming hindrances.* In short, one learned to sport within and amongst the barrier fences. From the writer's point of view, freedom came with the perfect mastery of rule. When a mind as lissome as Cicero's had completed such a course of verbal gymnastics, it would prove to have been 'a Good Thing,' for there seemed nothing that Cicero could not manage to say, and say with grace, fire, sincerity, or wit as he wished. But, over the years, as grammatical rule hardened and rhetorical bolts were tightened, less facile mouths and less inventive pens succumbed to the pressures and so droned on in their ponderous anticipatable modes. Livelier minds, however, rebelled. (The rebels will be dealt with shortly.)

Rhetoric's formalized system of values retained a firm and lasting grip on educational processes. It infused all literary prose, which quickly developed its own aesthetics, which in time became a governance almost as rigid and finicky as that for poetry, yet no less valid.[10] A student would learn both. He would also learn that the rules for both beautiful poetry and beautiful prose were at odds with the language of philosophy, which, purporting to deal only in truths, disdained aesthetic treatment of any kind and, instead, boasted a separate, nonpolite way of expression. Logic being the driving force of philosophy, philosophers fiercely disputed rhetoric's right to exist. In Isocrates and Plato's day, before rhetorical rigidity had become so dominant, philosophy (logic) and rhetoric (art for both poetry and prose) were seen as one. After literacy was an accepted fact of cultured life and Hellenistic language analysis had become the rage, philosophy and rhetoric separated. It was not until Dionysius of Halicarnassus (late in the first century BCE) that 'purport with style' became the announced goal.

For a final gasp at the strenuous training eventually required of a Roman student of rhetoric, here following is Professor Marrou's rendering of the protocol for an encomium (a statement of eulogy to honor someone either because he is dead, or because he has done some marvelous thing—perhaps won a race, or fought bravely to save the city).[11] One should bear in mind that this was just one of many types of oratory that a rhetor was expected to inculcate into the heads of his pupils. The materials for such an encomium would have been divided into 36 categories, arranged in the following way:

I   Exterior excellence

(a) Noble birth

(b) Environment
     1. Native city
     2. Fellow citizens
     3. Excellence of the city's political regime
     4. Parents and family

(c) Personal advantages
     1. Education
     2. Friends
     3. Fame
     4. Public service
     5. Wealth
     6. Children, number and beauty of
     7. Happy death

II   Bodily Excellences
     1. Health
     2. Strength
     3. Beauty
     4. Bubbling vitality and capacity for deep feeling

III Spiritual Excellences

(a) Virtues
     1. Wisdom
     2. Temperance
     3. Courage

And so on.

This overall 'system' of rhetorical rule was passed down through the centuries, from generation to generation. In the face of so much else to learn, its demands have gradually relaxed—which is good, some say, while others say not.

Varro: A Meticulous Grammarian

During his long reign (from 27 BCE to 14 CE), the Emperor Augustus brought a period of peace to the world, making it possible for the public to attend to the finer things of life—art, architecture, oratory, and literature. The result was a surge of aesthetic and pedagogical effort that sharpened the Latin language and enhanced its developing literature. By then, the Roman grammarian Varro (whose long life overlapped the birth and death of Cicero) had done more explicitly, expansively, and systematically for fast-growing Latin what the *Techne* of Dionysius Thrax had earlier done for Greek. Varro's 25 books, *De lingua latina* (most of which have been lost), were in effect a massive treatise on Latin philology and grammar. Sometimes penetrating, sometimes naïve, and sometimes even absurd, the highly acclaimed *De lingua latina* bravely dealt with the etymology, word meanings, inflections, grammar, and other mysteries and complications of the Latin language.

With Varro, we are deep into the thought processes of a logic-driven mind—a mind that sought to explain the origins and purpose of all the variables of his topic. His method of explication was to divide his topic into ever-smaller bits, to explain the effects of each, and to discuss its application—all in a very direct, very plain (logic-driven) writing style. Clarity was his goal. In reading Varro's works, one feels to be in the hands of a wise and knowing schoolmaster, whose attention is fixed on explaining matters, step-by-step, so that his reader may follow his argument. Varro's study of the Latin language reveals a compulsive curiosity about the mechanics of language in general, as well as a soundly reasoned pedagogy that far outpaces that of Dionysius Thrax. It is sad that out of 25 books, only Books 5 to 10 remain complete (and even then somewhat imperfectly).[12]

For a taste of Varro, we look now at his Book 5, which he dedicates to his younger friend Cicero. This book is devoted to a discussion of vocabulary, which he promptly divides into two parts: 'what the Greeks call Etymology and what they call Semantics.' Every word partakes of both, says Varro: where it came from (etymology) and what it means (semantics). And on he goes from there, working his way through the dark corridors of ignorance into sudden sunlight, where even the modern mind can often enjoy fresh insight. In an intriguing moment of mental quaintness, he tells us that inflections are necessary to all languages, so that (for example) the word 'ship' may remain recognizably 'ship,' whatever use it is being put to in a sentence. He reasons that without inflections a totally new word would have to be invented for each of the ship's separate uses. Thus: The ship lay in the harbor; but when the wind blew it out to sea, the word 'ship' (now the object) would have to become 'xxx' (bobum? kitmat? jeg?); and for each of its possible uses (possessive, indirect object, etc.), yet another totally different word would be needed. The result of so many words—all different and unrelated in sound or sight to the original 'ship'—would be too great a burden for the human brain. Inflections eliminate the problem entirely.

Varro digs into the matter of Latin etymology with enthusiasm. The quoted paragraph below (again from Book 5) will give us another view of his analytic passions. Here, he is grouping words that derive from earlier single-core words (or radicals) and demonstrating how those offshoots produced their own offshoots. In this way, he hoped to demonstrate how Latin acquired its extensive vocabulary. He explains his theory thus:

> These relations are often rather obscure for the following reasons: Not every word that has been applied [used], still exists, because lapse of time has blotted out some. Not every word that is in use, has been applied [used] without inaccuracy of some kind, nor does every word which has been applied [used] correctly remain as it originally was; for many words are disguised by change of the letters. There are some whose origin is not from native words of our own language. Many words indicate one thing now, but formerly meant something else.[13] (Varro, *Ling.* 5.1.3)

There are few things that lapse of time fails either to distort or remove from existence, and words make no exception. One should begin the study of words by considering the two innate features of each and every one: that is, from what thing does the word come and to what thing does it now apply? (I.e., how is it now used?)

Continuing, Varro groups words into clusters to show, so he thinks, their ancestral relationships and how over time they spawned new words, or families of words:

> There are three *actiones* 'actions,' and of these the first is the *agitatus* 'motion' of the mind, because we must first *cogitare* 'consider' those things which we are *acturi* 'going to do,' and then thereafter say them and do them. Of these three, the common folk practically never thinks that *cogitatio* 'consideration' is an action; but it thinks that the third, in which we do something, is the most important. But also when we *cogitamus* 'consider' something and *agitamus* 'turn it over' in the mind, we *agimus* 'are acting.' Therefore from this the orator is said *agere* 'to plead' the case, and the augurs are said 'to practise' augury, although in it there is more saying than doing.
>
> *Cogitare* 'to consider' is said to come from *cogere* 'to bring together': the mind *cogit* 'brings together' several things into one place, from which it can choose. Thus from milk that is *coactum* 'pressed,' *caseus*

'cheese' was named; thus from men brought together was the *contio* 'mass meeting' called, thus *coemptio* 'marriage by mutual sale,' thus *compitum* 'cross-roads.' From cogitation 'consideration' came *concilium* 'council,' and from that came *consilium* 'counsel'; and the *concilium* is said *conciliari* 'to be brought into unity' like a garment when it *cogitur* 'is pressed' at the cleaner's.[14] (Varro, *Ling.* 8.11.26)

Similar nuggets of 'discovery' rise to the surface in Varro's analyses, and though sometimes tedious, all derive from reasoned analysis and are clearly expressed—even though they are sometimes a touch outrageous, or (just as likely) dead wrong. Yet many are both intriguing and entertaining. All speaking ought to be aimed at practical utility, said Varro, and "it attains this only if it is clear and brief: characteristics which we seek, because an obscure and longish speaker is disliked."[15] A very interesting Attic plea is that!—given that his very devoted friend was Cicero. They were both, however, fervent analogists—advocates for regularity in verb forms, word usage, and case endings.

For a final glimpse into Varro's analysis of the Latin language, here are some thoughts from Book 7.

[T]he man who has made many apt pronouncements on the origins of words, one should regard with favour, rather than find fault with him who has been unable to make any contribution; especially since the etymologic art says that it is not of all words that the basis can be stated—just as it cannot be stated how and why a medicine is effective for curing; and that if I have no knowledge of the roots of a tree, still I am not prevented from saying that a pear is from a branch, the branch is from a tree, and the tree from roots which I do not see. For this reason, he who shows that *equitatus* 'cavalry' is from *equites* 'cavalryman,' *eques* from *equus* 'horse,' even though he does not give the source of the word *equus*, still gives several lessons and satisfies an appreciative person.[16] (Varro, *Ling.* 7.1.4)

Varro's contribution to the organization and understanding of the Latin language was enormous and pioneering. His works, much admired during his lifetime, are evidence of how distant from an oral outlook the literate outlook had become. Varro's was the first major step into the unexplored waters of the Latin language, and many would soon follow his lead. The subsequent artistic flowering during the Augustan calm was rooted in linguistic development, which in turn ensured that the study of the Latin language would continue to supersede all other studies in Rome's ancient culture and medieval future.[17]

Varro's little book on agriculture and farming (the *Rerum Rusticarum*, written some 115 years later than Cato's) has survived the years in its entirety. Set side by side, this pair of treatises provide a measure of Latin's literary growth. The genial discussion of good farming put out by Varro makes a startling comparison with the raw agricultural data so awkwardly put together by Cato. In fact, all of Varro's categorizations of 'how-to' detail is as alien to the oral mindset as any that can be found in the history of literature.

The opening statement of Varro's *Rerum Rusticarum* is not only personal in tone and plain in language, but also carefully styled. The effect is one of affectionate sincerity, rather like that of a fond teacher addressing an eager novice—in Varro's case, his young wife Fundania, who, so Varro claims, has asked for advice about managing her recently bought estate. The Loeb edition emphasizes Varro's artful Plato-ish simplicity by breaking up what was more likely material for a lengthy opening *period*. But with his use of the connecting *for, to which end, and,* and *nor* particles to bind the *cola* of his introduction, one can be pretty sure that Varro was in fact constructing a *period* of some intricacy, despite its seemingly relaxed language. The earliest extant manuscript for the *Rerum Rusticarum* dates from the twelfth or thirteenth century—too late to certify any underlying intention: *period* or non*period*. Favoring the *period* side of this argument is the fact that Cicero, Livy, and Quintilian—all of whom followed Varro in time—kept to the custom of opening a prose treatise with the firework display of a complex *period*—an ancient feature, we remember, that Xenophon preferred to discard. We do not know how Varro began his *De lingua Latina* as the opening pages have been lost.

Varro's easy management of agricultural information avoids the tangles, missing pieces, and conceits of his predecessor Cato. Whereas Cato's stance is terse and haughty towards his reader-pupil, Varro communicates his material in a gentler, clearer, friendlier, and more thoughtful manner. In the interim years between the two, tremendous strides towards a supple prose style have been taken. Interestingly, Varro constructs his agricultural thesis by artistically framing it in an imagined conversation between himself and friends, as we saw Plato do in the *Phaedo*. In reading Varro's *Rerum Rusticanum*, one will note how explicit he is without being bossy (as Cato was); and how (unlike Cato), he does not engage in religious mysticism.

Varro's clear and inviting efforts were as important to the art of pedagogy as to the analysis of the Latin language. The subsequent flowering of Latin prose literature was rooted in his linguistic and grammatical studies. His contribution to the growth of public literacy and his demand for clarity and knowledge ensured that the study of language would continue to supersede all other scholarly studies in Rome's ancient and medieval future.[18]

Introducing Cicero: A Man of Genius

Once Cato and Varro had embraced Latin prose as a language of literary potential, intellectuals in the cosmopolitan circles of Rome followed along. Style in composition, appropriate structures for Latin syntax, and classification of Latin parts all became popular issues, for which every detail was thought to merit study and analysis. What the Greeks called *colon* was by the Latins called *membrum*, a word often defined in terms of syllables or metrical beats. The phrases that the Greeks called *commata* became *incisa*. As for the full *periodic* sentence (the *circuitus*), it continued to be perceived as an elaborately organized concatenation of related thoughts set into *cola* (*membra*), which themselves were made up of *commata* (*incisa*)—the whole assemblage ending with a sense of completeness. The Greeks, we remember, had called such an assemblage a *periodos*, a term appropriately derived from 'race course.' (For the sake of simplicity in this account, only the Greek forms will be used hereafter, as they were in fact taken up again in Latin.) Generally, we may now think of a *periodos* as a "full statement," controlled in principle by balance and form, but in practice exuberantly eager to overspill the boundaries set by pedagogical theorists. Though nothing palpable had been added to the contemporary Greek prescriptions for sentence structure, the Romans, with so much of their literary discussion surviving, somehow give us the feeling that we are well within the outskirts of our own modern linguistic responses. What they say about shaping, presenting, and arranging language for the page will seem progressively more confident and familiar.

At the center of all this linguistic activity was the great Cicero (106–43 BCE), who received his *toga virilis* (the toga signifying that he was no longer a child, but a man and a citizen of Rome) at age 15 after a rigorous early education in Rome. As an ambitious member of a prominent intellectual family, he then turned to the serious study of rhetoric. At age 27, after a spell in the military and some well-received oratory in the senatorial courts, he went abroad to pursue the highest elevations of that demanding art form. He attended the lectures of the great rhetors in Athens and on the island of Rhodes, where it is said that his mentor Molon cured him of a Gorgianic ornamental tendency. He returned to Rome fired with ambition, new skills, and much new knowledge, married the wealthy Terentia (possibly the daughter of Varro), and began a prominent public career in government. Over the years, he held various offices (some very high); he also practiced law both privately and in the Senate.

His was a time of much political controversy, conniving, and shifting allegiances as enemies turned into friends and then back again. Cicero was actively engaged in the doings of Julius Caesar and his once-friend, then enemy, Pompey. At the same time, he was energetically and prodigiously productive in both the literary world and in the Senate, while also being a concerned family man: a loving father (though a twice-disappointed husband), a caring brother, a supportive uncle, and an engaging friend. He was noted for being almost dangerously witty—skilled in repartee and biting retorts. Amid the hectic activity of his many commitments, he found his peace from the public eye in writing. He wrote poetry, which, alas, has been declared by most to border on the awful. His forte was prose. Besides writing his own many tracts of impeccable prose, he translated Greek prose into Latin prose and various poets' output into prose. Particularly noteworthy were his translations of Demosthenes's speeches, whom in practice Cicero was said to equal. Cicero's surviving prose works include many of his orations (undoubtedly polished after the fact), philosophic tracts, and a number of treatises on language and rhetoric. There are also his extant letters, of which several thousand have luckily survived the centuries.

Varro quite rightly dedicated Books 5 to 10 of his *De lingua latina* to Cicero, who, though 10 years younger than Varro, was fast becoming the star of the Roman rhetorical-literary explosion that we now address. Cicero's treatises *De oratore*, *Brutus*, and *Orator* tell us a great deal about contemporary oral and written language. Though he did not necessarily practice his own dictates for the craft, his critical writings—fortified by the example of his illustrious forensic and political career—survived to cast their influence over all future written expression.[19] *The Oxford Classical Dictionary* describes Cicero as having "moulded the Latin language into an incomparably clear and effective vehicle of thought," to the degree that his style would long affect future writers, and his rhythms become "stereotyped in the Papal Chancery."[20] For centuries after Cicero, no one could compose a literary statement without both author and reader being acutely aware of his great example, for many of his works "survived as textbooks in the grammar schools and models in the rhetorical schools."[21]

Cicero's grammatical and prosodic ideas are not considered to have been particularly innovative, but rather the highly thoughtful and clearly expressed culmination of previous rhetorical pedagogy and practices. Nevertheless, his pen was slick, and he used it persuasively to free prose from the smothering technical stiffness of contemporary argument and style imposed by Hellenistic doctrine. His own verbal skill, vast knowledge, quick intelligence, and personal authority led to a more generous conception of rhetoric and a larger vision of what written language might accomplish than did the established Hellenistic mechanisms. In short, while Cicero admired the Greeks and was himself an avid student of classical and Hellenistic literature and oratory, he was the one who loosened their hold. Though he preceded the Augustan period of quiet, he set the stage for the tremendous literary activity that it would shortly bring.

Along with his intellectual gifts and patricianly confidence, Cicero's character included a native inheritance, which was twofold. Not only did Romans view themselves in stoical outline—brave, puritanical, tersely spoken (like Cato)—they had also their inflammable *emozioni Italiani* to keep in check. And Cicero by no means lacked those. Being so facile, he could either quell his voracious poetic appetite, or let fly. His range was enormous—from his relaxed conversational correspondence to the rolling swells of his early oratory, from his sometimes plebeian word choices to the sophisticated Greek that came so easily to him. In any case, he is the only pre-Christian Roman whose acute attention to the effects of language has come down to us in comprehensible completeness.

Cicero at Work

By the time he had reached middle age, Cicero had decided that the middle style was best for prose expression—his own middle style, that is—by which he meant a logical progress that did not disregard charm and fullness of presentation. Eschewing the no-nonsense plainness of the Atticists' hero Lysias—and even that of his admired, tight-lipped Cato—Cicero recommended Demosthenes as being exemplary, for what Demosthenes said and wrote was direct and clear, yet stimulating and varied. Cicero described his own middle style as being more artistic than the plain or conversational style. It was smooth while being ornamental, allowing long *periods*, imagery, and all the delights of parallelism and antithesis; yet controlled, logical, and direct as well. The grand style—replete with beautiful words, bristling with imagery, and inclined to basic figures of thought (such as allegory or irony)—he reserved for moments when a display of passion was called for.[22]

Though Cicero advocated the middle-styled charms (as defined by him), his own writings were extensively varied, leaning sometimes to the Attic plain and sometimes to the Asian grand, according to what he was trying to do. Whereas his sentences were brief and quick in law-court dispute, they could be complexly structured in laying out an argument, or again, chummy and slack as in his letters to relatives and friends. Though he favored a stoical directness in logical debate, he rejected the Stoic's view that oratory should be unemotional. One should mold style to one's purpose, said clever Cicero. And this he could do better than anyone. In a time of considerable brilliance, Cicero was the most enduring and brilliant star.

Cicero's sentence structures (particularly in the openings to his senatorial speeches) are the bane of classroom translators. They could wind, rhythmically, magniloquently, on and on. Despite a seeming interminability, however, they kept their balance and made their meaning clear. *How?*

The following 66-word *period* from Cicero's speech *Pro lege Manilia* (*On the Manilian Law*) of 66 BCE (a speech written when he was 40 years old but which he used himself to illustrate the charms of the 'middle style') will show how he managed against all odds to control sentences of monstrous length and complication. In this example, the clauses come in parallels, with binding correlatives and particles to direct the listener-reader's progress,[23] and to lead him from A to B with an expectancy that is rewarded. The cadences that were needed in so long a passage are prefigured by the verb positions. Cicero was particularly attentive to the rhythmic beats of his *clausulae*,[24] which were standardly seen to lend polish to a finishing segment of wordage. (Details of the *clausulae* will be discussed more thoroughly a few pages hence.)

The passage has been laid out (with its crucial particle elements italicized) in *The Cambridge History of Classical Literature* (2:238). Those who enjoy a good struggle will find the Latin in the chapter's endnotes.[25] In the first of the following English translations, the Latin has been translated word-by-word. It is then repeated in the more polished form found in the Loeb edition. One can imagine how the carry of the voice might elicit the sense more forcefully than can this structure-exposing, dry-as-dust analysis.

When translated line by line, the construction emerges more visibly:

(1) Now since
(2) *both* of authority in me *as much* may be,
(3) *so much* as you wished to be by sending honors
(4) *both* through practising of the faculty *so much*
(5) *as* to an alert man from forensic use almost
(6) daily through speaking by practise could bring,
(7) certainly
(8) *both whatever* of authority in me is,
(9) among *those* to use *who it* to me gave,
(10) *both whatever* in saying to achieve I am able,
(11) *to them* showing most powerful *who to him also*
(12) the fruit by his judgement to be attributed they led.

Which the Loeb editor more gracefully unravels as follows:

And now, since I possess such a measure of influence as, by conferring office upon me, you have intended should be mine, and such a degree of skill in public speaking as an almost daily practise in pleading can bestow through his experience in the courts upon one anxious to learn, then assuredly any influence that may be mine I will exercise among those to whom I owe it, and any attainments I can achieve as an orator I will display most chiefly to those whose verdict has pronounced that oratory, too, is deserving of reward.[26] (Cic., *Leg. Man.* 1.2–3)

How this speech was first written down is not known, but it seems likely that the original text, along with its guiding particles and cadencing *clausulae*, incorporated some type of punctuation as well as some aerating division of words. As will be shown, Cicero himself was an advocate of opening up dense text and dealing it out in absorbable chunks. Inscriptions and extant papyri of the first century BCE tell us that Latin writers were not only dividing words, but broadly using *clausulae* and Alexandrian dot-puncts—though the conventions to govern them remained unsettled. We may assume that with his own private secretary to do his bidding, Cicero must have insisted that the manuscript of his works include some sort of aeration, for by the time of his death, literary sophisticates were seriously discussing the inconvenience of reading back from crammed texts. Word separation would in fact be highly recommended through the next century, though alas! philhellenic snobbery would prevail in the end. Respect for the Greeks, whose commentaries had always been, and were still, written in *scriptura continua* was profound and persistent. In the end, that respect undermined common sense and demolished for a very long time the possibility of a pleasurable, relaxing read. That backward move from clarity to murk seems quite astonishing to us today.[27]

Cicero gave considerable attention to the breaking up of text. Refining the Greek example, he recommended the use of rhythmical *clausulae* closures not only for the termination of a *periodic* statement, but also for its larger segments, whose features had been recognized though not yet defined in terms like 'noun' clauses, or 'relative' and 'nonrelative' clauses, as they later came to be. By demarking these larger segments, he said, the grammatical structure of a *period* would not only be illumined but would also allow a greater complexity and length. Furthermore, the opportunities for the show of cleverness and the practice of wit would be expanded. Cicero was far more explicit than Aristotle had been about what the specifics of those finishing metrical *clausulae* should be. Though focusing on the lucidity and sense of manuscript wordage, what he actually addressed in this instance were the satisfactions of the ear. Having seen how *clausulae* rhythms could advance the meaning of word groups in oratorical argument and keep that clarity in the transfer into writing, Cicero kept those *clausulae* intact—to be heard again when the tract was murmured internally or actually read aloud. Even in Cicero's time, consummate prose was considered to be the distillation of formal speech, as found namely in oratory.

In Cicero's extensive writings on rhetorical matters as they relate to division, rhythm, style, and closure in prose writing, the interesting word *interpungendi* arises. Though it is generally translated in the literature as 'punctuation,' it still seems rather vague. Did it offer some indication for word division, breath control when reading aloud, sense demarcation, or a medley of all? It is simplest to assume that Cicero had more or less in mind what we have more or less in mind when he spoke of *interpungendi* and we speak of *punctuation*— that is, making written lines intelligible by gathering up cohering word groups and distinguishing them at appropriate cadencing moments. As we have seen, rhetorical cadences can vary, depending on the emotions and perceptions of an ear-attentive speaker or writer. Logical cadencing, which is ruled by grammatical principles, seems the one most adhered to by Cicero.

The following section will give some relevant quotations taken from the Loeb Classical Library editions of Cicero's *De oratore*, *Brutus*, and *Orator*.[28] In this last treatise, written in 46 BCE, Cicero is defending his own copious verbosity against the groundswell grumbles of contemporary Atticists, who, we remember, derived their aspirations from the Ionic sophists and eastern stoics, and (more locally) from Cato. It would seem that in the history of written language, whenever the swell of verbiage became almost unbearable, human sensibilities reversed to clear the system of dross and scum.

Cicero's Thoughts on Rhythm in Prose Structures

Eloquence is a potent force that embraces all things in a graceful and flowing style. By acquiring it, one can both instruct and give pleasure. The old Greek masters, Isocrates most particularly, held the view that prose should contain rhythms just as does poetry. They thought that in speeches

> the close of the *period* ought to come not when we are tired out but where we may take breath, and to be marked not by the punctuation (*interpuncts*) of copying clerks but by the arrangement of the words and of the thought...designed to give pleasure to the ear. (*De oratore,* 137–9) (Cic., De or. 44.173)

To engage the ear, the Greek poets, who were in those days also musicians, thought it proper to transfer from poetry to rhetoric, insofar as was compatible with the severe character of oratory, the modulation of the voice and the arrangement of words in *periods*. For it is the mark of an ignorant speaker to pour out

> disorderly stuff as fast as he can with no arrangement, and end a sentence not from artistic considerations but when his breath gives out, whereas the orator links words and meaning together in such a manner as to unfold his thought in a rhythm that is at once bound and free. (*De oratore,* 139) (Cic., De or. 44.175–6)

> We must make our style conform to this law of rhythm both by practise in speaking and by using the pen, which is a good tool for giving style and polish. (*De oratore,* 151) (Cic., De or. 49.190)

Just as the sun and the moon and the seasons recur in an orderly, rhythmic way, so speech must be ordered too.

The *periodic* structure has its origins in the physical limitation of breath-ing, so that our ears are gratified only by what can be easily endured by the human lungs.

> For it is true that by some natural instinct the expression of a thought may fall into a periodic form and conclusion, and when it is thus gath-ered up in fitting words it ends often with a rhythmical cadence. The reason is that the ear itself judges what is complete, what is deficient, and the breath by natural compulsion fixes a limit to the length of the phrase. If the breath labors, not to say fails utterly, the effect is painful. (*Brut.* 41) (Cic., *Brut.* 8.34)

Art in prose writing demands subtlety and variation in the use of rhythms. Aristotle recommends to orators that they speak in heroic meters as are found in the great epics (that is, mostly dactyls: dee-de-de)—a legitimate thing to do provided one does not fall into downright verse or something resembling verse. Also, Aristotle approves the paeon meters: dee-de-de-de (as in 'Clamorously, the mobs...'; or 'Presciently, the commander withdrew') for the beginning of a *period*, and de-de-de-dee (as in 'bit *into the peach*,' or, 'flew *over the seas*') for the end. Prose, being less fettered than poetry, must apply its own self-control so that it neither falls into song nor gushes with-out pause. All utterance contains an element of rhythm, which can quite properly be reckoned as a merit in prose. A continuing series of words will be much more pleasing if it is divided up into *cola* and *commata*, the *com-mata* becoming shorter near the end (*pace* Demetrius, who advocated the opposite), in indication of the coming final break. This recommendation of using short phrasal breaks towards the end of the *periodos* is related to physiological need, i.e., the gasps of an emptied lung. The purpose is rooted in orality, and is of benefit particularly to the speaker. As we shall see, the idea that a *period* should contain both short and long phrases reappears in the writings of later grammarians, though sometimes the expounding stylist will advise his disciples to begin with the short groups and end with a long one, the purpose in this case being perhaps to round off the *period* with the weightiest thought in the collection. All these instructions for voice will of course be reflected in prose writing.

> Only let your habitual practise in writing and speaking be to make the thoughts end up with the words, and the combination of the words themselves spring from good long free meters, specially the dactylic

[dee-de-de] or the first paeon [dee-de-de-de] or the cretic [dee-de-dee], though with a close of various forms and clearly marked, for similarity is particularly noticed at the close; and if the first and last feet of the sentences are regulated on this principle, the metrical shapes of the parts in between can pass unnoticed, only provided that the actual period is not shorter than the ear expected or longer than the strength and the breath can last out.

However, the close of the sentence [*periodos, circuitus*] in my opinion requires even more careful attention than the earlier parts, because it is here that perfection of finish is chiefly tested. For with verse equal attention is given to the beginning and middle and end of a line, and a slip at any point weakens its force, but in a speech few people notice the first part of the sentences and nearly everybody the last part; so as the ends of the sentences show up and are noticed, they must be varied, in order not to be turned down by the critical faculty or by a feeling of surfeit in the ear. (*De oratore*, 153) (Cic., *De or.* 49.191–3)

Words when connected together embellish a style if they sustain a certain symmetry....[The] shrewd orator must avoid...clauses of equal length, with similar endings, or identical cadences. (*Orator*, 365) (Cic., *Orat.* 2.81)

The arrangement of words in the sentence has three ends in view: (1) that final syllables may fit the following initial syllables [the beginning syllables of the ensuing sentence] as neatly as possible, and that the words may have the most agreeable sounds; (2) that the very form and symmetry of the words may produce their own rounded period; (3) that the *period* may have an appropriate rhythmical cadence. (*Orator*, 423) (Cic., *Orat.* 44.149)

Accordingly, just as in the realm of poetry, verse was discovered by the test of the ear and the observation of thoughtful men, so in prose it was observed, much later to be sure, but by the same promptings of nature, that there are definite periods and rhythmical cadences. (*Orator*, 457) (Cic., *Orat.* 53.178)

[The] *circuitus* [the *period*]...is carried along by the rhythm in a vigorous movement until it comes to the end and stops. (*Orator*, 463) (Cic., *Orat.* 55.187)

A frequent inquiry is whether rhythm is to be used throughout the whole sentence or only at the beginning and at the end [i.e., more or less as Aristotle had advocated]; there are many in fact who hold that it is only at the end that a sentence should be rhythmical. It is true that the end is the most appropriate place, but not the only one; for the period must be brought to a close gently, and not with a sudden movement. Therefore, since the ear is always awaiting the end and takes pleasure in it, this should not be without rhythm, but the period ought even from the very beginning to move toward such a conclusion, and to flow from the start in such a way that at the end it will come naturally to rest. (*Orator*, 475) (Cic., *Orat.* 58.199)

But, to speak and write with perfect grace, we are also advised to use iambs (de-dee) in passages of a plain, simple conversational type, and dactyls (dee-de-de) along with paeons (one long syllable and three short ones in any order) for the more elevated style. In summary, there should be a judicious mingling and blending. Without these rhythms to provide an emotional element, the words and ideas lose their strength. The beginning of the *period* should reach towards the end in a natural and smooth way, without sudden movement, so that the ear may await the end with pleasure, as the orderly line of words "is brought to a close now with one, now with another rhythmical figure."

Symmetry is another consideration that comes to us through the poets. But the prose writer is not held and should not be held to the rigidity of equally balanced *cola* and *commata*, as Gorgias believed. Variation of the *periodos* and the rhythmical *clausulae* (rhythmic ending phrases) should be sought with an air of naturalness, and Cicero suggests a number of candidates beyond the paeon foot preferred by Aristotle. The modern reader may find it difficult to appreciate how aesthetically serious a *clausula* could be. Nevertheless, be assured that *it was serious*. The imperfect *clausulae* of clumsy speakers could evoke loud derision from an audience. On the other hand, on a much noted occasion, Carbo Gracchus, a master rhetorician famous for *clausulae*, is said to have brought down the house with a ravishing, perorative, double trochee!

Commata and *cola* make up the long periods. But they can also be used alone for a punchy effect ('like little daggers') in passages of demonstration or refutation, to sharpen the pace. Interestingly, the four examples of *commata* given by Cicero are all conceptually complete sentences: *Domus tibi deerat? at habebas. Pecunia superabat? at egebas.* (Did you lack a house? Yet you had one. Was there money left? Yet you were in want.) When standing alone as complete elements with subject and verb, *commata* do not deal with the divisional requirements brought about by a 'when,' a 'because,' or a 'which.' In classical Roman rhetorical practice, a full comprehensive *period* of good length comprises approximately four *cola*, each of which consists of approximately 12 to 17 syllables, that is, a full hexameter line. But the ear wants variety, and that is why rhythms and symmetry should be used to bind together in unobtrusive ways, to give form to what might otherwise be shapeless.

* * * * *

So advised Cicero. One sees how integrated with speech and the ear he considered writing to be. Modern writers are not so intent on the tightness of that connection. It is exhausting for us to think about all the things that one would have had to think about before opening one's mouth or lifting one's pen to communicate with the visuo-audio sensitive Cicero.

Notes

1. Marrou, *A History of Education in Antiquity*, 181. Music was the study of intervals (octaves, fifths, etc.) and rhythms, which could be quite complicated and were applied to words as well as to music. Most of the material in this section on education comes from this monumental work of Henri Irénée Marrou.
2. Ibid., 265–73, passim.
3. Ibid., 268–9.
4. Ibid.,168.
5. Ibid., 168.
6. Ibid., 172.
7. Ibid., 175.
8. Ibid., 173–4.
9. Ibid., 174.
10. Ibid., 204.
11. Ibid., 242–52.
12. In Varro's case, a book's length would equal approximately 30 Loeb pages. By way of comparison, Herodotus's books are closer to 50 Loeb pages, and Quintilian's to 80. In general, the same pamphlet-like lengths would apply to all the 'book' divisions of Greek and Latin treatises. It has been suggested that the so-called books of ancient writers were whatever a scroll of papyrus could contain, and that the scroll sizes would have differed.
13. Varro, *On the Latin Language*, trans. Roland G. Kent, Loeb Classical Library (Cambridge: Harvard University Press, 2006), 1:5.
14. Ibid., 2:391.
15. Ibid., 1:271.
16. Ibid., 1:271.

17. M. C. Howatson, "Varro.," in *The Oxford Companion to Classical Literature*, Oxford: Oxford University Press, 1990.

18. Ibid.

19. Wilkinson, "Cicero and the Relationship of Oratory to Literature," in *The Cambridge Companion to Classical Literature*, 2:234–5. We are also told that Cicero's reputation endured by the sheer good luck of manuscript discovery. As for his multitudinous letters, Petrarch (in 1345) discovered a good many of them in palimpsest (the erased but still visible writing on a reused sheet of parchment, papyrus, or paper).

20. *The Oxford Classical Dictionary*, s.v. "Cicero" and "Rhetoric, Latin" (Oxford: Clarendon Press, 1949).

21. *The Oxford History of the Classical World*, 455–6.

22. Cicero, *Orator*, trans. H. M. Hubbell, in *Cicero*, Loeb Classical Library (Cambridge: Harvard University Press, 1988), 5:375–99. Also useful here was *The Oxford History of the Classical World*, 2:454–9.

23. Correlatives are pairs of words that work together, such as, '*both* this *and* that,' '*neither* this *nor* that.' There are also the anaphoric forward-looking correlatives (as in When *it* is full of vegetables, *soup* is good) and the backward-looking cataphoric correlative (as in When *soup* is full of vegetables, *it* is good). These and other rhetorical devices are useful in integrating the sprawl of a lengthy statement. They help to track meaning in an expansive word structure.

24. A much-used word referring to the ultimate and penultimate metric feet of a *colon* or *period* that by common understanding brings termination. Well into the late Latinate Middle Ages, *clausulae* operated as a kind of punctuation.

25. (1) Nunc cum
    (2) *et* auctoritatis in me *tantum* sit
    (3) *quantum* vos honoribus mandandis esse voluistis,
    (4) *et* ad agendum facultatis *tantum*
    (5) *quantum* homini vigilanti ex forensi usu prope
    (6) cotidiana dicendi exercitatio potuit adferre,
    (7) certe
    (8) *et si quid* auctoritatis in me est,
    (9) apud *eos* utar *qui eam* mihi dederunt,
    (10) *et si quid* in dicendo consequi possum,
    (11) *iis* ostendam potissumum *qui ei* quoque rei
    (12) fructum suo iudicio tribuendum esse duxerunt.

26. Cicero, *Orations: Pro Lege Manilia*, in *Cicero*, trans. H. Grose Hodge, Loeb Classical Library (Cambridge: Harvard University Press, 1959), 9:17.

27. Kenney, "Books and Readers in the Roman World," in *The Cambridge History of Classical Literature*, 2:17.

28. All of the following excerpts are from the Loeb Classical Library: Cicero, *Brutus*, trans. G. L. Hendrickson, and *Orator*, trans. H. M. Hubbell, vol. 5 (Cambridge: Harvard University Press, 1939; rev. 1988); and Cicero, *De Oratore*, trans. H. Rackham, vol. 4 (Cambridge: Harvard University Press, 1982).

References

Cicero. *Brutus.* In Vol. 5 of *Cicero.* Translated by G. L. Hendrickson. Loeb Classical Library. Cambridge: Harvard University Press, 1988.

———. *De Oratore.* In Vol. 4 of *Cicero.* Translated by H. Rackham. Cambridge: Harvard University Press, 1982.

———. *Orations: Pro Lege Manilia.* In Vol. 9 of *Cicero.* Translated by H. Grose Hodge. Loeb Classical Library. Cambridge: Harvard University Press, 1959.

———. *Orator.* In Vol. 5 of *Cicero.* Translated by H. M. Hubbell. Loeb Classical Library. Cambridge: Harvard University Press, 1988.

Howatson, M. C. "Varro." *The Oxford Companion to Classical Literature.* Oxford: Oxford University Press, 1990.

Kenney, E. J. "Books and Readers in the Roman World." In Vol. 2 of *The Cambridge History of Classical Literature.* Edited by P. E. Easterling and Bernard M. K. Knox. Cambridge: Cambridge University Press, 1985.

Marrou, Henri Irénée. *A History of Education in Antiquity.* Translated by George Lamb. New York: Sheed and Ward, 1956.

The Oxford Classical Dictionary, s.v. "Cicero" and "Rhetoric, Latin." Oxford: Clarendon Press, 1949

The Oxford History of the Classical World. Edited by John Boardman, Jasper Griffin, and Oswyn Murray. Oxford and New York: Oxford University Press, 1988.

Varro. Vol. 1 of *On the Latin Language.* Translated by Roland G. Kent. Loeb Classical Library. Cambridge: Harvard University Press, 2006.

Wilkinson, L. P. "Cicero and the Relationship of Oratory to Literature." In Vol. 2 of *The Cambridge History of Classical Literature.* Edited by P. E. Easterling and Bernard M. K. Knox. Cambridge: Cambridge University Press, 1985.

· 1 3 ·

RELAXING THE RULE

Cicero and the Developing Art Form of Letter Writing

Before Cicero, there was Plato. Plato's letters, written to his friends in Athens during his imprisonment in Sicily, established the principles of a literary letter, that is, a letter that purports to convey a not-too-personal nugget of news and information, so that it may be read by others as well as the addressee. Such a letter would have been written with some care, as well as foresight concerning word choice and sentence structures, and again, would vary in degrees of familiarity and frankness. As it usually dealt with a limited topic, it was very like a modern essay. Down through the ages, such letters in their published bulk have come to be considered a genre.

At a time of developing cultural interests, letters that had been written in the mid-fourth century BCE by Athenian Plato were destined to set the standard for admiring Latins who thought to seek literary fame by that route. There is still considerable argument about the authenticity of Plato's letters, but the majority of scholars consider at least the seventh to be truly Plato's. This several-page seventh letter document is addressed as follows: "Plato to Dion's associates and friends wishes well-being" and continues in a vein of self-justification that was destined for circulation in Athens. It was an earnest and detailed letter, though in no way intimate. Genuine or not, Plato's 13 extant letters were long treasured by the world's literary intelligentsia. As a way of addressing many on a topic of concentrated focus, letters like Plato's became more frequent after the analytic Hellenistic years. Following Cicero, we find a burst of essayistic letter writing. Amongst the works of the Roman writers—Sallust, Seneca the Younger, Tacitus, and Pliny—are letters meant to be read by many, along with their hybridizing variations: short essays, written discussions on an announced topic, and historical monographs. The epistolary form, with its cautious informality, avoids the labor of having to discourse on all the peripheral extensions of an announced topic. At the same time it offers a convenient way to zero in on a single aspect of a subject without demanding too much in the way of introductory elaboration or organized structure. In short, it is a good quick way to fire off opinions, as did, for example, Alistair Cooke in his *Letters from America* and Lord Chesterfield to his son on the art of gentlemanly conversation.

But it was Cicero (and later Pliny the Younger) who set the exemplar for Renaissance and Enlightenment epistolography—an art form destined also to become a practice exercise for teaching would-be authors how to lay out their sentences in incisive, eye-grabbing ways, and expand their versatility in matters of style. In its ideal form, the full-blown letter appealed to the intellect with its offerings of insight and personal opinion. Still, for perfection, some sense of unity was required, and with that, a show of deep concentration. Wit was a welcome element. Until telephones, emails, and texting demolished the habit, one took time over the writing of such letters, for *one's words were the measure of one's worth* (which might still, alas, be the case today). Within the boundaries of a context familiar to both correspondent and recipient, transmission processes could be relatively informal.

Cicero's letters were saved after his death by Tiro, his secretary, whose skills seem to have included a self-devised shorthand, which itself suggests a high speed of dictation on the part of his master. The circumstances in which these letters were composed are not known, though as one leafs through them today, varying degrees of off-the-cuff brevity (suggesting haste) and *periodi*city (suggesting cogitation) lead one to imagine the possibilities. Cicero's letters to his friend Atticus range from urgency to speculation, from familiar to formal, and their long life in the precincts of literature set high standards. Many of Cicero's letters to his brother Quintus also survive, as do those to others. In total some 2,000 remain extant. Given Cicero's versatility with language, we are not surprised to see even the simplest of thoughts articulated facilely and with wit. What *may* surprise is to find Cicero himself, amongst family and close friends, so engaging, gentle, fun-loving, and lively. Quintilian, his subsequent literary admirer, tells us that Cicero, "the Prince of Orators," was regarded by some as being unduly addicted to jests, not only in private but in his public speeches as well. He was, wrote Quintilian, highly amusing. "Both in his daily conversation and in his court debates and examinations of witnesses, he produced more witty remarks than anybody."[1]

The first of the following excerpts comes from the tail end of a long, long letter (who would have time for so many pages today?), full of advice and gossip, to his younger and only sibling, Quintus, who, having been posted to Gaul in service to Caesar, has left his family more or less in the charge of Cicero. It is an intimate letter. We see here a moment of playfulness, conveyed in a relaxed but eloquent word-flow and cadenced in an almost conversational style. In it, Cicero refers to his brother's son, also called Cicero, who (being probably adolescent) has a voracious appetite. With bracketed explanations and modern punctuation, the passage is herewith translated word for word to elucidate its closeness to the tempo and word order of natural speech.

> Cicero as you ask, I love, both as he deserves, and as I ought. However I am sending him away from me, both lest from his teachers I should lead him away, and because [his] mother from Portia never departs [*that is, his mother is going away to stay with Portia*] without whom [*the mother*] the voracity of the boy I tremble at. But we are together nevertheless very much. I have answered to all things, my sweetest and best of brothers. Goodbye.[2] (Cic., *QFr.* 3.9.9)

Here now is an excerpt from a letter to his friend Volumnius, for which the structure becomes rather involved. As always, once outside the family circle, formalities tend to gather. The translation is again word-for-word.

> But nevertheless all things to me will be, if you come, cheering; yet you come, as you yourself understand, in of maximal almost confluence of business to do, which if as we would wish we will accomplish, I truly a big farewell to the forum will say, and to the senate house, and live with you much and with those common to both of us loving.[3] (Cic., *Ep. Fam.* 7.23.2)

In other words: I'll be happy to see you, but I'm going to be horribly busy untangling my affairs so that I can say good-bye to the forum and Senate and free myself to spend much more time with you and our dear friends [preferably at a much later date]. The construction of such an intricate sentence—one so carefully concocted both to inform tactfully, yet soothe with compliment—necessarily involves some nimble forethinking. But that was no problem for Cicero.

In Cicero's letters we find the real man. His private language, when freed of high formality, flows to fit the nature of his intent, whatever it may be. When he is not modeling himself for posterity, he becomes the consummate correspondent. Full of intellectual energy, he fills the pages with humor, personal opinion, unembarrassed affection, and gripe. He is, in short, totally capable, and when all is said and done—*whoever would have thought it?*—really quite lovable.

Sallust: Man of the Hour

An antidote to Cicero's complex 'middle-style' soon came along. Though Sallust (86–34 BCE) was younger than Cicero by some 20 years, he married the divorced Terentia (after her long marriage to Cicero),[4] and with that, set up shop to become a literary figure too. Being both intellectual and a man of action (like Cicero and so many of their aristocratic coevals), Sallust served Rome variously as soldier, politician, loyal adherent to Caesar, and finally, at the end of his life, as writer and historian.[5] Always something of a rebel, he rejected both Cicero's so-called 'middle-styled' expansive, rolling *periods*, as well as the tame standardizations of vocabulary and syntax that were beginning to come into fashion. Wanting to be different, exciting, and colorful, Sallust developed his own style, a style that soon became famous for its pungency and addiction to novelty. He modeled himself after Thucydides (whose daring linguistic experiments and compacted expression he quite rightly admired) and Cato (whose archaic language was seen to ring of truth-telling and founding fathers). While Sallust claimed to have done the research for his works carefully and conscientiously, inaccuracies throughout his histories are well noted. He professed impartiality without actually practicing it; for Rome's growing political corruption made him furious, and his depictions of it are clearly exaggerated and biased. Nevertheless, Sallust wrote with a literary masterfulness. And the language he used to do so was un*periodic*, un-Ciceronian, and in general suggestive of a bouncier, off-the-cuff, ear-bound way of putting words together.[6]

Cranky as well as inventive, Sallust showed an almost aggressive fondness for *and*-ridden parataxis. His abrupt asyndetic lists were in imitation of oral spontaneousness with all its hesitations and sudden afterthoughts—which, of course, shocked literates who had been educated to admire rolling, pre-thought-out *periodic* structures. Surprise was a favorite Sallustian tactic. Yet, however outrageous and irrepressible he may have seemed, he made good sense. Sallust, more than any other contemporary writer, prevented the clever, word-packed elaborations of Cicero from becoming canonical for all subsequent writers of prose. With his coined words, archaicisms, staccato phraseology, lurching structures, and a syntax reflecting a strong vernacular influence, Sallust extended the horizons of Latin prose and enriched it at a time when it was most in danger of becoming imitative and artificial.[7]

In the following excerpt, Sallust is (typically) putting a new spin on the heroics of the ancient Hellenes. He has told his readers that the Greeks had brilliant historiographers (namely Herodotus, Thucydides, and Xenophon) *to exalt their merely so-so deeds.* His own compatriots could (and did) do equally courageous things, he wrote, but, being modest and more given to action than words, Romans felt that their own brave deeds should be lauded by others rather than by themselves. In the lines below, Sallust describes the virtuous Romans of Cato's earlier time, before military success had created too much wealth, and wealth too much leisure. Along with his quirky rhythms to express all this, Sallust moves the old-hat mix of rhetorical ploys (antitheses, tautological couplings and triplings) into utilitarian wordage and sentence structures so uncomplicated and direct that inflection seems almost unnecessary. The first sentence, which has been translated word-for-word (with clarifying modern punctuation to illustrate how 'natural' the language is), will illustrate the straightforwardness of his word order. Though his novelties attracted attention and stretched the linguistic potentials of Latin, his adherence to the basics of rhetorical habit held all in place. Note the antithetical pairings *at home/militia, concord/avarice, laws/nature,* and the parallels *justice/goodness* (a case of semantic rhyming), and so on. Despite this bow to rhetorical convention, the purport of the statement and its stabbing sentence structures were intended to shock. And they did. Sallust's confrontational stance in these matters was the notable first move in an evolving corrective readjustment of Cicero's smooth and ornamental mechanisms. His incisive, freer prose style pushed Latin's literary pendulum back towards Atticism. A sample with its Loeb punctuation follows, after the first word-for-word sentence.

Accordingly, at home and in the militia good morals were cultivated, the greatest concord the least avarice there was, justice and goodness among them not by laws more than by nature prevailed. [*The passage now continues more gracefully under Mr. Rolfe's guidance.*] Quarrels, discord, strife were reserved for their enemies; citizen vied with citizen only for the prize of merit. They were lavish in their offerings to the gods, frugal in the home, loyal to their friends. By practising these two qualities, boldness in warfare and justice when peace came, they watched over themselves and their country.[8] (Sall. *Cat.* 9.1–3)

The term natural word order has been mentioned before, but perhaps needs to be pinned down more firmly. Its goal, in short, is to set forth clearly what is wanted to be conveyed by means of simplifying the presentation. By eschewing syntactical artistry, natural word order offers a more direct route to immediate understanding. It is what we use when we are (1) our most relaxed selves; or, (2) feeling an urgent need to be understood, as in a military action, or in a medical emergency. Sallust's move towards a more natural and orally inspired syntax brought relief from complexity, while his attraction to abstruse vocabulary remained a problem for those not quite up to it.

Sallust's work—despite accusations of his being called "a debauchee, a gormandizer, a spendthrift, and a tippler," as well as "an ignorant pilferer of the archaic language of Cato"[9]—came to be considered classic, a paradigm for 'How to do it.' Being readable and punchy instead of glitteringly complicated, he was avidly read through subsequent years and was immensely influential in the output of many diverse writers. With the exception of Cicero, he came to be the most cited of any Latin prose author. As in the case of so many undocumented female helpmates, we know very little about Terentia, except that she seemed a veritable fountain of literary inspiration, is thought to have been the daughter of Varro, and had a hankering for cash. We shall meet again with Sallust shortly.

Catching Up on Matters of Style

Fifth-century sophistic doctrine and Athenian democracy had put rhetoric at the center of classical education and thereby enhanced the natural volubility of the Greeks. Later, during the litigious, pre-Caesar heyday of the Republican Roman Senate, eloquent rhetoric (in Latin, this time) peaked again, but not for long. In both cases, the decline of democracy and the rise of imperial governments discouraged public deliberation of issues and thereby altered the character of oratory. The common populace was no longer invited to participate as a working partner in the highly charged cut-and-thrust of a political debating event. With fewer sparkling samples to inspire, high style gave way to vernacular habit and a more natural word order took hold. Defiant young writers came to view the art of ancient rhetoric as static and rarified, a lifeless bag of rules preserved as an expensive pedagogical subject, whose long lists of components were actually a detriment to *what they wanted their words to mean*.

In our Roman scene, even before Cicero had closed his mouth, the plain, middle, and grand styles were giving birth to sundry, equally fertile, hybrids—each with its tangle of specifications to complicate the studies of young would-be rhetoricians. One gets a sense of the developing profusion from Dionysius of Halicarnassus, the specialist of style, who arrived in Rome about 30 BCE, a decade after Cicero's demise. As something of an Atticist by nature, Dionysius was delighted to find that Roman lucidity was superseding the "brainless" dithyrambic prose of contemporary Greeks, who had by then, he claimed, fully embraced ornamental Asianism. Dionysius favored sensible prose, but when it came to writing it down, he followed the 'sophisticated' eastern habit of *not leaving spaces between words*. He was used to it, one imagines. Or perhaps he thought cramming more elegant. In any case, with his authority magnified by his divine Greekness, he set a bad example, because of which he is considered to have contributed to the full return of *scriptura continua* in Latin manuscripts.

For modern readers Dionysius is not an easy man to follow. Fortunately, there is no need to summarize in these pages his views on propriety, nor his analysis of the emotional impact of syllable quantities, the moral propensities of vowels, or word lengths in relation to their meanings. But a brief inspection of what the early big guns of rhetorical chat-rooms thought about the multiplying options for style is relevant to literary history. Down which of so many garden paths should student writers be urged to go?

Theophrastus (Aristotle's disciple) had kicked off with a list of four crucial qualities for every style: correct diction, lucidity, propriety, and ornamentation. The Stoics came up with brevity, to which they added charm, grandeur, and force. Demetrius (advocate of self-supporting vaulted domes, whose little textbook *On Style* is our only surviving detailed example of all this refined chatter) described his favorite four style options: the grand, the plain, the elegant, and the forceful. Then, in a final push for the season's championship, he also defined the faulty opposites of those choices (i.e., the frigid, the arid, the affected, the repulsive) in terms of form, content, diction, and word arrangement, for each of which he recounted many applications. The grand style should apply its rich diction and elaborate sentences to the narrative of battles and cosmic myths; the plain style to ordinary life; the forceful style to anger and invective; and the elegant style to the poetry of Sappho, to love, wedding songs, and garden roses. In writing letters to friends, he held that one should not set down pompous tracts or disjointed conversational talk. A letter should reflect the character of the writer, but keep to the propriety of its form. Demetrius, as we see, had many *many* ideas. They simmered along with all the other now-lost ideas about the Optimal Style, for the world of his time was truly interested in all this.

From Dionysius of Halicarnassus we learn that Lysias (the admired, unassuming, and straight-to-the-point Attic orator of classical times) had the essential charm but lacked grandeur and force; whereas Thucydides and Herodotus had grandeur—but of the two, Thucydides was the more forceful and Herodotus the more charming.[10] An approximate contemporary, Longinus (author of the influential *On the Sublime*), laid his money, as did Cicero, on Demosthenes. Demosthenes was the truly, truly most sublime. Dionysius agreed.

In the late second to early third centuries CE, we find Hermogenes of Tarsus, who in his *On Types of Style* picks up the conversation (in Greek) more or less as his predecessors had left it. His influence on the medieval view of these matters was fated by quirk of rediscovery (like Cicero's) to be both profound and lasting. The subject had enlarged only a little in the lost interim (at a minimum, figure two additional styles per century), for Hermogenes (again, no great innovator) could come up with only *seven* ranks of authorial considerations, though he wrote about them all expansively. They were clarity, grandeur, beauty, speed, ethos, verity, and brevity (the last being his own personal stumbling block).

One would have thought that the sheer boredom of categorizing all the vaporous properties of style would have laid the topic to rest forever. *But no.* There is something about tedious lists of literary considerations that *wants* to survive, and therefore does. Their appeal will still be strong in seventeenth-century England. Writers of that era had an erudite mastery of the classical languages that allowed them to consult, query, ponder, and admire the advice of these long-dead rhetoricians. The reverence for ancient precepts at a time when English was gathering its own linguistic confidence would substantially affect the future of English pedagogy.

Sampling the Output of Less Privileged Classes

It is interesting to speculate on the literary accomplishments of the late BCE Romans who were less privileged, or perhaps less inclined to pore over their wax tablets in the schoolroom. We are fortunate to have an example. It comes from the *Bellum hispaniense*, an account of Julius Caesar's campaigns in western Spain, written not by the elegant Caesar, but by one of his men, an officer in the field. The Loeb introduction to this little volume claims it to be "perhaps the most illiterate and exasperating book in classical literature"—in short, a treasure. Aside from the grammatical infelicities (which are rife), the literary style is uninstructed and monotonous. Colloquial expressions mix with exalted quotations from Ennius (the revered poet of early Roman times) and Homer. The word choice is dull as well as repetitious—*bene* (for 'very' or 'goodly') being a common example and unpleasantly remindful of Cato's avoidance of charm.

The following lines will give a flavor. Since the official translator was really too kind, herewith is a more direct English translation, with the word order mildly readjusted for modern ease of understanding. In the endnotes for this chapter, the punctuation of the Loeb Latin text has been removed (in order to play fair with history); but the verbs, which offered definitive deciphering clues to ancient readers, have been italicized. In the Loeb's translated English below, the word groups have been comma-ed off.[11]

> As we were approaching, when out of the town came a very big multitude intending to cut to pieces the cavalry, the riders, as we wrote above, descended from the horses and made such a big battle that out of an infinite number of men few got back to the town. (Caes., *BHis.* 4)

In the Latin endnotes excerpt, the adjectives with their nouns are generally juxtaposed, or nearly so—an unsophisticated structure by the rules of literary Latin. No subliminal urges for high style inform the retelling of this event—which, if you think about it, must have been rather spectacular. Except for the placement of *cum* (meaning 'when') in the second Latin line, the language is straightforwardly simple, the phrases internally compact to the degree that one might imagine them having been hastily spoken. The feel of the total is jumpy. The core message of these lines is merely that *a huge crowd came out of the town to fight but the dismounted [attacking] cavalry made such a fight that very few got back into town.*

Urgent messages and family letters are more likely to reveal natural language habits than are official reports of battle, where the officer-writer is subject to *at least some* literary self-consciousness as he reports to his superior. To give a feel for the difference that unself-consciousness makes, below is a portion of a CE second-century letter (recently dug up, with many others) at Vindolanda, a key site along the Roman northern frontier in England before the construction of Hadrian's Wall. All of the Vindolanda letters were written with stylus on thin tablets of waxed birch wood, alder, or oak, and reveal in their directness and formulation a considerable awkwardness of expression. Understandably, with the primitive instruments at hand, one did not wish to exclaim over colorful sunsets or how restorative the drenching Northumberland rains were to the sinuses. The literary levels of the correspondents did not invite gabble, though there is a range of difference amongst them.

The following is a portion of a letter (the first two of four tablets) from someone named Octavius to someone (possibly his brother) named Candidus. The matter under discussion is of urgent importance to Octavius, a fact that should have encouraged him to express his wishes with all the clarity that he could muster. That the letter is so lacking in this respect seems rather sad. Octavius, who probably stopped school well before finishing his grammar years, was counting on his recipient's knowledge of the context to fill out the meaning. Though the complete picture is sketchy, the details as given make the urgency clear.

The word-by-word sequence brings out the simplicity of this basic piece of correspondence. One should note that the end-of-line cuts do not represent any intended grammatical or rhetorical phrasings. They are there only in response to the recalcitrance of the original writing materials. In its original form, the spaces between words are in no way as apparent as they appear to be in the original Latin below.[12]

i

Octavius to his brother Candidus
Greetings.
For Marinus the hundred pounds of sinew
I will settle up and from the time when about
this matter you wrote no mention
to me he made several times to you
I wrote that ears of grain I have bought

about *modii* five thousand on ac
count of which money to me is necessary
unless you send me some of the money

                    ii
at least five hundred denarii the future
is that what deposit I gave I shall lose
denarios about three hundred and I will be embarrassed
thus I ask as soon as possible
some money to me send and the hides you write [about]
are at Cataractonium write
that they be given to me and the wagon about which
you write and what might be in that wagon
to me write already that I would have sought out
except that the beasts I did not care to injure
while the roads are bad see with Tertius
about the money...

                    i
octavius candido fratri suo
salutem
a Marino neri pondo centum
explicabo e quo tu de hac
re scripseras ne mentionem
mihi fecit aliquotiens tibi
scripseram spicas me emisse
prope m(odios) quinque milia prop
ter quod (denarii) mihi necessari sunt
nisi mittis mi aliquit (denariorum)

                    ii
minime quingentos futurum
est ut quod arre dedi perdam
(denarios) circa trecentos et erubes
cam ita rogo quam primum aliquit
(denariorum) mi mitte coria que scribis
esse Cataractonio scribe
dentur me et karrum de quo
scribis et quit sit cum eo karro

mi scribe iam illec petissem
nissi iumenta non curavi uexsare
dum viae male sunt uide cum Tertio
de (denariis)...

Without punctuation or the constancy of word order and word separation, the sense is not quickly accessed by an 'outsider.' Nevertheless, we may imagine brother Candidus hard at work upon receipt of his letter, sounding out the words as he recognized them, identifying the verbs and then the word groups—and perhaps wishing that Octavius had stuck it out another year with his teachers. It is impossible for us to know how difficult to read the message might have seemed to Candidus. Though undoubtedly representative of the commoners' habits of his day and presumably intelligible to him, it is plainly *not* the polished Latin of the literates of that period.

The Senecas

And now back again to Rome. The pre-Augustan decades had been marked by a reinforced tendency to regulate the rules of rhetoric. As a result, speechmaking lay beyond all claim of spontaneity. By the early CE years, however, the serious subject matters for declamation that Cicero had practiced (both in Greek and in Latin and well into old age) had yielded to the easier subjects that prosperity inspires. Politics and philosophy gave way to fun. Like charades or a sing-song around the piano, declamation contests became the highlight parlor focus of a social occasion. Emboldened by wine no doubt, participants strove to demonstrate their skills at argument and persuasion. In such a festive atmosphere, the old-fashioned Ciceronian school-exercise topics for debate—topics that had dealt with law, war, religion, and aesthetics—were dropped for more titillating subject matter. Among the subjects on which party guests might debate were murders, disinheritance, the rights of nasty stepmothers, mistaken identities, captured maidens, the punishment of pirates, and so on—all of which tended to turn intellectual verbal sparring into performance extravaganzas that had less and less to do with the somber stuff of government and law, and more and more to do with tear-jerking, hair-raising, psychological dilemma.

The published *Controversiae* and *Suasoria* (arguments and advisements) of Seneca the Elder (55 BCE–39 CE) were essentially his remembrances (requested by his sons) of the exercises in declamation that he, as a well-known rhetor, had known (or invented) and taught in past years to relieve the tedium of professional pedagoguery and lure dull students out of their stupors. The original intention of declaiming workouts was to hone the arguing and persuading skills that a youth was expected to master for a career in the Senate or the courts of law. The historian Suetonius (a plain-styled writer of the late first century CE) tells us that in earlier times teachers of rhetoric would review fine speeches with regard to their rhetorical figures, incidents, and illustrations. Sometimes they would translate Greek works, and praise or censure distinguished men. Suetonius continues:

> [They would] compose narratives sometimes in a condensed and brief form, again with greater detail and flow of words. Sometimes they would translate Greek works, and praise or censure distinguished men. They would show that some practices in everyday life were expedient and essential, others harmful and superfluous. Frequently they defended or assailed the credibility of myths, an exercise which the Greeks call "destructive" and "constructive" criticism. But finally all these exercises went out of vogue and were succeeded by the debate.[13] (Suet., *Rhet.* 1.25)

Concerning those judicial and political debates, Suetonius continues with some interesting pedagogical examples that were used to stir up practice argument. Here is one:

> Some young men from the city went to Ostia in the summer season, and arriving at the shore, found some fishermen drawing in their nets. They made a bargain to give a certain sum for the haul. The money was paid and they waited for some time until the nets were drawn ashore. When they were at last hauled out, no fish were found in them, but a closed basket of gold. Then the purchasers said that the catch belonged to them, the fishermen that it was theirs. (Suet., *Rhet.* 1.25)

And another:

> When some dealers were landing a cargo of slaves from a ship at Brindisium, they dressed a handsome and high-priced young slave in the amulet and fringed toga [the dress of a freeborn youth of good family] for fear of the collectors of customs, and their fraud easily escaped detection. When they reached Rome, the case was taken to court and

a claim was made for the slave's liberty, on the ground that his master had voluntarily freed him.[14] (Suet., *Rhet.* 1.25)

With such fictions to debate, inanity was only a step away. Declaiming objectives deteriorated yet another notch, shamelessly turning the action into party games with topics suitable for a modern soap opera. A quick glance at one of these inglorious but popular contesting exercises will render the general flavor. Herewith is the case of "The Blind Mother Who Would Not Let Her Son Go," recorded by Seneca the Elder. For this, the thesis is: Children must support their parents, or be imprisoned.

A man with a wife and son by her set out abroad. Captured by pirates, he wrote to his wife and son about a ransom. The wife's weeping blinded her. She asks support from her son as he goes off to ransom his father; she demands that he should be imprisoned because he will not stay.[15] (Sen., *Controv.* 7.4)

Once the case is stated, the to-ing and fro-ing begins. One team defends the mother, the other argues for the son. Stupid remarks fly amongst the wiser ones. Says Buteo, a player on the son's team and speaking in character for the son: "At least I shall pluck out my eyes—so that I shan't have done less for my father than a wife did for her husband." (To be fair to his memory, it should be added that in the prefaces to his *Controversiae* and *Suasoria*, Seneca the Elder wrote in an easy, incisive prose, and also developed far saner themes for declamation.)[16]

In an atmosphere so densely unrealistic, old-fashioned Roman good sense paled, as had the Greek in its own time of excessive wealth and extravagance. But just as all seemed hopelessly unreal, Seneca's son, Seneca the Younger (4 BCE—CE 65), rose to his feet and called for a turnabout. Like his father, he too was devoted to the art of word usage, but fought for a serious, no-nonsense practice of it. Drawing on Sallust's example of half a century before, this Seneca Junior cut free from the rules and courtesies of earlier rhetorical habit and set out—a rebellious youth—on his own rough path. Highly inventive and blessed with a probing mind, he developed a style that, while brash, got quickly to the heart of matters. His direct manner appealed especially to the young, who were getting rather fed up, one imagines, with all the prancing about that they were supposed to be doing. In any case, suddenly, there he was—Seneca the Younger—under the spotlight, cheered by his contemporaries, and tushed by his elders.

Young Seneca was against the edicts of the older classical prose writers; against their labored progressions of smooth flowing, integrated sentences; and against their tedious trappings of connective particles, transitional structures, hierarchies of clausal architecture, and the required invention of *sententiae*, whose concisely stated generalities, like maxims, were considered the proof of one's wit. Possibly his only bow to the rhetoric his father had approved was the respect he showed for metrical clause endings (*clausulae*) with their powers of marking a cadence. Generally, his was the voice of speech—a farrago of questions and personal remarks, interspersed with jabs of sarcasm. Disdaining the rules of old-fashioned rhetoric (except for the *clausulae*), he kept his own sentences short and staccato. (Their energies are alive today. Indeed, for the young in heart, much of his writing is still fun to read.) A favorite Seneca Junior ploy was to juxtapose discordant materials for their shock value; and to draw metaphors from unpoetic areas such as military life, commerce, and medicine (remindful of T. S. Eliot's stark "patient etherized upon a table"). And that was not all. Young Seneca addressed his audience using the inflection for the second-person singular.[17] Using the familiar form *thou* for *you* would have been similar to our modern, informal custom of calling someone by his first name and discarding the titular Professor, Honored Guru, General, Mr., Mrs., Doctor, etc. *So crass*, said the friends of his parents. *So over-familiar!*

But for those who rather like this younger Seneca, the judgment can be that he wrote what he wrote in the language and style of a person intensely focused on matters of personal intellectual interest. His work is jumpy and shows him to have been a man of high irritability, an intense infighter over specific issues rather than a purveyor of panoramic views and a builder of big sentence structures to contain them. His gift lay in crystallizing his convictions with a few memorable words—a very Attic/Stoic thing to do—and delivering them in hot, on-off, speech-like, extemporaneous spurts. His favorite medium was the essay-letter, in which he could freely argue some few selected points.

His *Epistulae morales* (*Moralistic Letters*), addressed to his indulgent and philosophical friend from Naples, Lucilius, make up the extant collection of 124 short (three or four pages each), vibrantly oral (close to everyday speech), informal, and often combative treatises with titles like "On Drunkenness," "On Rest and Restlessness," "On the Natural Fear of Death," "On the Value of Advice," and so on. The following samples will demonstrate his distinctive quality, for Seneca was like no other:

You tell me (you say) to shun the crowd, to withdraw, to find my satisfaction in a good conscience? What happened to those famous [Stoic] doctrines of yours which tell us to die while doing? Really! Do you think that I am advising you just to be lazy? I have hidden myself away and barred the door for one reason only: to help more people. No day of mine expires in idleness; I claim possession of part of the nights for my studies. I leave no time for sleep; I only collapse under it. My eyes weary, they drop with sleeplessness, yet still I hold them to their work. I have withdrawn my presence not just from mankind but from business, my own business above all. My deals are done for our posterity.[18] (Sen., *Ep.* 8.1–2)

And again:

Nowadays, however, to what a stage have the evils of ill-health advanced! This is the interest which we pay on pleasures which we have coveted beyond what is reasonable and right. You need not wonder that diseases are beyond counting: count the cooks! All intellectual interests are in abeyance: those who follow culture lecture to empty rooms, in out-of-the-way places. The halls of the professor and the philosopher are deserted; but what a crowd there is in the cafes![19] (Sen., *Ep.* 95.23)

And later (about writing):

What is more unbecoming than the words, "A stream and a bank covered with long-tressed wood"? And see how "men plough the channel with boats and, touring up the shallows, leave gardens behind them." Or, "He curls his lady-locks, and bills and coos, and starts a-sighing, like a forest lord who offers prayers with down-bent neck."…Or, "A Genius could hardly bear witness to his own festival"; or "threads of tiny tapers and crackling meal"; "mothers and wives clothing the hearth."

Can you not at once imagine, on reading through these words that this was the man who always paraded through the city in a flowing tunic?…

And again:

"Just as luxurious banquets and elaborate dress are indications of disease in the state, similarly a lax style, if it be popular, shows that the mind (which is the source of the word) has lost its balance. Indeed you ought to wonder that the corrupt speech is welcomed not merely by the more squalid mob but also by our more cultured throng; for it is only in their dress and not in their judgments that they differ....

Let us now turn to the arrangement of words. In this department, what countless varieties of fault I can show you! Some are all for abruptness and unevenness of style, purposely disarranging anything which seems to have a smooth flow of language. They would have jolts in all their transitions; they regard as strong and manly whatever makes an uneven impression on the ear. With some others it is not so much an "arangement" of words as it is a setting to music; so wheedling and soft is their gliding style. And what shall I say of that arrangement in which words are put off and, after being long waited for, just manage to come in at the end of a period? Or again of that softly-concluding style, Cicero-fashion, with a gradual and gently poised descent, always the same and always with the customary arrangement of the rhythm! Nor is the fault only in the style of the sentences, if they are either petty and childish, or debasing, with more daring than modesty should allow, or if they are flowery and cloying, or if they end in emptiness, accomplishing mere sound and nothing more.

Some individual makes these vices fashionable—some person who controls the eloquence of the day; the rest follow his lead and communicate the habit to each other. Thus when Sallust was in his glory, phrases were lopped off, words came to a close unexpectedly, and obscure conciseness was equivalent to elegance.[20] (Sen., *Ep.* 114.5–17)

Lucilius, a patient man some 10 years younger than his irascible correspondent, was also the recipient of Seneca's *Quaestiones naturales* (*Questions about Nature*), set in the form of letters (again, each on a single topic), in which Seneca discusses such phenomena as comets, meteors, mirrors, oceans, earthquakes, and death. Seneca begins by telling Lucilius (rather vehemently) of his life-long addiction to natural philosophy:

If I had not been admitted to these studies it would not have been worthwhile to have been born. What reason would I have to be glad that I was placed among the living? In order that I might digest food and drink? In order that I might stuff this diseased and failing body [Seneca was always ailing], which would soon die unless it were filled continuously—and that I might live as an attendant on a sick man? In order that I might fear death, the one thing for which we are born?[21] (Sen., QNat. 1.4)

From another essay:

Now let us dismiss our teachers and begin to move on our own as we pass from what is agreed upon to what is doubtful. What is agreed upon? It is generally agreed that a lightning bolt is fire....[22] (Sen., QNat. 2.21)

And with that, he's off again, racing right to the point.

Seneca's epistolary attacks can be found in other of his essayistic pieces, such as his *Moral Essays*, or *Dialogi*, where he maintained his sharp edge by adopting a dialogue format: in which he rebutted the argumentative protests of a shadowy second person. It is sad that none of his oratory has survived. It would have been fun to watch him blow up a crowd. But even without that pleasure, we have much to rejoice over. Like a fly trapped in amber, young Seneca's verbal pungency, with all its jarring effects, is fixed in the body of extant Latin literature to stir complacent minds forever. His output was destined to be enormously influential throughout the subsequent centuries, to be taken up as front-page news in England's linguistically attentive seventeenth century. It was because of his acidulous, jagged mannerisms (often referred to as the 'pointed style') that the term 'Senecan' came to replace the term 'Attic.'

Led by Young Seneca, other masters of what C. S. Lewis called 'the verbal coup de théâtre' found fame in this period. Amongst them, most notably, was Young Seneca's nephew Lucan, 'the gloomy epigrammatist.'[23] With the confidence of youth and blue blood, these new-styled writers showered their wits and humors across a tired landscape and brought it to life again. By teasing and attacking the pomposity and rigidities of established literary regulation, they did it a timely service. It was they who rendered the written Latin language more flexible, more easy-going and natural—indeed, stretched it to simulate the vibrancy of lively conversational speech, a goal of Plato so long before.

Notes

1. See Quintilian, *The Orator's Education*, trans. H. E. Butler, Loeb Classical Library (Cambridge: Harvard University Press, 1985), 2:439–41.
2. Cicero, *Cicero: Letters to Quintus, Brutus, and Others*, trans. D. R. Shackleton Bailey, Loeb Classical Library (Cambridge: Harvard University Press, 2002), 28:610.

3. Ibid., *Letters to His Friends*, trans. W. Glynn Williams, Loeb Classical Library (Cambridge: Harvard University Press, 1979–83), 2:96.

4. Apparently, before shedding her, Cicero had disliked Terentia for some 10 years, and, moreover, was suspicious of her being dishonest in money matters (*The Oxford Classical Dictionary*, s.v. "Cicero").

5. Sallust was in fact the inventor of the historical monograph: that is, a short treatise on a specific historical topic, as opposed to the customary sweep of topics. The authenticity of his two extant letters (*Epistulae*) is not certain.

6. Despite Sallust's popularity and his obvious gifts, the conservative Quintilian in later years "expressly warns orators against taking him as a model." J. C. Rolfe, introduction to his translation of *Sallust*, Loeb Classical Library (Cambridge: Harvard University Press, 1931), xiv.

7. Rolfe, introduction to *Sallust* 1, xvii. See also F. R. D. Goodyear, "Sallust," in *The Cambridge History of Classical Literature*, 2:277–80.

8. Sallust, *Sallust* (*The War with Catiline*). trans. J. C. Rolfe, Loeb Classical Library (Cambridge: Harvard University Press, 1931), 17.

9. Suetonius, *On Grammarians*, in *Suetonius 2*, trans. J. C. Rolfe, Loeb Classical Library (Cambridge: Harvard University Press, 1997), 401.

10. D. C. Innes, "The Literature of the Empire," in *The Cambridge History of Classical Literature*, 1:648.

11. Appropinquantibus ex oppido bene magna multitudo ad equitatum concidendum cum *exissent* loricati ut supra *scripsimus* ex equis *descenderunt* et magnum proelium *fecerunt* sic uti ex infinita hominum multitudine pauci in oppidum se *reciperent*. Caesar, *The Spanish War*, trans. A. G. Way, Loeb Classical Library (Cambridge: Harvard University Press, 1955), 3:316–17.

12. Alan K. Bowman, *Life and Letters on the Roman Frontier* (London: British Museum Press, 1994), 84, 136–8, and 164.

13. Suetonius, *On Rhetoricians*, in *Suetonius 2*, trans. J. C. Rolfe, Loeb Classical Library (Cambridge: Harvard University Press, 2001), 417.

14. Ibid., 2:417–19.

15. Seneca, *Declamations*, trans. M. Winterbottom, Loeb Classical Library (Cambridge: Harvard University Press, 1974), 2:85–7.

16. C. J. Herington, "The Younger Seneca," in *The Cambridge History of Classical Literature*, 2:511–14. Seneca's style in his prefaces represents the beginning transition from the Ciceronian *periodic* to the sharper, shorter 'pointed style.'

17. Ibid., 2:511–19.

18. Seneca, *Epistulae morales*, 8.1–2. Translation taken from Herington, "The Younger Seneca," in *The Cambridge History of Classical Literature*, 2:518.

19. Seneca the Younger, *Epistles*, trans. Richard M. Gummere, Loeb Classical Library (Cambridge: Harvard University Press, 1925), 3:73.

20. Ibid., 3:303–13.

21. Ibid., *Natural Questions*, trans. Thomas H. Corcoran, Loeb Classical Library (Cambridge: Harvard University Press, 1971), 1:5.

22. Ibid., 1:107.

23. C. S. Lewis, *The Discarded Image* (Cambridge: Cambridge University Press, 1994), 29.

References

Bowman, Alan K. *Life and Letters on the Roman Frontier*. London: British Museum Press, 1994.

Caesar. Vol. 3. of *The Spanish War*. Translated by A. G. Way. Loeb Classical Library. Cambridge: Harvard University Press, 1955.

Cicero. *Letters to Quintus, Brutus, and Others*. Translated by D. R. Shackleton Bailey. Loeb Classical Library. Cambridge: Harvard University Press, 2002.

———. Vol. 2 of *Letters to His Friends*. Translated by W. Glynn Williams. Loeb Classical Library. Cambridge: Harvard University Press, 1979–83.

Goodyear, F. R. D. "Sallust." In Vol. 2 of *The Cambridge History of Classical Literature*. Edited by P. E. Easterling and Bernard M. K. Knox. Cambridge: Cambridge University Press, 1985.

Herington, C. J. "The Younger Seneca." In Vol. 2 of *The Cambridge History of Classical Literature*. Edited by P. E. Easterling and Bernard M. K. Knox. Cambridge: Cambridge University Press, 1985. Seneca's style in his prefaces represents the beginning transition from the Ciceronian *periodic* to the sharper, shorter 'pointed style.'

Innes, D. C. "The Literature of the Empire." In Vol. 1 of *The Cambridge History of Classical Literature*. Edited by P. E. Easterling and Bernard M. K. Knox. Cambridge: Cambridge University Press, 1985.

Lewis, C. S. *The Discarded Image*. Cambridge: Cambridge University Press, 1994.

Quintilian. Vol. 2 of *The Orator's Education*. Translated by H. E. Butler. Loeb Classical Library Cambridge: Harvard University Press, 1985.

Rolfe, J. C. Introduction to his translation of *Sallust*. Loeb Classical Library. Cambridge: Harvard University Press, 1931.

Sallust. *Sallust (The War with Catiline)*. Translated by J. C. Rolfe. Loeb Classical Library. Cambridge: Harvard University Press, 1931.

Seneca. *Declamations*. Translated by M. Winterbottom. Loeb Classical Library. Cambridge: Harvard University Press, 1974.

———. *Epistulae morales*. Translation taken from Herington, "The Younger Seneca." In Vol. 2 of *The Cambridge History of Classical Literature*. Edited by P. E. Easterling and Bernard M. K. Knox. Cambridge: Cambridge University Press, 1985.

Seneca the Younger. *Epistles*. Translated by Richard M. Gummere. Loeb Classical Library. Cambridge: Harvard University Press, 1925.

———. *Natural Questions*. Translated by Thomas H. Corcoran. Loeb Classical Library. Cambridge: Harvard University Press, 1971.

Suetonius. *On Grammarians*. In Vol. 2 of *Suetonius*. Translated by J. C. Rolfe. Loeb Classical Library. Cambridge: Harvard University Press, 1997.

———. *On Rhetoricians*. In *Suetonius* 2. Translated by J. C. Rolfe. Loeb Classical Library. Cambridge: Harvard University Press, 2001.

· 14 ·

LATIN PICKS UP STEAM

A Word or Two About Historiography

The word 'historiography' has developed new aspects of meaning over recent centuries. Modernly, it also includes the study of the methodology of historians and the development of history as a discipline. But its original and still-used meaning, *the writing of history* (Greek: *historia* 'history' or 'narrative'; *graphia* 'writing'), is the one that we shall be concerned with as we continue our story.

It is interesting to consider the different levels at which history may be written: from terse chronicles of notable events to the broader scopes of interpretation, where imagination, philosophy, and psychology play a part. One thinks of Thomas Carlyle's *The History of the French Revolution* and Thomas Macaulay's *History of England*, in which so much is made of so few absolute 'facts.' How best to report an event is a tricky problem, for there are so many ways. To what degree should the historian attempt to describe or interpret the causes of that event, or the circumstances surrounding it, or the subsequent human reactions to it? Are there lessons to be learned from it? Once the facts are there, ramifications of it naturally develop. That an earthquake kills 2,037 Kyrgyzstan peasants may be a fact, but as the event is presented for others to visualize, learn from, appreciate, or assess effectively, a fuller picture of the scene can be considered appropriate. According to Aristotle, an imagined expansion of detail will be acceptable if it is in keeping with *what might have been*. Thus, Thucydides's renditions of leadership speeches were legitimate in that they truly represented what Pericles or any of the other speechmakers might well have said under the circumstances. Anyone who recounts 'what happened' will be tempted to depict things *beyond what he actually knows or saw*, and to expand in accordance with *what might well have been*. The historiographer is particularly tempted to convey 'the whole scene'—both action and reaction—and from that to reach a broader public than can the 'historian researcher.' The historiographer is an interpreter. He reconstructs with credible likelihood. He is anxious to involve the reader in *what the event was like to experience*, and for that will choose to be a little less tangled in scholarly fastidiousness than is the 'academic historian.' That exercise of the imagination was a significant part of Roman historiography. The flying leap from the hardcore facts to credible likelihood was what made the historiographer's life so agreeably replete with opportunity both to teach and persuade.

There is little pleasure to be had in reading the works of the archaic Latin annalists, who year by year recorded the names of magistrates and events of cult importance. Such brief and date-ridden preciseness tends to be dry as toast. In ancient Rome—even down to the mid-second century BCE (Cato's era)—annalistic records remained more skeleton than flesh. Julius Caesar's mid-first century BCE *On the Gallic War* was more discursive and hence is more interesting to read. Yet Caesar's Attic clarity and much admired directness of expression leave modern appetites for 'reality' unsatisfied. *So much has been left unsaid*. What rich views of military life in early Gaul we might have had if Caesar had bothered to describe what his foragers had looted from village households, what crops they stole or set fire to in the fields, and what livestock they rustled. A reader cannot satisfactorily visualize the scene or appreciate the soldierly struggles without access to a richer array of particulars than Caesar was prepared to divulge. *What a loss!* He could have provided us with a host of missing facts and impressions. A reader, so far away in space and time, longs to know details—details of troop quarters, their jokes, songs, pastimes, and medical treatments; the commissarial and latrinal aspects of Roman camp life. When women were amongst the *impedimenta*, what passions raged in their domain? Was it a hive of squabble and jealousy, birthing howls, and the whines of small children? We are given no such details. Instead, Caesar wrote tersely of the struggles of bridge building, the habits of druids, and the general characteristics of Gauls and Germans. He tells us of grim, muddy marches to undefined places under conditions of blizzard or threat of ambush, and the sudden flooding of rivers unknown to us and never to be mentioned again—all of which, though interesting and informative to a degree, fails to enmesh us in the experience. Though his account is informative, we are left *lacking in satisfaction.*

Historiography thrives in an atmosphere of literacy and literature. It blossomed in Greece and in Rome as their languages developed and writing skills became more facile. As Olde England stumbled towards full-blown literacy, so their tight-lipped annalists yielded to laconic historians (like Bede), who in turn would yield (as had Tacitus) to the fuller historic treatments that linguistic and literary confidence encourages. The general reader of history today wants 'the whole experience'—a full picture, including surmises and likelihoods, of what happened and why: a truth for which the success of Hilary Mantel's *Cromwell Trilogy* bears witness. A glance at the *Anglo-Saxon Chronicle*, on the other hand, gives us a good idea of how tedious and skimpy annalistic history can be. Think what the historiographers Thomas Macaulay and Ms. Mantel might have made of the following entries (both given *in toto,* with the numerals marking the date):

> 958. Here in this year Archbishop Oda divorced King Eadwig and Aelfgifu because they were related.[1]

Or again:

> 978. Here in this year all the foremost councilors of the English race fell down from an upper floor at Calne, but the holy archbishop Dunstan alone was left standing upon a beam; and some were very injured there, and some did not escape it with their life.[2]

What most delights the general public are the details that support and illuminate an actual happening. Details give the sense of real life; whereas the mere chronicling of an event and a roll-call of its participants, though it may answer a query, will read like nothing more than a laundry list. With sound literary instincts, a gifted historiographer can 'bring a fact to life.' Only then, will Joe Average be willing to turn the page. That human yearning for fullness of detail (imagined or factual) was being well satisfied by the time that Augustus ruled over the Roman Empire.

As had Lysias, Sallust too recognized a popular interest in the mini-details of human life and (with the inspiring Terentia at his side) trained himself to exploit it. Despite his own various faults as a proper historian, he was in fact a lively depicter of character. His studies of Catiline, the suspected traitor, and Sempronia, the wanton, conniving wife of a Roman big shot, very definitely militate against a sound historical balance. Described with a vocabulary that is more acid than neutral, his portrayals etch unforgettable imprints on the reader's mental template. They are trenchant and gripping; but because they lack history's necessary cool, the basic truth of them is suspect. Sallust's introduction of Catiline reads in the Loeb translation as follows:

> In a city so great and so corrupt Catiline found it a very easy matter to surround himself, as by a bodyguard, with troops of criminals and reprobates of every kind. For whatever wanton, glutton or gamester had wasted his patrimony in play, feasting, or debauchery; anyone who had contracted an immense debt that he might buy immunity from disgrace or crime; all, furthermore, from every side who had been convicted of murder or sacrilege, or feared prosecution for their crimes; those, too, whom hand and tongue supported by perjury or the blood of their fellow citizens; finally, all who were hounded by disgrace, poverty, or an evil conscience—all these were nearest and dearest to Catiline.[3] (Sall., *Cat.* 14.1–4)

Gripping indeed, though the excess renders it suspect.

In the following Sallustian sample—his assessment of Sempronia—the balance of vituperation and admiration allow some credibility.

> Now among these women was Sempronia, who had often committed many crimes of masculine daring. In birth and beauty, in her husband also and children, she was abundantly favoured by fortune; well read in the literature of Greece and Rome, able to play the lyre and dance more skillfully than an honest woman need, and having many other accomplishments which minister to voluptuousness. But there was nothing which she held so cheap as modesty and chastity; you could not easily say whether she was less sparing of her money or her honour; her desires were so ardent that she sought men more often than she was sought by them. Even before the time of the conspiracy she had often broken her word, repudiated her debts, been privy to murder; poverty and extravagance combined had driven her headlong. Nevertheless she was a woman of no mean endowments; she could write verses, bandy jests, and use language which was modest,

or tender, or wanton; in fine, she possessed a high degree of wit and of charm.[4] (Sall., *Cat.* 25)

Though we read this with interest and are pretty much persuaded by the argument, we are still reluctant to bet on the pure truth of it. Sallust's strong personality is too much a participant.

Rome's interest in psychology derived from the Alexandrian focus on analysis and particularization, initially applied to textual matters. By the first century BCE, Roman sculptors were well into detailed and realistic replication. Eschewing the standardized paradigms of Eastern statuary, they had begun to depict individuals as they were. Puckered brows and retreating hairlines, warts, uneven alignment of features, worry lines, and bulbous noses—all became acceptable in the name of accuracy, for they bespoke the inner man and highlighted his individuality. Though overshooting the goal of true depiction, Sallust, too, sought to portray the differing details of character. Where we have seen Thucydides eliminate all signs of messy emotion, we now see Sallust and shall shortly see Tacitus pumping them back in. Their efforts were directed towards presenting a full 'reality'—with selective but 'likely' additives.

The many letters that survive from the first century BCE sustain the view of an enlarging focus on human variety. They conjure up a landscape of multitudinous personalities, sensibilities, and temperaments. They reveal an interest in people's characters and habits along with speculations as to what prompted them to be as they were.[5] In sum, the focus of artistic energy had moved from the stern religious ideals (of such as Cato) to the complexities that underlie appearances. Experiences and emotion were now seen as part and parcel of the total man; and because the language had sufficiently developed, their effects could be, and were, described in writing. Until the end of the nineteenth century when Leopold von Ranke persuasively recommended the use of primary sources only, historians more or less fed off the inherited materials of previous writers. A new account of 'what happened' required little more than a reinterpretation of a previous interpretation, with the addition of stimulating sideshow description. But the real success for those early historians lay mostly in the beauty of their writing. The more elegant the style, the more the result was acclaimed and accepted as true. We realize today, of course, that whatever historical 'truth' an author may choose to report, his selection of detail and even the order or choice of his words will tend to distort it. The interpreting human will always infect 'the truth,' for there is no keeping him entirely off the court.

It is hard to accept as *absolute fact* any historiographic episode; for in the mere setting down of 'what happened,' the historiographer begins to select. Since he or she cannot cover everything, some details must be left untouched, no matter how significant they might actually be. Too much description will always overwhelm the core report. The writer must choose, and what he/she chooses to describe may, simply by being mentioned, take on unwarranted emphasis. Whereas older practitioners laid claim to things they could never have proved and could almost be said to have written historical novels, modern historiographers have largely cleaned up their act. If they are smart and wish to be approved by fellow craftsmen, critics, and the public, they do not eliminate facts inconvenient to their thesis nor rearrange the sequence of events to suit their argument (as we shall shortly see Livy doing), for they are pretty sure someone will catch them out. The world of today wants history to deal in certifiable facts, not rich stories à la MGM. With outlooks so changed it is difficult to appreciate how much those old-timer historiographers were honored and believed. Yet they were—and all on *the grounds of their style and the swell of their narration*. Style was the historian's outstanding legitimate prerogative. For the great Aristotle had spoken thus: in telling a story, or giving an account, 'one could praise someone for doing something, even if there were no evidence, if he were the kind of person *who might have done it*.'[6] Still, the borderline between what has *actually been said* and what was *merely implied* is often hard to ascertain.

As grammatical elements settled and writing became more facile and ambitious, so style became more important. By the Augustan era, Roman historians were deeply engaged with matters of literary eloquence and beauty. Historical accounts were judged by the rhetorical charm they displayed. Until Leopold von Ranke's 'first-sources' edict, considerations of style would continue to magnetize the attentions of historians.

Livy as Historian-Historiographer

Titus Livius, or Livy (59 BCE–CE 17) first came to the profligate city of Rome as a talented, studious, well-heeled young man, trailing clouds of provincial austerity, idealistic dreams, and hopes for personal fame. Yet, as he dug into his new life, he found himself more and more appalled at the city's moral laxness. The impieties of those luxury-wallowing cosmopolitans shocked him. Worrying that their spendthrift wantonness might lose Rome her primacy amongst nations, he determined to reverse the situation with his pen. His personal wealth and high literary qualifications gave him a footing in the cultural life of the city, and before long his youthful public readings gained approval in imperial literary circles. The Emperor Augustus, a stoic idealist himself, was attracted by Livy's sterling northern character. He approved Livy's ambitious proposal to recount *with morally corrective intentions* the vast sweep of Rome's past, from its humble beginnings to its current gilded heyday. He agreed that a well-told saga, recalling Rome's ancient glories, the courage and sacrifices of the men who had made her great, might well inspire her arrogant, slothful, contemporary citizens to higher purpose.[7] The benefits of historical study, said Livy, lie in its application to life, in learning through examples of good and evil to make better choices and wiser decisions.

Livy was not a political animal. He was more of an academic interpreter of the doings of other people—an appraiser of good and bad. He had neither military credentials nor a grounding in political connivance. Unlike his predecessors—Thucydides, Demosthenes, Xenophon, Cato, Caesar, Cicero, Sallust—he could not speak from a background of practical experience. As a result, his writings show no familiarity with the inner workings of Roman government, no trace of personal political motive, no advocacy of policy, nor even much use of available government documents.[8] Unlike Thucydides, he did not view the writing of history as a disinterested and meticulous account of events, but rather as an exhortation to learn and improve. His use of secondary sources (often in preference to available original ones) and his reliance on 'information' from previous histories were not conducive to recounting what we think of as Actual Facts. His work, *Ab urbe condita* (*On the Founding of the City*), gives us a specimen view of the broad boundaries allowed to the working historian of his time.

As we see from his opening statement, Livy was well aware of the massiveness of his project. A modern reader of Livy is impressed by his conscientious authorial stance at the opening of his great work, for he begins with a modest assessment of what degree of success he might have. His tentative tone engages our interest. He opens his preface as follows, with the customary *period:* [Please ignore the Loeb punctuation.]

Whether I am likely to accomplish anything worthy of the labour,
if I record the achievements of the Roman people from the foundation
of the city, I do not really know, nor if I knew would I dare to avouch
it; perceiving as I do that the theme is not only old but hackneyed,
through the constant succession of new historians who believe either
that in their facts they can produce more authentic information, or
that in their style they will prove better than the rude attempts of the
ancients. Yet, however this shall be, it will be a satisfaction to have
done myself as much as lies in me to commemorate the deeds of the
foremost people of the world; and if in so vast a company of writers
my own reputation should be obscure, my consolation would be the
fame and greatness of those whose renown will throw mine into the
shade....[9] (*Livy*, I.1–3. Preface)

But what a nice man! We like this gentleman from the start. His task is so
huge. He does not know if he can manage it. Yet he will try. He will rely on
the power of his pen to make *his version* of the oft repeated account of Rome's
rise to greatness more vivid and more readable than had others before him.
And, indeed, this is what he did. The result of his efforts was a beautifully told
but unabashedly Augustan version of the way glory had come to Rome and
was likely in the future to fade unless society got a grip on itself.[10]

Livy's task required tremendous feats of imagination. Nevertheless, he
laid into the job with gusto. He opened his saga with the resurrection of
shadowy figures out of Rome's legendary past. Under his spell, Romulus
emerges from the mists of oral lore as a genuine person, a man of feeling,
courage, and forethought. Once he has polished off his twin brother Remus,
Livy turns him into a respectable figure, an alert and cunning leader, who
labors for the safety of his people in a hostile environment. Livy remodels
the Sabine women, too. He endows them with strong affections, as well as
the courage to stand up to their menfolk for the sake of peace. He transforms
them from screaming armloads of female flesh into sensitive human beings
with worries and griefs, with decisions to make and children to care for. In
elaborating the received wisps of legendary 'fact,' Livy held himself rigorously within the Aristotelian boundaries of psychological likelihood and withal
depicted a more complete and more likely rendition of how matters might
really have been.

Unlike the trenchantly positive Sallust, Livy made efforts to deal, both
equally and fairly, with heroes and villains alike. His readers will sense a prob-

ing after motive, a psychological interest in his characters' composition of faults, virtues, and ambitions under the pressures of circumstance—all those aspects of human reality that we now expect to read about when we pick up a history book. Here, by way of example, is Livy's famous description of Hannibal, Rome's preeminent and traditionally hated enemy. Had Sallust put his hand to Hannibal's portrayal, he would have made him an unmitigated villain. Livy's more equable portrayal rounds him out and makes of him a genuinely possible human.

> With Hannibal there was no campaigning that year. For neither did he invite attack, owing to his very recent wound...nor did the Romans provoke him so long as he remained inactive; such power they believed to be present in that one commander, even though everything else round him crashed. And I am inclined to think he was more marvelous in adversity than in success. For here he was, carrying on war in the enemy's land for thirteen years, so far from home with varying fortune, having an army not made up of his own citizens but a mixture of the offscourings of all nations, men who had in common no law, no custom, no language, differing from each other in bearing, in garb, in their arms, differing as to religious rites, sacred observances, one might almost say as to their gods. Yet he somehow bound them together by a single bond, so that no outbreak ensued among the men themselves nor any mutiny against their general. Yet in the enemy's country both money to pay them and supplies were often wanting—deficiencies which in the previous Punic war had given rise to many unspeakable acts on the part of commanders and soldiers....[W]ho would not find it a marvel that there was no outbreak in his camp? For added to everything else was this also, that he had no hope even of feeding his army except from the Bruttian region; and even supposing all of it to be under cultivation, it was nevertheless too small to feed so large an army. Moreover a great part of the young men, drawn off from the farming of the land had been claimed instead by the war and by their custom of training soldiers through brigandage, a practise viciously inbred in their nation. Furthermore, nothing was being sent from home, since they were concerned about their hold upon Spain, as though everything was succeeding in Italy.[11] (*Livy*, 28.12.1–9)

And so, with this outpouring of reasoned surmise, instead of an unequivocal villain we are shown an enemy of mysterious charisma—which, indeed, would seem more likely to have been the case.

Equally important to Livy's lasting reputation was his literary showmanship, for that was what imprinted his historical characters on the reader's mind.[12] His 'pictured prose' reveals a craftsman, daring yet restrained, skilled in variation, both in word use and in sentence structures; and more impressive yet, in his broadminded justification for the driving incentives of Rome's enemies. *Who were all these people? And why did they do what they did?* In accomplishing his feats of vivification, Livy availed himself of a range of rhetorical ploys. To fit the scenes of time long past, he used antiquated or poetic idiom. Again, if the speakers were from the lower classes, he would use coarse, provincial, and colloquial forms, or even words never found in classical prose authors but verified by the slave-talk found in the plays of Plautus and Terence.[13] In episodes of high drama, he would elevate his prose to near poetry. As his account progressed towards his own era, so his language subsided to levels more in keeping with contemporary usage, though he would still rework a known speech in order to emphasize some feature of the character he was dealing with. His vocabulary was astonishingly wide-ranging. Says *The Cambridge History of Classical Literature*: "Certainly no other Roman historian was so inventive."[14]

Livy pays close attention to the structure of his history. Given the length and breadth of it and the some-46 years that it took him to write it, one is not surprised to find that the style and internal arrangement of the 142 books (each ranging in the area of 100 Loeb pages and possibly even then unfinished at the time of his death at the age of 76) are not firmly the same. But with all its inner variations, the whole of it conforms with the Ciceronian requirements of varying color, appropriate words, and smooth and equable diction.[15] All in all, Livy's prose style was conservatively classical, for unlike Sallust or Seneca the Younger, Livy was an admirer of Cicero. It was Cicero who had claimed that, while the rhetorical rules that governed oratory must pertain in all subjects, both written and spoken, history—with all its mystique—was the one that was most demanding of eloquence. Livy seems to have taken this judgement to heart.

Livy launches new episodes with a series of complicated *periods* to describe the place and participants that he intends to discuss. He then jumps into the short, staccato sentences required by Aristotle for a *narratio*. Though Livy's *periods* are less formal, less driven by rule than those of Cicero, they are fully as intricate. Like so many of his literary forebears, Livy too stretched the power of his language with inventions of grammatical and syntactical elements.[16] For all these reasons, critics consider him a master of the Latin language. He is especially noted for his skill in shaping the emotional aspects of events and protagonists to fit his moral theme. Bringing events and people to life with psychological understanding and vivid description was to be his gift to historiographic tradition.

Livy covered the legendary founding and settlement of Rome in five- and ten-year segments. Each segment was dominated by a famous ruler or general, crisis or war, in keeping with old-fashioned, Latin annalistic custom. Later, when events led him into the confusions of his own time zone, he worked in larger thematic patterns: collecting disparate characters and far-flung incidents within the magnetic field of a prominent personage's character trait. Thus, for example, he tailored events to mesh with the 'ferocity' of Tullus Hostilius, the 'piety' of Camillus, the 'perfidy and impetuosity' of Hannibal, and so on. In handling themes in this way, he was responding to Aristotle's edict: art must mold the raw minutiae of history to secure a natural and logical flow in the narrative "so that each event seems to be motivated by its predecessor"—a very literacy-motivated instruction.[17]

Aristotle's authoritative mandate, which favored smooth, logical flow over historical exactitude, gave Livy license for fictional rearrangement and sequencing, for it diminished the necessity of recording time, place, or even character, with precision. As a result, Livy could, and did, mold his materials to fit his line of argument. Examples of Livy's molding efforts are ubiquitously manifest. The protagonists of early BCE years give detailed, entirely improbable Ciceronian orations whose content was sometimes (unlike Thucydides's renditions of speech-making) plainly out of keeping with historical likelihood. For the sake of character development, Livy allowed them to speak both indirectly and directly when in action.[18] Again, Livy showed prominent figures instigating things that they did not in fact instigate; he made the plague a direct cause of the Romans' inability to help their allies, which it was not; he modified actual dates where necessary, so as to smooth the sequence of events. He melded separate campaigns into one and eliminated altogether events and people that did not fit his patriotic scheme.[19] History, by Livy's rule, was driven by personality, and it was towards the revelation of personality that he focused his art by vigorously entering into the spirit of his characters.

Livy's success was both immediate and lasting. In his own era, his rich style, his un-Sallustian equability, his generosity, high-mindedness, and wisdom were perceived as the critical marks of a fine writer. He was praised by the aging Seneca, and later by Quintilian, Tacitus, and Plutarch. Eventually, an admiring Dante would refer to him as the man 'who did not err'; even Machiavelli would honor him.[20] Livy has generally been recognized through the ages as one of the world's great writers, and praise for his prose style can be found again and again in modern critical writings. His colossal masterpiece, *Ab urbe condita* (*On the Founding of the City*) became the standard source book from which future writers would draw their ancient materials. As a model for written prose, Livy's great history would come to share with the poet Vergil's *Aeneid* the honor of being the most widely read of Latin literary works.

By today's standards, of course, Livy was deficient in the essential requirements for the proper writing of history. He was not sufficiently critical. Where art collided with fact, he favored art. He was indifferent to original documents (*pace* von Ranke), many of which he could have consulted in the archives, particularly those pertaining to the more recent events of his day. His references to previous, perhaps more factual, annalists were casual. Nevertheless, the power of his story and the style of his prose were formidable. Withal, Livy changed the course of history for many centuries into the future. Any number of annalists could have told us what the Romans did; but, as Mr. Foster (in his introduction to the Loeb volumes of Livy) reminds us: it required genius to make us realize, as Livy does, what sort of people the Romans really were. "The People and the State are idealized no doubt by the patriotic imagination of this extraordinary writer,—but a people's ideals are surely not the least significant part of their history."[21]

Quintilian: The Rhetorical Peacemaker

During the first two hundred years CE—the so-called 'Second Sophistic Age'—a number of books and essays about rhetoric and famous rhetoricians were put forth. Out of these, a few survivors came to be studied, often diligently, throughout the Middle Ages, and in time influenced the course of English literary expression. Crucially important for its stabilizing response to Senecan radicalism was Quintilian's *Institutio oratoria* (*Education of an Orator*) in 12 books (each about 100 Loeb pages long), which was written post-Nero and post-Seneca the Younger, during the approximate years of 93–94 CE, after its author's long career of practicing law and teaching rhetoric in Rome.[22] The announced intent of this expansive treatise (like that of Cicero's *Orator* from which it draws admiringly) was to survey earlier well-known orators and writers in terms of their success and education, and to draw lessons therefrom for future rhetorical instruction. Actually, the volumes constitute the happy amalgam of a handbook on rhetoric and a treatise on the functions and goals of an orator, into which discussions of education and literature are generously blended.[23]

Having first cautioned his publisher, Trypho, to make his copies of the manuscript as correct as possible—for this was always an issue—Quintilian comes to the core of his subject: the training of an orator, which, oddly, we are told *must begin before birth*. For the parents—*yes, Mother, too*—must be educated first. That done, the couple may have a child, a boy-child if possible, so that Quintilian may more easily settle into his topic of 'boyhood education.' Apart from his suggestion that parents of a newborn baby hunt down the rhetorically ideal wet nurse for it—one who is, amongst the customary essentials, a moral philosopheress and an impeccable articulatrix of language—Quintilian imparts commonsensical advice—advice that is quite in keeping with modern perceptions.[24] Genial, wise, and moral in tone, the *Institutio* brought fresh popularity to Ciceronian graces, though it was in no way slavishly Ciceronian. Within its pages, Quintilian expounds no major revision of rhetorical theory. He himself writes with an easy elegance that leans towards the more traditional style, yet urges clear steerage between the possible extremes. Thoughtful and balanced though he was, Quintilian could on the rare occasion succumb to the pressures of too much to say. When that happened, his thoughts remained inextricable from the syntactic pileups. Though narrow in many respects and never the equal of Cicero for depth of analysis, Quintilian remained the quintessential authority on prose expression for many centuries, most particularly from the fifteenth to seventeenth centuries, when critics and pedagogues seemed to find a special rapport with his precepts.[25]

Quintilian purveyed the entire spectrum of education, with all its goals and possibilities. He outlined a sound intellectual training from inception to early adulthood, by which time a cultivated and aristocratic young man would have emerged to assume civic responsibility and to make a name for himself in law or politics. As we read Quintilian's opening chapters, we are impressed by how modern his pedagogical psychology seems. Such broadmindedness was the fruit of his long experience as a teacher. His mellow judgments seem as applicable today as they undoubtedly were in that first century after Christ.

Some hold that boys should not be taught to read till they are seven
years old, that being the earliest age at which they can derive profit
from instruction and endure the strain of learning....Those however
who hold that a child's mind should not be allowed to lie fallow for
a moment are wiser....I am well aware that during the whole period
of which I am speaking we can expect scarcely the same amount of
progress that one year will effect afterwards. Still those who disagree
with me seem in taking this line to spare the teacher rather than the
pupil. What better occupation can a child have so soon as he is able
to speak? And he must be kept occupied somehow or other. Or why
should we despise the profit to be derived before the age of seven,
small though it be? For though the knowledge absorbed in the previous years may be but little, yet the boy will be learning something
more advanced during that year, in which he would otherwise have
been occupied with something more elementary....

I am not however so blind to differences of age as to think that the
very young should be forced on prematurely or given real work to do.
Above all things we must take care that the child, who is not yet old
enough to love his studies, does not come to hate them and dread the
bitterness which he has once tasted, even when the years of infancy
are left behind. His studies must be made an amusement: he must
be questioned and praised and taught to rejoice when he has done
well; sometimes too, when he refuses instruction, it should be given
to some other to excite his envy, at times also he must be engaged in
competition, and should be allowed to believe himself successful more
often than not, while he should be encouraged to do his best by such
rewards as may appeal to his tender years.[26] (Quint., *Inst.* 1.1.13–20)

In the ninth book of the *Institutio*, Quintilian settles his attention on the interesting topic of textual division (punctuation), analyzing its benefits from a grammatical (logical) angle, but just as often euphuistically (rhetorically), in terms of
beguiling harmonies and rhythms. With benign diplomacy, he embraces both aspects for cadencing. He describes a *comma* as the expression of a thought lacking
rhythmical completeness (that is, it needed no ending *clausula*), though generally
writers up to his time had described it as only a portion of the *colon*. A *colon*, he
said, was "the expression of a thought which is rhythmically complete (with a
clausula), but...meaningless if detached from the whole body of the sentence." (It
is thus no longer a complete short sentence.) The *periodos*, meanwhile, could be

simple, i.e., a single thought, or a composite of thoughts conveyed in *commata* and *cola*, of such length as can be fueled by a single breath. Donning his logical cap, Quintilian added: "It is further essential that it (the *periodos*) should complete the thought which it expresses…be clear and intelligible and (pure Aristotle!)…not too long to be carried in the memory."[27] As for how to signal the completion of the sense, Quintilian recommended a verb wherever possible, as it is in the verbs that the real strength of language resides. But even this goal must give way (here, the euphuistic cap) to the demands of rhythm. Hyperbaton (the transposition of idiomatic word order) is a useful device where the selected word is recalcitrant to meter; however, (again, the logical cap) we should never abandon what is apt to our theme for the sake of smoothness.[28] Once the verb has been chosen, the *periodos* may round off to a close with a metronomical arrangement of rhythms (a *clausula*) to indicate that the group of thoughts has reached its natural limit and that a breather is being provided before recommencement of play. Additionally,

> not only must *commata* and *cola* begin and end becomingly, but even in parts which are absolutely continuous without a breathing space, there must be such almost imperceptible pauses. Who, for example, can doubt that there is but one thought in the following passage and that it should be pronounced without a halt for breath? Animadverti, iudices, omnem accusatoris orationem in duas divisam esse partes [Notice, judges, that every speech of the accuser is divided into two parts]. Still the groups formed by the first two words, the next three, and then again by the next two and three, have each their own special rhythms and cause a slight check in our breathing: at least such is the opinion of specialists in rhythm.[29] (Quint., *Inst.* 9.4.67–8)

Quite correctly, Quintilian spotted the fact that speech is replete with these scarcely noticeable little pauses.[30] Should they be recognized in writing? And if so, comma-ed off in respect to meaning, or rhythm, or emphasis, or to the needs of breathing? Their placements in speech can be quite varied and will depend in large part on the speaker's idiosyncratic mannerisms. Writing, in its response to grammatical habit, often ignores them. English speech reveals their presence most particularly after the introductory particle and the rush of a prepositional phrase (both herewith italicized) as follows, for example:

> *Furthermore* (mini-pause) it is interesting to note (mini-pause) that *in the early era of mass printing* (mini-pause) they were often a target (mini-pause) *for over-enthusiastic typesetters* (mini-pause) *in Britain.*

Quintilian has interesting things to say about the matter of language. Though he showed no direct knowledge of the major Greek writers, he does not refrain from comparing the Greek language with Latin. His remarks on the harshness of Latin sounds have been noted: its awkward fricatives, persistent plosives, and conglomerations of consonants, as well as its dearth of binding vowels between words, as in Cicero's massively constructed sentence beginning: 'Nunc cum' [Now since]—so ugly and awkward to say! Though Quintilian could not have known it, those word-ending vowels that bind are what make the Italian and Japanese languages so beautiful to hear. Instead, he complains that there are many things that have no Latin names, "so that it is necessary to express them by metaphor or periphrasis," whereas Greek may lay claim to an abundance of words. Furthermore, Greek is the more graceful of the two tongues; it allows for a greater delicacy of expression. *But enough of those Greeks!*

> The less help we get from our language, the more must we rely on inventiveness of thought to bring us through the conflict. We must discover sentiments full of loftiness and variety, must stir all the emotions and illumine our style by brilliance of metaphor. Since we cannot be so delicate, let us be stronger. If they beat us for subtlety, let us prevail by weight, and if they have greater precision, let us outdo them in fullness of expression.[31] (Quint., *Inst.* 12.10.36)

Quintilian, we see, is a patriot—perhaps another source of his contemporary popularity.

Continuing on to the matter of terseness, Quintilian refutes the Attic-Senecan purists who despise all ornaments in language on the grounds of their being unnatural, hence pretentious and insincere. Natural speech, says Quintilian in a cautionary remark against Seneca, is for the household. It contents itself with stark facts and the literal purpose of the mind. Though useful, that sort of talk is quite different from eloquence, and we should not confine ourselves to it alone. Nor should we, on the other hand, imitate the far-fetched phraseology once advocated by a certain class of speakers (the Asianists), who resembled poets rather than orators and regarded artificial methods of expression as positive merits. More reasonably than did Cicero, Quintilian describes a true middle way—namely, expression that delights when heard or read, yet makes plain its good sense. That kind of eloquence is granted to us, he says, from the same source as speech itself, and is therefore what should be cultivated and cherished.

One is today astonished by the intellectual agility and presence of mind demanded of ancient public speakers. It seems impossible that anyone, however alert and capacious of memory, could extemporize at the level that they seemed capable of reaching and maintaining. What is more certainly possible is that the impeccable written versions of what was said on the podium were amended afterwards for the page. "There is nothing of which our great politicians are so fond as writing speeches and bequeathing them to posterity," Socrates had grumbled in Plato's *Phaedrus*.[32]

Quintilian is unusual for his time in addressing, as well as approving, the symbiotic relationship between speaking and writing. Agreeing with Cicero, Quintilian urges that one should never for a moment be careless with language. He recommends the reading of good 'books' to acquire eloquence, and practice with a pen as well. He sees writing as related to profound thought, and the meditation required for its success as a coolant to the ardor of impulsive speech. He disparages empty loquacity and words 'born on the lips.' The practice of writing regularly in silence and seclusion, he says, will develop a resource of wisdom and well-formed expression on which to draw in the stress of speaking. "Indeed I am not sure that, if we practice both with care and assiduity, mutual profit will not result, and writing will give us greater precision of speech, while speaking will make us write with greater facility."[33]

Tacitus: The Historian-Historiographer

Tacitus (ca. 50–116 CE), who had himself been the pupil of Quintilian, was in turn the teacher of Pliny the Younger, whose writings will shortly be discussed. This trio of literary stars illumined an age of declining standards—a time of 'bad training and limited education,' as Tacitus lamented in his *Dialogue on Orators*. It was, moreover, an age that included the terrors of Nero's (54–68 CE) and Domitian's (81–96 CE) emperorships, as well as the more peaceable years of Nerva (96–98 CE) and Trajan (98–117 CE), during whose rule Tacitus's political career thrived.

Busy as he was with his onerous official responsibilities, Tacitus found time to write history, and thus to continue the line established by the notable Latin historians who preceded him: Julius Caesar, Sallust, and Livy. Tacitus shared with Sallust and Livy both a distaste for Rome's backsliding ways and an interest in the psychology of the personalities that had dominated the course of events. Tacitus was also alert to the psychology of his readers, whose instinctual appetite for the details of human travail he gratified by stepping up the lurid aspects of history's dramatic moments. His skills were spectacular. The men and women that he chose to write about were prominent figures, whom he portrayed with an impressive flourish in scenes of climactic drama.[34] Readers were stunned by his depictions of grief, passion, perversion, cruelty, and madness. *They were so real.* Rome, past and present, was replete with models for Tacitus to use.

All in all, the crown of Latin historiography belongs to Tacitus. In him are conjoined all the best of previous rivals. Unlike Livy, he was experienced in practical and civic affairs; indeed, he was one of the best civic orators of his time. He was a literary man too, highly trained and skilled in the arts of rhetoric—perhaps (so it was said), to the point of arrogance. His patriotic enthusiasms seem at times overwhelming, yet withal he maintained an objective demeanor, and "the actual facts which he record[ed] are generally accurate"—though he is known to have rearranged and highlighted certain aspects.[35] Whereas Livy had covered a more comprehensive range of historical information, Tacitus chose to focus on specific chunks of time, and sifted his source materials more selectively, shaping and introducing his 'facts' with the long-view perspective that literacy tends to develop. His discrimination proves him to have been the superior interpreter.[36] As for his style, it is helpful to remember that he lived after the time that the works of great Latin poets, dramatists, orators, declaimers, critics, and grammarians had been influencing aristocratic education for well over a century. Tacitus, in short, was riding the crest of a literary wave—a wave that would soon crash. Meanwhile, thanks to Quintilian, the antagonism between Senecans and Ciceronians had settled down, allowing new space and increased confidence for literary experimentation. The cultural climate being thus advantageous to his well-ripened skills, Tacitus bequeathed to posterity an informative view of life in Roman times, and a good read to boot.

In Tacitus's era, as well as before, writing history was considered an honorable activity. It was associated with patriotism, and offered the opportunity to nurture morals, display knowledge, and practice artistry. As such, it made a suitable pastime for ambitious, well-connected, well-heeled patriots of literary inclination. But what was history now to be? A list of facts? A chronicle of past doings? Ought it to be devoid of emotion, cleansed of authorial personality? Could it play with the imagination, as Livy had allowed? At this point, we should remind ourselves that in early Classical Greece, history had been viewed as an art form deriving from epic poetry, which was the prehistoric repository for tribal knowledge and *therefore sacred*. It still retained some of that mystical aura of eloquence and deeply felt national sentiment, *despite* the cautionary pleas for objective accuracy that had come from Thucydides and Aristotle. That is why, in Imperial Rome, history itself was generally viewed as an instructional adjunct to literature, *and in no way a science*.[37]

Realizing the power of excitement and empathetic involvement, Tacitus infused his histories with all the detail that Caesar's accounts had so noticeably lacked. By embroidering accepted facts with likely detail, he raised the level of popular interest. Separation, loss, vile weather, trickery, implacability, cruelty, and unbearable grief—all were more than just mentioned. They were described, and often described in detail. In this heightened atmosphere, Tacitus allowed his protagonists to respond both emotionally and logically to the dilemmas they faced; and by doing so, he swept his readers into full participation. His inclusion of feeling and mood into the factual sequence of historical events incited a sense of verisimilitude from which, he felt, readers could glean some helpful instruction and Rome could benefit. For like Sallust, Seneca the Younger, and Livy, Tacitus too believed that Roman morals were in need of correction. Though he certainly injected his own prejudices into his portraits of, say, heroic Germanicus and the tyrannical recluse Tiberius Caesar, Tacitus took pains to recount political and military arguments from both sides.

Tacitus played with language, much as Thucydides had done in his time, and Cicero and Livy in theirs. He experimented, condensed, expanded, invented, and shifted his style throughout his works. His various translators complain of the difficulty of rendering his Latin into English, for his language was so idiosyncratic and so terse that a "literal English translation in the same number of words is almost unintelligible."[38] Tacitus was an innovator, and clearly a consummate master of the technical aspects of the Latin language. While his style seems to shift constantly, all his writings are packed with epigrams, purple passages, alliteration, formal oratory, punchy statements, sarcasm, ironical remarks, verbal quips, and unexpected caprices.[39] In general, however, his word-flow followed traditional paths, and in his maturity, he avoided the extravagances of either Senecan roughness or Ciceronian expansiveness. All in all, he seemed mindful of what his mentor Quintilian had to say of history, which was this:

> History, which should move with speed and impetuosity, would have been ill-suited by the halts imposed by the rounding off of the *period*, by the pauses for breath inevitable in oratory, and the elaborate meth-

ods of opening sentences and bringing them to a close. It is however true that in the speeches inserted by historians we may note something in the way of balanced cadences and antitheses.[40] (Quint., *Inst.* 9.4.18) [Both Livy and Tacitus practiced this formality: in their histories, speech-makers spoke with Ciceronian completeness.]

In 98 CE, having already published (in the style of Cicero) the *Dialogus de oratoribus,* an expression of regret at the decadence of eloquence, Tacitus wrote the *Life of Julius Agricola,* a biography of his prominent father-in-law, who, as a general, had subdued Britain and become its governor. In this early short treatise of praise, we can see some reflection of the Attic mavericks, particularly Sallust, for its too-brilliant coloration, its portrayal of the stark and unsavory, the unusual vocabulary, the obvious avoidance of balanced phrases and rounded *periods,* the jumpy effects of asyndeton and short clausal structures— all of it by now popularly known as 'the pointed style.' Here, from the *Agricola,* is a sample of his early foray into style. Tacitus (though he was not there at the time) is depicting in great detail the piteous plight of the Britons after their defeat by the Romans. [The heavy punctuation is strictly modern.]

> Night was jubilant with triumph and plunder for the victors: the Britons, scattering amid the mingled lamentations of men and women, began to drag away their wounded, to summon the unhurt, to abandon their homes, and even, in their resentment, to set fire to them with their own hands. They selected hiding-places and as quickly renounced them: they took some counsel together, and then acted separately: sometimes they broke down at the spectacle of their loved ones, more often it excited them; it was credibly reported that some of them laid violent hands upon wives and children, as it were in pity. The morrow revealed more widely the features of the victory: everywhere was dismal silence, lonely hills, houses smoking to heaven.[41] (Tac., *Agr.* 38.1–2)

Tacitus described the *Agricola* as being the precursor of a projected work to be written "in artless and rough-hewn language," which rather suggests a Sallustian-Senecan treatment. But from that point on, no consistent development is discernible, for Tacitus seemed always to be striving to be different, original, and arresting in one moment, then sweeping and complete in the next, as though in reaction to the way he had just written what he had just written. Yet, as time passed, he toned down and varied the Sallustian elements he had earlier adopted. In *The Cambridge History of Classical Literature,* F. R. D. Goodyear tells us:

In general [Tacitus] avoids flat, lifeless and over-used words, and abstracts (especially when vivid and concrete synonyms are available)....Conversely, he likes words which, without being extraordinary, are yet fresh, graphic, and memorable. Tacitus [when presented the opportunity to use standard terms] sometimes replaces them simply to escape the tedium of repetition. Like most stylists, he is anxious not to bore his readers.[42]

Though Tacitus, as we see, could write with staccato abruptness, he was also known for distorting the Ciceronian *period* with appended thoughts (often in ablative absolute structures[43]) to a degree that overloaded and unbalanced its form, deliberately making what might have been graceful, lopsided and ungainly. A favorite trick was to reverse the customary sentence formula by transferring the weightier thoughts of a main clause to subsidiary clauses.[44] Tacitus is considered to have reached his best style in his *Histories* and *Annals* (the latter written at the end of his life). In both, having adapted the best of all the various styles to his own formidable individuality, he achieved the brilliance for which he is famous.

The prose tracts of Tacitus differ to accord with the varied intensity of his feelings. When relating routine business, he wrote with rapid narrative simplicity. For speeches, he diverged: his renditions of oratory contain a greater number of balanced clauses, and generally proceed in a comparatively flowing and expansive manner. He described oppression or moral decline in short abrupt sentences, in staccato phrases, in trenchant and surprising epigrams that were far removed from Ciceronian habit, let alone the common speech of his day. He could, at will, achieve a rich coloration by means of poetic clusterings, or resort to asyndeton for striking effects. His language is particularly contorted and difficult when he is himself emotionally involved, and then, his words and phrases acquire a sparkling semi-poetical quality.[45] Highly assured, Tacitus delivers his own commentary on this or that event, resorting as required to ironic comment or sarcasm, to exalted rhetoric or bossy exhortation. Variation seems a compulsion. Nevertheless, one senses that he unfailingly achieves the effects that he intended.

To illustrate one of his multifarious moments of style invention, beneath is a passage that is almost impressionistic in its dabs of informative handout. Because of that, it is difficult to interpret with precision, as can be seen in the two translations of the same passage from Book 1 of the *Annals*. The scene is the highlight moment after the golden-haired Germanicus, son of the emperor Tiberius, surrounded by his own rebellious troops and urged by his friends, decides at last that his pregnant wife Agrippina and their little son must be moved to safer places. John Jackson in the 1979 Loeb edition translates the scene as follows:

> He was long undecided, and Agrippina met the proposal with disdain, protesting that she was a descendant of the deified Augustus, and danger would not find her degenerate. At last, bursting into tears, he [Germanicus] embraced their common child, together with herself and the babe to be, and so induced her to depart. Feminine and pitiable the procession began to move—the commander's wife in flight with his infant son borne on her breast, and round her the tearful wives of his friends, dragged like herself from their husbands. Nor were those who remained less woe-begone.[46] (Tac., *Ann.* 1.40)

Michael Grant renders the same passage as follows:

> Germanicus was long hesitant. His wife scorned the proposal, reminding him that she was of the blood of the divine August and would live up to it, whatever the danger. Then he [Germanicus] burst into tears—and clasping to him the expectant mother and their child, persuaded her to go. It was a pitiable feminine company that set out. The supreme commander's own wife, a refugee, clutched his infant son to her breast. Her escorts, his friends' wives—forced to leave with her— were in tears. Those who remained were equally mournful.[47] (Tac., *Ann.* 1.40)

Both translators have remarked on the difficulties of translating Tacitus at all. It is interesting that they both ignored the use of the imperfect tense set up by Tacitus to compound the vividness of the scene: *This was happening*. Following the Latin version (with Jackson's punctuation), the same passage in a word-for-word rendition elucidates the difficulties of translation. Note the brevity of the passage: a total of seven Latin lines *vs.* 10 and 11 English ones.

> Diu cunctatus aspernantem uxorem, cum se divo Augusto ortam neque degenerem ad pericula testaretur, postremo uterum eius et communem filium multo cum fletu complexus, ut abiret perpulit. Incedebat muliebre et miserabile agmen, profuga ducis uxor, parvulum sinu filium gerens, lamentantes curcum amicorum coniuges, quae simul trahebantur; nec minus tristes qui manebant.

Diu = for a long time; *cunctatus* = he having delayed [subject]; *aspernantem uxorem* = disdaining wife [object]; *cum se* = since herself; *divo Augusto* = from divine Augustus; *ortam* = (she) risen; *neque* = and not; *degenerem* = (she) degenerate (i.e., of inferior stock, or soft); *ad pericula* = to peril; *testaretur* = (she/he) was protesting; *postremo* = at last; *uterum eius* = (her/his) belly (uterus); *et communem filium* = and communal son; *multo cum fleto* = much with weeping; *complexus* = having embraced; *ut abiret* = so that she/he would go away; *perpulit* = he/she forced. *Incedebat* [note the initiating verb!] = he/she/it was proceeding; *muliebre et miserabile agmen* = womanly and miserable group; *profuga ducis uxor* = fleeing of the leader wife; *parvulum sinu filium* = small at the breast son; [at this point the narration relaxes, to end less contortedly] *gerens* = carrying; *lamentantes* = (they) lamenting [subject]; *circum amicorum coniuges* = around of (masc.) friends mates; *quae* = who (fem.); *simul trahebantur* = at the same time they were being dragged; *nec minus tristes* = and not less sad; *qui manebant* = those who were remaining.

Agrippina was a favorite of Tacitus, as was her young husband, Germanicus. Because her life was fraught with dangers and never very peaceful, Tacitus's heroic descriptions of her tend to be gnarled in emotion. In the above passage, we are left to guess at many of the ideas suggested, for inflections, missing 'to be' verbs, and hyperbaton (shifted word order) have woven the elements of description very tightly. With Tacitus being a master hybridizer, the excerpt above gives neither a sampling of the Senecan pointed style (i.e., staccato full clauses) nor of the Ciceronian *periodic* architectures. It moves instead in a restless realm of its own, reflecting perhaps the author's tussle with his own sentiments.

So as to appreciate the vivid dramatic effects that Tacitus was able, again and again, to achieve, herewith is another passage. It too comes from the *Annals*, from the translating pen of John Jackson. We will forget linguistic gnarls for the moment and simply admire. Imagine, then, a dark plain in Germany, where battle-worn Romans are ensconced behind dirt embankments in a surround of gloomy mountain forests. The enemy occupies the dark hills above them. They have succeeded in diverting the mountain streams in order to flood the soils beneath the Roman encampment. Now restlessly, they watch for their moment to demolish the enemy for good. The time is ca. 70 CE.

It was a night of unrest....The barbarians, in high carousal, filled the low-lying valleys and echoing woods with chants of triumph or fierce vociferations; among the Romans were languid fires, broken challenges, and groups of men stretched beside the parapet or straying amid

the tents, unasleep but something less than awake....Arminius [the
German general], however, though the way was clear for attack, did
not immediately deliver his onslaught. But when he saw the [Roman]
baggage-train caught in the mire and trenches; the troops around it in
confusion; the order of the standards broken, and...every man quick
to obey his [own] impulse and slow to hear the word of command, he
ordered the Germans to break in....[Shouting insults] he [Arminius]
cut through the column with a picked band, [aiming blows] primarily at the horses. Slipping in their own blood and the marsh-slime,
the beasts threw their riders, scattered all they met, and trampled the
fallen underfoot....[Because of their greed, says Tacitus, the Germans
left the carnage to pursue the spoils and thereby gave the Romans a
moment to regroup and rebuild.] Tired as they were, a rampart had to
be raised and material sought for the earthwork; and most of the tools
for excavating soil or cutting turf had been lost. There were no tents
for the companies, no dressings for the wounded, and as they divided their rations, foul with dirt or blood, they bewailed the deathlike
gloom....[48] (Tac., *Ann.* 1.105)

Modern readers of Tacitus are often plagued by a sense of exaggerated drama,
for it is sometimes hard to accept as real the excitements or low motives being described. But to better appreciate his achievements, one should bear in
mind that historiographers of his period (like the sculptors) probably went
out of their way to emphasize the idiosyncrasies and minutiae of feature and
personality; and to invent or expand the details, *if the results were in keeping
with likelihood.* Sallust, Livy, and Tacitus—all three—had learned the lesson:
for being memorable, neither a sweeping generality nor an unexpanded hard
fact can compare with the elaboration of a well-selected detail. When handled with skill, the emotional impact can be immense. The Latin language
by the time of Tacitus was both pliable and capable. All in all, it seems quite
wonderful that he could mesh his literary heritage so engagingly with his own
contemporary, as well as modern, taste.

Tacitus was also admired—indeed, is still admired—for the *sententiae*
(aphorisms) that sparkle throughout his works. They are extremely terse, yet
noted for their polish as well as their content. Moreover, they seem true, and
in their brevity (often not more than a few words) retain both impact and
quotability. A good many remain famous today, even in English. Below are a
few samples.

Where they make a desert they call it peace. (*Agr.*, 30.4)

Discussion of rebellion is rebellion. (*Hist.*, 2.77.3)

The more corrupt a state, the more numerous its laws. (*Ann.*, 3.27.3)

Common opinion considered him capable of ruling until he actually ruled. (*Hist.*, 1.49)

The *sententiae* of Tacitus are universally considered to be the best to be found in Latin prose.

Appreciated in his own era, Tacitus was afterwards neglected, then rediscovered. By the fifteenth century, he was once again compelling the attention of scholars and thinkers, not only for his ripping accounts of historic happenings, but for his consummate style as well. He is now, of course, 'a classic'—required reading for advanced students of Latin (who must struggle, not only with the language but also with trying to keep the text, the dictionary, and the various undeclared English translations from sliding off the desk). His works are required reading as well for ancient history students (who may pleasurably and guiltlessly read him in English—and with their feet up as well).

Notes

1. George Norman Garmonsway, *Worcester Manuscript*, in *The Anglo-Saxon Chronicle*, trans. M. J. Swanton (London: J. M. Dent, 1996), 113.
2. Garmonsway, *Abingdon Manuscript*, *Anglo-Saxon Chronicle*, 123.
3. Sallust, *The War with Catiline*, trans. J. C. Rolfe, Loeb Classical Library (Cambridge: Harvard University Press, 1931).
4. Ibid., 45.
5. Betty Radice, introduction to her translation of *Younger Pliny's Letters* (London: Penguin Books, 1963), 21.
6. Aristotle, *The "Art" of Rhetoric*, 101. He was actually speaking of plots for tragic drama, but the purport of his advice was perceived to be applicable to all literary categories.
7. *The Oxford Classical Dictionary*, s.v. "Livius."
8. See B. O. Foster's introduction to his translation of *Livy, History of Rome, Book I*, Loeb Classical Library (Cambridge: Harvard University Press, 1936–1968), xxi.
9. *Livy, History of Rome*, 1:3.
10. P. G. Walsh, *Livy* (Oxford: Clarendon Press, 1974), 5. Because of his intimate friendships in high circles and the fact that his panoramic history was pointing the way towards a restoration of austerity, his detractors would accuse him of writing propaganda for the moral rehabilitation that Augustus was pressing to achieve. But this does not seem to have been

the case, for there is no sign of Livy's attempting to justify, or attack, the policies and aims of Augustus. Though always respectful, he was neither adulatory nor apologetic.

11. See Frank Gardner Moore's introduction to his translation of Livy, *History of Rome*, Book 8, Loeb Classical Library (Cambridge: Harvard University Press, 1936–1968), xxi.

12. Walsh, *Livy*, 35.

13. Two second-century BCE writers of popular comedy, and both good sources for street talk.

14. R. M. Ogilvie, "Livy," in *The Cambridge History of Classical Literature*, ed. P. E. Easterling and Bernard M. K. Knox (Cambridge: Cambridge University Press, 1985), 2:465–6. See also 464.

15. *The Oxford Classical Dictionary*, s.v. "Livy."

16. For more about Livy's style, see the analysis in Walsh, *Livy*, 23.

17. Ogilvie, "Livy," in *The Cambridge History of Classical Literature*, 2:463.

18. Walsh, *Livy*, 28, 29.

19. *The Cambridge History of Classical Literature*, 2:674.

20. B. O. Foster, introduction to *Livy, History of Rome, Book I*, xxiv.

21. Ibid., xxx–xxxi.

22. Interesting to history-of-academia buffs will be the fact that the Emperor Vespasian appointed Quintilian to the position of a salaried professor of rhetoric in Rome, ca. 86 CE (*The Oxford Classical Dictionary*, s.v. "Quintilian"). The word 'institutio' means 'a summary or plan of principles.'

23. F. R. D. Goodyear, "Rhetoric and Scholarship," in *The Cambridge History of Classical Literature*, 2:674.

24. Quintilian, *The Institutio oratoria*, trans. H. E. Butler, Loeb Classical Library (Cambridge: Harvard University Press, 1980), 1:21.

25. Goodyear, "Rhetoric and Scholarship," 2:676.

26. Quintilian, *Institutio*, 1:27–9.

27. Ibid., 3:577–9.

28. Ibid., 3:335–9.

29. Ibid., 3:545.

30. Try speaking the quoted passage aloud and loudly, as though throwing your voice to the back of a large room. You will find that you have made more pauses than you probably expected to make. 'Notice/ judges/ that every speech/ of the accuser/ is divided/ into two parts.' Somebody else might pronounce the same sentence with fewer mini-pauses: 'Notice/ judges/ that every speech of the accuser/ is divided into two parts.'

31. Quintilian, *Institutio*, 4:469.

32. Plato, *Phaedrus*, trans. B. Jowett (New York: Random House, 1937), 1:261.

33. Quintilian, *Institutio*, 4:149. We note here an echo of Cicero's comment on the mutually benefitting relationship between speech and pen.

34. Andrew Lintott, "Roman Historians," in *The Oxford History of the Classical World*, ed. John Boardman, Jasper Griffin, and Oswyn Murray (Oxford and New York: Oxford University Press, 1988), 646–50.

35. Tacitus, *The Annals of Imperial Rome*, trans. Michael Grant (London: Penguin, 1996), 20; F. R. D. Goodyear, "History and Biography," in *The Cambridge History of Classical Literature*, 2:649.

36. Walsh, *Livy*, 34.

37. Michael Grant, *The Annals of Imperial Rome*, rev. ed (1989; repr., London: Penguin, 1996), 20–1.
38. E. H. Warmington, introduction to Tacitus, *Agricola*, trans. Maurice Hutton, Loeb Classical Library (Cambridge: Harvard University Press, 1914; repr. 1980), 22.
39. Ibid., 23.
40. Quintilian, *Institutio*, 3:515.
41. Tacitus, *Agricola*, 97.
42. Goodyear, "History and Biography," in *The Cambridge History of Classical Literature*, 2:650–3, passim. This assessment tells us that Tacitus sidestepped the traditional advice repeated by his teacher Quintilian, as stated in his *Institutio* (9.4.145): "We should certainly never in our search for smoothness abandon for another any word that is apt and appropriate to our theme." Quintilian's advice is not in keeping with our modern-day preference for dodging the too-soon repetition of a potent word (noun, verb, or adjective). His statement suggests that first-century CE writers were avoiding the re-use of the same word to the degree that they needed correcting. This is the first notable evidence that 'repetition avoidance' was becoming an issue. It is known that the Classical Greeks felt no impatience if an apt word was repeated (though if repeated too often as in Cato's opening *period* or the officer's report from Spain, an awkwardness was perceived). Where we think of repeated wordage as tedious, Greeks thought it handsomely straightforward. But whether it was Tacitus who truly broke the spell is hard to say. In any case, starting from his time, prose writers often seem to be searching for a good substitute word for one that had just been used. As we shall shortly see, word variation would become a mania amongst early Celtic writers.
43. A grammatical structure containing a noun and a participle (both with ablative case endings) and used to substitute for a subordinate clause. It was a common grammatical tool, and similar to the Greek genitive absolute.
44. Goodyear, "History and Biography," 2:650.
45. Tacitus, *Annals*, trans. Grant, 25.
46. Ibid., *Annals*, trans. John Jackson, Loeb Classical Library (Cambridge: Harvard University Press, 1979), 3:313.
47. Ibid., *Annals*, trans. Grant, 56.
48. Ibid., *Annals*, trans. Jackson, 3:355–7.

References

Aristotle. *The "Art" of Rhetoric*. Translated by J. H. Freese. Loeb Classical Library. Cambridge: Harvard University Press, 1926.

Foster, B. O. Introduction to his translation of Vol. 1 of *Livy: History of Rome*. Loeb Classical Library. Cambridge: Harvard University Press, 1936–68.

Garmonsway, George Norman. *Abingdon Manuscript*. In *The Anglo-Saxon Chronicle*. Translated by M. J. Swanton. London: J. M. Dent, 1996.

Goodyear, F. R. D. "History and Biography." In Vol. 2 of *The Cambridge History of Classical Literature*. Edited by P. E. Easterling and Bernard M. K. Knox. Cambridge: Cambridge University Press, 1985.

————. "Rhetoric and Scholarship." In Vol. 2 of *The Cambridge History of Classical Literature*. Edited by P. E. Easterling and Bernard M. K. Knox. Cambridge: Cambridge University Press, 1985.

Lintott, Andrew. "Roman Historians." In *The Oxford History of the Classical World*. Edited by John Boardman, Jasper Griffin, and Oswyn Murray. Oxford and New York: Oxford University Press, 1988.

Moore, Frank Gardner. Introduction to his translation of Livy, *History of Rome*, Book 8. Loeb Classical Library. Cambridge: Harvard University Press; London, 1936–1968.

Ogilvie, R. M. "Livy." In Vol. 2 of *The Cambridge History of Classical Literature*. Edited by P. E. Easterling and Bernard M. K. Knox. Cambridge: Cambridge University Press, 1985.

The Oxford Classical Dictionary, s.v. "Livy." Oxford: Clarendon Press, 1949.

The Oxford Classical Dictionary, s.v. "Quintilian." Oxford: Clarendon Press, 1949.

Plato. Vol. 1 of *Phaedrus*. Translated by B. Jowett. New York: Random House, 1937.

Quintilian. *Institutio oratoria*. Translated by H. E. Butler. Loeb Classical Library. Cambridge: Harvard University Press, 1980.

Radice, Betty. Introduction to her translation of *Younger Pliny's Letters*. London: Penguin, 1963.

Sallust. *The War with Catiline*. Translated by J. C. Rolfe. Loeb Classical Library. Cambridge: Harvard University Press, 1931.

Tacitus, *Agricola*. Translated by Maurice Hutton. Loeb Classical Library. Cambridge: Harvard University Press, 1914. Reprinted in 1980.

————. *Annals*, Book 3. Translated by John Jackson. Loeb Classical Library. Cambridge: Harvard University Press, 1979.

————. *The Annals of Imperial Rome*. Translated by Michael Grant. London: Penguin, 1996.

Walsh, P. G. *Livy*. Oxford: Clarendon Press, 1974.

Warmington, E. H. Introduction to Tacitus, *Agricola*. Translated by Maurice Hutton. Loeb Classical Library. Cambridge: Harvard University Press, 1914. Reprinted in 1980.

· 1 5 ·

WINDING UP IN THE ANCIENT WORLD

Did You Hear From Pliny This Morning?

We have from Pliny the Younger (ca. 62–113 CE) some 247 extant letters, none of which offer the vivid personal touch, humor, or word-dexterity of Cicero. Pliny was more ponderous and guarded. Almost entirely, he wrote in the graceful, toned-down form recommended by Quintilian, and thus proceeded in the paths of *periodic* dictate with occasional forays into inappropriate, high-hat oratory. Nevertheless, says our *Cambridge History of Classical Literature*:

> By blending Ciceronian and modern ingredients Pliny created an apt medium for urbane and inhibited epistolography. In his letters we have the last flowering of classicism, before individual whim or the extravagances of the archaizers fatally infected prose style.[1]

A Pliny letter is to us a strangely disembodied object. For what purports to be a tête-à-tête communication is more essayistic than conversational, and generally encompasses only a single topic—one that has little to do with the activities or well-being of its recipient. Though friendly enough, its burden of courtesies, conceits, and uninspired philosophical commentary makes it the very reverse of intimate.

Pliny the Younger was neither a learned man (as was his polymath uncle, Pliny the Elder) nor a profound thinker. He was more of an educated literary aspirant and an earnest fan of culture. He labored over his writing and was proud to be known as an author and a close friend of Tacitus. Keen to capture inspiration whenever it should flutter by, he is said to have taken his writing materials with him wherever he went—even to the hunt.[2] One imagines him dropping out of the chase to record some beguiling phrase that had just come to mind.

Critics do not praise this Pliny for sublime thinking or beautiful prose, but rather, for having been *without major vices*. They praise him for his happy nature, for his depictions of wealthy lifestyles (he was himself extremely rich), for his dedicated love of the arts (he also wrote bad poetry), and particularly for restraining himself from using the antitheses, archaisms, mediocre epigrams, and alliterative sound effects that were dinning the air. The devices that most particularly mark his style are the two- and three-fold asyndeta: as in *quae sint inculcanda, infigenda, repetenda* ('which are to be inculcated, driven in, repeated'), and a strenuous avoidance of coming to grips with anything. He is bursting with sincere advice. More often, his efforts are concentrated on smooth phrasing, recurrent rhythmic patterns, and a well-balanced architecture of clause and *period*[3]—all the condiments for a thin slice of meat.

Overall, the difference between Pliny and his hero Cicero is more than one of genius. Where Cicero so often unlocked his heart to his correspondents in a semi-controlled blaze of emotion, Pliny—always conscious of an audience, whatever he was feeling—favored the lukewarmth of literary propriety. He not only published his letters himself, but composed them with an eye to publishing them. Though addressed to real people, they lie on the page like well-disciplined prose exercises. They fully complete the subject matter they initiate and rarely require a response. It is rather as though he were addressing a stone wall. After the opening salute, the flattered recipient—*Gee, a letter from Pliny!*—might as well be dead, for Pliny forgets him entirely as he busily sketches in the subject-to-be, then develops it, illustrates it with three examples (he liked doing things in threes),[4] and brings it to a polished close. Unlike the letters of Cicero, there is no sign of rush, ramble, passion, or after-thinking. Essayistic ambitions have replaced the human element that one usually associates with a letter from a friend.

Pliny does not grapple with hard problems, emotional or intellectual. (And one wonders how the no-longer-alive Young Seneca would have torn into him for that.) Instead, Pliny is mild-mannered and moderate in opinion—a true Edwardian gentleman, in that he keeps his distance and does not demonstrate much appetite for really anything. It would be nice if someone would discover (perhaps in the overlooked subcrypt of some musty medieval monastery) a cache of 'Passionate Pliny Productions,' but to date none have been found.[5] Nevertheless, his surviving letters are full of interest in that they contain much about the manners and habits of society in early Roman Empire times, as well as Pliny's own privileged life and deeds of generosity. We learn from his letters that he bought his old nurse a small farm; he gave money to a needy school friend, a dowry to an impecunious friend's daughter, and even a holiday abroad to a valued freed slave who was sick. He also gave enormous gifts to his hometown, Comum (Como), where he built a library and supported teachers and needy children.[6] These are the acts of a very nice man.

As a rich Roman, Pliny was acquainted with the highest and the best, the Emperor Trajan included; and his letters are a major source for the knowledge we have of custom and gossip in the late first and early second centuries CE. His attentive observations of the world around him, though presented to our modern eyes in a rather affected style, offer a fund of information—views of life in Rome that we might otherwise never have had. In the following excerpt, he describes the deplorable drop in attendance at public recitations of poetry and literary composition far more explicitly than did the young Seneca (some half century before). Pliny is astonished that literary pursuits in Rome can continue at all, when the public is so little disposed to listen to men of genius.

> Most of them sit about in public places, gossiping and wasting time when they could be giving their attention, and give orders that they are to be told at intervals whether the reader has come in and has read the preface, or is coming to the end of the book. It is not until that moment—and even then very reluctantly—that they come dawdling in. Nor do they stay very long, but leave before the end, some of them trying to slip away unobserved and others marching boldly out.[7]
> (Plin., *Ep.*, 1.13.2)

Pliny as a letter writer had no real successors in the ancient world. One will not find his true descendants until Mme. de Sévigné and Horace Walpole come along. But because Pliny's letters will be so admired in eighteenth-century England, another look at a few of his lines will be worthwhile. The following is an excerpt from a letter to Tacitus, as it appears in the Loeb edition of Pliny's letters. The Loeb translator has helped us with heavy pointing, but the Latin is easy to decipher in any case, since the word order is reasonably straightforward and the relationships amongst words and clauses plainly evident. The quoted passage is given here at some length, not only to illustrate the earnest blather of a Pliny composition, but also because his topic meshes rather neatly with discussions of style.

> I am always having arguments with a man of considerable learning and experience, who admires nothing in forensic oratory so much as brevity. I admit that this is desirable if the case permits, but if it means that points which should be made are omitted or hurried over when they should be impressed and driven home by repetition, one can only end by betraying one's client. Most points gain weight and emphasis by a fuller treatment, and make their mark on the mind by alternate thrust and pause, as a swordsman uses his steel.
>
> At this point he produces his authorities, and quotes me the Greek Lysias and our own Romans, the brothers Gracchus and Cato. It is true that most of their speeches are short and concise, but I counter Lysias with Demosthenes,…and Cato with Caesar…and above all Cicero, whose longest speech is generally considered his best. Like all good things, a good book is all the better if it is [a] long one; and statues, busts, pictures and drawings of human beings, many animals, and also trees, can be seen to gain by being on a large scale as long as they are well proportioned. The same applies to speeches; and when published they look better and more impressive in good-sized volume books, a large volume carries something of beauty and authority in its very size….
>
> Then it is argued that there is a great difference between a good speech as delivered and the written version. This is a popular view, I know, but I feel convinced (if I am not mistaken) that, though some speeches may sound better than they read, if the written speech is good it must also be good when delivered, for it is the model and prototype for the spoken type.[8] (Plin., *Ep.* 1.20.9–10)

To give a feel for the imperfect Latin-into-English exactness, below is the Latin of that above-quoted, gracefully translated, easy-flowing last paragraph. Its compacted Latinate path of some four lines needs a full six lines for a nearly word-for-word English. [N.b.: *Oration* here means the *written-down* version of a *speech* or *spoken* oration.]

> At aliud est actio bona, aliud oratio. Scio nonnullis ita videri, sed ego (forsitan fallar) persuasum habeo posse fieri, ut sit actio bona, quae non sit bona oratio, non posse non bonam actionem esse, quae sit bona oratio. Est enim oratio actionis exemplar, et quasi *archetupon*.

> But one thing is a good speech, another a [good written] oration. I know [it] to several thus to seem, but I (perchance I mistake) persuasion have that it is possible to become what may be good speech, which is not good written-oration, not possible that a not good speech may be what is a good written-oration. For the oration [is] the exemplar of speech, and almost the archetype.

The passage is succinct as well as artistically contrived with its inversion of ideas set in a nice plump (yet not obese) *period*. In any case, Pliny signs off eventually with the plea for a short response if Tacitus should agree with him on these matters; but if not, then a long, *really long* response explaining why. Poor Tacitus. Apparently, no answer now exists. Perhaps the thought of having to answer was too depressing.

Historically, as literacy increased, sentences continued to linearize. Once they had shed their tight vertical architectures, the need for inflection lessened. This general process towards unlabored, free-flowing expression would come to inform future ambitious epistolographers—sincerity being their big thing. Thus, it became wise to avoid *the appearance* of grammatical and lexical connivance since linguistic artistry destroys the feel of emotion, which is itself the soul of personality and the supreme element of a letter. The more a thought is squeezed into contorted grammatical constructions and exotic words, the less 'natural' it will seem and hence the less genuine—or indeed, friendly. As for Pliny, his letters are best described as short, often interesting, well-focused—though sometimes ponderous—essays.

The Victim Reader

From the earliest years of alphabetized communication, there seems always to have been some few scribes who tried, really tried, to compensate for the shortcomings of the written medium. Fragments of BCE manuscripts have not survived in quantity or size to tell us much about the early evolution of today's white spaces and pause-signaling marks. Nevertheless, a number of inscriptions and scraps of papyrus that have survived from those early times do show sporadic efforts towards the subdividing of text into topics marked with a *paragraphos*, or with *litterae notabiliores* ('more noticeable letters,' i.e., capital letters, often colored in red). Also, within a statement one can sometimes find various sorts of *interpungendi*, as well as spaces between word groups and even between words.

Over the years and centuries, consideration for the reader's comfort becomes more apparent. Evidence lies in all directions: in sophistic speculation about the nature of *cola* and *commata*; in the outpouring of treatises on grammar and sentence style; in the admiring references to Alexandrian editorial and librarial activities; in Cicero's studious commentary on manuscript pointing and language; and again, in Quintilian's *Institutio* with its recognition of the relationship and division of tasks between eye and ear. It would seem that Quintilian was the first to describe the eye as a separate physiological apparatus whose advance along the written track instructed its ear-mouth coordinate.[9]

The growth of linguistic analysis brought obvious benefits to the reader, and an interest in his ease also became more apparent as the years rolled on. Extant materials show Roman education bearing down on the schoolboy problems of picking out sense from the strangely persistent *scriptura continua* line, whose vagaries are addressed again and again in first millennium writings. Take *conspicitursus*, for example. Was it *a bear seeing* (*conspicit ursus*)? or *a sow being seen* (*conspicitur sus*)?[10] How could a novice be satisfactorily taught to distinguish?

The struggle towards literacy would always seem hard: a slow slog from letters to words, words to sentences, sentences to paragraphs, and onwards. Today, the process is easier, for we are bombarded with lettering on public signs from an early age, and our reading mothers, fathers, older siblings, and teachers are skillfully involved in our progress.

M. B. Parkes in *Pause and Effect* offers his readers a photograph plate of a scrap of papyrus (dating from the time of Christ). It is a 'practice text' from Cicero's Verrine speech, which had been anciently pointed (differentiated by marks) to aid its being read aloud. The copying scribe himself implanted both the interpuncts (separating dots in this case) between words and a 'K' to distinguish a *kaput* (or 'head' in the argument—that is, a signal often used to mark the commencement of a new *period*). Later, with a different pen, either teacher or student drew short oblique strokes over certain vowels (for pronunciation) and long oblique strokes (virgules) between phrases to indicate opportunities for pausing.[11]

More of such practice texts survive from the following years, revealing how persistently alien the writing medium was (indeed, *is*) to the human's inborn intellectual apparatus. Once a student had mastered his quota of texts in this way, more sophisticated and speedier options would begin to present themselves. The reader could begin to rely on his own feeling for sense, on terminating verbs, and on the *clausulae* rhythms to guide him through fresh, undifferentiated copy. Learning to drop the voice at a cretic-trochee (for which read: 'dee-de-dee-dee-de' as in *Eat the sweet pastries*) was a step towards high literacy. Cicero could do it. Even *we* could do it, if we put our minds to it.

Responding to the awe that Greekness seemed always to inspire, early Latin word division (long failing) was defunct by the fourth century CE, and *scriptura continua* returned in full force. Nevertheless, by then, Latin readers who could afford to buy manuscripts were somewhat literarily confident. They would expect the sectional divisions to be signaled by a *paragraphos* or a *littera nobilior*. In the output of some scriptoria, other symbols, or *notae* (perhaps what Cicero had called *interpungendi*), were also used to separate clauses and phrases, or to mark out items of particular significance. But this was apparently not standard. And so, the reader of a pristine manuscript tended to read with his pen in his hand so as to mark off word clusters and thereby illumine the sense. Before reading his purchase aloud to family and friends, he would emend errors of fact, spelling, and grammar according to his own perceptions; and add *scholia* (notes from his own store of knowledge) in the margins. In the early CE centuries, as Rome weakened and cultural degeneration set in, a paramount concern was the matter of preserving the shrinking body of classical wisdom for future generations. In learned circles, it became something of a mission to correct the misdoings of ignorant and careless scribes. Pointed manuscripts came to be known as *codices distincti* and were quite rightly prized.

The Last Word Is Pliny's

It is time now to concern ourselves with the Christian Latin prose as it developed under the aegis of churchly powers. To escort us into this new terrain, here once again is Pliny the Younger. It is rather surprising to discover that he was not only known for his epistolary musings, his wealth, and generosity, but also for his financial expertise and administrative skills.

In the tenth and final book of Pliny's collected letters are 121 official communications between Pliny and the Emperor Trajan in Rome. Pliny at the time was Trajan's representative in the Roman provinces of Bithynia and Pontus on the Black Sea, where his mission was to straighten out bothersome financial, judicial, and political matters. All the Book 10 letters relate to provincial matters as raised by Pliny and answered by Trajan. In writing as facile and assured as one could hope for even today, these letters detail worries and problems, and weigh the various options for solution. Pliny reveals himself as something of a Nervous Nelly, yet capable, earnest, and practical. His sensibilities, however, are rather repugnant to the modern mind. Trajan comes off as something of a political genius, both commanding and sage. The two voices make a splendid dialogue. However, it will be only Pliny we turn to now. He is requesting instruction for dealing with the droves of irksome Christians, who seem to be popping up like jacks-in-the-box, all over the territories of his jurisdiction. These last quotations from a Pliny letter will serve to transfer attention to the oncoming Christian era, as literacy yields to ignorance. Pliny writes:

> Nor am I at all sure whether any distinction should be made between them on the grounds of age, or if young people and adults should be treated alike; whether a pardon ought to be granted to anyone retracting his beliefs, or if he has once professed Christianity, he shall gain nothing by renouncing it; and whether it is the mere name of Christian which is punishable, even if innocent of crime, or rather the crimes associated with the name.
>
> For the moment this is the line I have taken with all persons brought before me on the charge of being Christians. I have asked them in person if they are Christians, and if they admit it, I repeat the question a second and third time, with a warning of the punishment awaiting them. If they persist, I order them to be led away for execution; for, whatever the nature of their admission, I am convinced that their stubbornness and unshakeable obstinacy ought not to go unpunished. There have been others similarly fanatical who are Roman citizens. I have entered them on the list of persons to be sent to Rome for trial. (Plin., *Ep.* 10.96.2–4)

Pliny speaks of the habits and beliefs of the Christians, and then, because all political societies were banned, he decided that it was all the more necessary to extract the truth by torture of two slave-women, whom they call deaconesses. I found nothing but a degenerate sort of cult carried to extravagant lengths.

I have therefore postponed any further examination and hastened to consult you...for a great many individuals of every age and class, both men and women, are being brought to trial, and this is like to continue. It is not only the towns, but villages and rural districts too which are infected through contact with this wretched cult.[12] (Plin., *Ep.* 10.96.8–9).

With that, we now enter a new world.

Notes

1. Goodyear, "History and Biography," *The Cambridge History of Classical Literature*, 2:659.
2. M. C. Howatson, "Pliny the Younger," *The Oxford Companion to Classical Literature* (Oxford: Oxford University Press, 1990), 446.
3. Goodyear, "History and Biography," 2:655–60, passim.
4. Ibid., 2:656.
5. The letter to his wife, Calpurnia, is an exception, both for its warmth and very obvious affection. See Pliny the Younger, *Letters and Panegyricus*, trans. Betty Radice, Loeb Classical Library (New York: Macmillan, 1969; repr. 1997), 1:411.
6. Radice, introduction to Pliny the Younger, *Letters*, 1:ix–xxvi.
7. Pliny the Younger, *Letters*, 1:41.
8. Ibid., 1:59–61.
9. Quintilian, *Institutio*, 4:139.
10. M. B. Parkes, *Pause and Effect: An Introduction to the History of Punctuation in the West* (Berkeley: Berkeley University Press, 1993), 10.
11. Ibid., 262.
12. Pliny the Younger, *Letters*, 2:287–91.

References

Goodyear, F. R. D. "History and Biography." In Vol. 2 of *The Cambridge History of Classical Literature*. Edited by P. E. Easterling and Bernard M. K. Knox. Cambridge: Cambridge University Press, 1985.

Howatson, M. C. "Pliny the Younger." *The Oxford Companion to Classical Literature*. Oxford: Oxford University Press, 1990.

Parkes, M. B. *Pause and Effect: An Introduction to the History of Punctuation in the West*. Berkeley: Berkeley University Press, 1993.

Pliny the Younger. *Letters* and *Panegyricus*. Introduced and translated by Betty Radice. Loeb
    Classical Library. New York: Macmillan, 1969. Reprinted in 1997.
Quintilian. *Institutio oratoria*. Translated by H. E. Butler. Loeb Classical Library. Cambridge:
    Harvard University Press, 1980.

·SECTION 4·

THE ROMAN CATHOLIC CHURCH

· 1 6 ·

CHRISTIAN INFLUENCES
ON LATIN LITERATURE

Early Christian Scholarship

During the social and political upheavals of early Christian times, the fear of heretical misguidance was real. A misinterpreted phrase caused by a mis-spelled word or a misplaced cadence could distort doctrine for the unwary— indeed, might even grease one's slide into hell. In an atmosphere of religious accusation and questioning of biblical interpretation, punctuational signals, grammar, word meaning, word division, and correct spelling acquired great status, for a textual error of any sort could induce a meaning that might not be holy. All aspects of textual precision became suddenly crucial. Because the Christian religion (like the Judaic one) was based on written materials, godli-ness derived from figuring out what they all meant.

Donatus

Aelius Donatus (fl. 353 CE in Rome) was the beloved teacher of St. Jerome and the author of his own two-volume *Ars grammatica*, the most used grammar (or 'donat,' as grammar books came to be called) of the middle ages. For cen-turies to come, no grammarian would be cited so often as was Donatus. He was to early Christian Latin what Dionysius Thrax had been to Greek—namely, a revered source of grammatical information and a source of inspiration. His writings, which were in no way as sophisticated as Varro's (four centuries earlier), reveal the reduced intellectual level of his times. They dealt simplistically with the elements of grammar, the eight parts of speech, and the failures and glories of language in general. The 11-page *Ars minor*, the beginner's section of his opus, is severely sparing in detail. Each item is introduced in the form of a question, just as a schoolmaster might ask:

> How many parts of speech are there? Eight. What are they? The *no-men* (noun), *praenomen, verbum, adverbium*, etc.

Donatus declines *hic magister* ('this teacher'), quickly explains a few terms, conjugates the verb *lego* ('I read; you read; he reads'), and gives some brief advice about pointing.[1] Though his instructions were little more than gleanings from all that had been said before him, his authority assured their continuing presence in the Latin-dominated West. As had Aristophanes of Byzantium and Dionysius Thrax, Donatus too used a three-tiered system of dots to differentiate the pauses, and he called these dots *positurae*, or *distinctiones*. They were (according to an early printed rendition of what might possibly have been close to his own words) to be used as follows:

> Distinctio. Subdistinctio. Media distinctio. The [distinctio] is where the full *sententia* [meaning] is finished for which we put the point [dot] at the top of the letter. The subdistinctio is where not much remains to be dealt with from the *sententia* yet something must quickly be subjoined, for which we put the point [dot] at the [base of the] letter. The media is where approximately as much of the *sententia* is left as we have already spoken and where breathing is required and its point [dot] we put at the middle of the letter. In a reading [text], the whole *sententia* is called a *periodos* whose parts are *cola* and *commata*. [Note: the word *sententia* here means 'full thought' or 'nugget of meaning,' as opposed to its earlier-mentioned usage for an epigrammatic or witty statement.]

The above translation comes from a very old text in the British Library. Printed in 1475 by an unidentified printer, it abbreviates words without uniformity, indeed leaves some out entirely; in addition to which, it does not itself follow the precepts that Donatus is proposing. The Latin is not supple, to say the least, and is hardly lucid. In reading it, one gains a glimpse

of a submerged world where information exchange is beclouded by authorial ineptness and inattention to the reader's possible interpretation of the
words set down. The scene is one that we shall come to know well before
this tale ends. Nevertheless, ideas are hinted at and sometimes conveyed.
Interestingly, Donatus stresses breathing as an element to be considered.
But unlike Aristotle, he speaks of it as being especially necessary for the
middle of a *period*.

Generally, the situation remained as has already been shown. A low-lying, on-the-line dot (a *subdistinctio*: that is, a dot that looks like a modern
period) came after a *comma* (a short word group, being especially useful after a
lengthy prepositional phrase, for example, 'After the retreating flood waters').
It signaled a minimal pause. The recommendation made earlier by Dionysius of Halicarnassus that the *subdistinctio* should break only into the opening
half of a full sentence and not interrupt the sustained climactic sense of the
second half (the wrap-around tail) seems to recede in importance as interest
mounts in other matters (like breathing) that relate to the ease or discomfort
of oral rerendering—evidence, surely, of retreat from Hellenistic literary ease.
With grammatical instruction turning back to the oral delivery of a text, we
may imagine an increased dependence on those who could read by those who
couldn't. In future, medieval writers will more often be invited to insert their
subdistinctio puncts in the latter part of a sentence, for which the given purpose is to help a gasping reader pump out the final phrases of a lengthy written
statement. Such instruction for implanting punctuation becomes more frequent in the succeeding centuries of barbarism.

As for the mid-lying dot (the *media distinctio*, written thus: •), there is less
to say. Deriving from old habits of Psalm-type dualism, it simply came after a
colon, that is, a bigger phrase-clause, whose internal sense, complete or not,
failed to accomplish the total idea. The *media distinctio* kept its 'middleness'
intact by lying both midway along the linear axis of a sentence and midway
between the high and low dot on the vertical axis. As it could indicate a pause
of almost any value—semicolon, colon, or comma—its powers of jurisdiction were extremely vague. Donatus recommended using it somewhere near
the middle of the *periodos*. Fifth-century grammarians refer to its presence as
spiritually refreshing.

Finally, a high-up, very visible dot (the *distinctio*, written thus: ˙) came at
the end of an unquestionably complete, fully formed, and utterly satisfying
periodos, in which the 'whole meaning' (*sententia*) was felt to have been cor-
ralled. Described in these vague terms of satisfaction, the *periodos* was itself

confusing, since a passage that some might consider 'to be complete' might not in all minds be absolutely complete. Nevertheless, that symbol of finish, the *distinctio*, was (like the *paragraphos*) a true sense marker. Corresponding (more or less) to our full stop, the *distinctio* offered the opportunity for a deep breath and a glance out the window.

As has been noted before, the actual 'distinction' dot marks were not, even in a majuscule *scriptura continua*, sufficiently distinct to be unfailingly helpful. Nevertheless, these Donatian puncts (or points)—all written as dots—were the ones most consistently advocated for centuries, though they were for the most part ignored or misapplied by scribes. As the purity and clarity of classical Latin receded, matters of breathing would become more prominent in discussions of how to set down text.[2]

Of the three dots, the most popular and easily adapted from oral reality was the *subdistinctio*, for it best represented the smallish units (noted by Quintilian) that we relaxedly use when we put our thoughts into groups of three or four spoken words. Whatever form that protean subdistinction would choose to adopt (whether dot, tailed-dot, dash, virgule, bracket, or empty space), it became the most popular and natural tool on the market to convert mouth noise into food for the eyes. In terms of modern perceptions of sentence structure, it was also the least controlled.

Overall, Donatus did not categorize Latin grammar in the most helpful way. He gave no comprehensive account of inflectional variation amongst the groups of nouns or verbs. Nouns, he grouped in accordance with gender, not declension. In his *Ars maior* (35 pages designed for the more advanced), he dealt with topics related to rhetoric—such as meters and general linguistic categories—as well as barbarisms, and the schemes and tropes. But alas! Paradigms, which would have clarified so many details, are lacking. To the modern student, for whom the pedagogical arts have broken all subject matters into discrete digestible pieces for quick and memorable consumption, he seems an archaically oral person. His ear is more alert than his eye. Nevertheless, both sections of his *Ars grammatica* dominated grammatical studies until the mid-ninth century, when at last they gave way to the more explicit work of Priscian.[3] Still (as mentioned before), even up through Shakespeare's time, a 'donat' meant 'a grammatical lesson.'

Colometry?

By the fourth century CE, Greek and Roman scribes had long been computing their output by numbers of verses (for poetry) and numbers of lines, or *stichoi* (meaning 'rows,' for prose). Indeed, stichometry, a Greek invention, appears to have been developed before Alexandrian Callimachus (third century BCE) and was quite likely coeval with literature itself. A *stichos* was essentially equivalent to the traditional hexameter line of poetry, that is, to a string of six dactylic beats—6 x dee-de-de (or its equivalent)—which would bring a complete *stichos* to some 16 to 18 syllables, as in the first line of the *Iliad*. (However, if made of iambic, de-dee lines, the *stichos* could shrink to a mere 12.) A syllabic measurement of this sort was very useful, for it laid out words on the page, so many per line, as best fitted the requirements of aesthetics or purse; and neither the scribe, who received his pay by the *stichos*, nor the purchaser, who bought by the sheet, would be in any doubt about how much money should be received or given.

In keeping with the length of the longer lines for which it was most commonly used, a *stichos* tended to equal a hexametric line, whose boundaries offered space for statement not very different from a short modern sentence.[4] The *stichos* thereby fell into a rather wobbly relationship with meaning, since decisions were required as to where the line should be lopped and another begun. Such decisions could be based on an exact syllable count or on an instinctual feel for a completed thought somewhere in the area of the 11th to 16th syllable.

Confusingly related to this commercial aspect of breaking up text was the development of a punctuational technique called colometry. Devised (so they say) by Aristophanes of Byzantium, its purpose was to lay out the passages of Greek tragedies according to the accepted meters (iambic for speech and dactylic for chorus), so that they were no longer seamlessly packed together as if they were prose. This technique (still in use today, in the layout of poetry or exchange of speech when set in writing) was thereafter adopted in a general way to aid anyone reading aloud (be it poetry or prose) in public. Colometry *means* 'the measuring out of *cola*,' with its singular form *colon* having grown to mean a mix of syllable count and a completed (but not necessarily independent) thought—a sort of limb, part, or member of a whole sentence. Thus, in very general terms, colometry marked off *cola* into short eye-catching lines, so that recitations of poetry, oratory, or church lessons might follow speech rhythms and, by that means, conjure up sense more easily.[5] Colometric layout usefully leavened textual word mass. In the lavish examples of early church books, we find an extravagant ratio of space to text, whose shorn lines (as we shall shortly see) had little to do with the sense.

Colometry thrived throughout the first Christian millennium. When first adopted by the prose camp, it adhered for a time to syllable counting: for the clauses (*cola*)—8 to 18 syllables; and for the phrases (*commata*)—8 syllables or less.[6] But since meaningful vocal effects generate more easily from clauses and phrases left intact, thoughtful scribes (of whom there were always *some*) took care where their new lines began. In their renderings, the succession of whole-line space-*stichoi* (for payment) would be numbered in the margins, and the broken colometric lines divided (one hoped) where cohesive word groups (sense-*stichoi*) seemed to dictate.

The great boost for the colometric sense line in prose literature came from St. Jerome, who advocated its use for the purpose of aerating and elucidating the difficult texts of Isaiah and Ezekiel in his Latin Vulgate Bible.

Jerome: A Saint, but Not Saintly

Religious paintings that attempt to portray St. Jerome (ca. 347–ca. 420) in his desert abode have rather ruined him for modern tastes; for all that unwashed sanctimony, those pleading oyster-moist eyes and protruding ribcage are not in these health-seeking times everyone's meat.[7] As for Jerome's character, recent scholarship reveals that it too was unpalatable. If one digs around in the literature, one stumbles quickly on a mass of his flaws. He was, it turns out, mean, haughty, mendacious, contentious, and (excepting that lion) a trial to all who knew him. His touted 'encyclopaedic knowledge,' it turns out, was derived (though he protested it was not) in large part from secondary materials and generalized commentary. The ideas he claimed for his own were frequently not his at all, nor were his sources what he said they were. The books he 'quotes' so learnedly from were often known to him only by reference and hearsay.

Nevertheless, we must endorse this man and forgive his wiles; forgive his overweening ego; all his 'sinful,' much-denied enthrallment with the Neoplatonists; the aspersions he cast on the Alexandrian Origen, whose works (from which he drew many ideas) he defamed as heretical; his censure of Ambrose for plagiarism (the very thing he was so expert at himself); his derision of Augustine's tenuous grasp of Greek—*so many things!* All in all, one might say that Jerome was almost everything that a saint is not supposed to be. Yet so voluminous were his writings,[8] and so well spun was his reputation for piety and learning that the folk of his time accepted his opinions with wide-eyed admiration. Nowadays, however, scholars have become critical of Jerome on the grounds that his rejection of myth-soaked pagan literature and his ridicule of the ancient philosophers (whose works he scarcely knew) contributed emphatically to the eventual closing down of all secular classical culture.[9]

Despite that serious charge, we accept his numerous rogueries in appreciation of his one enduring bequest from all those years of deceit and vindictiveness, for Jerome accomplished A Very Great Thing. Out of the mess of errant Greek, Latin, and Hebrew texts, he pieced together a new, more accurate and beautiful Latin Bible, known to us all as the Vulgate Bible. It was a job uniquely appropriate to his tenacity and very genuine talents, a labor of tremendous linguistic sensibility that not many of us, either then or today, would be equipped to perform. Though Latin was his maternal tongue, he had acquired over the years some considerable facility with Hebrew and Greek, and so became that rare bird for his times—a literate, erudite trilingual, and a Latinate defender of Hellenism, by which we do not mean the despised pagan literature, but rather the later Greek-speaking biblical exegetes, whose textual activities he drew upon (even while criticizing) and adopted as his own. His collation of disparate and disagreeing manuscripts for the Vulgate must have been a daunting task in those days of difficult travel. His eventual translation was not a stiffly 'word for word' one, but instead (for his pen was very pliant), gracefully 'sense for sense.' The result may be considered an act of compensation to subsequent generations for having been so persistently nasty to his own. In any case, his Vulgate Bible proved a daring move against the tight-fisted literalism of his Alexandrian-influenced times and a monument to linguistic deftness.[10]

But what can he be writing now on all those sheets of papyrus? Ah! He is writing his "Preface to Isaiah." He is enjoining Latin-speaking scribes to take up a "new kind of writing," a method that will arrange the words of a text in such a way as to divide and clarify biblical prose materials: *quod in Demosthene et Tullio solet fieri, ut per cola scribantur et commata* (i.e., that they write by *cola* and *commata* as is usually done with the works of Demosthenes and Cicero). The oratorical writings of Demosthenes and Cicero were by Jerome's time customarily written down in imitation of the poets: 'by clauses and phrases' (*per cola et commata*). Though it was no new thing that Jerome was recommending, his immense reputation as a scholar brought a world-wide response to his exhortation. Following Jerome, came a surge of colo-metric chic.

Colometry in Action

Ideally, colometry put groups of several whole words onto a number of sin-gle lines and indicated their collectiveness by indenting them under a cap-ital letter (*littera nobilior*) placed in the margin. Sometimes of a different color of ink, these *litterae nobiliores* were the eye-catchers that signaled for the reader the opening of what might be considered a small paragraph (or longish *periodos*), before which the reader might draw a new breath along with a glimpse of the jumps ahead. Where colometry divided prudently, sense was exposed. But then, prudence was not always available. All too often, scribes found the concept of phrasing for sense indefinite. As might be expected, a layout of biblical text into meaningful phrase bundles flagged by a *littera nobilior* was not consistently followed by all scribes or manuscript correctors.[11] The diversity in length of colometric 'sentences' drawn from the same textual material gives strong evidence of an infirm perception of a word group.

The following *per cola et commata* lines, which open the Gospel according to St. John, come from a sixth-century Book of Gospels written in Italian un-cials.[12] A portion has been italicized for easy comparison with the subsequent two samples. The differing division of words indicates how powerful a force page-design was in colometric decision making.[13]

INPRINCIPIOERAT	Inbeginningwas
UERBUM	word
ETUERBUMERAT	andwordwas
APUDDEUMETDEUS	withgodandgod
FUITHOMOMISSUS	was man sent
ERATUERBUM	wasword
HOCERATINPRIN	thiswasinbeg
CIPIOAPUDDEUM	inningwithgod
OMNIAPERIPSUM	allthingsthroughhim
FACTASUNT	madewere
ETSINEIPSOFACTUM	andwithouthimmade

ESTNIHIL	isnothing
QUODFACTUMEST	whatismade
INIPSOUITAERAT	inhimwaslife

The same words taken from a facsimile copy of the Lindisfarne Gospels (written probably some 150 years later, ca. 700) reads as follows.[14] (The italicized lines are those that will be repeated in the third sample). One should note that in the following case, except for PRIN/CIPIO, words are not split at the line's ending; moreover, in the actual manuscript, there are perceptible non-*scriptura continua* spaces between some words. Both these features are retained in the third example.

IN PRIN

    CIPIO

    ERATUERBUM

    ETUERBUMERAT

    APUDDEUMETDEUS

    ERATUERBUM *HOCERAT*

    INPRINCIPIO APUD DEUM

OMNIA PERIPSUM FACTA

    SUNT ETSINEIPSO

    FACTUM EST NIHIL

QUOD FACTUM ESTINIPSO

    UITA ERAT ETUITAERAT

Finally, picking up with HOC ERAT (This was) and noting the IM instead of IN before PRINCIPIO, we may again compare the same line cuts with those of the Echternach Gospels (early eighth century)[15]:

HOC ERAT IMPRINCI

    PIO APUDDEUM

    OMNIA PERIPSUM

    FACTA SUNT

ET SINE IPSO FACTUM

    EST NIHIL

QUOD FACTUM EST

    INIPSO VITA ERAT

Despite their discrepancies, Bibles rendered in this way invited the reader into an easy stride. Knowing the precious words from years of study, a priest could slide his finger down the columns of a *per cola et commata* biblical text (sheer grandeur!), and sense a joyous progress. The modern eye, on the other hand, is daunted by the steep chute of words, sometimes unseparated and sometimes strangely split (as in prin/cipio; and in other cases: ho/minum; comprehen/derunt, etc.). Perplexing, even in cases where the *paragraphos* was inserted to mark off topic divisions (as found, for example, in the *Codex Amiatinus*[16]), was when words remained unseparated while meaningful sense units were violated with impunity.[17] But such peccadillos were never a trouble to those who had memorized the text anyway.

The *per cola et commata* style of breaking up text persisted in Bible production until the ninth century. Its gift of clarity lay in its potential to create gobbets of word density that were easily assimilable to the human intellect. The device has been perfected and passed on to us in the line-by-line layout of modern-day speeches and for versification, in which the line endings are often fortified by puncts, but even when not, can intend some nuance of finish or meaning or instruction for voice control.

Literacy: Its Decline and Tenacity

Early Christianity was sorely affected by the doctrinal schism of East and West, and the incompatibility of Roman Catholicism with Greek Orthodoxy soon separated the Latin and Greek languages. Italy's former Latin-Greek bilingualism now became rare. While the Greeks, sitting atop their own mountain of cultural history, maintained some standards of worldly sophistication (for which, the knowledge of Greek was a must), Latin speakers fell victim to the homeland adversities of barbaric invasion and political disintegration. Western scholarship, which had for so many centuries included a solid grounding in Greek culture, was increasingly cut off from this major source of nourishment. In the press of more urgent matters, memorizing irregular Greek verbs became an extraneous activity. Unless you were born to rare privilege and could afford an educated Greek to teach you privately, Hellenistic polish was out of reach.

In the literary decline that came to prevail over the western end of the Mediterranean, the now-unpracticed Greek language took on an aura of untrustworthy exoticism. In place of frolicking, sin-drenched nymphs and satyrs, the Church recommended filling the mind with thoughts of God and hopes for an afterlife. When enemy fires are burning in your neighbor's orchard, it is time to put down irrelevant studies and begin to pray. Thus it was that Christianity won the day.

Though diminished in numbers and beleaguered, Hellenistic literaries persisted, and, with them persisted the use of punctuational signals—namely, the dots at differing heights that the Alexandrians had developed some two centuries before Christ. Origen, the great exegete of Christian doctrine in the century before Jerome, had used them in collating copies of the Septuagint.[18] With blessings from Donatus, they remained on stage after Jerome's time as well, so needful and handy had they proved to be. Augustine also favored them, despite the risk that they could be so easily changed, either in the copying process or by the misconstruings of an ignorant emender. Errors caused by punctuating with dots were particularly common in the dense, small lettering of less expensive manuscripts; whereas, a colometric layout did not submit to easy alteration. Colometry could lock a scriptural decision into place, more or less forever, and in that way, offer better protection against an inadvertent meander into heresy.

Augustine of Hippo: A Saintly Saint

Scholars are still uncertain about the Greek that Latin-speaking Augustine of Hippo (354–430 CE) actually knew, though it is clear that he got better and better at it as his life unfolded. While he would continue publicly to advocate the use of original texts over popular secondary sources (commentaries, summaries, and the like), there is little doubt that Greek was to him a troublesome animal that translations and *compendia* of extracts helped to subdue.[19] As a result of his deficient fluency, Augustine's own translations show a literal exactness far short of Jerome's free-flowing ease. Augustine's biblical exegeses and doctrinal treatises expose the labor behind them. They are unintuitive, awkward, distractingly given to the pursuit of minute accuracies, and on occasion, inclusive of unexpected linguistic barbarisms as well. It is thought that he may have allowed these lapses for the sake of matching the levels of his audience/readers in order to be better understood. Though highly admiring of Jerome's linguistic athleticism, Augustine was not too daunted to differ from him in matters of religious purport. His sympathy with the Neoplatonist camp made his writings more broadminded than Jerome's, more in keeping with modern notions of truth-seeking. His instruction was to make use of whatever the pagan philosophers and Platonists had to say that seemed both true and in harmony with Christian doctrine.[20] That benign advice (which, if taken, would have saved a lot of trouble) revealed a tolerance unusual for his times, and a personality more appealing and approachable than Jerome's.

During these early Christian years, grammatical understanding was increasingly viewed as being fundamental to scriptural study, for salvation lay in those often unpunctuated, imperfectly transmitted, puzzling words of God. As a possible tabernacle of sacred truths, a good manuscript was considered to be invaluable—a treasure to be preserved, copied, collated, and annotated by devoted scholars across Christendom. The ministry of the church was founded upon the words of the holy script, whose interpretation and derivative scholarship must adhere to what officialdom approved.

Here is an interesting sample of Augustine's writing on how a textual scholar should proceed in perfecting a translation.

> There is, again, an ambiguity arising out of the doubtful sound of syllables; and this of course has relation to pronunciation. For example, in the passage, "My bone [os meum] was not hid from Thee, which Thou didst make in secret," it is not clear to the reader whether he should take the word os as short or long. If he make it short, it is the singular of ossa [bones]; if he make it long, it is the singular of ora [mouths]. Now difficulties such as this are cleared up by looking into the original tongue, for in the Greek we find not stoma [mouth], but osteon [bone]. And for this reason the vulgar idiom is frequently more useful in conveying the sense than the pure speech of the educated. For I would rather have the barbarism, non est absconditum a te ossum meam, than have the passage in better Latin, but the sense less clear.[21] (August., Doc.Chr., 3.3.7)

Augustine's authoritative acceptance of backwater Latin became a powerful influence on subsequent writers. It was not only handy for correcting scholarly misapplication but also for getting through to the ignorant lower classes. Biblical pundits would come to lean heavily on his example to justify their own grammatical inelegances.

Augustine wrote of the difficult decisions that a religious textualist might have had to make. To assure the right conclusions, he offered the following advice: The biblical scholar must arm himself in a number of ways: (1) with a knowledge of languages "so as not to be stopped by unknown words and forms of speech"; (2) with the knowledge of certain necessary matters (like medicine, philosophy, and science), "so as not to be ignorant of the force and nature of those which are used figuratively"; and (3) with the assistance of accuracy in the texts, "which has been secured by skill and care in the matter of correction." When a man is thus prepared, then "let him proceed to the examination and solution of the ambiguities of Scripture." The guiding principle in general is this: No interpretation can be true that conflicts with the promotion of human or godly love, which is to say, *Interpret to your heart's content, but let nothing divert from accepted Christian principles.* In the following passage, Augustine is addressing the removal of ambiguities through punctuation.

> But when proper words make Scripture ambiguous, we must see in the first place that there is nothing wrong in our punctuation or pronunciation....
>
> Now look at some examples. The heretical pointing, "In principio erat verbum, et verbum erat apud Deum, et Deus erat," [which makes] the next sentence run, "Verbum hoc erat in principio apud Deum," arises out of unwillingness to confess that the Word *was* God. But this must be rejected by the rule of faith, which, in reference to the equality of the Trinity, directs us to say: "et Deus erat verbum"; and then to add: "hoc erat in principio apud Deum."[22] (August., *Doc.Chr.*,3.2.2).

Mistakes in such matters could well invite a spiritual disaster.

Throughout these early centuries, scholarly meticulousness became a special concern of the church. The biblical commentator became a kind of specialized *grammaticus*, whose task was to comb the Bible for the Word of God—to break open text and decode its divine riddles. Where choices surfaced, he would work hard to decide. Misplaced pauses and mistakenly separated syllables could generate a false interpretation of God's holy message. It was the grammarian's perceived responsibility to spot and correct such errors.

Notes

1. F. A. Wright and T. A. Sinclair, *A History of Later Latin Literature* (London: George Routledge & Sons, 1931), 39.
2. A good portion of this material comes from Walter J. Ong, "Historical Backgrounds of Elizabethan and Jacobean Punctuation Theory," *PMLA* 59, no. 2 (1944): 349–60.
3. Rosamund McKitterick, *The Carolingians and the Written Word* (Cambridge: Cambridge University Press, 1995), 14.

4. J. Rendel Harris, "Stichometry I," *American Journal of Philology* 4, no. 2 (1883): 135–9, 151. Harris tells us that well into the Middle Ages, especially at Bologna and in other university towns in Northern Italy, scribes were paid by the *pecia*, which measured off 16 columns, each of 62 lines, with 32 letters to the line.

5. L. D. Reynolds and N. G. Wilson, *Scribes and Scholars: A Guide to the Transmission of Greek and Latin Literature* (Oxford: Oxford University Press, 1968), 14.

6. Sir Edward Maunde Thompson, *An Introduction to Greek and Latin Paleography* (Oxford: Clarendon Press, 1912), 70.

7. Depictions of Jerome seem to fall into two camps. There is the scholarly, velvet-robed, gaunt but healthy Cardinal type (as in the manner of El Greco) and the desert variety. In the latter case, an undernourished, ragged, sunburnt, and hirsute Jerome (accompanied by his inexplicably glossy, well-fed lion) kneels in hot sand and raises his beseeching, moist eyes to the sky.

8. The works of Jerome fill 11 volumes of J. P. Migne's massive publication of both Greek and Latin theological literatures, known as the *Patrologia cursus completus*.

9. The claims made against Jerome in this section come primarily from the chapter "Christian Hellenism: St. Jerome," in Pierre-Paul Courcelle's *Late Latin Writers and Their Greek Sources*, trans. Harry E. Wedeck (Cambridge: Harvard University Press, 1969), 48–127, also 141–2.

10. Pierre-Paul Courcelle, *Late Latin Writers*, trans. Harry E. Wedeck (Cambridge: Harvard University Press, 1969), 54, 57.

11. Thompson, *Greek and Latin Paleography*, 70.

12. Uncial script has rounded letters, some shaped as modern capitals and others in cursive form; the style was much in use from the third to the tenth centuries CE.

13. This manuscript may be the one sent by Pope Gregory the Great to St. Augustine at Canterbury, in which case it probably dates from the late 500s. The text, as it stands here, comes from Peter Clemoes, "Liturgical Influence on Punctuation in Late Old English and Early Middle English Manuscripts," Occasional Papers No. 1, Cambridge University Department of Anglo-Saxon (Cambridge: Cambridge University, 1952); it was reprinted in the *Old English Newsletter* series Subsidia 4 (1980): 10. The actual manuscript (C.C.C.C. 286) is in the Parker Library at Corpus Christi College, Cambridge.

14. *Codex Lindisfarnensis*, facsimile edition, ed. T. D. Kendrick (Lausanne: Lars Graf, 1960), 1:211v.

15. *Codex Lindisfarnensis*, 2: pl. 7. Walter W. Skeat provides some interesting samples of how unemphatic the concept of a phrase break used to be. Two reproduced congenerous manuscripts (undated) have varying numbers of pausing line dots, though they compare exactly in verse layout and in the notable capitalizing of the *Fuit homo missus a deo* phrase. See Walter W. Skeat, *The Gospel According to St. John, in Anglo-Saxon and Northumbrian Versions* (Cambridge: Cambridge University Press, 1878), 12.

16. The *Codex Amiatinus* was transcribed in Northumbria, 716 CE, from Vivarium volumes brought north from Rome (see Courcelle, *Late Latin Writers*, 382). It is now in the keeping of the Biblioteca Medicea Laurenziana in Florence, Italy.

17. T. F. Husband and M. F. A. Husband, *Punctuation: Its Principles and Practise* (London: George Routledge and Sons, 1905), 16.

18. Parkes, *Pause and Effect*, 14. (The Septuagint is the earliest known translation of the Old Testament from the Hebrew into Greek.)

19. As for the Hebrew language, it escaped him entirely. Unless otherwise indicated, these biographical assessments of this African saint come from Pierre-Paul Courcelle, *Early Latin Writers and Their Greek Sources*, trans. Harry E. Wedeck (Cambridge: Harvard University Press, 1969), particularly pages 150–65 and 181–96.

20. Augustine of Hippo, *On Christian Doctrine*, trans. J. F. Shaw, *Nicene and Post-Nicene Fathers*, ed. Philip Schaff (Grand Rapids, MI: Wm. B. Eerdmans, 1956), 554.

21. Ibid., 558.

22. Ibid., 556–7. The Latin here translates: "In (the) beginning was (the) word, and (the) word was with God, and God was"—which makes the next sentence run as follows: "(The) Word this was in (the) beginning with God." Whereas it should read (in accordance with the Trinity): "And God was the word, this was in the beginning with God."

References

Augustine of Hippo. *On Christian Doctrine*. Translated by J. F. Shaw. *Nicene and Post-Nicene Fathers*. Edited by Philip Schaff. Grand Rapids, MI: Wm. B. Eerdmans, 1956.

Clemoes, Peter. *Liturgical Influence on Punctuation in Late Old English and Early Middle English Manuscripts*. Cambridge University Department of Anglo-Saxon. Cambridge: Cambridge University, 1952. Reprinted in the *Old English Newsletter* Series Subsidia 4 (1980): 10.

Codex Lindisfarnensis, 1. Facsimile edition. Edited by T. D. Kendrick. Lausanne: Lars Graf, 1960. l:211v.

Codex Lindisfarnensis, 2. Walter W. Skeat. *The Gospel According to St. John, in Anglo-Saxon and Northumbrian Versions*. Cambridge: Cambridge University Press, 1878.

Courcelle, Pierre. "Christian Hellenism: St. Jerome." In *Late Latin Writers and Their Greek Sources*. Translated by Harry E. Wedeck. Cambridge: Harvard University Press, 1969.

———. *Early Latin Writers and Their Greek Sources*. Translated by Harry E. Wedeck. Cambridge: Harvard University Press, 1969.

Harris, J. Rendel. "Stichometry I." *American Journal of Philology* 4, no. 2 (1883): 135–9, 151.

Husband, T. F., and M. F. A. Husband. *Punctuation: Its Principles and Practise*. London: George Routledge and Sons, 1905.

Kendrick, T. D., ed. *Codex Lindisfarnensis*, facsimile edition. Lausanne: Lars Graf, 1960.

McKitterick, Rosamund. *The Carolingians and the Written Word*. Cambridge: Cambridge University Press, 1995.

Ong, Walter J. "Historical Backgrounds of Elizabethan and Jacobean Punctuation Theory." *PMLA* 59, no. 2 (1944): 349–60.

Parkes, M. B. *Pause and Effect: An Introduction to the History of Punctuation in the West*. Berkeley: Berkeley University Press, 1993.

Reynolds, L. D., and N. G. Wilson. *Scribes and Scholars: A Guide to the Transmission of Greek and Latin Literature*. Oxford: Oxford University Press, 1968.

Skeat, Walter W. *The Gospel According to St. John, in Anglo-Saxon and Northumbrian Versions*. Cambridge: Cambridge University Press, 1878.

Thompson, Sir Edward Maunde. *An Introduction to Greek and Latin Paleography*. Oxford: Clarendon Press, 1912.

Wright, F. A., and T. A. Sinclair. *A History of Later Latin Literature*. London: George Routledge & Sons, 1931.

· 1 7 ·

SUNBLINK IN THE DUSK

A Brief Hellenistic Renaissance

For many years barbarians from the east and north invaded Roman Catholic lands, plundering the wealth of church and estates, disrupting the peace, and spreading fear. At last in the early part of the sixth century, 519 CE, Theodoric, king of the Ostrogoths and conquering master of the northern part of the Italic peninsula, warily and briefly accepted Byzantine authority under the Greek Orthodox emperor Justin—an astonishing turnaround for the cowering peoples on Italian terrain. Theodoric's truce with Orthodox Byzantium allowed a spell of welcome quiet. With the closure of the Greek-Roman ecclesiastical schism, Hellenistic pursuits blossomed once again in Italy—particularly in the south. Although Greek, the language of Orthodoxy, was no longer commonly understood (indeed had become suspect), the Latin intelligentsia once again turned its admiring attention to eastern culture, pagan knowledge, and Alexandrian scholasticism.

Boethius: A Victim of the Times

Under the clearing skies, Boethius (480–524 CE), a Latin Christian, determined to use his influence and skills to perpetuate ancient enlightenment so that the intellectual achievements of the past might be made useful to Rome. Being himself highly educated in both eastern and western cultures, he was uniquely positioned to pull together the two traditions, for his own prominent family in Rome had long had ties with the imperial East, most notably with Alexandria (which was still a cultural assembling point for foreigners). And so, with youthful confidence, Boethius took it upon himself to transpose the Greek *Arithmetic* of Nicomachus into Latin paraphrase, to clarify its obscurities and simplify its arithmetical ideas so that Latin speakers could become acquainted with the riches of Greek achievement; for Classical Greek culture had clearly become foreign material. That done, he turned to the works of Aristotle, but finished only his treatise on logic. His unattained ambitions included the translation with abridgments and commentary of Aristotle's *Ethics* and *Physics*, as well as all of Plato's works. Though Boethius was brave to tackle the prevailing public ignorance, his vision proved more enterprising than circumstances could tolerate.

Sadly, his cultural aspirations led Boethius into trouble. Christian church doctrine could not accommodate so much exposition of classical rationality, for it stimulated 'unseemly' inquiry into long-held religious tenets like the Virgin Birth and the Trinity. Along with the clerical frowns, came rumbles— like gathering tidal waves—of political disturbances throughout the land. Fear unsettled the capricious temperament of the Gothic king Theodoric. Always suspicious of treason, he suddenly turned against the sophisticated eastern-oriented circles within his domain. At his command, Boethius was locked up in a Pavian jail. There, grieving, Boethius wrote his famous *De consolatione philosophiae* (*On the Consolation of Philosophy*), a speculative, scientific, and dialectic inquiry into man's place in the universe. Fortunately for future generations, his keepers allowed him to finish this strangely un-Christian manifesto before putting him to death. He was only 44, yet his legacy would be lasting. Though it made no mention of Christ, in the subsequent centuries of the Christian world, *De consolatione* became one of the most influential books ever written in Latin. It was translated into Old High German, Italian, Spanish, French, and Greek; and into English, most famously by Alfred, Chaucer, John Walton, and even Queen Elizabeth I.[1]

Aside from his own fluent example, Boethius offered no particular advice for the progress of written language. Nevertheless, even his unfinished scholarly work had a lasting influence. The prevention of his worthy ambitions gives us a fair picture of the temper of his times. Intellectual pursuits that smacked of the East were dangerous. Culture was rapidly crumbling.

Cassiodorus

Another defender of culture in this era of decline was the immensely energetic Cassiodorus (490–585 CE). Like Boethius, he too felt the urgency of preserving and propagating the knowledge of Greek science and literature. He differed, however, on two important points. First, he believed that the *full* panoply of ancient studies (nymphs included) was an indispensable component of a perfect Christian education; and second, he was willing to use *practical means* and *political position* to ensure that the conquering boorish Ostrogoths would not destroy that knowledge. Unlike his fellow intellectual aristocrats (the cultivated relatives and friends of Boethius who lived in the southerly city of Rome), Cassiodorus, though learned and highborn too, had no fear of 'dirtying his hands' by dealing with the barbarians in their chosen northern capital, Ravenna. Whereas his horrified Roman compatriots watched the spread of ravaging Ostrogoths, but did little more than bite their nails and lament the decline of civilized dignities, he faced the situation in a more practical and courageous way: namely, by mingling with the conquerors in the north, gaining their confidence, and making himself useful to them *so as to change them and modify their wild habits.* As an accepted insider—an official in the royal Gothic household—he was able to analyze their motives, study their psychology, and thus position himself to be effective, not only in cooling the unpredictable tempers of their king, Theodoric, but also in restraining the ambitions and moderating the uncouth manners of Theodoric's governing court.[2]

Cassiodorus worked hard to channel the drift of Gothic energies away from villa-sacking and violence. When the antagonisms between Theodoric and the powerful Christian Emperor Justin in Constantinople first began to subside,[3] Cassiodorus, as quaestor to the barbarian court, found himself undertaking duties that were dauntingly multidirectional: secretarial, interpretational, pedagogical, advisory, and discretionary. We might think of him as a sort of *in loco parentis* prime minister, who was also the sleepless family flunkey.

In his description of a quaestor's responsibilities, Cassiodorus wrote that the office required one "to be the cupboard of laws…always ready for a sudden call." It was a job for which one must have "the authority in his tongue…to speak the King's words in the King's own presence" with a "knowledge of the law, wariness in speech, firmness of purpose, that neither gifts nor threats may cause him to swerve from justice."[4] In private conversations with the uneducated Theodoric, the learned Cassiodorus was enjoined to answer the king's naïve questions about scientific mechanisms (such as the water clock) and natural phenomena (medicines and disease, and perhaps even such things as why the wind blows, or how bees make honey.)[5] He had also to teach courtly courtesies and explain Roman administrative rule. He fashioned himself to be the benign, amiable, trustworthy, endlessly patient, always alert intermediary between cultivated Rome and her ruthless and rough-handed, Ravenna-based invaders—who, fortunately, were still in the mode of admiring their conquered prizes and wanted to learn how to behave in Ravenna as the Romans had done (and were still trying to do) in Rome. It was Cassiodorus who inspired in Theodoric the commendable (though brief) desire to be a Platonic philosopher-king.

Cassiodorus would seem to have been (like Cicero) the right man in the right place. He was sufficiently open-minded to have developed a sympathetic familiarity with the Ostrogothic character. He had noted the pride of these people, their penchant for violence, and their gratitude to benefactors.[6] For some 30 years, King Theodoric and his successors would rely on Cassiodorus both to teach them and to interpret (even reinvent for publication) their savage customs and uncouth behavior for reception in the civilized world. They left it to him to realize their (and his) euphoric vision of a new peaceful and united Latinate world: a bastion of administrative, commercial, and cultural expertise, which their fierce warrior power would fortify and defend. Essentially, the royal 'mission orders' to Cassiodorus, throughout his climb to higher official titles, were to make a functioning and effective whole of two disparate peoples. *How to begin?*

We may consider Cassiodorus to be amongst the world's most ambitious spin doctors, for his representations of Roman to Goth and Goth to Roman were outrageously exalted. His letters on behalf of the illiterate Theodoric were massively worded with syrupy rhetoric, elaborate courtesies, embellishments, and overdoses of Roman *dignitas*—all in the interests of mitigating the Ostrogothic churlish demeanor in the eyes of cowering Latin sophisticates. By encouraging his masters to revitalize old Roman institutions and culture,[7] he hoped to reduce both the chicanery of the current Romans and the violence of the Goths. It was a bold, diplomatic manipulation of facts, one that allowed him to "paint the delights of virtue and the terrors of vice" in such a way that "eloquence should almost make the sword of the magistrate needless."[8] Typical of his times was his faith in the power of words.

In his collected and still-extant official letters and documents, the *Variae*,[9] we see Cassiodorus hard at work, expounding the notion that Goths and Romans were born to help each other; that good emperors could love both peace and Goths; that collaboration, or some form of a *modus vivendi*, between the two dissimilar peoples would be advantageous to both; whereas mutual distrust could only mean trouble for both. He reasoned that diplomatic cordiality was more likely to bring peace than disdain and exclusion.

In keeping with this thinking, Cassiodorus wrote letters so droll, so ill-suited to the character of Theodoric, their supposed author, as to beggar credulity amongst the most credulous. Nevertheless, there they are, amongst his collection in the *Variae*. In the following excerpt we see Cassiodorus in full flamboyance. He has been ordered to reprimand a dawdling official who had failed to follow Theodoric's orders to ship corn immediately from Apulia to Rome. To that delinquent sluggard, on behalf of Theodoric (whose actual words were probably along the lines of *"Tell him to get the hell up to Rome with the corn or I'll carve his lazy guts out!"*), Cassiodorus lifted his pen and wrote:

> Why is there such great delay in sending your swift ships to traverse the tranquil seas? Though the south wind blows and the rowers are bending their oars, has the sucking-fish fixed its teeth into the hulls through the liquid waves; or have the shells of the Indian Sea, whose quiet touch is said to hold so firmly that the angry billows cannot loosen it, with like power fixed to their lips into your keels; idle stands the bark though winged by swelling sails; the wind favours her but she makes no way; she is fixed without an anchor, she is bound without a cable; and these tiny animals hinder more than all such prospering circumstances can help. Thus, though the loyal wave may be hastening its course, we are informed that the ship stands fixed on the surface of the sea, and by a strange paradox the swimmer [the ship] is made to remain immovable while the wave is hurried along by movements numberless. Or to describe the nature of another kind of fish,…[10] (Cassiod., *Var.* 1.35)

To explain the barbarians to Romans, or rather to recast their image, Cassiodorus also wrote a *History of the Goths* (alas, now lost),[11] in which he squeezed the Goths onto the same social registry of ancestry and birth as the ancient peoples of Greece and Rome. Under the spell of his minister's psychotherapy, the king's enlightened image seemed to advance quite well for a while. But then, during the terrible years of 524–526 CE, murmurings of Byzantine conspiracy and anti-heretical persecutions reached Theodoric's ears and shattered his aging nerves. It was during an absence of Cassiodorus from the court circle that Theodoric succumbed to suspicious rage and ordered the murder of the jailed Boethius and members of his family. The news of their deaths must have been a horrible shock to Cassiodorus, who amongst his other determined fantasies claimed a familial relationship to the elegant Boethius.

Despite these setbacks, Cassiodorus toiled on. His sway in political circles allowed him to establish a seat of Christian learning in Rome, namely a center for study and a gathering place for books and scholars. Sadly, that 'university' flourished only briefly, from 535 to 536 CE, when political strife and fresh waves of barbarians descended from the north, and quickly reversed all his achievements and hopes for a civilized Ostrogothic rule. When Theodoric himself died, Cassiodorus continued to help Theodoric's culture-loving daughter and his not-so-culture-loving grandson. Ever loyal, ever hopeful, he even served in the cabinets of their usurping successors. But when imperial Constantinople turned its efforts to exterminating the Goths once and for all, those semi-Italianized heathen hordes moved south from Ravenna and brought Rome fully to her knees.

At last, Cassiodorus gave up his political career (ca. 539 CE). After some 30 years of public service, he headed south for a further, 30-year career on his own quieter lands on the Gulf of Taranto. There, he established a monastery, Vivarium, for which he tirelessly gathered a library. The specific task he now set for himself was to make pagan learning the servant of Christian knowledge. Under his guidance, classical scholarship would become a continuing feature of monastic life, and the cloister would replace the court as a center of culture.[12] The realization of literary monasticism was his lasting gift to the world.

We know from the extant catalogue of the Vivarium library that Cassiodorus collected books from a broad spectrum. In addition to writing a great deal himself, he established a theological school and a manufactory for duplicating texts. Under his care, the Vivarium scriptorium became famous for the great accuracy with which both Christian and pagan works were copied—and this, one should note, at a time when churchly knowledge was restrictively inbred, when other monasteries were not widely responsive to Greek or classical Roman cultures. Seeking to broaden the horizons of all religious learning, Cassiodorus imported his first-generation Vivarium monks from the remnant sophisticates of Ravenna and Rome and set those elderlies to copying and translating Greek manuscripts into Latin, so that the knowledge contained therein might survive in the West. Through the energy and insight of Cassiodorus, Vivarium became a center of culture, a beehive of translation and scribal activity, where the preservation of eastern learning was a specific, tenacious endeavor and where the monks were exhorted not to emend the texts hastily, however plausible a correction might seem to be.[13] Caution and precision were to be the guiding principles of their labor.

Though the will to copy remained strong, the aging Cassiodorus was fighting a rearguard action.[14] As those imported first-generation monks died, untutored Calabrian initiates took their place. Cassiodorus did not try to teach Greek to these young, peasant, would-be monks—thinking, no doubt, that it was hopeless. Instead, he modified their monastic school curriculum with watered-down Latin abridgments of original texts. He left his strong imprint on all future European education with the program of study that he described in his famous *Institutiones divinarum et saecularium litterarum* (a plan or outline of the principles of divine and secular literature).[15] For this encyclopaedic compilation of the world's up-to-that-date scientific and literary knowledge, he selected and simplified important works and ideas. His goal was twofold: to introduce his pupils to the body of interpretative studies of the Holy Scripture; and to give them a compendious acquaintance with secular literature. As the *Institutiones* was intended to be a teaching book for the ignorant, he kindly abstained from *affectata eloquentia*, and instead, wrote sentences of striking clarity and simplicity. Certainly, his pedagogical style made a nice relief from the replete and turgid phraseology "in which the perverted taste of the times [had] caused him generally to shroud his meaning."[16]

Cassiodorus became quite bubbly as he described the sacred copy work being done by what he termed an *antiquarius* (meaning 'a scribe who saves the words of his elders'). To encourage and enlighten his young, unsophisticated trainees, he kept his sentences short and snappy. *What a lucky man is the antiquarius*, he said. *While he works, he may also wound the devil.*

[The *antiquarius*] may fill his mind with the Scriptures while copying the sayings of the Lord. With his fingers he gives life to men and arms them against the wiles of the devil. So many wounds does Satan receive as the *antiquarius* copies words of Christ. What he writes in his cell will be scattered far and wide over distant Provinces. Man multiplies the heavenly words, and by a striking figure—if I may dare so to speak—the three fingers of his hand express the utterances of the Holy Trinity. The fast-travelling reed writes down the holy words, and thus avenges the malice of the Wicked One, who caused a reed to be used to smite the head of the Saviour.[17] (Cassiod., *Inst.* 30.1)

At age 93, Cassiodorus succumbed to the request of his ink-stained monks, who complained of needing some guidance in spelling. To ensure their correct transmission of knowledge, he once again fired up his energies to produce a treatise, *De orthographia*, which was a compilation of the various rules set forth by an array of admired grammarians, most notably Donatus and Priscian. In this final work he is especially concerned about the breakup of classical Latin into dialects (later to become the Romance languages) and the confusion of *b* and *v*. If spoken Latin were allowed to stray so far from classical norm, he argued, there could be no accurate scholarship, for spelling is dependent on a nice discrimination of sound.[18] (As time passed, nice discriminations would be needed again, particularly amongst synonyms.)

Amongst his various pedagogical efforts, Cassiodorus included the matter of punctuation. Appropriate to the enveloping intellectual gloom, he likened the three *distinctii* to "paths of meaning and lanterns to words, as instructive to readers as the best commentaries."[19] Though we are glad to see that he recognized *three* distinctions, the image he stirs up of groping one's way through darkness tells us that Alexandrian sophistications are light-years away. For the actual form the points should take, Cassiodorus guided his scribes to the Donatus dot method, though in the case of the Vulgate he allowed them to use colometry, as recommended by Jerome.

Having prolonged the sixth-century period of intellectual enlightenment through his own writings, translations, and the careful copy work that he sponsored, Cassiodorus died, and his monastery seems to have died with him. In the turmoil of the times, its valuable books were dispersed. The informed conjecture is that they were incorporated into the Lateran Library and papal collections, from where they became widely disseminated by the Holy See. To this one man's liberality, skill, and passion for learning we owe the preservation of many Christian manuscripts as well as the continued availability of the pagan sciences, most notably medicine. But he could not do it all. By the beginning of the seventh century, Greek literary tradition was nonexistent in the West and stayed more or less that way until the Carolingian renaissance, ca. 800. Most of the surviving fifth- and sixth-century manuscripts that were written in the uncial script are believed to have come from the Vivarium monastic scriptorium.[20]

The sixth-century intellectual flowering, however brief, was not in vain. The secular literature that it had managed to preserve was passed on to a dwindling educated elite whose respect for Hellenistic textual precision was integral to later scholarly aspirations. Meanwhile, in the wake of the dying classicism, church oratory (particularly in the vernaculars) came to be less influenced by the rationale and patterns of classical rhetoric. The *codices distincti*, those texts with word separation and marked pauses, became expensive treasures, the possessions of the wealthy or of monastic libraries, where they were studied, admired, and copied—with imperfect understanding. Punctuation, in one form or another and in varying degrees of usefulness, was seen by this time to be necessary. Extant samples of the correction and revision of books show us that the practice of emendation became more common after Boethius, Cassiodorus, and Priscian. More texts begin to survive from this period; and the attempts made at pointing them become common.

Priscian

The historical reverence for the Greek language, with its melodious sounds and facile expression, were a worry to the papal West. Though the Church itself made use of the fact that Greece was the source and custodian of desirable things—the secrets of music, medicine, and those aspects of science acceptable to churchly doctrine—the Greek language continued to lose ground. In the end, Christianizing chauvinists put a finish to the fostering of all Greek culture. It was their claim that its history of analysis, reason, and philosophy—and its ties to pagan frolic and sin—made indecorous fare for Christians. As the doors to intellectual inquiry began to shut, and continued to shut, the old-timey teachings of Donatus simply carried on, without the benefit of fresh insight. In this time of linguistic incuriosity, Priscian (born in Romanized Spain and active in the mid-sixth century CE) now emerges as the only lasting Latin grammarian. In this bleak period of scholarly decline, he—a professor of Latin in Greek-speaking Constantinople—shone as a man of great learning.

It is intriguing that Priscian should have had such a high opinion of the contemporary work of Greek grammarians, about whom so little is known today, but he was strong in his admiration. The Greeks, he felt, had perfected the instruction of their own classical grammar, and it therefore behooved his fellow grammarians in Rome to study the Greek examples and follow suit in their own Latin language. Like Boethius, he lamented the decline of Rome's prestige, and longing to restore it, he advocated a revival of Greek knowledge. That Greece was the wellhead of all the liberal arts in the Latin world was still well recognized.

Spurred by his conviction, Priscian wrote *Institutiones grammaticae*, in which he summarized and adapted to Latin the critical works of recent prominent Hellenistic grammarians.[21] Designed for those few who knew both Latin and Greek, it was a certain nonseller. The world was not ready for it, unfortunately, though it unveiled many useful similarities between Greek and Latin; discussed matters of syntax, a topic heretofore unexamined by known grammarians; and hinted towards a Chomsky-like universal origin for all languages. In his *Institutiones*, Priscian also discussed and compared the declensions and conjugations in considerable detail. Yet, for centuries this eye-opening work would remain the silent chief-authority on correct Latin. Though Priscian's arguments were sound and would have been a stimulus to the teaching of grammar and rhetoric, his *Institutiones* took nearly three centuries (until Charlemagne's era) to really sink in. Meanwhile it came to be cherished by scholars for whom Latin was an acquired tongue—most notably the Anglo-Saxon Venerable Bede and Alcuin.[22]

More quickly successful was Priscian's *Institutio de nomine et pronomine et verbo*, which classified nouns by declension (in contrast to Donatus, who had classified them only by gender). Within decades this book would come to be amongst the best-known works on the grammatical market, with particular influence on Irish, Welsh, and Anglo-Saxon scholars. Though Priscian explained the forms of nouns, pronouns, and verbs and what they were, he still did not set them out as we do today: *amo, amas, amat, etc.*; nor did he provide rules for inflectional changes.[23] Nevertheless, his writings pressed towards the rigorous, eye-oriented, breakdown of grammatical analogies that had been initiated in Alexandria so many centuries before and that would eventually make life easier for both teachers and pupils.

Isidore of Seville: The Decline Accelerates

Isidore (ca. 560–636 CE) who was both the Bishop of Seville and the Archbishop of Toledo was the dwindling star in the decline of linguistic aptitude. This energetic theologian, who was the last of the western Latin Fathers and the first Christian encyclopedist,[24] generated an extraordinary succession of literary products, the outstanding item of which was his multivolumed encyclopaedia of all contemporary knowledge, the *Etymologiae, sive origines*. This opus, one of the most studied reference works in the so-called Dark and Middle Ages,[25] was an attempt to deal with

> the whole sum of knowledge, the world in general, its peoples and languages, the liberal arts and all the sciences, especially medicine and anatomy, the animal world, navigation, astronomy, geography, agriculture; religious knowledge, Church organisation and heresies, [all] sixty-eight of them. The chief impression of reading Isidore is surprise at the amount of erroneous or half-correct information which he conveys.[26]

The *Etymologiae* essentially consisted of a conglomeration of extractions from other works, including a wide scope of officially unapproved, ancient secular knowledge and naïve explanations of the origins of words.

In matters of grammar and rhetoric, Isidore is best defined as an industrious (frequently misinformed) compiler of (often skewed) information—an accolade, surely, of some distinction. Nevertheless, his writings offered his knowledge-starved contemporaries a kaleidoscopic peephole into the high-quality rhetoric of cultured antiquity.[27] Like most in the oppressive and authoritative early Christian era, Isidore was less an innovator than a follower. In the area of our focus now, namely his famous Book 10 on etymology and his linguistic studies (*Differentiarum libri*), he drew extensively from the works of Donatus. Concerning Isidore's disinclination to step out on his own, Mr. Brehaut, his eminent scholar, attaches an interesting footnote that demonstrates the temper of the times. To show how slavishly imitative each new grammarian tended to be, he lists in order of sequence a single phrase as it is taken up again and again, century after century. The exercise reveals an almost pathetic dependence on previous authority. Nobody, it seems, was about to sit down and rethink grammatical and rhetorical issues, let alone launch a fresh idea. Brehaut illustrates this lack of initiative with the repeated example of human voice-sound description as it appeared in an array of grammarians through the centuries. He begins with the earliest (though undated) sample. It comes from an obscure grammarian of the first century CE, who was referred to as 'Probus':

> *Vox sive sonus est aer ictus, id est percussus, sensibilis auditu quantum in ipso est*, meaning: [The voice or sound is air blown out, it is percussed, perceivable to the hearer as well as to himself (i.e., the one who is doing the percussing).]

Then, in Donatus (fl. 353 CE):

Vox est aer ictus sensibilis auditu, quantum in ipso est.

Then, in Sergius:

Vox est aer ictus sensibilis auditu, verbis emissa, et exacta sensus prolatio.

Then, in Marius Victorinus:

Vox est aer auditu percipibilis quantum in ipso est.

Then, in Maximius Victorinus:

Vox quid est? Aer ictus sensibilisque auditu quantum in ipso est.

Then, in Cassiodorus (sixth century):

Vox articulata est aer percussus sensibilis auditu quantum in ipso est.

And finally, in Isidore, some six centuries after Probus:

Vox est aer ictus sensibilis auditu, quantum in ipso est.

Isidore divided his *Differentiarium libri* into two books. The first, about the differences between similar word meanings, is particularly interesting, for its 610 alphabetically arranged word-pairs illuminate the subtle distinctions of meaning: for example, between *populus* and *plebs*, between *recens* and *novus*, between *religio* and *fides*, etc. Here, for example, one may learn the difference between *inquire* and *ask*. Isidore tells us that we *inquire* about things we are doubtful of; whereas we *ask* about things we don't know. Or, in the case of *voice* and *sound*: the first is used for humans and the second for the noise that boots make. Isidore also deals with the crucial matter of pronunciation, particularly *b* and *v* (as in *vis* and *bis*: one 'strength' and the other 'twice'; or *vivit* and *bibit*: one about living and the other about drinking);[28] and the effects of dropping inflections (as in *mare* for *marem*). The second book also deals with words, but with the emphasis on the things they are meant to represent, such as: What is the difference between the concepts of *deus* and *dominus*? or: How may a life of action compare with a life of contemplation?

Good for the *Differentiarium*! for it gave a push in the direction of needed exactitude. But in his *Etymologiae*, which aspired to cover all knowledge to date, this prone-to-be-wrong gentleman gives a fuller view of seventh-century misperceptions. The erroneous erudition that he presented in it would encumber successive scholarrs for centuries as they labored to resuscitate classical culture. Isidore did not discuss the tremendous mathematical achievements of the Greeks. He only addressed the mystical significance of numbers.[29] As for grammar, he did little to help with the understanding of punctuation, for though he adopted Donatus as a guide, he regularly used only two of the three available points, thereby failing in his own usage to differentiate between the pauses that follow *commata* and *cola*. He nevertheless claimed that the purpose of cadencing dots was to mark off the sense into *colons* (clauses), *commas* (phrases), and *periods* (sentences), where the voice "sets down"—thus a mix of vision and sound, and no real definition of anything.[30] This manner of sentence discussion became standard during the era's backsliding into orality, a time when very few people could actually read by themselves. Though sentence segments were recognized, the instruction for dealing with them remained very much riddled with breathing imperatives.

However, it is in the glossaries and explanations of word origins where Isidore's most intriguing unlikelihoods prevail. It is there that one can most plainly see the harm that unquestioned prestige might cause to illiterate ignorants in their acceptance of 'knowledge.' Isidore's etymologies, sedulously studied for centuries, were devised to correct mistakes in word usage. Words were his thing. Influenced by his studies of Varro, he claimed that all knowledge lay in words, whose true meanings could best be elucidated by reference to their origin rather than to the things they seemingly stood for. The blame for the misuse of words lay with the heathen writers and ancient poets who "disregarded the proper meanings of words under the compulsion of meter," so that (to project the matter into today's present tense) a flat wooden surface upon which one rests one's elbows is not truly a table, but more likely something else (a floor board? an oak tree? an acorn?), whose essential value can only be discovered by searching for what it once meant to the most ancient ancestor that could be found. (All of Isidore's commentary is riddled with antiquarian bias.) Thus, in the *Etymologiae*, he tells us that *homo* is derived from *humus*, because man is from the earth; and again, that *lutum* (meaning "mud") comes from lavare ("to wash") "since mud is not clean."[31]

In the encyclopedic section on language, Isidore simply incorporated the whole of Cassiodorus's textbook *De rhetorica* and did so without acknowledgement. This easy acceptance of the commonality of knowledge became more and more evident, as literacy faded and folk scrambled to preserve what they could of it. In such an atmosphere, personal responsibility for what was claimed to be true was diminished by the superior aura of Established Authority, particularly Church authority. In this matter of Isidore adopting Cassiodorus's work as his own, we sense not only the habit of the times, but also Isidore's distinctive ignorance and the unscholarly impatience deriving from it. Concerning the subject of elegant wordage, for example, Isidore tells us that it is easy enough for a reader to admire the rhetorical arts, but impossible to understand them; and in any case, once one has finished reading a book of rhetoric and laid it aside, "all recollection vanishes."[32] In other words, rhetorical study is both complicated and boring. So why bother?

Though we may find Isidore's childlike judgments amusing, it is rather sad to discover the difficulties that students in later times would have in trying to digest his strange pronouncements. Yet, despite all, Isidore's compilations turned out to be useful in keeping alive an interest in ancient attainments. They remain useful to modern scholars, too, as they follow the history of spoken language into writing. As for poor Isidore: he missed his target of being the Grand Scholar of the World by living at a time when secular learning was rapidly disappearing.

A Note on the Status of Bookmaking

It was during the early eighth century that Islam began its acquisitive rampage around the Mediterranean. With the upset of commerce and the spread of political strife, Egyptian papyrus was difficult to obtain and parchment became the staple for bookmaking. Good parchment was expensive, and the high cost of it encouraged the production of the homely, pocket-sized codex, especially popular for small Bibles. Increasingly thereafter, the dense, space-economizing, minuscule (small) lettering came to be used extensively for church materials. Minuscules were more suited to small pages than were the majestic uncials. As one can well imagine, the whole scene of small books with their abbreviations, crammed margins, unseparated words, glosses (i.e., interlinear translations to clarify outmoded or foreign vocabulary), tiny lettering, and ink-specks advising cadence—all these things slammed the door on easy reading. By this time, however, literacy and cultural knowledge were already close to extinction.

Notes

1. Courcelle, *Early Latin Writers*, 276 (from his chapter on Boethius, 273–330). These English renditions of *De consolatione* are more interpretive than exact, but interesting nevertheless, for they reveal the English language in several of its early phases.

2. Arnaldo Momigliano, "Cassiodorus and Italian Culture of his Time," *Proceedings of the British Academy* 41 (1955): 216; reprinted in Arnaldo Momigliano, *Studies in Historiography* (London: Weidenfeld and Nicolson, 1966).

3. Justin ruled over the eastern (Greek Orthodox) division of the once 'worldwide' dominions of Rome.

4. Thomas Hodgkin, *The Letters of Cassiodorus* (London: Henry Frowde, 1886), 301.

5. Ibid., 79–80.

6. Momigliano, "Cassiodorus," 224.

7. Ibid., 216–7.

8. Hodgkin, *Letters*, 301.

9. So called "because it was necessary that we who undertake to remind [or instruct] do not assume [only] one style." [Quia necesse nobis fuit stylum non unum sumere, qui personae variae suscepimus admonere.] That is, we should use different styles (of instructive writing) for different people. Cassiodorus followed this rule by simplifying his language for the less able. Cf. Wright and Sinclair, *Later Latin*, 91.

10. Hodgkin, "Introduction" to *Letters*, 17–18, 163.

11. This first attempt to place the history of the Goths within the framework of Roman history and civilization is also said to have been the last great work of Roman historiography.

12. Momigliano, "Cassiodorus," 225.

13. Hodgkin, *The Letters of Cassiodorus*, 60.

14. Courcelle, *Early Latin Writers*, 337. (Materials for this section have largely been drawn from Courcelle's chapters on Cassiodorus and Vivarium, 331–409). One-eighth of the total Vivarium collection was devoted to Greek MSS.

15. The second part of this work gives a brief exposition of the seven liberal arts, and was a kind of encyclopaedia of pagan learning, widely regarded in the Middle Ages as indispensable for understanding the Bible.

16. Hodgkin, *Letters*, 62–3.

17. Ibid., 58.

18. Ibid., 65–6.

19. Eadmer and R. W. Southern, *The Life of St. Anselm, Archibishop of Canterbury*, with introduction, notes, and translation (London: Thos. Nelson, 1962), xxxiii. In two short centuries down the line, Alcuin will be having to cajole his monks in a similar way.

20. Courcelle, *Early Latin Writers*, 401–9, 421.

21. McKitterick, *The Carolingians and the Written Word*, 14; and Courcelle, *Early Latin Writers*, 323–39.

22. Wright and Sinclair, *Later Latin Literature*, 94.

23. McKitterick, *The Carolingians and the Written Word*, 14.

24. See Ernest Brehaut, *Encyclopedist of the Dark Ages: Isidore of Seville* (London: P. S. King and Son, 1912), 7, passim. Mr. Brehaut, a prominent scholar of the era we now address, tells us

that as an encyclopaedist, Isidore was following in the footsteps of such as Varro (as in his origins of word meaning), Pliny the Elder, and Suetonius. Though few of his sources are extant today, he apparently had access to much recorded knowledge, since Spain had not suffered from barbarian raids as extensively as had Italy and France. Nevertheless, Brehaut and others have noted that a large part of Isidore's regurgitated information was in his own time not only antiquated but delivered in rather corrupt Latin.

25. Almost 1,000 medieval manuscripts of the *Etymologies* are still in existence today.
26. Wright and Sinclair, *Later Latin Literature*, 119.
27. *Encyclopaedia Britannica Micropaedia*, 15th ed., s.v. "Isidore of Seville."
28. Roger Wright, *Late Latin and Early Romance in Spain and Carolingian France* (Liverpool, UK: Francis Cairns, 1982), 83.
29. Brehaut, *Encyclopedist*, 29.
30. Walter J. Ong, "Historical Backgrounds," 349–60.
31. Brehaut, *Encyclopedist*, 100.
32. Ibid., 106.

References

Brehaut, Ernest. *Encyclopedist of the Dark Ages: Isidore of Seville*. London: P. S. King and Son, 1912.

Courcelle, Pierre. *Early Latin Writers and Their Greek Sources*. Translated by Harry E. Wedeck. Cambridge: Harvard University Press, 1969.

Eadmer, and R. W. Southern, *The Life of St. Anselm, Archibishop of Canterbury*, with introduction, notes, and translation. London: Thos. Nelson, 1962.

Encyclopaedia Britannica Micropaedia, 15th ed., s.v. "Isidore of Seville."

Hodgkin, Thomas. *The Letters of Cassiodorus*. London: Henry Frowde, 1886.

McKitterick, Rosamund. *The Carolingians and the Written Word*. Cambridge: Cambridge University Press, 1995.

Momigliano, Arnaldo. "Cassiodorus and Italian Culture of his Time." *Proceedings of the British Academy* 41 (1955): 216. Reprinted in Arnaldo Momigliano, *Studies in Historiography*. London: Weidenfeld and Nicolson, 1966.

Ong, Walter J. "Historical Backgrounds of Elizabethan and Jacobean Punctuation Theory." *PMLA* 59, no. 2 (1944): 349–60.

Wright, F. A., and T. A. Sinclair. *A History of Later Latin Literature*. London: George Routledge & Sons, 1931.

Wright, Roger. *Late Latin and Early Romance in Spain and Carolingian France*. Liverpool, UK: Francis Cairns, 1982.

·SECTION 5·

THE MEDIEVAL PERIOD
IN WESTERN EUROPE

· 1 8 ·

DIVING INTO PITCH

An Historical Overview

Scholars seem unable to agree on the start-up date for all the gloomy things that fall under the description of 'medieval.' Though the establishment of the Byzantine Empire in 300 CE defines a workable date for the East, our own Western-oriented interests make the collapse of Rome in 476 CE more useful,[1] for it was then that the northern tribes accelerated their devastation of Latin territories. In the subsequent confusion, civic order with its expectation of well-being came to an end, as did Rome's hitherto magisterial guardianship of the Latin language. As imperial power decomposed in each provincial area, so the sense of belonging to a greater whole gave way to a sense of local identity.[2] The uncertainties of living in such a shattered world did little to encourage the continuity of literary pursuits—let alone an adherence to classical Latin.

Looking at a map of fifth-century Europe, one can almost see the vast terrains of mountain and forest cracking apart like so many pieces of a geographical puzzle, as chunk by chunk the Roman Wall (which in its prime had included northern Africa, Scotland, Syria, and Spain) retracted its protective embrace. Once government rule and public wealth had been taken over by the boorish conquerors (whose strange clothing, strange speech, and strange gods were horrific to indigenous sensibilities), the Roman populace turned in droves to the Christian religion, where at least a stable afterlife was on offer. Under such circumstances, the Church reaped a harvest of believers. Their influx into its system enriched the papal power, with all its supporting retinue of priests, monks, and eventually, itinerant friars.

As intellectual life diminished on the public front, books and scholarship found their way into the increasingly numerous monasteries, where literacy was still being practiced. Since Christianity had been founded on the written words of the Bible, the art of reading was considered essential to those in position of clerical command. Thus, as Christianity spread, books spread with it, and monastic redoubts became the preservers and transmitters of both sacred and classical learning. Meanwhile, the new barbarian kings rather admired the cultural splendors of their victim peoples, and once they had firmly established their hold, took to surrounding themselves with Latin-speaking poets, rhetoricians, and jurists, through whom they gradually absorbed some of the educational and administrative legacies of Rome. In seeking to attain the cultural levels of those whom they must have felt to be superior company, they played a notable role in keeping Latin alive.

The ebb of Rome's supremacy encouraged the growth of dialects in outlying regions. Whereas the culture-stricken conquerors adopted the more traditional forms of Latin for running their governments, the Latin of ordinary folk in villages and towns became increasingly disparate. The *lingua franca* used for commercial communication was a rough Latin,[3] which in turn pressed the various provincial corruptions to become for practical purposes a somewhat unified, Latin-based amalgam of scattered popular vernaculars. Of these, a traveling merchant might easily have known several. Despite the constant change on the oral front, written-down Latin held dominion over the subsequent variations more or less up to the end of the ninth century, for it was not until then that civilized communities descended absolutely to rural levels, leaving culture entirely in the hands of the Church. With the retreat of public education, ignorance had its way. By the tenth century, ordinary people could not understand what the Latin-mumbling priests were reciting in Church.

Throughout this period, the West persisted in an ignorant, almost superstitious reverence for the vaguely perceived ancient Greek world: first, as it was seen through the Latinized interpretations of such as Ovid, Statius, Vergil, and Apuleius; and then, through the readapted productions of lesser poets, annalists, novelists, and epicists. Under Christian discipline, the regenerating distortions of ancient myth and legend went underground for centuries to re-emerge and feed the plots of pre-Renaissance romance cycles, starring Alexander the Great, Jason, and the indefatigable Helen of Troy. Although scholarly consensus is not firm, it is generally agreed that Latinate knowledge of the true Classical Athenian and Hellenic civilizations petered out sometime between 400 and 700 CE. Early in those years (in both East and West) pagan religious practice had become an offense to authority, and all pagan literature, along with its legacy of rhetorical subtleties, became suspect.

Not until Charlemagne's brief mini-renaissance (ca. 800) would the Romanic-Germanic peoples again experience (briefly experience) the splendors of true ancient learning. Thereafter would follow another lapse, a more profound lapse, thanks this time to the influx of rampaging Vikings. The succeeding calm following their absorption marked a time of the reaffirmation of cultural values, when ancient achievement and an interest in the written word began once more to take hold and grow. By the twelfth century, an irreversible passion for knowledge, inquiry, and experiment was flourishing. This, in broad outline, is the background story for what we will now examine.

On the Origins and Development
of the Romance Languages

For a few centuries after the fall of Rome in 476 CE, the common, often illiterate, masses remained acquainted with the traditional forms of the Latin language. Generally speaking, up into the late 800s, lowly Christian congregations were able to understand commentaries on the scriptures when they were read aloud. They could follow a recitation of the Latin text of the Gospels. Yet, during those several centuries, a slippage in the public's level of speech was being deplored in sophisticated circles. As we have already seen, Isidore of Seville's encyclopedic tomes (ca. 600 CE) are laden with linguistic commands intended to rectify the waywardness of expression. Conservative pedagogues were pressing to reintroduce correct classical Latin norms and to keep the small distinctions of Latin grammar from sliding out of sight. For without the knowledge of classical Latin, a man could neither access the magnificent literature of Rome nor appreciate the writings of the early Church fathers, who themselves had been bred on 'proper' Latin. There was a danger that all the store of Latin wisdom would be lost forever. Early lists of grammatical *vitia*, or 'improper ways of saying things,' give us our first glimpse of the centrifuging aspects of the proto-Romance languages. They reveal the accelerating post-imperial split between the written language (as reflected in the usage of the *eruditi*) and the practical street talk of uneducated commoners.

During this stage (i.e., the sixth, seventh, and eighth centuries), the Latin language should be perceived as a rather loosely constructed unity in a monolingual speech community. Despite its regional and stylistic variations, its basic elements still provided the primary means of interterritorial communication. The first real signs of decline in clerical literacy do not begin to show until the middle of the sixth century—that is, after Jerome, Augustine, and Ambrose—though the cultural atmosphere had plainly been on the skids for a good while. Not until Charlemagne's time do we have records in witness of the existence of two distinct languages in use: one (Latin) spoken and written by the educated, and the other (the proto-Romance 'rustica Romana lingua') by the illiterate. Though the privileged literates had probably long been using the words 'italiano' and 'français' to describe the breaking-away languages, there is no extant evidence before the beginning of the ninth century (Charlemagne's era) of any other *West European language name* than Latin. Throughout the first millennium that entire body of linguistic diversification was held together by the standardized written language used by a very small elite and associated with the enormously prestigious name of 'Latin.'

While classical Latin was loosening its hold, a sort of truce developed between the erudite grammarians and the ambitiously expanding Christian Church. Like everyone else, grammarians yearned for the bliss of an afterlife, to obtain which they needed the help of religious clerics. In return, the clerics needed the grammarians to resolve uncertainties in their sacred texts and emend what errors they might find so that the true dogma might be kept intact for teaching the public and saving themselves. Spiritual success was dependent on earthly success, which itself depended upon the conversion of heathens, the acquisition of wealth, and control over the masses. If the Church was to do the job it felt charged to do, namely save souls, then its message must be dispersed through readings and explanations to those from lower cultural settings. For that, priests in the pulpit would have to avoid oratorical pretensions, rare words, or long, complicated *periods*. The unlettered, ignorant folk, who filled the churches and swelled the Pope's dominion, were plainly more responsive when they were not being addressed in a hoity-toity language that they could not easily understand. Augustine's willingness to accept the linguistic 'aberrations' of the lower classes in order to spread the word had set an authoritative precedent that grew over time. In essence, it approved the

exchange of grammatical perfection for saved souls. Subsequent Church leaders, spotting the efficacy of this approach, popularized their language too, and
in doing so, set themselves up as the common man's friend. In the press of the
tide, erudites reluctantly followed suit.

Sixth-Century Latin:
The Crumbling of Classical Norms

A comparison of what is known of oral usage and written tradition exposes
an array of systemic differences, both lexical and grammatical. Though writing was applying the brakes and forcing change to slow its pace, it could not
stop how illiterate folk actually talked. In the end, the written word was itself
overwhelmed by the evolving speech sounds in the street. Of these, the most
lamented and crucial was the disappearance of the old, phonological opposition between short and long vowels. The resulting effect of all this must have
been similar to what we might initially feel if, say, nobody quite recognized
the differing 'o' sound-lengths in 'cop' and 'cope.' "Watch out! The copes
are coming!" is initially baffling, though of course we could all cop with it if
we tried. Of tremendous concern to the *educati* in these developing Christian years was the fact that 'careless' articulation was accelerating the loss of
the entire, ancient tradition of metric poetry and the cadencing (*clausulae*)
rhythms of prose. Both of these ancient joys were dependent upon the 'classical' vowel-duration system. One should remind oneself here that classical
vowel duration is quite specifically a time-related lengthening and shortening
of a vowel sound, as between (for example) *bat* and *baaat*. Classical longs and
shorts should not be confused with the modern stressed-unstressed drumbeats
that we find, for example, in Longfellow's *The Song of Hiawatha*. It is thought
that the classical longs and shorts emerged from song, and before that, from
dance. Indeed, they can easily be recognized and remembered by relating
them to the held and not-held differentiations possible for the voice (as for a
musical quarter-note opposed to a half-note) or to the short and long steps of
a dance.

The ancient long-short vowel distinctions were critical in another respect
as well. The disappearance of differentiated, time-oriented longs and shorts
confounded the inflectional system, and eventually broke it down. When one
could no longer tell which adjective modified which noun, or whether a vow-
eled word-ending indicated an ablative form (because it was long) or a voca-

tive form (because it was short), then some other indicator of how the words of a sentence fitted together was needed. For this, *word order proved the answer.*

Word ordering puts words into positions according to their syntactic and grammatical functions. It gathers words that are *bonded-by-meaning* and stabilizes the position of subjects, objects, and verbs. In the case of Latin, the subjects (with their modifying materials) customarily came early in the word string. Verbs (especially in formal writing) were generally the terminators, and all the rest came in between. By using inflections to denote relationships, the classical Latin writer had had the option of thwarting expectations by planting a word in a semantically alien phrase—with the resulting satisfaction of having achieved a better rhythm or smoother pronunciation or perhaps merely because that is where he wanted the word to be. Complication could sometimes seem a virtue. As inflections grew less stable, a speaker or writer was obliged to arrange his word strings in some anticipatable, standardized order; for if not, who would be able to tell what adjective went with which noun or whether that ablative absolute was to relate to this or to another portion of a sentence?

Without inflections, *position* became crucial, for semantic grouping is the default mode of *natural* (as opposed to *artistically crafted*) word use. Writing based on 'natural word-order' implies that the words have been set out to reflect in the most clear and direct manner possible what is meant. The 'natural' part of 'natural word-order' is supported by the flattering thought that to be clear is a natural human intent. Be that true or not, a straightforward word order presides in commonplace talk because it is easier to use and more quickly understood. We find its early footprint in the dialogue of early comedy (Aristophanes, Plautus, and Terence) and in the familial correspondence of Cicero. We are not surprised, then, to see early medieval writers increasingly arrange their *where, when,* and *how* phrases in a preposition-plus-modifier-plus-object formula (as in "*under* the fragrant shrubs," or "*on* his well-shod feet"). Even Thucydides, so long before, had sometimes taken that whole phrase option. As these open prepositional chains increased in number, so the ablative, genitive, and dative inflectional endings (which had previously allowed considerable separation between words that supported the same idea) became redundant, and could be, and eventually *were,* dropped.

In sum, prepositional constructs were replacing inflection and thereby changing an important mode of expression. Inflection had allowed speakers and writers to tighten their word strings for epigrammatic compactness of phrase. If a wordsmith wished to avoid a crowd of ungainly consonants (as in the groveling grizzly bear example) or to improve the rhythm of a line, then inflections enabled him to do so. With the demise of inflection, the emphasis of expression shifted from classical eloquence with its fondness for rhythm and terse complexity (as in Tacitus) to the ease of putting out and receiving straightforward, easy-to-grasp sense—that is, of communicating in 'natural speech.'

As far as one can tell from extant writings, the changes that Latin underwent during the very early medieval period were neither simultaneous nor regional. Some of the phenomena (like the appearance of the articles *the* and *a*, and the initial restructurings of the verb system) must have started up in relative antiquity. If one thinks back to Roman imperial times, when enormous power was wielded over vast outreaches of territorial and linguistic sprawl, it is easy to see how military and governing requirements would have had to allow grammatical slippage simply to get the job done.

Blatant regional effects on the Latin language did not emerge until the fifth century; and considerable awareness of linguistic unity was still alive in the sixth. The theory that there were at that time coexisting within the Latin-speaking world two linguistic strata, one truly 'Latin' and one truly 'Vulgar Latin' is now seriously questioned. More likely, the pre-Charlemagne Roman world was linguistically homogeneous in the sense that a form of Latin was mainly the norm and that variation from it was sufficiently held in check by it. In contrast, immediately after the beginning of the ninth century, there appears a clear realization of the unbridgeable rift between Latin and Romance. Though the public reverence for a pristine Mother Latin did not disappear, the erudite custodianship of her good health thereafter fell to the Church, with its special interest in appealing to the mobs. At the same time, commoners thought the speech habits of all who held power and bossed them around (mostly, the priests and Church administrators) best represented the exemplary classical norms, the very ones they should in their ambitions strive to follow. Secular rulers of the sixth and seventh centuries, despite their admiration of antiquity, could only minimally support the maintenance of genuine classical purity. As a class, those rulers were made up of uneducated people, often of German background, whose grasp of Latin was at best uncertain. Under these circumstances, the pace of Latin disintegration increased.

With disintegration, the practicalities of communication in local contexts took precedence. In each area, one of the early variants became the norm; each group made its own choice, bearing only in mind its own needs and those of the neighboring groups with which it communicated. It would seem a creditable probability that the situation was similar to that still evident in Italy, where a national government, aided by education, radio, and television, has brought peasants with very diverse dialects to a stage where they can also understand standard Italian. Though they may continue to converse in the old way amongst themselves and even, when doing so, feel themselves to be speaking Italian, yet they can recognize the difference.

Some Specifics of Change

Though rooted in classical soils, popular speech must have begun to slide away from the learned Latin norm long before the fourth century, for Jerome, Augustine, and Ambrose are clearly battling against entrenched habits when they remark on the laxity of common talk and the differences of pronunciation between the *docti* and the *indocti*.[4] Early Roman inscriptions bear them out, for common samplings were already showing serious grammatical subsidence. The most noticeable instances are the declensional errors, which resulted not only in certain cases no longer corresponding with their traditional functions, but also in new forms rising up to compensate while old ones were entirely dropped.[5] Such was the dropping of the 'm' from *castrum*, leaving only the uninflected *castro*, whose function in the sentence would then have to be guessed if position would not tell.

Also indicative of early decline were the erroneous verbal forms: a repeated example being the numerous graphic tombstone variants found for the simple form *quiescit* or *requiescit*, which could range from *quesquaet* to *requisqi*. The grammarians of the time tell us that the 'h' sound was disappearing and that the assibilation of 't' before 'i' (so that today for the word 'consolation,' we say: *consolayshun*, instead of *consolateeon*) had been in practice from the second to third centuries. The observant Consentius (whose work is known mostly through reference) listed a number of vulgarisms to be avoided. Amongst these we find *bobis* for *vobis*; *orator* with a short 'o' in the first syllable; *triginta* with the accent on the first syllable; the syncope form *socrum* instead of *socerum*, also *vilam* for *villa* and *mile* for *mille*; *onorem* for *honorem*, and so on. Grammarians repeatedly complained about the loss of traditional syllables within a word—as in today's *nucler* for *nuclear*, *partickler* for *particular*, *terrist* for *terrorist*, *militry* for *military*, *probly* for *probably*, etc. For if speakers could not speak, they complained, nor hearers hear, the full count of a metered line, how could they deal with classical texts? Confusion of single with double consonants and the transpositions of letters or syllables (metatheses) are invariably noted with disapproval. We may be sure that even in early post-Christ centuries, the *docti* were very much aware of the public's 'mistakes.'[6]

Throughout this period and later, 'acceptable' Latin vacillated.[7] Eighth-century extant manuscripts show correctly constructed legal and ecclesiastical documents with deviations from classical word formation as well as out-and-out vulgarisms. Often these were pure blunders, but as many again provide evidence of the ongoing contemporary street language. In all of this, syntactical change was slow to show its head; on the other hand, morphology and phonology were rapid in their response to common usage: for example, *suus* replaced *eius* (his) very suddenly in the mid-eighth century. Benedict of Nursia (d. ca. 547), who was both scholar and founder of the Benedictine Order as well as the monastery Monte Cassino, used striking vulgarisms, such as the genitive *talius* for *talis*, by analogy (presumably) with *ullius*, *ullius*, etc. Is such an adoption of common sixth-century speech habit to be explained by a companionable wish to be understood by the unlettered? Or, should one take such usage as evidence of a genuine laxity seeping into upper-crust ecclesiastical language?[8] The ninth century witnessed the firm establishment of the definite article. And so in this manner, the changes grew in number and took hold. In the prevailing political turmoil, the gap between the progressive spoken language and the conservative written language enlarged. School systems collapsed, and traditional grammatical and rhetorical learning became a rarity. All too soon, the masses no longer understood Latin.

Along with elitist grumbles over grammar 'mistakes' were the lexical laments. Throughout the sixth, seventh, and eighth centuries, words were being profusely coined—some no doubt abbreviated from lengthier constructions (like our 'good-bye' from 'God be with you,' or the British 'bloody,' probably from 'by Our Lady'); others probably remodeled from traditional usage to a new, more simple one. We see this same rollover of language in operation today: as when purists bewail the word 'hopefully' in a sentence like "Hopefully, it will rain." *Who is doing the hoping?* they snidely ask. *The speaker? It? The rain?* Yet with the passage of time (since the same objections pertain), purists have come to accept "Certainly, it will rain" (meaning: "I am certain it will rain," or "It is a certainty that it will rain"). The prevailing human tendency is towards more speed and ease for the tongue and less effort for the mind. But complaining is a hopeless activity. We all know that no matter what we do, street talk will blossom without reference to conservative habit or to the edicts of Webster, or Fowler, or really anybody of collegiate odor.

Street talk, in fact, gives us a colorful alternative vocabulary with which to clothe our thinking. Words like *nerd, geek, spam, creep, scumball, cool, jerk, bubblehead,* and street expressions like "What's shakin', baby?" "Get your ass outa here!" "Chill it!" and "Gimme five, man!" are highly expressive. They give relief to excessive energies and strong feelings. There is also military slang to draw on, naval slang, football slang, adolescent slang, musicianly slang, political slang, and household slang—all kinds of delicious, on-the-nose, descriptive, aberrant ways of saying things, and they are rarely sentimental.[9] Being high-spirited, often humorous, they can be injected (with caution) into higher level word-flow with vibrant effect. Since linguistic ebullience is so alive today, it seems reasonable to assume that common folk of long ago were equally inventive in playing about with language. In fact, during the centuries we now discuss, a dual vocabulary is known to have existed. Whereas highbrow expression was governed by austere written example, its lowly street-talk counterpart enjoyed a lively freedom. Hypothetical reconstructions from the agglomerate of early Romance languages suggest that hundreds of words and expressions, kept in the background by more distinguished and usually less specific written synonyms, lived in the language of the *vulgus.*

Classical Latin lost its muscle because of the scarcity of books, schools, and competent teachers. Conservative pedagogues, both within and outside the Church, associated the innovations of speech with schoolroom neglect of 'proper' Latin norms. They said their piece, but effected little. In the end, few grammarians were left who were capable of teaching the finicky classical paradigms, and even they in their ignorance seemed unable to agree on the rules. Nevertheless, however deficient they may seem to us today, their efforts held Latin together in a sufficiently recognizable form to outlast the first millennium, and thereby preserve a cache of its treasures to fuel the thirteenth-century European Renaissance.

Grammar: Queen of the Liberal Arts

As literary folk and educators became fewer and less sure of themselves, so they applied more strictly the grammatical rules that they knew. Reference to classical precepts offered a sense of certainty, a way to proceed and do it right. At the same time those inherited dictates invited the imposition of authority and a dependence on ancestral successes.

The liberal arts were 'liberal' because they constituted the education for a free man—a man, that is, who did not need to learn a trade. Grammar, rhetoric, dialectic (formal argument) made up what came to be known as the *trivium* (three roads) and were the initial subjects of study. Next to be mastered were arithmetic, geometry, music, and astronomy, collectively known (as early as Boethius) as the *quadrivium*. Of all these, the most exhaustively cultivated was grammar. Initially (in times of Plato and Aristotle), grammar meant only the art of reading and writing. In the wake of Alexandrian exegeses of poetry, Quintilian divided grammar into two parts: the science of correct speech and the interpretation of the poets. The importance of grammar in the Christian educational curriculum is reflected in Isidore of Seville's distribution of materials in his encyclopedia: namely, an entire book (58 modernly printed pages) for grammar; 20 pages for rhetoric; 21 for dialectic; 10 for arithmetic; 8 for geometry; 6 for music; and 17 for astronomy.[10] Out of all the subjects to be mastered, grammar induced the most formidable memories for all educated folk. We see the allegorical female figure of Grammar depicted again and again in medieval art and poetry, and on the façades of cathedrals. She is never a beauty. Grim-faced, gray-haired, and old, dressed in the Roman manner (suggestive of the historical and religious authority of Rome), she carries a casket, containing a knife and a file with which to excise surgically any grammatical error.

Up to 1200, when new grammars began to systematize materials logically, the medieval beginner of Latin was required to memorize Donatus's *Ars minor* (which in today's print comprises 10 or 11 pages). With that mastered, he (for he was almost always a 'he') proceeded to the *Ars maior* and/or Priscian's *Institutio grammatica* (two small volumes in modern print), which cited classical authors and thus provided a grounding in literature. Grammar instruction through Priscian's time was shaped by the philology practiced in the Greek stoa of Classical Athens. Its subjects included etymology, analogy, barbarism (errors in vocabulary and pronunciation), solecism (errors in construction), and metaplasm (deviation of grammatical forms for the sake of meter), and also discussed letters, syllables, and parts of speech.

Along with the analysis of poetry, the study of grammar also included the figures of speech (collectively called *schemata* by the Greeks). The *schemata* were perceived as dividing into (1) rhetorical figures, that is, tricky little ways of arranging words to provoke delight, as do, for example, simile, metaphor, litotes,[11] synecdoche[12] and oxymoron;[13] and (2) figures of thought, which remodel a perception: like allegory, or irony, or a comprehensive metaphor that would dominate the entire text. In later textbooks, the word *tropes* (from the Greek word meaning 'turns') was often used for many of these figures, but the terminology was never precisely settled, nor has it since been satisfactorily systematized. To describe the two kinds (rhetorical figures and figures of thought), the common phrase is '*schemes* and *tropes*.' For the pleasure of adding to the general fogginess of the concept, here is Isidore of Seville saying his piece on the matter of tropes. This statement, delivered to sustain posterity, is presented *in its entirety*.[14]

> Tropes are so named by the grammarian from a Greek word which in Latin means *modi lucutionum* ['ways of saying things']. They are turned from their own meaning to a kindred meaning that is not their own. And it is very difficult to comment on the names of them all, but Donatus gave for practise a list of thirteen selected from the whole number. [*Finis*] (Isidore, *Etymologies* 1.37.1)

Meter was also an important element in the study of grammar. Out of the many possible meters, the more common ones included the following: iambs (de-dee); trochees (dee-de); dactyls (dee-de-de); anapests (de-de-dee); spondees (dee-dee); and cretics (de-dee-de). A line of iambic trimeter would be counted out thus: de-dee/ de-dee/ de-dee—that is, three 'feet'[15] of iambs. A line of dactylic hexameter feet would be: dee de de, repeated six times. To clarify the difference between an ancient *vowel-lengthened* meter and its medieval and modern *accented* counterpart, Pau-Puk-Keewis's garments as described in Longfellow's "Hiawatha's Wedding-Feast" can offer clarifying help. This long poem is set in rarely varied trochaic tetrameters, that is, four accented trochaic feet per line, thus: de-de/ de-de/ de-de/ de-de—with de sounding out more emphatically. The modern accentual pronunciation is what so many of us chorused at school, coming down hard on the first, third, fifth, and seventh syllables, while the teacher whacked a ruler against her desk.

> Hé was dréssed in deér-skin léggings,
> Frínged with hédgehog quílls and érmine,
> Ánd in móccasíns of búck-skin,
> Thíck with quílls and béads embroídered.

Instead of pumping for bigger noise on the four stressed beats, a classical *grammaticus* would have had his pupils stretch out (incant) the sound of the stressed beats, thus:

He-e was **dre-essed** in de-e-er-skin **le-eg**gings,
Fri-inged with he-edgehog **qui-ills** and e-er**m**ine

In either mode grammar required hard work from its students, for its embrace of subtopics was large. Moreover, its details were tricky, and the required 'correctness' (according to the lights of the *grammaticus*) demanded unremitting drill. It is no wonder that 'privileged' young scholars—even into old age—would remember their grammatical days as days of drudgery.

Notes

1. Historians dealing with this period differ widely in their preferences for dates. For example, Arnold Toynbee preferred to think of the medieval era as running from the end of Charlemagne's brief renaissance to Gutenberg's invention of the printing press in 1440. Others, citing the enormous advance in intellectual and political matters beginning around 1075, preferred that as the ending date.

2. Roger Wright, ed., *Latin and the Romance Languages in the Early Middle Ages* (London and New York: Routledge, 1991). This book has been most helpful for explaining the concepts described in this chapter: in particular, Wright's introduction and the essays by Paul M. Lloyd, Tore Janson, Jozsef Herman, Alberto Varvaro, and Harm Inkster that appear in this book.

3. Meanwhile, the scene to the south and the east of Rome was quite different. From those directions came the Mohammedan Arabs, who eventually overspread the Mediterranean. Powering through Persia, Syria, Egypt, all of Roman Africa, and finally Spain, they dominated commerce and acquired vast wealth. Their purpose, unlike that of the northern barbarians, was religious—their goal was to convert the conquered peoples to Islam. A proud, fanatically religious people, they neither assimilated the Latin language nor adopted the customs of the peoples they subdued.

4. Even Pompeii graffiti of ca. 79 CE attest to linguistic breakaways from literary Latin. See Roger Wright, *Late Latin and Early Romance*, 48.

5. Jozsef Herman, "Spoken and Written Latin in the Last Centuries of the Roman Empire," in Wright's *Latin and the Romance Languages in the Early Middle Ages*, 24–36.

6. Ibid.

7. Einar Löfstedt, *Late Latin* (Cambridge: Harvard University Press, 1959), 3–4.

8. Ibid., 17.

9. For a delightful glimpse into the ingenious linguistic inventions of modern mankind, see Eric Partridge's copious studies on slang, catch phrases, and hobo language.

10. The material for this section comes primarily from Ernst Robert Curtius, *European Literature and the Latin Middle Ages*, trans. Willard R. Trask (Princeton: Princeton University Press, 1990), particularly 39–45.

11. A rhetorical figure using understatement and often expressed by the negative of its contrary, thus: 'not a little trinket' for a huge diamond ring; 'Her swimming pool was not just a hole in the ground.'
12. A figure of speech in which an aspect or part represents the whole: as in 'crown' for king, or 'sticks' for hockey team players.
13. A strong image made from seemingly contradictory elements, thus: "hot ice" or "rude charm."
14. Brehaut, *Encyclopedist*, 100–1.
15. This word, with its history of application to poetic meter, reveals its relation to prehistoric dance steps.

References

Brehaut, Ernest. *Encyclopedist of the Dark Ages: Isidore of Seville*. London: P. S. King and Son, 1912.

Curtius, Ernst Robert. *European Literature and the Latin Middle Ages*. Translated by Willard R. Trask. Princeton: Princeton University Press, 1990.

Herman, Jozsef. "Spoken and Written Latin in the Last Centuries of the Roman Empire." In *Latin and the Romance Languages in the Early Middle Ages*, by Roger Wright. London and New York: Routledge, 1991.

Löfstedt, Einar. *Late Latin*. Cambridge: Harvard University Press, 1959.

Wright, Roger. *Late Latin and Early Romance in Spain and Carolingian France*. Liverpool, UK: Francis Cairns, 1982.

·SECTION 6·

MOVING NORTH

· 1 9 ·

IN THE LANDS OF MIST

The Celts and Anglo-Saxons

Isolated behind monastic walls and dominated by Church authority, the intellectual and artistic life of Europe lost vitality. The exception to this trend took place in Ireland. Because Ireland had never been a part of the Roman Empire, being both out of the way geographically and undersupplied with desirable items to appropriate, its monastic culture was left free to flower on its own. In the seventh century, when all was bleak in continental scriptoria, Irish learning persisted vigorously, soon to become the wonder of the world. Irish monasteries were hives of industry, artistry, and intellectualism. The exotic beauty of the books they produced would in time (in the nick of time) revitalize scriptorial energies both on the continent and in England. How did this come to be? How did it happen that Ireland would possess the most extensive early vernacular literature in all of medieval Europe?[1] It is a complex story.

The Irish, who were always a word-loving people, had established from time immemorial an order of poets called the *filid* (this is the plural form), who, along with other designated cerebrals (such as judges), constituted the most elevated and revered segment of Irish society. The *filid*'s charge was to chronicle Irish heroics; record the native genealogical data; and, in the most gorgeous language they could muster, provide withal the entertainment so

necessary for survival in a wet and chilly climate. While poeticizing the ancestral glories of their race, the *filid* also took care to instill those guidelines of
belief and virtue that would instruct (and control) the restless young. It is no
wonder that the Irish public loved their *filid*, admired their skills, fussed over
them, and empowered them in a way that they did not even grant to their
chieftains and kinglets.

Because Ireland's geographical marginality had saved it from Roman conquest and political influence, its society never adopted the ways of Roman civilization. Ireland had no central government, and no unimpeachable crowning
authority. Instead, it was ruled by precepts of extreme antiquity, with social
laws similar to the Sanskrit laws of India—laws that emphasized the life of
the mind, self-control, endurance, and positive thinking. The reverence that
the Irish extended to their 'poet-historians' derived from attitudes associated with what is customarily (but misleadingly) known as 'ancestor worship.'[2]
Typically practiced in oral societies, ancestor worship is essentially a simultaneous past-future meld of perspectives. In practice, the living member of a
family fulfills his duty both to his ancestors and his progeny by celebrating the
past-future continuity. He honors his forebears by recounting (and no doubt
exaggerating) their virtues and heroic exploits so as to inspire his own young.
If he is Irish and a fully qualified *fili* to boot, he will make poetry of it. The
practicality of this past-future embrace has proved effective in controlling the
wild youths of oral and Eastern societies and might (or not) beneficially be
adopted by today's Western literate societies too. Apparently, a sense of pride
in what one inherits by way of genes and commendable ancestral example sets
up an ideal that can, once the diapers have been dispensed with, successfully
control behavior—or so it is claimed.

But back to the *filid*. As artistic refurbishers of a tribal past, they were
revered and rewarded in accordance with their prowess as poets, each rank
being allowed (by law) a certain number of official admirers for retinue. (The
filid, it should be noted, were unfailingly status-conscious and insistent on
their perks.) But aside from the job of admiring their leader, a poet's retinue
also served to protect him as he traversed the wild landscapes to instruct far-
apart communities on their common fog-ridden past. Crossing local boundaries with his poems and lyre, a *fili* interlaced the peripheral elements of Irish
dialect, working them centerwards towards a unity of expression that was easily understood countrywide. The fact that vernacular literary diction would
come to be so quickly smoothed into homogeneity is attributed to that initial
oral networking across the island. To such an extent had the *filid* integrated

the Celtic Irish tongue that by the sixth century CE very little significant dialect variation remained to be written down. (Compare this with Italy or England!) A standardized orthography was in place as well.

While congratulating Ireland on its linguistic unity and readiness to produce literature, it should be noted too that sixth-century Irish scholars had a considerable knowledge of Latin literature, including, it is thought, a number of ancient pagan writers. Of Christian literature, they knew the Bible from the Vulgate version of Saint Jerome as well as from pre-Vulgate Irish manuscripts dating from before the fifth century. They were familiar with Apocryphal writings such as the *Book of Enoch* and the *Apocalypse of Moses*, which had been forbidden in Romish Christendom. Also, they knew the writings of the Greek fathers in Latin translations; the writings of the four fathers of the Latin church (Ambrose, Jerome, Augustine, and Gregory the Great), including their commentaries and interpretations of scripture with sermons based on the same. They knew the lives of saints and martyrs, the rules ordering the daily life of monks, the penitentials prescribing penance for various degrees and kinds of sin, the hymns for use in the monastic offices of the church, and a great variety of religious poems and prayers.[3] The seventh century found the Irish religious establishment steeped in culture. The early writing down of *filid*-derived sagas had prepared the Irish for future extensive scholarship and given them an enormous self-confidence with their pens. It was a confidence so established and firm as to make them quite ready to take the world by the tail—which, in a sense, they did.

How did the Irish acquire their knowledge of Latin and their skills in reading and writing it? Evidence tells us that literacy was probably established in Celtic-speaking Ireland before Christ, and that its origins were Latinate, the result of early commerce. Loan words (probably coming through Roman Gaul or England) suggest considerable pre-Christian intermingling. Tacitus mentioned the activities of Romanized Celtic traders, probably from Gaul, doing business in Irish ports. There, luxury items—wine, glass, and fine cloth—from the south were exchanged for the rougher produce of rural Ireland. Irish traders (who had earlier been accustomed to making contracts orally and corroborating them with witnesses) found themselves on safer ground in bargaining with continental merchants when they adopted Roman ways of confirming a contract by written record. There is little doubt that some form of Latin was the *lingua franca* used for such commerce and that whatever agreements or tallies that needed to be made would have been written down using the Roman alphabet.

The situation in Ireland marks a contrast with that of nearby Britannia (the island site of England, Scotland, and Wales). There, Latin literacy developed effectively ca. 43 CE during the reign of Claudius. Tacitus reported that his father-in-law, while governing Britain (77/78–84 CE) set up Latin schools for the elite young Britons. After the Romans departed in 410 CE, the English aristocracy and the clerisy continued for a while to speak and write in Latin, while the lower classes went on with their native Celtic Brittonic, which was never transposed into fluid writing. In England's fifth and sixth centuries, civic instability replaced the era of Roman law and order. Amidst the succeeding turbulence and fear, the Roman church thrived. It opened its arms to threatened English aristocrats, who promptly moved themselves (with books and wealth) from their menaced country estates to the safety of monastic walls, where they settled comfortably into positions of priestly power. With a high sense of superiority, these upper-crust English *religiosi* (often becoming bishops) kept their arrogant distance from the common people and issued their edicts with their noses in the air.

In Ireland, during this period, things were different. At some point in the second or third century CE, the *filid* seem to have accepted writing as an auxiliary technique for assuring the permanency of their efforts. Meanwhile, not only Latin, but another kind of writing had developed. Though the early *filid* certainly knew about Latin and perhaps even used it, they grew uncomfortable with transcribing Celtic into a Latin alphabet that had little to do with the Irish phonesis (vocal sounds). To repair this failing, the old pre-Christian *ogam* alphabet (akin to runes) was resurrected and broadly put to use. Its strange, secretive appearance, very different from Roman lettering, might well have made ogam useful against the prying eyes of the Romans.[4] It is certainly thinkable that the integrity of the ogam's pledge to the Celtic language, lore, and beliefs contributed to the process that would culminate in the seventh-century efflorescence of a very un-Roman style of Latin literary expression. Latinity and literacy started to naturalize in Ireland no later than the fourth century, having developed out of a very early *Roman* (instead of a post-Christ atmosphere), as had been the case in Britannia and Gaul. In other words, educated Irish, particularly the *filid*, had been ready at a surprisingly early stage to study the early Christian texts. When in the fifth century CE Patrick came to evangelize Ireland, he wisely selected *filid* to be its bishops and left it to them to set up and direct Irish churchly affairs. This inspired move, so sensitively in keeping with native perceptions, was accepted, and the new *filid* bishops took on their fresh duties with great good will. As previous proud guardians of their own ancient past, the *filid* were unwilling to participate in the suppression of their national lore. Instead, they accommodated it. Unlike the clampdown that took place in Romanized Anglo-Saxon England (where the bishops were so haughty), the mutual appreciation of Irish pagans and Romanized Christian evangelists allowed the vernacular culture to thrive in freedom. Its continuing presence in the Irish literary landscape contributed hugely to the widened scope for native writers. Promoted to Christian sanctity, the *filid* merely dumped the burden of their former pagan iniquities onto the shoulders of the lower-caste, hocus-pocus druids. With that, we see the Irish church now safely delivered into the hands of an intellectually broad-minded elite that was composed of the learned classes from a recent heathen society. The satisfying result has been referred to as "the positively embarrassing riches of vernacular Irish culture."[5] Those riches included, of course, artistic design as well as an artistic prose style, both of which were fraught with exuberant, self-assured complexity.

What is additionally remarkable about the Irish conversion to the Christian religion is that the fifth-century *filid*-turned-bishops not only retained their allegiance to their own history but also bequeathed their sentiments to descendent bishops, who continued proudly to trace their genealogies to the great poets of their past. That the Roman Catholic Church, seated in faraway Rome and rather known for oppressive tactics, could insinuate its precepts into pagan Ireland in this unobtrusive way was Patrick's triumph. While the Church had impressed the *filid* deeply with its message of salvation, it could not overawe them with the Christian accompaniment of literacy, because to a notable extent, the *filid* had it already. Since Christianity was dependent on literacy, and literacy was dependent on knowledge of Latin, Irish literates simply applied their vernacularly-arrived-at skills to the writing of Latin religious tracts.

There is no doubt that the Christianization of Ireland brought with it a vast increase in the amount of writing that went on there. It is very likely that the Irish missionaries, who replaced and multiplied copies of Christian texts throughout the barbarian-battered continent, advanced the technology of writing in major ways. As smooth papyrus and parchment with flowing ink superseded knife and wood, so the action of writing became easier. Nevertheless, the preparation of a 'worthy manuscript'—with gilded illustrations and puzzling networks of knotted serpentine decoration—was a slow and complex matter. Clearly the Irish loved their pens, for as the quantity of writing grew, so did the complexity of their manuscript decoration and the contortion of their language. It would seem that the Irish love of artistic visual detail was closely related to their love of verbal embellishment. Complication was their specialty.

Abounding with metaphor, imagery, borrowings from foreign languages and pagan literatures, Irish Latin prose has a very noticeable exuberance and fondness for complexity, which, as we shall soon see, reached its seventh-century literary culmination with the highbrow output of England's Irish-trained Aldhelm. His ornate style stretched the boundaries of ordinary Latin prose, allowing the incorporation of much information—and too many words per thought—within the confines of a sentence. At that point, the weight of incomprehensibility drew the 'writing pendulum' back towards simplicity, and the directness of Senecan (Attic) principles once again took hold. To achieve that newly wanted clarity, the English Anglo-Saxon Venerable Bede would none too soon step on stage. But for the moment we must thank Ireland for all it did to preserve knowledge and enhance verbal expression in the turmoiled centuries of early northern Christendom.

The Church Is Established in Ireland: St. Patrick

Patrick,[6] the man who brought the Bible to Ireland, considered himself to be unlearned and rough, for his education had never reached the high level of classical rhetoric. Coming from a well-to-do family in Britain, he had grown up speaking Latin and studying how to read and write it. His schooling ended when, at age 16, he was dragged from his father's villa by Irish marauders and enslaved as a shepherd on a lonely Irish heath. Eight years passed before he escaped to his homeland. Once back, he became a devout Christian, and returned voluntarily to Ireland to evangelize. It was he who initiated the practical details of establishing the Christian Church in Ireland.

In the early ninth-century Book of Armagh,[7] there are preserved two unquestionably authentic pieces of Patrick's composition: his *Confessio* (which is very moving and soul-baring) and his *Epistula* (a letter written to British Christians who had been subdued and maltreated by their Roman governor Coroticus). Every stumbling sentence of these two 'rustic' Latin compositions shines with Patrick's moral and spiritual intensity. Though the unorthodox inflections and peculiar repetition of ideas make it difficult to translate gracefully, the following word-for-word opening of his epistle will at least reveal how very plain Patrick's language and syntax were. The short phrasing is particularly worth mentioning. The punctuation follows the modernized text from which the Latin came.

> Patrick sinner uneducated (it is evident) in Ireland located that I am bishop I confess. Most certainly I think from God I accepted what I am: amongst barbarians thus I live as proselytizer and fugitive on account of love for God. Witness is he, so thus it is.[8]

On the Spread of Irish Ebullience

In the following century, Columcille (521–597 CE), better known as St. Columba, set out to build on Patrick's conversion successes. As a pious and educated man from a family with royal connections, Columcille was particularly effective in strengthening the Irish church and in bridging the divide between Celtic secular and Latin ecclesiastic interests.[9] After founding schools of learning in Ireland, Columcille established a mother-house for monks on the Hebridean island of Iona. From there, scholars, missionaries, and experienced scribes initiated a massive exportation of Irish Latin literacy. Their work proved to be a worldwide stimulant for the creation and preservation of books. It was by traveling this northern route—from Rome to Ireland, to Iona, to Anglo-Saxon Britain, and finally back to the demoralized continent—that ancient literature escaped annihilation. Because of Irish monastic ministrations, a large part of Roman and Greek cultural legacy was destined to survive and, though somewhat changed by travel, would once again flourish and spread.

Owing to the abstruse Latinity that had evolved in Ireland's Christendom, Celtic literary dominance (though briefly powerful) lasted only some 30 years. In contrast to continental Latin, Irish Latin was not anchored in the traditions of rigorous classical Latin. While Irish scholars could be quite accepting of classical pagan literature, they tended to adapt rather freely the Latin that contained it. Religious asceticism, a penchant of the Celtic spirit, had led them to imitate *uncritically* and to elaborate on the 'impure' fourth-century language of the Vulgate Bible, which had become the revered and authoritative biblical version throughout the Christian world. Jerome had deliberately liberated his Vulgate Bible by dispensing with the absolutes of classical sentential constructions and word usage. He had not only tolerated common words and speech patterns in his masterpiece, but eschewed the complexities of translating the biblical books into Latin verse. For the sake of harvesting souls, he had rendered the Greek and Hebrew originals into unmetered Latin *prose*, not *verse*—later expressing regret (along with abhorrence) that now "The Holy Scripture is like a beautiful body concealed by a dirty gown!" Later commentators on grammar and style (even Isidore of Seville) would come to remark on the unclassical awkwardnesses to be found in the Vulgate phrasings. But to the Irish, Jerome's rejection of classical metered poetry and his relaxed grip on rhetorical-grammatical rules offered a luscious liberty. Free of these ancient details, Irish prose took flight on its own—an exotic bird with a fondness for invention.

Despite the Vulgate's linguistic laxities, the fact remains that the entire body of Latinate religious literature (including the Vulgate Bible) was rife with ancient rhetorical adornments. To appreciate its sacred message, one needed to understand these beautifying, though sometimes obfuscating, mechanisms. As already noted, these were allegory, antithesis, parallelism, alliteration, and metaphor, along with a variety of subsidiary decorative devices: synecdoche, simile, personification, and so on. As a group, they were still referred to as the rhetorical *artes*. Though devised and bequeathed by pre-Christ Greek and Roman pagans, such elements had long been used to enhance Christian materials too.

Irish writers not only accepted the lowered linguistic levels of the Vulgate Bible, but, being unaffected by Rome's classical pull, felt at liberty to expand their own exuberant tastes as well. They were in love with words and keen to experiment with them. If something else could possibly be said on the subject at hand, they said it. Their extensions and subextensions of basic ideas swelled with paraphrase and extravagant illustration. They juggled and romped with the classical schemes and tropes. The result was excess mixed with confusion. For when they applied the rhetorical *artes* to their own structurally more relaxed Vulgate-derived word-flow, they did it with so little feel of gravity, with such tremendous gusto and compulsion, that in the end they isolated themselves from the dogmatic literary standards familiar to the remaining erudite folk on the Romanized continent. Thus, while Ireland's ebullient and intricate artwork continued to be admired throughout the Christian world, its written language proved too complex and unwieldy. To the classically-oriented Anglos and continentals, it seemed an incomprehensible jargon.

Nevertheless, within that period of brief ascendancy, Irish missionaries— most notably St. Columcille (St. Columba) and St. Columban—succeeded in transmitting their literary, artistic, and ascetic passions beyond Anglo-Saxon England to the continent. The monasteries of St. Gall in Bavaria and Bobbio in Northern Italy owe their origins to the far-ranging labors of Columba and his disciples. The St. Gall Foundation (established in 612 by St. Gall, a follower of Columban) thrived to become (in 720) a Benedictine abbey, which up to the eleventh century supported the most important educational institution north of the Alps, including a scriptorium to support its world-famed library.[10] Bobbio was founded (also in 612) by St. Columban himself. It, too, became a center of medieval culture and learning, and was especially renowned for its great library.[11]

Britannia: Home of the Mysterious Gildas

Though insulting to the kings and clergy of his own time, Gildas has been gracious to the scholars of ours. The uncertainties that might have engendered his unique writing style have opened exciting frontiers for exploration and speculation. That his early years were spent in the Celtic north of Britain (i.e., Scotland); that he wrote his famous 'epistle,' *De excidio Brittannia* (*The Ruin of Britain*) in the year 540 CE; and that, having become a saintly monastic, he died in 570 CE in Celtic-speaking Morbihan in French Brittany are all agreed-upon facts. Thereafter, uncertainty descends, and the various possibilities multiply ferociously. Nevertheless, as Gildas is considered to have been a pivotal author in the emergence of literary English prose, one should (along with the puzzled historians and ecclesiastics) at least try to understand the influences that fed his aspirations, and thereby gain some feel for the sixth-century linguistic and pedagogical renaissance as it developed in northern Celtic areas.

First, it must be noted that Gildas's single extant work, *The Ruin of Britain*, quickly became a highly regarded treatise. It was admired for its style and command of late Latin, which was the language of upper-crust literates in the tri-lingual Britain of his time.[12] Literary tradition has considered *The Ruin* to have been the preponderant influence on the seventh-century English Aldhelm. Since Gildas was 'known' (if such a word may apply) to have been educated (at least partially) in South Wales and Ireland (both being purely Celtic in speech and habit), his turgid style was presumed for many years to be entirely Celtic-derived and uninfluenced by Anglo-Saxon idiom or Latinate rhetoric. Though this opinion is currently under scholarly bombardment, it seems to be surviving. Nevertheless, caution is urged, for accounts of his life are permeated with phrases like *if we may say, perhaps, as seems likely, must be the case*. A universally accepted premise, however, is that Gildas's style is unique to the world of his time. The game starts there. Where did this 'unique' style come from? Should one search for Celtic and Anglo-Saxon precedents,[13] or investigate the pages of continental contemporaries, such as the eminent Cassiodorus?

Argument necessarily hovers over Gildas himself. Was he a native Latin speaker, or a speaker of Anglo-Saxon British, or some mix of both? Was his the apical performance of a settled tradition, or, of a Thucydidean experiment to test new space? To what extent was he educated? Had he worked only through the Latin grammar (like Patrick), or had he reached higher levels with a rhetor? And if the latter, how had he managed to find one? For in the wake of Rome's retreat from Britain, law and government had changed their shape. Rhetorical schools, where the art of declamation had been taught to young men seeking executive status in government administration, had been superseded by monasticism, whose driving urge was *not to declaim* but to retreat from the practical world entirely. Romish officialdom frowned upon secular culture, and in stricter circles actually forbade its being taught. Yet strangely, traces of rhetorical training pervade *The Ruin*. Gildas's work is full of anomalies and unanswerable questions. Who indeed was he?

In the mid-sixth-century, when *The Ruin* first appeared, Britain was not a happy place. The law and order of Roman rule had evaporated. The tensions between the now-settled Anglo-Saxon immigrants and the indigenous Celts had opened up to warfare and were (according to Gildas) bringing the country to ruin. In strong, vituperative language Gildas condemns the disruptions and exhorts his countrymen—especially the bullying kings and the thickheaded clergy—to stop the turmoil and reinstate peace. In reviewing the causes of these gloomy affairs, Gildas was probably working from distant memories, for he is hazy about the sequence of historical events. In addition to that, his prose style seems antiquated. He apportions his text and feeds out his thoughts with no firm sense of termination.[14] His sentence structures are roughhewn and meandering. His vocabulary is unusual: almost a quarter of the words are rare or single-time usages. To top it off, he poeticizes extravagantly. He is fond of internal rhyming and alliteration—ancient ploys to abet memorization for oral delivery. All in all, *The Ruin* seems at best to be a grand and unusual performance.

The Ruin of Britain: A Primitive Snarl?

Because its grammatical baseline is so foggy, *The Ruin* at first glance seems something of a shapeless lump, and is exceedingly hard to take in. The *system* that holds it together is remindful of ancient literary devices used by Hero-

dotus in that the components of the treatise are controlled by punctuational substitutes of a deep-lying structural nature. In particular, upon proposing
an idea, he antithesizes it and then, to be sure we get his point, he presents
a parallel for more contrast. Thus, "Britain has kings, but they are tyrants"
(27.1). This theme is expanded, until we are led to consider a parallel issue:
the clergy. They are even more awful: "Britain has priests, but they are fools."
(66.1) The succeeding denunciations of each of these two villainous types of
potentates follow a pattern as well. First, Gildas expresses his own disapproval,
and then turns to the Bible for authority and protection. In Professor Winterbottom's words:

> The passages are not chosen at random, nor arranged without order.
> Gildas works through Old and New Testament according to a fixed,
> though idiosyncratic scheme; and most of the passages he chooses are
> obviously to his point without his own added comment....
> This is structure on the grand scale, conscious and calculated.[15]

Gildas's sentences are equally 'grand.' He thinks in large paragraphs, whose
content he presents in long *periodic* sentences that swell with peripheral rel-
evances. The phrases expressing the mini-ideas of the corporate whole are
woven together with the clear intention of expanding the statement's content
until it is as complete and global as words can make it.

Professor Winterbottom is of the opinion that Gildas expounds without
regard to the classical rules prevalent in the writings of contemporaneous south-
ern-trained writers; that he frequently fails to parcel out his inflated rhetoric
in clauses and *periods* according to the accepted continental way: that is, by
vowel-lengthened, *metrical* cadences (*clausulae*)—which were still in use, even
when accompanied by puncts. Though Gildas *must* have known about this
well-established, prepointing method for dividing sentence parts (a method
so highly prized by Cicero, discussed by Quintilian, and regularly deployed by
Cassiodorus), he ignores it. Instead, he seems to use *accentual* ('Hiawathan') cadences to secure his rhythms at the end of clauses—but even then, not always.

Gildas also ignores the habits of classical word order. (All the critics agree
on that.) Coeval continental writers (still steeped in the classical use of declension differentiation) made considerable use of *hyperbaton* (word transposition) to improve the resonance of their sentences; but their ingrained sense
of a Latin prose line held them back from overload, from too much shrouding
of meaning with literary trickery. We shall shortly see how, one hundred and
some years later, Aldhelm (who was trained in both Irish and Roman-orient-

ed Canterburgian schools, and was just as verbose and even more poetry-loving) stayed in closer touch with continental literaries and thereby attained a grasp of sentence structure that Gildas never mastered. To remind us of the antiquity of modern straight-talk principles, Professor Winterbottom calls our attention to Quintilian's irritated reaction to Maecenas for his (Maecenas's) airy transpositions of the word order within sentences.

To elucidate Quintilian's complaint, here is his sample of a Maecenas line: *inter se sacra movit aqua fraxinos* (rerendered word for word: 'among itself sacred moved water ash trees'). The assimilability of this statement, he points out, is vastly increased by joining words that belong together: thus, *aqua sacra inter fraxinos (se) movit*, or, 'water sacred among ash trees (itself) moved.'[16] Gildas seemed intent on avoiding this simple and (even by his time) pretty well established 'natural' norm of relaxed simplicity. Although convinced that he was conveying matters of extreme importance, he chose to underline that importance by *elevating* his tone rather than *clarifying* his message, which he might easily have done by restructuring his sentences. The path he chose, one feels, was an archaic one that was generated by oral-poetic instincts, tempered perhaps with a touch of educated aristocratic pride. Though the separation of word-units has always been acceptable for versifying or high-flying prose (either written or oral), in extreme forms it is incompatible with the urgent, information-bearing communication.

In his article "Gildas's Prose Style and Its Origins," Neil Wright gives a handsome example of Gildasian word ordering.

> Quare *tantas* peccaminum regiae cervici sponte, ut ita dicam, *ineluctabiles*, celsorum ceu montium, innectis *moles*?

A word-for-word translation reduces this to

> Why *so many* of sins on your royal neck willingly, as it were, *unavoidable*, of high like mountains, do you put *masses*?

The italicized words are semantically related, yet physically widely separated. Mr. Wright translates it more gracefully:

> Why do you willingly encircle your royal neck with such, as thus I will say, inescapable masses of sin, like lofty mountains?

How much easier it might have been to glean the sense if the words that contributed meaning to an idea had maintained some degree of proximity! Mr.
Wright improves the arrangement as follows:

> Quare *tantas* ineluctabiles, ut ita dicam, *moles* peccaminum ceu cel-
> sorum montium regiae cervici sponte innectis?[17]

> Why so many inescapable, as thus I will say, masses of sin like lofty
> mountains on your royal neck willingly do you put?

The more natural word order assures the intake of intended meaning, which
is, after all, the true goal of communicating in the first place.

Some Resolutions (Perhaps) to Quandary

When taking everything into account (including his wayward syntax), we
cannot say that Gildas sprang from a totally 'oral' background, nor that he
showed any sign of being unfamiliar with the literary canon of his day. Quite
the contrary, for he seems to have been quite well read. In *The Ruin* he quotes
from both the Bible and from Vergil, and shows a firm acquaintance with
Jerome. Though he wallows in alliteration and puns (both being joys of the
spoken word), he also sprinkles his pages with sophisticated Greek. Michael
Lapidge in his "Gildas's Education and the Latin Culture,"[18] draws many
persuasive conclusions about the Latinity of Gildas, some of which will be
helpful in imagining the particularly bleak atmosphere that barely sustained
Irish-British prose writing during the sixth century.

Gildas himself describes his Latin as *lingua nostra*, suggesting comfort
and companionability, but then proceeds to employ that Latin *lingua* in a
classically correct manner: that is, without the numerous phonological and
morphological vulgarisms (like the dropping of *m* from *castrum*) that we find
disfiguring the Latin of his Roman-British predecessor Patrick. The *Ruin* betrays no influence of colloquial speech. More often than not, readers are faced
with the classical diction of pedagogical edict. Nor does Gildas misuse forms
of Latin words as did so many non-native Latin-speaking authors who tended
to draw their vocabulary from glossaries or word lists without a firm knowledge of connotation. There are no idiosyncratic quirks of meaning or usage in
Gildas. Such linguistic purity will not be found in Aldhelm, who, in the late
seventh century, would come to supply us with many deviations attributable
to colloquial habit. Gildas's fastidious word use points to the probability that

he was a privileged, educated native Latin speaker, for whom Latin was indeed a living language.

But to what level was he educated? Mr. Lapidge is quite convincing in his claim that Gildas must have surpassed (by then[19]) the up-to-age-16 grind with a *grammaticus*, under whose supervision he would have tackled Vergil (along with other venerated curricular authors) and line by line have scrutinized word meanings and the effects of meter and hyperbaton (inversion of word-order), alliteration, antithesis, parallelism, and so on. Gildas's verbatim quotations are admittedly not many, but he alludes to classical materials in a way that shows he had absorbed them and was not quoting with a finger on the parent text. His ease with classical secular materials supports the conjecture that at the very least he received training from a genuine Roman *grammaticus*. Lapidge goes further. He discovers that the belabored syntax of *The Ruin*, though described as an 'epistle' by the author, follows the pattern of a full-bodied classical Roman declamation—complete with *exordium*, *narratio*, *propositio*, *argumentatio*, and *epilogus*—the mastery of which had once been the necessary route to forensic and administrative stardom. What strange things have we unearthed here? an epistle in the form of a speech? by Gildas, who was a monastic, and would shortly become a miracle-working saint?

Those unexpected contradictions can be quickly laid to rest, for we are told that in late antiquity, epistolography had come to occupy a central position in the study of rhetorical declamation. Even as early as the first century CE, the great grammarian, rhetorician, and pedagogue Quintilian was proclaiming the marriage of writing and speaking—the fact that they mirror each other and are so deeply interrelated that the practice of one benefits the other. Later, as Christian influence grew stronger, oral declamation declined; whereas its offspring epistolography—a quieter, monastically acceptable activity—came to be practiced broadly.

The Ruin, then, should be perceived as a public letter, a sort of *written* rhetorical declamation, which by custom followed the outmoded principles of *oral* declamation—in this case, of vituperative oral declamation. And indeed, on inspection, Gildas's violent invective is similar to what Cicero sometimes mustered when seized by anger. Lapidge views *The Ruin* as an epistolary declamation directed by an (imagined) prosecution (namely Gildas) against a vice-ridden country, for which the authoring Gildas uses a full arsenal of rhetorical figures of speech: apostrophes to the tyrannical kings; outbursts of indignation and violent language; the starkness of *asyndeton*; sharp question and answer sequences (*brachylogia*); as well as the correct classical legal terms. From all these bits of evidence, Lapidge concludes that Gildas had somehow undergone training at the hands of a classical *rhetor* in preparation for a career in legal administration.

If this interesting theory were true, then an adjustment of date for the disappearance of rhetorical study on British soil would be needed, and the Roman literary heritage would seem more enduring than scholars had previously thought. As no schools of rhetoric were still operating in mid-sixth-century Gaul (where experience with Roman government and the military outlasted that of Britain), it is interesting that Gildas might have had such training. Without assurance that Gildas had even once traveled deep into southern papal terrain, Lapidge speculates that he might well have trained with a private rhetor somewhere on British soil—Ireland being unlikely since its Roman connections were so tenuous. Classical rhetorical skills, then, must still have been prized by the dwindling British elite to the extent that they could be acquired through private means. Given that, we must conclude that in Gildas's sixth century, rhetors went where the money was (as had the peripatetic sophists of ancient Greece), or moved about seeking fame (like the wandering Irish *filid*). However it happened, it would seem likely that Gildas was not the only contemporary British literate to appreciate these ancient arts, for he was writing to persuade and impress a large audience; and many readers in succeeding generations approved his argument.[20]

Giovanni Orlandi, in his essay "*Clausulae* in Gildas's *De Excidio Britanniae*,"[21] supports this taught-by-rhetor likelihood with a careful study of the cadencing devices that Gildas actually used—namely, a mix of the previously-discussed *clausulae* and the newborn ("Hiawathan"-style) *cursus*, both of which are so very foreign to contemporary perceptions of punctuation. Unfortunately for us moderns with our obtuse-ear affliction, their presence will linger on in prose writing throughout the lifetime of spoken Latin. Dealing with them seems always a pain, but because they are important to our discussion, the following user-friendly review is offered.

The classical *clausulae* were (usually) the last two words of a *colon* or a *period*. Such words were chosen for their rhythms to signal termination. The rhythms themselves were measured *in terms of time* by vowel-sound lengths appropriate to the song or dance movements from which they derived. Over the early Christian centuries, they gradually modified to become something quite different. The evolving device, which was less various, less measured, and less dependent on carefully articulated speech, co-existed for a while with the classical *clausulae*. Called the *cursus*, this later device polished off clauses and full statements with the same sorts of syllables, but *accented* in thumpety-thump ('Hiawathan') style. In an environment of decaying inflections (caused by imprecise speech-sounds pushing classical norms towards 'natural speech'), the early *clausulae* were dropped and the blatant *cursus* took over.

Put briefly, Orlandi discovered in Gildas evidence of numerous accented *cursus* closures, where others had previously found only wisps and suspicions of the classical quantitative *clausulae* closures. It would seem then that Gildas was more conscious of the requirements of cadencing than earlier scholars had thought. With that accepted, *The Ruin* no longer seems quite the antiquated lump that it had originally appeared to be. Instead, we may think of Gildas now as truly literate and reasonably well trained in the arts of rhetoric, a man who on occasion chose to put the *cursus* into action at a time when the traditions of classical prosody, though fading, were still somewhat alive—and definitely alive in pockets, as manifested in the writings of his contemporary, Cassiodorus.

What is additionally interesting in Orlandi's discussion is the correspondence he finds among the three most-used classical *clausulae* and their derivative three *cursus*. In each case, the accented beats of the *cursus* exactly tally with the positions of the long-vowel syllabic quantities of the ancient *clausulae*. In other words, the signaling rhythms produced by *clausulae* and *cursus* are alike, though effected by differing means. The drag of vowel sound (developed first in incanted epic poetry and surviving in formal Greek oratory and later in Greek and classical Latin literature) was simply converted into stressed beats for the less discriminating prosal 'natural language' output.

It is very likely (says Orlandi) that the two types of measure, the one withering as the other came into flower, would have existed in parallel before the new could preponderate entirely. The changeover seems to have started up in the fifth and sixth centuries. Thus, the *cursus* was gaining acceptance at the very time that classical Latin was losing its hold in the provinces and when ecclesiastical usage, increasingly yielding to colloquial influence, was adopting simplified linguistic structures (as in reliance on word order in place of inflections and the adoption of full prepositional phrases in place of ablative and dative case endings).

We see then that Gildas in the sixth-century north *was* punctuating— innovatively (if erratically) punctuating both with *cursus* and some few *clausulae*—while rigidly holding on to his inflections and classical diction. Orlandi concludes that, beginning in late antiquity and continuing during a span of some 150 years, the system of formally calling attention to the termination of a written worded thought was in a period of flux. Though mysteries continue, we may surmise from his previously unnoticed use of the *cursus* in *The Ruin* that Gildas was an 'educated' man, while yet the product of his turbulent times.

A Tentative *Curriculum Vitae*

There are conflicting accounts of the whereabouts and doings of the living Gildas. In the eleventh century (that is, some 500 years into his future), an unknown Breton monk at the Abbey of Rhuys (founded by Gildas on a peninsula point in France's Brittany) wrote a "Life of Saint Gildas." A century later, a Welshman wrote another. In piecing together the harmonizing parts of these *vitae* along with notations from Welsh manuscripts and the accounts of various historians and *religiosi* of the period, *The Catholic Encyclopedia* has constructed a coherent sequence,[22] which of course must not be swallowed whole, for other opinions emerge constantly to challenge the verity of the tale.

All agree, however, that Gildas was born into a noble British family somewhere in the Firth of Clyde region of southern Scotland. He is said to have received his early education in Wales under the tutelage of King Arthur's cousin St. Illtyd, whose monastic foundation, like others throughout Wales, was becoming a huge sanctuary of holiness and a home for sacred learning that catered literally to thousands. It is said to have been one of the most famous religious houses in Britain, a veritable monastic university, made up, as are Oxford and Cambridge, of numerous colleges. (In imagining all this, one must not think in terms of handsome buildings with gardens and cloistered quadrangles, but rather of people camping in groups on hillsides, each with a faculty of several admired figures.) This expansive community of some estimated 3,000 members included many later saints and scholars of note, amongst whom was the young Gildas. According to the *Cambria sacra* (the sacred chronicle of Wales), the course of studies in Iltyd's community included Latin, Greek, rhetoric, philosophy, theology, and mathematics.

It was later, in Ireland, that Gildas took priestly orders, spending some time at Armagh before his return to North Britain, where he became famous for having his teachings allegedly confirmed by miracles. In later life, he returned to Ireland, and from there, most interestingly, is said by some to have made a pilgrimage to Rome. Afterwards, on his way back north (if indeed he ever went so far south), he retired into hermithood on the uninhabited Isle d'Houat off the coast of Brittany. It was there that he wrote his famous epistle to the British kings and priests, founded the monastery at Rhuys on the mainland, and died in the year 570 CE.

About the Celtic Style

It would seem most likely from this shadowy account that Gildas had numerous connections with Celtic-speaking peoples, not many of whom would have been his sort of aristocratic native Latin-speaker. His Celtic rapport seems additionally supported by his end-of-life predilection for hermithood, for the Welsh were noted for their bias towards eremitic hardship.

Gildas might possibly have acquired his knowledge of literary formalities in the classical atmosphere of Rome, if indeed he actually went there. But his penchant for interwoven sentence structures most probably came from the pervasive influence of Celtic literary complexity and the oral bias of the ambiances in which he spent so much of his time. His mix of Celtic ornateness with bookish Latin reflects the disruption in the Britain of his time. Whether he might better have combined the two had he been trained in rigorous Roman-oriented monastic establishments must remain a teasing possibility.

As we shall soon see, shades of Gildasian mannerisms pop up again in later authors, leading some to suspect that Gildas, who was highly admired in his era, may have had considerable influence on the subsequent 'Celtic style' of writing. It has been noted, for example, that the extreme intricacies of his interlacing word-order *formulae* are repeated by later writers. Interlacing (a type of hyperbaton) is the rearrangement of adjective-noun pairs—wherein, for example, adjective *a* is followed by noun *B* (which it does not modify) followed by the noun *A* (which it does modify) followed by the adjective *b* which modifies *B*. Interlacing is also found in an *ab*+verb+*AB* pattern.

From examples of interlacing, it has been reasoned that Gildas provided the inspiration for a phenomenon typical of Celtic Latinity, as seen in the writings of St. Columban, Adomnan of Iona, the later *Hisperica Famina* (Irish Tales), and finally England's Aldhelm. However, on other grounds, the notion of Gildasian influence on the style of Aldhelm is increasingly disputed. In short, Gildas's style and its influence on later writers are continuing to churn up lusty speculation. With all that said, we now have a look. What is this 'Celtic style'?

The following sample will serve our purpose. It is a word-for-word translation of the first few lines of Gildas's opening description of Britain. The entire piece, a statement some 20 lines long, constitutes in its earliest extant form a single paragraphic sentence—a Celtic version of the classical introductory *period*, of which we now inspect only a small portion. The target of the exercise, for which our fragment will suffice, is to demonstrate the impenetrable turgidness of Gildas's prose style. As it is unlikely that *The Ruin* was initially punctuated in the modern sense of the word, modern commas and semicolons have been removed and slashes (virgules) inserted to indicate the breaks between word groups. Attached too are *a*'s and *b*'s to denote which displaced words must go with which. By these means, it is hoped that some sense of meaning will emerge from the seeming disorder.

> Brittannia island in extreme almost of the sphere at the limit of the northwest and west towards/ the divine(a) (as it is said) balance(A) of the earth entirely at the mark from Africa northern more inclining stretched(a) at the axis/ of 800 in length thousand/ of 200 in width space/ with exceptions(A) of diverse(b) many(a) promontories(B) extended (a)/ which with bow-shaped(c) of ocean with bays(C) are encircled...etc.

To make smoother sense of this, Professor Winterbottom's rendition breaks the parts into sentences of readier illumination. Herewith is the whole of that same segment of sentence as he has seen fit to translate it.

> The island of Britain lies virtually at the end of the world, towards the west and north-west. Poised in the divine scales that (we are told) weigh the whole earth, it stretches from the south-west towards the northern pole. It has a length of eight hundred miles, a width of two hundred: leaving out of account the various large headlands that jut out between the curving ocean bays.

To illustrate the willfulness of prosal habit, we now jump ahead to an early seventeenth-century 'modern' English version of the same completed passage, which remains persistently (and perversely) of-a-whole-piece, namely, a single rambling, unstoppable, engorged *periodic* boa constrictor. The translator (unnamed, but probably William Cooke) claims to present to his reader a rendering of the true Gildas that is (says he) "still the same though in his apparell fashioned to the time."

> The Iland of *Britaine* placed in the balance of the divine poising hand (as they call it) which weigheth the whole world, almost the uttermost bound of this earth towards the *South* and *West*; extending it selfe from the *South West*, out towards the *North* Pole, eight hundred miles in length, and containing two hundred in bredth, besides the farre outstretched Forelands of sundry Promontaries, embraced by the embowed bosomes of the Ocean Sea; with whose most spacious, and on every side (having only the Southerne streights, by which we saile to *Gallebelgicke*) impassable enclosure (as I may call it) shee is strongly defended; enriched with the mouths of 2. Noble Floods, *Thames* and *Severne*, as it were two armes (by which outlandish commodities have in times past beene transported into the same) besides other Rivers of lesser account, strengthened with eight and twenty Cities, and some other Castles, not meanely fenced with Fortresses of Wals, embattelled Towers, Gates, & buildings (whose roofes being raised aloft with threatening hugenesse, were mightily in their aspiring toppes compacted) adorned with her large spreading fields, pleasant seated hils, even framed for good husbandry, which overmastereth the ground, and mountains most convenient for the changeable Pastures of cattell (whose flowers of sundry collours, troden by the feete of men, imprint no unseemely picture on the same) as a spouse of choice, decked with divers jewels; watered with cleere Fountaines, and sundry Brookes, beating on the snow white sands together with silver streames sliding forth with soft sounding noise, and leaving a pledge of sweet savours on their bordering bankes, and lakes gushing out abundantly in cold running Rivers.[23]

It seems very possible that Gildas's early-post-classical, high-toned, content-packed sentences were motivated by his ambitious aspirations to prove himself 'literary' in an atmosphere that was more 'oral' than erudite. In the works of Aldhelm, and much later in those of Thomas More, we find more of this drive to impress the less educated with their sentence-flooding verbal prowess. Like so many scholarly folk of his era, Gildas was in love with words. It was as if too many could never be enough.

This rather detailed section on Gildas will end with the following thought about the matter of cadency. The realization that 'It's time to stop!' is triggered by the requirements of the meanings of words as well as the order (syntax) in which they are laid—in short, by lexical custom and grammatical dictate. Grammar, being the apparatus (or system) by which we can transform our private thinking into word structures for communication, works in partnership with our physiological limitations. It deals in rules for breaking the *continuum* of speech sound into segments that our lungs can sustain and our minds absorb. If that grammar, upon which we depend to make ourselves intelligible to one another, is not manifest amongst the words of silent prose, all will turn to sludge. As has been noted earlier, speech, with its powers of gesture, facial expression, and tonal adjustment can often pinch-hit for grammar; *whereas* written words that lack grammatical support cannot be counted on to convey the intended meaning.

The *Hisperica Famina*

It is time now to come to grips with what is meant by the term 'Celtic influence,' for it crops up again and again in critical assessments of British late-Latin literary development. What specifically were the defining features of Irish (or Welsh) tradition? The mid-seventh-century *Hisperica Famina*, a document that marks the closing down of Ireland's explosive influence on medieval literature, is the most-quarried body of literature for enlightenment in response to that question. Its 600 some lines are replete with elements that distinguish northern manuscripts from continental ones of the same period. The *Famina* is like nothing found elsewhere. Though it is clearly concerned with student life in pre- and early Christian culture in Great Britain, nobody knows exactly what the action is about, where it takes place, or (without the benefits of punctuation) whose voice belongs to whom, or even for what purpose the so-called 'faminator' composed it.

The *Hisperica Famina* comprises a series of people-populated scenes, with additional materials (such as ode-like descriptions of sky and sea), expressed in language (Latin) that lies midway between poetry and prose. In the opening section we are presented with the voice of a young scholar, whose native tongue was probably Anglo-Saxon.[24] Somewhere within his pugnacious opening aria, more voices begin to give vent. While all are vibrating more or less in the same semantic field, they remain individually unidentified. We learn from their talk how as seekers of knowledge they had banded together to rove the countryside (most likely Ireland, but quite possibly Wales or even Scotland) in search of good teachers; and how at the same time they had to hunt down food and shelter, like mendicants, to sustain their cultural endeavors.

After a good feed at the hands of the admiring illiterates whose lands they traversed (and probably plucked clean), they would work the rest of the day at their books in order to win prizes and become famous. We gain this information from the combative braggadocio that the voices engage in and the insults they hurl at each other during the sociabilities of mealtime. Oratorical sparring is their youthful hobby; but their passion to refine and extend their language is the dominating theme of the piece. Surprisingly, there is no mention of church, priests, or prayer. The feel of countryside, the struggle for livelihood, the hurly-burly of ambitious boy-men on the make are ancillary aspects of the central topic—along with a sense of deep, almost rabbinical, reverence for learning. For the modern reader, a strange experience is unfolding.

Generally, the *Famina* is thought to have been written for pedagogical purposes: that is, to provide an exemplar for expert word manipulation, the crowning achievement of a Celtic education in the arts. By demonstration of heightened rhetorical practice, it teaches the would-be scholar numerous difficult words and linguistic tricks with which to adorn his word-flow; or, should the need arise, to hang it with barbs—the better to *demolish* competitors. The supposition seems to have been that by acquiring these aggressive linguistic techniques, by one way or the other, the student would fit himself for scholarly acclaim.

As there is no fixed arrangement of rhyme or assonance (rhyming only by vowel sounds, as in *made* and *cake*) and no fixed quantity of syllables either before or after a posited *caesura* (where the beat of a foot and a word both come to an end, thus causing an unwanted pause of sound), Professor Michael Herren, our directing guru for this subject, deems it unlikely that the piece was poetically conceived, even though later manuscripts have doled it out in colometric lines. In any case, most of those colometric lines are fully developed, scannable mini-sentences with verb (usually active) included. As such, they have the power to conjure up complete and vivid images, one after the other, with a bing-bing-bing persistence. In the absence of strict verse, punctuation, or even (to some extent) expectable syntax, the most notable thing left for critical examination is *the vocabulary*. And here the difficulty begins. Every sentence seems trip-wired with obscure and exceptional word specimens. They throng the *Famina*, as though in exuberant experiment, and their usage is far from standard. The turgid detail that they stir up distracts both reader and listener. Herren tells us that

> a sword is never *gladius*, but always *spatha, framea*, and occasionally *ensis*; one does not wear just "clothes," but always a *trabea, stola, chlamys*, or *armilausa*...often with little regard to the appropriateness of the garment mentioned. It is not the sun that rises, but the *titaneus arotus*, the *febeus proritus*, or the *phetoneum incendium*....One does not get caught in a stiff *uento*, but in a *zephiro, austro, euro* or *noto*....The parts of the body are frequently expressed by metaphor: mouths are *forcipes*, feet are *basses*, eyes are *conae*, hands are *cupae*.[25]

Where unwonted words are used to embellish or replace ordinary words; where ordinary words are used in exceptional senses; where new words result from a confusion of forms or some misunderstanding of a gloss, or derive from too assiduous (or too lax) a bonding with their etymology—in such places lies the stuff of Celtic invention. Though oddities of this nature do not always inhibit the fluency, they are alien to the customs of the established Latin language. They make awkward hurdles for the reader. In the case of the *Famina*, they tell us that the authoring faminator was ignorant of the rules of traditional Latin word formation in respect to the meanings of both stems and suffixes.

But there is more to say about the traces of Celtic authorship in the *Hisperica Famina*. A man with an enormous word hoard is inclined to show what he can do with it. Pride eggs him on to match his capability with that of others and, if possible, to outdo them. We sense something of this contesting attitude in the faminator's display of versatility, in his reinforcement of an image by a more exacting rewording of it. The first exposure of a basic thought is given a follow-up second—a fresh focus in fresh language. Each rephrased line is intended to heighten the message of the one before it, to fulfill it by adding elements that render it more graphic, more detailed and thrilling. Little is left for the reader to imagine, for it has all been done for him. To exercise such a parenting control, the author needs to have an armory of verbal choices. In the following example, a three-liner description of the sea, we are told of three ways in which land meets sea.

> The spuming sea encircles the shores of the world,
> It pounds against the margins of the land with its aged tides,
> It rushes into the rocky hollows with masses of water.[26]

Again, the faminator begins his ode-like piece on the sky as follows:

> Regarding the huge firmament of the heaven I shall produce an abun-
> dance of words in measured tones.

and then, continuing, he describes the sun:

> The Titanian star inflames the ceiling of heaven and illuminates the
> sea with its warm exhalation; it traverses the sky in fiery brilliance and
> ascends the vault of the bountiful firmament.[27]

Despite what Mr. Herren's smoothed-out, user-friendly rendition may suggest, the *Famina* makes for a tedious uphill read. There is little variety of syntax. In their Latin form, the lines end with a noun. The verb lies in the mid-section of each colon and not at the end, leaving the nouns with their modifiers to orbit around it. That these modifiers are sometimes adjacent to their nouns and sometimes not so adjacent is a most unclassical set-up as well. There are few particles to be seen, and the presence of absolute ablatives to abbreviate is rare. The sequencing bonds of cause and effect are not in play. Thus, we are presented with tremendous semantic variety and very little of the syntactical kind. With such an imbalance of formula, the words necessarily stand out. The sparkling precision of image that they conjure up by means of reinforcing synonyms dominates the reader's attention. To give a modern reader a more realistic sense of the paraphrased word-bumpiness to be found in the *Famina*, here are the opening lines translated by the candid pen of E. K. Rand.

> Ample jubilation swells the caverns of my breast, and scorching grief I
> pluck from my lungs, and I imprison in the arteries of my chest a beating
> storm of joy, when I behold the famous lords of wisdom who down their
> throats swallow the glorious liquor of an urbane culture, who weave the
> vipery syllogisms that men of letters understand. Over the stretches of the
> three-cornered earth, the flower-laden troop of rhetoricians guide their
> chariots and leave far, far behind the bournes of the vasty foundation,
> whether they broach themselves of fable from their lips or fierce battle is
> rife among the sons of disputation.[28]

In differentiating Celtic bias from traditional mainstream Latin, one should note how anxious the faminator was to avoid the repetition of words. As we have already seen, the avoidance of word repetition was a goal much disdained by the classical Greeks and Romans—a silly waste of time according to Quintilian, though not so much to Tacitus. In Celtic culture, *word repetition was considered to be deadening*. Fresh synonyms signaled erudition and a fertile imagination. The faminator scored high on word-fertility charts, for he was whole-hog into the business of supplanting an already used word with a striking, even esoteric, substitute. The change of focus caused by synonym substitution with its accompanying effect of enlarging mental perception is *the critical feature* to remember in association with what is thought to be 'the Celtic style.' Another, though it is less agreed upon, is the already discussed interlacing word order.

Celtic departures from classical rule persisted not only in semantic and structural matters, but in phonetics, morphology, and word formation. Though the *Famina*'s accumulation of oddities argues for an Irish-Celtic (over a Welsh or Scottish) origin, the clinching detail lies in its profusion of glossary words.[29] Their presence betrays an insularity foreign to the Welsh,[30] and instead points firmly to Ireland and the oblique relationship that it maintained with the Roman-influenced literary standards that prevailed elsewhere. In the *Famina*'s case, the eager author has clearly plucked words from books and word lists without a practiced knowledge of their 'received' usage. He has skewed their connotations to fit his private meaning. It is as though a foreigner might say in modern English: *His girlfriend was suggestive that they go to the movies*—which, of course, is decipherable but disturbing, and in any event, lexically wrong. Aside from its many glossary words, one should remember that the *Famina* also includes invented words, foreign borrowings, hybrids, and words of mutated etymology—in short, words that are remindful of the grotesqueries set forth as truths in Isidore's *Etymologiae*. Interestingly, by the faminator's time the published Isidorian corpus had recently arrived on the shores of Ireland and is known to have stirred up immediate intellectual activity.

That the *Famina* author seemed strangely 'out of it' may also be noted in his misapplication of Vergilian glosses. In Herren's analysis of these matters, we are shown how the faminator borrowed Vergil's vocabulary not only for his own Vergilian adaptations but for their surrounding lines as well. This slavish attendance to classical paradigm does not bespeak a comfortable familiarity, such as Gildas was proved to have had. More evidence yet for the Irishness of the *Famina* lies in its orthographic peculiarities (the duplications of consonants and the dropping of syllables) and its persistent immunity to classical rhythms.

From these many clues, one may justly reason that the faminator was working beyond the boundaries of his own linguistic homeland, consulting lexicons and hunting down useable items, somewhat in the manner of an amateur herbalist collecting rare specimens. The overall oddness of his composition tallies with Ireland's history of having been, from the very first, outside the circle of Roman influence, both artistically and politically. In sum, the *Famina* is thought to have been the work of a clever, even learned, book-oriented, noncontinental (probably Irish) writer, whose core features of style were a gushing word-flow supplied by naïve book scavenging, along with displays of unneeded synonyms embedded in a monotonous syntax.

Herren conjectures that the Celtic line of heritage may have developed out of Wales, where in the mid-500s (when Gildas wrote his *De excidio*) rhetors and scholars were known to be striving for rarified diction. The same love of recherché words quickly took fire in Ireland, passed to Iona and Scotland, then back to Ireland to reach its peak near the middle of the seventh century (ca. 650–660). Gildas's *De excidio Britannia* and the *Hisperica Famina* have many lexical correspondences. Because so much of the Hisperic material that we possess is secular in tone, an interesting speculation is that the "Hisperic craze" might represent some action for keeping the proud *filid* heritage intact by means of a hieratic language accessible to only the honored, erudite few—those few who had access to books.[31]

Given the brief florescence of this Irish literary activity (no more than 30 years), one might think that the movement was stamped out by some drastic natural occurrence: plague, meteor fallout, invasion of vipers—who can know? But also to be considered is the possibility that papal oppression played a part.[32] Whatever the cause of its final demise, aspects of Irish literary achievements lived on, most especially through the writings of Aldhelm, who plundered words and whole phrases from Gildas's *De excidio* and the *Hisperica Famina* alike.

Notes

1. Jane Stevenson, "The Beginnings of Literacy in Ireland," *Proceedings of the Royal Irish Academy: Archaeology, Culture, History, Linguistics, Literature* 89C (1989): 127–65, is an important source for these early Irish materials. Another is her article "Literacy in Ireland: The Evidence of the Patrick dossier in the Book of Armagh," in *The Uses of Literacy in Early Mediaeval Europe*, ed. Rosamond McKitterick (Cambridge: Cambridge University Press, 1990), 11–35.

2. The Japanese concept of *Oe* provides a useful parallel, for it incorporates a similar respect for, and unity of feeling with, the previous members of one's family. *Oe* can most easily be described as a kind of mystical family hierarchy, suggesting aspects similar to the symbolism of a totem. In the *Oe* case, the living present-tense member is enjoined to uphold the family spirit by teaching young members about those who have come before.

3. Eleanor Shipley Duckett, *Anglo-Saxon Saints and Scholars* (New York: Macmillan, 1947), 19–20.

4. The ogam letters, formed originally from carved straight lines (visually similar to the Germanic-Roman-based rune), were alphabetically sequenced in consonant and vowel clusters, as opposed to our less scientifically organized ABC series, where the vowels pop up randomly amongst an already random series of consonants. Nobody knows the details of the actual invention of the Celtic ogam alphabet, but it was used only in the British Isles, most prominently in Ireland, and had given way entirely to the Latin alphabet by the seventh century. Modern scholars have noted similarities of the ogam arrangement with phonetic principles established by the late Roman grammarians of the Varro-Donatus line.

5. Stevenson, "Beginnings of Literacy in Ireland," 151–2.

6. Patrick was born in the late fourth century and probably died around CE 460.

7. Armagh is an ancient city near Belfast and the historic primatial center of Ireland's Catholic Church. The *Book of Armagh* is now in Dublin's Trinity College. It lies under glass cover and is diligently guarded.

8. Whitley Stokes, ed., "Epistola S. Patricii Ad Christianos Corotici Tyranni Subditos," in *The Tripartite Life of Patrick, with Other Documents Relating to that Saint, Chronicles and Memorials of Great Britain and Ireland During the Middle Ages* 89 (London: Her Majesty's Stationery Office, 1887): 2:375.

9. Maire Herbert, *Iona, Kells, and Derry: The History and Hagiography of the Monastic Family of Columba* (Oxford: Clarendon Press, 1988), 27–35.

10. St. Gall's former monastic buildings are still standing, and its library (a subsequent rococo edifice) still operates. It contains about 2,000 precious manuscripts, as well as numerous incunabula and books dating from the Carolingian and Ottonian empires.

11. During the decline of monasteries in the fifteenth century, however, the collections of approximately 700 tenth-century manuscripts were dispersed, most of them going to the Vatican. Though monastic activities were suppressed in 1803 by the French, Bobbio's fifteenth- and seventeenth-century buildings survive, including the tomb of Saint Columban, whose relics are preserved in the museum.

12. The three languages of Britain were the indigenous Gaelic (Celtic), the Latin of the conquering first-century CE Roman imperialists, and the Anglo-Saxon brought in by the invasions of fifth- and sixth-century Danish hordes.

13. Christopher Abram, "In Search of Lost Time: Aldhelm and *The Ruin*," *Quaestio: Selected Proceedings of the Cambridge Colloquium in Anglo-Saxon, Norse and Celtic* 1 (Cambridge: University Department of Anglo-Saxon, Norse and Celtic, 2000), 23–44.

14. Gildas, "*The Ruin of Britain and Other Works*," ed. and trans. Michael Winterbottom, Arthurian Period Sources 7 (London: Phillimore, 1978). Mr. Winterbottom's introduction is extremely helpful for understanding the stylistic features in Gildas.

15. Winterbottom, introduction to *Ruin of Britain*, 6.

16. Ibid., 9; and Quintilian, *Institutio oratoria*, 3:521.

17. Neil Wright, "Gildas's Prose Style and Its Origin," in *Gildas: New Approaches*, ed. Michael Lapidge and David Dumville, Celtic History 5 (Suffolk, UK: Boydell Press, 1984), 27–50.

18. Much of this information about the educational background of Gildas comes from *Gildas: New Approaches*, ed. Michael Lapidge and David Dumville, Celtic History 5 (Suffolk, UK: Boydell Press, 1984), 27–50.

19. As grammar took on more and more of the contents of rhetoric, so the age of a grammar graduate would have increased. In earlier times, it had been closer to 14.

20. Rosamond McKitterick, in her essay "Latin and Romance: An Historian's Perspective," in Roger Wright, *Latin and the Romance Languages*, 130–45, persuades us that even into the ninth century, those who were privileged to learn their letters at all, learned them in Latin, and thereafter, in reading and writing followed as best they could the traditions of a Latin education.

21. Giovanni Orlandi, "*Clausulae* in Gildas's *De Excidio Britanniae*," in *Gildas: New Approaches*, ed. Michael Lapidge and David Dumville (Suffolk, UK: Boydell Press, 1984), 27–50.

22. *Catholic Encyclopedia*, ed. Charles George Herbermann, s.v. "Gildas."

23. From *The Epistle of Gildas*, trans. unknown (London: William Cooke, 1638) 1–4.

24. My primary source for the materials in this section is the commentary and translation of Michael Herren, in his *Hisperica Famina: I. The A-Text* (Toronto: Pontifical Institute of Mediaeval Studies, 1974). The bands of (probably English) students described here would have had some minimal ability in 'tourist' Celtic, and probably coped in their travels, too, with local versions of the common Latin-based *lingua franca*.

25. Herren, *Hisperica Famina*, 46–7. With this, we are reminded of the ancient criticisms of archaic and abstruse word usage (as of Sallust, who is said to have hired others to seek them out on his behalf). One wonders if this longing was in deliberate opposition to the ancient precept of 'not being afraid to use a word immediately again *if it is the right word.*'

26. Ibid., 15.

27. Ibid., 91–3.

28. Ibid., 56.

29. Glossary words were the words that a reader would write above a manuscript's textual line to translate (perhaps into his own dialect) a word he did not know or was unsure of. The implication here is that the ambitious young scholar would pluck a novel synonym from wherever he could.

30. Both Wales and Scotland were more influenced by Rome than was Ireland. Of the two, Wales was more famously focused on scholarship.

31. Herren, *Hisperica Famina*, 43.

32. Ibid., 43.

References

Abram, Christopher. "In Search of Lost Time: Aldhelm and *The Ruin*." In *Quaestio: Selected Proceedings of the Cambridge Colloquium in Anglo-Saxon, Norse and Celtic* 1. Cambridge: University Department of Anglo-Saxon, Norse and Celtic, 2000.

The Catholic Encyclopedia. Edited by Charles George Herbermann, s.v. "Gildas."

Duckett, Eleanor Shipley. *Anglo-Saxon Saints and Scholars*. New York: Macmillan, 1947.

Gildas. *The Epistle of Gildas*. Translator unknown. London: William Cooke, 1638.

————. *The Ruin of Britain and Other Works*. Edited and translated by Michael Winterbottom. Arthurian Period Sources 7. London: Phillimore, 1978.

Herbert, Maire. *Iona, Kells, and Derry: The History and Hagiography of the Monastic Family of Columba*. Oxford: Clarendon Press, 1988.

Herren, Michael. *Hisperica Famina: I. The A-Text*. Toronto: Pontifical Institute of Mediaeval Studies, 1974.

Lapidge, Michael, and David Dumville. *Gildas: New Approaches*. Celtic History 5. Suffolk, UK: Boydell Press, 1984.

McKitterick, Rosamond. "Latin and Romance: An Historian's Perspective." In *Latin and the Romance Languages in the Early Middle Ages*, 130–45. Edited by Roger Wright. University Park, PA: Pennsylvania State University Press, 1996.

Orlandi, Giovanni. "*Clausulae* in Gildas's *De Excidio Britanniae*." In *Gildas: New Approaches*. Edited by Michael Lapidge and David Dumville. Suffolk, UK: Boydell Press, 1984.

Quintilian. Vol. 3 of *Institutio oratoria*. Translated by H. E. Butler. Loeb Classical Library. Cambridge: Harvard University Press, 1980.

Stevenson, Jane. "The Beginnings of Literacy in Ireland." *Proceedings of the Royal Irish Academy: Archaeology, Culture, History, Linguistics, Literature* 89C (1989): 127–65.

————. "Literacy in Ireland: The Evidence of the Patrick Dossier in the Book of Armagh." In *The Uses of Literacy in Early Mediaeval Europe*. Edited by Rosamond McKitterick. Cambridge: Cambridge University Press, 1990.

Stokes, Whitley, ed. "Epistola S. Patricii Ad Christianos Corotici Tyranni Subditos." In Vol. 2 of *The Tripartite Life of Patrick, with Other Documents Relating to that Saint, Chronicles and Memorials of Great Britain and Ireland During the Middle Ages* 89. London: Her Majesty's Stationery Office, 1887.

Winterbottom, Michael. Introduction to his translation of *The Ruin of Britain and Other Works*. Arthurian Period Sources 7. London: Phillimore, 1978.

Wright, Neil. "Gildas's Prose Style and Its Origin." In *Gildas: New Approaches*. Edited by Michael Lapidge and David Dumville. Celtic History 5. Suffolk, UK: Boydell Press, 1984.

· 2 0 ·

ENGLAND BESTIRS ITSELF

Introducing the Great Aldhelm

Aldhelm (639–709 CE) has been described as the 'first man of English letters' and was, in early opinion, 'the best' as well. The glosses of tenth- and eleventh-century copies of his works show how persistently important Aldhelm remained in the pre-Norman English curriculum of authors—that is, the authors on whom young scholars focused to perfect their own diction, vocabulary, and syntax. The goal of Aldhelm's style was *to fill to the brim with detail*; whereas Bede's (which is so much more accessible, let alone appealing to modern tastes) is more classical, more Attic (or Senecan), which is to say, clear-cut and lean.[1]

In seeking the provenance for Aldhelm's exuberant idiosyncrasies, scholars have come up with a variety of possibilities, of which the most prominent tie him (1) to Gorgias, (2) to late classical epistolography, (3) to patristic traditions, and (4) to Anglo-Saxon vernacular poetry; but, most persistently, (5) to Irish complexity. In the hope of uncovering some irrefutable line of influence, scholars have totted up instances in his writing of synonymous doublets (pairs of words meaning essentially the same thing, such as 'favorable and harmonious' or 'dark and nocturnal'), esoteric words, repetitions of phrasal rhythms, presence of homoeoteleuton (rhyming by inflections—a Gorgianic predilection), avoidance of homoeoteleuton (an Irish bias), assonance (rhyming with vowel sounds—Irish), paraphrasings (Gorgias again and Irish), interlaced word order (Irish), quantitative meters (Roman), accented rhythms (late continental Latin), alliteration (Anglo-Saxon, but also everybody else)—all of that, accompanied by learned musings on Aldhelmic syntax and how it knots and twines like Irish pictorial design with all its pagan resonances. Actually, Aldhelm has been an ongoing topic among literary academics for a very long time. Despite the all-out effort, nothing has come to light that truly succeeds in resolving arguments about the sources of his style. Answers scarcely hit the table before they begin to propagate new questions.

Perhaps the best way, then, to deal with Aldhelm's writing style is to accept that it emanated from a man of broad learning who had a background in both Celtic and Roman educational traditions. Historians describe Aldhelm as the earliest of the three most eminent scholars from the seventh and eighth golden-period centuries of northern culture. Moreover, his influence on Anglo-Latin literature, especially on verse, is universally acknowledged to have been profound. Bede and Alcuin (both from Britain's Northumbria) followed through on Aldhelm's initial moves, and successively all three managed to establish for England a formidable reputation for learning. Bede, who was himself erudite, admired Aldhelm "for being a man of great learning in all ways"—and a sparkling stylist to boot.[2]

More than his predecessor Gildas, Aldhelm was responsive to the requirements of a cadenced syntax. For the most part, even his most bulging structures can be made to scan. Scholars have noted that he took considerable care over the balance of sentential parts, and that he could terminate his *colons* and *periods* either by the long-voweled, classical meters (*clausulae*) or accentually (by *cursus*). In contrast to these achievements, a Gildas sentence seems (despite the proclaimed presence of cadences) shapeless—unkempt, burdened with antithesis and parallelism, minimally rhythmic, and dependent for its power on savage strong words, invective, and metaphor. Though a luxuriant Aldhelm sentence lacks the feel of pure classical Latin,[3] yet its parts are controlled and in accordance with continental mode. For that blessing we must give credit to Roman influence.

Some Historical Background

In the mid-seventh century, Irish missionaries from the Isle of Iona brought Christianity and learning to Northumbria, as they had done in Aldhelm's southwestern Wessex. For a time, Roman-oriented Canterbury and Celt-ic-oriented Iona advanced their influences equably into Anglo-Saxon territo-ry, so that Christian English youths were sent both to Romish seats of culture and to Ireland to study. But the religious practices of the two cultures were sufficiently different that they soon came into conflict. To resolve their differ-ences and to decide which of their separate ecclesiastical views (particularly the date for Easter) would predominate in all the land, prelates from both the Celtic and Roman churches came together in 663–664 at Whitby on the northeast coast of England for a period of discussion and dispute that was fa-mously known as the Synod of Whitby. In the end, the Celtic church (noted for asceticism, fervor, simplicity, and scholarship) lost the debate, and with it, gradually, its political and administrative authority. To ensure its position of primacy, the Anglo-Roman church then carved the land into dioceses and parishes, and, since the Celtic bishops and priests were inclined like the *filid* to wander, ruled that all clergy stay put within their allotted boundaries. That move gave particular impetus to the future buildup of power and wealth in the English extension of papal Rome. Thereafter, throughout Britain, new monasteries sprang up, and with them scriptoria and libraries—all responsive to the customs and edicts of Rome.

Amongst the Bees With Aldhelm

For uninitiated readers of Aldhelm, the difficulty comes in those moments when he elaborates his primary message with exaggerated, over-dramatic sim-ile or paraphrase—for the purpose (one assumes) of heightening the overall glitter. No statement is left in pristine simplicity. What he says gets said again and again with increasing complication. When unleashed entirely, Aldhelm's grandiloquence strains the syntax to a degree that can make decipherment diffi-cult—though the clues are usually there. A significant element of that grandilo-quence is his vocabulary, which in many respects reminds us of the faminator's: to wit, a lavish display of Greekisms, neologisms, personal inventions, and ar-chaisms exhumed from scholarly glossaries. In both refinement and deluge, Ald-helm's literary output was beyond the ordinary. Aldhelm refers to his own prose style (with apparent pride) as a *densa Latinitatis silva* ('a dense Latinate forest'). Michael Lapidge describes the exercise of reading Aldhelm's prose:

Aldhelm's Latin is extremely difficult, and sometimes impenetrable. His sentences are tediously long and complicated; his vocabulary is often bizarre and arcane, sometimes inscrutable. Indeed, Aldhelm's love of verbiage for its own sake—he calls it 'verbose garrulity or garrulous verbosity'—must often exasperate the well-intentioned reader who, having penetrated the lexical and syntactical obscurities of a two-page long sentence, finds that he is left with a trivial apothegm of the merest banality.[4]

In unraveling the tangle of Aldhelm's literary roots we get very little help from what we know of his life, for there too lies a blend of possible influence. Aldhelm came from Wessex, and in that western-English setting was trained initially by migrating Irish scholars. With his basic education completed under a Celtic regimen, he (ca. age 30) studied for some two more years in Canterbury at the famous monastic Abbey School, under the supervision of the learned Abbot Hadrian and Archbishop Theodore, both of whom spoke Greek as well as Latin. While there in Canterbury, Aldhelm himself probably learned to speak Greek fluently. He also submerged himself in Roman law; in complicated calculations in arithmetic; in the mysteries of astrology; in sacred and profane literatures (the latter, of course, for the sake of the former); in classical verse forms with all the many meters to master; and in music, for which there was not only the problem of melodies to remember, but the problem, too, of determining how the words and syllables would fit harmoniously within their measures.[5] This industrious sojourn in Romanized Canterbury, though draining to his health, became the highlighted memory of his life once he returned to his Irish-oriented monastery in Wessex.

Aldhelm learned a great deal from his Celtic and Roman experiences, and in both sets of scholarly circles gained an enormous eminence. As the differences between the two religious outlooks were developing, Aldhelm might easily have led the English Church into either camp. But with a bow to the Celtic, he seems to have favored the Roman, for in the end, he wholly supported papal preferences, as much for literary scholarship as for the dates of Easter and the styles of tonsure. As abbot of scholarly Malmsbury and then bishop of Sherborne (where, in hall, the schoolboys and girls still sing of his fame), Aldhelm vigorously protested the Irish acceptance of the profane works of antiquity, though he himself as a youth had studied, admired, and perhaps even relished them. Nevertheless, in his ultimate adherence to papal Rome, he accepted and propounded the same old view that ancient culture was not to be enjoyed, but only analyzed for the purpose of better interpreting the rhetoric of the Bible—a difficult task, but perhaps feasible in a thick-walled, piety-controlled monastic library. There, it was presumed possible (though it might have been wiser to doubt it) for a young male scholar to inspect the nuzzlings of Aeneas and Dido, or even Ovid's metamorphic *affaires* (let alone his instructions for making love), *if* he (the aforementioned young scholar) would keep his nose to the grindstone and focus solely on classical tropes, meters, syntax, etymologies, and similarly frail entertainments.

Aldhelm's eventual biographer, William of Malmesbury (ca. 1090–1143), expressed his regret that Aldhelm "has always been esteemed less than he ought, and always, because of people's indolence, lain hidden and uncelebrated."[6] Devotion to saintly memory did not allow this William to think the unthinkable thoughts that come to us so easily today, namely: that confronting Aldhelm, with his spigots on full blast, tends to induce an irresistible longing to lie down. One cannot imagine anyone, however anxious to improve his spiritual self, receiving a letter from Aldhelm and saying *"Oh what a joy! I can't wait to figure out what he's trying to tell me!"*

That the Lapidge and Herren team managed to derive such explicit sense from Aldhelm's famously quoted letter to Heahfrith is altogether a triumph. Here is an excerpt from that letter, a sample of Aldhelm at his unfathomable worst. It is thought that he was trying to dissuade the young Heahfrith (ca. 680) from seeking out glib Irish rhetors by demonstrating how glib he, Aldhelm, the polished product of the Roman-English educational system, could be when it came to Latinate *copia verborum*. Interestingly, in Aldhelm's Latin original, 15 out of the first 16 words begin with a 'P,' making of it (but why?) a sort of Peter-Piper-Picked exhibit of hyper-alliteration.

> Likewise I do not hesitate in the least to disclose from the depths of my heart to your propitious Blessedness that this [your return] has come about especially for the increase of joy among deacons and priests, nay rather, for the glory of the name of the Lord, because—rumour aside—by the proclamation of those dwelling on Irish soil, on whose companionship you relied for a little while [actually, for 'thrice two years'] for the purpose of sucking 'on the teat of wisdom,' was our hearing shaken, as if by a kind of bellow of thunder issuing from a clashing of clouds, and common opinion bruited it abroad through so many and such large measures of the land of learning and to the parishes and provinces that the wandering hither and thither and back and forth of those traversing the abysses of the sea on ship-path is as busy as a kind of kindred swarm of bees skillfully manufacturing

[their nectar]. For just as the honey-flowing swarm [of bees]—when the mist of night departs in its course and Titan [the sun] emerges from the sea up to the peak of heaven—clothed in yellow vestments carries its burden through the flowering tops of blooming lindens to the graceful honey-combs, in like fashion, if I am not mistaken, a mass of ravenous scholars and an avid throng of sagacious students, the residue from the rich fields of Holy Writ, thirstily seize and swallow not only the grammatical geometrical arts—to say nothing of the twice-three [a favorite Hisperic feature for numbering] scaffolds of the art of physics—but also, the fourfold honeyed oracles of allegorical or rather tropological disputation of opaque problems in aetherial mysteries, conceal and store them away to be conserved until death with perpetual meditation in the beehives of learning, from the catalogue of which an excellent report has bruited it that your Sagacity emerged burdened with booty and drenched and overflowing with floods of the sacred torrent.[7]

One wonders how Heahfrith responded.

Alternatively, Aldhelm could be quite charming. His sincerity *almost* always outshines his verbosity splurges. His best moments seem to come when he is being a little less coiled and a little more direct; or, to put it in terms we have heretofore associated with ancient literatures—a little less decorative (Asian) and a little more straightforward (Attic-Senecan). However, a poetic instinct is manifest in all his writing, for Aldhelm had a prosodic knowledge that was supreme for his time. In his youth, his aural sensibilities had been cultivated by Anglo-Saxon and Celtic poetry and then sharpened in his Canterbury studies of classical prosody. Poetry was both his joy and his consolation for an arduous life. To show his stuff and to exercise his accumulated skills must have been a constant temptation, for there was nobody around who could outdo him.

So that we do not leave Aldhelm everlastingly tainted by his letter to Heahfrith, here is another prose sample, this time a letter to the Abbots of Wilfrid, who were dithering over what to do about their contentious leader's deposition from office. Should they stay with him, or scatter to find security? Aldhelm is firm. *Stay*, says he. The translation is again by the courageous Lapidge and Herren. We see in these lines that, though Aldhelm once more enmeshes himself in eager swarms of nectar-yearning bees, his manner is gracious, his tone mild, his admonishments gentle, and his reasoning sound. His poetic instincts are in full display and (except for the threat of buzzing bees) under control.

Recently a raging and tempestuous disturbance—as you learned from experience—has shaken the foundations of the Church in the manner of a gigantic earthquake, the noise of which has resounded far and wide like a thunderclap through the various regions of the land. Wherefore, I beg of you, sons of the same tribe, with bended knee and hopeful prayer, to be in no wise scandalized by the deceit of this disturbance, lest anyone of you grow sluggish in a faith of lazy inactivity, since the necessity of event requires that you along with your own bishop who has been deprived of the honour of his office, be expelled from your native land and go to any transmarine country in the wide world that is suitable. What harsh or cruel burden in existence, I ask, would separate you and hold you apart from that bishop, who like a wet-nurse gently caressed you, his beloved foster-children, warming you in the folds of his arms and nourishing you in the bosom of charity, and who brought you forward in his paternal love by rearing, teaching, and castigating you from your very first exposure to the rudiments (of education) and from your early childhood and tender years up to the flower of your maturity? Examine carefully, I beseech you, the order of creation and the nature divinely planted within it, so that by comparing the very least things, you may comprehend with Christ's help the unchanging pattern of life. (See) how swarms of bees eagerly emerge from their hives, yearning for nectar, when warm heat descends from the sky, and, when their leader departs, the cohorts thronging in swift flight heap up to the aether their winter shelters of close-packed *etc.*, *etc.*[8]

Prose or Poetry? The Ambidextrous Master

Aldhelm's most revered work was his *De virginitate*, which he wrote first in prose to fortify the nuns of Barking (in Essex) in their virginal resolves, and then distilled to poetry for their further inspiration. A comparison of his prosal and poetic styles is rather interesting. In the case of the episode about Thecla (Thecla was a virgin of superhuman rectitude), we note that the initial prose version is only half the length of the later poem version, though its contents are essentially the same. Whereas the prose comprises four sentences only, the poem contains 10 shorter and far more accessible ones—which suggests that the nuns didn't quite get it the first time around. Most likely, being unable to read,

they needed to memorize it with the help of prosodic mnemonics. It is interesting that "while Aldhelm in his prose [version] is at pains to vary the length
of the constituent parts of every sentence, his verses are practically all end-
stopped, and, within the line, strictly divided into three main metrical units…
[and] composed in a continuous series of staccato phrases of fixed length."[9] The
poem's short and easily scanned lines with their repetitious metrical units, their
sustained alliteration and artfully constructed imagery were designed to please
simple but sensitive minds whose favored method of information-intake was
aural. The poem's total effect is that of a kindly pastoral statement.

The more intricate and varied prose version (likewise kindly and thoughtful) recounts the same tale in a weightier, more eye-appealing way. While giv-
en to the density of poetic effects that one might expect from classical Latin,
the prose version of Thecla's trials seems also to follow the Vulgate's book of
linguistic rules—which is to say that, although it may seem enormously more
complicated, its syntax does more or less follow the lineaments of the natural
word order usual to common speech. Its sophisticated verbiage, on the other
hand, was boldly different from the contemporary, less artful Vulgate-Church
usage that was so effective for communication with humble folk. One must
admire Aldhelm's versatility: that he could gracefully write in so many styles
and successfully address so many levels of society.

Interestingly, Aldhelm was highly conscious of homoeoteleuton (as in
Puellae pulcherae paratae et volentae sunt: 'The beautiful girls are ready and
willing'), which he used to create rhymes in his poetry, but avoided resolutely
in prose. In prose, when he wanted a noun and its associated adjective to be
in close proximity, he chose words from different declensions to circumvent
that mesmerizing homoeoteleuton effect. This anti-jingling-rhyme ploy was
a prominent feature of the close-to-contemporary Hiberno-Latin *Hisperica
Famina*; and Aldhelm's self-imposed adoption of it suggests a notable strain
of Celtic influence in his work. The impulse to avoid the singsong of home-
oteleuton may well account for the baroque vocabulary that characterizes the
prose works of all three writers: Gildas, the faminator, and Aldhelm.[10]

An Hisperic spirit imbues the semantic superstructure of all Aldhelm's
writing. Though generally his word choice is somewhat less startling than
that of Gildas,[11] it is true that Aldhelm extensively 'borrowed' both words and
phrases from *The Ruin* and the *Hisperica Famina*. Overall, we are not surprised
to discover Aldhelm's affinity to Gildas, for both were Celtic-Roman trained,
Latin-writing authors. Of the two, Gildas was more pedantically classical in
diction but syntactically confusing, and Aldhelm was more Vulgate in diction

but more inclined to be classically sound in matters of syntax and cadence. Yet the prose of both reveals a strong poetic inclination, as manifested in alliteration, imaginative striving for vocabulary, and a deep probing focus into every aspect of a single idea.

Of the two, Aldhelm is considered more poetry-driven than Gildas—a judgement that derives from his expansive ornamental propensities (as in his bee similes) as well as his sense of balance and his easeful planting of *cursus* (or even the classical *clausulae*) to reinforce the rhythms. Aldhelm also showed a penchant for semantic doublets (like 'dreich and dreary'—always a sign of rhetorical elevation) and revealed as well a sensitive poetic perception in his avoidance of homoeoteleuton in his prose works. He too played with unnatural word order (hyperbaton), particularly through the interlacing (or 'enveloped') separation of adjectives from their related nouns. In fact, he seems as fond of hyperbaton as was Gildas. This last feature, when coupled with fierce semantic and syntactic displays (as was common to both writers), is considered to be highly Celtic. In sum, it would seem that Aldhelm's prose, most of which was written in his later years, might well be termed *all*-inclusive: that is to say, inclusive of his wide reading, of his Celtic and Roman educations, and his daily experiences in an essentially Anglo-Saxon environment. To the delight of his countrymen, he seemed to have mastered it all. For some five generations beyond his lifetime, everybody who could manage to read him would unite in thinking him literature's triumphant joy.

Celtic religious dominance on the island of Britain diminished during the lifetime of Aldhelm, and was gradually replaced, almost totally, by the Rome-oriented, Anglo-Saxon Christian culture. Once Irish foundations had relaxed their own ambitions to lead the Christian world and had pledged their allegiance to the Pope instead, they applied their energies to evangelizing the illiterate continentals back to literary enlightenment. The Irish legacy was the preservation of books and knowledge, and along with that, a broadened vocabulary and a flamboyant artistry in using words. In James Joyce, Brendan Behan, Sean O'Faolain, Flann O'Brian, and others, Irish literary pride continues to ride high, and deservedly so. But what we must note for the moment in our tale is this: the direction of style from Gildas to the faminator (whoever he was) to Aldhelm shows a steady firming of statement towards clarity—despite some wild daring.

As we shall shortly see, the Anglo-Saxon Bede will bring plain-speaking Atticism back on stage. Under his guidance, the literary pendulum will reverse its swing, and simplicity will rule once again over complexity.

In Northumbria With the Venerable Bede

Benedict Biscop, like so many of the Church fathers (one thinks especially of Jerome, Ambrose, Gregory, and Augustine of Hippo), had probably enjoyed an aristocratic Roman-based education. He had worked with Hadrian and Theodore in Canterbury and was an avid importer and transporter of books from the Vatican in Rome to Northumbria. It was he who had founded (in 673 CE) the combined monasteries known as Wearmouth and Jarrow near Sunderland in Durham. His scholarly reputation, his passion for books, and his repeated trips to Rome in search of them suggest an early premonastic acquaintance with the South and a tentative acceptance of the secular values of ancient literatures.[12] Benedict's fame was such that the kinfolk of a seven-year-old Saxon orphan, named Bede (later to become 'Venerable') sought out this renowned double monastery so as to have their young charge brought up by its learned and book-loving founder. The scholarly establishment at Wearmouth and Jarrow became Bede's home for the rest of his life, which ended in 735 CE. There, as Bede would in time report, the library's acquisitions were doubled by Benedict's successor.

The Venerable Bede (we may now call him) was the most profound scholar of his era. He knew Latin, Greek, and probably some Hebrew. His delight, he tells us, was in learning, teaching, and writing. In accordance with the Benedictine practice of nurturing culture, he was relieved of daily household and farmyard chores, and encouraged to pursue the intellectual activities for which he was so remarkably gifted. The Northumbrian Jarrow Monastery library, where he worked and read, was unusual for the times, being copiously fed by a stream of new books from Rome as well as those borrowed through the very active network of exchange with other monastic libraries.

Bede impresses the modern world not only for the humility with which he handled his extensive learning, but also for his love of truth and accuracy, and his courage in tackling difficult subjects. His *The Reckoning of Time*, for example, became the

> most influential computus textbook of the Middle Ages. Synthesizing liturgical, historical, and astronomical conceptions of time, it covered, besides Easter, everything from fractions and finger-reckoning (a means to perform basic arithmetic on one's hands) to tides and shadows to AntiChrist and Judgment Day.[13]

Bede was meticulous in rejecting common hearsay in favor of authoritative sources; and—most unusual for his time—in giving credit where he could. His explication of doctrine is set in straightforward 'natural' language so as to benefit a broader readership. In describing an 'ideal teacher,' one would include many of Bede's virtues—kindness, gentleness, patience, passion for knowledge, personal modesty, and a focus on what the pupil will be able take in. In a period of prevailing ignorance, Bede's primary concern was to find the facts as best he could and to pass them on in the clearest possible form to his pupils and readers. "I would not that my children should read a lie," he was famously said to have said.[14] Bede's combination of lucid writing skills, scholarship, and plain-spoken honesty is a rare thing in the world's literature. Self-preening displays of cleverness are not to be found in his legacy to the world, nor is pompous pedagogy. In the history of writing, he was a rare bird. Though attentive to style and correctness of speech (as we shall shortly see), he was willing to go more than halfway to meet his reader. For 13 centuries, critics have praised his learning and industry, his quest for veracity, and his self-effacing simplicity.

Bede's clarity, even in his sometimes discursive *periods*, will be appreciated by the modern reader. The following Latin quotation, which comes (with the Loeb punctuation) from his most famous work, *Ecclesiastical History of the English Nation*, tells the story of the poet Caedmon. To illustrate the easy comprehensibility of Bede's style, a style open to the least able of readers, the following passage has been translated, word for word, from the Loeb's Latin text, with the addition of virgules to mark off the *colon* endings. To be noted especially are the unpretentious vocabulary and the bias towards natural word order. Also notable is the fact that a verb regularly finishes each *colon*, so that in reading the passage aloud, one can expect to breathe comfortably at rhythmically and semantically established times, knowing that the relevant idea is complete, and usually so in a mere handful of syllables. Herewith is a word-for-word English translation (see Loeb's Latin in the notes):[15]

> And indeed too others after him [Caedmon] in the English race religious poems to make were trying / but no one him to equal could / for he neither by men nor by man the singing art did he learn / but divinely aided freely for singing the gift received / because of which never of frivolous or vacuous poems to make was he able / but those of such a kind that to religion pertained / [and to] religious his tongue were befitting.[16] (Bede, *Hist. eccl.* 4.24)

Note that the final line of the Latin verse ends with a trochaic-cretic finishing *clausula*, thus: *linguam decebant* (dee-de / de-dee-de).

Remembering the prose of Aldhelm, one should especially appreciate the refreshing directness of Bede's address. Within a single page, one senses the profound sincerity of this author. His avoidance of egoistic display is manifest throughout his writings. Bede always puts himself in the shoes of his readers. He reaches out to them, encouraging them and inviting them to understand. The message itself is the impelling feature of his output—not the style nor his personal cleverness, though he is always careful to be correct. To ensure that the message is clear to all, he keeps his grammar and vocabulary as simple as possible. Bede's scholarship, his accessible language, and his advocacy of historical truth brought a refreshing breeze through the annals of early Christian Latin prose. Joining hands with previous humble instructors (like Gregory and Benedict—and even Cassiodorus once he had settled into the monastic activity of teaching the ignorant), Bede guided Britain's prose writing into freer, more honest spaces. His enormous scholarly reputation and literary leadership deflected the continuing influences of Celtic complication and lingering Roman rigidities. It made simplicity respectable. We may say that, thanks to Bede, written prose advanced yet another mile. It was because of him that Latinate England's prose became truly and freely expressive, as had Greek prose with Xenophon, Classical Roman prose with Seneca the Younger, and finally, as had Catholic Church prose under the gentle auspices of Pope Gregory the First ("Pastoral Care") and St. Benedict ("Benedictine Rule").[17]

Again, to emphasize the pliancy of Bede's style as well as his dramatic powers, herewith is another translated passage. Once again, this excerpt comes from the Caedmon episode (in Bede's *Ecclesiastical History of the English Nation*) and is presented more or less word for word. In this passage, Bede has chosen not to stay in the verb-ending-the-colon mode. Instead, he has swung out to capture the sudden drama with the verbal phrase *adstitit ei* ('there stood next to him'—*pow!*). By planting the verbal phrase *at the beginning* of the colon, and *not* at the customary end, Bede makes the vision come to Caedmon like a burst of lightning. This line, the next 'limbs he had given to sleep' and the final one, 'Caedmon he said sing to me something'—all suggest a burgeoning desire to free the verb from its classically constrained, finalizing position. This relaxation from ancient principle would seem to have developed from the tendencies of common oral speech. In this passage (with the verbs set in boldface) Bede is recounting how the miraculous gift of song first came to the humble Caedmon:

*…et relicta domo convivii **egressus esset***
…and abandoning [the] house of feasting he went out

*ad stabula iumentorum quorum ei custodia nocte illa **erat***
delegata
to the stable of animals of which to him as custodian on that night he
had been assigned

*ibique hora competenti membra **dedisset** sopori*
and there at an hour suitable [his] limbs he had given to sleep

***adstitit** ei quidam per somnium eumque salutans ac suo appellans nomine*
stood next to him someone in [his] sleep and him greeting and calling
him by his name

*Caedmon **inquit canta** mihi aliquid*
Cadmon he said sing to me something.[18] (Bede, *Hist. eccl.* 4.24)

Besides his better known writings on history, theology, chronology, and natural phenomena, Bede also wrote on matters that relate specifically to the interests of writers. His *De orthographia* is set in the form of a random collection
of pedagogical notes filed under the letters of the alphabet. Being much more
than a mere treatise on spelling, it more closely resembles a glossary,[19] with
grammatical comments, etymologies, and semantic distinctions of his own devising, along with improved rephrasings of Isidore of Seville. Bede also wrote
about meter and the figures of speech. His little book on meter includes a
discussion of Latin versification, for which he compiled commentaries on Donatus made by previous grammarians. It is replete with examples from Vergil
and Christian poets, and gives an ample account of the bulk of Latin classical
and postclassical metrical usage.[20]

Professor Lapidge, in the publication of his Jarrow Lecture of 1993, tells us
that Bede had all the instincts of a poet and that he engaged in critical analysis of it as well as composing it himself. Bede's *De arte metrica*, surviving in
more than a hundred manuscripts, served as the standard introduction to that
subject throughout the Middle Ages. It was later printed and went through
11 editions before 1600. He also wrote epigrams in hexameters and elegiac
couplets (now lost), a collection of hymns (some extant and identified), and a
poeticized version (*Vita metrica S. Cuthberti*) of an anonymous prosaic version
of Saint Cuthbert's life by an earlier Lindisfarne monk. This work was 'widely

studied and imitated, not only by his successors in England, such as Alcuin...,
but [also] by a host of Carolingian poets.'[21] Furthermore, says Lapidge:

> As befits a work intended for meditation and rumination, the diction
> of Bede's poem is tightly compressed. The metre of the poem is tech-
> nically excellent, even by classical standards (an unusual achievement
> among medieval Latin poets)....Bede in his hexameters uses frequent
> elision but avoids hiatus altogether. His verse has a higher percentage
> of dactyls than any other Anglo-Saxon poet and he avoids the monot-
> onous repetition of metrical patterns more noticeably than any of his
> contemporaries (the graceful movement of his verse stands in stark
> contrast to the repetitive, spondaic monotony of Aldhelm's verse).[22]

It is clear that we are engaging here with a consummate wordsmith, a man
of refinement and subtlety, who rejected the diction of recent writers, avoided recherché vocabulary and verbal pyrotechnics, and worked and reworked
whatever he wrote. The references, in both his prosal and poetic writings,
were oblique rather than intrusive. To give an idea of Bede's poetic quality,
Professor Lapidge suggests a similarity between Bede's skills and those of seventeenth-century George Herbert, a very great poet indeed. Both were scholars, profound in their knowledge of Latin, and meticulous with words and
meter. It is Lapidge's idea that Bede's prosal simplicity developed from his
practice of poetic distillation.

> For a scholar who in all his writings—historical, exegetical, scientif-
> ic—was concerned with clarity and economy of exposition, poetry
> may have seemed the highest form of expression, a goal to which all
> his other writing unconsciously tended.[23]

In his little treatise *De schematis et tropibus*, Bede listed the 17 classical *schemata* and the 13 *tropi* mentioned by Donatus in the last two sections of
his *Ars grammatica*. Drawing heavily on the Bible, Bede furnished for each
scheme and trope a definition and at least one example (which he usually
explained and in some cases copiously explained),[24] for he believed that the
Latin Vulgate Bible was superior to all other writings not only in authority,
in utility and antiquity, but in artistic supremacy as well. He discussed its
urbanity of phrase. Though plainly acquainted with the works of ancient pagan writers, Bede, who had had all his education within northern monastic
walls, preferred to illustrate his works with quotations from the Christian
poets.[25] Where the great Roman and early Christian grammarians had relat-

ed the rhetorical figures to classical pagan orators, poets, and prosists, Bede almost entirely related them to biblical study. Says the scholarly Mr. Curtius, it was a principle that "prevailed and was to grow like mustard-seed."

It was Bede

> who carried to its logical conclusion the transference of antique rhetoric to the text of the Bible, for which…Augustine and Cassiodorus prepared the way. He was able to do so because, for him as for Aldhelm, *the grammatico-aesthetic objections to [Vulgate] Bible Latin had lost their validity.*[26] [Italics are added.]

Time had dimmed all the detailed post-Jerome scholarship, so much of which was disdainful of the Vulgate's aberrations from classical standard. Bede's world fully accepted Vulgate idiosyncrasies as paradigmatic of ancient rhetorical perfection.

In the preface to his great *Ecclesiastical History of the English Nation*, Bede paid homage to the Pope and to the school at Canterbury, and listed his sources with gratitude. Unlike Gildas, he took great pains to make his chronology correct. He claimed to have gathered his information from documents and epistles brought back from Rome, and from the notes of monastic librarians and revered bishops in the provinces—of whom he named many. In accounting for his information, he speaks, too, of innumerable faithful witnesses:

> but partly also [I] have been careful to add skillfully thereunto such things as I could learn myself by the sure testimony of men of good credit. And I humbly beseech the reader, that if he shall find anything set down otherwise than truth in this that I have written, he will not impute it unto us, as [we] have endeavored with all sincerity to put in writing to the instruction of our after comers such things as we have gathered by common report, which is the true law of history.[27] (Bede, *Ecclestical History*, Preface)

It would seem from this, that Bede, though he reputedly never traveled, was the epicenter of a massive correspondence and mail-service program.

Bede Passes the Torch to Alcuin

News of Anglo-Latin intellectual achievements traveled widely. It inspired and guided the brief Carolingian Renaissance that we next address. As missionaries from Britain's north traversed the barbarian-ridden continent, preaching, converting, founding monasteries, and visiting Holy Rome, they initiated a south-moving flow of fervor for literacy and a liberal intellectual outlook. They fortified the perception that a well-stocked, accurately and legibly copied, well-balanced library was beneficial to ecclesiastical education. Bede's writings, the pride of Anglo-Saxon Northumbria, traveled with these evangelists. Spreading broadly into monastic schools and scriptoria, his literary legacy took hold and endured, often in the form of curricular texts. Eventually, his work on the schemes and tropes, and his exquisitely contrived hymns and poetry would come to influence traditions of stylistic rhetoric and poetic imagery in England. If Bede had not lived to turn things around, writers might still be trailing along behind Aldhelm, flicking their hankies at bees.

Egbert, who was one of Bede's most eminent pupils, founded a cathedral school at York, where he fostered the traditions of Bede's teaching. In time, York became, throughout Europe, the most respected educational center of its day. It was there that Alcuin (735–809 CE) became first a pupil, then a deacon, and in 767, the headmaster. Later, when Alcuin was in his 50s and a much-experienced educator, renowned for scholarship and admired also for having two Roman pilgrimages under his belt, Charlemagne (rightly impressed by the Anglo-Saxon reputation for teaching rustics how not to be so rustic) persuaded him to join his royal court circle. There, Alcuin found himself a member of an elite group of grammarians and scholars, whom Charlemagne had managed to import from wherever he could find them—Italy, Spain, England, and Ireland. Joined by the avid-for-knowledge king, they formed a kind of academy where learned discussion took place and plans were laid for reforming the Frankish church, teaching the masses, and improving the management of government. Alcuin's assignment was to run the palace school at Charlemagne's capital city, Aachen (now Aix-la-Chapelle), and to advise the king on ecclesiastical and educational matters.

Interestingly, before leaving York to join the assault against continental ignorance, Alcuin wrote a poeticized catalogue, listing the books held in York's cathedral library. Since a glancing selection of York's librarial holdings will give a sense of the cultural climate that had nurtured Alcuin and his northern fellow scholars, here is a list of the better known authors that the catalogue mentions: Jerome, Ambrose, Augustine, Gregory the Great, Cassiodorus, Aldhelm, and Bede (of course). Also mentioned are poets and grammarians of whom some were Christian (Donatus and Priscian) and some not Christian. To be noted, particularly, is the fact that the York library was not entirely given to theological works, for it included a significant number of pagan writers. Amongst these are Boethius (who, though Christian, had supplanted Christ with Philosophy in his famous *Consolatio*), Pliny, Aristotle, Cicero, Vergil, Lucan, Statius,[28] and many more masters of classical standing. Though it is thought that Alcuin knew only the rudiments of Greek and no Hebrew whatsoever,[29] the magnitude of his list bespeaks the possible breadth of his own cultural horizon. It is known that Alcuin himself was educated to levels above a scholar's standard for his day.

Charlemagne did well to entice Alcuin (in 782 CE) to be his intellectual aide-de-camp. In the landscape where Alcuin found himself transplanted, ignorant rusticity was abundantly available for practicing his powers of pedagogy.[30] He would soon prove himself up to the job, for he turned out to be not only an efficient teacher (which we already knew), but also a sound organizer and a trustworthy advisor. The Carolingian renaissance would owe much to his perspicacity and diligence.

Notes

1. The information for this chapter is drawn extensively from the introductory materials of Michael Lapidge and Michael Herren, *Aldhelm: The Prose Works* (Cambridge and New York: Rowan and Littlefield, 1979) and from Michael Winterbottom, "Aldhelm's Prose Style and Its Origins," *Anglo-Saxon England* 6 (1977): 39–76. Also instructive and useful were Andy Orchard, *The Poetic Art of Aldhelm*, Cambridge Studies in Anglo-Saxon England 8 (Cambridge, UK: Cambridge University Press), and E. R. Curtius, *European Literature and the Latin Middle Ages*.
2. Bede, *Ecclesiastical History of the English Nation*, trans. J. E. King, Loeb Classical Library (Cambridge: Harvard University Press, 1963), 2:296–7.
3. Curtius, *European Literature and the Latin Middle Ages*, 46.
4. Lapidge and Herren, *Aldhelm: The Prose Works*, 4.
5. Duckett, *Anglo-Saxon Saints*, 38–9.
6. Orchard, *Poetic Art*, 2.
7. Letter from Aldhelm to Heahfrith (C–D), in Lapidge and Herren, *Aldhelm: The Prose Works*, 161.
8. Letter from Aldhelm to the Abbots of Wilfrid, in Lapidge and Herren, *Aldhelm: The Prose Works*, 169.
9. Orchard, *Poetic Art*, 14, and, generally, 11–16.
10. Orchard gives credit to Michael Herren for this observation. One should remember, too, when comparing Early Irish propensities with those of 'classical' writers, that those high-minded Greeks and early Romans saw no aesthetic benefit in avoiding the repetition of a word, *if that was the word that best portrayed what they really meant*. In later centuries the opposite policy governed prose composition—and particularly that of the early Irish. Our contemporary literary critic and writer Martin Amis has chosen the ancient way as

the better one (see his book *The War Against Cliché*). Being the young Seneca of our day, he frowns on this kind of squirming around for synonyms, all for the sake of eloquence. Interestingly, his father, Kingsley Amis, author of (amongst other things) *The King's English*, was a no-repetition man. The last hundred years seem to have been a turnover time for rethinking the issue.

11. Curtius, *European Literature and the Latin Middle Ages*, 42–6.

12. George Hardin Brown, *Bede the Venerable* (Boston: Twayne, 1987), 29.

13. Ian F. McNeely with Lisa Wolverton, *Reinventing Knowledge: From Alexandria to the Internet* (New York: W. W. Norton, 2008), 70–1.

14. J. E. King, introduction to his translation of Bede's *Ecclesiastical History* 1:xv.

15. Text from the Loeb edition of Bede's *Ecclesiastical History*, trans. King, 2:140–2. Et quidem et alii post illum in gente Anglorum religiosa poemata facere tentabant; sed nullus eum aequiparare potuit. Namque ipse non ab hominibus, neque per hominem institutus canendi artem didicit; sed divinitus adiutus gratis canendi donum accepit. Unde nihil unquam frivoli et supervacui poematis facere potuit; sed ea tantummodo quae ad religionem pertinent, religiosam eius linguam decebant.

16. We find in the Latin of this passage a further instance of changing habit in the phrases *religiosa poemata* and *divinitus adiutus*, which are instances of adjectives preceding their nouns, as they habitually do in English and French (but not in Italian). In these cases, the context is not established first, but because the adjectives are smack against the noun they modify, they keep their unity and hence their transparency. Moreover, the particles (et *quidem* = 'and indeed'; *sed*, appearing three times = 'but'; *namque* = 'for'; *non–neque* = 'neither nor'; *unde* = 'therefore') make the line of argument absolutely clear at a time when pointing marks were still unsettled.

17. Neither Gregory nor Benedict, in their instructions for simpler folk, wrote in the classical styles that the educated clerics in the papal chancery would normally have sought to emulate.

18. Text from Loeb edition of Bede's *Ecclesiastical History*, 2: 142. Note the position of the verbs in the last three lines.

19. A glossary was a primitive form of dictionary, usually a list of difficult or foreign words, with explanations of usage and origin. The orthographical information presented here comes from Roger Wright, *Late Latin and Early Romance*, 101.

20. Brown, *Bede the Venerable*, 32. Interestingly, Professor Brown also tells us that there is no evidence of Quintilian in the Wearmouth-Jarrow libraries (29).

21. Michael Lapidge, "Bede the Poet," in *Bede and His World*, The Jarrow Lectures, 1979–1993 (Jarrow, UK: Variorum, 1994), 2:929.

22. Ibid., 940–1.

23. Ibid., 944.

24. Brown, *Bede the Venerable*, 34.

25. His occasional classical references were mostly to Vergil who, because of Vergil's prediction of a savior in his Fourth Eclogue, was honored as a prophetic 'almost-Christian.' Bede seemed also to approve a wise (cautious) use of Cicero's rhetorical ideals. Brown, *Bede the Venerable*, 30–1.

26. Curtius, *European Literature*, 47.

27. Bede, *Ecclesiastical History*, trans. King, 1:9–11.
28. A first-century CE poet, whose works dealt mostly with mythological sagas. He was much admired in later centuries. Dante regarded him as a potential Christian, influenced by Vergil.
29. Elizabeth L. Eisenstein, *The Printing Press as an Agent of Change* (Cambridge: Cambridge University Press, 1985), 1:339.
30. Reynolds and Wilson, *Scribes and Scholars*, 80.

References

Aldhelm to the Abbots of Wilfrid. In Lapidge and Herren. *Aldhelm: The Prose Works*. Cambridge and New York: Rowan and Littlefield, 1979.

Aldhelm to Heahfrith (C–D). In Lapidge and Herren, *Aldhelm: The Prose Works*. Cambridge and New York: Rowan and Littlefield, 1979.

Bede. Vol. 2 of *Ecclesiastical History of the English Nation*. Translated by J. E. King. Loeb Classical Library. Cambridge: Harvard University Press, 1963.

Brown, George Hardin. *Bede the Venerable*. Boston: Twayne, 1987.

Curtius, Ernst Robert. *European Literature and the Latin Middle Ages*. Translated by Willard R. Trask. Princeton: Princeton University Press, 1990.

Duckett, Eleanor Shipley. *Anglo-Saxon Saints and Scholars*. New York: Macmillan, 1947.

Eisenstein, Elizabeth L. Vol. 1 of *The Printing Press as an Agent of Change*. Cambridge: Cambridge University Press, 1985.

King, J. E. Introduction to his translation of Bede, *Ecclesiastical History of the English Nation*. Loeb Classical Library. Cambridge: Harvard University Press, 1963.

Lapidge, Michael. "Bede the Poet." In Vol. 2 of *Bede and His World*. The Jarrow Lectures, 1979–1993. Jarrow, UK: Variorum, 1994.

Lapidge, Michael, and Michael Herren. Introduction to *Aldhelm: The Prose Works*. Cambridge and New York: Rowan and Littlefield, 1979.

McNeely, Ian F., with Lisa Wolverton. *Reinventing Knowledge: From Alexandria to the Internet*. New York: W. W. Norton, 2008.

Orchard, Andy. *The Poetic Art of Aldhelm*. Cambridge Studies in Anglo-Saxon England 8. Cambridge: Cambridge University Press, 2006.

Reynolds, L. D., and N. G. Wilson. *Scribes and Scholars: A Guide to the Transmission of Greek and Latin Literature*. Oxford: Oxford University Press, 1968.

Winterbottom, Michael. "Aldhelm's Prose Style and Its Origins." *Anglo-Saxon England* 6 (1977): 39–76.

Wright, Roger. *Late Latin and Early Romance in Spain and Carolingian France*. Liverpool, UK: Francis Cairns, 1982.

·SECTION 7·

THE CAROLINGIAN RENAISSANCE

NORTHERN ACHIEVEMENTS INFLUENCE THE CONTINENT

Charlemagne Domesticates the Uncouth Franks

Though highly intelligent and avid to learn, Charlemagne (742–814 CE) was not fully literate. Moreover, Latin was not his mother tongue. His native speech was an Old High German idiom, and it is thought that he also understood the Old French dialect spoken by many of his Frankish subjects. As a grown man, he came to know Latin, and some Greek as well, along with the rudiments of mathematics and astronomy. When it came to difficult texts (perhaps theological or historical), he enjoined scholars to read aloud to him whatever passages he wished to broach.[1] As an ardently Christian king, he was alert to the sanctitude as well as the power and prestige that literate culture might bring to his realm.

Charlemagne had inherited a territory that included many tribes, dialects, and differing customs—a territory predominated by a scattered and rustic economy that was sorely in want of organization. To better his people and unify his holdings, he instigated an ambitious program of education, for the practical needs of government were urgent. Estates had to be managed and administrative details kept track of. To handle these matters, his imperial clerks and palace staff needed to know how to read, write, and keep accounts. But there were spiritual needs as well. Charlemagne's Christian conscience prompted him to prepare his subjects for their (and his) entry into heaven. As leader of the Church (as well as the state), the newly enthroned Charlemagne was appalled to discover what poor Latin his abbots and bishops were using in their correspondence. *How could they possibly understand the Bible* when their letters to him, "though they were often very correct in sentiment were very incorrect in grammar"?[2]

Charlemagne's concern was justified, for Christianity, both as a religion and as an institution, had sunk to levels approaching the ludicrous. Extant reports of clerical ignorance and confusion are many. Upon taking up the throne, Charlemagne found himself ruling over a kingdom rife with linguistic malfunction, a delightful example of which was recounted by the English missionary Boniface, a predecessor to Alcuin. Boniface tells of having heard a Frankish priest, during the motions of baptizing, bless his infant victim in the following unstandard way: *In nomine patria et filia et spiritus sancti* ("in the name of the father, and the daughter, and the holy spirit"). Did he not even know that he was talking of Jesus, the male offspring of Mary? Apparently not. Indeed, sexual differentiation seems to have eluded the Frankish priesthood more frequently than one might have predicted, for other churchly sources refer to St. Columba as a *virgo* and Venus as a man.[3]

Such errors had been allowed to infest Christian instruction because there was no one around to refute or correct them. In central Europe, during the two centuries before Charlemagne, classical Latin literature had virtually ceased to be known, and what there was, if not hidden in the musty recesses of unfrequented libraries, existed mostly in palimpsests.[4] It was a time when those who knew no better would tear their books apart and use the pages for wrappings.[5] With the schools essentially defunct, there seemed no possible redress.

Ignorance was on the loose. Street language was infecting—let alone demeaning and misrepresenting—ecclesiastical and governmental dictates. Administrative affairs were in chaos. Church buildings had fallen into ruin, and were sometimes so crumbled that they could only be used as barns.[6] All in all, Charlemagne's inherited Frankish clergy were unmethodical, slovenly, abjectly trained, and backward. They were unprepared to administer the holy sacrament, to preach, teach, or manage ecclesiastical property. Even the Bible they used was riddled with error—error commonly aggravated by the unintelligible, local pronunciations of those rendering it aloud in worship.

Charlemagne plunged into all this intellectual pollution with vigor and high intention. He was determined to raise the cultural level of the clergy whether by persuasion or compulsion. His thinking was this: that once the priests had been straightened out, they in turn would educate the laity. Since it was plain that, to interpret the Holy Scriptures, one must have a command of correct language and a fluent knowledge of the Latin tongue, Charlemagne ordered, in his capitulary (royal command) of 789 CE,[7] that in every bishopric and in every monastery the psalms, music (notes and chants), calculation (arithmetic), and grammar should be taught, and carefully corrected books be made available. Moreover,

> Since it is our concern to improve the state of our churches, let us work hard to repair, with a careful study of the letters [literature], the training institutions [i.e., educational programs] which were almost forgotten through the idleness of our predecessors, *and by avidly pursuing the study of the liberal arts*, let us by our example urgently invite whom we can [to follow suit].[8] [The italics have been added.] (*Epist. gen.*, MGH. *Capit.* 1.2.80)

Given the glaring decay of literacy, the first step was to improve the quality of Latin in use and to force it back into stable classical (or at least Vulgate) mode so that it might once again be written down in a uniform way and thereby rendered able to communicate meaning to distant places for future reference. Latin must no longer be subject to dialectal differences or allowed to vacillate in form and usage. Noun cases must be used correctly, and verbs be properly inflected. Spelling must be unvarying and pronunciation standardized. Script must be made legible. Words must be separated for ease of comprehension, and word meanings stabilized. Punctuation too must be regularized and effectively applied. All the ancient rhetorical repertoire of literary devices must be understood, and the conventions for using them forced back into being. Those who would administer law and government, keep track of imperial edicts, and run the churches would by royal decree be educated away from their regional dialects and in future aspire to reach the old papal levels of chancellery letter-writing and bookkeeping. Classical Latin, at least to the level of the Vulgate Bible, was what people should strive to attain.

Charlemagne's educational directives were broadly effective. In response to his edicts, the priests and government administrators jacked up their standards and improved their knowledge of 'correct' Latin. For that, books were the obvious necessity. Libraries were set up, as well as scriptoria, for the maintenance and reproduction of manuscripts.[9] Biblical, old liturgical, and classical manuscripts were urgently sought for scribes to copy. Here lay fresh trouble, for at that time the bulk of copying in scriptoria was being done by boys or young monks who were chosen for these intellectually undemanding labors for the very reason that *they were not* much given to study or reading. Copying was considered only in terms of being a physical chore, requiring, in particular, strong hands and muscular stick-to-itiveness. Charlemagne, spotting the folly of this, in 789 issued his *Admonitio generalis* (a general admonishment), which stipulated that important religious books be copied by men of mature age; for dependability was the key to scribal success, not animal energy, nor even intellectual creativity.[10] Within that same *Admonitio*, Charlemagne decreed that every monastery should set up a school for teaching boys *from every station in life* to read and write and calculate.[11]

Charlemagne recognized the importance of broad intellectual training. The elimination of sloppy wordage would not only keep heresy at bay, but also civilize his people and glorify his name. His embrace of classical literary tradition (schemes and tropes included) and the reforms he initiated in reference to them progressively included pagan authors as appropriate sources of study.[12] "Since the Holy Scripture is strewn with figures of speech, no one can doubt that every reader will the more quickly understand it spiritually, the more fully he has been instructed in the art of letters."[13] Implicit was this thought: *Though often vile, pagan writers too have much to offer.* Again and again over the years, Charlemagne would urge his clerics not to neglect the study of the ancient classics.

Such broadmindedness not only invited the clergy to resume the study of books, but also pressed them to reinspect ancient literatures for revelation about the Bible. The adoption of this freer attitude, which was somewhat at odds with the more restrictive principles of papal Rome, became the foundational feature of the Frankish educational and political structure.

At this point, one wonders what relics of usable material Charlemagne initially found to work with, given the apparent uncouthness of the Frankish masses, and their deficient linguistic standards? *How was one to achieve culture in an atmosphere of corrupt and variable language?* We now look more closely into the matter. When Charlemagne was gathering the reins of government into his own hands, the language being spoken was more or less the composted product of Germanic-Frankish dialects and the existing endemic Latinoid; and yet it seems plain that the ghost of ancestral Latin was somewhere hovering to provide the occasional glimmer as to how to proceed. Of primary importance in this respect was the Church. Though discrepancies in common speech had plainly increased by Charlemagne's time, scholars today lean to the opinion that even up to ca. 800 CE, the common laity, through force of habit, could understand the Latin used in the Christian service. Thus, we may say that Church recitation preserved some seminal sense of Vulgate Latin useful to the fragile growth of linguistic improvement.

Also critical was the heritage of aristocratic habit, for it too had set life-lines for the future expansion of Latin tradition. It is now thought possible that deep in the fabric of Romanized Gaul, the late-Roman aristocratic education survived in the far-flung redoubts of the elite, even up to Charlemagne's time. Though the old Roman-style rhetorical schools had disappeared, it is known that some remaining aristocratic nonclerics could easefully read and had genuine intellectual interests.[14]

Meanwhile, those who were destined to become officiates or *notariats* in any of the regional or local seats of power must have continued to receive some professional instruction, probably in the courts of kinglets. There is some testimony, too, of youngsters of high birth being accepted into monastic establishments to learn the elements of reading and writing along with the prospective novitiates. Again, some may have learned their letters with tutors at home, while sons of less wealthy families may even have been taught locally in some kind of school for boys. Yet, these possible instances of endeavor are far more rare than common. Extant scraps of evidence tell us that while education may have continued, it was rudimentary, inconstant, and primarily practical in its aims.

Particularly fortifying to traditional Latin were the necessities of government. Because late Roman Gaul had transmitted to the young Frankish kingdom its legal structure and administrative patterns (all of it dependent on the written Latin word), a recently existing legacy of precedence and form was in place to receive fresh content.[15] It was Charlemagne's wish to put that fresh content into clear and permanent form, so that he might effectively administer his government and keep track of his disparate Germanic-Frankish peoples. As his political and military successes enlarged his empire, he increasingly relied on available document specimens of administrative and legal procedures that the Romans had once used in governing Gaul. The continued use of Latin as an executive language offered the advantage of providing to some extent a common tongue for all of Charlemagne's polyglot realm.

With the three givens of Church, aristocratic tradition, and the procedures of long-ago governments, how hard was it, actually, to resuscitate 'proper' Latin for the proletariat? As there was no contesting tongue to offer even the most rudimentary literacy, all elementary exercises in reading and writing had to be done in Latin. Rosamond McKitterick, a prominent scholar of these matters, surmises that in the Latinate regions of southeastern and central Gaul, one was merely learning to read the formal written version of one's dialect. In the German-speaking areas to the east (a major segment of the Merovingian-Carolingian kingdom), one was learning the correct and written form of a language encountered at every level of public life and worship. Latin was therefore, she claims, not the obstacle to literacy that it has hitherto been assumed to be.[16]

The numerous Donatus and Priscian Latin grammars, extant from Charlemagne's period, offer an overview of the situation. They tell us that amongst the continental educated, Latin was to some degree still an understood medium. The original Donatus and Priscian grammars were not handbooks to teach a foreign language, so much as discussions of Latin principles for the nonbeginner—for whom as time passed, new versions often included extra material on inflection and declension. Alongside these and probably issuing from the palace scriptorium itself, were the newer, insular grammars from England and Ireland, just beginning their continental career. These manuals of Latin grammar were specifically designed to teach Latin as a foreign language, for they dealt in detail with the basics of Latin structure and form.[17]

As we have seen, there was a goodly crowd whose classical-free backgrounds needed the push that a manual could give them for jumping the ditch to culture. Yet, even as they jumped, they left behind an underprivileged multitude of folk to do the chores and talk like hicks. The more Charlemagne's program for classical education spread, the more it rigidified the rules of 'proper' Latin, rules that illiterate folk could not follow. Thus, Latin improved and stabilized for the use of the educated, while amorphous dialects continued in use for those who could not afford a manual or attend a Latin-based school. As a consequence, each side of the divide became more consolidated within itself and less transparent to the other. With the spread of the writing capability, the conventions of each linguistic mode normalized its own word meanings and settled its own syntactical rules and spellings. Finally, at some time during the ninth century, *Français* was broadly considered to be a true and separate language.[18]

Not only did the Carolingians reimpose strict rules on the written Latin language, but they also conventionalized its pronunciation, for the Latin spoken in far-flung localities could often sound very different to local ears. It was even the case that eighth- and ninth-century Latin-speaking English and Irish missionaries could only make their spoken Latin understood in papal Rome by writing it out for others to read.[19] The success of Charlemagne's speech-sound standardization secured the separation of Young French from Late Latin. It firmly distinguished the homely chatter of farmyard and village from what the administrative and clerical elite were speaking.[20]

Given the state of the language when Charlemagne took up the throne, it is quite marvelous to see how he induced such a groundswell of intellectual activity. It has been noted that, during his reign, even his own decrees were at first written out rather imprecisely, but with increasing articulation during the last two decades of his reign. The clearest and most famous clarification of the royal attitude to spiritual understanding and perfect utterance was the *Epistula de litteris colendis* (a note about cultivating letters, ca. 784–785), probably compiled by Alcuin. The epistle's central argument lies in the assertion that the right faith—indeed, every right thought—must be clothed in appropriate form and language, lest it be falsified. Thus, the clergy are reminded again not to

> neglect the study of literature, but with a humble effort well pleasing to God seek learning with all your might, so that you may be able the more easily and correctly to penetrate the mysteries of God's Book. In its sacred pages you will find inserted many figures of speech, turns of rhetoric, and such like things; and there can be no doubt that the more fully a man has been instructed in literary knowledge the more quickly will he understand the spiritual meaning of what he reads. So let such men be chosen for this task as have the will and power to learn, and also have the desire to teach others.[21]

This was the kickoff for intensive study of classical literatures for all Carolingian monastic and cathedral schools.

With culture at last in the ascendency, the *lingua mixta* that had been creeping into manuscripts became no longer acceptable. The purification of written Latin made it negotiable throughout the kingdom. Precision of wordage was valued as crucial to record-keeping, crucial to prosperity, and certainly crucial to spiritual aspiration.[22] As educational successes proliferated and took hold, one sees the Latin of extant manuscripts from Charlemagne's period readjusting to classical pattern. To a large extent, traditional norms *did* become reinstated.[23]

Charlemagne's wisdom, foresight, and energies animated the regeneration of classical literature and the meaningfulness of written words. His elevation of scholars and scholarship, his interest in books, libraries, schools, and scriptoria freed the human mind from penumbral ignorance and readied it for a fresh reawakening after its next retreat into hibernation.

Alcuin and the All-Too-Brief Carolingian Renaissance

As Charlemagne's chief assistant for educational and church reform, Alcuin focused his efforts on consolidating the norms of pronunciation and stabilizing punctuation, manuscription, and spelling. His success was enormous, for uniformity in speech and writing not only eased communication across the Frankish territories but also encouraged the pursuit of literacy (in the vernaculars as well), all of which in turn brought order.

We are told that Alcuin was especially interested in creating a uniform pronunciation because he himself could not understand the Latin speech of his new continental friends. His native Germanic Anglo-Saxon vernacular tongue had accustomed his ear to a different Latin sound-mode from that being spoken by the clerisy from more southerly regions. And so, Alcuin, amongst other corrections, 'corrected' the accent of his pupils' Latinoid renderings by closely relating their sounds to spelling—thus bringing aural comprehension into line with the visual.

Alcuin's work in making the alphabet letters correspond with their spoken Germanic sounds is interesting. Frederick Wright's study of it includes a text that was circulated in Britain in the eighth century and was probably the basis for Alcuin's methods. Below are a few samples from Wright's list of instructions for the 23 letters used in Latin.

> **B** labris per spiritus impetum reclusis edicimus.
> [We pronounce **B** through the impetus of the breath through closed lips.]
> **K** faucibus palatoque formatur.
> [**K** is formed with the fauces[24] and palate.]
> **O** rotundi oris spiritu comparatur.
> [**O** is achieved with breath of a rounded mouth.]
> **S** sibilum facit dentibus verberatis.
> [**S** makes a hissing sound with the teeth vibrating.]
> **X** quicquid C atque S formavit exsibilat.
> [**X** ejects with a hiss what C and S formed.]

The description of each letter's pronunciation was plainly a textual instruction for those unfamiliar with the Latin language. (*You see a B: then what do you do? You close your lips and force breath through them. And so on.*) Trained in York, Alcuin himself must have learned to follow instructions such as these in reading Latin aloud, and finding it useful, appropriated the method for teaching continental speakers. These continental folk, when young, would naturally have picked up the 'tongue of the town.' That would have been a vernacular, derived from Latin but variously pronounced. Guided by Alcuin, however, they were enabled to spell the related original Latin words and pronounce them in the "correct" and uniform way.[25]

Alcuin also advanced the need for punctuational rule, for up to his time, manuscript pointing was often erratic and unhelpful when it existed at all. Like most people who choose to write about punctuation for the yawning proletariat, he too felt the need to add a little zip. In the form of a metered mnemonic, he described to his scribes what they might achieve with a thoughtful injection of puncts in a text. Herewith, his famous jingle:

> Per cola distinguant proprios et commata sensus
> Et punctos ponant ordine quosque suo;
> Ne vel falsa legat, taceat vel forte repente
> Ante pios fratres lector in ecclesia.

> They should bring out the proper sense by clause and phrase and put their points in place so that the reader [who would be reading aloud] does not read falsely nor by chance fall into sudden silence before his pious brothers in the church.[26]

As we see, when constrained by meter, Alcuin, like so many, played with the word order. Considering the case for clarity and easy intake, the first line's phrase *per cola et commata* which was usually kept intact has been divided by *distinguant proprios*. Nevertheless, under the guidance of inflection and the relaxed placement of verbs, the poem reads easily. As for the recipients of its message, they might have enjoyed the little jolt produced by the rearrangement of the *per cola et commata* phrase. In any case, they seem to have got something from the instruction of the lines; for the extant manuscripts in the major scriptorial center of Tours (where Alcuin spent so much of his time) show no evidence of a clear punctuating system before he had arrived there, whereas during his time and for a short time after, they uniformly improved.

Punctuation improvements were effected by a more or less constant battle on the teaching front. With a very uncertain sense of what constitutes the *cola* and *commata*, the rustic scribes at Tours seemed to find that *even under instruction* punctuating was very hard. Without reminders, they could not apparently recognize the delicacy of distinctions and subdistinctions, or the relationship they bore to meaning. To Alcuin's particular disgust, they were devotedly fond of the medial stop, for, he complained, they accorded it the duty of marking indiscriminately both half pauses and whole pauses (i.e., sentence endings). In time, they mastered the *distinctio* (the mark of full stop); but the wispy *subdistinctio* (think comma) was too much.

Many manuscripts from St. Martin's scriptorium in Tours bear punctuational corrections in another ink, though it is impossible to say when these corrections were made. E. K. Rand conjectures that they were inserted "by the director or a corrector especially assigned to the task, who would return the new book *requisitum et distinctum*" (pointed as required). It would have seemed

> unreasonable to expect the scribe while at work to solve the often delicate questions of punctuation; his mind [was not to be] diverted from his proper task of reproducing in clear and beautiful forms the letters and words of the original with little attention to their sense.[27]

There is, however, one surviving manuscript that was made under Alcuin's certain direction and to his apparent satisfaction. In it, one sees that a new punctuating system (one used by many subsequent Turonian correctors down to the end of the ninth century[28]) has been put into operation. Interestingly, since Charlemagne himself founded a school of song and personally supervised the work done there, the system deployed two new symbols drawn from musical notation. Of these, the rising stroke ($\checkmark$ = a half pause) and the descending stroke (either $\wedge$ or $\cdot$ = *a whole pause*), indicated where the reading voice should raise or lower its pitch.[29] This easy 'up-down' vocal system addressed the special needs of hinterland monastic communities, where unenlightened monks might stumble over Latin archaicisms but were well accustomed to chant. In truth, it reflects our own general tendencies today, when we give voice to a complex sentence, such as the following.

> When his horse failed the first jump$\checkmark$
> I held my breath for the second $\cdot$

One of Alcuin's finest deeds was to bring about the universal acceptance of the clear, rounded, noncursive script known as the 'Carolingian minuscule' (i.e., small-lettered), which would, to the relief of the world, eventually supersede the less easily deciphered Gothic and uncial (see fig. 21.1), with all their over-decorated brother and sister scripts.[30] Pre-Carolingian scripts came in at least a dozen varieties, of which most were not easy to read. Clear, separate, immediately recognizable letters, each written as an independent unit and standardly shaped, made reading much easier. In the Carolingian minuscule (see fig. 21.2), words were no longer irregularly separate, nor, as before, arbitrarily split. Moreover, difficult-to-interpret contractions and meldings of words to save space became less frequent.[31]

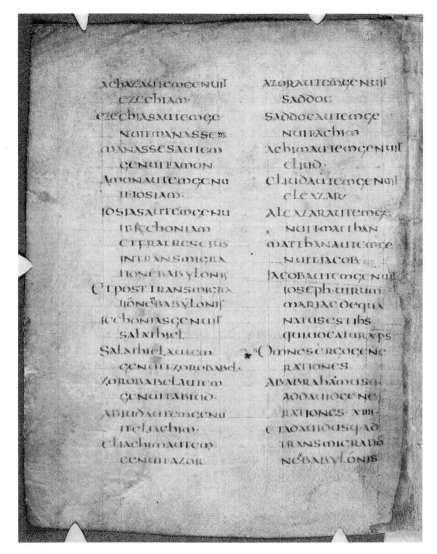

Fig. 21.1: Sample of uncial script

This page of uncial script (a script that in time would yield to the superior Carolingian clarity) comes from the famous manuscript known as the St. Augustine Gospels (MS286), a late sixth-century gospel book. Pope Gregory the Great is thought to have given it to Augustine of Canterbury to carry with him when he came to Christianize the English in 597. True or not, it almost certainly came to England with one of the early waves of Roman missionaries. Courtesy of Parker Library, Corpus Christi College, Cambridge.

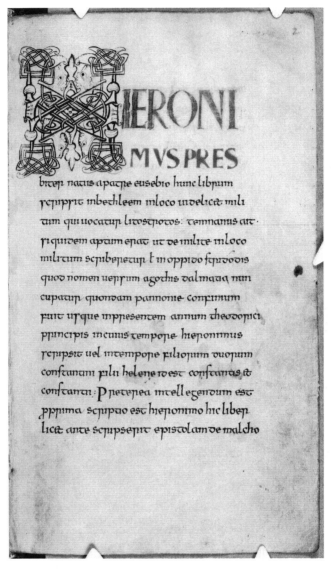

Fig. 21.2: Carolingian minuscule

Here is a sample of a late variety of Carolingian minuscule, a script that was noted for its clarity and regularity of form. It is the opening page of a volume (MS389) written at St. Augustine's Abbey, Canterbury, in the late tenth century. The volume contains Jerome's Life of St. Paul the First Hermit and the Life of St. Guthlac by Felix of Crowland (composed in the eighth century). Courtesy of Parker Library, Corpus Christi College, Cambridge.

It was in his last few years that Alcuin was granted Charlemagne's permission to quit his duties in the capital city of Aachen and retire to Tours. There, in monastic quietude, he continued to write, instruct, and monitor scriptorial standards. From 796 to 804, during the time that he presided as abbot, the monastery of St. Martin of Tours along with the scriptoria of St. Gatian's and Marmoutier (also in Tours) became principal centers for the tremendous spate of Carolingian publication, and for the reformation and dissemination of all the scribal arts.

Alcuin enjoyed Charlemagne's esteem to the end of his life, and worked diligently to please his royal master. His achievements lay particularly in educational improvements and in his studious revision of the Frankish liturgy and Bible. Alcuin was neither a great poet nor an inventive intellect. His teachings (including his famous observation that 'digging vines was not as holy a thing to do as digging words') seem to us today to have been somewhat simplistic, though evidence tells us they were effective.[32]

With an almost mystical reverence, Alcuin had stressed the value of books, and the result was that books and libraries became almost sacrosanct. His teachings supported the return to health of the wilting written word and endowed it with a prestidigital glow that would endure up to the invention of email and texting. Though the 'sanctification' of the ancient rhetorical *artes* was often credited to him, he should more accurately be honored for resuscitating the work of Cassiodorus, who had preceded him by some 250 years.

And so, despite the irritatingly slow wits of his scribes and pupils, Alcuin was able to leave behind sound standards of spelling, punctuation, pronunciation, grammar, and manuscription. His presence in Tours made it an important center for all scribal training. For some decades after his death, the schools that he had helped to establish throughout Charlemagne's kingdom carried on the great work of preserving books, nurturing the intellect, and exhorting clerical scholars to study the classical literatures so as to reinstate the traditional Latin language with its freight of rhetorical ploy. All had been in keeping with Charlemagne's command:

> We, in company with our *fideles*, have thought it desirable that bishoprics and monasteries, entrusted to us to be governed by the Grace of Christ, should emphasize, in addition to the observance of monastic discipline and the practise of holy religion, the study of *litterae* [i.e., letters, words, texts, literature] for those who by God's grace are able to learn.[33]

What the Carolingian Regeneration Did for the World

During the Carolingian Age, a staggering amount of parchment was consumed, for which large holdings of livestock were required. The spate of publication produced in monastic and royal scriptoria included all manner of types and genres: contemporary poetry; history; biography; hagiography; theology; philosophy; biblical exegeses; and handbooks on rhetoric, dialectic, metrics, and grammar—to name only some.[34]

Numerous private Carolingians left behind them abundant evidence of the respect that they, individually, had for intellectual activities. The extant wills of those with wealth reflect broad interests, both sacred and profane; for happily, under Charlemagne, the written word was more than a vehicle for the Christian faith. Recorded bequests include not only saints' lives and guides to a Christian life, but also history books and historical miscellanies. Interesting too are the many bequeathals of poetry sheets that were customarily passed around the court in times of solemnity or celebration. Writing and reading aloud a poem of one's own devising (be it in classically-oriented Latin or in the unpretentious vernacular) was considered a social diversion. Private wills also mention practical handbooks on agriculture, personal devotional books, religious instruction, psalters, prayer books, law books, and tracts on war—*for a total of some 50,000 known publications owned and produced by Carolingians*. The publication records for each passing year show an increase of secular materials.

Again, Carolingian catalogues from monastic, cathedral, and lay libraries, and their lists of desiderata tell us of an immense church-driven scholarly activity. Among these inventories, we find manuscripts compiled for the purpose of organizing librarial materials, with instructions for binding, gathering, and copying manuscripts—in short, a collection of bibliographical and management handbooks. The existence of these alone testifies to the Carolingian initiative in organizing the knowledge hoard of its day. Particularly notable in this respect were their library guides for the retrieval of books, though not (as one might have wished) by alphabetic classification. To find a book, one worked first by topic, and thereafter by the chronological ordering of authors. That inconvenient custom would last in Europe until the wake-up call from the more enduring twelfth-century renaissance.

Against so much evidence of literary zeal, one cannot insist on the total illiteracy of the laity. Rosamond McKitterick tells us, in fact, that the Carolingian laity, for a considerable way down the social scale, became literate.[35]

Both male and female members of the Carolingian nobility and well-to-dos, too, were cultivated literates. Inspired by Alcuin's reverential attitude towards books, the superior claims of intellectual and spiritual study over manual labour appear to have become stronger from the Carolingian period onwards. Books became cherished *per se* and were passed on to one's heirs as treasures. Invested with an aura of awe, knowledge, and holiness, they incited a desire to understand their contents.

The Carolingian renaissance was sadly short-lived. It flashed like a beacon over the spreading gloom, but was too brief for a continuing advancement of learning. Nevertheless, in their great monastic strongholds—one thinks particularly of the monasteries Reichenau, Fulda, St. Gall, St. Riquier, and the royal monastery of Lorsch with its extensive collection of classical authors—Carolingians consolidated and re-established an intellectual culture, and with that laid the foundations for subsequent developments in education and scholarship throughout Europe.[36]

Rosamond McKitterick ends her scholarly assessment of the Carolingian contribution to the world most eloquently. Quoted, herewith, is the final paragraph of her study *The Carolingians*.

> The written word, moreover, was used by the Carolingians on an apparently larger scale than ever before in the barbarian kingdoms of western Europe. Books themselves were accorded a new status and that new status had repercussions on how this kind of wealth was safeguarded, replenished, augmented and distributed. To the Franks in the eighth and ninth centuries, and to their successors, literacy, and the Latin culture that went with it, were essential elements of a civilized Christian society. Carolingian society was thus not simply one where rather more people than used to be thought were literate to some degree, even if not necessarily learned. It was a society to which the written word was central. The written word was used, moreover, in such a way as to indicate that it was not just a tool, a weapon or a means of communication, but was also a resource, a guide, a key and an inspiration.[37]

In the Years After

Though the monastic and cathedral schools and the scriptoria established by Charlemagne and Alcuin were in place to save what they could of the

small harvest, no printing press existed to promulgate it. Thus, when rapa-
cious foreign hordes and its own internal political disagreements fragmented
Charlemagne's empire in 843 CE, ignorance resumed its sway. Books fell into
disuse, and scriptorial output became increasingly defective. Error once again
defiled knowledge. One needs only to glance at the French, the medieval Latin, and Anglo-Saxon interlinear glosses in manuscripts of the tenth to thirteenth centuries to realize how desperately ignorant of the classical tongues
the would-be literate folk had become. As speech once again became the pre-
dominant communicative mode, and the Benedictine spirit of learning faded,
society again lapsed into a state where reading was for the elite, and writing
no more than a scribal craft. Testamentary evidence of the personal collections of books eased off in the mid-ninth century. The tenth and eleventh
centuries were, in layman terms, years of darkness. Perched in some shadowy
monastic recess, the Human Intellect once again folded its wings and closed
its eyes—unwilling to witness the misrepresentations of truth that had begun
to litter the world.

In those several centuries following Charlemagne, literates and clerics
became more and more the minority. Books remained sacred in principle,
whereas those who could read them were few. With illiteracy on the loose,
monastic libraries accepted some interesting manuscript tomes for their
shelves. Among these were Ovid with his love-making revelations; Apuleius
the novelist; and even the sixth-century Maximus, who elegized not only on
the sexual highlights of his distant youth but also on those of his salacious
old age. With the passage of time, the fading study of grammar and rhetoric
had come to include a broad (and surprising) array of 'acceptable' curriculum
authors.

By the end of the twelfth century, a period known as the High Middle
Ages, respect for *any of the classical authors* was very nearly absolute.[38] Indeed,
the medieval reverence for the *auctores* (authors) had gone far beyond what
critical sense could possibly approve. Without the stabilizing ability to read
written-down facts, oral imaginations took wing. The legends and strange
tales we are left with from this period are so counter to possibility, so illogical
in their claims, that they are nothing if not laughable to modern literate perceptions. Amongst these jewels, we find Statius, the ancient epicist and successor to Vergil, a suddenly baptized Christian (as in Dante); and the declaiming Seneca the Elder in unlikely cahoots with St. Paul. We are told the story
of the traveling Plato: how when he could not answer a simple question asked
of him by the sailors on his ship, he was so overwhelmed with shame that he

could no longer face himself in the mirror (*what mirror?*), and so jumped over-board into the dancing waves and drowned.

But the best known of these soap operas with classical protagonists was the constantly embellished medieval saga of Vergil, who in mythologized ig-norance was submitted to a dizzying series of role changes as he progressed from benign savior of Naples to omniscient necromancer, to lubricious wom-anizer, to becoming "the son of Gorgilius, King of Bugia in Libya," and cli-mactically (and anachronistically) to expounding the Christian faith. Jean d'Outremeuse, a romancer during the final years of this credulous age, goes further than most. In his tales, Vergil delivers long discourses, not only in Rome but also in Egypt, on the doctrine of the Trinity and the articles of the creed, by which he converts large numbers to the faith that historically was yet to be. When Vergil, still prone to necromancing, saw that his own death was imminent, he sent away the devils who had served him and humbled himself before God, making confession of his faith.

> After this he writes a book on Christianity, gives a final banquet, at which he inculcates its doctrines, has himself provisionally baptized and finally settles himself to die, holding in his hand a work on theol-ogy and being seated in an arm-chair on which he had with his own hand depicted all the events of the New Testament, from the Annun-ciation to the Assumption. And there he remained sitting till St. Paul came in search of him and pulled his mantle, whereupon he fell into dust. The apostle was grieved, thinking that he had died a pagan, but consoled himself on reading the work he had left behind him.[39]

Come England's fourteenth century, literacy (with its regard for truth and fact) commenced yet another season of springtime bloom. In time, with the invention of the printing press, education democratized. Common folk could read, buy books, write, and classify, rework, and rewrite ideas. By the twen-ty-first century, studies of meaning, cognition, and linguistics were well into engaging the public's attention.

The transfer of a holistic thought into a linear word string has become a popular topic, inspiring publications both scientific and general. Also, there are many available books that discuss the most acceptable style. In the mean-time, punctuation seems hopelessly enmeshed in a humorous tangle, while complaints about the crumbling of old grammatical dictates multiply. As for semantic studies, there are books and articles galore on offer: some complaining, others exulting in correction. With such a wealth of opinion accessible, this story of early invention will come to an end.

But to balance the scales, we will next very briefly address a few modern deficiencies.

Notes

1. *Encyclopaedia Britannica*, 15th ed., s.v. "Charlemagne, Emperor."
2. *Encyclopaedia Britannica*, 15th ed., s.v. "Education, History of."
3. McKitterick, *Carolingians and the Written Word*, 175; also see Reynolds and Wilson, *Scribes and Scholars*, 80.
4. Because parchment was expensive, the previous writing on a page was often erased so that it might be used again. Palimpsest is the original writing that, though palely, still shows through. Many classical materials have survived in palimpsests.
5. See McKitterick, *Carolingians*, 155.
6. Curtius, *European Literature*, 47.
7. *Encyclopedia Britannica*, 15th ed., s.v. "Education, History of."
8. Reynolds and Wilson, *Scribes and Scholars*, 80. The Latin reads as follows: Igitur quia curae nobis est ut nostrarum ecclesiarum ad meliora proficiat status, oblitteratam paene maiorum nostrorum desidia reparare vigilanti studio litterarum satagimus officinam, et ad pernoscenda studia liberalium artium nostro etiam quos possumus invitamus exemplo (*Epist. gen.*, MGH. Capit. 1.2.80). Interesting to note are the several word groups in which related words are set side by side; and the several instances where the exact opposite pertains. An example of artistic disarrangement lies in the last six words, in preparation for the *cursus*. There, *nostro* belongs with *exemplo*. For the cadencing beat (the *clausula* or *cursus*) we get *-amus exemplo*, a trochee plus a cretic: **dee**-de/de-**dee**-de.
9. *Encyclopaedia Britannica*, 15th ed., s.v. "Education, History of."
10. Löfstedt, *Late Latin*, 4, 14.
11. McKitterick, *Carolingians*, 220.
12. Curtius, *European Literature*, 48–50.
13. Translation from Charlemagne's letter to Abbot Baugulf at the monastery of Fulda. Cf. Curtius, *European Literature*, 48.
14. McKitterick, *Carolingians*, 214–15.
15. Ibid., 2–3.
16. Ibid., 21–2.
17. Ibid., 13, 17–18.
18. Ibid., 11. On p. 21, McKitterick describes the diglossia we see in the Carolingian realm as not really representing two distinct languages, but rather two registers or levels of the same language, with intercomprehension remaining assured. Not all would agree with this.
19. Ibid., 11. Interestingly, in the eighth century there was an established English community in Rome.
20. Ibid., 11–12.
21. Wright and Sinclair, *Later Latin Literature*, 139.

22. McKitterick, *Carolingians*, 2–3, 155.

23. For example, *illut que* reverted correctly to *illud quod, pristetirunt* to *praestiterunt*; and *ipsius monastiriae* to *ipsius monasteri*. Cf. Reynolds and Wilson, *Scribes and Scholars*, 72–4.

24. The area at the back of the mouth, where the throat begins.

25. For these materials on Anglo-Saxon-oriented pronunciation, see Roger Wright, *Late Latin*, 100–9.

26. Clemoes, "Liturgical Influence," 11.

27. E. K. Rand, *A Survey of the Manuscripts of Tours* (Cambridge: Medieval Academy of America, 1929), 1:29. Also, Rand, *Manuscripts of Tours*, 1:30.

28. Ibid., 1:31.

29. R. W. Southern, foreword to Geoffrey Bosanquet's translation of *Eadmer's History of Recent Events in England* (London: Crescent Press, 1964), xxxiii.

30. Reynolds and Wilson, *Scribes and Scholars*, 81–7.

31. Roger Wright, *Late Latin and Early Romance*, 114–15.

32. The thought comes in the concluding lines to Alcuin's poem on scribes: "It is better to write books than to dig vines/ one fills the belly but the other serves the soul." Hraban Maur, Alcuin's intellectual colleague in the Charlemagne circle, wrote, "Only letters are immortal and ward off death, only letters in books bring the past to life." McKitterick, *Carolingians*, 150.

33. Roger Wright, *Late Latin and Early Romance*, 113.

34. Reynolds and Wilson, *Scribes and Scholars*, 87.

35. This section with its assessment of the Carolingian legacy owes much to McKitterick, *Carolingians*, 151, 163–9, 197–8, 249–70, passim.

36. McKitterick, *Carolingians*, 184.

37. Ibid., 272–3.

38. Curtius, *European Literature*, 52.

39. Domenico Comparetti, *Vergil in the Middle Ages*, trans. E. F. M. Benecke (London: Swan Sonnenschein, 1895), 293, 326, 359–61.

References

Clemoes, Peter. *Liturgical Influence on Punctuation in Late Old English and Early Middle English Manuscripts*. Cambridge University Department of Anglo-Saxon. Cambridge: Cambridge University, 1952. Reprinted in the *Old English Newsletter* Series Subsidia 4 (1980): 10.

Comparetti, Domenico. *Vergil in the Middle Ages*. Translated by E. F. M. Benecke. London: Swan Sonnenschein, 1895.

Curtius, Ernst Robert. *European Literature and the Latin Middle Ages*. Translated by Willard R. Trask. Princeton: Princeton University Press, 1990.

Encyclopaedia Britannica, 15th ed., s.v. "Charlemagne, Emperor."

Encyclopaedia Britannica, 15th ed., s.v. "Education, History of."

Löfstedt, Einar. *Late Latin*. Cambridge: Harvard University Press, 1959.

McKitterick, Rosamund. *The Carolingians and the Written Word*. Cambridge: Cambridge University Press, 1995.

Rand, E. K. *A Survey of the Manuscripts of Tours*. Cambridge: Medieval Academy of America, 1929.

Reynolds, L. D., and N. G. Wilson. *Scribes and Scholars: A Guide to the Transmission of Greek and Latin Literature*. Oxford: Oxford University Press, 1968.

Southern, R. W. Foreword to Geoffrey Bosanquet's translation of Eadmer's *History of Recent Events in England*. London: Crescent Press, 1964.

Wright, F. A., and T. A. Sinclair. *A History of Later Latin Literature*. London: George Routledge & Sons, 1931.

Wright, Roger. *Late Latin and Early Romance in Spain and Carolingian France*. Liverpool, UK: Francis Cairns, 1982.

·SECTION 8·

THE SCENE TODAY

· 2 2 ·

A QUICK REVIEW
OF THE WRITING ARTS TODAY

A Comparison: Now and Earlier

Faced with the here-now excitements of TV, the internet, and pantechnic film, today's verbal constructs for the static page are more likely to attract if kept simple and short. Modern readers are impatient with old-fashioned literary artistry, whose fullness of expression, Latinate vocabulary, clever turns of phrase, prosodic rhythms, and agglomerating sequences were once so pleasing.

Textbooks for budding journalists are recommending short sentences of 15 to 20 words and vertical lists for 'a clear layout' of complicated materials. They instruct that to be successful, authors need not embellish every sentence with a verb, nor, in fact, worry very much about the dictates of grammar. Language should be pitched to suit the sophistication levels of the reading masses, of whom there are an estimated 77 million incompetents lurking in the United Kingdom and the United States alone. Such are the guiding directives for practicing writers, and by extension, for editors, publishers, and booksellers, all of whom are scrambling, not to sustain, but to accommodate the public, be successful, and make money.

The human, we remember, is physiologically constituted to speak and hear, not write and read. Nevertheless, so powerful an extension of our natural selves did literacy prove to be that, even in its infancy, it began to reorganize our thinking. Writing gave a special opportunity to wordmongers. It trained the public mind to accept a tighter weave of detailed information and to appreciate the sense of permanency and accuracy it offered. It initiated a demand for dictionaries, with a result that deepened our sense of linguistic history by prolonging the lifetime of 'outmoded' words and recording their etymologies. Withal, it increased the semantic and metaphoric possibilities for expressing exactly what is meant. To ease the reader's intake, writers instituted textual conventions that worked like traffic signals to keep their public on track. They perfected punctuation, whose task became trifold: to clarify structure; disambiguate semantic confusion; and restore (when possible) the emotional subtleties of speech that contribute so much to meaning: emphasis, intonation, and rhythm. In time, they augmented the range and coherency of a statement beyond the common limits of an oral one. The deliberation required to couch a thought in written words has for centuries pressed the mind to 'think again' in search of precision. During the centuries needed to develop its powers, writing came to discard the relaxed ramble of voice patterns and then, by mirrored reflection, became itself the ordered, often complex exemplar for 'educated' speech, whose early champion was Quintilian and whose best-documented proponent was Samuel Johnson. The scene is now changing and the things one *writes* are what one might say—*even casually say*. Writing no longer sets the pace for elegance, let alone clarity. Speech, any kind of speech, has become the common exemplar for written prose matter.

Though outmoded, multifaceted, and challengingly vocabularized sentences may require more effort to read, they are worth something, for they concentrate the minds of both author and reader. They reject gush. They align and expose relationships. They suggest nuances. Their digressions and inclusions (when expertly handled) induce a pleasing suspense for their outcome. Along with their promise of wit, insight, and reach to give pleasure, they impart a sense of exploration. The creative labor that sustains such writing is not generally expended in these rushed, informal days. In our modern world, where recreational excitements are everywhere available and worldwide 'information' floods the cranial cavity like water from a fire hydrant, publishers press their writers to style their prose for a quicker intake. One is expected to punch the half-chewed message directly into the circuitry behind the reader's eye and thereby enliven those old-fashioned word-ghosts stamped on the page. The push to make reading a competitively fun, easygoing experience has forced our written language to discard complication and to behave, in so far as it can, like ordinary street talk.

The decline of the expansive *periodic* style has been precipitous. Along with the educational practices of the 1930s, the shortened, vigorous, 'plain-spoken' sentences that marked the twentieth-century publishing output (one thinks especially of Ernest Hemingway) encouraged a massive change. Simplicity became essential to the nourishment of an author's bank account. Once an artistic tool, simplicity switched allegiance and became a marketing tool. Had Thucydides been around to read Samuel Beckett's opening lines to *The Lost Ones* (published in 1972), he would have frowned with discomfort. Pure objectivity is too close to silence.

> Abode where lost bodies roam each searching for its lost one. Vast enough for search to be in vain. Narrow enough for flight to be in vain. Inside a flattened cylinder fifty metres round and sixteen high for the sake of harmony. The light. Its dimness. Its yellowness.[1]

The convention-busting grammar of so fine an artist as Beckett was one of many such encouragements for simplified journalistic novelty. Short, full-stopped word clusters (that were in Beckett's case directed to echo the jumpy responses of a perceiving mind) became negotiable coin for many purposes—including authorial relaxation. Nevertheless, when handled with true artistry, unencumbered and sharp sentence fragments can be splendidly telling. The more vibrantly they stir the senses, the better they sock home. The ploy descends from its ancient ancestor, asyndeton.

Raymond Carver wrote searing stories in full but short, simple sentences occasionally joined by 'and.' Though they too suggested more than they exposed, they were nothing if not user friendly. Whatever readers could supply from their own imaginations Carver left unsaid. He counted on the common schemes of human experience to keep his tales pared to the bone. In the following instance, a marriage has fallen apart (a situation, whose scheme we react to because it is so common); no job (again: common), sitting on a stool and drinking beer in a bar (again so); two women—familiar types—engage him in conversation. With no further elaboration, we see it all, though more has been left out than was stated. Most of Carver's work concerned the imperfect communication of those who are inarticulate, financially unfortunate, and abnormally laid back. Guilt and regret prevail amongst his themes.

> My marriage had just fallen apart. I couldn't find a job. I had another girl. But she wasn't in town. So I was at a bar having a glass of beer,

and two women were sitting a few stools down, and one of them began to talk to me.[2]

The marketing successes of such literary artists as Beckett and Carver (and so many others like them) tell us that the old goals of sentence structuring are losing their glamor, as is the habit of intellectual application required to appreciate them. Elaborate syntax with variegated vocabulary no longer appeals to the average reader. No matter what meaningful insights and joys it may offer, he or she will simply not 'get it.' A study of the change in popular writing shows that between 1936 and 1996 sentence lengths in best-selling books decreased by some two-fifths, while dialogue (rarely artful) increased by a third. As for punctuation, its range of use has been essentially halved and only the full stop seems to be holding its own.

In matters of cultural intake, it is plain that the passive, film-watching mode of ingesting a book's content is now the more popular one. The critical bits of excitement, the pared-down plot—those are what the public wants. While the characters rampage about on our screens, burbling love and killing each other, our thumping hearts surrender to the visual excitement that has supplanted hard analysis. Why, indeed, should we push our brains along the bumpy byways of prolonged, outmoded sentences—those mazes of dry description and wispy nuance—when quicker-to-take-in communication services beep, thump, and flicker at us, pressing us to watch some Charles Dickens as interpreted by third parties? or to enjoy ourselves while we gape at what's going on in Syria? Though it may claim to inform us, filmed commentary is generally brief, unprobing, and vague. It is sensation-oriented, and relates to little but itself. Addressing the ear, it is blaring and unsubtle; addressing the eye, it is kaleidoscopic. Being so fidgety, it can hardly touch on serious, complicated matters for more than the flash of a few seconds. Entertainment is its 'thing.'

Modern technology, it would seem, has triumphed over our sensibilities. It has lured us like small children into dark precincts, where an experience must be had if the equipment supports it. There, in the land of distortion, the music is louder, the pixel count higher, the colors more vibrant, and the voices more urgent. All these wonderments of virtual 'reality' pluck at the human sensorium, stimulating hyperkinetic mental images that shatter the inner quiet that we used to enjoy to our benefit. The bedlam in our heads does not encourage in-depth thinking, argument, discourse, or the acute examination of motive or 'truth.' We no longer deal with verbal precision. Most TV commentary is headline stuff, brief snippets of verbiage shaped not for content, but for potential camera theatrics. Film narrative is impatient with logical sequence and historical fact, choosing instead to blow the mind with pulsating music and panoramic photography. Reading, by contrast, must limp along without the aid of screen or sound, let alone the additives of hot 'technology.' Lengthy sentence structures are impediments to speed—and speed is everything these days. Uncommon vocabulary and complicated grammatical constructions are not sufficiently fun, nor does exactitude of fact cut much of a figure in current popular amusement choices. Reading—being so patently vicarious, so *un*virtual—requires cerebral effort, and to be successful, it must 'grab' you. The electronically revved-up mind has not the patience to follow a lengthy written line. It *hates* patience. It *hates* to be alone. It particularly *hates* the silence conducive to focused thinking.

Can it be possible that we are yearning, like bored school children, for that Eden-like dream-garden where we can just jig around snapping our fingers and be our sub-basic selves? If it is to be the case that our hard-earned, read-write capability is no longer used for cerebral or aesthetic stimulation but only for utilitarian communication, then we are back to a new Middle Age. All the richness of literary artistry will go down the drain, and individual expression, through lack of practice and striving, will take on an ugly sameness. With each increment of electronic sensation, we become that bit less responsive to delicately reasoned distinctions and less patient with all the pastimes and pleasures that require intellectual concentration.

In Abraham Lincoln's time (and even down to Roosevelt's), national issues were addressed in words strung into full-blown sentences—sentences that were listened to with full attention as well as discrimination. Political matters are now evaluated by selected film-footage views of participants, few of whom seem willing (or able) to articulate their reasoning with any grace. Guitar performances, anecdotal chitchat, jokes, and even belly-dancing (yes!) have tended to replace serious theological and ethical topics as appropriate fare for church congregations. The warmth of 'togetherness' is enough. As evidenced in the texting habits of our offspring, everybody these days wants to cuddle up with everybody else. They want to know NOW, without a second's delay, what each of their vast acquaintance is doing, eating, playing at, feeling—which, of course, rather limits the need for careful commentary. As for our 'educated' lawyers and judges, they are rarely the guardians of lucid language that they used to be. The overall decline in speaking skills is sustaining the market for fast-paced books, from which all verbal complexity has been bowdlerized. The beauty of incisive expression and the give-and-take of well-reasoned political debate is beyond the ken of today's man-on-the-street. He is more comfortable on his sofa at home, enjoying his popcorn and beer, while 'watching' the news.

All in all, we are letting go of something precious; we are ignoring the gift of ancestral expositors who worked at their craft like tigers. We fail to respond to a well-cut statement. Its flash of beauty, its sparkling vocabulary and reach for clarity are not noticed. We haven't the knowledge to appreciate it, let alone the skill to produce it ourselves. Our talk is careless, and by reflection so is the way we write. All the fine flair of language, polished through centuries and bequeathed to us with pride, is now sliding out of sight. Before long, that flair will be irretrievable. And all because we are so mentally lazy! We do not practice accuracy, nor expend the effort needed to create beauty in our speech. Our vocabularies are small and our sentence structures monotonous. We prefer generalities over particulars. Yes, we are indeed lazy, as much in public oratory as in our social chatter.

It is important that we sharpen up about what is happening to our levels of speech and from there to our levels of writing. To illustrate from a thousand other possible examples, I have chosen some sadly uninspiring words extracted from a Sam Brownback speech to the American Senate. It was a very important occasion. But when he lifted his head from the guiding pages of his script, this is what he said:

> We go at Iraq and it says to countries that support terrorists, there remain six in the world that are as our definition state sponsors of terrorists, you say to those countries: 'We are serious about terrorism, we're serious about you not supporting terrorism on your own soil.'[3]

How sad that Mr. Brownback could think such a feeble comment would add to his argument! His listeners, bred on modern education, TV, and newspapers, were too accepting. Senators of a half century ago would have frowned at a public statement of that quality. They were used to greater rhetorical craft, one that included a clear logical exposure of meaning, and with a dash of grace as well.

And now, because he is impossible to avoid, here from our current scene is President Trump. He is, we are being told, hoping to reach an agreement with Beijing on his next meeting with Mr. Xi.

> We're going to try to make a deal with China because I want to have great relationships with President Xi, as I do, and also with China.[4]

A good instructional exercise for university students would be to rewrite the above two political garbles so as to render the intended sense (in so far as one can discern it) with appropriate grammatical support, a tighter connection of related parts, a more challenging vocabulary, and—for extra credit?—perhaps a dash of hyperbaton and a smidge of brachylogia.

Why can't our leaders talk or write with dignity anymore? An adherence to grammar and logic with a rousing choice of words and an intensifying build-up of argument—all these things stir the receiving human mind. One wonders how Demosthenes might have handled today's critical moments. When we read about the political controversy of previous times, we are impressed by the verbal capabilities of even our recent ancestors. The words and the purport of the American Constitution and Lincoln's Gettysburg address stun us with their impact. More recently, we are pleased to find that F. D. Roosevelt, too, was sensitive to the potentials of language and to the attractions of interesting sentence construction. In the following statement, the balanced opposition of 'abundance' with 'too little' shadows the dictates of an Aristotelian *period*. Its balanced negative/positive arrangement makes it rather attractive. And that in turn makes it memorable—which, no doubt, was Roosevelt's hope.

> The test of our progress is not whether we add more to the abundance
> of those who have much; it is whether we provide enough for those
> who have too little.[5]

So epigrammatic! Even Tacitus might have approved. Roosevelt would have been surprised to learn that, in less than a century after his death, 'educated' American diction had dropped to the mundane levels that we are willing to live with today.

As the world well knows, Churchill, too, was sensitive to the power of rhythm and well-chosen words. Below is a portion of the famous statement he delivered first to his Parliamentarian colleagues and later growled over the radio to his British compatriots at the beginning of the Second World War. Elements of classical rhetoric fuel its driving force. But what should be most appreciated is its effectiveness. Against overwhelming odds, Churchill *prevailed*—and that alone should be an enticement to our improvement. These were his words:

> I have, myself, full confidence that if all do their duty, if nothing is
> neglected, and if the best arrangements are made, as they are being
> made, we shall prove ourselves once again able to defend our Island

home, to ride out the storm of war and to outlive the menace of tyr-
anny, if necessary for years, if necessary alone.[6]

We will pause here to consider what Britain's fate might have been, if, at that
crucial moment in Parliament, Churchill had risen to say instead:

> Hey, you guys! We gotta man up and fight! On the beaches, and in
> the pubs—wherever. We gotta lock arms and kick those Helmuts and
> Heinrichs and whatevers off our territorial inheritances. We gotta
> teach them some old-fashioned geography, like this island's ours, see?
> And it's been ours ever since our ancestors can remember!

With a speech like that, the discriminating British public might not have
been so easily rallied to follow his lead. Fortunately, Churchill knew how
to use words to full effect. And did so, on that crucial day. Using judicious
amounts of beguilement and emotion, he pumped out his sentence parts in
a powerful rhythmic crescendo of encouragement and resolve—so Demosthenes!—and in that manner stiffened the spines of his indecisive public and
persuaded it to resist.

As for Trump: his rambling rants get less and less parsable. So perhaps he
doesn't matter after all.

*   *   *   *   *

Sentences are the building blocks for the thoughts that a writer wants to
convey or for a story he wants to tell. In times past, a sentence could carry
much freight and do so with transparency and grace. The successful writer was
practiced at keeping his words in focus so that the beginning led appropriately
to the end. Composing a sentence was an exercise in harnessing considerable
information and arranging it to inform the reader in the clearest and most
pleasing manner. Wit, vocabulary, turn of phrase, digestible flow of information, incremental buildup of argument—all these things could play a part in
the success of a statement. An author worked hard for his effects. It was accepted as fact that a well handled sentential construction could offer a bag of
delights.

To see what caviar the general book-reading public is missing these days,
let us look for a few moments at some of those 'old-fashioned' English-lan-
guage sentence types to assess their word choices and construction—their
rhythms, and frequent fireworks of wit. Do the pleasures they offer recom-
pense the exertion required to write them, let alone read them? The following samples have been chosen to illustrate the possible 'charm factor' of a

so-called difficult 'big sentence.' One should notice the quality and variety of vocabulary, the titillating effects of delayed impact, the sometimes eye-catching use of rhetorical figures, and the unabashed confidence in handling words.

Here, then, is an excerpt from Edward Gibbon, author of *The Decline and Fall of the Roman Empire*. It comes from his *Memoirs of My Life*, written in 1791.

> Since I have escaped from the long perils of my childhood, the serious advice of a physician has seldom been requisite. 'The madness of superfluous health' I have never known; but my tender constitution has been fortified by time; the play of the animal machine still continues to be easy and regular; and the inestimable gift of the sound and peaceful slumbers of infancy may be imputed both to the mind and body.[7]

Again, a sentence (from *Emma*) written by Jane Austen in 1816. The author is directing Emma's internal musings as she weighs the matrimonial chances of her friend, the less discerning Harriet:

> He was reckoned very handsome; his person much admired in general, though not by her [Emma], there being a want of elegance of feature which she could not dispense with:—but the girl [Harriet] who could be gratified by a Robert Martin's riding about the country to get walnuts for her, might very well be conquered by Mr. Elton's admiration.[8]

Here is a sentence from Charles Dickens's *Bleak House*, published in 1853. Its topic is an umbrella:

> She never puts it [the umbrella] up, having the greatest reliance on her well-proved cloak with its capacious hood; but generally uses the instrument as a wand with which to point out joints of meat or bunches of greens in marketing, or to arrest the attention of tradesmen by a friendly poke.[9]

And here, a sentence from George Eliot's *Adam Bede*, published in 1859:

> Mrs. Poyser would probably have brought her rejoinder to a further climax, if every one's attention had not at this moment been called to the other end of the table, where the lyrism, which had at first only manifested itself by David's sotto voce performance of "My love's

a rose with a thorn," had gradually assumed a rather deafening and complex character.[10]

In 1891 Alice James, the sister of Henry James, spent her declining years on an invalid's couch "composing sentences" for her journal. The following was written in 1891.

> She was a refined mortal, and although fifty years of age, embodied still, as K. said, the Wordsworthian maiden, having that wearying quality which always oozes from attenuated purity.[11]

There is something unaccountably pleasurable about incorporative, well-architectured statements. Perhaps it is the suspense they sometimes build by inserting fresh materials as they reach for the finish line; for they do not deal in instant gratification. Luckily, there are some contemporary readers who (being sufficiently experienced to be at ease with wily sentential construction) continue to experience delight from a lengthy unwind of information. Statistics of sales tell us that financial reward can still be had by writers who are skillful enough to manipulate an extended sentence, to adjust its balance, and time the moment for the telling punch. Bernard Levin, who died not so long ago, was a successful example of a modern stylist who managed to reanimate classical tradition. In his web of complexity, one should note how determinedly he kept track of the grammar. The following comes from one of his book reviews:

> Mr. Harrison begins by declaring that 'it's books that I'm into' and goes on to make clear that he is interested in what his local community 'is all about and where it's at'—a statement of faith which hardly leads to a belief that it is literacy that Mr. Harrison is into or that the English Language is where he's at.[12]

Long sentences of today are less likely to be embedded in the comfy crooks and crannies of conservative grammar. For the grand finale of this exercise, we now inspect some examples from three 'modern' novelists who, despite writing richly vocabularied, complex sentences in an Age of Instantaneous Gratification, have achieved success in the marketplace. The notable characteristic of this rejuvenating 'modernly formal' style seems to lie in the meltdown of Latinate hierarchical formalization into tack-on rivulets of modification, whose comfortable meanderings (directed usually by commas and dashes) elicit the impression of 'listening in' on the talk of an intimate mental voice. The classical tropes and schemes have given way to new complexities, which are equally informing, full of intellectual challenge, and pleasurable to follow for those not glued to their iPhones. Heartwarming is the fact that all three authors have enjoyed commercial respect.

In the following sentence from Tim Park's *Europa*, we feel close to the thought processes that crowd his hero's head. However hectic they may seem, they can be easily absorbed by the reader, since the author has managed to stay within the vastly stretched but still acceptable boundaries of grammatical English sentence structure.

> We filed into the Chambers Service Station, built as was to be expected in the ubiquitous Euro-architecture of curved cement-and-glass surfaces, with a generous bristle of flagpoles outside displaying the colours of every nationality the franchise-holders hope to take money from and inside a sense of disorientation generated by flights of steps and walkways and signs that are no longer in any language but just cups and knives-and-forks and wheelchairs and crossed-out dogs all presented in stylized white lines on plastic blue squares, and in fact the moment we're through the steamy swing doors, heavy against the cold, almost all the girls none of whom is wearing a skirt, follow the sign displaying a human figure distinguishable from another human figure precisely and exclusively because it is wearing a skirt or dress, rather than trousers, reminding me of something I read not so long ago in *Corriere della Sera* where a woman contributing to one of those *déjà vu* debates about the discrimination against the fairer sex inherent in the insufficient provision of lavatory facilities in public spaces remarked, against the swim of the debate, that as she saw it…[We are at this point about two-thirds through this sentence, and must in the interests of time and space move on.][13]

And now again, another excerpt, voiced in the words of a reacting narrator; this time from Thomas Pynchon's *Mason & Dixon*.

> Conrad has a lot invested in the Door, which he's carpenter'd, carrv'd, and hung all with his one set of hands,—he watches, not yet able to believe that these men he thought he knew could become a Band of Raiders who mean him harm, and his Grand-son as well, it seems, for now in this ear-batt'ring Kitchen Melee the Baby is suddenly become a Ball in a Game, being toss'd in short high arcs from one Party to

another 'bout the House, as the Shelbyites go beating upon anyone in
their Reach, injuring some so badly they won't make it into Court.[14]

But no one can beat William Faulkner for swollen sentence structures, so
many of which (and there are lots) are replete with subsidiary extensions that
carry on unabashedly in the narrator's nonparticipating descriptive voice for
a page or two. Teeming with relative clauses and dashes for apposition or refinement, they engulf and swell (and frequently obscure) the specific matter
under focus. Mr. Faulkner's style is heavily freighted with interruption, readjustment, and then addition. The sample Faulkner sentence beneath comes
from his novel *Absalom, Absalom!* It gives us a complicated three-sided view
of the spectating horsemen, the architect, and the general as they oversee
activity at the site of a turmoiled house construction. Compared to so many
others of Faulkner, it is not particularly long.

> They worked from sunup to sundown while parties of horsemen rode
> up and sat their horses quietly and watched, and the architect in his
> formal coat and his Paris hat and his expression of grim and embit-
> tered amazement lurked about the environs of the scene with his air
> something between a casual and bitterly disinterested spectator and
> a condemned and conscientious ghost—amazement, General Comp-
> son said, not at the others and what they were doing so much as at
> himself, at the inexplicable and incredible fact of his own presence.[15]

Novels that count extensively on dialogue can smack too much of indolence.
They tend to skim, not dive. But even then, if anything too subtle or abstruse
is advanced, a slack connection may develop between the writer's intention
and the reader's cognition. *But not to worry!* It is there, in that abyss of possible
misalignment, where the ambitious aspirer to modern authorship may yet find
his pot of gold. His pals, the geeks, will help him, of course. According to contract, they will invent a typography that heightens laconic ardor with music
and (for some mega-bucks extra) will emit personality-reinforcement aromas
so that uncertain readers may determine which of the characterless characters
to like and which to hate.

With all the excitement of flying speech-fragments to distract us, it is
scarcely surprising that we have grown less confident in dealing with the older, more disciplined style of silent verbal expression. We are less willing to
test ourselves against its special requirements of concentration, discipline, and
solitude. For the most part our knowledge of grammar is not up to it. But since

our cultural history is essentially preserved in the complex *periodic* medium, much will be lost if popular novelists and journalists cannot sometimes redeem the old style, and readers contrive to handle it. If eloquent, full-bodied sentential exposition is to survive at all, then young writers will have to remodel their sentence structures (as did Park, Pynchon, and Faulkner) to make the new style as tellingly complete as was the old. Ancient rhetorical tricks are still useful—if only as patterns for cutting new fashion. While the future is plainly precarious, true writers with magical keyboards and a passion for language continue to exist. We must hope for them and wish them well.

Notes

1. Samuel Beckett, "The Lost Ones," *The Complete Short Prose*, 1929–1989 (New York: Grove Press, 1929–1989), 202.
2. Raymond Carver, "Night School," *Will You Please Be Quiet, Please* (New York: McGraw-Hill, 1976), 92.
3. Sam Brownback, quoted in Emily Eakin, "Going at the Changes in, Ya Know, English," *New York Times*, November 15, 2003, https://www.nytimes.com/2003/11/15/books/going-at-the-changes-in-ya-know-english.html.
4. Donald Trump, quoted in Glenn Thrush, "U.S. Trade Advisor Issues Warning of No Quick Deal in Rift with China," *New York Times*, November 10, 2018.
5. Franklin Delano Roosevelt (inaugural address, Four Freedoms Park, Roosevelt Island, New York City, January 20, 1937), https://www.history.com/speeches/franklin-d-roosevelts-first-inaugural-address.
6. Winston Churchill. "We Shall Fight on the Beaches," speech delivered to the House of Commons of the Parliament of the United Kingdom, June 4, 1940, and later broadcast to the public.
7. Edward Gibbon, *Memoirs of My Life* (London: Penguin Books, 1984), 174.
8. Jane Austin, *Emma* (London: Penguin Popular Classics, 1994), 28.
9. Charles Dickens, *Bleak House* (New York: Bantam Books, 1983), 440.
10. George Eliot, *Adam Bede*, Everyman's Library (New York: Knopf, 1992), 579.
11. Alice James, *Her Brothers, Her Journal* (New York: Dodd, Mead, 1934), 205.
12. Bernard Levin, *Times* (London), November 19, 2018.
13. Tim Parks, *Europa* (London: Martin Secker and Warburg, 1997), 55–6.
14. Thomas Pynchon, *Mason & Dixon* (New York: Henry Holt, 1997), 578.
15. William Faulkner, *Absalom, Absalom!* (New York: Vintage International, 1986), 28.

References

Austin, Jane. Emma. London: Penguin Popular Classics, 1994.
Beckett, Samuel. "The Lost Ones." The Complete Short Prose, 1929–1989. New York: Grove Press, 1929–1989.

Brownback, Sam. Quoted in Emily Eakin, "Going at the Changes in, Ya Know, English," New York Times, November 15, 2003. https://www.nytimes.com/2003/11/15/books/going-at-the-changes-in-ya-know-english.html.

Carver, Raymond. "Night School," Will You Please Be Quiet, Please. New York: McGraw-Hill, 1976.

Churchill, Winston. "We Shall Fight on the Beaches," speech delivered to the House of Commons of the Parliament of the United Kingdom, June 4, 1940, and later broadcast to the public.

Dickens, Charles. Bleak House. New York: Bantam Books, 1983.

Eliot, George. Adam Bede, Everyman's Library. New York: Knopf, 1992.

Faulkner, William. Absalom, Absalom!. New York: Vintage International, 1986.

Gibbon, Edward. Memoirs of My Life. London: Penguin Books, 1984.

James, Alice. Her Brothers, Her Journal. New York: Dodd, Mead, 1934.

Levin, Bernard. Times (London), November 19, 2018.

Parks, Tim. Europa. London: Martin Secker and Warburg, 1997.

Pynchon, Thomas. Mason & Dixon. New York: Henry Holt, 1997.

Roosevelt, Franklin Delano. Inaugural address, Four Freedoms Park, Roosevelt Island, New York City, January 20, 1937. https://www.history.com/speeches/franklin-d-roosevelts-first-inaugural-address.

Trump, Donald. Quoted in Glenn Thrush, "U.S. Trade Advisor Issues Warning of No Quick Deal in Rift with China." New York Times, November 10, 2018.

· 2 3 ·

TERMINATION

How Will We Know When We've Reached the End?

The finishing boundary of a sentence is a troublesome spot. For some two thousand years grammarians have struggled to come up with a surefire definition for a 'completed sentence.' Being 'instinctually recognizable' instead of actually described, the full stop was felt to be more akin to a harmonic resolution than to an ending post. Traditionally, a 'sentence' was seen as a series of words that arranged ideas in a circuit that ended where it began, as does a racecourse, which was the source of its ancient names (*periodos* in Greek and *circuitus* in Latin). The pattern of beginning and ending with the same idea, or even the same word—as in ring composition—must have been common in archaic Greek oral composition, for it was plainly flourishing in Homer, Herodotus, and Thucydides. Today's sentential unit is perceived as being linear—a straight (or even zigzagged) run down the field to the finish line. There, at its termination, whatever the route that was taken, a mysterious tonal repose will be sensed. The mind is pulled to the mat and there it rests. *But why?* How can we verify that an utterance has come to an end? This question, so long a puzzle to the literary world, has modernly been *almost* answered by a swell of grammatical, cognitive, neurological, and physiological contributions, as well as the several probing explorations of writers. Their responses suggest at least a semi-definitive possible answer.

To appreciate how dense the forests behind us once were, let us quickly review our slow advance through them, keeping in mind the likelihood that defining sentential endings was not a sought-after specific of grammatical study until after writing got under way. Before then, termination was determined by the ear. As we well know, the word-spurts of oral language with their jagged rises and drops do not always tally with today's authorized 'grammatical principles.' That the feel of a perfectly finished grammatical sentence is innate seems worth exploring. Science has accepted the assertion that we humans develop neural-network extensions for dealing with new skills—skills such as driving in traffic or handling complicated aeronautical or electronic equipment—and yes, writing too.

Under the stimuli of need and desire, the primate brain will accommodate a tremendous degree of change. We have seen in these pages some verification of the neural-network-extension hypothesis: first, in the cognitive modifications that humans underwent when our primitive brains developed the ability to assemble our thoughts in sequences and our primitive larynxes reshaped to transmit them; then again, when the invention of alphabet letters shifted our communicating powers to the eye. Writing gave a push to our linear impulses, to a sense of cause and effect that in turn initiated an expectation of conclusion, once the words were felt (*and seen*) to have finished a 'completed' thought. Similar changes are rearranging our mental world today, as electronic and photographic invention turns us back towards primitive immediacies. It would seem that huge numbers of ordinary people are being profoundly remodeled as the benefits of instantaneousness displace those of contemplation. Nevertheless, as long as we remain literate, our current feel for sentence integrity is likely to prevail.

Again and again, in various places and times, the surfacing of literary consciousness has revealed a pattern. As writers became more experienced and confident, their initial confusion about the shape and conclusion of sentences gradually subsided. With the passing decades, in each of the emerging literate civilizations herein discussed, writing grew to become more malleable and clear—more responsive to thought, more easily reeled out, and more easily understood. Though grammarians had more or less conquered verb forms, syntax, lexical meanings, uniform pronunciation, spelling, and the like, they did nothing more than accept the assumption that everyone knows instinctively where the end of a sentence lies. They could find no way to define or explain

that feel of termination. To view the pattern of writing development in relation to our own language, we now look at sixteenth century Renaissance
England—a time when English was developing literary fluency, and style had
become a consideration.

During that early period the visual objectivity that writing and reading
inspire was still egressing from an oral-aural mindset. Scholastic influence
was encouraging imitation of Latin's ability to incorporate much information
within the confines of a single sentence. This, Englishmen were ill-equipped
to do, for the English 'sentence' structure was innately simple, forward-mov-
ing, and notably freer of inflection than any of its continental cousins. Nevertheless, to demonstrate his superior sophistication in this uncomplicated,
young, and free-swinging language, an 'educated' Englishman achieved his
literary ambitions by distending the core message of his sentences with serial
attachments—relative clauses, appositions, and prepositional phrases—to the
detriment of clarity. The following example of an off-course trek comes from
a 1522 letter from Sir Thomas More to Cardinal Wolsey:

> After this, whan I was goone from His Highnes, hit lyked hym to
> send agayne for me in to his Prevy Chambre, abowte 10 of the clok-
> ke; and than commaunded me to advertise Your Grace, ferther, that
> he had considered with hym selfe how loth the Low Cuntreis be, to
> have eny warre with hym; and that hym selfe and Your Grace, if it
> may be voided, wold be as lothe to have eny warre with theym; and,
> for that cause, His Grace thinketh it good, that albeit he wold, there
> were no slakkenes in putting of my Lord Sandes, and his cumpany, in
> a redynesse, yit they shold not over hastely be sent over, leste those
> Low Cuntreis, being put in more dowte and fere of His Graces en-
> tent and purpose toward theym, for some exploit to be done by land,
> myght be the rather moved to retayne and kepe stil the goodes of
> his merchauntes, and to begynne also somme busynes upon the Eng-
> lishe pale; which thing, the mater thus hanging, without ferther fere
> or suspicion added, His Highnes verily thinketh that they will not
> attempte, but rather, in good hope of peace, accelerate the delivery
> of his merchauntes goodes; namely, perceiving the discharge of the
> Spanyardes, whom, by Your Graces moost prudent advice, His High-
> nes hath condescended shortely to sett at libertie and fre passage.[1]

When More was writing his piece, he was addressing someone in his own educated inner circle and probably complicating his message deliberately to im-

press his correspondent with his classical knowledge and ability with words. In short he was striving to parade his elegance in the manner of his day. Gildas, we remember, did more or less the same thing. Nevertheless, More seemed troubled by the endlessness of some of his statements, for he sometimes (as though suddenly tired) would bring all to a full-stopped halt and begin anew with the very conjunction that was the obvious link to the preceding segment. At which point, we find ourselves reminded of Herodotus.

Although the English public was to remain puzzled for some time, grammarians settled matters of clausal and phrasal relationships quite rapidly during the next century, the seventeenth. Nevertheless, the essential boundaries of a sentence remained throughout undefined. Exactly what did constitute a sentence? Ben Jonson in his little grammar book did not attempt to reason about the full stop at the end of a sentence. As opposed to the clause or the phrase, it was simply "in all respects perfect.[2] "A perfect distinction closes a perfect sense and is marked with a round punct," proclaimed Alexander Hume in his *Of the Orthographie and Congruitie of the Britan Tongue* (1617).[3] And that was that. Other grammarians of the period did no better, and definitions (despite the ever more controlled structures such as those of Milton, Hooker, and Clarendon) continued through the seventeenth century in terms of "laying it down," "lowering the voice," "feeling a satisfaction," "resting the spirit," and so on. Grammatical elements were discussed, but always the 'sentence' eluded.

During the Enlightenment, as ear dependencies were giving way to eye-ish ones, writing concerns became more syntactical and less rhetorical. Sentence parts were being described with more precision. Though clarity was fast becoming a literary issue, termination was not. Samuel Johnson in his dictionary of 1755 could offer nothing but a roundabout of interdependencies. A sentence, he wrote, is a "short paragraph; a *period* in writing."[4] At the same time a *period* is "a complete sentence from one full stop to another." A full stop is "a point in writing by which sentences are distinguished." In short, because it is a glorious and 'perfect thing,' *we all recognize a sentence when we meet one.* In his assessment of 1823, William Cobbett presciently declared that the "Full-Point" was to be used at the "end of every collection of words, which make a full and complete meaning, and is not necessarily connected with other collections of words." But what exactly is to be made of that 'not necessarily connected'?[5]

During the early post-Gutenberg centuries, the sense of sentence unity grew stronger. Nevertheless, instead of a consummate definition, the finished sentence acquired an aspect of mystery that did not become vigorously addressed until, in the nineteenth century, psychology became a recognized academic and medically useful pursuit. Instructions for pointing and guidelines for relative pronouns, particles, prepositional phrases, spelling, word-use, and participles became decade by decade more precise. It is elucidating to compare More's ramble with the following (only a century and a half later) 1666 sample from Henry Oldenburg's introduction to the first issue of the Royal Society's *Philosophical Transactions*.

> Whereas there is nothing more necessary for promoting the improvement of Philosophic Matters, than the communicating to such, as apply their Studies and Endeavours that way, such things as are discovered or put in practise by others, it is therefore thought fit to employ the *Press*, as the most proper way to gratifie those, whose engagement in such Studies, and delight in the advancement of Learning and profitable Discoveries, doth entitle them to the knowledge of what this Kingdom, or other parts of the World, do, from time to time, afford, as well of the progress of the Studies, Labours, and attempts of the Curious and Learned in things of this kind, as of their complete Discoveries and performances: To the end, that such Productions being clearly and truly communicated, desires after solid and usefull knowledge may be further entertained, ingenious Endeavours and Undertakings cherished, and those, addicted to and conversant in such matters, may be invited and encouraged to search, try, and find out new things, impart their knowledge to one another, and contribute what they can to the Grand design of improving Natural knowledge, and perfecting all *Philosophical Arts*, and *Sciences*.[6]

As public education, printed matter, and the edicts of the Enlightenment spread, so the English written language steadied, to become less exclusively the property of Members of the Club Only. The more folk read, the more easily they could unravel elaborate sentences. At the same time, popular speech habits, influenced by printed constructions, were growing more complicated and perforce more attentive to the rules of the language. Punctuation and grammar (with guiding particles such as *on the one/ other hand, furthermore, then, but, because*, etc.) proved to be manageable tools that could nudge the sentential elements towards the completion of an overarching idea. The argument-controlling links that worked above the sentence level (such as *contrary to expectation, quite apart from the internet, be it resolved that, whereas, as we were saying before*), though largely semantic, became quasi-grammatical tools in that they worked to direct attention and mark a path through the larger tracts. In addition, the public was sprouting, like little horns, the requisite neural stuff to cope.

In its full-blown written form, the ancient *period* (often of paragraphic length) had constituted a semantic and constructive whole, which was sometimes marked off with a *paragraphos* in the margin. By the eighteenth century CE, an educated Englishman wishing to impress tended to organize his thoughts into grammar-controlled structures before uttering them. By their own accounts, Edward Gibbon, Samuel Johnson, and Winston Churchill, having trained themselves to do so from childhood, regularly thought through (and in Churchill's case wrote down) an entire complicated sentence before speaking it.

Although some contemporary authors are composing well-turned complex sentences for their diminishing numbers of appreciative readers, most writers nowadays aim only to penetrate the pachydermic resistance to written words of a possibly neurally un-re-wired populace. With the familiar publishing houses now nesting under some eight big roofs and throwing money at a handful of 'big-name' authors, a more concerted hold over fashion in word style is being exercised than ever. The intention is neither aesthetic nor intellectual. Escape, relaxation, thrills, and money are the goals. The schooling of journalists and popular writers deals frankly with the salability of reading products to a nonreading public.

But back to our muttons. By the turn of the twentieth century, deeper thoughts about what a sentence might be began to appear. A new notion had floated to the surface, namely this: that within a well-formed sentence some difficulty is presented and resolved. Herewith is Robert Louis Stevenson's analysis of the action:

> Communication may be made in broken words, the business of life be carried on with substantives alone; but that is not what we call literature; and the true business of the literary artist is to plait or weave his meaning, involving it around itself; so that each sentence, by successive phrases, shall first come into a kind of knot, and then, after a moment of suspended meaning, solve and clear itself. In every properly constructed sentence there should be observed this knot or hitch; so that (however delicately) we are led to foresee, to expect, and then to welcome the successive phrases.[7]

Stevenson is suggesting that a disturbance contained in the initial 'given' creates a tension, which is the effect of incompleteness and unsupported dependencies. That effect fades when relationships settle into fresh balance, bringing symmetry and calm. It was that feel of calm that had for centuries been called 'perfection.'

Only a few years before, Ernest Fenollosa's 1908 essay on Chinese kanji (posthumously translated and annotated by Ezra Pound, but not published until the mid-1930s) presented to the English-speaking world a number of intriguing speculations about the sentence.

> I wonder how many people have asked themselves why the sentence form exists at all, why it seems so universally necessary *in all languages?*...
>
> I fancy the professional grammarians have given but a lame response to this inquiry. Their definitions fall into two types: one, that a sentence expresses a "complete thought"; the other, that in it we bring about a union of subject and predicate.

Fenollosa discards the 'complete thought' idea on the grounds that everything is interdependent. All acts

> are successive, even continuous; one causes or passes into another.... All processes in nature are interrelated; and thus there could be no complete sentence (according to this definition) save one which it would take all time to pronounce.

He rejects the subject-predicate definition as an accident of man's ego, for man selects and arranges his subject and predicate where and how he wants to, that is, arbitrarily, according to his own point of view. A more accurate definition of a sentence, then, according to Fenollosa, will come from science.

> Valid scientific thought consists in following as closely as may be the actual and entangled lines of forces as they pulse through things.... The sentence form was forced upon primitive men by nature itself. It was not we who made it; it was a reflection of the temporal order in causation. All truth has to be expressed in sentences because all truth is the *transference of power.*[8]

So then, a sentence is like a flash of lightning that passes between two terms. In its most primitive form it tells of a redistribution of force: from agent, through action, to object—as in 'Farmer pounds rice'—and so corresponds to the universal form of action in Nature through the order of cause and effect. As does all Aryan etymology, both farmer and rice have evolved from original verb concepts. Thus the farmer farms, and the rice is what grows in its special way. Farmer and rice are the noun-out-of-verb terms that define the extremes of the pounding. In this way we learn that in the end everything reduces to action. Under the metaphorical superstructures of English words (be they nouns, adjectives, or adverbs), one can to this day identify primitive Sanskrit verb roots. In the case of the Chinese kanji, the trained eye can track the actual history of a verb's evolution.

The decades that preceded World War II brought a flux of insight to challenge the practicing stylist. The integrity of a sentence—its shape and carrying power—became matters of accelerating concern. Writers were pressed to say their piece against a background of commentary about what 'natural' or 'effective' ought to mean. The peculiarities that separate what is written from what is spoken, and both from what is thought, were being more precisely described. In this period of exploration, we find examples of short, disconnected, full-stopped spurts of 'mentalese' à la James Joyce and the rat-a-tat stream-of-consciousness phrases à la Virginia Woolf. Later, Faulkner added his twist, putting forth phrases and clauses separated by commas, dashes, semicolons, and colons in long chains that could have been broken into sentences—but audaciously weren't. Hemingway was influential in popularizing short, easy-to-follow descriptive sentences, which he frequently connected with simple *ands*. D. H. Lawrence was especially devoted to short sentences to register passion and urgency. All these diminished structures dodged the wide-scanning, formally organized sentence of descriptive prose with its inviting opportunities for wit. Brevity was the mode of emotion, and for attracting attention. Convolution was the mode of intellectuality. With the falling off of the reading habit (and the impending shrinkage of the neural network extensions that support it), the cerebral province of library-quiet has daily grown smaller. Anarchic speech is our default mode. The very 'naturalness' of it is the effect that writers now seek. Their cut-and-thrust style is especially suitable for the emotional side of human nature, for when a person gives vent to strong feeling, he does not stop to ponder the logic of his expression. Emotion is best for best-sellers.

The frequency of the full stop in modern texts owes much to the rhythms of grammar-disinterested, casual speech. In relaxed discussion, we let go our adherence to classroom decree. We don't like being regulated, even though *how* we say what we are saying is sometimes a plague to our hearers. But, as anyone knows who has tried to parse an ad-libbed statement on TV, or to follow a route supplied by a passing pedestrian, that's the way we are these days. Transcripts of our talk are replete with evidence of grammatical lapse.

But back to the matter of terminating sentences. In 1968, Barbara Strang, the esteemed professor of English language and general linguistics at the University of Newcastle upon Tyne, defined the completed sentence as a linguistic sequence that has internal but no external grammatical relations—a description not too far from Cobbett's. It is, therefore, a grammatical, self-contained structure. She describes it thus:

> the disjunction of what is grammatically self-contained from what is not is one of the most absolute in the language.

But even so, she continues: the term 'sentence' (representing a completed thing) continues to generate much dissatisfaction, as is

> indicated by the number of attempts at definition…, for there is no need to redefine a term unless you are dissatisfied with your predecessors' use of it.[9]

In 1985, Randolph Quirk et al. in their *Comprehensive Grammar of the English Language* had this to say:

> 'What counts as a grammatical English sentence?' is not always a question which permits a decisive answer; and this is not only because of the difficulty of segmenting a discourse into sentences but because questions of grammatical acceptability inevitably become involved with questions of meaning, with questions of good or bad style, with questions of lexical acceptability, with questions of acceptability in context, etc.[10]

Stephen Pinker in his *The Language Instinct* offers a simple recipe for composing the 'standardly complete' sentence. To perform the act of utterance (that is, the 'outering' of thought into words), he says, the human mind must balance lexicographic instructions with the rules of grammar—a complicated business, but our adaptable neurons take it in stride. The first word of an utterance will introduce a trail of requisite follow-ups that must be slotted in along the grammatical line in keeping with their lexicographic constraints. Thus, each determiner must have (and accord with) its noun, each adjective also must have (and accord with) its noun, nouns that are subjects must have their suitable verbs, each transitive verb a suitable object, and so on. As we begin our sentence, "The cat and the dog ate their dinners," the very first "the" forces us onward through every unfulfilled element until we reach fulfillment. But, say we, *What drives 'cat' to 'and'?* As the sentence stands, it is indeed a neatly tied knot with the word 'their' requiring a plural subject. In this case the Pinker definition is not truly applicable except with a single subject and a singular pronoun in the predicate. If that pertains, then each word *will* need the next to match its lexicographic requirements.

> When memory has been emptied of all its incomplete dangling branches, we experience the mental 'click' that signals that we have just heard a complete grammatical sentence.[11]

Of course, we may then decide to attach more: with a *whom, because, when, where,* or *a full apposition*—so many choices! Note the continuing possibilities:

> I hit John./, *whom* I have always disliked./, *because* of his rudeness to my uncle./, *when* we were celebrating Marjorie's acceptance into law school./—*the very* school *that* she once had no hope of attending./, because…etc. [Conceivably forever!]

When we begin to make sentences like that, new considerations will kick in to stop us: style, for one, and a concern for the ease with which we will be understood. Communicating, we discover, is a savage sport, played on a field of sinkholes and slime.

And that being the case, we will now cease to engage in it.

Notes

1. Letter from Sir Thomas More to Cardinal Wolsey (1523?), *Luminarium: Anthology of English Literature*, http://www.luminarium.org/renlit/morewolsey1523.htm.
2. Ben Jonson, *The English Grammar* (London, 1640), 76.
3. Alexander Hume, *Of the Orthographie and Congruitie of the Britan Tongue* (1617) (London, 1891), 34.
4. Samuel Johnson, *A Dictionary of the English Language* (London, 1755), s.v. "Sentence."
5. William Cobbett, *A Grammar of the English Language* (London, 1823), 74.
6. Henry Oldenberg, introduction to *Philosophical Transactions of the Royal Society*, vol. 1, 1666, Project Gutenberg e-book.
7. Robert Louis Stevenson, *The Art of Writing and Other Essays* (London: Chatto & Windus, 1905), 9–10.

8. Ernest Fenollosa, *The Chinese Written Character as a Medium for Poetry*, ed. Ezra Pound (San Francisco: City Lights Books, 1936), 10–14.
9. Barbara M. H. Strang, *Modern English Structure* (London: Edward Arnold, 1968), 71–2.
10. Randolph Quirk, Sidney Greenbaum, Geoffrey Leech, and Jan Svartvik, *A Comprehensive Grammar of the English Language* (London and New York: Longman, 1985), 47.
11. Stephen Pinker, *The Language Instinct: How the Mind Creates Language* (New York, William Morrow, 1994), 200.

References

Cobbett, William. *A Grammar of the English Language*. London, 1823.

Fenollosa, Ernest. *The Chinese Written Character as a Medium for Poetry*. Edited by Ezra Pound. San Francisco: City Lights Books, 1936.

Hume, Alexander. *Of the Orthographie and Congruitie of the Britan Tongue* (1617). London, 1891.

Johnson, Samuel, s.v. "Sentence." In *A Dictionary of the English Language*. London, 1755.

Jonson, Ben. *The English Grammar*. London, 1640.

More, Sir Thomas, to Cardinal Wolsey (1523?). In *Luminarium: Anthology of English Literature*. http://www.luminarium.org/renlit/morewolsey1523.htm.

Oldenberg, Henry. Introduction to Vol. 1 of *Philosophical Transactions of the Royal Society*, 1666, Project Gutenberg e-book.

Pinker, Stephen. *The Language Instinct: How the Mind Creates Language*. New York, William Morrow, 1994.

Quirk, Randolph, and Sidney Greenbaum, Geoffrey Leech, and Jan Svartvik. *A Comprehensive Grammar of the English Language*. London and New York: Longman, 1985.

Stevenson, Robert Louis. *The Art of Writing and Other Essays*. London: Chatto & Windus, 1905.

Strang, Barbara M. H. *Modern English Structure*. London: Edward Arnold, 1968.

INDEX

E

F

G

X

Y

Z